BUSINESS
IN ACTION

BUSINESS IN ACTION

with Real-Time Updates

FOURTH EDITION

Courtland L. Bovée

Professor of Business Administration

C. Allen Paul Distinguished Chair

Grossmont College

John V. Thill

Chief Executive Officer

Global Communication Strategies

PEARSON

Prentice Hall

Upper Saddle River, New Jersey 07458

Library of Congress Cataloging-in-Publication Data

Bovée, Courtland L.

Business in action : with real-time updates / Courtland L. Bovée, John V. Thill. — 4th ed.

p. cm.

Earlier editions lack subtitle.

ISBN 978-0-13-615408-2

1. Business. 2. Commerce. 3. Industrial management. I. Thill, John V. II. Title.

HF1008.B685 2008

650—dc22   2007044134

VP/Publisher: Natalie E. Anderson
AVP/Executive Editor: Print: Jodi McPherson
Director, Product Development: Pamela Hersperger
Editorial Project Manager: Claudia Fernandes
Development Editor: George Dovel
Editorial Assistant: Kate Horton
Editorial Media Project Manager: Lisa Rinaldi
Technical Analyst: Dave Moles
Production Media Project Manager: Lorena Cerisano
Marketing Manager: Andrew Watts
Marketing Assistant: Justin Jacob
Senior Managing Editor: Cynthia Zonneveld
Production Project Manager: Lynne Breitfeller
Manager of Rights & Permissions: Charles Morris
Senior Operations Director: Nick Sklitsis
Operations Director: Natacha St. Hill Moore

Senior Art Director: Jonathan Boylan
Interior Design: GGS Information Services
Cover Design: GGS Information Services
Cover Illustration/Photo: © George Doyle/Stockbyte/Getty Images, Inc.
Illustration (Interior): GGS Information Services
Director, Image Resource Center: Melinda Patelli
Manager, Rights and Permissions: Zina Arabia
Manager: Visual Research: Beth Brenzel
Manager, Cover Visual Research & Permissions: Karen Sanatar
Image Permission Coordinator: Joanne Dippel
Photo Researcher: Kathy Ringrose
Composition: GGS Information Services
Full-Service Project Management: GGS Information Services
Printer/Binder: Courier/Kendallville
Typeface: 10.5/12 Minion Roman

Credits and acknowledgments borrowed from other sources and reproduced, with permission, in this textbook appear on pages 421–426.

Pearson Education LTD.
Pearson Education Singapore, Pte. Ltd
Pearson Education, Canada, Ltd
Pearson Education–Japan

Pearson Education Australia PTY, Limited
Pearson Education North Asia Ltd
Pearson Educación de Mexico, S.A. de C.V.
Pearson Education Malaysia, Pte. Ltd.

10 9 8 7 6 5 4 3 2 1
ISBN-13: 978-0-13-615408-2
ISBN-10: 0-13-615408-5

Contents in Brief

Preface   xv

Prologue: Are You Ready for Success?   xxiii

Part 1   Developing a Business Mind-Set   1

Chapter 1   The Fundamentals of Business and Economics   1
Chapter 2   Ethics and Corporate Social Responsibility   29
Chapter 3   The Global Marketplace   56
Chapter 4   Business Systems   80

Part 2   Organizing the Business Enterprise   110

Chapter 5   Business Structures   110
Chapter 6   Small Business and Entrepreneurship   133

Part 3   Managing for Profitability   158

Chapter 7   Accounting and Financial Management   158
Chapter 8   Banking and Securities   186

Part 4   Creating and Satisfying Customers   213

Chapter 9   Marketing Concepts and Strategies   213
Chapter 10   Products and Pricing   242
Chapter 11   Distribution and Customer Communication   268

Part 5   Leading and Supporting Employees   296

Chapter 12   Management Functions and Skills   296
Chapter 13   Organization, Teamwork, and Motivation   321
Chapter 14   Human Resources   348

Appendixes

Appendix A   The U.S. Legal System and Business Law   379
Appendix B   Personal Finance: Getting Set for Life   388

Contents

Preface   xv
Prologue: Are You Ready for Success?   xxiii

PART 1
Developing a Business Mind-Set   1

Chapter 1   The Fundamentals of Business and Economics   1

Behind the **Scenes:** Making Dollars and Sense of Online Music at Apple iTunes   2

Developing a Business Mind-Set: How This Course Will Help Your Career   2
  How This Affects You   3
  Understanding What Business Does   3
  Recognizing the Various Types of Businesses   4
Understanding Economic Systems   6
  Free-Market Systems   8
  Planned Systems   9
Microeconomics: Understanding the Forces of Demand and Supply   9
  Understanding Demand   9
  Understanding Supply   11
  Understanding How Demand and Supply Interact   11
Macroeconomics: Understanding How an Economy Operates   12
  Competition in a Free-Market System   12
  Government's Role in a Free-Market System   13
    Fostering Competition   13
    Regulation and Deregulation   14
    Protecting Stakeholders   14
    Contributing to Economic Stability   15
How a Free-Market System Monitors Its Economic Performance   18
  Watching Economic Indicators   18
  Measuring Price Changes   19
    Inflation and Deflation   19
    Price Indexes   19
  Measuring a Nation's Output   20
The Challenges You'll Face in the Global Economy   20
SUMMARY OF LEARNING OBJECTIVES   22

Behind the **Scenes:** Moving the Music at Apple iTunes   23

KEY TERMS   24
TEST YOUR KNOWLEDGE   24
PRACTICE YOUR KNOWLEDGE   24
EXPAND YOUR KNOWLEDGE   25
SEE IT ON THE WEB   26
  Check Out This 24-Hour Business Library   26
  Step Inside the Economic Statistics Briefing Room   26
  Discover What's in the CPI   26
COMPANION WEBSITE   26
VIDEO CASE: Helping Business Do Business: U.S. Department of Commerce   26
▪ *Is Web 2.0 the Future or the Past Revisited?   5*
▪ *Learning from Business Blunders   21*

Chapter 2   Ethics and Corporate Social Responsibility   28

Behind the **Scenes:** Protestors Pour on the Trouble for PepsiCo in India   29

Ethics and Social Responsibility in Contemporary Business   29
  What Is Ethical Behavior?   30
    Competing Fairly and Honestly   30
    Communicating Truthfully   31
    Not Causing Harm to Others   31
  Factors Influencing Ethical Behavior   32
    Cultural Differences   32
    Knowledge   32
    Organizational Behavior   33
  How Do You Make Ethical Decisions?   34
  Corporate Social Responsibility   35
    The Relationship Between Business and Society   36
    Perspectives on Corporate Social Responsibility   37
    Philanthropy Versus Strategic CSR   39
Business's Efforts to Increase Social Responsibility   41
  Responsibility Toward Society and the Environment   41
    Efforts to Reduce Pollution   42
    The Trend Toward Sustainability   43
  Responsibility Toward Consumers   44
    The Right to Buy Safe Products   44
    The Right to Be Informed   45
    The Right to Choose Which Products to Buy   46
    The Right to Be Heard   46
  Responsibility Toward Investors   46

vii

Responsibility Toward Employees   46
  The Push for Equality in Employment   47
  Occupational Safety and Health   48
Ethics and Social Responsibility Around the World   49
SUMMARY OF LEARNING OBJECTIVES   49

Behind the Scenes: **PepsiCo Responds to Protests over Water Usage and Product Safety   50**

KEY TERMS   51

TEST YOUR KNOWLEDGE   52

PRACTICE YOUR KNOWLEDGE   52

EXPAND YOUR KNOWLEDGE   53

SEE IT ON THE WEB   53
  Build a Better Business   54
  Surf Safely   54
  Learn About Environmental Protection   54

COMPANION WEBSITE   54

VIDEO CASE: **Doing the Right Thing: American Red Cross   54**

■ *Wow, That Sure Was Nice of Kathy to Give Us Those Free Coupons!   31*

■ *Lead Your Team with Ethical Behavior   34*

■ *Learning from Business Blunders   47*

Chapter 3   The Global Marketplace   56

Behind the Scenes: **MTV Base Africa: Extending the Reach of One of World's Biggest Media Brands   57**

Fundamentals of International Trade   57
  Why Nations Trade   58
  How International Trade Is Measured   59
  Free Trade and Fair Trade   59
  Trade Restrictions   61
  Agreements and Organizations Overseeing International Trade   62
    The General Agreement on Tariffs and Trade (GATT)   62
    The World Trade Organization (WTO)   62
    The International Monetary Fund (IMF)   63
    The World Bank   63
  Trading Blocs   63
    North American Free Trade Agreement (NAFTA)   63
    European Union (EU)   63
    Asia-Pacific Economic Council (APEC)   65
  Foreign Exchange Rates and Currency Valuations   65
The Global Business Environment   66
  Cultural Differences in the Global Business Environment   66
  Legal Differences in the Global Business Environment   68
  Forms of International Business Activity   68
    Importing and Exporting   70
    International Licensing   70
    International Franchising   70
    International Strategic Alliances and Joint Ventures   70
    Foreign Direct Investment   71

Strategic Approaches to International Markets   72
Terrorism's Impact on the Global Business Environment   73
SUMMARY OF LEARNING OBJECTIVES   74

Behind the Scenes: **Adapting an American Cultural Icon to the African Market   75**

KEY TERMS   76

TEST YOUR KNOWLEDGE   76

PRACTICE YOUR KNOWLEDGE   77

EXPAND YOUR KNOWLEDGE   78

SEE IT ON THE WEB   78
  Navigating Global Business Differences   78
  Going Global   78
  Banking on the World Bank   78

COMPANION WEBSITE   79

VIDEO CASE: **Entering the Global Marketplace: Lands' End and Yahoo!   79**

■ *Studying Other Cultures   67*

■ *Learning from Business Blunders   72*

Chapter 4   Business Systems   80

Behind the Scenes: **Fulfilling Customized Dreams at Carvin Guitars   81**

An Introduction to Systems Thinking   81
  What Is a System?   81
  Principles of Systems Thinking   83
  The Business Model   85
Production Systems   86
  Value Chains and Value Webs   86
  Supply Chain Management   87
    Supply Chains Versus Value Chains   88
    Supply Chain Systems and Techniques   89
  Production and Operations Management   90
    Facilities Location and Design   90
    Forecasting and Capacity Planning   90
    Scheduling   91
    Lean Systems   91
  Mass Production, Customized Production, and Mass Customization   93
  The Unique Challenges of Service Delivery   93
  Product and Process Quality   94
    Statistical Quality Control and Continuous Improvement   95
    Total Quality Management and Six Sigma   95
    Global Quality Standards   96
Information Systems   96
  How Businesses Use Information   97
  Types of Business Information Systems   98
    Operational Systems   98
    Professional and Managerial Systems   99
  The Internet Revolution   99
  Information Systems Management Issues   100
    Ensuring Security and Privacy   101
    Protecting Property Rights   102
    Guarding Against Information Overload   102

Monitoring Productivity 103
Managing Total Cost of Ownership 103
Developing Employee Skills 104
Maintaining the Human Touch 104
SUMMARY OF LEARNING OBJECTIVES 104

Behind the **Scenes:** Carvin's Production System Satisfies Demanding Guitarists 105

KEY TERMS 106
TEST YOUR KNOWLEDGE 106
PRACTICE YOUR KNOWLEDGE 107
EXPAND YOUR KNOWLEDGE 108
SEE IT ON THE WEB 108
Make Quality Count 108
Follow This Path to Continuous Improvement 108
Stay Informed with CIO 108
COMPANION WEBSITE 108
VIDEO CASE: Managing Production Around the World: Body Glove 109

▪ *Offshoring: Profits, Yes, But at What Cost?* 88
▪ *Advanced Technology on the Factory Floor* 92
▪ *Learning from Business Blunders* 101

PART 2
Organizing the Business Enterprise 110

Chapter 5 Business Structures 110

Behind the **Scenes:** Google Searches for a Solution to the Display Advertising Business 111

Choosing a Form of Business Ownership 111
Sole Proprietorships 113
Advantages of Sole Proprietorships 113
Disadvantages of Sole Proprietorships 113
Partnerships 113
Advantages of Partnerships 114
Disadvantages of Partnerships 114
Keeping It Together: The Partnership Agreement 115
Corporations 115
Ownership 115
Advantages of Corporations 117
Disadvantages of Corporations 117
Special Types of Corporations 118
Corporate Governance 119
Understanding Mergers, Acquisitions, and Alliances 121
Mergers and Acquisitions 121
Advantages of Mergers and Acquisitions 123
Disadvantages of Mergers and Acquisitions 124
Trends in Mergers and Acquisitions 124
Merger-and-Acquisition Defenses 125
Strategic Alliances and Joint Ventures 125
SUMMARY OF LEARNING OBJECTIVES 127

Behind the **Scenes:** Google Buys a Major Stake in the Online Display Ad Business 127

KEY TERMS 128
TEST YOUR KNOWLEDGE 129
PRACTICE YOUR KNOWLEDGE 129
EXPAND YOUR KNOWLEDGE 130
SEE IT ON THE WEB 131
Choose a Form of Ownership 131
Follow the Fortunes of the *Fortune* 500 131
Build a Great Board 131
COMPANION WEBSITE 131
VIDEO CASE: Doing Business Privately: Amy's Ice Creams 131

▪ *Learning from Business Blunders* 123
▪ *Hey, Wanna Lose a Few Billion? Do We Have a Deal for You* 126

Chapter 6 Small Business and Entrepreneurship 133

Behind the **Scenes:** GeniusBabies.com Builds a Smart Business 134

Understanding the World of Small Business 134
Economic Roles of Small Businesses 135
Characteristics of Small Businesses 136
Factors Contributing to the Increase in the Number of Small Businesses 136
E-Commerce and Other Technologies 136
Growing Diversity in Entrepreneurship 136
Downsizing and Outsourcing 138
Starting a Small Business 138
Characteristics of Entrepreneurs 138
Importance of Preparing a Business Plan 140
Small-Business Ownership Options 141
The Franchise Alternative 143
Types of Franchises 143
How to Evaluate a Franchise 143
Advantages of Franchising 144
Disadvantages of Franchising 145
Why New Businesses Fail 145
Sources of Small-Business Assistance 146
Government Agencies and Nonprofit Organizations 146
Business Partners 147
Mentors and Advisory Boards 147
Print and Online Media 147
Networks 148
Business Incubators and Accelerators 148
Financing a New Business 149
Seeking Private Financing 149
Banks and Microlenders 149
Venture Capitalists 150
Angel Investors 150
Credit Cards 151
Small Business Administration Assistance 151
Going Public 151
SUMMARY OF LEARNING OBJECTIVES 152

Behind the **Scenes:** Another Web-Based Dream Becomes Reality at GeniusBabies.com 152

KEY TERMS   153

TEST YOUR KNOWLEDGE   154

PRACTICE YOUR KNOWLEDGE   154

EXPAND YOUR KNOWLEDGE   155

SEE IT ON THE WEB   155
   Guide Your Way to Small-Business Success   155
   Start a Small Business   156
   Learn the ABCs of IPOs   156

COMPANION WEBSITE   156

VIDEO CASE: Managing Growth at
Student Advantage   156

■ *Blueprint for an Effective Business Plan   142*

■ *Learning from Business Blunders   146*

PART 3

Managing for Profitability   158

Chapter 7 Accounting and Financial Management   158

Behind the **Scenes:** Microsoft Looks for Ways
to Unload a Mountain
of Cash   159

Understanding Accounting   159
   What Accountants Do   160
   The Rules of Accounting   161
      GAAP   161
      Sarbanes-Oxley   163

Fundamental Accounting Concepts   164
   The Accounting Equation   164
   Double-Entry Bookkeeping and the Matching Principle   165

Using Financial Statements   166
   Understanding Financial Statements   167
      Balance Sheet   167
      Income Statement   169
      Statement of Cash Flows   171
   Analyzing Financial Statements   172
      Trend Analysis   172
      Ratio Analysis   173
      Types of Financial Ratios   173

Understanding Financial Management   175
   Developing and Implementing a Financial Plan   176
   Monitoring Cash Flow   176
   Developing a Budget   176
      Securing Financing   177
      Length of Term   177
      Cost of Capital   177
      Debt Versus Equity Financing   178

SUMMARY OF LEARNING OBJECTIVES   179

Behind the **Scenes:** Microsoft Hands Out Cash to
Happy Shareholders   180

KEY TERMS   181

TEST YOUR KNOWLEDGE   181

PRACTICE YOUR KNOWLEDGE   182

EXPAND YOUR KNOWLEDGE   183

SEE IT ON THE WEB   183
   Link Your Way to the World of Accounting   183
   Sharpen Your Pencil   184
   Think Like an Accountant   184

COMPANION WEBSITE   184

VIDEO CASE: Accounting for Billions of Burgers:
McDonald's   184

■ *Learning from Business Blunders   160*

■ *Putting Accountability Back into Public
Accounting   162*

■ *How to Read an Annual Report   172*

Chapter 8 Banking and Securities   186

Behind the **Scenes:** Charles Schwab Takes
on the Titans of Wall
Street   187

Money and Financial Institutions   187
   Characteristics and Types of Money   188
      Checking and Savings Accounts   188
      Credit Cards, Debit Cards, and Smart Cards   188
   Financial Institutions and Services   189
      Deposit and Nondeposit Financial Institutions   189
      Loans   190
      Electronic Banking   190
   Bank Safety and Regulation   191
   The Evolving U.S. Banking Environment   191

Types of Securities Investments   193
   Stocks   193
      Common Stock   193
      Preferred Stock   193
   Bonds   193
      Corporate Bonds   194
      U.S. Government Securities and Municipal Bonds   195
   Mutual Funds   195

Securities Markets   197
   Evolution of Securities Markets   197
   Regulation of Securities Markets   198
      SEC Filing and Disclosure Requirements   199
      Securities Fraud   199

Investment Strategies and Techniques   200
   Establishing Investment Objectives   200
   Creating an Investment Portfolio   201
   Buying and Selling Securities   201
      Securities Brokers   201
      Orders to Buy and Sell Securities   202
   Analyzing Financial News   202
      Watching Market Indexes and Averages   203
      Interpreting the Financial News   204

SUMMARY OF LEARNING OBJECTIVES   207

Behind the **Scenes:** Schwab Innovates All
the Way Back to Its
Roots   208

KEY TERMS   209

TEST YOUR KNOWLEDGE   210

PRACTICE YOUR KNOWLEDGE   210

EXPAND YOUR KNOWLEDGE   211

SEE IT ON THE WEB   211
    Tour the U.S. Treasury   211
    Stock Up at the NYSE   211
    Invest Wisely—Like a Fool   212
COMPANION WEBSITE   212
VIDEO CASE: **Learn More to Earn More with Motley Fool** 212
▪ *Is an Index Fund Right for Your Financial Future?*   196
▪ *Learning from Business Blunders*   200
▪ *Put Your Money Where Your Mouse Is*   203

PART 4
Creating and Satisfying Customers   213

Chapter 9   Marketing Concepts and Strategies   213

Behind the **Scenes:** Toyota Scion: Connecting with a New Generation of Car Buyers   214

Marketing in a Changing World   215
  The Role of Marketing in Society   216
    Needs and Wants   216
    Exchanges and Transactions   216
    The Four Utilities   216
  The Marketing Concept   217
  Marketing on the Leading Edge   218
    Involving the Customer in the Marketing Process   218
    Making Marketing More Accountable   219
    Balancing Technology and the Human Touch   219
    Marketing with Greater Concern for Ethics and Etiquette   220
Understanding Today's Customers   221
  The Consumer Decision Process   222
  The Organizational Customer Decision Process   223
  Marketing Research and Market Intelligence   224
Planning Your Marketing Strategies   225
  Step 1: Examining Your Current Marketing Situation   225
    Reviewing Performance   226
    Evaluating Competition   226
    Examining Internal Strengths and Weaknesses   226
    Analyzing the External Environment   226
  Step 2: Assessing Your Opportunities and Setting Your Objectives   227
  Step 3: Developing Your Marketing Strategy   228
    Dividing Markets into Segments   228
    Choosing Your Target Markets   229
    Positioning Your Product   230
    Developing Your Marketing Mix   231

SUMMARY OF LEARNING OBJECTIVES   236

Behind the **Scenes:** Scion's New-Generation Marketing Strategy Pays Off   237

KEY TERMS   238

TEST YOUR KNOWLEDGE   238

PRACTICE YOUR KNOWLEDGE   239

EXPAND YOUR KNOWLEDGE   239

SEE IT ON THE WEB   240
    Join the Conversation on Social Media   240
    Get Some Marketing Power   240
    Learn to Think Like Your Customers   240
COMPANION WEBSITE   240
VIDEO CASE: **In Consumers' Shoes: Skechers USA   240**
▪ *Mining Your Deepest Secrets*   220
▪ *Learning from Business Blunders*   223
▪ *Questionable Marketing Tactics on Campus*   234

Chapter 10   Products and Pricing   242

Behind the **Scenes:** Allergan Stumbles onto a Billion-Dollar Product   243

Characteristics of Products   243
  Types of Products   244
    Service Products   244
    Consumer Products   244
    Industrial and Commercial Products   245
  The Product Life Cycle   246
    Introduction   247
    Growth   248
    Maturity   248
    Decline   248
  Product Enhancements and Makeovers   248
The New-Product Development Process   249
Product Identities   251
  Brand Name Selection   251
  Brand Sponsorship   252
  Packaging   252
  Labeling   252
Product-Line and Product-Mix Strategies   253
  Product Lines   253
  Product Mix   253
  Product Expansion Strategies   255
  Product Strategies for International Markets   256
Pricing Strategies   256
  Cost-Based Pricing   257
  Price-Based Pricing   258
  Optimal Pricing   259
  Skim Pricing   260
  Penetration Pricing   260
  Loss-Leader Pricing   260
  Auction Pricing   261
  Price Adjustment Strategies   261
    Price Discounts   261
    Bundling   261
    Dynamic Pricing   262

SUMMARY OF LEARNING OBJECTIVES   262

Behind the **Scenes:** Allergan Puts a New Face on Cosmetic Medicine   263

KEY TERMS   264

TEST YOUR KNOWLEDGE   264

PRACTICE YOUR KNOWLEDGE   264

EXPAND YOUR KNOWLEDGE   265

SEE IT ON THE WEB   266
   Be a Sharp Shopper   266
   Protect Your Trademark   266
   Uncover Hidden Costs   266
COMPANION WEBSITE   266
VIDEO CASE: Sending Products into Space: MCCI   266
■ *Designing Safer Products*   *247*
■ *Learning from Business Blunders*   *248*
   ■   *Ringing Up Business in Creative New Ways*   *250*

Chapter 11   Distribution and Customer Communication   268

Behind the **Scenes:**   Costco Makes the Good Life More Affordable   269
Developing Distribution Strategies   269
   Understanding the Role of Marketing Intermediaries   *270*
      Wholesalers   *270*
      Retailers   *271*
   Selecting Your Marketing Channels   *275*
      Channel Length   *276*
      Market Coverage   *276*
      Cost   *277*
      Control   *277*
      Channel Conflict   *277*
   Managing Physical Distribution   *277*
Developing Customer Communication Strategies   *278*
   Setting Your Communication Goals   *279*
   Defining Your Message   *279*
   Deciding on Your Market Approach   *281*
   Selecting Your Communication Mix   *281*
      Personal Selling   *281*
      Advertising   *282*
      Direct Marketing   *284*
      Sales Promotion   *286*
      Public Relations   *287*
      Social Media   *287*
      Postsales Communication   *288*
   Respecting Ethics, Etiquette, and Regulations   *289*
SUMMARY OF LEARNING OBJECTIVES   290

Behind the **Scenes:**   Costco Pushes Its Supply Chain to Satisfy Customers   291

KEY TERMS   292
TEST YOUR KNOWLEDGE   292
PRACTICE YOUR KNOWLEDGE   293
EXPAND YOUR KNOWLEDGE   293
SEE IT ON THE WEB   294
   Explore the World of Wholesaling   294
   Learn the Consumer Marketing Laws   294
   See How the Pros Put Marketing to Work   294
COMPANION WEBSITE   294
VIDEO CASE: Revving Up Promotion: BMW Motorcycles   295
■ *Learning from Business Blunders*   *279*
■ *Hey! Where Did Everybody Go?*   *285*

PART 5
Leading and Supporting Employees   296

Chapter 12   Management Functions and Skills   296

Behind the **Scenes:** Wegmans Satisfies Customers by Putting Employees First   297
The Four Basic Functions of Management   297
   The Planning Function   *298*
      Understanding the Strategic Planning Process   *298*
      Planning for a Crisis   *304*
   The Organizing Function   *304*
   The Leading Function   *304*
      Developing an Effective Leadership Style   *307*
      Coaching and Mentoring   *308*
      Managing Change   *309*
      Building a Positive Organizational Culture   *310*
   The Controlling Function   *311*
Management Skills   312
   Interpersonal Skills   *312*
   Technical Skills   *313*
   Conceptual Skills   *313*
   Decision-Making Skills   *314*
SUMMARY OF LEARNING OBJECTIVES   315

Behind the **Scenes:** Customers Believe in Wegmans Because Wegmans Believes in Its Employees   316

KEY TERMS   317
TEST YOUR KNOWLEDGE   317
PRACTICE YOUR KNOWLEDGE   317
EXPAND YOUR KNOWLEDGE   318
SEE IT ON THE WEB   319
   Become a Better Manager   319
   Linking to Organizational Change   319
   Learn from the Best   319
COMPANION WEBSITE   319
VIDEO CASE: Creative Management: Creative Age Publications   319
■ *Do You Have What It Takes to Be a Leader?*   *306*
■ *Creating the Ideal Culture in Your Company*   *310*
■ *Learning from Business Blunders*   *312*

Chapter 13   Organization, Teamwork, and Motivation   321

Behind the **Scenes:** Reinventing the Retail Experience at The Container Store   322
Designing an Effective Organization Structure   322
   Identifying Job Responsibilities   *323*
   Defining the Chain of Command   *324*
   Organizing the Workforce   *326*
      Functional Structures   *326*
      Divisional Structures   *327*
      Matrix Structures   *327*
      Network Structures   *327*
      Hybrid Structures   *328*

Working in Teams   328
  What Is a Team?   328
  Types of Teams   329
  Advantages and Disadvantages of Working in Teams   329
  Characteristics of Effective Teams   330
  Stages of Team Development   332
  Team Conflict   333
    Causes of Team Conflict   333
    Solutions to Team Conflict   334
  Productive Team Meetings   334
Motivating Employees   335
  What Is Motivation?   335
  Theories of Motivation   336
    Maslow's Hierarchy of Needs   336
    Herzberg's Two-Factor Theory   337
    Theory X, Theory Y, and Theory Z   338
    Equity Theory   338
    Expectancy Theory   339
  Motivational Strategies   340
    Setting Goals   340
    Reinforcing Behavior   340
SUMMARY OF LEARNING OBJECTIVES   342

Behind the Scenes: Teaming Up for Success at The Container Store   343

KEY TERMS   344

TEST YOUR KNOWLEDGE   344

PRACTICE YOUR KNOWLEDGE   345

EXPAND YOUR KNOWLEDGE   345

SEE IT ON THE WEB   346
  Learn from Leaders in Collaborative Work   346
  Be Direct   346
  Resolve Conflict Like a Pro   346

COMPANION WEBSITE   346

VIDEO CASE: **Juicing Up the Organization: Nantucket Nectars**   346

  ▪ *Learning from Business Blunders*   326

  ▪ *Which Theory Will Solve the Problem of Employee Theft?*   339

Chapter 14 Human Resources   348

Behind the Scenes: Brewing Up People Policies for Chainwide Success   349

Keeping Pace with Today's Workforce   349
  Staffing Challenges   350
  Demographic Challenges   350
    Workforce Diversity   351
    Diversity Initiatives   353
  Alternative Work Arrangements   353
Planning for a Company's Staffing Needs   354
  Forecasting Supply and Demand   354
  Evaluating Job Requirements   355

Recruiting, Hiring, and Training New Employees   355
  The Hiring Process   357
  Training and Development   358
Appraising Employee Performance   360
Administering Compensation and Employee Benefits   362
  Salaries and Wages   362
  Incentive Programs   363
  Employee Benefits and Services   364
    Insurance   364
    Retirement Benefits   365
    Stock Options   366
    Family Benefits   367
    Other Employee Benefits   368
Overseeing Changes in Employment Status   368
  Promoting and Reassigning Employees   368
  Terminating Employees   369
  Retiring Employees   369
Working with Labor Unions   369
  Union Organization   370
  The Collective Bargaining Process   371
  The Labor Movement Today   372
SUMMARY OF LEARNING OBJECTIVES   373

Behind the Scenes: Perking Up the Perfect Blend at Starbucks   374

KEY TERMS   375

TEST YOUR KNOWLEDGE   376

PRACTICE YOUR KNOWLEDGE   376

EXPAND YOUR KNOWLEDGE   377

SEE IT ON THE WEB   377
  Explore the Latest Workforce Management Ideas   377
  Digging Deeper at the Bureau of Labor Statistics   378
  Maximizing Your Earning Potential   378

COMPANION WEBSITE   378

VIDEO CASE: **Channeling Human Resources at Showtime**   378

  ▪ *Learning from Business Blunders*   355

  ▪ *When Employees Turn on Each Other*   358

  ▪ *Somebody's Watching (and Listening and Reading and Monitoring and Recording)*   362

Appendixes

Appendix A   The U.S. Legal System and Business Law   379

Appendix B   Personal Finance: Getting Set for Life   388

References   405
Glossary   427
Name/Organization/Brand/Company Index   439
Subject Index   443

Preface

Meeting the real-life needs of business educators with unparalleled instructional support

Constant Currency: Only with *Business in Action with Real-Time Updates*

Business in Action with Real-Time Updates, Fourth Edition, integrates print and online media in unprecedented ways to create a standout instructional package. Until now, it was virtually impossible to keep text content up to date and to provide instructors with lecture material on late-breaking business events and trends. A unique new electronic update service, *Business in Action with Real-Time Updates,* uses web and newsfeed technologies to meet both challenges. First, the authors provide weekly online updates to key content areas, so students and instructors are always kept up to date on important topics. At strategic points in every chapter, students are directed to the "Real-Time Updates" website to learn about the latest news or a major event pertaining to a particular aspect of the chapter.

Second, when important, late-breaking events occur that affect the world of business, the authors quickly prepare podcasts for students to download from the site and accompanying PowerPoints for instructors to use immediately. The PowerPoints, accompanied by lecture notes, are delivered via newsfeed to instructors' desktops.

The website's newsfeeds are tied directly to the textbook, so the online content is an integral part of the text itself, not just an end-of-chapter exercise. The instructor website (www.prenhall.com/bovée) is also a blog, with all the interactive immediacy that blogging offers. If you want to make a suggestion or are having a problem about the presentation of a concept, simply go to the website and send a comment or a query to the authors.

Faster Assessment and Remediation: MyIntroBusinessLab.com

MyIntroBusinessLab.com simplifies the assessment experience for instructors and improves the remediation experience for students.

For instructors, MyIntroBusinessLab provides a rich and flexible set of course materials, along with course-management tools that make it easy to deliver all or a portion of your course online:

- *Spend less time grading and more time teaching.* With the powerful Homework and Test Manager, it's easy to create, import, and manage online homework assignments, quizzes, and tests that are automatically graded. Create assignments from

The unique Real-Time Updates feature, available only with Business in Action, *offers automated online delivery of new content throughout the course.*

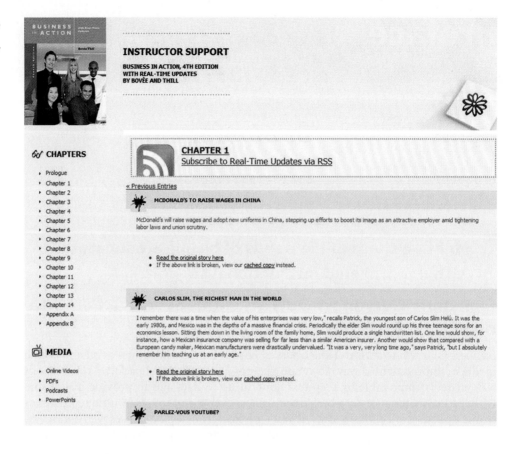

online exercises directly correlated to the textbook. You can choose from a wide range of assignment options, including time limits, proctoring, and maximum number of attempts allowed.

- *Automatically track students' progress.* Comprehensive gradebook tracking lets you monitor your students' results on tests, homework, and tutorials and gives you control over managing results and calculating grades. The MyIntroBusinessLab Gradebook provides a number of views of student data and gives you the flexibility to weight assignments, select which attempts to include when calculating scores, and omit or delete results for individual assignments. All grades can be exported to a spreadsheet, too.

- *Easily manage multiple sections and work with TAs.* MyIntroBusinessLab Coordinator Courses help you manage multiple sections and work with multiple TAs. After your course is set up, it can be copied to create sections or "member courses." Changes to the Coordinator Course ripple down to all members, so changes need to be made only once.

For students, MyIntroBusinessLab provides a personalized interactive learning environment where they can learn at their own pace and measure their progress along the way:

- *Get unlimited opportunities for practice and mastery.* Homework and practice questions are correlated to the textbook. Helpful feedback coaches students whenever they enter incorrect answers.

- *Create a self-paced learning plan.* MyIntroBusinessLab generates a personalized study plan for each student based on his or her test results, and the study plan links directly to interactive, tutorial exercises for topics the student hasn't yet mastered. Students can monitor their own progress, letting them see at a glance exactly which topics they need to practice.

What's New in This Edition

■ *Streamlined coverage of management topics.* Current adopters of *Business in Action* asked us to streamline the coverage of management and business administration topics, both to free up time for other subject areas and to reduce the overlap with other business courses. We responded by compressing the four management-related chapters in the previous edition into three chapters in this edition. The chapters still provide a solid introduction to management skills, strategic planning, organization, teamwork, motivation, and human resources, but they do so in a more efficient manner, with greater emphasis on the "big picture."

■ *Adaptable coverage of marketing topics.* You also asked for some flexibility in covering the marketing area, so we created a new introductory marketing chapter that can serve as standalone coverage for the entire topic. This approach can free up time to concentrate on other subject areas or work on special projects, such as business plans or service projects. Instructors who wish to explore marketing in greater depth can continue with the two additional marketing chapters, one that covers products and pricing and one that covers distribution and customer communication.

■ *"How This Affects You" theme.* Few instructional efforts pay off as big as helping students engage with the content on a personal level. Toward that end, the fourth edition weaves the theme of "How This Affects You" throughout the text, in both critical thinking checkpoints and end-of-chapter analysis questions. As one example, students learn the connection between decisions made by the Federal Reserve Bank and the size of the houses they'll be able to buy after graduation.

■ *Unique new chapter on business systems.* This new chapter explains the importance of systems thinking and introduces students to three essential business systems: the value chain, supply chain management (including an overview of the production of goods and services), and e-commerce.

■ *Thorough content updates.* The fourth edition covers the latest thinking and best practices in business today. For example, Chapter 2 covers the ongoing controversy about corporate social responsibility, Chapter 9 discusses the shift in thinking from unilateral "promotion" to bilateral "customer communication" as part of the marketing mix, and Chapter 11 explains how leading-edge companies are incorporating the newest social media in their marketing strategies.

A Complete Teaching and Learning Solution

Business in Action offers a complete set of pedagogical features that simplify teaching, promote active learning, and stimulate critical thinking. These components work together at four levels to provide seamless coverage of vital knowledge and skills:

■ *Previewing.* Each chapter prepares students with clear learning objectives and a brief "Behind the Scenes" vignette featuring a company facing a critical challenge that involves the business concepts the student is about to learn.

■ *Developing.* Chapter content develops, explains, and elaborates on concepts with a concise, carefully organized presentation of textual and visual material. "How This Affects You" checkpoints help students understand how their own lives are influenced by the world of business—and how they can apply these ideas to their careers.

■ *Enhancing.* Compelling examples from a carefully chosen selection of companies bring business concepts to life. Special feature boxes add additional depth to key concepts by exploring extended examples or intriguing business issues and controversies.

■ *Reinforcing.* The case study solution to the "Behind the Scenes" chapter-opening vignette shows students how each company met its challenge by applying concepts covered in the chapter. An extensive array of questions, exercises, and activities then help students "take ownership" of chapter principles through review, analysis, and application.

At every stage of the learning experience, *Business in Action* provides the tools that instructors and students need in order to succeed (see table following page).

Building on Proven Pedagogy

Business in Action with Real-Time Updates provides a wealth of features that facilitate both guided instruction and students' own reading (see table on page xx).

Additional Teaching and Learning Support

OneKey Online Courses

OneKey offers the best teaching and learning online resources in one place, with all the tools and resources that instructors need in order to plan and administer courses. OneKey also offers students anytime, anywhere access to online course material, including Learning Modules (section reviews, learning activities, and pretests and posttests), PowerPoints, and Research Navigator (four exclusive databases of reliable source content to help students understand the research process and complete assignments).

Conveniently organized by textbook chapter, these compiled resources save time and help students reinforce and apply what they have learned. Use OneKey for convenience, simplicity, and success. *OneKey is available in three course-management platforms: Blackboard, CourseCompass, and WebCT.*

Instructor's Resource Center Available Online, in OneKey, or on CD-ROM

The Instructor's Resource Center, available on CD, at www.prenhall.com/irc, or in your OneKey online course, provides presentation materials and other classroom resources. Instructors can collect the materials, edit them to create powerful class lectures, and upload them to an online course-management system.

The Instructor's Resource Center offers a variety of faculty resources:

- **PowerPoints**

  Choose from a traditional set of PowerPoints or Classroom Response System (CRS) PowerPoints. CRS is a wireless polling system that enables instructors to pose questions to students in a PowerPoint presentation, record results, and display those results instantly in the classroom. Students answer the questions using a clicker that can be bundled with the textbook.

- **TestGen Test-Generating Software**

  The test bank contains approximately 100 questions per chapter, including true/false, multiple choice, fill-in, and essay questions.

- **Instructor's Manual**

  The Instructor's Manual makes it easy to plan lectures and incorporate all resources offered with *Business in Action*. Each chapter contains a chapter overview, a variety of classroom activities, answers to all end-of-chapter exercises, answers to all box feature questions, and answers to the video case.

- **Test Item File**

  Microsoft Word files with test bank questions.

Companion Website

The text website at www.prenhall.com/bovée features chapter quizzes and PowerPoints, which are available for review or can be conveniently printed three to a page for in-class note taking.

FEATURES THAT HELP STUDENTS BUILD ESSENTIAL KNOWLEDGE AND SKILLS	PREVIEWING	DEVELOPING	ENHANCING	REINFORCING
Learning Objectives (beginning of chapter)	•			
Behind the Scenes vignettes (beginning of chapter)	•			
Concise presentations of fundamentals (within chapter)		•		
How This Affects You checkpoints (within chapter)		•		
Real-life examples (within chapter)			•	
Highlight boxes (within chapter)			•	
Learning from Business Blunders (within chapter)			•	
Key term definitions (within chapter)				•
Behind the Scenes case study solution (end of chapter)				•
Summary of Learning Objectives (end of chapter)				•
Test Your Knowledge questions (end of chapter)				•
Apply Your Knowledge questions (end of chapter)				•
Practice Your Knowledge activities and exercises (end of chapter)				•
Expand Your Knowledge web resources (end of chapter/online)				•
Video Cases (end of chapter)				•
Business Plan Pro exercises (online)				•

Study Guide

The study guide includes review questions and study quizzes, including multiple-choice, true/false, matching, and critical thinking questions. Suggested answers to the review questions and quizzes are included.

VangoNotes.com

Students can study on the go with VangoNotes—chapter reviews from this text in downloadable MP3 format. Students can purchase VangoNotes for the entire textbook or for individual chapters. For each chapter, VangoNotes contains:

- **Big Ideas** The "need to know" for each chapter.
- **Key Terms** Audio "flashcards" to help students review key concepts and terms.
- **Rapid Review** A quick drill session—to use right before taking a test.

FEATURE	MAJOR BENEFITS	EXAMPLES
Learning Objectives	Measurable learning objectives prepare students by framing the content of each chapter and establishing instructional expectations.	p. 1, 110, 296
Behind the Scenes chapter-opening vignette	Chapter-opening vignette offers a slice-of-life look at a successful manager or entrepreneur; over two-thirds of the vignettes are new in this edition, including MTV's launch in Africa, Pepsi's troubles in India, Carvin Guitar's mass customization strategy, and Google's acquisition of DoubleClick.	p. 29, 81, 322
Behind the Scenes chapter-closing case study	Each chapter ends with a case that expands on the chapter-opening vignette. The case includes three critical-thinking questions that require students to apply the concepts covered in the text. Plus, students can find out more about the company featured in the case by completing the "Learn More Online" exercise.	p. 50, 105, 343
Special highlight boxes	Make the world of business come alive with current examples to further enhance student learning. Each box includes two critical-thinking questions that are ideal for developing team or individual problem-solving skills.	p. 5, 31, 247
Learning from Business Blunders	Finds the lesson in such errors as Northwest Airlines inadvertently insulting laid-off employees, McDonald's giving away virus-infected music players, and Amp'd Mobile growing itself right into bankruptcy.	p. 21, 47, 101
How This Affects You checkpoints	Present students with several critical-thinking questions to help them understand how chapter material applies to their personal and professional lives.	p. 17, 62, 314
Summary of Learning Objectives	Briefly review the chapter material that addresses each learning objective, giving students an effective way to judge their understanding and retention of chapter content.	p. 49, 179, 342
Sharpening Your Communication Skills	Communication skills are one of the top concerns among today's hiring managers; this exercise lets students practice listening, writing, and speaking in a variety of real-life scenarios.	p. 77, 239, 264
Building Your Team Skills	Teaches students important team skills, such as brainstorming, collaborative decision making, developing a consensus, debating, role playing, and resolving conflict.	p. 52, 329, 376
Improving Your Tech Insights	Introduces students to such revolutionary developments as nanotechnology, location and tracking technologies, and assistive technologies for people with disabilities; students are directed to summarize an important technical development and explain its business implications.	p. 77, 107, 318
Discovering Career Opportunities	Gives students the opportunity to explore career resources on campus, observe businesspeople on their jobs, interview businesspeople, and perform self-evaluations to assess their own career skills and interests.	p. 25, 78, 345
Developing Your Research Skills	Familiarizes students with a wide variety of business reference material and offers practice in developing research skills.	p. 53, 131, 211
See It on the Web	Acquaints students with the wealth of information on the web that relates to the content of each chapter; includes online research and analysis activities.	p. 54, 131, 346
Video Case	Takes students behind the scenes at a wide variety of small, medium, and large companies; each includes a synopsis, five discussion questions, and an online exploration exercise.	p. 132, 212, 240

Videos

Exciting and relevant custom videos are available to instructors to expand upon themes discussed in the chapters. Video discussion questions are available in the student text and answers are found in the Instructor's Manual.

CourseSmart eTextbook

CourseSmart Textbooks Online is an exciting new choice for students looking to save money. As an alternative to purchasing the print textbook, students can subscribe to the same content online and save up to 50 percent off the suggested list price of the print text. With a CourseSmart eTextbook, students can search the text, make notes online, print out reading assignments that incorporate lecture notes, and bookmark important passages for later review. For more information, or to subscribe to the CourseSmart eTextbook, visit www.coursesmart.com.

Personal Acknowledgments

A very special acknowledgment goes to George Dovel, whose superb editorial skills, distinguished background, and wealth of business experience assured this project of clarity and completeness. Recognition and thanks go to Jackie Estrada for her outstanding skills and excellent attention to details. Paul Staley's professionalism and keen eye for quality were invaluable.

The supplements package for *Business in Action with Real-Time Updates* has benefited from the able contributions of numerous individuals. We would like to express our thanks to them for creating a superb set of instructional supplements.

We want to extend our warmest appreciation to the devoted professionals at Prentice Hall. They include Jerome Grant, president; Natalie Anderson, publisher; Jodi McPherson, executive editor; Claudia Fernandes, project manager; Andrew Watts, marketing manager; all of Prentice Hall Business Publishing; and the outstanding Prentice Hall sales representatives. Finally, we thank Cynthia Zonneveld, senior managing editor of production; Jonathan Boylan, senior art director; and Lynne Breitfeller, production project manager, for their dedication; and we are grateful to Doug Bell, senior production editor at GGS Book Services; and Charles Morris, permissions supervisor, for their superb work.

Courtland L. Bovée

John V. Thill

Prologue

Are You Ready for Success?

Your Future in Business Starts Right Now

You might not be thinking about your long-term career path as you dive into this business course, but this is actually the perfect time to start planning and preparing. Even though you may not have decided which area of business interests you the most, it's never too early to start accumulating the skills, experiences, and insights that will give you a competitive advantage when it's time to enter (or reenter) the business job market. By thinking ahead about the qualifications you'd like to have on your résumé when you graduate, you can select courses, seek out part-time employment and internship opportunities, and pursue extracurricular activities that will give you the professional profile that top employers look for.

This Prologue offers an overview of all the steps you'll need to take as you research, plan, and prepare for the job search process. First you'll answer some questions that will help you figure out just what you'd like to do in the world of business, then you'll find brief overviews of the major career categories within business. The two sections following that offer up-to-date advice on preparing your résumé and getting ready for job interviews. The final section offers some tips on keeping your career momentum going after you join the workforce.

Looking Ahead to Your Career

Finding the right job at every stage of your career is a lifelong process of seeking the best fit between what you want to do and what employers are willing to pay you to do. For instance, if money is more important to you than anything else, you can certainly pursue jobs that promise high pay; just be aware that most of these jobs require years of experience, and many produce a lot of stress, require frequent travel, or have other drawbacks you'll want to consider. In contrast, if location, lifestyle, intriguing work, or other factors are more important to you, you may well have to sacrifice some level of pay to achieve them. The important thing is to know what you want to do, what you have to offer, and how to make yourself more attractive to employers.

What Do You Want to Do?

Economic necessities and the vagaries of the marketplace will influence much of what happens in your career, of course; nevertheless, it's wise to start your employment search by examining your own values and interests. Identify what you want to do first, then see whether you can find a position that satisfies you at a personal level while also meeting your financial needs.

■ *What would you like to do every day?* Research occupations that interest you. Find out what people really do every day. Ask friends, relatives, or alumni from your school. Read interviews with people in various professions to get a sense of what their careers are like.

- *How would you like to work?* Consider how much independence you want on the job, how much variety you like, and whether you prefer to work with products, machines, people, ideas, figures, or some combination thereof. Constant change or a predictable role?

- *What specific compensation do you expect?* What do you hope to earn in your first year? What's your ultimate earnings goal? Are you willing to settle for less money in order to do something you really love?

- *Can you establish some general career goals?* Consider where you'd like to start, where you'd like to go from there, and the ultimate position you'd like to attain.

- *What size company would you prefer?* Do you like the idea of working for a small, entrepreneurial operation or a large corporation?

- *What sort of corporate culture are you most comfortable with?* Would you be happy in a formal hierarchy with clear reporting relationships? Or do you prefer less structure? Do you like a competitive environment?

- *What location would you like?* Would you like to work in a city, a suburb, a small town, an industrial area, or an uptown setting? Do you favor a particular part of the country? Another country?

What Do You Have to Offer?

Knowing what you *want* to do is one thing. Knowing what you *can* do is another. You may already have a good idea of what you can offer employers. If not, some brainstorming can help you identify your skills, interests, and characteristics. Start by jotting down 10 achievements you're proud of, such as learning to ski, taking a prize-winning photo, tutoring a child, or editing your school paper. Think carefully about what specific skills these achievements demanded of you. For example, leadership skills, speaking ability, and artistic talent may have helped you coordinate a winning presentation to your school's administration. As you analyze your achievements, you'll begin to recognize a pattern of skills. Which of them might be valuable to potential employers?

Next, look at your educational preparation, work experience, and extracurricular activities. What do your knowledge and experience qualify you to do? What have you learned from volunteer work or class projects that could benefit you on the job? Have you held any offices, won any awards or scholarships, mastered a second language?

Take stock of your personal characteristics. Are you aggressive, a born leader? Or would you rather follow? Are you outgoing, articulate, great with people? Or do you prefer working alone? Make a list of what you believe are your four or five most important qualities. Ask a relative or friend to rate your traits as well.

If you're having difficulty figuring out your interests, characteristics, or capabilities, consult your college placement office. Many campuses administer a variety of tests to help you identify interests, aptitudes, and personality traits. These tests won't reveal your "perfect" job, but they'll help you focus on the types of work best suited to your personality.

How Can You Make Yourself More Valuable?

While you're figuring out what you want from a job and what you can offer an employer, you can take positive steps toward actually building your career. You can do a lot before you graduate from college and even while you are seeking employment:

- *Keep an employment portfolio.* Collect anything that shows your ability to perform, whether it's in school, on the job, or in other venues. Your portfolio is a great resource for writing your résumé, and it gives employers tangible evidence of your professionalism. An *e-portfolio* is a multimedia presentation of your skills and experiences (see Exhibit 1).[1] Think of it as a website that contains your résumé, work samples, letters of recommendation, articles you may have written, and other information about you and your skills. Be creative. For example, a student who was pursuing a degree in meteorology added a video clip of himself delivering a

EXHIBIT I
Professional Portfolio
Claudia Volpi, a creative director and writer based in Santa Monica, California, uses Portfolios.com to host her professional portfolio. From the thumbnail images on the front page, viewers can click to see samples of her work, such as this television commercial. They can also click to learn more about her background and qualifications.

weather forecast.[2] The portfolio can be burned on a CD-ROM for physical distribution or, more commonly, posted online—whether it's a personal website, your college's site (if student pages are available), or a networking site such as www.collegegrad.com or www.portfolios.com.

- *Take interim assignments.* As you search for a permanent job, consider temporary jobs, freelance work, or internships. These temporary assignments not only help you gain valuable experience and relevant contacts but also provide you with important references and with items for your portfolio.[3] Considering applying your talents to *crowdsourcing* projects, in which companies and nonprofit organizations invite the public to contribute solutions to various challenges. For example, Fellowforce (www.fellowforce.com) posts projects involving advertising, business writing, photography, graphic design, programming, strategy development, and other skills.[4] Even if your contributions aren't chosen, you still have solutions to real business problems that you can show to potential employers as examples of your work.

- *Continue to polish and update your skills.* Join networks of professional colleagues and friends who can help you keep up with your occupation and industry. Many professional societies have student chapters or offer students discounted memberships. Take courses and pursue other educational or life experiences that would be hard to get while working full-time.

Seeking Employment Opportunities and Information

Whether your major is business, biology, or political science, once you know what you want and what you have to offer, you can start finding an employer to match. If you haven't already committed yourself to any particular career field, review the career tables in the *Occupational Outlook Handbook,* a nationally recognized source of career information published by the U.S. Bureau of Labor Statistics. Revised every two years, the handbook (available in print and online at www.bls.gov/oco) describes what workers do on the job, working conditions, the training and education needed, earnings, and expected job prospects in a wide range of occupations.[5]

Here is a brief overview of the future outlook for a number of careers in business:

- *Careers in management.* Today's business environment requires the skills of effective managers to reduce costs, streamline operations, develop marketing strategies, and supervise workers. As you'll read in Chapter 12, managers perform four basic functions: planning, organizing, leading, and controlling. Facing increased competition, many businesses are becoming more dependent on the expertise of outside management consultants—one of the fastest-growing occupations of all jobs. Outside management consultants perform many important tasks, but chief among them is evaluating operating conditions and making recommendations to improve effectiveness. To find out more about what you can do with a degree in management and the typical courses management majors take, log on to the Prentice Hall Student Success SuperSite at www.prenhall.com/success/MajorExp/mgmt.html.

- *Careers in human resources.* As Chapter 14 discusses, human resources managers plan and direct human resource activities that include recruiting, training and development, compensation and benefits, employee and labor relations, and health and safety. Additionally, human resources managers develop and implement human resources systems and practices to accommodate a firm's strategy and to motivate and manage diverse workforces. Large numbers of job openings are expected in the human resources field in the near future. Efforts to recruit quality employees and to provide more employee training programs should create new human resources positions. With a vast supply of qualified workers and new college graduates, however, the job market for human resources is likely to remain competitive.

- *Careers in computers and information systems.* Job opportunities abound for trained information technology workers. As competition and advanced technologies force companies to upgrade and improve their computer systems, the number of computer-related positions continues to escalate. Within the computer field, only two categories of jobs are expected to decrease: computer operators and data-entry clerks. More user-friendly computer software has greatly reduced the need for operators and data-entry processors, but displaced workers who keep up with changing technology should have few problems moving into other areas of computer support. To find out more about careers in computer science and information systems, log on to the Prentice Hall Student Success SuperSite at www.prenhall.com/success/MajorExp/CSImajors.html, then explore the various specialties listed.

- *Careers in sales and marketing.* Increasing competition in products and services should create greater needs for effective sales and marketing personnel in the future. Employment opportunities for retail salespersons look good because of the need to replace the large number of workers who transfer to other occupations or leave the workforce each year. Opportunities for part-time work should be abundant. Employment for insurance and real estate agents, however, is expected to grow more slowly than average. Computer technology will allow established agents to increase their sales volume and eliminate the need for additional marketing personnel in these fields. For additional information on the types of courses marketing majors take and what you can do with a degree in marketing see

Chapters 9 through 11 and log on to the Prentice Hall Student Success SuperSite at www.prenhall.com/success/MajorExp/mktg.html.

- *Careers in finance and accounting.* As Chapters 7 and 8 point out, accountants and financial managers are needed in every industry. Most positions in finance and accounting are expected to grow as fast as the average for all occupations in the near future, as continued growth in the economy and population is expected to create more demand for trained financial personnel. To find out more about careers in finance and accounting, log on to the Prentice Hall Student Success SuperSite at www.prenhall.com/success/MajorExp/acct.html, and select finance or accounting.

- *Careers in economics.* As Chapter 1 discusses, economists study how society distributes scarce resources such as land, labor, raw materials, and machinery to produce goods and services. They conduct research, collect and analyze data, monitor economic trends, and develop forecasts. Economists are needed in many industries and spend time applying economic theory to analyze issues that are important to their firms. For example, they might analyze the effects of global economic activity on the demand for the company's product, conduct a cost-benefit analysis of the projects the company is considering, or determine the effects of government regulations or taxes on the company. Employment of economists is expected to grow about as fast as the average for all occupations, with the best opportunities in private industry—especially research, testing, and consulting firms—as more companies contract out for economic research services. To find out more about what you can do with a degree in economics and the typical courses economics majors take, log on to the Prentice Hall Student Success SuperSite at www.prenhall.com/success/MajorExp/econ.html.

- *Careers in communications.* As businesses recognize the need for effective communications with their customers and the public, employment of communications personnel is expected to grow as fast or faster than the average for all occupations in the near future. Recent college graduates may face keen competition for entry positions in communications as the number of applicants is expected to exceed the number of job openings. Newly created jobs in the ever-expanding computer world—such as graphic designers for websites or technical writers for instruction manuals—are expected to improve the career outlook for new communications graduates.

Exhibit 2 lists the business occupations (including management positions) that are projected to grow the fastest between now and 2014. Keep in mind that most of the high-growth jobs require college degrees, and many of the hottest jobs in today's business world demand technological and computer skills. Even if you're interested in finance, human resources, or marketing positions, you'll need basic computer skills to snare the best jobs in your desired field of work.

Staying Abreast of Business and Financial News

Thanks to the Internet, staying on top of business news is easy today. In fact, your biggest challenge will be selecting new material from the many available sources. To help you get started, here is a selection of periodical websites that offer business news (in some cases, you need to be a subscriber to access all of the material, including archives):

- *Wall Street Journal:* http://online.wsj.com/public/us
- *New York Times:* www.nyt.com
- *BusinessWeek:* www.businessweek.com
- *Business 2.0:* www.business2.com
- *Fast Company:* www.fastcompany.com
- *Fortune:* www.fortune.com
- *Forbes:* www.forbes.com

EXHIBIT 2 The 25 Fastest-Growing Business Occupations

According to government estimates, these 25 business occupations are expected to grow the fastest between 2004 and 2014. (The list does not include technical specialties such as engineering or computer programming.)

JOB CATEGORY	EMPLOYMENT 2004 (THOUSANDS)	EMPLOYMENT 2014 (THOUSANDS)	PERCENT INCREASE
Employment, recruitment, and placement specialists	182	237	30.5
Business operation specialists	897	1,139	27.0
Computer and information systems managers	280	353	25.9
Personal financial advisors	158	199	25.9
Training and development managers	37	47	25.9
Human resources, training, and labor relations specialists	166	206	24.1
Actuaries	18	22	23.2
Public relations specialists	188	231	22.9
Appraisers and assessors of real estate	102	125	22.8
Emergency management specialists	10	13	22.8
Accountants and auditors	1,176	1,440	22.4
Meeting and convention planners	43	52	22.2
Public relations managers	58	70	21.7
Compensation and benefits managers	57	70	21.5
Training and development specialists	216	261	20.8
Marketing managers	188	228	20.8
Compensation, benefits, and job analysis specialists	99	119	20.4
Industrial-organizational psychologists	2	3	20.4
Advertising and promotions managers	64	77	20.3
Management analysts	605	727	20.1
Sales managers	337	403	19.7
Market research analysts	190	227	19.6
Sales representatives, services, all other	380	452	18.7
Sales and related workers, all other	226	267	18.4
Cost estimators	198	234	18.2

In addition, numerous bloggers and podcasters now offer news and commentary on the business world. To identify those you might find helpful, start with directories such as Technorati (www.technorati.com/blogs/business) for blogs or Podcast Alley (www.podcastalley.com; select the "business" genre) for podcasts. For all these online resources, be sure to use a newsfeed aggregator to select the type of stories you're interested in and have them delivered to your screen automatically.

Of course, with all the business information available today, it's easy to get lost in the details. Try not to get too caught up in the daily particulars of business. Start by examining "big picture" topics—trends, issues, industry-wide challenges, and careers—before delving into specific companies that look attractive.

In addition to gaining detailed information about prospective employers, you can use the web to look for and respond to job openings. Most companies, even small firms, offer at least basic information about themselves on their websites. Look for the "About Us" or "Company" part of the site to find a company profile, executive biographies, press releases, financial information, and information on employment opportunities. You'll often find information about an organization's mission, products, annual reports, and employee benefits. Plus, you can often download annual reports, brochures, and other materials. Any company's website is going to present the firm in the most positive light possible, of course, so look for outside sources as well, including the business sections of local newspapers and trade publications that cover the company's industries and markets.

Exhibit 3 (page xxx) lists some of the many websites where you can learn more about companies and find job openings. Start with The Riley Guide, www.rileyguide.com, which offers links to hundreds of specialized websites that post openings in specific industries and professions. Your college's career center placement office probably maintains an up-to-date list as well.

Networking

Networking is the process of making informal connections with a broad sphere of mutually beneficial business contacts. According to one recent survey, networking is the most common way that employees find jobs.[6] Networking takes place wherever and whenever people communicate: at industry functions, at social gatherings, at sports events and recreational activities, in online newsgroups, at alumni reunions, and so on. Increasingly, business-oriented social networking sites such as LinkedIn (www.linkedin.com) and Ryze (www.ryze.com) have become important ways to get connected with job openings. Some of these sites are even linked to job posting websites, and when you apply for a job at a particular company, you can see a list of people in your network who work at that company.

To find helpful networks, both the in-person and online variety, read news sites, blogs, and other online sources. Participate in student business organizations and visit *trade shows* that cater to an industry you're interested in. You will learn plenty about that sector of the workplace and rub shoulders with people who actually work in the industry.[7] Don't overlook volunteering in social, civic, and religious organizations. As a volunteer, you not only meet people but also demonstrate your ability to solve problems, plan projects, and so on.

Novice job seekers sometimes misunderstand networking and unknowingly commit breaches of etiquette. Networking isn't a matter of walking up to strangers at social events, handing over your résumé, and asking them to find you a job. Rather, it involves the sharing of information between people who might be able to offer mutual help at some point in the future. Think of it as an organic process, in which you cultivate the possibility of finding that perfect opportunity. Networking can take time, so start early and make it part of your lifelong program of career management.

To become a valued network member, you need to be able to help others in some way. You may not have any influential contacts yet, but because you're actively researching a number of industries and trends in your own job search, you probably have valuable information to share. Or you might simply be able to connect one person with another who can help. The more you network, the more valuable you become in your network—and the more valuable your network becomes to you.

Seeking Career Counseling

College placement offices offer individual counseling, credential services, job fairs, on-campus interviews, and job listings. They can give you advice on résumé-writing software and provide workshops in job search techniques, résumé preparation, interview techniques, and more.[8] You can also find job counseling online. You might begin your self-assessment, for example, with the Keirsey Temperament Sorter, an online personality test at www.advisorteam.com. For excellent job-seeking pointers and counseling, visit college- and university-run online career centers. Major online job boards such as Monster.com also offer a variety of career planning resources.

EXHIBIT 3 Netting a Job on the Web

Use these helpful sites to gather information for your job search.

WEBSITE*	URL	HIGHLIGHTS
The Riley Guide	www.rileyguide.com	Vast collection of links to both general and specialized job sites for every career imaginable; don't miss this one—it'll save you hours and hours of searching
CollegeRecruiter.com	www.collegerecruiter.com	Focused on opportunities for graduates with less than three years of work experience
Monster.com	www.monster.com	One of the most popular job sites, with hundreds of thousands of openings, many from hard-to-find smaller companies; extensive collection of advice on the job search process
MonsterTrak	www.monstertrak.com	Focused on job searches for new college grads; your school's career center site probably links here
Yahoo! HotJobs	http://hotjobs.yahoo.com	Another leading job board, formed by recent merger of HotJobs and Yahoo! Careers
CareerBuilder.com	www.careerbuilder.com	Fast-growing site affiliated with more than 100 local newspapers around the country
USA Jobs	www.usajobs.opm.gov	The official job search site for the U.S. government, featuring everything from economists to astronauts to border patrol agents
IMDiversity	www.imdiversity.com	Good resource on diversity in the workplace, with job postings from companies that have made a special commitment to promoting diversity in their workforces
Dice.com	www.dice.com	One of the best sites for high-technology jobs
Net-Temps	www.net-temps.com	Popular site for contractors and freelancers looking for short-term assignments
InternshipPrograms.com	www.internships.wetfeet.com	Posts listings from companies looking for interns in a wide variety of professions
SimplyHired.com Indeed.com	www.simplyhired.com www.indeed.com	Specialized search engines that look for job postings on hundreds of websites worldwide; find many postings that aren't listed on "job board" sites such as Monster.com

*Note: This list represents only a small fraction of the hundreds of job-posting sites and other resources available online; be sure to check with your college's career center for the latest information.

Preparing Your Résumé

A **résumé** is a structured, written summary of a person's education, employment background, and job qualifications. Although many people have misconceptions about résumés (see Exhibit 4), the fact is that a résumé is a form of advertising. It is intended to stimulate an employer's interest in you—in meeting you and learning more about you. A successful résumé inspires a prospective employer to invite you to interview with the company. Thus, your purpose in writing your résumé is to create interest—*not* to tell readers every little detail.[9]

Your résumé is one of the most important documents you'll ever write. You can help ensure success by remembering four things: First, treat your résumé with the respect it

Career fairs give companies the chance to meet potential employees—and for you to learn more about career opportunities.

deserves. Until you're able to meet with employers in person, your résumé is all they have of you. Until that first personal contact occurs, you *are* your résumé, and a single mistake or oversight can cost you interview opportunities. Second, give yourself plenty of time. Don't put off preparing your résumé until the last second and then try to write it in one sitting. Let this special document stew and try out different ideas and phrases until you hit on the right combination. Also, give yourself plenty of time to proofread the résumé when you're finished—and ask several other people to proofread it as well. Third, learn from good models. You can find thousands of sample résumés online at college websites and job sites such as Monster.com. Fourth, don't get frustrated by the conflicting advice you'll read about résumés; they are more art than science. Consider the alternatives and choose the approach that makes the most sense in your specific situation.

By the way, if anyone asks to see your "CV," they're referring to your *curriculum vitae*, the term used instead of *résumé* in some professions and in many countries outside the United States. Résumés and CVs are essentially the same, although CVs can be more detailed. If you need to adapt a U.S.-style résumé to CV format, or vice versa, Monster.com has helpful guidelines on the subject.

Gathering Pertinent Information

If you haven't been building an employment portfolio thus far, you may need to do some research on yourself at this point. Gather all the pertinent personal history you can think of, including all the specific dates, duties, and accomplishments of any previous jobs you've held. Collect every piece of relevant educational experience that adds to your qualifications—formal degrees, skills certificates, academic awards, or scholarships. Also, gather any relevant information about personal endeavors: dates of your membership in an association, offices you may have held in a club or professional organization, any presentations you might have given to a community group. You probably won't use every piece of information you come up with, but you'll want to have it at your fingertips before you begin composing your résumé.

Selecting the Best Medium

Selecting the medium for your résumé used to be a simple matter: it was typed on paper. These days, though, your job search might involve various forms, including an uploaded Word document, a plain-text document that you paste into an online form, or a multimedia résumé that is part of your online e-portfolio. Explore all your options and

EXHIBIT 4

Fallacies and Facts About Résumés

Many people incorrectly believe that a good résumé will get them the job they want; the real purpose of a résumé is to secure an invitation to a job interview.

FALLACIES	FACTS
The purpose of a résumé is to list all your skills and abilities.	The purpose of a résumé is to generate interest and an interview.
A good résumé will get you the job you want.	All a résumé can do is get you in the door.
Your résumé will be read carefully and thoroughly.	In most cases, your résumé needs to make a positive impression within 30 or 45 seconds; moreover, it may be screened by a computer looking for keywords first—and if it doesn't contain the right keywords, a human being may never see it.
The more good information you present about yourself in your résumé, the better.	Recruiters don't need that much information about you at the initial screening stage, and they probably won't read it.
If you want a really good résumé, have it prepared by a résumé service.	You have the skills needed to prepare an effective résumé, so prepare it yourself—unless the position is especially high-level or specialized. Even then, you should check carefully before using a service.

choose those that (a) meet the requirements of target employers and (b) allow you to present yourself in a compelling fashion. For instance, if you're applying for a sales position, in which your personal communication skills would be a strong point, a video podcast showing you making a sales presentation (even a mock presentation) could be a strong persuader.

No matter how many media you eventually use, it's always a good idea to prepare a basic paper résumé and keep copies on hand. You'll never know when someone might ask for it, and not all employers want to bother with electronic media when all they want to know is your basic profile. In addition, starting with a traditional paper résumé is a great way to organize your background information and identify your unique strengths.

Keeping Your Résumé Honest

At some point in the writing process, you're sure to run into the question of honesty. A claim may be clearly wrong ("So what if I didn't get those last two credits—I got the same education as people who did graduate, so it's OK to say that I graduated too"). Or a rationalization may be more subtle ("Even though the task was to organize the company picnic, I did a good job, so it should qualify as 'project management'"). Either way, the information is dishonest.

Somehow, the idea that "everybody lies on their résumés" has crept into popular consciousness, and dishonesty in the job search process has reached epidemic proportions. As many as half of the résumés now sent to employers contain false information. And it's not just the simple fudging of a fact here and there. Dishonest applicants are getting creative—and bold. Don't have the college degree you want? You can buy a degree from one of the websites that now offer fake diplomas. Better yet, pay a computer hacker to insert your name into a prestigious university's graduation records, in case somebody checks. Aren't really working in that impressive job at a well-known company? You can always list it on your résumé and sign up for a service that provides phony employment verification.[10]

Applicants with integrity know they don't need to stoop to lying to compete in the job market. If you are tempted to stretch the truth, bear in mind that professional recruiters have seen every trick in the book, and employers who are fed up with the dishonesty and are getting more aggressive at uncovering the truth. Roughly 80 percent now contact references and conduct criminal background checks, and many do credit checks when the job involves financial responsibility.[11] And even if you get past these filters with fraudulent information, you'll probably be exposed on the job when you can't live up to your own résumé. Such fabrications have been known to catch up to people many years into their careers, with embarrassing consequences.

To maintain a high standard of honesty in your résumé, subject any questionable entries to two simple tests: First, if something is not true, don't include it—don't try to rationalize it, excuse it, or make it sound better than it is; simply leave it out. A second and more subtle test, helpful for those borderline issues, is asking whether you'd be comfortable sharing a particular piece of information face-to-face. If you wouldn't be comfortable saying it in person, don't say it in your résumé. These tests will help ensure a factual résumé that represents who you are and lead you toward jobs that are truly right for you.

Organizing Your Résumé Around Your Strengths

As you compose your résumé, try to emphasize the information that has a bearing on your career objective, and minimize or exclude any that is irrelevant or counterproductive. To interest potential employers in your résumé, call attention to your best features and downplay your weaknesses—but be sure you do so without distorting or misrepresenting the facts.[12] Do you have something in your history that might trigger an employer's red flag? Following are some common problems and some quick suggestions for overcoming them:[13]

- *Frequent job changes.* Reasonable employers understand that many otherwise stable employees have been forced to job hop in recent years. Group all contract and temporary jobs under one heading if they're similar.

- *Gaps in work history.* Mention relevant experience and education gained during time gaps, such as volunteer or community work. If gaps are due to personal problems such as drug, alcohol abuse, or mental illness, offer honest but general explanations about your absences ("I had serious health concerns and had to take time off to fully recover").

- *Inexperience.* Do related volunteer work. List relevant course work and internships. Offer hiring incentives such as "willing to work nights and weekends."

- *Overqualification.* Tone down your résumé, focusing exclusively on pertinent experience and skills.

- *Long-term employment with one company.* Itemize each position held at the firm to show "interior mobility" and increased responsibilities. Don't include obsolete skills and job titles.

- *Job termination for cause.* Be honest with interviewers. Show you're a hard-working employee and counter their concerns with proof such as recommendations and examples of completed projects.

- *Criminal record.* You don't necessarily need to disclose a criminal record or time spent incarcerated on your résumé, but you may be asked about it on a job application form. Laws regarding what employers may ask (and whether they can conduct a criminal background check) vary by state and profession, but if you are asked and the question applies to you, you must answer truthfully or you risk being terminated later if the employer finds out.

To focus attention on your strongest points, adopt the appropriate organizational approach—make your résumé chronological, functional, or a combination of the two. The "right" choice depends on your background and your goals.

The Chronological Résumé

In a **chronological résumé**, the work-experience section dominates and is placed in the most prominent slot, immediately after the name and address and optional objective. You develop this section by listing your jobs sequentially in reverse order, beginning with the most recent position and working backward toward earlier jobs. Under each listing, describe your responsibilities and accomplishments, giving the most space to the most recent positions. If you're just graduating from college with limited professional experience, you can vary this chronological approach by putting your educational qualifications before your experience, thereby focusing attention on your academic credentials.

The chronological approach is the most common way to organize a résumé, and many employers prefer it. This approach has three key advantages: (1) Employers are familiar with it and can easily find information, (2) it highlights growth and career progression, and (3) it highlights employment continuity and stability.[14] As vice president with Korn/Ferry International, Robert Nesbit speaks for many recruiters: "Unless you have a really compelling reason, don't use any but the standard chronological format. Your résumé should not read like a treasure map, full of minute clues to the whereabouts of your jobs and experience. I want to be able to grasp quickly where a candidate has worked, how long, and in what capacities."[15]

The chronological approach is especially appropriate if you have a strong employment history and are aiming for a job that builds on your current career path (see Exhibit 5).

The Functional Résumé

A **functional résumé**, sometimes called a *skills résumé*, emphasizes your skills and capabilities, identifying employers and academic experience in subordinate sections. This pattern stresses individual areas of competence, so it's useful for people who are just entering the job market, want to redirect their careers, or have little continuous career-related experience. The functional approach also has three advantages: (1) Without having to read through job descriptions, employers can see what you can do for them, (2) you can emphasize earlier job experience, and (3) you can de-emphasize any lack of career progress or lengthy unemployment. However, you should be aware that not all employers like the functional résumé, perhaps partly because it can obscure your work history and partly because it's less common. In any event, many seasoned employment professionals are suspicious of this résumé style, and some assume that candidates who use it are trying to hide something. In fact, Monster.com lists the functional résumé as one of employers' "Top 10 Pet Peeves."[16] If you don't have a strong, uninterrupted history of relevant work, the combination résumé might be a better choice.

The Combination Résumé

A **combination résumé** includes the best features of the chronological and functional approaches. Nevertheless, it is not commonly used, and it has two major disadvantages: (1) It tends to be longer, and (2) it can be repetitive if you have to list your accomplishments and skills in both the functional section and the chronological job descriptions.[17]

As you look at a number of sample résumés, you'll probably notice variations on the three basic formats presented here. Study these other options in light of effective communication principles; if you find one that seems like the best fit for your unique situation, by all means use it.

Producing Your Résumé

With less than a minute to make a good impression, your résumé needs to look sharp and grab a recruiter's interest in the first few lines. A typical recruiter devotes 45 seconds to each résumé before tossing it into either the "maybe" or the "reject" pile. Few recruiters read every résumé from top to bottom; most give them a quick glance to look for key words and accomplishments. If yours doesn't stand out—or stands out in a negative way—chances are a recruiter won't look at it long enough to judge your qualifications.[18]

EXHIBIT 5 Chronological Résumé

Roberto Cortez calls attention to his most recent achievements by setting them off in list form with bullets. The section titled "Intercultural and Technical Skills" emphasizes his international background, fluency in Spanish and German, and extensive computer skills—all of which are important qualifications for his target position.

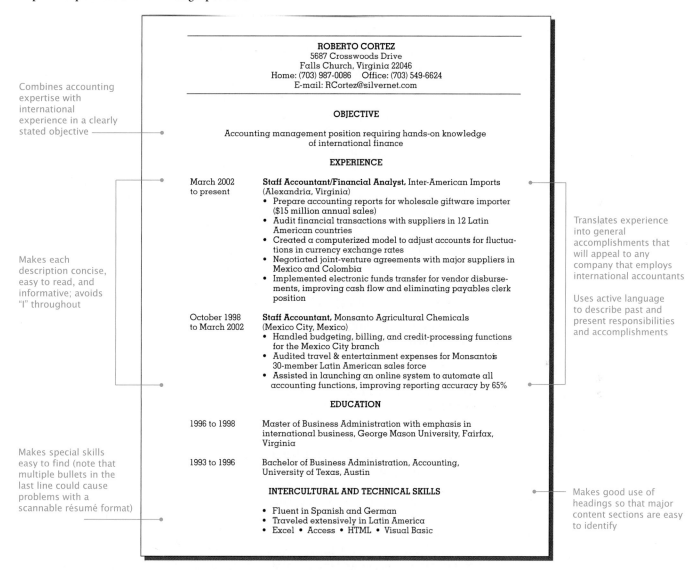

Combines accounting expertise with international experience in a clearly stated objective

Makes each description concise, easy to read, and informative; avoids "I" throughout

Makes special skills easy to find (note that multiple bullets in the last line could cause problems with a scannable résumé format)

Translates experience into general accomplishments that will appeal to any company that employs international accountants

Uses active language to describe past and present responsibilities and accomplishments

Makes good use of headings so that major content sections are easy to identify

---

ROBERTO CORTEZ
5687 Crosswoods Drive
Falls Church, Virginia 22046
Home: (703) 987-0086   Office: (703) 549-6624
E-mail: RCortez@silvernet.com

OBJECTIVE

Accounting management position requiring hands-on knowledge
of international finance

EXPERIENCE

March 2002 to present — **Staff Accountant/Financial Analyst,** Inter-American Imports (Alexandria, Virginia)
- Prepare accounting reports for wholesale giftware importer ($15 million annual sales)
- Audit financial transactions with suppliers in 12 Latin American countries
- Created a computerized model to adjust accounts for fluctuations in currency exchange rates
- Negotiated joint-venture agreements with major suppliers in Mexico and Colombia
- Implemented electronic funds transfer for vendor disbursements, improving cash flow and eliminating payables clerk position

October 1998 to March 2002 — **Staff Accountant,** Monsanto Agricultural Chemicals (Mexico City, Mexico)
- Handled budgeting, billing, and credit-processing functions for the Mexico City branch
- Audited travel & entertainment expenses for Monsanto's 30-member Latin American sales force
- Assisted in launching an online system to automate all accounting functions, improving reporting accuracy by 65%

EDUCATION

1996 to 1998 — Master of Business Administration with emphasis in international business, George Mason University, Fairfax, Virginia

1993 to 1996 — Bachelor of Business Administration, Accounting, University of Texas, Austin

INTERCULTURAL AND TECHNICAL SKILLS

- Fluent in Spanish and German
- Traveled extensively in Latin America
- Excel • Access • HTML • Visual Basic

Good design is a must, and it's not hard to achieve. Good designs feature simplicity, order, plenty of white space, and straightforward typefaces such as Times Roman or Arial (keep in mind that many of the fonts on your computer are not appropriate for a résumé). Make your subheadings easy to find and easy to read, placing them either above each section or in the left margin. Use lists and leave plenty of white space. Color is not necessary by any means, but if you add color, make it subtle and sophisticated, such as in a thin horizontal line under your name and address. If any part of the design "jumps out at you," tone it down. An amateurish design could end your chances of getting an interview. As one experienced recruiter put it recently, "At our office, these résumés are rejected without even being read."[19]

Depending on the companies you apply to, you might want to produce your résumé in as many as six forms:

■ *Printed traditional résumé.* Format your traditional résumé simply but elegantly to make the best impression on your employer. Naturally, printed versions must be delivered by hand or by mail.

- *Printed scannable résumé.* Prepare a printed version of your résumé that is unformatted and thus electronically scannable so that employers can store your information in their database.

- *Electronic plain-text file.* Create an electronic plain-text file to use when uploading your résumé information into web forms or inserting it into e-mail messages.

- *Microsoft Word file.* Keep a Microsoft Word file of your traditional résumé so that you can upload it on certain websites.

- *HTML format.* By creating an HTML version, you can post your résumé on your own website, on a page provided by your college, or some of the many job board sites now available. (If you don't have HTML experience or other means to create an HTML version, you can save your résumé as a webpage from within Word. This method won't necessarily create the most spectacularly beautiful webpage, but it should be functional at least.)

- *PDF file.* This is an optional step, but a portable document format (PDF) file of your traditional résumé provides a simple, safe format to attach to e-mail messages. Creating a PDF version of your résumé is a simple procedure, but you need the right software. Adobe Acrobat (not the free Acrobat Reader) is the best known program, but many others are available, including some free versions. You can also use Adobe's online service at http://createpdf.adobe.com to create PDFs without buying software.

Producing most of these formats is a straightforward task, but printing a scannable résumé and creating a plain-text file require careful attention to some important details.

Printing a Scannable Résumé

To cope with the flood of unsolicited paper résumés in recent years, many companies now optically scan incoming résumés into a database that hiring managers can search for attractive candidates. Whether they use simpler key word matching or sophisticated linguistic analysis, these systems display lists of possible candidates, each with a percentage score indicating how closely the résumé reflects a given position's requirements.[20] Nearly all large companies now use these systems, as do many midsized companies and even some smaller firms.[21]

The emergence of such scanning systems has important implications for your résumé. First, computers are interested only in matching information to search parameters, not in artistic attempts at résumé design. In fact, complex designs can cause errors in the scanning process. Second, *optical character recognition (OCR)* software doesn't technically "read" anything; it merely looks for shapes that match stored profiles of characters. If the OCR software can't make sense of your fancy fonts or creative page layout, it will enter gibberish into the database (for instance, your name might go in as "W<$..3r ?00!#" instead of "Walter Jones"). Third, even the most sophisticated databases cannot conduct a search with the nuance and intuition of an experienced human recruiter.

For job searchers, this situation creates two requirements for a successful scannable résumé: (1) use a plain font and simplified design, and (2) compile a **key word summary** that lists all the terms that could help match your résumé to the right openings. Other than the key word summary, a scannable résumé contains the same information as your traditional résumé but is formatted to be OCR-friendly (see Exhibit 6):[22]

- Use a clean sans serif font such as Optima or Arial, and size it between 10 and 14 points.

- Make sure that characters do not touch one another (whether numbers, letters, or symbols—including the slash [/]).

- Don't use side-by-side columns.

- Don't use ampersands (&), percent signs (%), foreign-language characters (such as é and ö), or bullet symbols (use a hyphen or dash, not a lowercase *o*, in place of a bullet symbol).

- Put each phone number and e-mail address on its own line.

- Print on white, plain paper.

EXHIBIT 6 Scannable Résumé

Because some of his target employers will be scanning his résumé into a database, and because he wants to submit his résumé via e-mail or post it on the Internet, Roberto Cortez created a scannable résumé by changing his formatting and adding a list of key words. However, the information remains essentially the same.

Removes all boldfacing, nontext characters such as bullets, and two-column formatting

Includes carefully selected keyword list derived from descriptions of target jobs

Uses a dash instead of bullet point character in bulleted lists

Uses ample white space to help ensure accurate scanning

Roberto Cortez
5687 Crosswoods Drive
Falls Church, Virginia 22046
Home phone: (703) 987-0086
Office phone: (703) 549-6624
E-mail: RCortez@silvernet.com

KEYWORDS

Financial executive, accounting management, international finance, financial analyst, accounting reports, financial audit, computerized accounting model, exchange rates, joint-venture agreements, budgets, billing, credit processing, online systems, MBA, fluent Spanish, fluent German, Excel, Access, Visual Basic, team player, willing to travel

OBJECTIVE

Accounting management position requiring hands-on knowledge of international finance

EXPERIENCE

Staff Accountant/Financial Analyst, Inter-American Imports (Alexandria, Virginia), March 2002 to present
— Prepare accounting reports for wholesale giftware importer ($15 million annual sales)
— Audit financial transactions with suppliers in 12 Latin American countries
— Created a computerized model to adjust for fluctuations in currency exchange rates
— Negotiated joint-venture agreements with major suppliers in Mexico and Colombia
— Implemented electronic funds transfer for vendor disbursements, improving cash flow and eliminating payables clerk position

Staff Accountant, Monsanto Agricultural Chemicals (Mexico City, Mexico), October 1998 to March 2002
— Handled budgeting, billing, and credit-processing functions for the Mexico City branch
— Audited travel & entertainment expenses for Monsanto's 30-member Latin American sales force
— Assisted in launching an online system to automate all accounting functions, improving reporting accuracy by 65%

EDUCATION

Master of Business Administration with emphasis in international business, George Mason University (Fairfax, Virginia), 1996 to 1998

Bachelor of Business Administration, Accounting, University of Texas (Austin, Texas), 1993 to 1996

INTERCULTURAL AND TECHNICAL SKILLS

— Fluent in Spanish and German
— Traveled extensively in Latin America
— Excel, Access, HTML, Visual Basic

Your scannable résumé will probably be longer than your traditional résumé because you can't compress text into columns and because you need plenty of white space between headings and sections. If your scannable résumé runs more than one page, make sure your name appears on every subsequent page (in case the pages become separated). Before sending a scannable résumé, check the company's website or call the human resources department to see whether it has any specific requirements other than those discussed here.

When adding a key word summary to your résumé, keep your audience in mind. Employers generally search for nouns (because verbs tend to be generic rather than specific to a particular position or skill), so make your key words nouns as well. Use abbreviations sparingly and only when they are well-known and unambiguous, such as *MBA*.

List 20 to 30 words and phrases that define your skills, experience, education, and professional affiliations as they relate to your target position (review job descriptions to find words most relevant to a given position). Place this list right after your name and address.

If you're tempted to toss in impressive key words that don't really apply to you, don't. Increasingly sophisticated résumé analysis systems can now detect whether your key words truly relate to the job descriptions and other information on your résumé. If a system suspects you've padded your key word list, it could move you to the bottom of the ranking or delete your résumé.[23]

Creating a Plain-Text File of Your Résumé

An increasingly common way to get your information into an employer's database is by entering a **plain-text version** (sometimes referred to as an *ASCII text version*) of your résumé into an online form. This approach has the same goal as a scannable résumé, but it's faster, easier, and less prone to errors than the scanning process. If you have the option of mailing a scannable résumé or submitting plain text online, go with plain text.

In addition, when employers or networking contacts ask you to e-mail your résumé, they'll often want to receive it in plain-text format in the body of your e-mail message. Thanks to the prevalence of computer viruses these days, many employers will refuse to open an e-mail attachment. Plain text is also helpful when you're completing online application forms; simply copy and paste from your plain-text file into the appropriate fields.

Plain text is just what it sounds like: no font selections, no bullet symbols, no colors, no lines or boxes, and so on. A plain-text version is easy to create with your word processor. Start with the file you used to create your traditional printed résumé, use the Save As choice to save it as "plain text" or whichever similarly labeled option your software has, then verify the result.

The verification step is crucial because you can never be quite sure what happens to your layout. Open the text file to view the layout, but don't use your word processor; instead, open the file with a basic text editor (such as Microsoft's Notepad) so that the text doesn't get reformatted in any way. If necessary, adjust the page manually, moving text and inserting spaces as needed. For simplicity's sake, left justify all your headings, rather than trying to center them manually. You can put headings in all caps or underline them with a row of dashes to separate them from blocks of text.

Preparing Your Application Letter

Whenever you submit your résumé, accompany it with an *application letter* or *cover letter* to let readers know what you're sending, why you're sending it, and how they can benefit from reading it. Because your application letter is in your own style (rather than the choppy, shorthand style of your résumé), it gives you a chance to show your communication skills and some personality.

Always send your résumé and application letter together, because each has a unique job to perform. The purpose of your résumé is to get employers interested enough to contact you for an interview. The purpose of your application letter is to get employers interested enough to read your résumé.

Before drafting a letter, learn something about the organization you're applying to; then focus on your audience so that you can show you've done your homework. Imagine yourself in the recruiter's situation, and show how your background and talents will solve a particular problem or fill a specific need the company has. The more you can learn about the organization, the better you'll be able to capture the reader's attention and convey your interest in the company. During your research, find out the name, title, and department of the person you're writing to. Reaching and addressing the right person is the most effective way to gain attention. Avoid phrases such as "To Whom It May Concern" and "Dear Sir."

When putting yourself in your reader's shoes, remember that this person's in-box is probably overflowing with résumés and cover letters. So respect your reader's time. Steer clear of gimmicks, which almost never work, and include nothing in your cover letter that already appears in your résumé. Keep your letter straightforward, fact-based, short, upbeat, and professional (see Exhibit 7). Note that these guidelines also apply if you're applying by e-mail. The e-mail message serves as your cover letter, so treat it with the same formality that you would a printed letter.

Following Up on Your Application

If your application letter and résumé fail to bring a response within a month or so, follow up with a second letter to keep your file active. This follow-up letter also gives you a chance to update your original application with any recent job-related information. Even if you've received a letter acknowledging your application and saying that it will be kept on file, don't hesitate to send a follow-up letter three months later to show that you are still interested. Such a letter can demonstrate that you're sincerely interested in working for the organization, that you're persistent in pursuing your goals, and that you're upgrading your skills to make yourself a better employee. And it might just get you an interview.

EXHIBIT 7 Application Letter

In her unsolicited application letter, Glenda Johns manages to give a snapshot of her qualifications and skills without repeating what is said in her résumé.

457 Mountain View Rd.
Clear Lake, IA 50428
June 16, 2008

Ms. Patricia Downings, Store Manager
Wal-Mart
840 South Oak
Iowa Falls, IA 50126

Dear Ms. Downing:

Gains attention in the first paragraph by speaking directly to the reader's needs

You want retail clerks and managers who are accurate, enthusiastic, and experienced. You want someone who cares about customer service, who understands merchandising, and who can work with others to get the job done. When you're ready to hire a manager trainee or a clerk who is willing to work toward promotion, please consider me for the job.

Points out personal qualities that aren't specifically stated in her résumé

Working as a clerk and then as an assistant manager in a large department store has taught me how to anticipate customer problems and deliver the type of service that keeps customers coming back. Moreover, my recent BA degree in retailing, which encompassed such courses as retailing, marketing, management, and business information systems, will provide your store with a well-rounded associate. (Please refer to my enclosed résumé for more information.) You'll find that I'm interested in every facet of retailing, eager to take on responsibility, and willing to continue learning throughout my career.

Builds the reader's interest by demonstrating knowledge of the company's policy toward promotion

I understand that Wal-Mart prefers to promote its managers from within the company, and I would be pleased to start out with an entry-level position until I gain the necessary experience. Could we meet in the near future to discuss my qualifications for the next available associate position? I will phone you early next Wednesday to arrange a meeting at your convenience.

Focuses on the reader and displays the "you" attitude, even though the last paragraph uses the word "I"

Sincerely,

Glenda Johns

Glenda Johns

Enclosure

Interviewing with Potential Employers

An **employment interview** is a formal meeting during which you and the prospective employer ask questions and exchange information. These meetings have a dual purpose: (1) The organization's main objective is to find the best person available for the job by determining whether you and the organization are a good match, and (2) your main objective is to find the job best suited to your goals and capabilities. Most employers conduct two or three interviews before deciding whether to offer a person a job. The first interview, generally held on campus or online, is the **preliminary screening interview**, which helps employers eliminate unqualified applicants from the hiring process. Those candidates who best meet the organization's requirements are invited to visit company offices for further evaluation. Some organizations make a decision at that point, but many schedule a third interview to complete the evaluation process before extending a job offer.

Many companies now conduct part of the interviewing process online. These virtual interviews can range from simple structured interviews to sophisticated job simulations that are similar to working interviews. People applying for teller positions at SunTrust, a regional bank based in Atlanta, interact with video-game-like characters while performing job-related tasks. These job simulations not only identify better candidates but also reduce the risk of employment discrimination lawsuits because they closely mimic actual job skills.[24] The latest innovation in simulators uses prerecorded video of real people asking questions and records the candidate's answers on video as well.[25]

Because the interview process takes time, start seeking interviews well in advance of the date you want to start work. Some students start their job search as early as nine months before graduation. Early planning is even more crucial during downturns in the economy because many employers become more selective when times are tough. Whatever shape the economy is in, try to secure as many interviews as you can, both to improve the chances of receiving a job offer and to give yourself more options when you do get offers.

What Employers Look For

The interview process gives them a chance to go beyond the basic information on your résumé to answer two essential questions: Will the candidate be a good fit with the organization, and can he or she handle the responsibilities of the position?

To determine whether a candidate will be compatible with the other people in the organization, some interviewers may ask you questions about your interests, hobbies, awareness of world events, and so forth. Others may consider your personal style. You're likely to impress an employer by being open, enthusiastic, and interested. Still others may look for courtesy, sincerity, willingness to learn, and a style that is positive and self-confident. All of these qualities help a new employee adapt to a new workplace and new responsibilities.

When you're invited to interview for a position, the interviewer already has some idea of whether you have the right qualifications, based on a review of your résumé. But during the interview, you'll be asked to describe your education and previous jobs in more depth so that the interviewer can determine how well your skills match the requirements. When describing your skills, be honest. If you don't know how to do something, say so. In many cases, the interviewer will be seeking someone with the flexibility to apply diverse skills in several areas.

What You Should Look For

What things should you find out about the prospective job and employer? By doing a little advance research and asking the right questions during the interview (see Exhibit 8), you can probably find answers to these questions and more:

- Are these my kind of people?
- Can I do this work?
- Will I enjoy the work?

1. What are the job's major responsibilities?
2. What qualities do you want in the person who fills this position?
3. How do you measure success for someone in this position?
4. What is the first problem that needs the attention of the person you hire?
5. Would relocation be required now or in the future?
6. Why is this job now vacant?
7. What makes your organization different from others in the industry?
8. How would you define your organization's managerial philosophy?
9. What additional training does you organization provide?
10. Do employees have an opportunity to continue their education with help from the organization?

EXHIBIT 8

Ten Questions to Ask the Interviewer

Learn as much as you can about potential employers by asking these questions.

- Is this job what I want?
- Does the job pay what I'm worth?
- What kind of person would I be working for?
- What sort of future can I look forward to with this organization?

How to Prepare for a Job Interview

It's perfectly normal to feel a little anxious before an interview. Don't worry too much, however; preparation will help you perform well. Learning about the organization and the job is important because it enables you to consider the employer's point of view. Here are some pointers to guide that preparation:

- *Think ahead about questions.* Most job interviews are essentially question-and-answer sessions: You answer the interviewer's questions about your background, and you ask questions of your own to determine whether the job and the organization are right for you. By planning for your interviews (see Exhibit 9), you can handle these exchanges intelligently. Of course, you don't want to memorize responses or sound overrehearsed.

- *Bolster your confidence.* By overcoming your tendencies to feel self-conscious or nervous during an interview, you can build your confidence and make a better impression. If some aspect of your background or appearance makes you uneasy, correct it or exercise positive traits to offset it, such as warmth, wit, intelligence, or charm. Instead of dwelling on your weaknesses, focus on your strengths so that you can emphasize them to an interviewer.

- *Polish your interview style.* Confidence helps you walk into an interview and give the interviewer an impression of poise, good manners, and good judgment. You're more likely to be invited back for a second interview or offered a job if you maintain natural eye contact, smile frequently, sit in an attentive position, and use frequent hand gestures. These nonverbal signals convince the interviewer that you're alert, assertive, dependable, confident, responsible, and energetic.[26] Work on eliminating speech mannerisms such as "you know," "like," and "um." Speak in your natural tone, and try to vary the pitch, rate, and volume of your voice to express enthusiasm and energy. Practice interviewing with friends or use an interview simulator if you have access to one.

- *Plan to look good.* Physical appearance is important because clothing and grooming reveal something about a candidate's personality, professionalism, and ability to sense the unspoken "rules" of a situation. When it comes to clothing, the best policy is to dress conservatively. Wear the best-quality businesslike clothing you can,

EXHIBIT 9

Twenty-Five Common Interview Questions

Prepare for an interview in advance by thinking about your answers to these questions.

QUESTIONS ABOUT COLLEGE

1. What courses in college did you like most? Least? Why?

2. Do you think your extracurricular activities in college were worth the time you spent on them? Why or why not?

3. When did you choose your college major? Did you ever change your major? If so, why?

4. Do you feel you did the best scholastic work you are capable of?

5. Which of your college years was the toughest? Why?

QUESTIONS ABOUT EMPLOYERS AND JOBS

6. What jobs have you held? Why did you leave?

7. What percentage of your college expenses did you earn? How?

8. Why did you choose your particular field of work?

9. What are the disadvantages of your chosen field?

10. Have you served in the military? What rank did you achieve? What jobs did you perform?

11. What do you think about how this industry operates today?

12. Why do you think you would like this particular type of job?

QUESTIONS ABOUT PERSONAL ATTITUDES AND PREFERENCES

13. Do you prefer to work in any specific geographic location? If so, why?

14. How much money do you hope to be earning in 5 years? In 10 years?

15. What do you think determines a person's progress in a good organization?

16. What personal characteristics do you feel are necessary for success in your chosen field?

17. Tell me a story.

18. Do you like to travel?

19. Do you think grades should be considered by employers? Why or why not?

QUESTIONS ABOUT WORK HABITS

20. Do you prefer working with others or by yourself?

21. What type of boss do you prefer?

22. Have you ever had any difficulty getting along with colleagues or supervisors? With instructors? With other students?

23. Would you prefer to work in a large or a small organization? Why?

24. How do you feel about overtime work?

25. What have you done that shows initiative and willingness to work?

preferably in a dark, solid color. Wearing clothes that are appropriate and clean is far more important than wearing clothes that are expensive. Avoid flamboyant styles, colors, and prints. Even in companies in which interviewers may dress casually, it's important to show good judgment by dressing—and acting—in a professional manner. Even minor points of etiquette can make a lasting impression on recruiters.

- *Be ready when you arrive.* Be sure you know when and where the interview will be held. Take a small notebook, a pen, a list of your questions, a folder with two copies of your résumé, an outline of your research findings about the organization, and any correspondence about the position. You may also want to take a small calendar, a transcript of your college grades, a list of references, and, if appropriate, samples of your work. After you arrive, relax. You may have to wait, so bring something to read that is related to the company or industry.

At every step, even before you meet your interviewer, show respect for everyone you encounter. If the opportunity presents itself, ask a few questions about the organization or express enthusiasm for the job. Refrain from smoking before the interview (non-smokers can smell smoke on the clothing of interviewees), and avoid chewing gum or otherwise eating or drinking in the waiting room. Anything you do or say while you wait may well get back to the interviewer, so make sure your best qualities show from the moment you enter the premises.

How to Follow Up After the Interview

Touching base with the prospective employer after the interview, either by phone or in writing, shows that you really want the job and are determined to get it. It also brings your name to the interviewer's attention again and reminds him or her that you're waiting to know the decision.

The two most common forms of follow-up, the thank-you note and the inquiry, are generally handled by letter or e-mail. But a phone call can be just as effective, particularly if the employer favors a casual, personal style. Express your thanks within two days after the interview, even if you feel you have little chance for the job. In a brief message, acknowledge the interviewer's time and courtesy, convey your continued interest, and ask politely for a decision. If you're not advised of the interviewer's decision by the promised date or within two weeks, you might make an inquiry, particularly if you don't want to accept a job offer from a second firm before you have an answer from the first. Assume that a simple oversight is the reason for the delay, not outright rejection.

Make a positive first impression with careful grooming and attire. You don't need to spend a fortune on new clothes, but you do need to look clean, prepared, and professional.

Building Your Career

Having the right skills is vital to your success at every stage of your career. Employers seek people who are able and willing to adapt to diverse situations, who thrive in an ever-changing workplace, and who continue to learn throughout their careers. In addition, companies want team players with strong work records and leaders who are versatile. Many companies encourage managers to get varied job experience.[27] In some cases, your chances of being hired are better if you've studied abroad or learned another language. Many employers expect college graduates to have a sound understanding of international affairs, and they're looking for employees with intercultural sensitivity and an ability to adapt in other cultures.[28]

Even after an employer hires you, continue improving your skills to distinguish yourself from your peers and to make yourself more valuable to current and potential employers:[29]

- Acquire as much technical knowledge as you can, build broad-based life experience, and develop your social skills.

- Learn to respond to change in positive, constructive ways; this will help you adapt if your "perfect" career path eludes your grasp.

- Keep up with developments in your industry and the economy at large; read widely and subscribe to free e-mail newsletters.

- Learn to see each job, even so-called entry-level jobs, as an opportunity to learn more and to expand your knowledge, experience, and social skills.

- Take on as much responsibility as you can outside your job description.
- Share what you know with others instead of hoarding knowledge in the hope of becoming indispensable; helping others excel is a skill, too.
- Understand the big picture; knowing your own job inside and out isn't enough any more.
- Understand that what counts isn't only who you know but also what you know and who knows you.

BUSINESS IN ACTION

PART 1

Developing a Business Mind-Set

CHAPTER 1
The Fundamentals of Business and Economics

CHAPTER 2
Ethics and Corporate Social Responsibility

CHAPTER 3
The Global Marketplace

CHAPTER 4
Business Systems

CHAPTER 1

The Fundamentals of Business and Economics

LEARNING OBJECTIVES
After studying this chapter, you will be able to

1 Define what a business is and identify four vital social and economic contributions that businesses make

2 Differentiate between goods-producing and service businesses and list five factors contributing to the increase in the number of service businesses

3 Differentiate between a free-market system and a planned system

4 Explain how supply and demand interact to affect price

5 Discuss the four major economic roles of the U.S. government

6 Explain how a free-market system monitors its economic performance

7 Identify five challenges you will face as a business professional in the coming years

Behind the Scenes

Making Dollars and Sense of Online Music at Apple iTunes

www.apple.com/itunes

Success in business is often a matter of connecting the dots: looking at your own strengths and weaknesses, exploring customer needs, and analyzing the various legal, technical, and social forces at work in the marketplace. You consider what you're capable of doing, what your competitors might do, what customers would like you to do—and what forces are reshaping the business landscape. Then you look for connections and opportunities. How can you capitalize on changing markets? What can you do to meet customer needs better than anyone else?

Apple Computer CEO Steve Jobs has spent his career connecting those dots, leading the development of innovative products that have changed the way people work and play, including the way people listen to music. Although Apple didn't start out in the music business, by 2003 the company had become a significant force in music, at least indirectly. Many musicians and creative professionals favored Apple computers, and the company's sleek new iPod portable music players were a must-have item for trendsetting music fans everywhere.

Outside the company, though, the music industry was in a state of turmoil. Music fans, tired of buying entire CDs

Apple CEO Steve Jobs spotted an opportunity in linking online music sales with his company's popular iPod music players.

for just one or two favorite songs, were downloading millions of songs for free from the Internet. However, many people consider this practice unethical and the recording industry considers it illegal. Performers, songwriters, and music companies were all looking for better ways to address customer complaints about the music industry while protecting their legal rights and financial assets. As is often the case, technology seemed to be one step ahead of business strategy. Everybody agreed that online distribution was central to the future of the music business, but nobody had quite figured out how to make it work.

Jobs wasn't the only person pondering this situation, of course. A diverse group of companies, from Wal-Mart and Sony to RealNetworks and a reborn Napster, wanted a piece of the new online music market. Amazon.com, eBay, and other companies had proven the potential for selling over the Internet, but was it possible to make money selling something as inexpensive as an individual song? If you were Steve Jobs, how would you approach the challenges and opportunities of online music? How would you connect the dots between Apple's strengths and the complex dynamics of the marketplace?[1] ∎

Developing a Business Mind-Set: How This Course Will Help Your Career

No matter where your career plans take you, the dynamics of business will affect your work and life in innumerable ways. If you aspire to be a manager or an entrepreneur like Steve Jobs (profiled in the chapter opener), knowing how to run a business is vital, of course. If you plan a career in a professional specialty such as law, engineering, or finance, knowing how businesses operate will help you interact with clients and colleagues more effectively and thereby contribute to your career success. Even if you plan to work in government, education, or some other noncommercial setting, business awareness can help you as well; many of these organizations look to business for new ideas and leadership techniques. And in your role as a consumer and taxpayer, knowing more about business will help you make better financial decisions.

You'll develop a basic business vocabulary that will help you keep up with the latest news and make more-informed decisions. By participating in classroom discussions and completing the chapter exercises, you'll gain some valuable critical-thinking, problem-solving, team-building, and communication skills that you can use on the job and throughout your life.

This course will also introduce you to a variety of jobs in business fields such as accounting, economics, human resources, management, finance, and marketing. You'll see how people who work in these fields contribute to the success of a company as a whole. You'll gain insight into the types of skills and knowledge these jobs require—and you'll discover that a career in business today can be fascinating, challenging, and rewarding.

In addition, a study of business management will help you appreciate the larger context in which businesses operate and the many legal and ethical questions managers must consider as they make business decisions. Both government regulators and society as a whole have many expectations regarding the ways businesses treat employees, shareholders, the environment, other businesses, and the communities in which they operate.

Even if this course is your first formal exposure to the business world, you already know a great deal about business, thanks to your experiences as a consumer. You understand the impact of poor customer service, for example—or great customer service. You have a sense for product value and why some products meet your needs but others don't. You're an expert in the entire experience of searching for, purchasing, and owning products.

As you progress through this course, though, you'll begin to look at things through the eyes of a business professional rather than those of a consumer. Instead of thinking about the cost of buying a particular product, you'll start to think about the cost of making it, promoting it, and distributing it. You'll think about what it takes to make a product stand out from the crowd. You'll recognize the importance of finding opportunities in the marketplace and meeting the challenges companies encounter as they pursue those opportunities. You'll begin to see business as an integrated system of inputs, processes, and outputs. You'll start to develop a *business mind-set* as you gain an appreciation for the myriad decisions that must be made and the many problems that must be overcome before companies can deliver the products that satisfy customer needs (see Exhibit 1.1).

How This Affects You

In addition to helping you see the world from a manager's perspective, this book helps you understand how forces in the business world affect your life. In each chapter, you'll encounter several critical-thinking checkpoints called "How This Affects You" to help you relate what you're learning to your personal and professional lives. By taking a moment to think about these questions, you'll not only increase your understanding of chapter concepts but also come away with practical insights that can help you for years to come.

Understanding What Business Does

The term *business* is used in a number of ways:

- As a label for the overall field of business concepts, as in "I plan to major in business."
- As a collective label for the activities of many companies, as in "This legislation is viewed as harmful to American business."
- As a way to indicate specific activities or efforts, as in "Our furniture business earned record profits last year, but our housewares business has lost money for the third year in a row."
- As a synonym for *company*, as in "Apple is a successful business."

EXHIBIT 1.1
The Business Mind-Set

Your experiences as a consumer have taught you a great deal about business already; now the challenge is to turn those experiences around and view the world from a manager's perspective. Here is a small sample of how a business professional approaches some of the questions you've asked as a consumer.

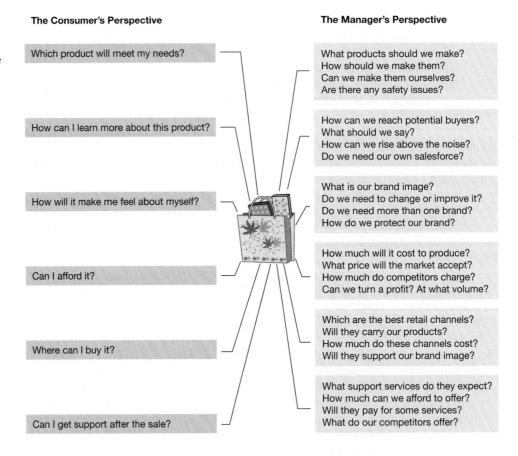

The Consumer's Perspective

Which product will meet my needs?

How can I learn more about this product?

How will it make me feel about myself?

Can I afford it?

Where can I buy it?

Can I get support after the sale?

The Manager's Perspective

What products should we make?
How should we make them?
Can we make them ourselves?
Are there any safety issues?

How can we reach potential buyers?
What should we say?
How can we rise above the noise?
Do we need our own salesforce?

What is our brand image?
Do we need to change or improve it?
Do we need more than one brand?
How do we protect our brand?

How much will it cost to produce?
What price will the market accept?
How much do competitors charge?
Can we turn a profit? At what volume?

Which are the best retail channels?
Will they carry our products?
How much do these channels cost?
Will they support our brand image?

What support services do they expect?
How much can we afford to offer?
Will they pay for some services?
What do our competitors offer?

---

business
A profit-seeking organization that provides goods and services that a society wants or needs

In this last sense, a **business** is any profit-seeking organization that provides goods and services designed to satisfy customers' needs. Through its iTunes service, for example, Apple satisfies an important aspect of consumers' entertainment needs. Businesses (1) provide a society with necessities such as housing, clothing, food, transportation, communication, health care, and much more; (2) provide people with jobs and a means to prosper; (3) pay taxes that fund government services that benefit society such as transportation infrastructure, education, and scientific research; and (4) reinvest their profits in the economy, thereby creating a higher standard of living and quality of life for society as a whole.

profit
Money left over after expenses and taxes have been deducted from revenue generated by selling goods and services

nonprofit organizations
Firms whose primary objective is something other than returning a profit to their owners

The driving force behind most businesses is the prospect of earning a **profit**—money that remains after all expenses have been deducted from the sales revenue the business has brought in. Such a prospect is commonly referred to as a *profit motive*. Businesses may keep and use their profits as they wish, within legal limits. Still, not every organization exists to earn a profit. **Nonprofit organizations** or *not-for-profit organizations* such as museums, public schools and universities, symphonies, libraries, and charities exist to provide society with a social, educational, or other service. The American Red Cross, for example, provides relief to victims of disasters and helps people prevent, prepare for, and respond to emergencies. Although nonprofit organizations do not have a profit motive, to meet their primary missions they must operate in financially efficient ways. All nonprofit organizations, from a student club with only a few dozen members to a multibillion-dollar operation such as the Red Cross, can learn from business opportunities, challenges, and activities discussed throughout this course.

Recognizing the Various Types of Businesses

goods-producing businesses
Businesses that produce tangible products

Most businesses can be classified into two broad categories. **Goods-producing businesses** primarily produce tangible goods by engaging in activities such as manufacturing, construction, mining, and agriculture. Because they require large amounts of

Is Web 2.0 the Future or the Past Revisited?

Take your pick: (a) It unleashes the power of the individual while harnessing the collective wisdom of crowds; it shifts the web from consumption to contribution; and far into the future it "will be recognized as the largest, most complex, and most surprising event on the planet." (b) It is a load of baloney that at best is meaningless marketing nonsense and at worst is an attempt to repackage failed business models from the dot-com boom of the late 1990s.

"It" is Web 2.0. Defining Web 2.0 is difficult, and estimating the extent of its eventual impact on business is even harder. Web 2.0 could be described as a shift in the philosophy and technology of the World Wide Web, from static, isolated, and tightly controlled websites to connected, interactive, user-driven services. However, the term is used so widely and so loosely that no accepted definition has yet emerged.

Technologies often included under the Web 2.0 umbrella include blogging, podcasting, wikis, newsfeeds, tagging, and virtual worlds. Among the companies frequently cited as examples of the Web 2.0 approach are the news-tagging website Digg.com (www.digg.com), which allows users to tag the most important news stories from around the world; the social bookmarking site del.icio.us (http://del.icio.us), which helps web surfers find interesting and useful websites; and YouTube (www.youtube.com), the wildly popular video sharing service. YouTube in particular is a good example of *user-generated content*, in which individual consumers create a website's content.

Web 2.0 detractors generally don't dispute the value of these sites and tools; rather, they question whether Web 2.0 is really the profound philosophical shift in human behavior that some of its proponents seem to claim—and whether a whole class of profitable businesses can be built around the concept. However, some observers say the Web 2.0 phenomenon is unlike the "irrational exuberance" that was the hallmark of the dot-com era in the late 1990s, when unproven managers with untested business plans and untried technologies could secure millions of dollars in start-up financing on their way to billion-dollar stock offerings—before crashing to Earth when investors woke up and realized these companies might never be profitable. These observers say that Web 2.0 entrepreneurs learned from the lessons of the dot-com crash and are building more sustainable companies based on sound business ideas. Many also aim to sell out to Google, Microsoft, or another tech titan, rather than taking their chances on the stock market.

While that debate rages on, look for ways to take advantage of these powerful new tools in your business without getting too caught up in what exactly Web 2.0 means or where it might be going. (For the latest information on Web 2.0, visit www.prenhall.com/bovée and click on "Real-Time Updates" in the upper right-hand corner.)

Questions for Critical Thinking

1. Why would a company such as Digg offer its services for free? How can it expect to stay in business?
2. In the case of a company such as YouTube, what are some of the risks of relying entirely on website visitors to voluntarily provide the content that is vital to the success of your company?

---

money, equipment, land, and other resources to get started and to operate, goods-producing businesses are often **capital-intensive businesses**. The capital needed to compete in these industries is a **barrier to entry**, a resource or capability a company must have before it can start competing in a given market. Other barriers to entry include government testing and approval, tightly controlled markets, strict licensing procedures, limited supplies of raw materials, and the need for highly skilled employees.

Rather than creating tangible goods, **service businesses** perform activities for customers. This category includes finance, insurance, transportation, utilities, wholesale and retail trade, banking, entertainment, health care, repairs, and information. Nordstrom, Jiffy Lube, and eBay are examples of service businesses. Service businesses tend to be **labor-intensive businesses**, in that they rely more on human resources than buildings, machinery, and equipment to prosper. However, the Internet and other technologies have reduced the labor required to operate many types of service businesses. Consider Target and Wal-Mart, two well-run retail chains that do some business online but do most of their business through labor-intensive retail stores. In one recent year, the two stores generated roughly $168,000 and $184,000 per employee, respectively. Compare those figures to Amazon.com, which sells exclusively online: That same year it sold $715,000 per employee.[2] Although the product lines of the three stores don't overlap entirely, the dramatic difference in revenue per employee highlights the selling efficiency that the Internet can provide.

capital-intensive businesses
Businesses that require large investments in capital assets

barrier to entry
A critical resource or capability a company must possess before it can enter a particular market or industry

service businesses
Businesses that perform useful activities for customers

labor-intensive businesses
Businesses in which labor costs are more significant than capital costs

Goods and services are useful categories, but as more and more manufacturers focus on servicing and supporting their products and customers, it becomes increasingly difficult to classify many companies as either goods-producing or service businesses. For example, IBM is well known as a manufacturer of computers and other technological goods, but roughly half the company's sales now come from services such as systems design, consulting, and product support.[3]

Over the past few decades, the U.S. economy has undergone a profound transformation from being dominated by manufacturing to being dominated by services. The service sector now accounts for 70 to 80 percent of the nation's economic output, and service businesses will continue to create the vast majority of new jobs.[4] The service sector is growing for a number of reasons:

- *Many consumers have more disposable income.* The 76 million baby boomers in the United States (people born between 1946 and 1964) are in their peak earning years and look for services to help them invest, travel, relax, and stay fit.

- *Services target changing demographic patterns and lifestyle trends.* As the population changes, businesses find opportunities in providing services that people can't or don't do for themselves, from in-home care for an increasingly aging population to self-storage units for people who've used their increasing incomes to buy more stuff than they can fit in their homes.

- *Services are needed to support complex goods and new technology.* From home theaters to automated production systems, many goods now require specialized installation, repair, user training, or extensive support services.

- *Companies are increasingly seeking professional advice.* Many firms turn to professional advisers for help as they seek ways to cut costs, refine processes, expand internationally, and harness the power of the Internet and other technologies.

Understanding Economic Systems

Whether you produce goods or services, running a successful company requires a firm understanding of basic economic principles. **Economics** is the study of how a society uses its scarce resources to produce and distribute goods and services. The study of economic behavior among consumers, businesses, and industries who collectively determine the quantity of goods and services demanded and supplied at different prices is termed **microeconomics**. The study of a country's larger economic issues, such as how firms compete, the effect of government policies, and how an economy maintains and allocates its scarce resources, is termed **macroeconomics**.

All societies must deal with how limited economic resources, or *factors of production,* should be used to satisfy the society's needs. These five factors are natural resources, human resources, capital, entrepreneurs, and knowledge. **Natural resources** are things that are useful in their natural state, such as land, forests, minerals, and water. **Human resources** are people—anyone from company presidents to grocery clerks who works to produce goods and services. **Capital** includes resources such as money, computers, machines, tools, and buildings that a business needs in order to produce goods and services. **Entrepreneurship** is the spirit of innovation, the initiative, and the willingness to take the risks involved in creating and operating new businesses (see Exhibit 1.2). **Knowledge** is the collective intelligence of an organization. *Knowledge workers* are

economics
The study of how society uses scarce resources to produce and distribute goods and services

microeconomics
The study of how consumers, businesses, and industries collectively determine the quantity of goods and services demanded and supplied at different prices

macroeconomics
The study of "big picture" issues in an economy, including competitive behavior among firms, the effect of government policies, and overall resource allocation issues

natural resources
Land, forests, minerals, water, and other tangible assets usable in their natural state

human resources
All the people who work for an organization

capital
The physical, human-made elements used to produce goods and services, such as factories and computers; can also refer to the funds that finance the operations of a business

entrepreneurship
The combination of innovation, initiative, and willingness to take the risks required to create and operate new businesses

knowledge
Expertise gained through experience or association

EXHIBIT 1.2 Entrepreneurial Success Stories

Many great companies start from humble beginnings.

THE COMPANY	ITS START
Amazon.com	In 1994 Jeff Bezos came across a report projecting annual web growth at 2,300 percent. So Bezos left his Wall Street job, headed to Seattle in an aging Chevy Blazer, drafting his business plan as his wife drove. His e-business, Amazon.com, initially focused on selling books over the Internet, but Bezos later expanded his product offerings to include toys, consumer electronics, software, home improvement products, and more. Today, Amazon.com generates billions of dollars in annual sales and helped legitimize the entire concept of e-commerce.
Clorox	In May 1913, five men pooled $100 each and started Clorox. The group had no experience in bleach-making chemistry but suspected that the brine found in salt ponds in San Francisco Bay could be converted into bleach.
Coca-Cola	Pharmacist John Pemberton invented a soft drink in his backyard in 1886. Asa Chandler bought the company for $2,300 in 1891. Current sales now exceed $20 billion every year.
Google	The web's best-known search engine and one of the most influential companies in modern business got its start in a dorm room at Stanford University when founders Larry Page and Sergey Brin put their heads together to develop a new way to find information online.
Marriott	Willard Marriott and his fiancée-partner started a nine-seat A&W soda fountain with $3,000 in 1927. They demonstrated a knack for hospitality and clever marketing from the beginning, eventually building one of the world's leading hotel and resort chains.
Nike	In the early 1960s, Philip Knight and his college track coach sold imported Japanese sneakers from the back of a station wagon. Start-up costs totaled $1,000.
The Limited	In 1963, 26-year-old Leslie Wexner left his family's retail store after having an argument with his father. He opened one small store in a strip mall in Columbus, Ohio. Today the company operates thousands of stores across the United States.
United Parcel Service	In 1907 two Seattle teenagers scraped together $100 to began a message and parcel delivery service for local merchants. UPS now circles the globe with a massive fleet of trucks and aircraft.
Wrigley's Gum	In 1891 young William Wrigley Jr. started selling baking soda in Chicago. To entice new customers, he threw in two packages of chewing gum with every sale. Guess what the customers were more excited about?

employees whose primary contribution to their companies involves the acquisition, analysis, and application of information.

Traditionally, a business or a country was considered to have an advantage if its location offered plentiful supplies of natural resources, human resources, capital, and entrepreneurs. In today's global marketplace, however, intellectual assets are often the key. Companies can now obtain capital from one part of the world, purchase supplies from another, and locate production facilities in still another. They can relocate their operations to wherever they find a steady supply of affordable workers. Thus, countries with the greatest supply of knowledge workers and ones with economic systems that give workers the freedom to pursue their own economic interests will have an advantage in the new economic landscape (see Exhibit 1.3).

The role that individuals and government play in allocating a society's resources depends on the society's **economic system**, the basic set of rules for allocating resources to satisfy its citizens' needs. Economic systems are generally categorized as either *free-market systems* or *planned systems,* although these are really theoretical extremes; virtually every system in use today exhibits aspects of both approaches.

economic system
Means by which a society distributes its resources to satisfy its people's needs

EXHIBIT 1.3 What's New About the New Economy?

Influenced dramatically by innovations in networking, telecommunications, and other technologies, the "new economy" differs from the old, pre-Internet economy in a number of key ways. Besides being faster and more volatile, it's highly dependent on the use of information to gain a competitive advantage.

CHARACTERISTIC	OLD ECONOMY	NEW ECONOMY
Competitive advantage	Competitive advantage based on physical assets	Competitive advantage based on intellectual assets
Financial strategy	Profits maximized by controlling costs	Profits maximized by adding value to goods and services
Technology	Mechanical technology is main influence on economic growth	Information technology is main influence on economic growth
Workforce	Job-specific skills	Transferable skills and lifelong learning
Geography	Firms locate near resources to reduce costs	Firms locate near collaborators and competitors to boost innovation
Capital	Debt financing	Venture capital
Communication with customers	Mass media, with companies controlling a one-way conversation	Fragmented, personalized media, with customers talking back to companies and to each other through multiple conversations

Free-Market Systems

free-market system
Economic system in which decisions about what to produce and in what quantities are decided by the market's buyers and sellers

capitalism
Economic system based on economic freedom and competition

In a **free-market system**, individuals are free to decide what products to produce, how to produce them, whom to sell them to, and at what price to sell them. In other words, they have the chance to succeed—or to fail—by their own efforts. **Capitalism** and *private enterprise* are the terms most often used to describe the free-market system—one in which individuals own and operate the majority of businesses and where competition, supply, and demand determine which goods and services are produced. Capitalism owes its philosophical origins to eighteenth-century philosophers such as Adam Smith. According to Smith, in the ideal capitalist economy (pure capitalism), the *market* (an arrangement between buyer and seller to trade goods and services) serves as a self-correcting mechanism—an "invisible hand" to ensure the production of the goods that society wants in the quantities that society wants, without regulation of any kind.[5]

Because he believed the market is its own regulator, Smith was opposed to government intervention. He held that if anyone's prices or wages strayed from acceptable levels set for everyone, the force of competition would drive them back. In modern practice, however, the government often intervenes in free-market systems to accomplish goals that leaders deem socially or economically desirable. This practice of limited intervention is characteristic of a *mixed economy* or *mixed capitalism*, which is the economic system of the United States and most other countries. For example, federal, state, and local governments intervene in the U.S. economy in a variety of ways, such as influencing particular allocations of resources through tax incentives, prohibiting or restricting the sale of certain goods and services, or setting *price controls*. Price controls can involve maximum allowable prices (such as limiting rent increases or capping the price on gasoline or other products during emergencies and shortages) and minimum allowable prices (such as supplementing the prices of agricultural goods to ensure producers a minimum level of income or establishing minimum wage levels).[6]

Mixed economies, particularly those with a strong capitalist emphasis, offer opportunities for wealth creation but usually attach an element of risk to the potential reward. For instance, it's relatively easy to start a company in a mixed economic system such as the United States, but you could lose all of your start-up money if the company isn't successful. Entrepreneurs and investors willing to face these risks are a vital force in capitalist economies, and they can be rewarded handsomely when they are successful.

Planned Systems

In a **planned system**, governments largely control the allocation of resources and limit freedom of choice in order to accomplish government goals. Because social equality is a major goal of planned systems, private enterprise and the pursuit of private gain are generally regarded as wasteful and exploitative. The planned system that allows individuals the least degree of economic freedom is **communism**, which still exists in a few countries, most notably China. (Keep in mind that even though communism and socialism are discussed here as economic systems, they can be political and social systems as well.) Although pure communism still has its supporters, the future of communism is dismal. As economists Lester Thurow and Robert Heilbroner put it, "It's a great deal easier to design and assemble the skeleton of a mighty economy than to run it."[7] As you'll read in Chapter 3, even as its government remains strongly communist, China has embraced many concepts of capitalism in recent years and has become one of the world's most powerful and important economies as a result.

Socialism lies somewhere between capitalism and communism. Like communism, socialism involves a relatively high degree of government planning and some government ownership of capital resources. However, government involvement is focused on industries considered vital to the common welfare, such as transportation, utilities, medicine, steel, and communications. Private ownership is permitted in industries that are not considered vital, and in these areas both businesses and individuals are allowed to benefit from their own efforts.

Over the past several decades, a number of governments around the world have taken steps to sell or lease existing public facilities to private businesses (or to allow businesses to build these facilities themselves), a practice known as **privatization**. In the United States, private companies now own or operate a number of highways, bridges, ports, prisons, and other infrastructure elements. The primary reason for this trend is the belief that private firms motivated by the profit incentive can do a more efficient job of running these facilities.[8]

Microeconomics: Understanding the Forces of Demand and Supply

At the heart of every business transaction is an exchange between a buyer and a seller. The buyer wants or needs a particular service or good and is willing to pay the seller in order to obtain it. The seller is willing to participate in the transaction because of the anticipated financial gains. In a free-market system, the marketplace (composed of individuals, firms, and industries) and the forces of demand and supply determine the quantity of goods and services produced and the prices at which they are sold. **Demand** refers to the amount of a good or service that customers will buy at a given time at various prices. **Supply** refers to the quantities of a good or service that producers will provide on a particular date at various prices. Simply put, *demand* refers to the behavior of buyers, whereas *supply* refers to the behavior of sellers. Both work together to impose a kind of order on the free-market system.

Understanding Demand

The airline industry offers a helpful demonstration of supply and demand. A **demand curve** is a graph showing the relationship between the amount of product that buyers will purchase at various prices, all other factors being equal. Demand curves typically slope downward, which means that lower prices generally attract more customers. The black line labeled "Initial demand" in Exhibit 1.4 shows a possible demand curve

---

planned system
Economic system in which the government controls most of the factors of production and regulates their allocation

communism
Economic system in which the government owns and operates all productive resources and determines all significant economic choices

socialism
Economic system characterized by public ownership and operation of key industries combined with private ownership and operation of less-vital industries

privatization
The conversion of public ownership to private ownership

demand
Buyers' willingness and ability to purchase products

supply
Specific quantity of a product that the seller is able and willing to provide

demand curve
Graph of the quantities of product that buyers will purchase at various prices

EXHIBIT 1.4

Demand Curve

The demand curve (black line) for economy seats on one airline's Chicago to Denver route shows that the higher the ticket price, the smaller the quantity demanded, and vice versa. Overall demand is rarely static, however; market conditions can shift the entire curve to the left (decreased demand at every price, red line) or to the right (increased demand at every price, green line).

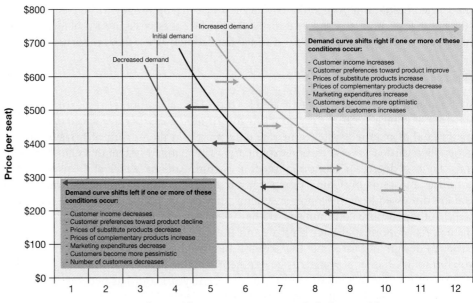

for the monthly number of economy tickets (seats) for an airline's Chicago to Denver route at different prices. You can see that as price decreases, demand increases and vice versa. If demand is strong, airlines can keep their prices consistent or perhaps even raise them. If demand weakens, they can lower prices to stimulate more purchases. (In fact, airlines use sophisticated *yield management* software to constantly adjust prices in order to keep average ticket prices as high as possible while also keeping their planes as full as possible.)

This movement up and down the demand curve is only part of the story, however. Demand at all price points can also increase or decrease in response to a variety of factors. If demand for air travel decreases, the entire demand curve moves to the left (the red line in Exhibit 1.4). If overall demand increases, the curve moves to the right (the green line). The bullet lists in Exhibit 1.4 indicate the effects of some of the major factors that can cause overall demand to increase or decrease:

- customer income
- customer preferences toward the product (fears regarding airline safety, for example)
- the price of *substitute products* (products that can be purchased instead of air travel, including rail tickets, automobile travel, or web conferencing)
- the price of *complementary goods* (such as hotel accommodations or restaurant dining for the airline industry)
- marketing expenditures (for advertising and other promotional efforts)
- customer expectations about future prices and their own financial well-being

For example, if the economy is down and businesses and consumers have less money to spend, overall demand for air travel is likely to shrink. Conversely, if customers have more money to spend, more of them are likely to travel for business or leisure, thereby increasing overall demand. Similarly, if the price of substitute products increases, the demand for air tickets could increase as train travelers look for cheaper alternatives. The price of complementary products can affect air travel demand as well. If the hotels in Denver started a price war, Chicagoans looking for a vacation in the Mile High City might decide it's time to travel.

Understanding Supply

Demand alone is not enough to explain how a company operating in a free-market system sets its prices or production levels. In general, a firm's willingness to produce and sell a good or service increases as the price it can charge and its profit potential per item increase. In other words, as the price goes up, the quantity supplied generally goes up. The depiction of the relationship between prices and quantities that sellers will offer for sale, regardless of demand, is called a **supply curve**. Movement along the supply curve typically slopes upward. So as prices rise, the quantity that sellers are willing to supply also rises. Similarly, as prices decline, the quantity that sellers are willing to supply declines. Exhibit 1.5 shows a possible supply curve for the monthly number of economy tickets (seats) supplied on an airline's Chicago to Denver route at different prices. The graph shows that increasing prices for economy tickets on that route should increase the number of tickets (seats) an airline is willing to provide for that route, and vice versa.

supply curve
Graph of the quantities that sellers will offer for sale, regardless of demand, at various prices

As with demand, supply is dynamic and is affected by a variety of internal and external factors. These include the cost of inputs (such as wages, fuel, and planes for the airlines), the number of competitors in the marketplace, and advancements in technology that allow companies to operate more efficiently. A change in any of these variables can shift the entire supply curve, either increasing or decreasing the amount offered at various prices, as Exhibit 1.5 suggests.

Understanding How Demand and Supply Interact

Customers and suppliers clearly have opposite goals: Customers want to buy at the lowest possible price, and suppliers want to sell at the highest possible price. Neither side can "win" this contest. Customers might want to pay $100 for a ticket from Chicago to Denver, but airlines aren't willing to sell many, if any, at that price. Conversely, the airlines might want to charge $1,000 for a ticket, but customers aren't willing to buy many, if any, at that price. So the market in effect arranges a compromise known as the **equilibrium price**, at which the demand and supply curves intersect (see Exhibit 1.6). At the equilibrium price point, customers are willing to buy as many tickets as the airline is willing to sell.

equilibrium price
Point at which quantity supplied equals quantity demanded

Since the supply and demand curves are dynamic, so is the equilibrium point. As variables affecting supply and demand change, so will the equilibrium price. For example, increased concerns about passenger safety or longer lines at airport security checkpoints

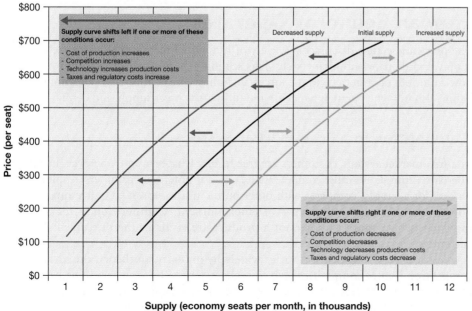

EXHIBIT 1.5

Supply Curve

This supply curve, again in this case for economy seats on the Denver to Chicago route, shows that the higher the price, the more tickets (seats) the airline would be willing to supply, all else being equal. As with demand, however, the entire supply curve can shift to the left (decreased supply) or the right (increased supply) as producers respond to internal and external forces.

EXHIBIT 1.6

The Relationship Between Supply and Demand

The equilibrium price is established when the amount of a product that suppliers are willing to sell at a given price equals the amount that consumers are willing to buy at that price.

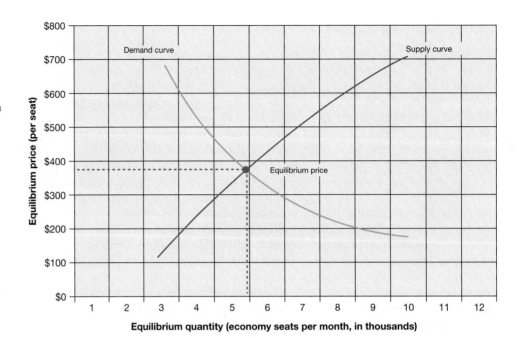

could encourage travelers to make alternative economic choices such as automobile travel or web conferencing, thus reducing the demand for air travel at every price and moving the equilibrium point as well. Suppliers might respond to such a reduction in demand by either cutting the number of flights offered or lowering ticket prices in order to restore the equilibrium level.

Questions of supply, demand, and equilibrium pricing are among the toughest issues you'll face as a manager. Imagine that you're a concert promoter planning for next year's summer season. You have to balance the potential demand for each performer across a range of prices in the hope of matching the supply you can deliver (the seating capacity of each venue and the number of shows)—and you have to make these predictions months in advance. Predict well, and you'll make a tidy profit. Predict poorly, and you could lose a pile of money. You'll learn more about pricing in Chapter 10.

Macroeconomics: Understanding How an Economy Operates

The previous section discussed a variety of individual factors that affect the forces of supply and demand simultaneously. This section expands that discussion by showing how a number of larger economic forces, including competition and government regulation, also influence market behavior and ultimately affect supply and demand.

Competition in a Free-Market System

In a free-market system, customers are free to buy whatever and wherever they please. Therefore, companies must compete with rivals for potential customers. Apple's iTunes service, for example, competes with other online music stores, CDs, live music, illegal downloads, and even other types of entertainment. **Competition** is the situation in which two or more suppliers of a product are rivals in the pursuit of the same customers.

The nature of competition varies widely by industry. In theory, the ideal type of competition is **pure competition**, which is characterized by three conditions: a marketplace of multiple buyers and sellers, a product or service with nearly identical features such as wheat or cotton, and low barriers of entry. When these three conditions exist, no

competition
Rivalry among businesses for the same customer

pure competition
Situation in which so many buyers and sellers exist that no single buyer or seller can individually influence market prices

single firm or group of firms in an industry becomes large enough to influence prices and thereby distort the workings of the free-market system. At the other extreme, in a **monopoly** there is only one supplier of a product in a given market, and that supplier thus is able to determine the price (within regulatory limits).

Most industries exist somewhere between the extremes of pure competition and pure monopoly. For instance, commercial aircraft manufacturing is dominated by only a few suppliers (primarily Boeing and Airbus Industries), a situation known as an **oligopoly**. Like monopoly suppliers, oligopoly suppliers can sometimes exercise a degree of power over customers, based simply on the customers' lack of alternatives.

Most of the competition in advanced free-market economies is **monopolistic competition**, in which a large number of sellers (none of which dominates the market) offer products that can be distinguished from competing products in at least some small way. Toothpaste, cosmetics, soft drinks, Internet search engines, and restaurants are examples of products that can vary in the features each offers.

When markets become filled with competitors and products start to look alike, companies use price, speed, quality, service, or innovation to gain a **competitive advantage**—something that sets one company apart from its rivals and makes its products more appealing to consumers. For example, Google competes on the quality of its search results, Southwest Airlines competes on price, and Jiffy Lube competes on speed. The risk/reward nature of capitalism promotes constant innovation in pursuit of competitive advantage, rewarding companies that do the best job of creating appealing goods and services.

monopoly
Market in which there are no direct competitors so that one company dominates

oligopoly
Market dominated by a few producers

monopolistic competition
Situation in which many sellers differentiate their products from those of competitors in at least some small way

competitive advantage
Ability to perform in one or more ways that competitors cannot match

Government's Role in a Free-Market System

Although the free-market system generally works well, it's far from perfect. If left unchecked, the economic forces that make capitalism succeed may also create severe problems for some groups or individuals. In an attempt to correct these types of problems, government serves four major economic roles: It enacts laws and creates regulations to foster competition, it regulates and deregulates certain industries, it protects stakeholders' rights, and it intervenes to contribute to economic stability.

Fostering Competition

Because competition generally benefits the U.S. economy, the federal government and state and local governments create thousands of new laws and regulations every year to preserve competition and ensure that no single enterprise becomes too powerful. For instance, if a company has a monopoly, it can harm consumers by raising prices, cutting output, or stifling innovation. Furthermore, because most monopolies have total control over certain products and prices and the market share for those products, it's extremely difficult for competitors to enter markets where monopolies exist. For these reasons, over the last century or so, a number of laws and regulations have been established to help prevent individual companies or groups of companies from gaining control of markets in ways that restrain competition or harm consumers.

Antitrust Legislation   *Antitrust* laws limit what businesses can and cannot do to ensure that all competitors have an equal chance of producing a product, reaching the market, and making a profit. Some of the earliest government moves in this arena produced such landmark pieces of legislation as the Sherman Antitrust Act, the Clayton Antitrust Act, and the Federal Trade Commission Act, which generally sought to rein in the power of a few huge companies that had financial and management control of a significant number of other companies in the same industry. Usually referred to as *trusts* (hence the label *antitrust legislation*), these huge companies controlled enough of the supply and

The potential rewards available in a free-market economy encourage innovators to create new and exciting products such as Apple's iPod players and iTunes service.

distribution in their respective industries, such as Standard Oil in the petroleum industry, to muscle smaller competitors out of the way.

In recent years, software giant Microsoft has been the target of antitrust activity by the U.S. government and the European Union (EU) over allegedly using its dominance in the operating systems market (through Microsoft Windows) to unfairly influence competition and customer choice in the application software market (where it offers such products as Word and Excel). At one point, a U.S. federal judge even ordered that Microsoft be split into two independent companies so that other application software companies could compete against it more effectively. This decision was overturned the following year, but the issues didn't fade away. Antitrust regulators in the EU ordered the company to "unbundle" its Windows Media Player software from the Windows operating system. The EU asserted that making the media software part of the operating system put other media software companies (such as RealNetworks) at a competitive disadvantage.[9]

Merger and Acquisition Approvals   To preserve competition and customer choice, governments may occasionally prohibit two companies in the same industry from combining through a merger or acquisition. When Whole Foods (based in Austin, Texas) announced a deal to acquire Wild Oats (based in Boulder, Colorado), another natural foods grocery chain, the Federal Trade Commission sued to block the purchase, claiming the merger would reduce nationwide competition to the degree that prices would increase and quality would decrease.[10] Another alternative is to force the companies to *divest* (sell) parts of the newly combined company. For instance, the U.S. Department of Justice recently required Monsanto and Delta & Pine Land Company to divest a seed company in order to preserve price competition in the cottonseed market.[11]

Regulation and Deregulation

As part of their mandate to ensure fair competition, ethical business practices, safe working conditions, and general public safety, government bodies at the federal, state, and local levels impose a variety of regulations on many industries. In a *regulated industry,* close government control is substituted for free competition, and competition is either limited or eliminated. In extreme cases, regulators may even decide who can enter an industry, what customers they must serve, and how much they can charge. For years, the telecommunications, airline, banking, and electric utility industries fell under strict government control. However, the trend over the past few decades has been to open up competition in regulated industries by removing or relaxing existing regulations. Hopes are that such *deregulation* will allow new industry competitors to enter the market, create more choices for customers, and keep prices in check. But the debate is ongoing about whether deregulation achieves these goals. After an experiment with partial deregulation in the electric market in California went disastrously awry, leading to skyrocketing prices and unstable supply, many states are now looking at varying degrees of regulation in key industries.[12]

Protecting Stakeholders

stakeholders
Individuals or groups to whom business has a responsibility

In addition to fostering competition, another important role the government plays is to protect the stakeholders of a business. Businesses have many **stakeholders**—groups that are affected by (or that affect) a business's operations, including colleagues, employees, supervisors, investors, customers, suppliers, and society at large. In the course of serving one or more of these stakeholders, a business may sometimes neglect the interests of other stakeholders in the process. For example, managers who are too narrowly focused on generating wealth for shareholders might not spend the funds necessary to create a safe work environment for employees or to reduce waste. Similarly, a publicly traded company that withholds information about its true financial performance hampers the ability of investors to make informed decisions.

EXHIBIT 1.7 Major Government Agencies and What They Do

Government agencies protect stakeholders by developing and promoting standards, regulating and overseeing industries, and enforcing laws and regulations.

GOVERNMENT AGENCY OR COMMISSION	MAJOR AREAS OF RESPONSIBILITY
Consumer Product Safety Commission (CPSC)	Regulates and protects public from unreasonable risks of injury from consumer products
Environmental Protection Agency (EPA)	Develops and enforces standards to protect the environment
Equal Employment Opportunity Commission (EEOC)	Protects employees from discriminatory employment practices
Federal Aviation Administration (FAA)	Sets rules for the commercial airline industry
Federal Communications Commission (FCC)	Oversees communication by telephone, telegraph, radio, and television
Federal Energy Regulatory Commission (FERC)	Regulates rates and sales of electric power and natural gas
Federal Highway Administration (FHA)	Regulates vehicle safety requirements
Federal Trade Commission (FTC)	Enforces laws and guidelines regarding unfair business practices and acts to stop false and deceptive advertising and labeling
Food and Drug Administration (FDA)	Enforces laws and regulations to prevent distribution of harmful foods, drugs, medical devices, and cosmetics
Interstate Commerce Commission (ICC)	Regulates and oversees carriers engaged in transportation between states: railroads, bus lines, trucking companies, oil pipelines, and waterways
Occupational Safety and Health Administration (OSHA)	Promotes worker safety and health
Securities and Exchange Commission (SEC)	Protects investors and maintains the integrity of the securities markets
Transportation Security Administration (TSA)	Protects the national transportation infrastructure

To protect consumers, employees, shareholders, and the environment from the potentially harmful actions of business, the government has established numerous regulatory agencies (see Exhibit 1.7). Many of these agencies have the power to pass and enforce rules and regulations within their specific area of authority. Such regulations are intended to encourage businesses to behave ethically and in a socially responsible way. Chapter 2 takes a closer look at society's concerns for ethical and socially responsible behavior, specific government agencies that regulate such behavior, and the efforts by businesses to become better corporate citizens.

Contributing to Economic Stability

A nation's economy is always in a state of change, expanding or contracting in response to the combined effects of such factors as technological breakthroughs, changes in investment patterns, shifts in consumer attitudes, world events, and basic economic forces. *Economic expansion* occurs when the economy is growing and people are spending more money. Consumer purchases stimulate businesses to produce more goods and services, which in turn stimulates employment and wages, which then stimulate more consumer purchases. *Economic contraction* occurs when such spending declines. Businesses cut back on production, employees are laid off, and the economy as a whole slows down.

recession
Period during which national income, employment, and production all fall

recovery
Period during which income, employment, production, and spending rise

business cycles
Fluctuations in the rate of growth that an economy experiences over a period of several years

monetary policy
Government policy and actions taken by the Federal Reserve Board to regulate the nation's money supply

If the period of downward swing is severe, the nation may enter into a **recession**, traditionally defined as two consecutive quarters of decline in the *gross domestic product*, a basic measure of a country's economic output (see page 20). When a downward swing or recession is over, the economy enters into a period of **recovery**: Companies buy more, factories produce more, employment is high, and workers spend their earnings. These up-and-down swings are generally known as **business cycles**, although many economists prefer *economic fluctuations* because "cycle" implies a sense of regular repeatability that real economies do not exhibit.[13]

Monetary Policy   While you're busy pondering your company's health during the ups and downs of economic fluctuation, federal economists and bankers will be making their own predictions and "pulling the strings" of the national economy through monetary policy and fiscal policy. Every economy has a certain amount of "spendable" money in it at any given time, a quantity known as the *money supply*. **Monetary policy** involves adjusting the nation's money supply by increasing or decreasing interest rates. In the United States, monetary policy is controlled primarily by the Federal Reserve Board (often called "the Fed"), a group of appointed government officials who oversee the country's central banking system.

The Fed influences the money supply to make certain that enough money and credit are available to fuel a healthy economy. However, it must act carefully, because altering the money supply affects interest rates, inflation, and the economy. When the money supply is increased, more money is available for loans, so banks can charge lower interest rates to borrowers. On the other hand, an increased money supply can lead to more consumer spending and can result in the demand for goods exceeding supply. When demand exceeds supply, sellers may raise their prices, leading to inflation. In turn, inflation can slow economic growth—a situation the Fed wants to avoid.

The Fed can use four basic tools to influence the money supply (see Exhibit 1.8):

- *Changing the reserve requirement.* All financial institutions must set aside *reserves,* sums of money equal to a certain percentage of their deposits. The Fed can change the *reserve requirement,* the percentage of deposits that banks must set aside, to influence the money supply. However, the Fed rarely uses this technique because a small change can have a drastic effect. Increasing the reserve requirement slows down the economy: Banks have less money to lend, so businesses can't borrow to expand and consumers can't borrow to buy goods and services. Conversely, reducing this requirement boosts the economy, because banks have more money to lend to businesses and consumers.

- *Changing the discount rate.* The Fed can also change the *discount rate*, the interest rate it charges on loans to commercial banks and other depository institutions.

EXHIBIT 1.8

Influencing the Money Supply

The Federal Reserve uses four tools to influence the money supply as it attempts to stimulate economic growth while keeping inflation and interest rates at acceptable levels.

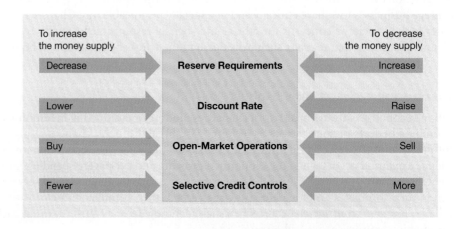

When the Fed raises the discount rate, member banks generally raise the *prime interest rate*, the lowest interest rate on short-term loans to preferred borrowers. This discourages loans, and in so doing tightens the money supply, which can slow down economic growth. By contrast, lowering the discount rate results in lower lending rates, which can encourage more borrowing and stimulate economic growth.

▪ *Conducting open-market operations.* The tool the Fed uses most often to influence the money supply is the power to buy and sell U.S. government bonds (a *bond* is a mechanism for borrowing money). Because anyone can buy these bonds on the open market, this tool is known as *open-market operations.* If the Fed is concerned about inflation, it can reduce the money supply by selling U.S. government bonds, which takes cash out of circulation. And when the Fed wants to boost the economy, it can buy back government bonds, putting cash into circulation and increasing the money supply.

▪ *Establishing selective credit controls.* The Fed can also use *selective credit controls* to set the terms of credit for various kinds of loans. This tool includes the power to set *margin requirements,* the percentage of the purchase price that an investor must pay in cash when purchasing a stock or a bond on credit. By altering the margin requirements, the Fed is able to influence how much cash is tied up in stock market transactions.

Monetary policy affects many aspects of the economy, such as when higher interest rates dampen demand for new housing.

A good example of the Fed's influence on your life as a consumer and a business manager is its manipulation of the *discount rate,* the interest rate it charges commercial banks to borrow money. When you borrow money from a bank to buy a house or new manufacturing equipment, the interest rate you pay is heavily influenced by the discount rate, and your interest rate can have a profound effect on your purchasing behavior. For instance, if you can handle $2,000 a month for a house payment and interest rates are at 7 percent, you can afford a $300,000 house, roughly speaking. However, if rates climb to 10 percent, your price range suddenly drops to around $230,000. At 16 percent, you'll be shopping for a $150,000 house—only half the house you can buy with a 7-percent loan.

In addition to the initial impact that a change in the money supply can have, money injected into the economy has a *multiplier effect* as it makes its way through the system. For example, if a company spends money to build a large office complex, thousands of construction workers will be gainfully employed and earn wages. If some of these workers decide to spend their extra income to buy new cars, car dealers will have more income. The car dealers, in turn, might invest their increased revenue in new equipment for the service department, and the sales staff (who earn commissions on the car sales) might buy new clothes, and so on. This *circular flow* of money through the economic system links all elements of the U.S. economy by exchanging goods and services for money, which is then used to buy more goods and services in a never-ending cycle.

fiscal policy
Use of government revenue collection and spending to influence the business cycle

Fiscal Policy   **Fiscal policy** involves changes in the government's revenues and expenditures to stimulate a slow economy or dampen a growing economy that is in danger of overheating. On the revenue side, governments can adjust the revenue they bring in by changing tax rates and various fees collected from individuals and businesses (see Exhibit 1.9). When the federal government lowers the income tax rate, for instance, it does so with the hope

---

How This Affects You

1. As a consumer, how do you benefit from competition among the companies that supply you with the goods and services you need? Does this competition have any negative impact on your life?

2. Would it be wise for the government to put price controls on college tuition? Why or why not?

3. How is the federal budget deficit likely to affect you? What about your children as they grow up?

EXHIBIT 1.9

Major Types of Taxes

Running a government is an expensive affair. Here are the major types of taxes that national governments, states, counties, and cities collect to fund government operations and projects.

TYPE OF TAX	LEVIED ON
Income taxes	Income earned by individuals and businesses. Income taxes are the government's largest single source of revenue.
Real property taxes	Assessed value of the land and structures owned by businesses and individuals.
Sales taxes	Retail purchases made by customers. Sales taxes are collected by retail businesses at the time of the sale and then forwarded to the government.
Excise taxes	Selected items such as gasoline, tobacco, and liquor. Often referred to as "sin" taxes, excise taxes are implemented to help control potentially harmful practices.
Payroll taxes	Earnings of individuals to help fund Social Security, Medicare, and unemployment compensation. Corporations match employee contributions.

that consumers and businesses will spend and invest the money they save by paying lower taxes.

On the expenditure side, local, state, and federal government bodies constitute a huge market for goods and services, with billions of dollars of collective buying power. Governments can stimulate the economy by increasing their purchases, sometimes even to the point of creating new programs or projects with the specific purpose of expanding employment opportunities and increasing demand for goods and services.

Fiscal policy decisions nearly always involve discussions of budget deficits, both annual deficits (when the government spends more than it takes in during any given year) and the accumulating national debt (the result of the many years in which the government spends more than it receives). The U.S. national debt is now heading toward $10 trillion, and the interest payments alone on this debt cost U.S. taxpayers several hundred billion dollars a year, money that could be spent on health care, education, lower taxes, or dozens of other areas. Unless the government is able to bring its revenues and expenses closer in line, future generations will be forced to pay higher taxes, accept a lower level of government services—or both.[14]

How a Free-Market System Monitors Its Economic Performance

economic indicators
Statistics that measure variables in the economy

Economic indicators are statistics such as interest rates, unemployment rates, housing data, and industrial productivity that are used to monitor and measure economic performance. Statistics that point to what may happen to the economy in the future are called *leading indicators;* statistics that signal a swing in the economy after the movement has begun are called *lagging indicators.*

Watching Economic Indicators

Economists monitor the performance of the economy by watching a variety of indicators. Unemployment statistics, for example, signal future changes in consumer spending. When unemployment rises, people have less money to spend, and the economy suffers. Housing starts, another leading indicator, show where several industries are headed. When housing starts drop, builders stop hiring and may even lay off workers. Meanwhile, orders fall for plumbing fixtures, carpets, and appliances, so manufacturers decrease production and workers' hours. Home-improvement and furniture retailers, real estate agents, and others dependent on housing-related transactions begin to feel the pinch as well. Following the circular flow concept, these cutbacks ripple through the economy and lead to slower income and job growth and weaker consumer spending. Since all the expenditures related to housing make up roughly 15 percent of the nation's economy, a slowdown in housing can be bad news for a wide swath of the U.S. economy.[15] Another leading indicator is durable-goods orders, or orders for goods that typically last more than three years (which can mean everything from desk chairs to airplanes). A rise in durable-goods orders is a positive indicator that business spending is turning around. In addition to all these indicators, economists closely monitor price changes and national output to get a sense of how well the economy is working.

Measuring Price Changes

Price changes, especially price increases, are another important economic indicator. In a period of rising prices, the purchasing power of a dollar erodes, which means that you can purchase fewer things with today's dollar than you could in a prior period. Over time, price increases tend to lead to wage increases, which in turn add pressures for higher prices, setting a vicious cycle in motion.

Inflation and Deflation

Inflation is a steady rise in the prices of goods and services throughout the economy. When the inflation rate begins to decline, economists use the term *disinflation*. **Deflation**, on the other hand, is the sustained fall in the general price level for goods and services. It is the opposite of inflation; that is, purchasing power increases because a dollar held today will buy more tomorrow. In a deflationary period, investors postpone major purchases in anticipation of lower prices in the future. Keep in mind that although prices in the overall economy tend to increase year after year, not all industries and product categories necessarily follow this trend. The average price of a new computer might drop while the price of the electricity needed to power it goes up.[16]

Price Indexes

Price indexes offer a way to monitor the inflation or deflation in various sectors of the economy. The best known of these, the **consumer price index (CPI)**, measures the rate of inflation by comparing the change in prices of a representative "basket" of consumer goods and services, such as clothing, food, housing, and utilities. A numerical weight is assigned to each item in the basket to adjust for each item's relative importance in the marketplace. The CPI has always been a hot topic because it is used by the government to index Social Security payments, and it is widely used by businesses in various contracts to calculate cost-of-living increases. However, like most economic indicators, the CPI is not perfect. Although it is based on data from thousands of retail establishments across the country, the representative basket of goods and services may not reflect the prices and consumption patterns of the area in which you live or of your specific household. The U.S. Bureau of Labor Statistics periodically adjusts the mix of products used in the CPI, but the CPI should always be viewed as a general indicator of price trends, not as a specific measurement.[17]

In contrast to the CPI, the **producer price index (PPI)** measures price at the producer or wholesaler level. (Although the PPI is usually referred to as a single index, it is actually a family of more than 600 industry-specific indexes.) PPI calculations cover virtually the entire goods-producing segment of the U.S. economy and many service sectors as well. In recent years, economists have noticed an important

inflation
Economic condition in which prices rise steadily throughout the economy

deflation
Economic condition in which prices fall steadily throughout the economy

consumer price index (CPI)
Monthly statistic that measures changes in the prices of about 400 goods and services that consumers buy

producer price index (PPI)
A statistical measure of price trends at the producer and wholesaler levels

Food is one of the major elements of the consumer price index.

change in the relationship between the PPI and the CPI. Historically, cost increases at the producer level were generally passed along to the consumer level. For instance, if automakers had to pay more for steel, they would work that increase into the price of new cars. As global competition heats up, however, producers find they can't always pass along price increases and remain competitive. The alternative is to accept lower profit levels or else find ways to improve productivity, such as by investing in more-efficient factories or clamping down on labor costs.[18]

Measuring a Nation's Output

gross domestic product (GDP) Value of all the final goods and services produced by businesses located within a nation's borders; excludes receipts from overseas operations of domestic companies

The broadest measure of an economy's health is the **gross domestic product (GDP)**. The GDP measures a country's output—its production, distribution, and use of goods and services—by computing the sum of all goods and services produced for *final* use in a market during a specified period (usually a year). The products may be produced by either domestic or foreign companies as long as the production takes place within a nation's boundaries. Sales from a Honda assembly plant in California, for instance, would be included in the U.S. GDP, even though Honda is a Japanese company. Although far from perfect, the GDP enables a nation to evaluate its economic policies and to compare its current performance with prior periods or with the performance of other nations.

gross national product (GNP) Value of all the final goods and services produced by domestic businesses that includes receipts from overseas operations and excludes receipts from foreign-owned businesses within a nation's borders

GDP has largely replaced an earlier measure called the **gross national product (GNP)**, which excludes the value of production from foreign-owned businesses within a nation's boundaries and includes receipts from the overseas operations of domestic companies. GNP considers *who* is responsible for the production; GDP considers *where* the production occurs.

The Challenges You'll Face in the Global Economy

globalization Tendency of the world's economies to act as a single interdependent economy

No matter which direction the various elements of the economy move in the coming years, two things are certain. First, the U.S. economy is inextricably tied to the larger global economy. **Globalization**—the increasing tendency of the world to act as one market instead of a series of national ones—opens new markets for a company's goods and services and new sources of natural resources, labor, and skills. Second, as an employee, a manager, or an entrepreneur in this global business scenario, your success will depend on how well you can handle some key challenges:

Successful businesses recognize not only the need to support and embrace an increasingly diverse workforce but also the advantage of having multiple perspectives to help make decisions and communicate with diverse customer bases.

■ *Producing quality goods and services that satisfy customers' changing needs.* Today's customer has access to considerable amounts of information about product choices and often has a wide range of goods and services from which to choose. For many businesses, competing in the global economy means competing on the basis of *speed* (getting products to market sooner), *quality* (doing a better job of meeting customer expectations), and *customer satisfaction* (making sure buyers are happy with every aspect of the purchase, from the shopping experience until they're through using the product). Success isn't a one-time event, either. To be successful, companies must work constantly to keep satisfying customers. Friendster helped revolutionize online communication when it launched the first successful social networking website, but performance problems and limitations on what people could do with their pages began to frustrate users. When MySpace and others jumped in with more appealing solutions, Friendster users left in a stampede. But MySpace can't rest, either; some of its users are now migrating to Ning, Vox, Esnips, and other sites that offer even more customization and personal control.[19]

- *Thinking like an entrepreneur, even if you're an employee in a large company.* Given the uncertainty and multiple challenges of today's economic environment, it is more important than ever to have entrepreneurial skills—embracing new ideas, finding and creating opportunities, taking decisive action even when faced with limited information, focusing with laser intensity on the core activities of the business, and directing all your energy toward satisfying customers and outperforming competitors.

- *Thinking globally and embracing a culturally diverse workforce.* Globalization opens new markets for a company's goods, increases competition, and changes the composition of the workforce into one that is more diverse in race, gender, age, physical and mental abilities, lifestyle, culture, education, ideas, and background. As population patterns evolve and businesses continue to reach across national and cultural borders, companies must also embrace the increasingly diverse workforce—both to support the needs of everyone in the workforce and to realize the benefits of having workers who represent a wider range of cultural backgrounds.

- *Behaving in an ethically and socially responsible manner.* With global expansion and technological change, businesses face an increasing number of ethical and social issues (as Chapter 2 discusses). Topics of current concern include the marketing of unhealthful products, the use of questionable accounting practices to compute financial results, and the pollution of the environment. In the future, businesses can expect continued pressure from environmental groups, consumers, employees, and government regulators to act ethically and responsibly.

- *Keeping pace with technology and electronic commerce.* Everywhere we look, technology is reshaping the world. The Internet and innovations in computerization, miniaturization, and telecommunication have made it possible for people anywhere in the world to exchange information and goods. Such technologies are collapsing boundaries and changing the way customers, suppliers, and companies interact. At the same time, technology can introduce new problems, from the loss of privacy to the economic damage caused by computer viruses.[20] In short, the Internet has touched every business and industry and is changing all facets of business life.

As these challenges suggest, doing business in the twenty-first century means working in a world of increasing uncertainty where change is the norm, not the exception. In the coming chapters, you'll explore specific challenges that businesses are facing in the global economy and learn how to apply the lessons of real-world companies to your own aspirations as an executive or entrepreneur.

Learning from Business Blunders

Oops: Hey, look what came with today's newspaper: a quarter of a million credit card numbers! After a well-intentioned effort to reduce waste by recycling used office paper to wrap bundles of newspapers delivered to carriers and retailers, the *Boston Globe* and the *Telegram & Gazette* in Worcester, Massachusetts, discovered that some of the used paper contained the credit and debit card numbers of 240,000 newspaper subscribers.

What You Can Learn: This mistake could've been prevented or at least minimized at several stages. First, any documents with sensitive customer data should never have been placed in regular recycling bins. Any such paperwork needs to be disposed of using secure methods in which documents are kept under lock and key until they are destroyed. Second, the overall system of using recycled paper for the bundle wraps should have been analyzed before being implemented to uncover potential problems such as this. Third, the employees handling the bundled newspapers might've noticed that something was amiss and immediately alerted superiors (presumably, this is how the error was discovered, but not before 9,000 bundles had been delivered). Particularly in light of the potential costs of identity theft, every business has a strict ethical obligation to protect all sensitive customer data.

How This Affects You

1. If you're currently working, how might a decrease in the employment rate in your city or region affect your job? (If you're not currently working, pick a job in the local economy and make the same analysis.)

2. In your multiple economic roles as a consumer, employee, and investor, is inflation a good thing, a bad thing, or both? Explain your answer.

3. If you're currently working, how could you think more like an entrepreneur to help your company and boost your career? (If you're not currently working, pick a job in the local economy and make the same analysis.)

Summary of Learning Objectives

1 **Define what a business is, and identify four vital social and economic contributions that businesses make.**

A business is a profit-seeking activity that provides goods and services to satisfy consumers' needs. The driving force behind most businesses is the chance to earn a profit; however, non-profit organizations exist to provide society with a social or educational service. Businesses make four vital contributions: They provide society with necessities; they provide people with jobs and a means to prosper; they pay taxes that are used by the government to provide services for its citizens; and they reinvest their profits in the economy, thereby increasing a nation's wealth.

2 **Differentiate between goods-producing and service businesses, and list five factors contributing to the increase in the number of service businesses.**

Goods-producing businesses produce tangible goods and tend to be capital intensive, whereas service businesses produce intangible goods and tend to be labor intensive. The number of service businesses is increasing because (1) consumers have more disposable income to spend on taking care of themselves; (2) many services target consumers' needs brought about by changing demographic patterns and lifestyle trends; (3) consumers need assistance with using and integrating new technology into their business operations and lifestyles; (4) companies are turning to consultants and other professionals for advice to remain competitive; and (5) in general, barriers to entry are lower for service companies than they are for goods-producing businesses.

3 **Differentiate between a free-market system and a planned system.**

In a free-market system, individuals have a high degree of freedom to decide what is produced, by whom, and for whom. Moreover, the pursuit of private gain is regarded as a worthwhile goal. In a planned system, governments limit the individual's freedom of choice in order to accomplish government goals, control the allocation of resources, and restrict private ownership to personal and household items. The pursuit of private gain is nonexistent under a planned system. Nearly all modern economies fall somewhere between purely free-market and purely planned.

4 **Explain how supply and demand interact to affect price.**

In the simplest sense, supply and demand affect price in the following manner: When the price goes up, the quantity demanded goes down, but the supplier's incentive to produce more goes up. When the price goes down, the quantity demanded increases, whereas the quantity supplied may (or may not) decline. When the interests of buyers and sellers are in balance, an equilibrium price is established. However, adjusting price or supply to meet or spur demand does not guarantee profitability; business may not be able to adjust costs and price far enough and quickly enough. The important thing to remember is that in a free-market system, the interaction of supply and demand determines what is produced and in what amounts.

5 **Discuss the four major economic roles of the U.S. government.**

First, the U.S. government fosters competition by enacting laws and regulations, by enforcing antitrust legislation, and by approving mergers and acquisitions, with the power to block those that might restrain competition. Second, it regulates certain industries where competition would be wasteful or excessive. Third, it protects stakeholders from potentially harmful actions of businesses. Finally, it contributes to economic stability by regulating the money supply and by spending for the public good.

6 **Explain how a free-market system monitors its economic performance.**

Economists evaluate economic performance by monitoring a variety of economic indicators, such as unemployment statistics, housing starts, durable-goods orders, and inflation. They compute the consumer price index (CPI) to keep an eye on price changes—especially inflation. In addition, economists measure the productivity of a nation by computing the country's gross domestic product (GDP)—the sum of all goods and services produced by both domestic and foreign companies as long as they are located within a nation's boundaries.

7 **Identify five challenges you will face as a business professional in the coming years.**

The five challenges identified in the chapter are (1) producing quality products and services that satisfy customers' changing needs; (2) thinking like an entrepreneur, even if you're an employee in a large company; (3) thinking globally and embracing a culturally diverse workforce; (4) behaving in an ethically and socially responsible manner; and (5) keeping pace with technology and electronic commerce.

Behind the Scenes

Moving the Music at Apple iTunes

When Steve Jobs surveyed the marketplace for online music, he no doubt liked some of the things he saw more than others. On the plus side, Apple was a well-known and highly regarded presence in both the computer and music industries, so almost anything the company chose to do would have the support and respect of many consumers and potential business partners. Plus, 2 million people were already walking around with an Apple iPod, the enormously popular portable music player. Moreover, Apple's design team had a proven knack for making technology easier to use, a critical issue in the technically complicated arena of digital music.

On the minus side, Jobs knew there would be serious challenges in any effort to turn online music into a successful business venture. The technology would be complex, starting from the need to collect and store hundreds of millions of songs and to make them easily available to millions of online customers at once. The technology might've been the easiest part of the whole problem, however. The music business is a complex stew of strong personalities, strong traditions, tangled legal contracts, and lots of people who want a piece of the financial action, including performers, songwriters, music publishers, and record companies. Some artists refuse to sell songs individually out of fear it will hurt CD album sales (and a few refuse to sell their music online at all). As a result, Apple and other companies often need to negotiate deals one song at a time—all of which takes time and costs money. To complicate matters even further, contractual terms differ from country to country, requiring a new round of negotiations for each place. Then there are the millions of music listeners who were already in the habit of simply making copies of pirated songs. How could they be convinced to pay for a product that they'd already been taking for free?

After 25 years of doing commercial battle with the likes of IBM and Microsoft, though, Steve Jobs has never been one to back down from a challenge. He added up those pluses and minuses, then decided to lead Apple into the fray. The result is iTunes.com, the web-based music site that millions of listeners now count on for getting the music they love. True to Apple form, iTunes combines style with simplicity, making it easy for anyone with an iPod or the iTunes player on their computer to load up on their favorite songs at $0.99 each (a separate category of songs without usage restrictions began selling for $1.29 in 2007). The store now offers millions of songs plus podcasts, audio books, TV shows, movies, games, and even college course lectures.

Measured by sales volume, at least, it's hard to say that iTunes has been anything other than a success, having sold several billion songs so far, plus 50 million TV shows and more than a million movies. And it has helped the company sell over 100 million iPods, which in turn has created an entire industry of accessories, with more than 4,000 complementary products.

Is iTunes a profitable business venture, though? After all, when you're selling something for $0.99, you'd better run a pretty tight ship if you're going to make any money. Skeptics abounded when iTunes was launched. When Apple collects those $0.99 for each song it sells, it first hands over $0.70 to whichever company controls the rights to the song. (This company then has to divide $0.70 among music publishers, performers, and songwriters.) From the $0.29 Apple keeps, it needs to cover its costs for advertising, staffing, computer systems, and other business expenses. A single nationwide advertising campaign can cost millions of dollars, so you can get an idea of how hard it is to stretch $0.29 to cover costs and turn a profit.

However, the company has said it just about breaks even on iTunes, and one financial analyst concluded that it might make as much as $0.10 per song. Now, $0.10 won't buy you anything these days, but $0.10 multiplied by several billion certainly will.[21]

Critical Thinking Questions

1. If Steve Jobs decided to let iTunes operate at a loss to generate more sales of iPods, does iTunes still qualify as a profit-seeking business? Explain your answer.
2. Is iTunes a goods-producing business or a service business? Why?
3. What barriers to entry did iTunes have to overcome to enter the online music business?

LEARN MORE ONLINE

Visit the iTunes website at www.apple.com/itunes. What does the website do to appeal to customers? What goods and services are offered? In what ways does the website encourage visitors to make purchases?

(For the latest information on iTunes, visit www.prenhall.com/bovée and click on "Real-Time Updates.") ■

Key Terms

barrier to entry (5)	entrepreneurship (6)	monopoly (13)
business (4)	equilibrium price (11)	natural resources (6)
business cycles (16)	fiscal policy (17)	nonprofit organizations (4)
capital (6)	free-market system (8)	oligopoly (13)
capital-intensive businesses (5)	globalization (20)	planned system (9)
capitalism (8)	goods-producing businesses (4)	privatization (9)
communism (9)	gross domestic product (GDP) (20)	producer price index (PPI) (19)
competition (12)	gross national product (GNP) (20)	profit (4)
competitive advantage (13)	human resources (6)	pure competition (12)
consumer price index (CPI) (19)	inflation (19)	recession (16)
deflation (19)	knowledge (6)	recovery (16)
demand (9)	labor-intensive businesses (5)	service businesses (5)
demand curve (9)	macroeconomics (6)	socialism (9)
economic indicators (18)	microeconomics (6)	stakeholders (14)
economic system (7)	monetary policy (16)	supply (9)
economics (6)	monopolistic competition (13)	supply curve (11)

Test Your Knowledge

Questions for Review

1. Why do businesspeople study economics?
2. Why are knowledge workers a key economic resource?
3. How is capitalism different from communism and socialism in the way it achieves economic goals?
4. Why is government spending an important factor in economic stability?
5. Why might a government agency seek to block a merger or acquisition?

Questions for Analysis

6. Why is it often easier to start a service business than a goods-producing business?
7. Why is competition an important element of the free-market system?
8. Why do governments intervene in a free-market system?
9. How do countries know if their economic system is working?
10. Ethical Considerations. Because knowledge workers are in such high demand, you decide to enroll in an evening MBA program. Your company has agreed to reimburse you for 80 percent of your tuition. You haven't revealed, however, that once you earn your degree, you plan to apply for a management position at a different company. Is it ethical for you to accept your company's tuition reimbursement, given your intentions?

Questions for Application

11. Company sales are skyrocketing, and projections show that your computer consulting business will outgrow its current location by next year. What factors should you consider when selecting a new site for your business?
12. How would a decrease in Social Security benefits to the elderly affect the economy?
13. Graph a supply and demand chart for the iTunes pricing structure. Make up any data you need, but show the equilibrium price for an individual song to be $0.99.
14. How This Affects You. Assume that many financial experts currently predict the Fed will gradually raise the discount rate several times over the next few years. How might this affect you, both on the job and in your personal financial life?

Practice Your Knowledge

Sharpening Your Communication Skills

Select a local service business you are familiar with. How does that business try to gain a competitive advantage in the marketplace? Write a brief summary, as directed by your instructor, describing whether the company competes on speed, quality, price, innovation, service, or a combination of those attributes. Be prepared to present your analysis to your classmates.

Building Your Team Skills

Economic indicators help businesses and governments determine where the economy is headed. You may have noticed news headlines such as the following, each of which offers clues to the direction of the U.S. economy:

1. Housing Starts Lowest in Months
2. Fed Lowers Discount Rate and Interest Rates Tumble
3. Retail Sales Up 4 Percent Over Last Month
4. Business Debt Down from Last Year
5. Businesses Are Buying More Electronic Equipment
6. Industry Jobs Go Unfilled as Area Unemployment Rate Sinks to 3 Percent
7. Telephone Company Reports 30-Day Backlog in Installing Business Systems

Discuss each of those headlines with the other students on your team. Is each item good news or bad news for the economy? Why? What does each news item mean for large and small businesses? Report your team's findings to the class as a whole. Did all the teams come to the same conclusions about each headline? Why or why not? With your team, discuss how these different perspectives might influence the way you interpret economic news in the future.

Improving Your Tech Insights: Instant Messaging

If you're a serious user of instant messaging (IM), do you remember what it was like those first few times you communicated through IM? Chances are it changed the way you interacted with friends and family. IM may have started as a way for individual computer users to stay in touch, but it quickly became a major communication tool for businesses worldwide. For both routine communication and exchanges during online meetings, IM is now widely used throughout the business world and is beginning to overtake or even supplant e-mail for internal communication in many companies. Businesses use IM to replace in-person meetings and phone calls, to supplement online meetings, and to interact with customers. Key benefits include rapid response to urgent messages and lower cost than phone calls and e-mail. *Enterprise IM*, systems created specifically for businesses, go beyond typical consumer systems with such features as remote display of documents, remote control of other computers, advanced security, message archiving, newsfeeds from blogs and websites, and even automated *bot* capabilities in which computers mimic human beings to help with basic customer service tasks.

Research one company's use of IM for either internal communication among employees or external communication with customers and business partners. To learn more about how IM works, you can check out http://computer.howstuffworks.com/instant-messaging.htm. For the latest on the business applications of IM, log on to www.instantmessagingplanet.com. In a brief e-mail message to your instructor, describe the company's use of IM and explain how it has changed the way the company does business.[22]

Expand Your Knowledge

Discovering Career Opportunities

Thinking about a career in economics? Find out what economists do by reviewing the *Occupational Outlook Handbook* in your library or online at www.bls.gov/oco. This is an authoritative resource for information about all kinds of occupations. Search for "economists," then answer these questions:

1. Briefly describe what economists do and their typical working conditions.
2. What is the job outlook for economists? What is the average salary for starting economists?
3. What training and qualifications are required for a career as an economist? Are the qualifications different for jobs in the private sector as opposed to those in the government?

Developing Your Research Skills

Gaining a competitive advantage in today's marketplace is critical to a company's success. Use Bovée and Thill's Business Search page or search the *Business in Action Real-Time Updates* archives at www.mybusinesslab.com to find an article about a company whose strategies and tactics have given it an advantage over its competitors.

1. What products or services does the company manufacture or sell?
2. How does the company distinguish its goods or services from those of its competitors? Does the company compete on price, quality, service, innovation, or some other factor?
3. What evidence do you find that the company is taking advantage of newer communication technologies such as blogging and podcasting?

See It on the Web

Visit these websites and answer the following questions for each one. (Up-to-date links for all websites mentioned in this chapter can be found on the Textbook Resources page for Chapter 1 at www.mybusinesslab.com. Please note that links to sites that become inactive after publication of the book will be removed from the Featured Websites section.)

1. What is the purpose of this website?

2. What kinds of information does this website contain? Please be specific.

3. How is the information provided at this website useful for businesspeople? Consumers?

4. How did you expand your knowledge of economics by reviewing the material at this website? What new things did you learn about this topic?

Check Out This 24-Hour Business Library

The Internet Public Library is a great place to start your research into any business and economics topic. Click on "Business" in the Subject Collections, then explore the two dozen subject areas ranging from accounting and entrepreneurship to taxes. You can even submit questions for the IPL staff. www.ipl.org

Step Inside the Economic Statistics Briefing Room

Want to know where the economy is headed? Visit the Economic Statistics Briefing Room to get the latest economic indicators compiled by a number of U.S. agencies. Click on "Federal Statistics" by category to enter the room, and check out the stats and graphs for new housing starts; manufacturers' shipments, inventories, and orders; unemployment; average hourly earnings; and more. Are monthly housing starts, unemployment, and annual median household income increasing or decreasing? Make your own projections about which direction the economy is heading. www.whitehouse.gov/fsbr/esbr.html

Discover What's in the CPI

The CPI is an important tool that allows analysts to track the change in prices over time. But the CPI doesn't always match a given individual's inflation experience. Find out why by visiting the website maintained by the U.S. Bureau of Labor Statistics (look for Consumer Price Index). Be sure to check out how the CPI measures homeowners' costs, how the CPI is used, what goods and services it covers, and whose buying habits it reflects. http://stats.bls.gov

Companion Website

Learning Interactively

Log onto www.prenhall.com/bovée, locate your text, and then click on its Companion Website. For Chapter 1, take advantage of the interactive Chapter Quiz to test your knowledge of the chapter. Get instant feedback on whether you need additional studying. Also, you'll find an abundance of valuable resources that will help you succeed in this course, including PowerPoint presentations and Web Links.

Video Case

Helping Business Do Business: U.S. Department of Commerce

LEARNING OBJECTIVES

The purpose of this video is to help you:

1. Understand world economic systems and their effect on competition

2. Identify the factors of production

3. Discuss how supply and demand affect a product's price

SYNOPSIS

The U.S. Department of Commerce seeks to support U.S. economic stability and help U.S.-based companies do business in other countries. In contrast to the planned economy of the People's Republic of China, the United States is a market economy where firms are free to set their own missions and buy from and sell to any other business or individual. In the United States, companies must comply with government regulations that set standards such as minimum safety requirements. When doing business in other countries, they must consider tariffs and other restrictions that govern imports to those markets. In addition, supply and demand affect a company's ability to set prices and generate profits.

Discussion Questions

1. *For analysis:* If a U.S. company must pay more for factors of production such as human resources, what is the likely effect on its competitiveness in world markets?

2. *For analysis:* Is the equilibrium price for a company's product likely to be the same in every country? Explain your answer.

3. *For application:* To which factors of production might a small U.S. company have the easiest access? How would this affect the company's competitive position?

4. *For application:* Is a company likely to see more competitors enter a market when supply exceeds demand or when demand exceeds supply?

5. *For debate:* Should the U.S. Department of Commerce, funded by citizens' tax payments, be providing advice and guidance to U.S. companies that want to profit by doing business in other countries? Support your chosen position.

ONLINE EXPLORATION

Visit the U.S. Department of Commerce (DOC) website at www.commerce.gov and follow some of the links from the home page to see some of this government agency's resources for businesses. Also follow the link to read about the DOC's history. What assistance can a U.S. business expect from this agency? How have the agency's offerings evolved over the years as the needs and demands of business have changed?

CHAPTER 2

Ethics and Corporate Social Responsibility

LEARNING OBJECTIVES
After studying this chapter, you will be able to

1 Discuss what it means to practice good business ethics and highlight three factors that influence ethical behavior

2 Identify three steps that businesses are taking to encourage ethical behavior and explain the advantages and disadvantages of whistle-blowing

3 List four questions you might ask yourself when trying to make an ethical decision

4 Explain the difference between an ethical dilemma and an ethical lapse

5 Explain the controversy surrounding corporate social responsibility

6 Discuss how businesses can become more socially responsible

7 Define *sustainable development* and explain the strategic advantages of managing with sustainability as a priority

Protestors Pour on the Trouble for PepsiCo in India

www.pepsico.com

Every business wants consumers to feel passionate about its products—but not the sort of passion where they set fire to cardboard replicas of the products during public demonstrations or issue press releases calling the products dangerous and the company's corporate communication efforts dishonest.

Such is the situation that PepsiCo, the global beverage and snack food giant based in Purchase, New York, recently faced in India. For several years, the company has been the target of a publicity campaign organized and led by the small nonprofit Centre for Science and Environment (CSE) and its director, Sunita Narain, a well-known activist.

After a nonprofit organization accused Pepsi of selling tainted beverages in India, protesters burned Pepsi products in effigy.

The issue of product contamination is less clear but no less volatile. Pesticides and industrial chemicals in the soil have been seeping into groundwater supplies for years, and after government studies showed those contaminants were moving into the food supply, CSE tested a variety of beverages made in India by Pepsi and Coke. Although the level of contaminants it found was far lower than those found previously in the milk supply, Narain announced in a press conference in 2003 that pesticides in Pepsi's brands of bottled water were 36 times higher and Coke's were 30 times higher than European safety standards (which were used for comparison because the Indian government hadn't set its own safety standards).

The protests focus on two issues, the use of water and the safety of Pepsi bottled waters and sodas. Water is in short supply in much of India. For millions of Indians, acquiring safe water to drink and enough water to serve a family's daily needs is a major challenge. Critics such as Narain accuse Pepsi and other businesses of overusing a scarce resource that belongs to the people. Pepsi acknowledged it could do better in this respect: To make 24 eight-ounce bottles of beverage—a gallon and a half—the company's production process used over nine gallons of water.

Narain's awareness campaign had an immediate effect, with protesters taking to the streets and local governments around India banning or restricting sales of Pepsi products. As sales dropped and Pepsi's reputation eroded, one of the Pepsi executives responsible for responding to the situation was ironically also a prominent woman with roots in India. Indra Nooyi, Pepsi's president and chief financial officer at the time, had vivid memories of water shortages while growing up in India. She was deeply sensitive to the water and safety issues but was adamant that CSE's tests were flawed and that Pepsi's products were safe. If you were Nooyi, how would you respond?[1] ∎

Ethics and Social Responsibility in Contemporary Business

Like PepsiCo's Indra Nooyi (profiled in the chapter opener), thousands of managers today wrestle with the sometimes-competing demands of running a profitable business and running a socially responsible company. As a future business leader, you will face some of the challenges discussed in this chapter, and your choices won't always be easy. You may struggle to find ethical clarity in some situations, to even understand what your choices are and how each option might affect your company's various stakeholders. You may need to muster the courage to stand up to colleagues, bosses, or customers if you think ethical principles are being violated. Fortunately, by having a good understanding of what constitutes ethical behavior and what society expects from business today, you'll be better prepared to make these tough choices.

However, be aware that you are likely to face skeptical audiences from time to time, even when you do make ethical choices. Daniel Yankelovich, a respected researcher who has been studying public opinion since the 1950s, explains that business leaders have lost the benefit of the doubt in recent years. His surveys indicate that people perceive business loyalty as a "one-way street"—businesses expect loyalty from customers, communities, and employees but don't show them any loyalty in return.[2]

In discussions of *social responsibility* and *ethics,* you'll often hear the two terms used interchangeably, but they are not the same. **Corporate social responsibility (CSR)** is the idea that business has obligations to society beyond the pursuit of profits. **Ethics,** by contrast, is defined as the principles and standards of moral behavior that are accepted by society as right versus wrong. *Business ethics,* then, is the application of moral standards to business situations.

Thanks to a number of high-profile scandals involving finances and product safety, corporate social responsibility and managerial ethics have been pushed to center stage in recent years. Several of these scandals have painfully demonstrated that corporate responsibility and ethics are not just intriguing philosophical questions but real-life issues, where unethical behavior by just a handful of people can erase billions of dollars of shareholder value (including the life savings of many employees), destroy tens of thousands of jobs, and affect families and communities for years.

The news is not all bad, of course. When you hear about illegal—or legal but unethical—behavior on the part of a few managers, bear in mind that the vast majority of businesses are run by ethical managers and staffed by ethical employees whose positive contributions to their communities are unfortunately overshadowed at times by headline-grabbing scandals. Companies around the world help their communities in countless ways, from sponsoring youth sports teams to raising millions of dollars to build hospitals.

Moreover, even when companies are simply engaged in the normal course of business—and do so ethically—they contribute to society in such ways as making useful products, providing gainful employment, and paying taxes. Business catches a lot of flak these days, some of it rightly deserved, but overall, its contributions to the health, happiness, and well-being of society are practically beyond measure.

What Is Ethical Behavior?

Wanting or claiming to be an ethical corporate citizen isn't enough; people in business must actively practice ethical behavior. In business, besides obeying all laws and regulations, practicing good ethics means competing fairly and honestly, communicating truthfully, and not causing harm to others.

Competing Fairly and Honestly

Businesses are expected to compete fairly and honestly and not knowingly deceive, intimidate, or misrepresent themselves to customers, competitors, clients, or employees. Practices that raise ethical questions include hiring employees from competitors to gain *trade secrets*, engaging in *industrial espionage* to spy on other companies, and *pretexting*—essentially lying about who you are (such as posing as a journalist) in order to gain access to information that you couldn't get otherwise.[3]

For example, the co-founder of a private intelligence firm known as Diligence posed as a British government agent to convince an employee of the accounting firm KPMG to hand over confidential information about a financial audit KPMG was conducting on another firm. While it's unclear yet whether Diligence broke any laws, KPMG successfully sued Diligence for fraud. The firm being audited, a Bermuda-based company called IPOC, has also sued Diligence and the powerful Washington, D.C., lobbying firm that hired Diligence on behalf of a Russian company that was competing with IPOC on a big acquisition deal.[4]

corporate social responsibility (CSR)
The idea that business has obligations to society beyond the pursuit of profits

ethics
The rules or standards governing the conduct of a person or group

Communicating Truthfully

Today's companies communicate with a wide variety of audiences, from their own employees to customers to government officials. Communicating truthfully is a simple enough concept: Tell the truth, the whole truth, and nothing but the truth. However, matters sometimes aren't so clear. For instance, if you plan to introduce an improved version of a product next year, do you have an obligation to tell customers who are buying the existing product this year? Suppose you do tell them, and so many decide to delay their purchases that you end up with a cash flow problem that forces you to lay off several employees. Would that be fair for customers but unfair for your employees?

Whenever you face a dilemma about what to say and when to say it, think about the decisions your audience is facing. Business communication ethics often involves the question of **transparency**, the opportunity for affected parties to observe relevant aspects of transactions or decisions. What information do they need in order to make an intelligent decision? You may encounter situations when, for a valid reason such as protecting confidential financial information, you can't give people all the information they'd like to have. However, by focusing on your audience's needs, you'll find it much easier to clarify what constitutes truthful communication.

transparency
The degree to which affected parties can observe relevant aspects of transactions or decisions

Not Causing Harm to Others

All businesses have the capacity to cause harm to employees, customers, other companies, their communities, and investors. Problems can start when managers make decisions that put their personal interests above those of other stakeholders, underestimate the risks of failure, or neglect to consider potential effects on other people and organizations. Harm can also result even when managers have acted ethically—but they're still responsible for these negative outcomes.

Wow, That Sure Was Nice of Kathy to Give Us Those Free Coupons!

Has a friend or classmate ever encouraged you to try a product, and perhaps even given you discount coupons or free samples—for no apparent reason?

Chances are, there was a reason. Hundreds of thousands of people across the United States now help promote products to their friends in exchange for free goods and services, inside information about upcoming products, and other benefits. More than 200,000 unpaid teenagers spread marketing messages for Tremor and more than a half million mothers promote products on behalf of Vocalpoint, both promotional businesses started by Procter & Gamble (P&G), the consumer goods giant. Tremor and Vocalpoint run campaigns for other companies as well, including record companies and movie studios. These efforts are part of a recent wave of *stealth marketing, buzz marketing, viral marketing*, and various other attempts to reach potential buyers without traditional advertising techniques.

Neither Tremor nor Vocalpoint requires its participants to disclose that they are discussing products on behalf of a company. P&G says that is the ethical way to handle the situation—to let each participant decide whether to disclose the connection when talking to their friends. However, the Word of Mouth Marketing Association (WOMMA at www.womma.org), an organization that represents companies using these marketing tactics, urges mandatory disclosure in its code of ethics.

The rapid growth of blogs is presenting a similar issue online. If a company pays a blogger to write about its products, does the blogger have an ethical obligation to share that fact with his or her audience? Can companies create fictitious bloggers to write about their own products? Both WOMMA and marketing consultants such as David Meerman Scott are clear on this point: Bloggers should always tell their readers if they are writing on behalf of a company. Scott says he always discloses the connection whenever he writes about products from one of his clients, and he urges bloggers to disclose any potential conflict of interest.

Perhaps WOMMA sums it up best: "Consumers come first, honesty isn't optional, and deception is always exposed."

Questions for Critical Thinking

1. Do you agree with P&G or WOMMA on the question of whether to disclose the true nature of stealth marketing campaigns?

2. If Tremor and Vocalpoint paid their participants in cash instead of free samples and other nonmonetary rewards, would that change your opinion on the issue of disclosure? (For the latest information on stealth marketing and viral marketing, visit www.prenhall.com/bovée and click on "Real-Time Updates.")

insider trading
The use of unpublicized
information that an individual
gains in the course of his or her
job to benefit from fluctuations in
the stock market

conflict of interest
Situation in which a business
decision may be influenced by
the potential for personal gain

In nearly every company, the manner in which employees and executives handle information is one key to avoiding harm to others. Because these people often have access to information that outsiders don't have, they have a responsibility not to take advantage of the situation. Specifically, buying or selling a company's stock based on information that outside investors lack is known as **insider trading**, which is not only unethical but also illegal. Insider trading is a good example of the ethical trouble that businesspeople can get into when they face a **conflict of interest**, a situation in which a choice that promises personal gain compromises a more fundamental responsibility. If you're in charge of buying a new computer system for your company and you select the vendor who gave you Super Bowl tickets instead of the vendor who offered a better deal for your company, you would be guilty of a conflict of interest.

As business and technology grow ever more complex, the potential for harm increases. For instance, U.S. food companies frequently import meat, produce, and a variety of food ingredients from other countries, but only 1 percent of those imports are inspected by the Food and Drug Administration (FDA). A former FDA commissioner says that the "food-safety system in this country is broken." Experts say that while companies such as Kraft and Nabisco do a thorough job of monitoring the quality of ingredients all the way back to the source, not all companies are so careful.[5]

Harm doesn't necessarily have to involve physical damage, either. Sony outraged leaders of the Church of England when it used a photorealistic representation of Manchester Cathedral in a violent, shootout-style video game that takes place within a church. Church leaders were particularly upset because the city of Manchester has a serious problem with gang-related gun violence, and the church has been active in addressing that problem. The Very Reverend Rogers Govender, dean of the cathedral, characterized Sony's actions as "beyond belief, and in our view highly irresponsible." For its part, Sony sent a letter of apology but contended that the game's science fiction setting is clearly unrelated to real-life issues in the city.[6]

Factors Influencing Ethical Behavior

Although a number of factors influence the ethical behavior of businesspeople, three in particular appear to have the most impact: cultural differences, knowledge, and organizational behavior.

Cultural Differences

Globalization exposes businesspeople to a variety of cultures and business practices. What does it mean for a business to do the right thing in Thailand? In Nigeria? In Norway? What may be considered unethical in the United States may be an accepted practice in another culture. Managers may need to consider a wide range of issues, including acceptable working conditions, minimum wage levels, product safety issues, and environmental protection. Chapter 3 explores these issues in more detail.

Knowledge

As a general rule, the more you know and the better you understand a situation, the better your chances are of making an ethical decision. In the often frantic churn of daily business, though, it's easy to shut your eyes and ears to potential problems. However, as a business leader, you have the responsibility to not only pay attention but to actively seek out information regarding potential ethical issues. Ignorance is never an acceptable defense in the eyes of the law, and it shouldn't be in questions of ethics, either.

With information in hand, your next responsibility is to act in a timely and effective manner. After MySpace received numerous complaints that adult pedophiles were posing as teenagers as a way to make friends on the popular social networking site, the company hired Hemanshu Nigam, a former federal prosecutor, to establish systems and policies to protect underage users. Every week, MySpace now deletes 8,000 profiles of people who lied about their ages. Artificial intelligence software patrols the site now, too, looking for words and phrases that child molesters tend to use. As Nigam puts it, "We have to forge the way for an entire industry."[7]

Organizational Behavior

The foundations of an ethical business climate are ethical awareness and clear standards of behavior. Organizations that strongly enforce company codes of conduct and provide ethics training help employees recognize and reason through ethical problems. Similarly, companies with strong ethical practices set a good example for employees. At United Technologies (www.utc.com), an aerospace and defense conglomerate based in Hartford, Connecticut, ethical behavior starts at the top, where executives are responsible for meeting a number of clearly defined ethical standards and their annual compensation is tied to how well they perform.[8] In sharp contrast, companies that commit unethical acts in the course of doing business open the door for employees to follow suit.

To help avoid ethical breaches, many companies proactively develop programs designed to improve their ethical conduct, often under the guidance of a chief ethics officer or other top executive. These programs typically combine training, communication, and a variety of other resources to guide employees. More than 80 percent of large companies have also adopted a written **code of ethics**, which defines the values and principles that should be used to guide decisions (see Exhibit 2.1 for an example). By itself, however, a code of ethics can't accomplish much. To be effective, a code must be supported by employee communications efforts, a formal training program, employee commitment to following it, and a system through which employees can get help with ethically difficult situations.[9]

code of ethics
Written statement setting forth the principles that guide an organization's decisions

Codes of ethics are so important that according to the Federal Sentencing Guidelines (1991), a company found to be violating federal law might not be prosecuted if it has the proper ethics policies and procedures in place.[10] Another way companies support ethical behavior is by establishing a system for reporting unethical or illegal actions at work, such as an ethics hotline. Companies that value ethics will try to correct reported problems. United Technologies, for instance, has long had an ethics hotline as part of a comprehensive ethics communication program. During the last two decades, employees have made nearly 60,000 queries, and more than 40 percent of these queries led to some sort of change by the company.[11]

If a serious problem persists, or in cases where management may be involved in the act, an employee may choose to blow the whistle. **Whistle-blowing** is an employee's disclosure to the media or government authorities of illegal, unethical, or harmful practices by the company. At Enron and WorldCom, where two monumental cases of fraud cost thousands of employees their jobs and much of their life savings, unethical behavior came to light

whistle-blowing
The disclosure of information by a company insider that exposes illegal or unethical behavior by others within the organization

EXHIBIT 2.1 eHealth Code of Ethics

The Internet Healthcare Coalition, which represents companies and organizations that provide online health-care information, encourages its members to abide by these ethical principles.

Candor	Disclose information that if known by consumers would likely affect consumers' understanding or use of the site or purchase or use of a product or service.
Honesty	Be truthful and not deceptive.
Quality	Provide health information that is accurate, easy to understand, and up to date.
	Provide the information users need to make their own judgments about the health information, products, or services provided by the site.
Informed consent	Respect users' right to determine whether or how their personal data may be collected, used, or shared.
Privacy	Respect the obligation to protect users' privacy.
Professionalism	Respect fundamental ethical obligations to patients and clients.
	Inform and educate patients and clients about the limitations of online health care.
Responsible partnering	Ensure the organizations and sites with which they affiliate are trustworthy.
Accountability	Provide meaningful opportunity for users to give feedback to the site.
	Monitor their compliance with the *eHealth Code of Ethics*.

through the efforts of whistle-blowers: Sherron Watkins at Enron and Cynthia Cooper at WorldCom. (Both women strongly dislike the term *whistle-blower*, by the way; they don't see themselves as tattle-tales but as good employees doing their jobs.)[12]

Whistle-blowing can bring high costs: Public accusation of wrongdoing hurts the business's reputation, requires attention from managers who must investigate the accusations, and damages employee morale. Moreover, whistle-blowers risk being fired or demoted, and they often suffer career setbacks, financial strain, and emotional stress. The fear of such negative repercussions may allow unethical or illegal practices to go unreported.

How Do You Make Ethical Decisions?

Determining what's ethically right in any given situation can be difficult, as you've no doubt experienced from time to time in your personal life. For instance, is it right to help a friend get a passing grade, even though you know he or she doesn't understand

Lead Your Team with Ethical Behavior

A written code of ethics, an ethics hotline, employee training, and other tactics are important parts of any effort to ensure strong ethics in your company, but nothing is more crucial than the behavior of the company's owners and managers—and if you're the top executive, you're the most important part of the equation. Your actions say more about the company's virtues than any program or poster.

The gap between talk and action has led to a credibility crisis in U.S. companies. In one survey, more than 80 percent of top managers said they consider ethics in their decision making, but 43 percent of employees expressed the belief that managers routinely overlook ethics. When leaders make decisions that show profits winning out over ethics, employees not only lose faith in their leaders but begin to assume that all the glorious talk about ethics is just that—talk. And in an era when many corporate executives can earn staggering sums of money in pay and bonuses based on company profits and stock prices, skeptical employees might just assume that the unethical behavior is done is pursuit of personal gain.

Moreover, questionable behavior at the top creates an environment ripe for ethical abuse throughout the organization. If employees see that bending or breaking the rules is not only accepted but the best way to succeed, some will be tempted to start emulating their leaders. Then, as other employees see those people getting away with their behavior and getting ahead, they'll jump on the bandwagon. The unethical bandwagon doesn't need too many people on it to bring down an entire corporation, either, as WorldCom, Enron, and others have shown.

As a leader, you have a moral—and in many cases, legal—responsibility for the actions of your organization.

- *Lead by example.* Again, nothing is more important than demonstrating your commitment to ethics by behaving ethically yourself.
- *Don't tolerate unethical behavior.* At the same time, you have to show that bad decisions won't be accepted. Let

one go without correction, and you'll probably see another one before long.

- *Inspire concretely.* Tell employees how they will personally benefit from participating in ethics initiatives. People respond better to personal benefits than to company benefits.
- *Acknowledge reality.* Admit errors. Discuss what went right, what went wrong, and how the company can learn from the mistakes. Solicit employee opinion and act on those opinions. If you only pretend to be interested, you'll make matters worse.
- *Communicate, communicate, communicate.* Ethics needs to be a continuous conversation, not a special topic brought up only in training sessions or when a crisis hits. Harold Tinkler, the chief ethics and compliance officer at the accounting firm Deloitte & Touche, says that "Companies need to turn up the volume" when it comes to talking about ethics.
- *Be honest.* Tell employees what you know as well as what you don't know. Talk openly about ethical concerns and be willing to accept negative feedback.
- *Hire good people.* Alan Greenspan, former chairman of the Federal Reserve Board, put it nicely: "Rules are no substitute for character." If you hire good people (not people who are good at their jobs, but people who are good, period) and create an ethical environment for them, you'll get ethical behavior. If you hire people who lack good moral character, you're inviting ethical lapses, no matter how many rules you write.

Questions for Critical Thinking

1. How does building trust, even when you've done so by admitting mistakes, encourage your employees to be more ethical?
2. How can you balance the business need to inspire employees to compete aggressively with the moral need to avoid competing unethically?

what's going on in the class? One helpful approach is to measure your choices against standards. These standards are usually grounded in universal teachings such as "Do not lie" and "Do not steal" that are aimed at assuring **justice**—the resolution of ethical issues in a way that is consistent with those generally accepted standards of right and wrong. Another place to look for ethical guidance is the law. If saying, writing, or doing something is clearly illegal, you have no decision to make; you obey the law.

Even though legal considerations will resolve some ethical questions, you'll often have to rely on your own judgment and principles. For example, what are your motives in a given situation? If your intent is honest, the decision is ethical; however, if your intent is to mislead or manipulate, your decision is unethical. Don't automatically assume you're viewing a situation fairly and objectively, either. Psychological research suggests that many people are influenced by unconscious biases that may even run counter to their stated beliefs.[13] Moreover, don't assume that other people think the way you do. The time-honored "Golden Rule" of treating others the way you want to be treated can get you into trouble when others don't want to be treated the same way you do. You might also consider asking yourself a series of questions:

1. Is the decision legal? (Does it break any laws?)
2. Is it balanced? (Is it fair to all concerned?)
3. Can you live with it? (Does it make you feel good about yourself?)
4. Is it feasible? (Will it actually work in the real world?)

When you need to determine the ethics of any situation, these questions will get you started. The decision-making tools in the right-hand column of Exhibit 2.2 can also help. One of the most practical and widely accepted methods is **utilitarianism**, an approach that seeks the greatest good for the greatest number of people involved. The approaches in the list are not mutually exclusive. On the contrary, most businesspeople combine them to reach decisions that will satisfy as many stakeholders as possible without violating anyone's rights or treating anyone unjustly.

When making ethical decisions, keep in mind that most ethical situations can be classified into two general types: ethical dilemmas and ethical lapses. An **ethical dilemma** is a situation in which one must choose between two conflicting but arguably valid sides. All ethical dilemmas have a common theme: the conflict between the rights of two or more important groups of people. The second type of situation is an **ethical lapse**, in which an individual makes a decision that is clearly wrong, such as divulging trade secrets to a competitor. Be careful not to confuse ethical dilemmas with ethical lapses. A company faces an ethical dilemma when it must decide whether to continue operating a production facility that is suspected, but not proven, to be unsafe. A company makes an ethical lapse when it continues to operate the facility even after the site has been proven unsafe.

justice
The resolution of ethical questions and other dilemmas in a manner that is consistent with generally accepted standards of right and wrong

utilitarianism
A decision-making approach that seeks to create the greatest good for the greatest number of people affected by the decisions

ethical dilemma
Situation in which both sides of an issue can be supported with valid arguments

ethical lapse
Situation in which an individual or group makes a decision that is morally wrong, illegal, or unethical

Corporate Social Responsibility

Corporate social responsibility has been a hot topic in recent years, with hundreds of companies announcing new initiatives or publishing reports describing their efforts and progress.[14] In fact, judging from the number of publications, conferences, and consultants now in the field, one might think CSR has become a mini-industry of its own. There is a widespread assumption these days that CSR is both a moral imperative for business as well as a good thing for society, but the issues aren't quite as clear as they might seem at first glance.

How This Affects You

1. In your current job (or any previous job you've held), in what ways does your employer contribute to society?
2. Have you ever encountered an ethical dilemma in your work? If so, how did you resolve it?
3. If you go to work tomorrow morning and your boss asks you to do something you consider unethical, what factors will you take into consideration before responding?

EXHIBIT 2.2 Guidelines for Making Ethical Decisions

Companies with the most success in establishing an ethical structure are those that balance their approach to making decisions.

IS THE DECISION ETHICAL?	DOES IT RESPECT STAKEHOLDERS?	DOES IT FOLLOW A PHILOSOPHICAL APPROACH?
IS IT LEGAL?	WILL OUTSIDERS APPROVE?	IS IT A UTILITARIAN DECISION?
Does it violate civil law?	Does it benefit customers, suppliers, investors, public officials, media representatives, and community members?	Does it produce the greatest good for the greatest number of people?
Does it violate company policy?		DOES IT UPHOLD INDIVIDUAL, LEGAL, AND HUMAN RIGHTS?
IS IT BALANCED?	WILL SUPERVISORS APPROVE?	Does it protect people's own interests?
Is it fair to all concerned, in both the short and the long term?	Did you provide management with information that is honest and accurate?	Does it respect the privacy of others and their right to express their opinion?
CAN YOU LIVE WITH IT?	WILL EMPLOYEES APPROVE?	Does it allow people to act in a way that conforms to their religious or moral beliefs?
Does it make you feel good about yourself?	Will it affect employees in a positive way?	
Would you feel good reading about it in a newspaper?	Does it handle personal information about employees discreetly?	DOES IT UPHOLD THE PRINCIPLES OF JUSTICE?
IS IT FEASIBLE?	Did you give proper credit for work performed by others?	Does it treat people fairly and impartially?
Does it work in the real world?		Does it apply rules consistently?
Will it improve your competitive position?		Does it ensure that people who harm others are held responsible and make restitution?
Is it affordable?		
Can it be accomplished in the time available?		

The Relationship Between Business and Society

Questions about the social responsibility of business start with the relationship between business and society. What is the nature of this relationship—and what should it be? Is it inherently antagonistic or more interdependent? What does business owe society, and what does society owe business?

Any attempt to understand and shape this relationship needs to consider four essential truths:

1. Consumers in contemporary societies enjoy and expect a wide range of benefits, from education to health care to products that are safe to use. Most of these benefits share an important characteristic: They require money.

2. Businesses operating in free-market systems such as the U.S. economy generate the vast majority of the money in a nation's economy, either directly or indirectly. When companies pay taxes or pay for the right to use a public asset (such as a mobile phone company buying the right to use part of the radio spectrum), they directly contribute to the nation's economic well-being. When companies pay employees, those employees spend money on goods and services and pay income taxes on what they earn as well as a variety of other taxes on what they buy and own. Either way, profit-seeking companies are the economic engine that powers modern society. People who expect

"the government" to pay for something need to remember that the government gets most of its income from taxpayers, both businesses and individuals.

3. Aside from money, much of what we consider when assessing a society's standard of living, from medication to building materials, involves goods and services created by profit-seeking companies.

4. Conversely, companies cannot hope to operate profitably without the many benefits provided by a safe and relatively predictable business environment—talented and healthy employees, a transportation infrastructure, opportunities to raise money, protection of assets, and customers with the ability to pay for goods and services, to name just a few.

Taking these four factors into account, it is clear that business and society need each other—and each needs the other to be healthy and successful. Generally speaking, when one suffers, the other suffers, and when one succeeds, the other succeeds. Looking around the world, you will notice a strong correlation between the economic well-being of a country and the social well-being of its citizens. In the words of Professors Michael Porter and Mark Kramer (see "Philanthropy Versus Strategic CSR" on page 39), "The most important thing a corporation can do for society, and for any community, is contribute to a prosperous economy."[15]

Of course, this is a "big picture," long-term view of the relationship between business and society. It doesn't necessarily account for the behavior of individual companies or the behavior of one society toward another, particularly when it comes to short-term behaviors that benefit one company or one group but have detrimental effects for everyone in the long term. For instance, a single company can behave in an unethical and antisocial manner without immediately suffering the consequences. Suppose a meat-packing plant subjects its employees to unsafe working conditions while offering them no health insurance. When those employees inevitably need health care as a result of their unsafe work environment, they are then forced to use hospital emergency rooms for even routine care because they can't afford regular doctor visits—and U.S. hospitals are bound by law to provide emergency health care to anyone who needs it. However, the costs of that care aren't borne by the unethical employer, but rather by the hospitals and by everyone else who buys health insurance or medical care (since the costs of caring for the uninsured raise costs for everyone). So these employees, other companies, consumers, and society as a whole suffer, but this one company doesn't.

Similar inequities can occur between countries. Imagine a U.S.-based multinational company that is a respectable corporate citizen here at home but exploits workers or depletes natural resources in another country, even if it adheres to all applicable laws in both countries. American society won't necessarily be harmed by this company's overseas behavior—and the company's customers will probably benefit from lower prices. However, the society in that other country will be harmed.

Inequalities don't need to be caused by unethical behavior, either. For instance, to help alleviate a chronic shortage of information technology (IT) professionals, Microsoft is investing $50 million to help U.S. community colleges improve their IT training programs.[16] Microsoft stands to benefit from this effort because it needs more IT specialists, students clearly benefit, and society will benefit when these students move into good-paying jobs and eventually pay higher taxes. However, many other companies, including Microsoft's competitors, also stand to benefit by hiring from a larger pool of qualified IT candidates. Is it fair for these companies to reap the benefit without making the investment? If society as a whole benefits, should society as a whole pay?

Perspectives on Corporate Social Responsibility

To encourage ethical behavior and promote a mutually beneficial relationship between business and society, it is clearly necessary to establish expectations about how businesses should conduct themselves. However, both business and society are still grappling with exactly what those expectations should be. Approaches to CSR can be roughly categorized into four perspectives (see Exhibit 2.3):

■ *Minimalist.* According to what might be termed the *minimalist* view, the only social responsibility of business is to pay taxes and obey the law. In a 1970 article that is still widely discussed today, Nobel Prize–winning economist Milton Friedman articulated this view by saying, "There is only one social responsibility of business: to use its resources and engage in activities designed to increase its profits so long as it stays within the rules of the game, which is to say, engages in open and free competition without deception or fraud."[17] This view, which tends to reject the stakeholder concept described in Chapter 1, might seem selfish and even antisocial, but it raises a couple of important questions. First, any business that operates ethically and legally provides society with beneficial goods and services at fair prices. Isn't that meeting the business's primary social obligation? Second, should businesses be in the business of making social policy and spending the public's money? Proponents of the minimalist view claim this is actually what happens when companies make tax-deductible contributions to social causes. Assume a company makes a sizable contribution that nets it a $1 million tax break. That's $1 million taken out of the public treasury—where voters and their elected representatives can control how money is spent—and put into whatever social cause the company chooses to support. Would it be better for society if companies paid full taxes and let the people decide how the money is spent?

■ *Defensive.* Many companies today find themselves facing pressure from a variety of activists and **nongovernmental organizations (NGOs)**, nonprofit groups that provide charitable services or promote causes, from workers' rights to environmental protection. One possible response to this pressure is to engage in CSR activities as a way to avoid further criticism. In other words, the company takes positive steps to address a particular issue but only because it has been embarrassed into action by negative publicity.

■ *Cynical.* Another possible response is purely cynical, in which a company accused of irresponsible behavior promotes itself as being socially responsible without making

nongovernmental organizations (NGOs)
Nonprofit groups that provide charitable services or promote social and environmental causes

---

EXHIBIT 2.3

Perspectives on Corporate Social Responsibility

The perspectives on CSR can be roughly divided into four categories, from minimalist to conscientious. Companies that engage in CSR can pursue either generic *philanthropy* or *strategic CSR*.

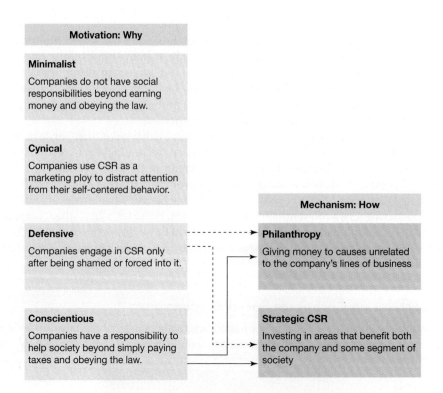

substantial improvements in its business practices. For example, environmental activists use the term *greenwash* (a combination of *green* and *whitewash*, a term that suggests covering something up) as a label for publicity efforts that present companies as being environmentally friendly when their actions speak otherwise. Ironically, some of the most ardent antibusiness activists and the staunchly probusiness advocates of the minimalist view tend to agree on one point: that many CSR efforts are disingenuous. Thirty-five years after his provocative article, Friedman said he believed that "most of the claims of social responsibility are pure public relations."[18]

■ *Conscientious.* In the fourth approach to CSR, company leaders believe they have responsibilities beyond making a profit, and they back up their beliefs and proclamations with action—without being prompted to by outside forces. John Mackey, CEO of Whole Foods Market, is a strong proponent of this view: "I believe that the enlightened corporation should try to create value for all of its constituencies," which he identifies as customers, employees, vendors, investors, communities, and the environment. From its inception, the company has given 5 percent of profits to a variety of causes. "Whole Foods gives money to our communities because we care about them and feel a responsibility to help them flourish as well as possible." Mackey says the minimalist view and Adam Smith's invisible hand guiding the marketplace (see Chapter 1) are based on a "pessimistic and crabby view of human nature." Note that his approach doesn't have to compromise profits or returns for investors, either: Whole Foods is the most profitable large grocery chain in the United States.[19]

So what's the right answer? Of these four perspectives, we can instantly eliminate the cynical approach simply because it is dishonest and therefore unethical. Beyond that, the debate is less clear, but the opinions are certainly strong. Some proponents of the minimalist view equate CSR with *collectivism*, a term that suggests communism and socialism. Some consider CSR demands from NGOs and other outsiders to be little more than extortion.[20] Professor Alexei Marcoux of Loyola University in Chicago says that CSR is "fundamentally antagonistic to capitalist enterprise."[21] At the other extreme, some critics of contemporary business seem convinced that corporations can never be trusted and that every CSR initiative is a cynical publicity stunt.

A two-tiered approach to CSR can yield a practical, ethical answer to this complex dilemma. At the first tier, companies must take responsibility for the consequences of their actions and limit the negative impact of their operations. This can be summarized as "do no harm," and it is not a matter of choice. Just as it has a right to expect certain behavior from all citizens, society has a right to expect a basic level of responsible behavior from all businesses, including minimizing pollution and waste, minimizing the depletion of natural resources, being honest with all stakeholders, offering real value in exchange for prices asked, and avoiding exploitation of employees, customers, suppliers, communities, and investors. Some of these issues are covered by laws, but others aren't, thereby creating the responsibility of ethical decision making by all employees and managers in a firm.

At the second tier, moving beyond "do no harm" does become a matter of choice. Companies can choose to help in whatever way that investors, managers, and employee see fit, but the choices are a matter of free will. Even John Mackey of Whole Foods says that decisions to help the community should be voluntary and companies should not be coerced into them.[22] (For the latest information on CSR, visit www.prenhall.com/bovée and click on "Real-Time Updates.")

Philanthropy Versus Strategic CSR

Companies that engage in CSR activities can choose between two courses of action, general philanthropy or strategic CSR. **Philanthropy** involves the donation of money, employee time, or other resources to various causes without regard for any direct business benefits for the company. For instance, a company might support the arts in its hometown in the interest of enhancing the city's cultural richness. In addition to free

philanthropy
The donation of money, time, goods, or services to charitable, humanitarian, or educational institutions

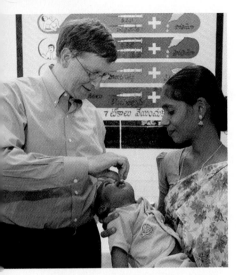

Bill Gates originally made his name as the co-founder and guiding force behind Microsoft, but in recent years he and his wife Melinda (not pictured) have become increasingly well known for their generous contributions to world-wide health care and education.

strategic CSR
Social contributions that are directly aligned with a company's overall business strategy

---

products, employee time, use of company facilities, and other noncash contributions, U.S. companies donate billions of dollars to charity every year.[23]

In contrast to generic philanthropy, **strategic CSR**, a concept championed by Michael Porter and Mark Kramer, involves social contributions that are directly aligned with a company's overall business strategy. In other words, the company helps itself and society at the same time. This approach can be followed in a variety of ways. A company can help develop the workforce, as in the Microsoft example cited earlier, or in the case of the hotel chain Marriott providing job training to chronically underemployed workers. A company can also help develop markets for its goods and services, as the British firm Thames Water did by assisting groups trying to improve water supplies in Africa.[24] And a company can make choices that position it favorably in the minds of target customers and give it a competitive advantage. Toyota's decision to invest in hybrid automotive technology helps reduce environmental damage (its hybrid engines consume half the fuel while reducing harmful emissions by up to 90 percent) and gave Toyota a commanding lead in a major new segment of the car market.[25]

Strategic CSR makes more sense than general philanthropy or an antagonistic business-versus-society mind-set, for several reasons. First, because business and society are mutually dependent, choices that weaken one or the other will ultimately weaken both. Second, investments that benefit the company are more likely to be sustained over time. Third, making sizable investments in a few strategically focused areas, rather than spreading smaller amounts of money around through generic philanthropy, will yield greater benefits to society.[26] Thames Water CEO Bill Alexander emphasizes that "Philanthropy won't be enough. To achieve real scale we need a new business model."[27]

Exactly how much can or should businesses contribute to social concerns? This is a difficult decision because all companies have limited resources that must be allocated to a number of goals, such as upgrading facilities and equipment, developing new products, marketing existing products, and rewarding employee efforts, in addition to contributing to social causes. As Exhibit 2.4 suggests, stakeholders' needs sometimes conflict, requiring managers to make tough decisions about resource allocation.

EXHIBIT 2.4

Balancing Business and Stakeholders' Rights

Balancing the individual needs and interests of a company's stakeholders is one of management's most difficult tasks.

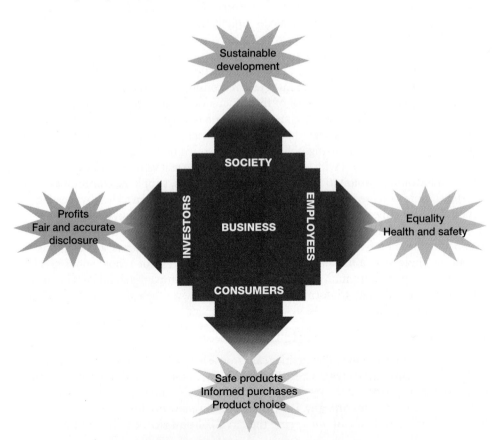

Business's Efforts to Increase Social Responsibility

Companies that are trying to manage CSR investments often begin with a **social audit**, a systematic evaluation and reporting of how the company's activities affect its various stakeholders. With the social audit as a guide, owners and managers can then decide how and where they would like to make a difference. In some cases, the effort will be purely charitable, such as donating money to a favorite cause. In others, the effort will be linked in some way to the company's own business efforts, bringing benefits to the business and to one or more groups in society. A common approach is *cause-related marketing*, in which a portion of product sales helps support worthy causes (see page 216).

Similarly, managers can make business decisions that affect other businesses or communities in a positive way. For instance, in response to pressure from environmental activists, Home Depot persuaded its lumber suppliers in Chile to adopt tree farming methods that protected native forests. By using its power as a huge customer (the company buys 10 percent of the wood exported from Chile, for example), Home Depot was able to influence other companies for a positive outcome.[28]

Responsibility Toward Society and the Environment

In the past few decades, few issues in the public dialog have become as politicized and polarized as pollution and resource depletion. Environmentalists and their political allies sometimes portray business leaders as heartless profiteers who would strip the Earth bare for a few bucks. Corporate leaders and their political allies, on the other hand, sometimes cast environmentalists as "tree huggers" who care more about bunnies and butterflies than human progress. As is often the case, the shouting match between these extreme positions obscures real problems—and opportunities for real solutions.

To ensure a clearer understanding of this situation, keep three important points in mind. First, the creation and delivery of products that society values virtually always generates pollution and consumes natural resources. Think that web-based businesses are "clean" because there is no visible pollution? Think again: The Internet and all the computers attached to it have a voracious appetite for electricity, and the generation of electricity nearly always affects the environment—over 70 percent of the electricity used in the United States is generated by burning coal, oil, or natural gas (see Exhibit 2.5).[29] According to Mark H. Mills, a physicist and investor in the energy industry, "The information and digital parts of our economy consume the energy equivalent of 700 million barrels of oil a year."[30] Moreover, computers, MP3 players, and other electronic devices are packed with toxic materials that must somehow be disposed of whenever people upgrade to newer models.

social audit
Assessment of a company's performance in the area of social responsibility

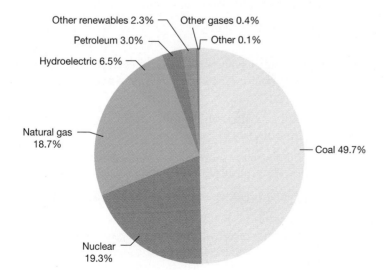

Other renewables 2.3% — Other gases 0.4%
Petroleum 3.0% — Other 0.1%
Hydroelectric 6.5% —
Natural gas 18.7%
Coal 49.7%
Nuclear 19.3%

EXHIBIT 2.5

Sources of Electricity in the United States

More than 70 percent of the electricity used in the United States is produced by burning coal, petroleum, or natural gas. Nuclear and hydroelectric power provides most of the rest.

Second, we all consume natural resources and generate pollution, so we are all part of the problem. For example, the United States has made relatively little progress toward reducing smog in the last 10 to 15 years, and the Environmental Protection Agency blames the continuing popularity of vehicles with low gas mileage and a dramatic increase in the miles being driven.[31]

Third, "environmental" causes are often as much about human health and safety as they are about forests, rivers, and wildlife. The quality of our air, water, and soil affects everyone in society, not just people concerned with wild spaces.

Efforts to Reduce Pollution

ecology
Study of the relationships among living things in the water, air, and soil, their environments, and the nutrients that support them

Concerns over pollution have been growing since the dawn of the Industrial Age in the nineteenth century. However, widespread concern for the environment really dates to the 1960s when **ecology**, the study of the relationship between organisms and the natural environment, entered mainstream public discussion. The conversation has been contentious from the beginning, too. When Rachel Carson published *Silent Spring* in 1962, which called attention to the dangers of pesticide use, she was attacked by the chemical industry, by many in the news media, and even by some government officials.[32]

In 1963, federal, state, and local governments began enacting laws and regulations to reduce pollution (see Exhibit 2.6). In 1970, the federal government established the

EXHIBIT 2.6 Major Federal Environmental Legislation

Since the early 1960s, major federal legislation aimed at the environment has focused on providing cleaner air and water and reducing toxic waste.

LEGISLATION	PROVISION
National Environmental Policy Act (1999)	Establishes a structure for coordinating all federal environmental programs
Clean Air Act and amendments (1963, 1965, 1970, 1977, 1990)	Assists states and localities in formulating control programs; sets federal standards for auto-exhaust emissions; sets maximum permissible pollution levels; authorizes nationwide air-pollution standards and limitations to pollutant discharge; requires scrubbers in new coal-fired power plants; directs EPA to prevent deterioration of air quality in clean areas; sets schedule and standards for cutting smog, acid rain, hazardous factory fumes, and ozone-depleting chemicals
Solid Waste Disposal Act and amendments (1965, 1984)	Authorizes research and assistance to state and local control programs; regulates treatment, storage, transportation, and disposal of hazardous waste
Resource Recovery Act (1970)	Subsidizes pilot recycling plants; authorizes nationwide control programs
Federal Water Pollution Control Act and amendments (1972)	Authorizes grants to states for water-pollution control; gives federal government limited authority to correct pollution problems; authorizes EPA to set and enforce water-quality standards
Safe Drinking Water Act (1974, 1996)	Sets standards of drinking-water quality; requires municipal water systems to report on contaminant levels; establishes funding to upgrade water systems
Noise Control Act (1972)	Requires EPA to set standards for major sources of noise and to advise Federal Aviation Administration on standards for airplane noise
Toxic Substances Control Act (1976)	Requires chemicals testing; authorizes EPA to restrict the use of harmful substances
Oil Pollution Act (1990)	Sets up liability trust fund; extends operations for preventing and containing oil pollution

Environmental Protection Agency (EPA) to regulate air and water pollution by manufacturers and utilities, supervise the control of automobile pollution, license pesticides, control toxic substances, and safeguard the purity of drinking water. A landmark piece of legislation, the Clean Air Act, was also passed that year. Many individual states and cities have also passed their own tough clean-air laws.

However, even with many laws and regulations in place, air pollution remains a global problem, as evidenced by the threat of **global warming**, a gradual rise in average temperatures around the planet that has been linked to increases in atmospheric carbon dioxide (one of the major components of engine exhaust). According to the American Geophysical Union, www.agu.org, a nonprofit, nonpartisan organization whose membership includes more than 40,000 scientists in 130 countries, "It is virtually certain that increasing atmospheric concentrations of carbon dioxide and other greenhouse gases will cause global surface climate to be warmer."[33]

In contrast to air pollution, a good deal of progress has been made in reducing water pollution, thanks in large part to the Clean Water Act passed in 1972. As with the Clean Air Act, though, the conflict between environmental and commercial forces rages on when it comes to such issues as the dumping of mining wastes into rivers and streams and the annual discharge of millions of gallons of animal waste from large "factory" farms.[34] Drinking water quality has improved somewhat in the past couple of decades but still varies considerably around the country.[35] On the negative side, reports of mercury pollution in rivers and lakes, which is primarily the result of air pollution from coal-burning power plants and waste incinerators, are on the rise.[36]

The complex war on toxic waste on land has marked a number of successes over the years, although as with air and water pollution, overall results are mixed. The EPA's Superfund program, designed to clean up the worst toxic waste dumps in the country, still has more than a thousand sites left to clean.[37] Electronics waste is a growing problem that has only recently been given serious attention. For example, more than 100 million mobile phones are tossed out in the United States every year. Fewer than 5 percent of them are currently recycled, but Motorola, Nokia, and other phone manufacturers are now pushing recycling initiatives.[38]

Many of the electronics products thrown out in the United States end up in environmentally unsound reclamation centers such as this one near the Lianjiang River in China.

global warming
A gradual rise in average temperatures around the planet; caused by increases in carbon dioxide emissions

sustainable development
Operating business in a manner that minimizes pollution and resource depletion, ensuring that future generations will have vital resources

green marketing
Efforts by companies to distinguish themselves by practicing sustainable development and communicating these efforts to consumers

The Trend Toward Sustainability

In recent years, many business leaders have shifted their thinking on pollution and resource depletion toward the notion of **sustainable development**, which the United Nations has defined as development that "meets the needs of the present without compromising the ability of future generations to meet their own needs."[39] For example, according to the Millennium Ecosystem Assessment, a comprehensive study of resource usage in 95 countries, 60 percent of the natural resources that human life relies on either directly or indirectly (such as air, drinking water, forests, and fish stocks) are either being degraded or used in unsustainable ways.[40]

Businesses that recognize the link between environmental performance and sustained financial well-being are discovering that spending now to prevent pollution can end up saving more money down the road (by reducing cleanup costs, litigation expenses, and production costs). From building eco-industrial parks to improving production efficiency, these activities are a part of the **green marketing** movement, in which companies distinguish themselves by reducing pollution, cutting waste, and curbing resource depletion—and then communicate these efforts to consumers. Besides addressing

Recycling is a key part of Patagonia's efforts to minimize pollution and resource depletion. The company even recycles buildings when it can. Its Portland, Oregon, store is housed in a building that dates from 1895; when it was remodeled, 97 percent of the building materials were reclaimed or recycled.

ethical and financial concerns, such efforts can help companies build goodwill with customers, communities, and other stakeholders.

In addition to better stewardship of shared natural resources, sustainable development is also a smart business strategy. By taking a broad and long-term view of their companies' impact on the environment and stakeholders throughout the world, managers can ensure the continued availability of the resources their organizations need and be better prepared for changes in government regulations and shifting social expectations. In fact, some experts believe sustainability is a good measure of the quality of management in a corporation. According to investment researcher Matthew J. Kiernan, companies that take a sustainable approach "tend to be more strategic, nimble, and better equipped to compete in the complex, high-velocity global environment."[41]

General Electric (GE) and Dow Chemical, two corporations long criticized for their environmental practices, now appear to be embracing sustainability as core business strategies. Both companies are investing heavily in wind and solar power, hybrid engines, water treatment, and other technologies aimed at sustainability. According to Dow CEO Andrew N. Liveris, "There is 100% overlap between our business drivers and social and environmental interests."[42]

Responsibility Toward Consumers

consumerism
Movement that pressures businesses to consider consumer needs and interests

The 1960s activism that awakened business to its environmental responsibilities also gave rise to **consumerism**, a movement that put pressure on businesses to consider consumer needs and interests. (Note that some people use *consumerism* in a negative sense, as a synonym for *materialism*.) Consumerism prompted many businesses to create consumer affairs departments to handle customer complaints. It also prompted state and local agencies to set up bureaus to offer consumer information and assistance. At the federal level, President John F. Kennedy announced a "bill of rights" for consumers, laying the foundation for a wave of consumer-oriented legislation (see Exhibit 2.7). These rights include the right to safe products, the right to be informed, the right to choose, and the right to be heard.

The Right to Buy Safe Products

As mentioned previously, doing no harm is one of the foundations of corporate social responsibility. The United States and many other countries go to considerable lengths to ensure the safety of the products sold within their borders. The U.S. government imposes many safety standards that are enforced by the Consumer Product Safety Commission (CPSC), as well as by other federal and state agencies. Theoretically, companies that don't comply with these rules are forced to take corrective action. Moreover, the threat of product-liability suits and declining sales motivates companies to meet safety standards. After all, a poor safety record can quickly damage a hard-won reputation. However, unsafe goods and services remain a constant concern, given the ever-changing array of products available and the sheer magnitude of the monitoring effort.

identity theft
Crimes in which thieves steal personal information and use it to take out loans and commit other types of fraud

Product safety concerns range from safe toys, food, and automobiles to less-tangible worries such as online privacy and **identity theft**, in which criminals steal personal information and use it to take out loans, request government documents, get expensive medical procedures, and commit other types of fraud. According to Federal Trade Commission estimates, some 9 million Americans are victims of identity theft every year.[43] Companies play a vital role in fighting this crime because they frequently collect the information that identity thieves use

EXHIBIT 2.7 Major Federal Consumer Legislation

Major federal legislation aimed at consumer protection has focused on food and drugs, false advertising, product safety, and credit protection.

LEGISLATION	PROVISION
Food, Drug, and Cosmetic Act (1938)	Puts cosmetics, foods, drugs, and therapeutic products under Food and Drug Administration's jurisdiction; outlaws misleading labeling
Cigarette Labeling Act (1965)	Mandates warnings on cigarette packages and in ads
Fair Packaging and Labeling Act (1966, 1972)	Requires honest, informative package labeling; labels must show origin of product, quantity of contents, uses or applications
Truth-in-Lending Act (Consumer Protection Credit Act) (1968)	Requires creditors to disclose finance charge and annual percentage rate; limits cardholder liability for unauthorized use
Fair Credit Reporting Act (1970)	Requires credit-reporting agencies to set process for assuring accuracy; requires creditors to explain credit denials
Consumer Product Safety Act (1972)	Creates Consumer Product Safety Commission
Magnuson-Moss Warranty Act (1975)	Requires complete written warranties in ordinary language; requires warranties to be available before purchase
Alcohol Labeling Legislation (1988)	Requires warning labels on alcohol products, saying that alcohol impairs abilities and that women shouldn't drink when pregnant
Nutrition Education and Labeling Act (1990)	Requires specific, uniform product labels detailing nutritional information on every food regulated by the FDA
American Automobile Labeling Act (1992)	Requires carmakers to identify where cars are assembled and where their individual components are manufactured
Deceptive Mail Prevention and Enforcement Act (1999)	Establishes standards for sweepstakes mailings, skill contests, and facsimile checks to prevent fraud and exploitation
Controlling the Assault of Non-Solicited Pornography and Marketing Act (2003)	Known as CAN-SPAM, attempts to protect online consumers from unwanted and fraudulent e-mail

to commit their fraud, including credit card and Social Security numbers. Any company that collects such information has a clear ethical obligation to keep it safe and secure.

The Right to Be Informed

Consumers have a right to know what they're buying, how to use it, and whether it presents any risks to them. They also have a right to know the true price of goods or services and the details of any purchase contracts. For example, the availability of *subprime* home loans—loans extended to people with weaker credit ratings who don't qualify under regular lending criteria—has increased dramatically in the last decade. Such loans used to be rare, making up only 1 or 2 percent of all home loans in the United States, but by 2006 they made up more than 20 percent of home loans. Many of these were also riskier types of loans, including loans with monthly payments that start out quite low but then increase dramatically overnight—sometimes doubling or tripling.[44]

When thousands of consumers who signed these loans got into financial trouble because they couldn't make the payments, many claimed that the risks weren't fully explained to them. The nation's biggest subprime lender, Ameriquest, was investigated by 49 states after borrowers claimed the company lied to them, obscuring the true costs and risks of financing. The company settled out of court with the states; part of the settlement included random monitoring of phone calls to make sure Ameriquest loan

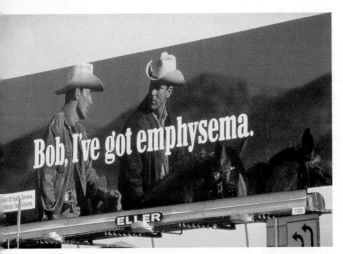

Using advertising such as this billboard that plays off the macho image of the Marlboro Man, health advocates campaign against smoking. However, cigarettes remain a legal product in the United States.

officers communicate truthfully. Borrowers have also filed a class-action lawsuit against the company. Responding to the growing crisis, in 2007 six national banking trade groups agreed on a set of lending principles that included better disclosure of loan terms.[45]

The Right to Choose Which Products to Buy

Especially in the United States, the number of products available to consumers is truly amazing. But how far should the right to choose extend? Are we entitled to choose products that are potentially harmful, such as cigarettes, alcoholic beverages, guns, or even cars with low gas mileage? Should the government take measures to make such products illegal, or should consumers always be allowed to decide for themselves what to buy?

Consider cigarettes. Scientists determined long ago that the tar and nicotine in tobacco are harmful and addictive. In 1965, the Federal Cigarette Labeling and Advertising Act was passed, requiring all cigarette packs to carry the Surgeon General's warnings. Over the years, tobacco companies have spent billions of dollars to defend themselves in lawsuits brought by smokers suffering from cancer and respiratory diseases. Lawsuits and legislative activity surrounding tobacco products continue to this day—and are likely to continue for years. Meanwhile, consumers can still purchase cigarettes in the marketplace. As RJR Nabisco Chairman Steve Goldstone put it, "Behind all the allegations . . . is the simple truth that we sell a legal product."[46]

The Right to Be Heard

The final component of consumer rights is the right to be heard. Fortunately, communication technology has made this easier in recent years, with online comment forms, real-time customer service IM chat, blog comments, and e-mail links. Companies can use such feedback to improve their products and services and to make informed decisions about offering new ones.

Responsibility Toward Investors

Whether companies solicit funds directly from venture capitalists and other investors or sell shares to the public through the stock market, they have an ethical responsibility to use that money carefully and to communicate honestly. As noted earlier in the chapter, much of the controversy surrounding CSR stems from the conflict over investors' rights versus the rights of other shareholders. In a corporation, investors are represented by the *board of directors*, who are responsible for making the major decisions that affect the company. After some of the financial scandals of the past decade, in which thousands of investors suffered significant losses, comprehensive new financial regulations made directors more accountable for the actions of their companies. You'll read more about corporate boards in Chapter 5.

Responsibility Toward Employees

The past few decades have brought dramatic changes in the attitudes and composition of the global workforce. These changes have forced businesses to modify their recruiting, training, and promotion practices, as well as their overall corporate values and behaviors. Chapter 14 offers a closer look at contemporary employment practices; this section discusses some key responsibilities that employers have regarding employees.

The Push for Equality in Employment

The United States has always stood for economic freedom and the individual's right to pursue opportunity. Unfortunately, in the past, many people were targets of economic **discrimination**, were relegated to low-paying, menial jobs, and were prevented from taking advantage of many opportunities solely on the basis of their race, gender, disability, or religion.

The Civil Rights Act of 1964 established the Equal Employment Opportunity Commission (EEOC), the regulatory agency that addresses job discrimination. The EEOC is responsible for monitoring the hiring practices of companies and for investigating complaints of job-related discrimination. It has the power to file legal charges against companies that discriminate and to force them to compensate individuals or groups who have been victimized by unfair practices. The Civil Rights Act of 1991 extended the original act by allowing workers to sue companies for discrimination and by granting women powerful legal tools against job bias.

Affirmative Action   In the 1960s, **affirmative action** programs were developed to encourage organizations to recruit and promote members of groups whose economic progress had been hindered through legal barriers or established practices. Affirmative action programs address a variety of situations, from college admissions to executive promotions to conducting business with government agencies (businesses that want to sell goods or services to the federal government are generally required to have an affirmative action program in place, for instance). Note that while affirmative action programs address a variety of population segments, from military veterans with disabilities to specific ethnic groups, in popular usage, "affirmative action" usually refers to programs based on race.

Affirmative action remains one of the most controversial and politicized issues in business today, with opponents claiming it creates a double standard and can encourage reverse discrimination against white males, and proponents saying that it remains a crucial part of the effort to ensure equal opportunities for all. One of the key points of contention is whether affirmative action programs are still needed, given the various antidiscrimination laws now in place. Opponents assert that everyone has an equal shot at success now, so the programs are unnecessary and if anything, should be based on income, not race; proponents argue that laws can't remove every institutionalized barrier and that discrimination going back decades has left many families and communities at a long-term disadvantage.[47]

Political debates aside, well-managed companies across the country are finding that embracing diversity in the richest sense is simply good business. You'll read more about *diversity initiatives* in Chapter 14.

People with Disabilities   In 1990, people with a wide range of physical and mental difficulties got a boost from the passage of the federal Americans with Disabilities Act (ADA), which guarantees equal opportunities in housing, transportation, education, employment, and other areas for the estimated 50 to 75 million people in the United States with disabilities. As defined by the 1990

discrimination
In a social and economic sense, denial of opportunities to individuals on the basis of some characteristic that has no bearing on their ability to perform in a job

affirmative action
Activities undertaken by businesses to recruit and promote members of groups whose economic progress had been hindered through either legal barriers or established practices

Learning from Business Blunders

Oops: As Northwest Airlines began laying off thousands of workers, it gave them a booklet that contained a list titled "101 Ways to Save Money." Sounds like helpful advice for anyone who has just lost his or her job, but several points struck many observers as crass, such as this admonition: "Don't be shy about pulling something you like out of the trash." Telling former employees to dig through the garbage for things they can no longer afford was offensive, particularly when CEO Doug Steenland was set to receive nearly $2 million in compensation that same year. A representative of the employees' union called the booklet "disgraceful" and "insulting." After receiving numerous complaints and being lambasted in the media, Northwest revised the booklet to remove the list.

What You Can Learn: Even though the effort to help laid-off employees save money was surely well intentioned, the list struck many people as a sign of the company's disrespect for its employees—including those who still had their jobs. In volatile situations such as this, take extra care to make sure feelings don't get bruised. If Northwest managers had privately polled a few employees about the list before distributing it, they would've found out how offensive it was and saved themselves a lot of embarrassment.

law, *disability* is a broad term that protects not only those with physical handicaps but also those with cancer, heart disease, diabetes, epilepsy, HIV/AIDS, drug addiction, alcoholism, emotional illness, and other conditions. In most situations, employers cannot legally require job applicants to pass a physical examination as a condition of employment. Employers are also required to make reasonable accommodations to meet the needs of employees with disabilities, such as modifying work stations or schedules.[48]

Occupational Safety and Health

Every year 5,000 to 7,000 U.S. workers lose their lives on the job and thousands more are injured (see Exhibit 2.8).[49] During the 1960s, mounting concern about workplace hazards resulted in the passage of the Occupational Safety and Health Act of 1970, which set mandatory standards for safety and health and which established the Occupational Safety and Health Administration (OSHA) to enforce them. These standards govern everything from hazardous materials to *ergonomics*, the study of how people interact with machines. For instance, a major ergonomics issue in recent years has been the risk of repetitive stress injuries such as carpal tunnel syndrome, which can develop after prolonged use of computer keyboards and other devices that require repeated wrist action.

Raising the visibility of such issues is often key to creating change, a notion that even the best-run U.S. companies take care to follow. At computer chip maker Intel, for instance, the CEO receives a report within 24 hours whenever an Intel employee suffers an injury that results in even a single day of lost time. Thanks to the executive-level attention that workplace safety gets at Intel, the injury rate among the company's 80,000 employees is 25 times lower than the industry average. The company is also active in such areas as studying the relationship between workplace stress, heart disease, and depression.[50]

Concerns for employee safety can extend beyond a company's own workforce, and this concern is particularly acute for the many U.S. companies that contract out production to factories in Asia, Latin America, and parts of the United States to make products under their brand names. A number of these companies have been criticized for doing business with so-called *sweatshops*, a disparaging term applied to production facilities that treat workers poorly. Some of these factories have been accused of forcing employees to work 24 hours or more at a time, employing young children in unsafe conditions, or virtually imprisoning workers in conditions that have been compared to slavery.[51]

Mattel, Reebok, Patagonia, Liz Claiborne, Gap, and Nike are among the industry leaders that have responded to the poor working conditions in these factories.[52] Gap sends

EXHIBIT 2.8

Workplace Killers

In 2005, 5,702 American workers lost their lives on the job; transportation accidents are the leading cause of death in the workplace.

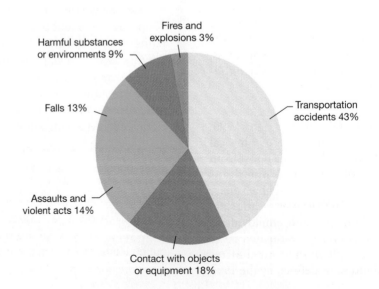

inspectors around the globe to make sure contract manufacturers follow the company's *Code of Vendor Conduct*. The company also learned that by improving its own processes, such as reducing last-minute change orders, it can reduce overtime and stress on factory employees.[53] Nike, meanwhile, realized that setting standards and monitoring operations wasn't improving conditions in its contract factories sufficiently and is now working closely with vendors to improve their operations and practices. Nike also intends to engage other companies, including its competitors, in a shared effort to create lasting change in these factories around the world.[54]

Why don't these other countries do more to protect their own citizens? They're caught in a competitive battle just as companies are. For instance, the government of Mexico is reluctant to increase the costs of doing business there for fear that even more production work will move to places such as China, leaving its citizens with fewer jobs. And as China continues its economic development, it, too, is facing cost competition from countries such as Thailand and Vietnam. As long as wage differences exist between various regions of the world, these problems will persist at least to some degree. Meanwhile, a number of groups, such as the Fair Labor Association (www.fairlabor.org), are working to address these issues. American colleges have played an important role in this effort, by the way: More than 200 schools have joined the Fair Labor Association to ensure that school-logo products are manufactured in an ethical manner.[55]

Ethics and Social Responsibility Around the World

As complicated as ethics and social responsibility can be for U.S. businesses, these issues grow even more complex when cultural influences are applied in the global business environment. Corporate executives may face simple questions regarding the appropriate amount of money to spend on a business gift or the legitimacy of a payment to "expedite" business. Or they may encounter out-and-out bribery, environmental abuse, and unscrupulous business practices. As you read about global business in Chapter 3, you'll have the opportunity to see how a country's ethical codes of conduct, laws, and cultural differences are indeed put to the test as more companies transact business around the globe.

Summary of Learning Objectives

1 Discuss what it means to practice good business ethics and highlight three factors that influence ethical behavior.

Businesspeople who practice good business ethics obey all laws and regulations, compete fairly and honestly, communicate truthfully, and avoid causing harm to others. Of the many factors that influence ethical behavior, the three most common are cultural differences, knowledge of the facts and consequences involving a decision or action, and the ethical practices and commitment to ethical behavior at one's place of work.

2 Identify three steps that businesses are taking to encourage ethical behavior and explain the advantages and disadvantages of whistle-blowing.

Businesses are adopting codes of ethics, appointing ethics officers, and establishing ethics hotlines. In spite of these efforts, if illegal, unethical, or harmful practices persist, an employee may need to blow the whistle or disclose such problems to outsiders. Doing so may force the company to stop the problematic practices. But bringing these issues into the public eye has consequences. It can hurt the company's reputation, take managers' time, damage employee morale, and impact the informant's job with the company.

3 List four questions you might ask yourself when trying to make an ethical decision.

When making ethical decisions, ask yourself: (1) Is the decision legal? (Does it break any law?) (2) Is it balanced? (Is it fair to all concerned?) (3) Can you live with it? (Does it make you feel good about yourself?) (4) Is it feasible? (Will it work in the real world?)

4 Explain the difference between an ethical dilemma and an ethical lapse.

An ethical dilemma is an issue with two conflicting but arguably valid sides, whereas an ethical lapse occurs when an individual makes a decision that is illegal, immoral, or unethical.

5 Explain the controversy surrounding corporate social responsibility.

The minimalist view of CSR holds that companies fulfill their responsibilities to society simply by following the law and maximizing their profits. Proponents of this view believe that companies should not use investors' or taxpayers' money to promote social causes. The conscientious view, in contrast, holds that companies have a broader reason for existing than simply maximizing profits. In addition, both probusiness and antibusiness critics sometimes assert that CSR efforts are simply public relations efforts that lack substance or try to distract attention away from companies' misdeeds.

6 Discuss how businesses can become more socially responsible.

Companies can start by conducting social audits to assess whether their performance is socially responsible. Based on that information, they can choose to contribute through either philanthropy (general donations of time, money, or other resources) or strategic CSR (social investments that align with the company's business goals). Companies can protect and improve the environment by taking a variety of actions to reduce pollution. They can become good citizens by considering consumers' needs and respecting their four basic rights: the right to safe products; the right to be informed—which includes the right to know a product's contents, use, price, and dangers; the right to choose which products to buy; and the right to be heard, such as the right to voice a complaint or concern. They can look out for a company's investors and protect the value of their interests. And they can foster good employee relationships by treating employees fairly and equally and by providing a safe working environment.

7 Define *sustainable development* and explain the strategic advantages of managing with sustainability as a priority.

The United Nations provided a compelling definition of sustainable development as that which "meets the needs of the present without compromising the ability of future generations to meet their own needs." In other words, businesses should operate in ways that minimize pollution and resource depletion so that future generations have a habitable world with sufficient resources. Managing with sustainability in mind can help a company plan for and respond to changes to government regulations or social expectations, instead of being caught on the defensive.

Behind the Scenes

PepsiCo Responds to Protests over Water Usage and Product Safety

After tests conducted and publicized by the Centre for Science and Environment (CSE) in 2003 claimed that the beverages Pepsi manufactured and sold in India had unsafe levels of pesticides, the company responded in several ways, starting with a joint press conference with archrival Coke to dispute CSE's findings. Over the next couple of years, Pepsi executives met with CSE director Sunita Narain and Indian government officials in an attempt to iron out safety standards for beverages.

Just as an agreement was about to be finalized, the government deferred, saying more research was required.

Narain angrily accused the government of caving in to corporate pressure. CSE then conducted more tests and in August 2006 released new data claiming that pesticide levels in Pepsi products were 30 times higher than the proposed Indian safety standards. Protests flared again, and some local governments once again banned Pepsi and Coke products.

Indra Nooyi, who had been playing a key role in Pepsi's efforts to counter CSE's campaign, was promoted to chief executive officer of Pepsi shortly after. Her response to CSE's new round of accusations was blunt: "For somebody to think that Pepsi would jeopardize its brand—its global brand—by doing something stupid in one country is crazy." Soon after becoming CEO, she traveled to India to discuss Pepsi's side of the story with the news media. The fact that she is a woman from India who grew up to become the CEO of one of the world's top companies and one of the most powerful women in American business garnered Nooyi much adoration in her home country, which probably helped improve public opinion regarding Pepsi products.

Other Pepsi communication efforts included advertisements featuring Indian celebrities endorsing Pepsi beverages and tours of the water treatment facility in its beverage plant that highlight steps taken to ensure product safety. Pepsi also aggressively attacked its own water consumption problem, reducing its usage to a mere one-quarter of the previous level. And the company continues to assist local communities around the country with new wells and water conservation efforts.

At least for the time being, the response seems to be working, halting the sales decline and quieting the critics somewhat. However, as of mid-2007, the government still hadn't finalized safety standards, so the issue is not yet fully resolved.

Narain freely admits that she chose Pepsi as a target partly because attacking a huge multinational corporation—particularly an American one—would draw attention to the problem of pesticide contamination in India's water supply. While she refused to meet with Nooyi during the Pepsi CEO's trip to India, she did say, "It's great to have an Indian woman in such a high-profile position."

Meanwhile, Nooyi also says she could've handled the situation better by traveling to India as soon as the controversy erupted back in 2003. She realizes that Pepsi must continue to educate consumers and the media about the company's products and its efforts to be a responsible corporate citizen. As water and other resources grow scarce in many regions and critics of globalization complain about "corporate colonialism" by multinational companies, Nooyi and other executives will continue to face the challenge of ensuring their organizations act responsibly—and communicate effectively.[56]

Critical Thinking Questions

1. Pepsi asserts that its products meet all applicable government safety standards. From an ethical perspective, is this a sufficient response to concerns about consumer safety? Why or why not?

2. Was it ethical for Sunita Narain to single out Pepsi as a protest target, when the problems of industrial water usage and groundwater contamination involve thousands of companies, farmers, and municipalities? Why or why not?

3. Indra Nooyi stressed in an interview that bottled water and soda consume only 0.04 percent of the total water used by all industries throughout India. Explain whether or not you think this specific point is a valid response to the water-usage criticism.

LEARN MORE ONLINE

Visit the Pepsi India website at www.pepsiindia.co.in. Click on "Community Initiatives" and read the company's corporate social responsibility statement. Also, click on "Tour Our Plant" to view a short video and read testimonial statements from people who have visited the plant in person. You can also read several press releases related to the water-usage and product safety issues. Do you think the company does an effective job of responding to its critics? Does visiting the website change your opinion of the company?

(For the very latest information on Pepsi's CSR activities, visit www.prenhall.com/bovée and click on "Real-Time Updates.") ■

Key Terms

affirmative action (47)
code of ethics (33)
conflict of interest (32)
consumerism (44)
corporate social responsibility
  (CSR) (30)
discrimination (47)
ecology (42)
ethical dilemma (35)

ethical lapse (35)
ethics (30)
green marketing (43)
global warming (43)
identity theft (44)
insider trading (32)
justice (35)
nongovernmental organizations
  (NGOs) (38)

philanthropy (39)
social audit (41)
strategic CSR (40)
sustainable development (43)
transparency (31)
utilitarianism (35)
whistle-blowing (33)

Test Your Knowledge

Questions for Review

1. Who shapes a company's ethics?
2. What is a conflict-of-interest situation?
3. How do companies support ethical behavior?
4. How are businesses responding to the environmental issues facing society?
5. What can a company do to assure customers that its products are safe?

Questions for Analysis

6. Why can't legal considerations resolve every ethical question?
7. How do individuals employ philosophical principles in making ethical business decisions?
8. Why does a company need more than a code of ethics to be ethical?
9. Why is it important for a company to balance its social responsibility efforts with its need to generate profits?
10. **Ethical Considerations.** Is it ethical for companies to benefit from their efforts to practice corporate social responsibility? Why or why not? How can anyone be sure that CSR efforts aren't just public relations ploys?

Questions for Application

11. You sell musical gifts on the web and in quarterly catalogs. Your 2-person partnership has quickly grown into a 27-person company, and you spend all your time on quality matters. You're losing control of important environmental choices about materials suppliers, product packaging, and even the paper used in your catalogs. What steps can you take to be sure your employees continue making choices that protect the environment?
12. **How This Affects You.** Based on what you've learned about corporate social responsibility, what effect will CSR considerations have on your job search?
13. **Integrated.** Chapter 1 identified knowledge workers as a key economic resource of the twenty-first century. If an employee leaves a company to work for a competitor, what types of knowledge would it be ethical for the employee to share with the new employer and what types would be unethical to share?
14. **Integrated.** Is it ethical for state and city governments to entice businesses to relocate their operations to that state or city by offering them special tax breaks that are not extended to other businesses operating in that area?

Practice Your Knowledge

Sharpening Your Communication Skills

All organizations, not just corporations, can benefit from having a code of ethics to guide decision making. But whom should a code of ethics protect, and what should it cover? In this exercise, you and your team are going to draft a code of ethics for your school.

Start by thinking about who will be protected by this code of ethics. What stakeholders should the school consider when making decisions? What negative effects might decisions have on these stakeholders? Then think about the kinds of situations you want your school's code of ethics to cover. One example might be employment decisions; another might be disclosure of confidential student information.

Next, using Exhibit 2.1 as a model, draft your school's code of ethics. Write a general introduction explaining the purpose of the code and who is being protected. Next, write a positive statement to guide ethical decisions in each situation you identified earlier in this exercise. Your statement about promotion decisions, for example, might read: "School officials will encourage equal access to job promotions for all qualified candidates, with every applicant receiving fair consideration."

Compare your code of ethics with the codes drafted by your classmates. Did all the codes seek to protect the same stakeholders? What differences and similarities do you see in the statements guiding ethical decisions?

Building Your Team Skills

Choosing to blow the whistle on your employees or coworkers can create all kinds of legal, ethical, and career complications. Here are five common workplace scenarios that might cause you to search your soul about whether or not to go public with potentially damaging charges. Read them carefully and discuss them with your teammates. Then decide what your team would do in each situation.[57]

1. You believe your company is overcharging or otherwise defrauding a customer or client.
2. With all of the headlines generated by sexual harassment cases lately, you'd think employees wouldn't dare break the law, but it's happening right under your company's nose.
3. You discover that your company, or one of its divisions, products, or processes, presents a physical danger to workers or to the public.
4. An employee is padding overtime statements, taking home some of the company's inventory, or stealing equipment.
5. You smell alcohol on a coworker's breath and notice that individual's work hasn't been up to standard lately.

Improve Your Tech Insights: Location and Tracking Technologies

Location and tracking technologies cover a wide range of capabilities. Radio frequency identification (RFID) technology uses small scannable tags attached to products or even people and pets. RFID is being implemented extensively in retail and wholesale distribution systems to enhance inventory management. Parents and caregivers can also use RFID to check on elderly relatives, pets, or children. The Great America amusement park in Santa Clara, California, offers RFID bracelets for $5 so parents and children can reconnect if they get separated in the crowds. The FDA has approved an implantable device that stores medical information that emergency personnel could retrieve with a quick scan, even if the patient is unconscious.

The Global Positioning System (GPS) can pinpoint any location on Earth using a network of satellites and small transceivers. Trucking fleets use GPS to keep track of all their vehicles to optimize scheduling and make sure drivers stay on assigned routes. Some rental car companies use GPS to see whether drivers break the speed limit or venture outside of permitted rental territories. *Enhanced 911*, or *E911*, uses either GPS or mobile phone towers to let emergency personnel pinpoint the location of people calling on mobile phones.

Using online research tools, identify at least one emerging business opportunity that could take advantage of location and tracking technologies. In an e-mail message to your instructor, describe the opportunity and briefly explain how the technology would be used.[58]

Expand Your Knowledge

Discovering Career Opportunities

Businesses, government agencies, and not-for-profit organizations offer numerous career opportunities related to ethics and social responsibility. How can you learn more about these careers?

1. Search the *Occupational Outlook Handbook* at www.bls.gov/oco for *occupational health and safety specialists and technicians,* jobs concerned with a company's responsibility toward its employees. What are the duties and qualifications of the jobs you have identified? Are the salaries and future outlooks attractive for all of these jobs?

2. Select one job from the *Handbook* and search blogs, websites, and other sources to learn more about it. Try to find real-life information about the daily activities of people in this job. Can you find any information about ethical dilemmas or other conflicts in the duties of this position? What role do you think people in this position play within their respective organizations?

3. What skills, educational background, and work experience do you think employers are seeking in applicants for the specific job you are researching? What keywords do you think employers would search for when reviewing résumés submitted for this position?

Developing Your Research Skills

Articles on corporate ethics and social responsibility regularly appear in business journals and newspapers. Look in recent issues (print or online editions) to find one or more articles discussing one of the following ethics or social responsibility challenges faced by a business:

- Environmental issues, such as pollution, acid rain, and hazardous-waste disposal
- Employee or consumer safety measures
- Consumer information or education
- Employment discrimination or diversity initiatives
- Investment ethics
- Industrial spying and theft of trade secrets
- Fraud, bribery, and overcharging
- Company codes of ethics

1. What was the nature of the ethical challenge or social responsibility issue presented in the article? Does the article report any wrongdoing by a company or agency official? Was the action illegal, unethical, or questionable? What course of action would you recommend the company or agency take to correct or improve matters now?

2. Which stakeholders are affected? What lasting effects will be felt by (a) the company and (b) these stakeholders?

3. Writing a letter to the editor is one way consumers can speak their mind. Review some of the letters to the editor in newspapers or journals. Why are letters to the editor an important feature for that publication?

See It on the Web

Visit these websites and answer the following questions for each one. (Up-to-date links for all websites mentioned in this chapter can be found on the Textbook Resources page for Chapter 2 at www.mybusinesslab.com. Please note that links to sites that become inactive after publication of the book will be removed from the Featured Websites section.)

1. What is the purpose of this website?

2. What kinds of information does this website contain? Please be specific.

3. How is the information provided at this website useful for businesspeople? Consumers?

4. How did you expand your knowledge of ethics and social responsibility in business by reviewing the material at this website? What new things did you learn about this topic?

Build a Better Business

One way to distinguish your business as an ethical organization is to join the Better Business Bureau (BBB). Members of this private, not-for-profit business group agree to maintain specific standards for operating ethically and addressing customer complaints. The BBB website is packed with information about the organization, member businesses, and programs that benefit businesses and consumers alike. You can find reports on companies, register complaints, get help with consumer problems, and access publications on all kinds of consumer issues, such as avoiding business scams and investigating charitable organizations. www.bbb.org

Surf Safely

Although the majority of telemarketing and online businesses are legitimate, unethical businesses bilk consumers out of billions of dollars every year. Fortunately, the National Fraud Information Center (NFIC) can help consumers fight back. The center was established by the National Consumers League (NCL) to safeguard consumers against telemarketing and Internet fraud. Resources on the center's website include reports about current online and telephone scams, tips for online safety, advice on how to file a fraud report, statistics about telemarketing fraud, and special advice for seniors, who are targeted by con artists. Even if you consider yourself a savvy consumer, the site contains a lot of valuable information to help you avoid being ripped off. www.fraud.org

Learn About Environmental Protection

For more than 30 years, the U.S. Environmental Protection Agency (EPA) has been working for a cleaner, healthier environment for the American people. Visit the agency's website to get the latest information on today's environmental issues. Become familiar with the major environmental laws and proposed regulations and learn how to report violations. Expand your knowledge about air pollution, ecosystems, environmental management, and hazardous waste. Visit the EPA newsroom to get regional news. Read the current articles and follow the links to hotlines, publications, and more. This site is a must for all businesses. www.epa.gov

Companion Website

Learning Interactively

Log onto www.prenhall.com/bovée, locate your text, and then click on its Companion Website. For Chapter 2, take advantage of the interactive Chapter Quiz to test your knowledge of the chapter. Get instant feedback on whether you need additional studying. Also, you'll find an abundance of valuable resources that will help you succeed in this course, including PowerPoint presentations and Web Links.

Video Case

Doing the Right Thing: American Red Cross

LEARNING OBJECTIVES

The purpose of this video is to help you:

1. Identify some of the social responsibility and ethics challenges faced by a nonprofit organization

2. Discuss the purpose of an organizational code of ethics

3. Understand the potential conflicts that can emerge between an organization and its stakeholders

SYNOPSIS

Founded in 1881 by Clara Barton, the American Red Cross is a nonprofit organization dedicated to helping victims of war, natural disasters, and other catastrophes. The organization's 1,000 chapters are governed by volunteer boards of directors who oversee local activities and enforce ethical standards in line with the Red Cross's code of ethics and community norms. Over the years, the Red Cross has been guided in its use of donations by honoring donor intent. This helped the organization deal with a major ethical challenge after the terrorist attacks of September 11, 2001. The Red Cross received more than $1 billion in donations and initially diverted some money to ancillary operations such as creating a strategic blood reserve. After donors objected, however, the organization reversed its decision and—honoring donor intent—used the contributions to directly benefit people who were affected by the tragedy.

Discussion Questions

1. *For analysis:* What are the social responsibility implications of the American Red Cross's decision to avoid accepting donations of goods for many local relief efforts?
2. *For analysis:* What kinds of ethical conflicts might arise because the American Red Cross relies so heavily on volunteers?
3. *For application:* What can the American Red Cross do to ensure that local chapters are properly applying the nonprofit's code of ethics?
4. *For application:* How might a nonprofit such as the American Red Cross gain a better understanding of its stakeholders' needs and preferences?
5. *For debate:* Should the American Red Cross have reversed its initial decision to divert some of the money donated for September 11 relief efforts to pressing but ancillary operations? Support your chosen position.

ONLINE EXPLORATION

Visit the American Red Cross site at www.redcross.org and scan the headlines to read about the organization's response to recent disasters. Also look at the educational information available through links to news stories, feature articles, and other material. Next, carefully examine the variety of links addressing the needs and involvement of different stakeholder groups. What kinds of stakeholders does the American Red Cross expect to visit its website? Why are these stakeholders important to the organization? Do you think the organization should post its code of ethics prominently on this site? Explain your answer.

CHAPTER 3

The Global Marketplace

LEARNING OBJECTIVES
After studying this chapter, you will be able to

1   Discuss why nations trade

2   Explain why nations restrict international trade and list four forms of trade restrictions

3   Highlight three protectionist tactics nations use to give their domestic industries a competitive edge

4   Explain the role of trading blocs in international business

5   Highlight the opportunities and challenges of conducting business in other countries

6   List five ways to improve communication in an international business relationship

7   Identify five forms of international business activity

8   Discuss terrorism's impact on globalization

MTV Base Africa: Extending the Reach of One of the World's Biggest Media Brands

www.mtvbase.com

Children everywhere grow up fighting—fighting over toys, homework, bedtime, a turn at the video game. But many, too many, of the young people in Alex Okosi's target audience grew up fighting, period. Of the estimated 300,000 child soldiers in the world, more than a third live in Africa, the region Okosi calls both home and his target market.

After years of colonialism, warfare, famine, widespread poverty, and rampant health problems ranging from malnutrition to the AIDS epidemic, Africa might not strike the average businessperson as a promising market. But Okosi saw reasons for hope, with economies showing signs of recovery in Angola, Uganda, Kenya, and elsewhere.

A native of Nigeria, Okosi immigrated to the United States as a boy, and after college in Vermont he wound up out West, working for Viacom, the parent company of MTV Networks. However, a trip home in 2000 convinced him that his future was in Africa, not in selling Viacom channels to cable operators in Idaho, Nevada,

Alex Okosi combined his entrepreneurial spirit and his love of music to lead the successful launch of MTV Base Africa.

and Wyoming. And when he returned to Africa, he would bring MTV with him.

After some market research suggested that advertising, the lifeblood of any television business, was growing as local economies expanded, he knew the time was right. "If you had any entrepreneurial spirit at all," he explained, "You'd say, 'Okay, I can do this.'" After several years of making contacts throughout the company, he transferred to MTV International's headquarters in London, ready to put his plans into action.

By this time, MTV had already launched nearly 100 country-specific channels around the world, so it was no stranger to doing business in the global marketplace. But none of those markets presented the challenges that Africa did. If you were in Alex Okosi's shoes, what steps would you take to bring MTV to Africa? How would you build a consumer market in a region where many people were still learning to adjust to the notion of a modern consumer economy?[1] ∎

Fundamentals of International Trade

Wherever you're reading this, stop and look around for a minute. You might see cars that were made in Japan running on gasoline from Russia or Saudi Arabia, mobile phones made in South Korea, food from Canada or Mexico or Chile, a digital music player made in China, clothing from Vietnam or Italy, industrial equipment made in Germany—and dozens of other products from every corner of the globe. Conversely, if you or a family member work for a midsize or large company, chances are it gets a significant slice of its revenue from sales to other countries. In short, we live and work in a global marketplace.

Just as employees compete with one another for jobs and companies compete for customers, countries compete with one another for both. The ability of firms such as Viacom, the company that owns MTV (profiled in the chapter opener), to conduct business across national borders depends on the complex economic relationships the United

States maintains with other countries. Naturally, the U.S. government promotes and protects the interests of U.S. companies, U.S. workers, and U.S. consumers. Other countries are trying to do the same thing. As you might expect, the many players in world trade sometimes have conflicting goals, making international trade a never-ending tug of war.

Why Nations Trade

International trade is a fact of life for all countries, for two reasons. First, no single country, even a country as vast as the United States, has the resources and capabilities to produce everything its citizens want or need at prices they're willing to pay. In some cases, it's a matter of simply not having these resources or capabilities. For instance, the United States doesn't produce enough oil to meet its needs, so we buy oil from Russia, Saudi Arabia, Venezuela, and other countries that produce more than they can use. Conversely, most countries lack the ability to make commercial aircraft, so many of them buy planes from Boeing, a U.S. company, or Airbus, a consortium of companies based in Europe. In other cases, buyers prefer products made in other countries even though similar products are available from domestic companies. In recent years, for example, Japanese youth culture has become a significant force in fashion and consumer product design. Designers in other countries can even monitor Japanese youth trends online at Japanese Streets (www.japanesestreets.com).

The second major reason countries trade is that many companies have ambitions too large for their own backyards. Well-known U.S. companies such as Microsoft and Boeing would be a fraction of their current sizes if they were limited to the U.S. marketplace. Overseas companies view the U.S. market as a giant, tasty target as well. In fact, competition can strike a company from just about anywhere. Romania is a leader in antivirus software, Israel is a leader in software that protects computer networks, and there's a good chance the disk drive in your computer came from Singapore.[2]

All this international activity involves more than just sales growth. By expanding their markets, companies can benefit from **economies of scale** when they purchase, manufacture, and distribute in higher quantities.[3] If you build a thousand cars a year, you can't afford to invest in automated factories, large advertising campaigns, and a vast network of dealers. However, if you build a million cars a year, you can do all these things, which allows you to produce and sell each car for less money. In addition to helping companies, international trade also helps consumers by giving them more options and lower prices, and it helps governments by generating more revenue.

The motivation to trade is clear, but how does a country know which products it should make and which it should trade for with other countries? If a country can produce something more efficiently than every other country, or it has a natural resource that no other country has, it would have an **absolute advantage** in the world marketplace. In practice, however, virtually no country has an absolute advantage in any industry. Instead, **comparative advantage theory** suggests that each country should specialize in those areas where it can produce more efficiently than other countries, and it should trade for goods and services that it can't produce as economically. The basic argument behind the comparative advantage theory is that such specialization and exchange will increase a country's total output and allow both trading partners to enjoy a higher standard of living.

Comparative advantage is both relative and dynamic. In other words, no matter how good you are, you have an advantage only if you are better than someone else, and no advantage is preordained to last forever. The U.S. auto industry was once the unquestioned world leader, but over the course of just a couple of decades, Japan was able to reduce that advantage with quality products at lower prices, and Toyota is now the world's largest auto company.[4] South Korea is repeating the Japanese strategy with its own brands, most notably Hyundai. The United States remains one of the world's most competitive countries, to be sure, but dozens of other countries now compete for the same employees, customers, and investments (see Exhibit 3.1).

economies of scale
Savings from buying parts and materials, manufacturing, or marketing in large quantities

absolute advantage
A nation's ability to produce a particular product with fewer resources per unit of output than any other nation

comparative advantage theory
Theory that states that a country should produce and sell to other countries those items it produces most efficiently

RANK	COUNTRY	RANK	COUNTRY
1.	Switzerland	6.	United States
2.	Finland	7.	Japan
3.	Sweden	8.	Germany
4.	Denmark	9.	Netherlands
5.	Singapore	10.	United Kingdom

EXHIBIT 3.1

The World's Most Competitive Countries

According to the World Economic Forum, Switzerland, Finland, and Sweden are currently the world's most competitive countries, based on their ability to sustain economic growth.

The comparative advantage theory has been a cornerstone of economic thinking for 200 years, but a few economists are starting to question whether it still holds true in a world that has been transformed by technology. For example, over the past few decades, globalization has had a traumatic impact on much of the U.S. manufacturing sector. Many lower-skilled jobs in labor-intensive industries disappeared when U.S. manufacturers either moved their operations to lower-wage countries or stopped trying to compete in those industries altogether. Conventional economic thinking acknowledged that this job loss was temporarily painful for those U.S. workers and companies but positive for the economy overall, since those people could then focus on higher-skilled, higher-paying work in computer programming, aerospace engineering, medical technology, and other areas where the United States holds a comparative advantage. However, when *those* jobs started to move to lower-wage countries as well, some economists started to wonder whether all this rampant globalization is really going to be good for the United States after all. The question is still unanswered, but it affects thousands of companies and millions of workers, so you can expect it to be a hot topic in the coming years.[5] (For the latest information on the movement of jobs in the global economy, visit www.prenhall.com/bovée and click on "Real-Time Updates.")

How International Trade Is Measured

Chapter 1 discussed how economists monitor certain key economic indicators to evaluate how well a country's economic system is performing, and several of these indicators measure international trade. As Exhibit 3.2 illustrates, the United States imports more goods than it exports, but it exports more services than it imports. Two key measurements of a nation's level of international trade are the *balance of trade* and the *balance of payments*.

The total value of a country's exports *minus* the total value of its imports, over some period of time, determines its **balance of trade**. In years when the value of goods and services exported by a country exceeds the value of goods and services it imports, the country has a positive balance of trade, or a **trade surplus**. The opposite is a **trade deficit**, when a country imports more than it exports.

The **balance of payments** is the broadest indicator of international trade. It is the total flow of money into the country *minus* the total flow of money out of the country over some period of time. The balance of payments includes the balance of trade plus the net dollars received and spent on foreign investment, military expenditures, tourism, foreign aid, and other international transactions. For example, when a U.S. company buys all or part of a company based in another country, that investment is counted in the balance of payments but not in the balance of trade. Similarly, when a foreign company buys a U.S. company or purchases U.S. stocks, bonds, or real estate, those transactions are part of the balance of payments.

Free Trade and Fair Trade

The benefits of the comparative advantage model are based on the assumption that nations don't take artificial steps to minimize their own weaknesses or to blunt the advantages of other countries. Trade that takes place without these interferences is known as **free trade**.

balance of trade
Total value of the products a nation exports minus the total value of the products it imports, over some period of time

trade surplus
Favorable trade balance created when a country exports more than it imports

trade deficit
Unfavorable trade balance created when a country imports more than it exports

balance of payments
Sum of all payments one nation receives from other nations minus the sum of all payments it makes to other nations, over some specified period of time

free trade
International trade unencumbered by restrictive measures

EXHIBIT 3.2 U.S. Exports and Imports Since 1990

The U.S. trade deficit has been growing dramatically in recent years. Although the United States maintains a trade surplus in services (middle graph), the international market for services isn't nearly as large as the market for goods. Consequently, the trade deficit in goods (top graph) far outweighs the trade surplus in services, resulting in an overall trade deficit (bottom graph).

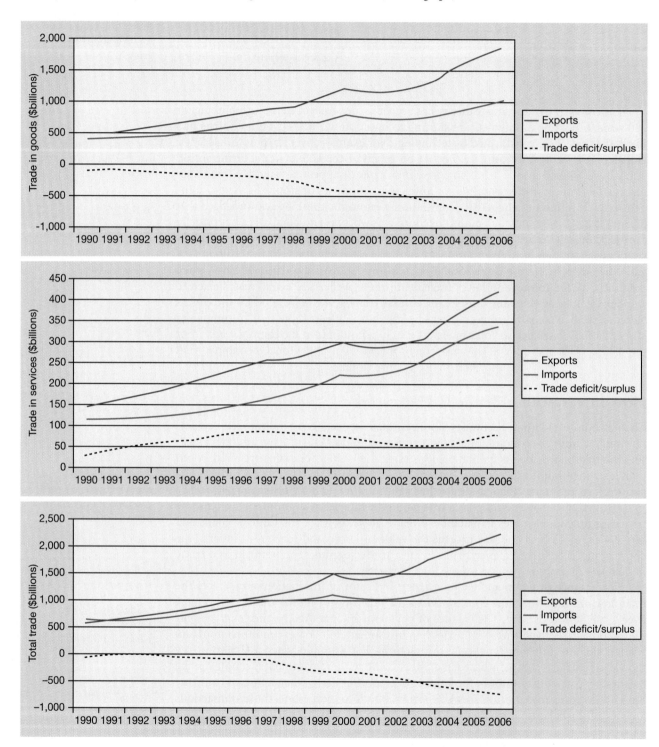

Free trade is not a universally welcomed concept, in spite of the positive connotation of the word *free*. Supporters claim it is the best way to ensure prosperity for everyone, but detractors call it unfair to too many people and a threat to the middle class.[6] In addition, some critics argue that free trade makes it too easy for companies to exploit workers around the world by pitting them against one another in a "race to the bottom," in which production moves to whichever country has the lowest wages and fewest restrictions regarding worker safety and environmental protection.[7] This complaint has been at the heart of recent protests over free trade and globalization in general. However, this criticism is rebutted by some researchers who say that companies prefer to do business in countries with stable, democratic governments. Consequently, says this camp, less-developed nations are motivated to improve their economic and social policies.[8]

One common example of the criticism of free trade involves the negotiating advantages that large international companies can have when buying from small farmers and other producers in multiple countries. The result, it is argued, is that prices get pushed so low that those producers struggle to earn enough money to survive because somebody, somewhere is always willing to work for less or sell for less. One response to this situation is the concept of **fair trade**, in which buyers voluntarily agree to pay more than the prevailing market price in order to help producers earn a *living wage*, enough money to satisfy their essential needs.[9]

Trade Restrictions

Unlike fair trade, which is a voluntary reaction to perceived inequalities in international free trade, governments can also mandate official restrictions on various aspects of international trade. These restrictions are collectively known as **protectionism,** since they often seek to protect a specific industry or groups of workers. Governments can also take protectionist steps to shield industries that are key to their national defense, to protect the health and safety of their citizens, and to give new or weak industries an opportunity to grow and strengthen before facing the full brunt of international competition.[10]

Are trade restrictions a good idea or a bad idea? While they can help in the short term, many protectionist measures actually end up hurting the groups they were intended to help. When an industry is isolated from real-life competition, it can fail to develop and become strong enough to compete on its own.[11]

The most commonly used trade restrictions are *tariffs, quotas, embargoes,* and *sanctions.*

- *Tariffs.* **Tariffs** are taxes, surcharges, or duties levied against imported goods. Sometimes tariffs are levied to generate revenue for the government, but more often they are imposed to restrict trade or to punish other countries for disobeying international trade laws.

- *Quotas.* **Quotas** limit the amount of a particular good that countries can import during a given year. The United States puts ceilings on a variety of agricultural products, including many types of dairy goods.[12]

- *Embargoes.* In its most extreme form, a quota becomes an **embargo**, a complete ban on the import or export of certain products or even all trade between certain countries. For instance, the United States has had a trade embargo against Cuba for nearly a half century.

- *Sanctions.* Sanctions are politically motivated embargoes that revoke a country's normal trade relations status; they are often used as forceful alternatives short of war. Sanctions can include arms embargoes, foreign-assistance reductions and cutoffs, trade limitations, tariff increases, import-quota decreases, visa denials, air-link cancellations, and more. For instance, the United States recently imposed sanctions against several government officials in Sudan for their role in the violence in the Darfur region.[13] Most governments (including the United States) use sanctions

fair trade
A voluntary approach to trading with artisans and farmers in developing countries, guaranteeing them above-market prices as a way to protect them from exploitation by larger, more-powerful trading partners

protectionism
Government policies aimed at shielding a country's industries from foreign competition

tariffs
Taxes levied on imports

quotas
Limits placed on the quantity of imports a nation will allow for a specific product

embargo
Total ban on trade with a particular nation (a sanction) or of a particular product

Automobiles are just one of the many products that have been subject to trade restrictions by various governments over the years.

dumping
Charging less than the actual cost or less than the home-country price for goods sold in other countries

sparingly, because studies show that sanctions are ineffective at getting countries to change.[14]

In addition to restricting foreign trade, governments sometimes give their domestic producers a competitive edge by using these protectionist tactics:

- *Restrictive import standards.* Countries can assist their domestic producers by establishing restrictive import standards, such as requiring special licenses for doing certain kinds of business and then making it difficult for foreign companies to obtain such a license. Some countries restrict imports by requiring goods to pass special tests.

- *Subsidies.* Rather than restrict imports, some countries subsidize domestic producers so that their prices can compete favorably in the global marketplace. Subsidies continue to be one of the most hotly contested aspects of international business, and farm subsidies often top the list of the most disputed items. A number of countries complain that subsidy payments to U.S. farmers allow them to export crops at artificially low prices and, therefore, make it difficult for other countries to compete on the world market.[15]

- *Dumping.* The practice of selling large quantities of a product at a price lower than the cost of production or below what the company would charge in its home market is called **dumping**. This tactic is most often used to try to win foreign customers or to reduce product surpluses. If a domestic producer can demonstrate that the low-cost imports are damaging its business, most governments will seek redress on their behalf through international trade organizations. Dumping is often a tricky situation to resolve, however; buyers of the product being dumped benefit from the lower prices, and proving what a fair price is in the country of origin can be difficult.[16]

Agreements and Organizations Overseeing International Trade

Solving business disputes within a country is fairly simple, since all parties are subject to the rules of the same government. However, disputes between countries are another matter entirely, often involving complicated negotiations that can take years to resolve. In an effort to ensure equitable trading practices and iron out the inevitable disagreements over what is fair and what isn't, governments around the world have established a number of important agreements and organizations that address trading issues, including GATT, WTO, IMF, and the World Bank.

The General Agreement on Tariffs and Trade (GATT)

The General Agreement on Tariffs and Trade (GATT) is a worldwide pact that was first established in the aftermath of World War II. The pact's guiding principle is nondiscrimination: Any trade advantage a GATT member gives to one country must be given to all GATT members, and no GATT nation can be singled out for punishment. In 1995, GATT established the World Trade Organization (WTO), which has replaced GATT as the world forum for trade negotiations.

The World Trade Organization (WTO)

The World Trade Organization (WTO), www.wto.org, is a permanent forum for negotiating, implementing, and monitoring international trade procedures and for mediating trade disputes among its roughly 150 member countries. The organization's primary goal is to improve the welfare of people worldwide by helping international trade function more efficiently. Critics of globalization and free trade often direct their ire at the WTO, but the organization says these criticisms are unjustified and based on misunderstandings of what the WTO does.[17]

The International Monetary Fund (IMF)

The International Monetary Fund (IMF), www.imf.org, was established in 1945 to foster international financial cooperation. Its primary functions are monitoring global financial developments, providing short-term loans to countries that are unable to meet their financial obligations, and providing training.[18]

The World Bank

The World Bank (www.worldbank.org) is a United Nations agency owned by its 184 member nations. It was founded to finance reconstruction after World War II and is now involved in hundreds of projects around the world aimed at addressing poverty, health, education, and other concerns in developing countries.[19]

Trading Blocs

Trading blocs, or *common markets*, are regional organizations that promote trade among member nations. Although specific rules vary from group to group, their primary objective is to ensure the economic growth and benefit of members. As such, trading blocs generally promote trade inside the region while creating uniform barriers against goods and services entering the region from nonmember countries. Three of the largest trading blocs are the North American Free Trade Agreement (NAFTA), the European Union (EU), and Asia-Pacific Economic Cooperation (APEC). Exhibit 3.3 shows the members of these three and several other blocs around the world.

trading blocs
Organizations of nations that remove barriers to trade among their members and that establish uniform barriers to trade with nonmember nations

North American Free Trade Agreement (NAFTA)

In 1994, the United States, Canada, and Mexico formed a powerful trading bloc, the North American Free Trade Agreement (NAFTA). The agreement paved the way for the free flow of goods, services, and capital within the bloc through the phased elimination of tariffs and quotas.[20]

Has NAFTA been a success? That depends on where you look and whom you ask. For instance, Mexican exports are up dramatically, and U.S. and other foreign companies have invested billions of dollars in the country. Some Mexican companies are thriving, thanks to those export opportunities, while others, particularly in agriculture, have been hurt severely by low-cost imports from the United States. Many of the manufacturing jobs Mexico hoped to attract wound up in China instead. And outside the business sphere, hoped-for improvements in education and health care in Mexico haven't materialized to the extent NAFTA backers expected, either, although they place the blame on government inaction, not on the free-trade agreement. In the United States, critics of NAFTA claim that much of the promised benefits of lower consumer prices and steady export markets for small farmers didn't materialize, and that benefits of NAFTA have gone mostly to huge agribusiness corporations.[21]

European Union (EU)

One of the largest trading blocs is the European Union (EU), www.europa.eu, whose membership now encompasses more than two dozen countries and a half billion people. EU nations have eliminated hundreds of local regulations, variations in product standards, and protectionist measures that once limited trade among member countries. Across the

EXHIBIT 3.3 Members of Major Trading Blocs

As the economies of the world become increasingly linked, many countries have formed powerful regional trading blocs that trade freely with one another but place restrictions on trade with other countries and blocs.

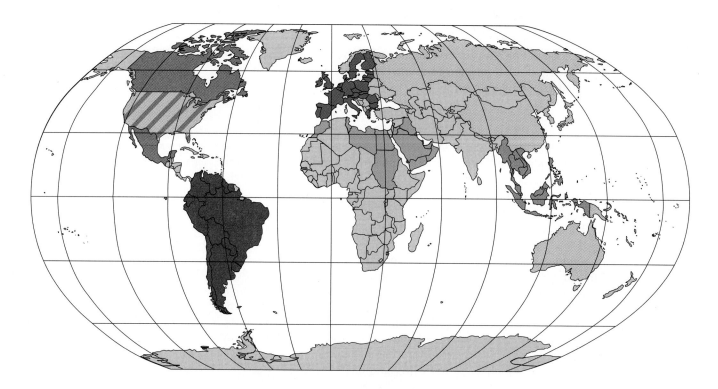

European Union (EU)	North American Free Trade Agreement (NAFTA)	Association of Southeast Asian Nations (ASEAN)	Union of South American Nations	Asia-Pacific Economic Cooperation (APEC)	Greater Arab Free Trade Area (GAFTA)
Austria	Canada	Brunei	Argentina	Australia	Jordan
Belgium	Mexico	Cambodia	Bolivia	Brunei Darussalam	Bahrain
Bulgaria	United States	Indonesia	Brazil	Canada	United Arab Emirates
Cyprus		Laos	Chile	Chile	Tunisia
Czech Republic		Malaysia	Colombia	China	Saudi Arabia
Denmark		Myanmar	Ecuador	Hong Kong	Syria
Estonia		Philippines	Guyana	Indonesia	Iraq
Finland		Singapore	Paraguay	Japan	Oman
France		Thailand	Peru	Republic of Korea	Qatar
Germany		Vietnam	Suriname	Malaysia	Kuwait
Greece			Uruguay	Mexico	Lebanon
Hungary			Venezuela	New Zealand	Libya
Ireland				Papua New Guinea	Egypt
Italy				Peru	Morocco
Latvia				Philippines	Sudan
Lithuania				Russian Federation	Yemen
Luxembourg				Singapore	Palestine
Malta				Chinese Taipei	
Netherlands				Thailand	
Poland				United States	
Portugal				Viet Nam	
Romania					
Slovakia					
Slovenia					
Spain					
Sweden					
United Kingdom					

EU, trade now flows among member countries in much the same way as it does among states in the United States. The EU's reach extends far beyond the borders of Europe, in fact; to simplify design and manufacturing for world markets, many companies now create their products to meet EU specifications. If you've seen the "CE" marking on any products you may own, that stands for *Conformité Européenne* and indicates that the product has met EU standards for safety, health, and environmental responsibility.[22]

The EU has taken a significant step beyond all other trading blocs in the area of money by creating its own currency, the **euro**, which has been adopted by roughly half the member states of the EU. By switching to a common currency, these countries vastly simplify commerce for both consumers and businesses by removing the hassle and expense of changing money, maintaining catalogs with multiple currencies, calculating prices for online orders, and completing other financial tasks.

The euro eases price comparisons for products sold in the member countries of the European Union.

Asia-Pacific Economic Council (APEC)

Asia-Pacific Economic Cooperation (APEC), www.apec.org, is an organization of 21 countries that is making efforts to liberalize trade in the Pacific Rim (the land areas that surround the Pacific Ocean). Among the member nations are the United States, Japan, China, Mexico, Australia, South Korea, and Canada. Its long-term goal is to eliminate all tariffs and trade barriers among industrialized countries of the Pacific Rim by 2010 and among developing countries by 2020.[23]

euro
A unified currency used by roughly half the nations in the European Union

Foreign Exchange Rates and Currency Valuations

The euro was designed to solve one of the most complex issues that bedevil international commerce: exchange rates and currency valuations. When companies buy and sell goods and services in the global marketplace, they complete the transaction by exchanging currencies. For instance, if a Japanese company borrows money from a U.S. bank to build a manufacturing plant in Japan, it must repay the loan in U.S. dollars. Or if a South Korean car manufacturer imports engine parts from Japan, it must pay for them in yen (Japan's currency). The process is called *foreign exchange,* the conversion of one currency into an equivalent amount of another currency. The number of units of one currency that must be exchanged for a unit of the second currency is known as the **exchange rate** between the currencies.

Most international currencies operate under a *floating exchange rate system,* meaning that a currency's value or price fluctuates in response to the forces of global supply and demand. The supply and demand of a country's currency are determined in part by what is happening in the country's own economy. Moreover, because supply and demand for a currency are always changing, the rate at which it is exchanged for other currencies may change a little each day. Japanese currency might be trading at 123.4 yen to the U.S. dollar on one day and 124.09 on the next.

A currency is called *strong* relative to another when its exchange rate is higher than what is considered normal and called *weak* when its rate is lower than normal ("normal" is a relative term here). A *strong dollar* means that relative to most currencies around the world, the U.S. dollar buys more units of those other currencies than it has in the recent past. For instance, if a dollar bought 125 yen in January and 130 yen in March, it would be strengthening or rising relative to the yen. A *weak dollar* means the opposite. Note that "strong" isn't necessarily good, and "weak" isn't necessarily bad when it comes to currencies, as Exhibit 3.4 illustrates. Exchange rates can dramatically affect a company's financial results by raising or lowering the cost of supplies it imports and raising or lowering the price of goods it exports.

Even though most governments let the value of their currency respond to the forces of supply and demand, sometimes a government will intervene and adjust the exchange

exchange rate
Rate at which the money of one country is traded for the money of another

EXHIBIT 3.4

Strong and Weak Currencies: Who Gains, Who Loses?

A strong dollar and a weak dollar aren't necessarily good or bad; each condition helps some people and hurts others.

	STRONG DOLLAR	WEAK DOLLAR
How it helps	U.S. buyers pay less for imported goods and services	U.S. products more price-competitive in foreign markets
	Lower-cost imports help keep inflation in check	U.S. firms under less price pressure from imports in U.S. market
	Travel to other countries is cheaper	Overseas tourists encouraged to visit the U.S.
	Foreign investments are cheaper	Investments in U.S. stocks and bonds more attractive to international investors
How it hurts	U.S. exports more expensive to buyers in other countries	Prices of imported products are higher for U.S. consumers and businesses
	U.S. companies must compete with lower-priced imports in the U.S. market	Higher import prices raise cost of living; contribute to inflation
	Overseas tourists discouraged from visiting the U.S.	International travel more expensive for U.S. residents
	International investors less likely to invest in the U.S. capital markets (stocks, bonds, etc.)	Expansion and investment in other countries more difficult for U.S. firms and investors

devaluation
A move by one government to drop the value of its currency relative to the value of other currencies

rate of its country's currency. **Devaluation**, a move by one government to drop the value of its currency relative to the value of other currencies, can at times boost a country's economy because it makes the country's products and services more affordable in foreign markets while it increases the price of imports, as Exhibit 3.4 indicated.

The Global Business Environment

Doing business internationally is neither easy nor simple, but it has become essential for thousands of U.S. companies. Venturing abroad can be a boon, but it also presents many challenges. Every country has unique laws, customs, consumer preferences, ethical standards, labor skills, and political and economic forces. All these factors can affect a firm's international prospects. Furthermore, volatile currencies, international trade relationships, and the threat of terrorism can make global expansion a risky proposition. Still, in most cases the opportunities of the global marketplace greatly outweigh the risks.

Not every business is a candidate for international sales. Some industries, such as consumer electronics and apparel, are highly globalized. These products are easy to make just about anywhere, and they don't cost much to ship. Others, including products that are expensive to ship relative to their sales value (such as steel) are less globalized. Services are among the least-globalized product categories, given the obvious costs and difficulties of delivering most services at long distances.[24]

Cultural Differences in the Global Business Environment

Cultural differences present a number of challenges in the global marketplace. Successful companies recognize and respect differences in language, social values, ideas of status, decision-making habits, attitudes toward time, use of space, body language, manners, and ethical standards. Above all else, businesspeople dealing with other

Studying Other Cultures

Effectively adapting your communication efforts to another culture requires not only knowledge about the culture but also the ability and the motivation to change your personal habits as needed. In other words, it's not a simple task. Unfortunately, a thorough knowledge of another culture and its communication patterns (both verbal and nonverbal) can take years to acquire. Fortunately, you don't need to learn about the whole world all at once. Many companies appoint specialists for specific countries or regions, giving you a chance to focus on fewer cultures at a time. Some firms also provide resources to help employees prepare for interaction with other cultures. On IBM's workforce diversity website, for instance, employees can click on the GoingGlobal link to learn about customs in specific cultures.

Even a small amount of research and practice will help you get through many business situations. In addition, most people respond positively to honest effort and good intentions, and many business associates will help you along if you show an interest in learning more about their cultures.

Try to approach situations with an open mind and a healthy sense of humor. When you make a mistake, simply apologize if appropriate, ask the other person to explain the accepted way, and then move on. As business becomes ever more global, even the most tradition-bound cultures are learning to deal with outsiders more patiently and overlook the occasional cultural blunder.

Numerous websites and books offer advice on traveling to and working in specific cultures. Also try to sample newspapers, magazines, and even the music and movies of another country. For instance, a movie can demonstrate nonverbal customs even if you don't grasp the language. However, be careful not to rely solely on entertainment products. If people in other countries based their opinions of American culture only on Hollywood's silly teen flicks and violent action movies, what sort of impression do you imagine they'd get?

Questions for Critical Thinking

1. What steps could you take to help someone from another country adapt to U.S. business culture?
2. If you repeatedly commit cultural blunders in front of business associates in another country, what is likely to happen to your relationship? Why?

---

cultures must avoid falling into the twin traps of stereotyping and ethnocentrism. **Stereotyping** is assigning a wide range of generalized (and often superficial or even false) attributes to an individual on the basis of membership in a particular culture or social group without considering the individual's unique characteristics, while **ethnocentrism** is the tendency to judge all other groups according to one's own group's standards, behaviors, and customs.

The best way to prepare yourself for doing business with people from another culture is to study that culture in advance. Learn everything you can about the culture's history, religion, politics, and customs—especially its business customs. Who makes decisions? How are negotiations usually conducted? Is gift giving expected? What is the proper attire for a business meeting? In addition to the suggestion that you learn about the culture, seasoned international businesspeople offer the following tips for improving intercultural communication:

- *Be alert to the other person's customs.* Expect the other person to have values, beliefs, expectations, and mannerisms that may differ from yours.
- *Deal with the individual.* Don't stereotype the other person or react with preconceived ideas. Regard the person as an individual first, not as a representative of another culture.
- *Clarify your intent and meaning.* The other person's body language may not mean what you think, and the person may read unintentional meanings into your message. Clarify your true intent by repetition and examples. Ask questions and listen carefully.
- *Adapt your style to the other person's.* If the other person appears to be direct and straightforward, follow suit. If not, adjust your behavior to match.
- *Show respect.* Learn how respect is communicated in various cultures—through gestures, eye contact, and actions. For example, standing too close when introducing yourself can make a British colleague uncomfortable, whereas standing too far away can offend a Spanish colleague.[25]

stereotyping
Assigning a wide range of generalized attributes, which are often superficial or even false, to an individual based on his or her membership in a particular culture or social group

ethnocentrism
Judging all other groups according to your own group's standards, behaviors, and customs

These are just a few tips for doing business in the global marketplace. Successful international businesses learn as much as they can about political issues, cultural factors, and the economic environment before investing time and money in new markets. Exhibit 3.5 can guide you in your efforts to learn more about a country's culture before doing business abroad.

Legal Differences in the Global Business Environment

Differences in national legal systems may not be as immediately obvious as cultural differences, but they can have a profound effect on international business efforts. For instance, the legal systems in the United States and the United Kingdom are based on *common law*, in which tradition, custom, and judicial interpretation play important roles. In contrast, the system in countries such as France and Germany is based on *civil law*, in which legal parameters are specified in detailed legal codes. One everyday consequence of this difference is that business contracts tend to be shorter and simpler in civil law systems, since the existing legal code outlines more aspects of the transaction or relationship. A third type of legal system, *theocratic law*, or laws based on religious principles, predominates in such countries as Iran and Pakistan. Beyond the differences in legal philosophies, the business of contracts, copyrights, and other legal matters can vary considerably from one country to another.

Perhaps no issue in international business law generates as much confusion and consternation as bribery. In some countries, payments to government officials are so common that they are considered by some businesspeople to be standard operating practice. These payments are used to facilitate a variety of actions, from winning contracts for public works projects (such as roads or power plants) to securing routine government services (such as customs inspections) to getting preferential treatment (such as the approval to raise prices).[26] These payment systems discourage much-needed investment in developing countries, weaken trust in government, raise prices for consumers by inflating business costs, and can even present security risks by essentially making officials' actions up to the highest bidder. Some businesspeople have argued that critics of such payoffs are trying to impose U.S. values on other cultures, but Transparency International, a watchdog group that works to reduce business–government corruption around the world, discredits that argument by saying that all countries have laws against corruption, so it can hardly be considered a cultural issue.[27] (To learn more about Transparency International's work, visit www.transparency.org.)

All U.S. companies are bound by the Foreign Corrupt Practices Act (FCPA), which outlaws payments with the intent of getting government officials to break the laws of their own countries. However, the FCPA does allow payments that expedite actions that are legal, such as clearing merchandise through customs, although critics such as Transparency International consider this behavior unethical as well because it permits private profits to be gained from public trust.[28] Other types of payments can also be considered forms of influence but aren't covered by the FCPA, such as foreign aid payments from one government to another, made with the intent of securing favorable decisions for business.

Following the FCPA, the Organisation for Economic Co-Operation and Development (OECD), an international body dedicated to fostering economic prosperity and combating poverty, established antibribery guidelines for its member nations as well.[29] The good news is that more laws and expectations are in place around the world; the bad news is that enforcement is still spotty.[30]

Forms of International Business Activity

Beyond cultural and legal concerns, companies that plan to go international also need to think carefully about the right organizational approach to support these activities. The five common forms of international business are *importing and exporting, licensing, franchising, strategic alliances and joint ventures,* and *foreign direct investment*, and each has a varying degree of ownership, financial commitment, and risk.

EXHIBIT 3.5 Checklist for Doing Business Abroad
Use this checklist as a starting point when investigating a foreign culture.

ACTION	DETAILS TO CONSIDER
Understand social customs	✓ Is the society homogenous or heterogeneous?
	✓ How do people react to strangers? Are they friendly? Hostile? Reserved?
	✓ How do people greet each other? Should you bow? Nod? Shake hands?
	✓ How do you express appreciation for an invitation to lunch, dinner, or someone's home? Should you bring a gift? Send flowers? Write a thank-you note?
	✓ Are any phrases, facial expressions, or hand gestures considered rude?
	✓ How do you attract the attention of a waiter? Do you tip the waiter?
	✓ When is it rude to refuse an invitation? How do you refuse politely?
	✓ What topics may or may not be discussed in a social setting? In a business setting?
Learn about clothing and food preferences	✓ What occasions require special clothing?
	✓ What colors are associated with mourning? Love? Joy?
	✓ Are some types of clothing considered taboo for one gender or the other?
	✓ How many times a day do people eat?
	✓ How are hands or utensils used when eating?
	✓ Where is the seat of honor at a table?
Assess political patterns	✓ How stable is the political situation?
	✓ Does the political situation affect business in and out of the country?
	✓ What are the traditional government institutions?
	✓ Is it appropriate to talk politics in social or business situations?
Understand religious and folk beliefs	✓ To which religious groups do people belong?
	✓ Which places, objects, actions, and events are sacred?
	✓ Is there a tolerance for minority religions?
	✓ How do religious holidays affect business and government activities?
	✓ Does religion require or prohibit eating specific foods? At specific times?
Learn about economic and business institutions	✓ What languages are spoken?
	✓ What are the primary resources and principal products?
	✓ Are businesses generally large? Family controlled? Government controlled?
	✓ Is it appropriate to do business by telephone? By fax? By e-mail?
	✓ What are the generally accepted working hours?
	✓ How do people view scheduled appointments?
	✓ Are people expected to socialize before conducting business?
Appraise the nature of ethics, values, and laws	✓ Is money or a gift expected in exchange for arranging business transactions?
	✓ Do people value competitiveness or cooperation?
	✓ What are the attitudes toward work? Toward money?
	✓ Is politeness more important than factual honesty?

Importing and Exporting

importing
Purchasing goods or services from another country and bringing them into one's own country

exporting
Selling and shipping goods or services to another country

Importing, the buying of goods or services from a supplier in another country, and **exporting**, the selling of products outside the country in which they are produced, have existed for centuries. In the last few decades, however, the increased level of these activities has caused the economies of the world to become tightly linked.

Exporting, one of the least risky forms of international business activity, permits a firm to enter a foreign market gradually, assess local conditions, then fine-tune its product offerings to meet the needs of foreign consumers. In most cases, the firm's financial exposure is limited to the costs of researching the market, advertising, and either establishing a direct sales and distribution system or hiring intermediaries. Such intermediaries include *export management companies,* which are domestic firms that specialize in performing international marketing services on a commission basis, and *export trading companies,* which are general trading firms that will buy your products for resale overseas as well as perform a variety of importing, exporting, and manufacturing functions. Still another alternative is to use foreign distributors.

Working through a foreign distributor with connections in the target country is often helpful to both large and small companies because such intermediaries can provide you with the connections, expertise, and market knowledge you will need to conduct business in a foreign country.[31] In addition, many countries now have foreign trade offices to help importers and exporters that are interested in doing business within their borders. Other helpful resources include professional agents, local businesspeople, and the International Trade Administration of the U.S. Department of Commerce (www.export.gov). This trade organization offers a variety of services, including political and credit-risk analysis, advice on entering foreign markets, and financing tips.

International Licensing

licensing
Agreement to produce and market another company's product in exchange for a royalty or fee

Licensing is another popular approach to international business. License agreements entitle one company to use some or all of another firm's intellectual property (patents, trademarks, brand names, copyrights, or trade secrets) in return for a royalty payment.

Many firms choose licensing as an approach to international markets because it involves little out-of-pocket cost. A firm has already incurred the costs of developing the intellectual property to be licensed. Pharmaceutical firms, for instance, routinely use licensing to enter foreign markets. Once a pharmaceutical firm has developed and patented a new drug, it is often more efficient to grant existing local firms the right to manufacture and distribute the patented drug in return for royalty payments. Of course, licensing agreements are not restricted to international business. A company can also license its products or technology to other companies in its domestic market.

International Franchising

Some companies choose to expand into foreign markets by *franchising* their operations. Chapter 6 discusses franchising in more detail, but briefly, franchising involves selling the right to use a business system, including brand names, business processes, trade secrets, and other assets. For instance, there are roughly 31,000 McDonald's restaurants around the world, but McDonald's owns only 25 percent of those. The rest are owned and operated by independent franchisees.[32] Franchising is an attractive option for many companies because it reduces the costs and risks of expanding internationally.

International Strategic Alliances and Joint Ventures

strategic alliance
Long-term relationship in which two or more companies share ideas, resources, and technologies in order to establish competitive advantages

A **strategic alliance** is a long-term partnership between two or more companies to jointly develop, produce, or sell products in the global marketplace. To reach their individual but complementary goals, the companies typically share ideas, expertise, resources, technologies, investment costs, risks, management, and profits. In some cases, a strategic alliance might be the only way to gain access to a market, which was the reason Viacom (which owns CBS, MTV, and other media) decided to form an alliance with Beijing Television in order to expand its presence in China.[33]

Strategic alliances are a popular way to expand globally. The benefits of this form of international expansion include ease of market entry, shared risk, shared knowledge and expertise, and synergy. Companies that form a strategic alliance with a foreign partner can often compete more effectively than if they entered the foreign market alone. When the French retail giant Carrefour attempted to enter the Japanese market without a local partner, it had trouble getting land for new stores. Land in Japan is often held in complex partnerships that outsiders find difficult to penetrate. The company pulled out of Japan within five years.[34]

A **joint venture** is a special type of strategic alliance in which two or more firms join together to create a new business entity that is legally separate and distinct from its parents. In some countries, foreign companies are prohibited from owning facilities outright or from investing in local business. Thus, establishing a joint venture with a local partner may be the only way to do business in that country. In other cases, foreigners may be required to move some of their production facilities to the country to earn the right to sell their products there.

joint venture
Cooperative partnership in which organizations share investment costs, risks, management, and profits in the development, production, or selling of products

Foreign Direct Investment

Many firms prefer to enter international markets through partial or whole ownership and control of assets in foreign countries, an approach known as **foreign direct investment (FDI)**. To enter the Chinese market, for instance, Amazon.com purchased Joyo, an established e-commerce company. The company is now known there as Joyo Amazon.cn (www.amazon.cn).[35] Some facilities are set up through FDI to exploit the availability of raw materials; others take advantage of low wage rates; others minimize transportation costs by choosing locations that give them direct access to markets in other countries. In almost all cases, at least part of the workforce is drawn from the local population. Companies that establish a physical presence in multiple countries through FDI are called **multinational corporations (MNCs)**.

foreign direct investment (FDI)
Investment of money by foreign companies in domestic business enterprises

multinational corporations (MNCs)
Companies with operations in more than one country

Yahoo! Japan is just one of the many U.S. companies that have expanded internationally through foreign direct investment.

FDI typically gives companies greater control, but it carries much greater economic and political risk and is more complex than any other form of entry in the global marketplace. Consequently, most FDI takes place between the industrialized nations (a group that includes such large, stable economies as the United States, Canada, Japan, and most countries in Europe), which tend to offer greater protection for foreign investors. The top three countries in which U.S. companies own facilities through FDI are the United Kingdom, Canada, and the Netherlands, and the top three countries whose companies invest in U.S. facilities through FDI are the United Kingdom, Japan, and the Netherlands.[36]

Strategic Approaches to International Markets

Choosing the right form of business to pursue is the first of many decisions that companies need to make when moving into other countries. Virtually everything you learn about in this course, from human resources to marketing to financial management, needs to be reconsidered carefully when going international. Some of the most important decisions involve products, customer support, promotion, pricing, and staffing:

- *Products.* You face two primary dilemmas regarding products. First, which products should you try to sell in each market? For instance, before China and Russia began to liberalize their economies, it made little sense for luxury goods suppliers to offer many products there. Now, with personal incomes on the rise in both countries, luxury brands from Gucci to Ferrari are racing in with new stores and expanded product offerings.[37] Second, should you *standardize* your products, selling the same product everywhere in the world, or *customize* your products to accommodate the lifestyles and habits of local target markets? Customization seems like an obvious choice, but it can increase costs and operational complexity, so the decision to customize is not automatic. The degree of customization can also vary. A company may change only the product's name or packaging, or it can modify the product's components, size, and functions. Of course, understanding a country's regulations, culture, and local competition plays into the decisions. For instance, LG Electronics, a South Korean appliance maker, markets refrigerators in India with extra-large vegetable compartments (catering to India's many vegetarians), a different version in Saudi Arabia that has a special cooler for dates (which are popular there), and yet another version in South Korea with a sealed compartment for *kimchi* (to keep the richly aromatic dish from interacting with other foods).[38]

- *Customer support.* Cars, computers, and other products that require some degree of customer support add another layer of complexity to international business. Many customers are reluctant to buy foreign products that don't offer some form of local support, whether it's a local dealer, a manufacturer's branch office, or a third-party organization that offers support under contract to the manufacturer.

- *Promotion.* Advertising, public relations, and other promotional efforts also present the dilemma of standardization versus customization. After years of trying to build global brands, many U.S. companies are putting new emphasis on crafting customized messages for each country. As one British advertising executive put it, "One size doesn't fit all. Consumers are more interesting for

---

Learning from Business Blunders

Oops: The nature of social behavior varies among cultures, sometimes dramatically. Wal-Mart learned this lesson the hard way when the giant retailer tried to expand into Germany. Store clerks resisted the company requirement of always smiling at customers—a cornerstone of customer relationship strategies in the United States—because doing so was sometimes misinterpreted by customers as flirting. Wal-Mart dropped the requirement but, after a number of other cultural and strategic missteps, eventually left the German market.

What You Can Learn: Wal-Mart's mistake regarding smiling is not uncommon for Americans traveling and working in other countries. American culture tends to be friendly and open, and smiling is used to build rapport with strangers. However, this habit is not shared by all cultures, and Wal-Mart erred by assuming it was.

their differences rather than their similarities."[39] Pepsi-Cola didn't catch on in India until the company started featuring Indian movie star Shahrukh Khan and cricket player Sachin Tendulkar in its TV commercials.[40]

- *Pricing.* Even a standardized strategy adds costs, from transportation to communication, and customized strategies add even more costs. Before moving into other countries, businesses need to make sure they can cover all these costs and still be able to offer competitive prices.

- *Staffing.* Depending on the form of business a company decides to pursue in international markets, staffing questions can be major considerations. Many companies find that a combination of U.S. and local personnel works best, mixing company experience with local knowledge and connections. In Latin American markets, U.S. companies such as Home Depot, Payless, and Marriott have been successful in transferring Spanish-speaking employees, many of whom are immigrants from Latin America, from the United States back to the region to establish and manage facilities.[41]

Even with the worldwide power of the Disney brand, the company learned that it needed to adapt its products and services to the local tastes of the European market.

Given the number and complexity of the decisions to be made, you can see why successful companies plan international expansion with great care.

Terrorism's Impact on the Global Business Environment

The continuing threat of terrorist acts is a concern for business managers in nearly every industry. The attacks on September 11, 2001, specifically targeted a well-known symbol of global commerce, the World Trade Center in New York City, and were partly intended to wreak havoc on the economies of Western countries. However, the impact of terrorism reaches far beyond the overt acts of violence; terrorism affects business in many ways:

- *Government expenditures.* Every year, the federal government spends billions of dollars on homeland security, and this amount doesn't include additional costs related to military activities or a wide variety of added expenses incurred by local and state governments—money that could have been spent on education, research, health care, lower taxes, and other areas that benefit business and society. At the same time, much of this money did flow to businesses through contracts for security-related products and services.

- *Business expenditures.* Beefing up security also costs money, whether it's the small, private police force that FedEx set up to guard the company's operations or more routine items such as increased background checks on new employees, vulnerability assessments by security consultants, or backup facilities for corporate computer systems.[42] Wall Street investment banks now spend three or four times as much on security as they did before September 11.[43] Joseph Coleman, CEO of RiteCheck Financial Service Centers, a small chain of check-cashing stores in New York, estimates he now spends an extra $100,000 a year to comply with the record-keeping provisions of the Uniting and Strengthening America by Providing Appropriate Tools Required to Intercept and Obstruct Terrorism (USA PATRIOT) Act, a set of antiterrorism laws passed in the wake of September 11.[44]

- *Transportation.* The U.S. economy depends heavily on the flow of goods across its borders, but it's impossible to inspect every one of the thousands of shipments that enter the country every day via ship, air, train, or truck. By doing a better job of securing distribution channels from end to end, officials hope to improve security without the massive costs and delays that would result from 100-percent inspection. For instance, the Customs and Trade Partnership Against Terrorism offers expedited border crossings from Canada for companies that can prove they have measures in place to help ensure the security of their suppliers, warehouses, and other transportation components.[45]

■ *Banking.* Cutting off terrorists' financial support is a key element in the fight against terror, but the sometimes-murky world of international banking makes this a challenge. For instance, Citigroup, the U.S. financial giant, discovered that a bank in Saudi Arabia that it managed and co-owned had allegedly been funneling payments to terrorist groups. Unable to verify the charges because of Saudi secrecy laws, Citigroup sold its interest in the bank and pulled out of a country where it had been doing business for 50 years.[46]

■ *Staffing.* Immigration remains a contentious issue in American politics, and it remains an important issue for American business. For example, the H-1B visa, which you'll read more about in Chapter 14, allows U.S. companies to hire highly skilled temporary employees from other countries as long as they can demonstrate skills that are not available in the resident workforce. Before the September 11 attacks, 200,000 of these visas were made available every year, but that number soon dropped to only 65,000. Business leaders such as Microsoft's Bill Gates say that restricting the number of these valuable employees is hurting the competitiveness of U.S. companies.[47]

In spite of these costs and obstacles, the U.S. economy, thousands of U.S. companies, and millions of U.S. workers are too dependent on international trade to retreat behind our national borders. In fact, expanding international trade may itself be a helpful deterrent in battling terrorism by bringing countries closer together in the pursuit of safety and freedom.

Summary of Learning Objectives

1 Discuss why nations trade.

Nations trade to obtain raw materials and goods that are unavailable to them or too costly to produce. International trade benefits nations by increasing a country's total output, offering lower prices and greater variety to its consumers, subjecting domestic oligopolies and monopolies to competition, and allowing companies to expand their markets and achieve production and distribution efficiencies.

2 Explain why nations restrict international trade and list four forms of trade restrictions.

Nations restrict international trade to boost local economies, to shield domestic industries from head-to-head competition with overseas rivals, to save specific jobs, to give weak or new industries a chance to grow strong, and to protect a nation's security. The four most commonly used forms

of trade restrictions are tariffs (taxes, surcharges, or duties levied against imported goods), quotas (limitations on the amount of a particular good that can be imported), embargoes (the banning of imports and exports of certain goods), and sanctions (politically motivated embargoes).

3 Highlight three protectionist tactics that nations use to give their domestic industries a competitive edge.

From time to time countries give their domestic producers a competitive edge by imposing restrictive import standards, such as requiring special licenses or unusually high product standards, by subsidizing certain domestic producers so they can compete more favorably in the global marketplace, and by dumping or selling large quantities of a product at a lower price than it costs to produce the good or at a lower price than the good is sold for in its home market.

4 **Explain the role of trading blocs in international business.**

Trading blocs are regional groupings of countries within which trade barriers have been removed. These alliances ease trade among bloc members and strengthen barriers for non-members. Critics of trading blocs fear that as members become more protective of their regions, those not in the bloc could suffer. Proponents see them as a way to help smaller or younger nations compete with producers in more-developed nations. Three of the most significant trading blocs today are the North American Free Trade Agreement (NAFTA), the European Union (EU), and the Association of Southeast Asian Nations (ASEAN).

5 **Highlight the opportunities and challenges of conducting business in other countries.**

Conducting business in other countries can provide such opportunities as increased sales, operational efficiencies, exposure to new technologies, and consumer choices. At the same time, it poses challenges such as the need to learn unique laws, customs, and ethical standards. Furthermore, it exposes companies to the risks of political and economic instabilities, volatile currencies, international trade relationships, and the threat of global terrorism.

6 **List five ways to improve communication in an international business relationship.**

To improve international communication, learn as much as you can about the culture and customs of the people you are working with; keep an open mind and avoid stereotyping; anticipate misunderstandings and guard against them by clarifying your intent; adapt your style to match the style of others; and learn how to show respect in other cultures.

7 **Identify five forms of international business activity.**

Importing and exporting, licensing, franchising, strategic alliances and joint ventures, and foreign direct investment are five of the most common forms of international business activity. Each provides a company with varying degrees of control and entails different levels of risk and financial commitment.

8 **Discuss terrorism's impact on globalization.**

Terrorism could prompt companies to withdraw from the global marketplace and focus more on doing business within their national borders. But the likelihood of moving in that direction is remote. Most multinational organizations have too much at stake to move backward; they see globalization as the key to their future. Global terrorism, however, does pose new challenges to world trade. Tighter security, border crossing delays, cargo restrictions, and higher transportation costs are having an impact on the free flow of goods in the global marketplace. These obstacles are forcing some companies to rethink their inventory and manufacturing strategies.

Behind the Scenes

Adapting an American Cultural Icon to the African Market

By the time Alex Okosi was ready to launch MTV in Africa, the company had already set up 99 other versions of the music and entertainment channel around the world. International experience was not a problem. However, no market could've presented the challenges that Africa presented. From low consumer income to limited availability of television, the hurdles to success would require a unique approach.

On the positive side, Africa did present a potentially huge opportunity as countries up and down the continent began to develop stronger consumer economies. Moreover, Okosi wasn't the only African émigré who wanted to return home; while working in the United States he had met a number of other people from African countries who wanted to return and help rebuild their respective countries.

Then there was the incredibly rich music culture and the millions of people who were passionate about their music.

The musical connection between Africa and America goes back centuries, actually, when the ancient singer-songwriter tradition from countries such as Mali found its way to the United States as a consequence of the slave trade. The music eventually evolved into American blues and jazz, which then inspired rock, soul, R&B, hip-hop, and other styles. Meanwhile, today's African popular music is a vibrant blend of traditional local styles and contemporary imports. For instance, the *hip-life* style popular in Ghana combines hip-hop with *highlife*, a jazzy, guitar-driven dance sound that dates from the 1920s.

The musical tradition was rich, but music television needs quality videos, and those were few and far between. To increase the supply, Okosi nurtured local talent, even visiting some aspiring directors in their homes to help them learn how to create broadcast-quality videos.

After several years of work, Okosi and his colleagues were ready to launch, and in 2005, MTV Base went live with "African Queen" by the popular Nigerian artist 2Face Idibia. Will Smith and Ludacris were among the American celebrities who helped launch the new channel at dance parties and other events around Africa.

MTV Base combines videos and shows produced in Africa with content imported from the United States. Locally produced videos now account for 40 percent of the channel's musical fare, and Okosi wants to raise that to at least 50 percent in the near future. He describes the channel's goal as showcasing "the creativity and diversity of contemporary music in Africa, giving an international platform to African genres such as Kwaito, Hip-Life, Mbalax, and Zouk and putting African artists in the spotlight alongside their international peers." MTV Base is also active in health and social causes, such as offering educational programming about HIV protection.

As a business venture, MTV Base looks to be a success. By 2007, it had 50 million subscribers, and Okosi expects to reach 75 million by 2010. The channel is profitable and attracts a variety of local and international advertisers. And it has already become an exporter: videos produced in Africa are now shown in a special program on MTV in the United Kingdom, and rising African stars such as D'Banj have appeared on MTV in the United States.[48]

Critical Thinking Questions

1. Why would MTV use the MTV brand name for its launch in Africa, rather than coming up with a new name more closely identified with the target market, such as African Music Television?
2. What ethical responsibilities does MTV have relative to its expansion into Africa? Why?
3. Do global media such as MTV have the potential to improve international relations? Do they have the potential to harm international relations? Explain your answers.

LEARN MORE ONLINE

Visit the MTV Base website at www.mtvbase.com. Compare the site with MTV's U.S. home page at www.mtv.com. What differences and similarities do you see? How much American culture do you see reflected on the MTV Base website, as either content on the site itself or content on the cable channel that is described on the website? How many artists currently listed in the MTV Base Top Ten are from Africa?

(For the latest information on MTV's global efforts, visit www.prenhall.com/bovée and click on "Real-Time Updates.") ■

Key Terms

absolute advantage (58)	euro (65)	multinational corporations (MNCs) (71)
balance of payments (59)	exchange rate (65)	protectionism (61)
balance of trade (59)	exporting (70)	quotas (61)
comparative advantage theory (58)	foreign direct investment (FDI) (71)	stereotyping (67)
devaluation (66)	fair trade (61)	strategic alliance (70)
dumping (62)	free trade (59)	tariffs (61)
economies of scale (58)	importing (70)	trade deficit (59)
embargo (61)	joint venture (71)	trade surplus (59)
ethnocentrism (67)	licensing (70)	trading blocs (63)

Test Your Knowledge

Questions for Review

1. How can a company use a licensing agreement to enter world markets?
2. What two fundamental product strategies do companies choose between when selling their products in the global marketplace?
3. What is the balance of trade, and how is it related to the balance of payments?
4. What is dumping, and how does the United States respond to this practice?
5. What is a floating exchange rate?

Questions for Analysis

6. Why would a company choose to work through intermediaries when selling products in a foreign country?
7. How do companies benefit from forming international joint ventures and strategic alliances?
8. What types of situations might cause the U.S. government to implement protectionist measures?
9. How do tariffs and quotas protect a country's own industries?
10. **Ethical Considerations.** Should the U.S. government more closely regulate the practice of giving trips and

other incentives to foreign managers to win their business? Is this bribery?

Questions for Application

11. Suppose you own a small company that manufactures baseball equipment. You are aware that Russia is a large market, and you are considering exporting your products there. What steps should you take? Who might be able to give you assistance?

12. **How This Affects You.** How has your current employer or any previous employer been affected by globalization? For instance, does your company compete with lower-cost imports? (If you don't have any work experience, ask a friend or family member.)

13. **Integrated.** Review the theory of supply and demand discussed in Chapter 1. Using this theory, explain how a country's currency is valued and why governments sometimes adjust the values of their currency.

14. **Integrated.** You just received notice that a large shipment of manufacturing supplies you have been waiting for has been held up in customs for two weeks. A local business associate tells you that you are expected to give customs agents some "incentive money" to see that everything clears easily. How will you handle this situation? Evaluate the ethical merits of your decision by answering the questions outlined in Exhibit 2.2 on page 36.

Practice Your Knowledge

Sharpening Your Communication Skills

Languages never translate on a word-for-word basis. When doing business in the global marketplace, choose words that convey only their most specific denotative meaning. Avoid using slang or idioms (phrases that can have meanings far different from their individual components when translated literally). For example, if a U.S. executive tells an Egyptian executive that a certain product "doesn't cut the mustard," chances are that communication will fail.

Team up with two other students and list ten examples of slang (in your own language) that would probably be misinterpreted or misunderstood during a business conversation with someone from another culture. Next to each example, suggest other words you might use to convey the same message. Make sure the alternatives mean exactly the same as the original slang or idiom. Compare your list with those of your classmates.

Building Your Team Skills

In today's interdependent global economy, fluctuations in a country's currency can have a profound effect on the flow of products across borders. The U.S. steel industry, for example, has been feeling intense competition from an influx of Korean, Brazilian, and Russian steel imports. After the currencies of those countries plummeted in value, the price of steel products exported to the United States dropped as well, making U.S. steel much more expensive by comparison.

Fueled by low prices, steel flooded into the United States, hurting sales of U.S. steel. Over the course of several months, the volume of steel imports nearly doubled. Stung, U.S. steelmakers slashed production and laid off more than 10,000 U.S. workers. U.S. trade officials charge that the cheap imported steel is being dumped, and they are considering protectionist measures such as imposing quotas on steel imports.[49]

With your team, brainstorm a list of at least four additional ways the United States might handle this situation. Once you have your list, consider the probable effect of each option on these stakeholders:

- U.S. businesses that buy steel
- U.S. steel manufacturers
- U.S. businesses that export to Korea, Brazil, or Russia
- Employees of U.S. steel manufacturers

On the basis of your analysis and discussion, which option will your team recommend? Select a spokesperson to explain your selection and your team's reasoning to the other teams. Compare your recommendation with those of your classmates.

Improving Your Tech Insights: Telepresence

Telepresence systems start with the basic idea of videoconferencing but go far beyond with imagery so real that colleagues thousands of miles apart virtually appear to be in the same room together. The audio and visual quality of the latest systems comes very close to duplicating the nuanced experience of communicating in person. The ability to convey nonverbal subtleties such as facial expressions and hand gestures makes these systems particularly good for negotiations, collaborative problem-solving, and other complex discussions.

The number of companies that use telepresence has been doubling every year, and some experts predict that nearly all major companies will use it within the next ten years.

Conduct research to identify a company that has installed a telepresence system. What kinds of meetings does the firm use the telepresence system for? What advantages does the system give the company?[50]

Expand Your Knowledge

Discovering Career Opportunities

If global business interests you, consider working for a U.S. government agency that supports or regulates international trade. For example, here are the duties performed by an international trade specialist at the International Trade Administration of the U.S. Department of Commerce: "The incumbent will assist senior specialists in coordination and support of government trade programs and events; perform research and analysis of trade data and information on specific topics or issues within a larger project or assignment; and disseminate trade information and materials on government products/services to U.S. businesses and associations. Incumbent will attend meetings and engage in other activities for developmental purposes. As a condition of employment, applicants must be available for reassignment and relocation within the United States."[51]

1. On the basis of this description, what education and skills (personal and professional) would you need to succeed as an international trade specialist? Why? How does this job description fit your qualifications and interests?

2. Given their duties, where would you expect international trade specialists to be situated or transferred? Would you be willing to move to another city or state for this type of position?

3. What sources would you contact to locate trade-related jobs with government agencies such as the International Trade Administration?

Developing Your Research Skills

Companies involved in international trade have to watch the foreign exchange rates of the countries in which they do business. Use your research skills to locate and analyze information about the value of the Japanese yen relative to the U.S. dollar. As you complete this exercise, make a note of the sources and search strategies you used.

1. How many Japanese yen does one U.S. dollar buy right now? (You can find the foreign exchange rate for the yen at www.x-rates.com and many similar sites.)

2. Investigate the foreign exchange rate for the yen against the dollar over the past month. Is the dollar growing stronger (buying more yen) or growing weaker (buying fewer yen)?

3. If you were a U.S. exporter selling to Japan, how would a stronger dollar be likely to affect demand for your products? How would a weaker dollar be likely to affect demand?

See It on the Web

Visit these websites and answer the following questions for each one. (Up-to-date links for all websites mentioned in this chapter can be found on the Textbook Resources page for Chapter 3 at www.mybusinesslab.com. Please note that links to sites that become inactive after publication of the book will be removed from the Featured Websites section.)

1. What is the purpose of this website?

2. What kinds of information does this website contain? Please be specific.

3. How is the information provided at this website useful for businesspeople? Consumers?

4. How did you expand your knowledge of doing business in the global economy by reviewing the material at this website? What new things did you learn about this topic?

Navigating Global Business Differences

In today's global marketplace, knowing as much as possible about your international customers' business practices and customs could give you a strategic advantage. To help you successfully conduct business around the globe, navigate the resources at the U.S. Government Export Portal. Start at www.export.gov, then click on "Country Information." Click anywhere on the world map to learn more about each country. www.export.gov

Going Global

Have you ever thought about getting into the world of exporting? Where would you go for information and help? Many small and large companies have gotten valuable export assistance from online material such as the *Basic Guide to Exporting*, offered by the U.S. Department of Commerce. Visit www.export.gov and navigate to the "Export Basics" section and find "Basic Guide to Exporting" for a wealth of information about export procedures; foreign markets, industries, companies, and products; export financing; unfair trade practices; trade statistics; and more. www.export.gov

Banking on the World Bank

The World Bank plays an important role in today's fast-changing, closely meshed global economy. Do you know what this organization of five closely associated institutions does? Do you know who runs the bank, where the bank gets its money, and where the money goes? Learn how this organization's programs and financial assistance help poorer nations as well as affluent ones. Log on to the World Bank website and find out why global development is everyone's challenge. www.worldbank.org

Companion Website

Learning Interactively

Log onto www.prenhall.com/bovée, locate your text, then click on its Companion Website. For Chapter 3, take advantage of the interactive Chapter Quiz to test your knowledge of the chapter. Get instant feedback on whether you need additional studying. Also, you'll find an abundance of valuable resources that will help you succeed in this course, including PowerPoint presentations and Web Links.

Video Case

Entering the Global Marketplace: Lands' End and Yahoo!

LEARNING OBJECTIVES

The purpose of this video is to help you:

1. Understand the different reasons that businesses undertake international expansion
2. Identify the financial and marketing issues of selling goods and services internationally
3. Recognize the influence of culture on business decisions in an international firm

SYNOPSIS

Yahoo! is an Internet company headquartered in Santa Clara, California, with offices around the world. The company's service offerings have expanded from a search engine and web directory to a wide array of content and e-commerce offerings. Lands' End began in 1963 by selling sailing equipment by catalog. Today the firm is one of the largest apparel brands in the United States, with a variety of catalogs and a high-volume e-commerce site. This video segment shows how these two very different companies approached the same goal: expansion into international business. You will see how each copes with cultural, financial, monetary, and marketing differences as well as differences in language and method of payment. See whether you can identify those areas in which each firm chose to adapt to the needs and expectations of the international marketplace, and where it maintained its original product or policy.

Discussion Questions

1. *For analysis:* Compare the different reasons why Lands' End and Yahoo! decided to expand internationally.

2. *For analysis:* How did Lands' End succeed in establishing itself in the United Kingdom and Japan?
3. *For application:* In addition to hiring local employees in countries such as France and China, how could Yahoo! help educate U.S. employees about the nuances of doing business in these countries?
4. *For application:* How should Lands' End alter its online marketing efforts in countries that have different expectations of personal modesty?
5. *For debate:* Both Yahoo! and Lands' End expect their employees to behave in an ethical manner in all business dealings. However, experienced managers recognize that definitions of ethical behavior can vary from country to country? Should both companies demand a consistent ethical code in all cases across all regions of the world? Why or why not?

ONLINE EXPLORATION

Visit Yahoo!'s website (www.yahoo.com) and explore some of the features and functions that appeal to you. Then select one of the international sites listed at the bottom of the Yahoo! home page and compare it to the U.S. site. Identify the changes that have been made to suit the particular country's language and customs, and observe what elements of the site have *not* been changed. What do you think is the motivation behind the design and content choices Yahoo! made in the overseas site? Do you think it is successful in its market?

CHAPTER 4

Business Systems

LEARNING OBJECTIVES

After studying this chapter, you will be able to

1 Identify eight principles of systems thinking that can improve your skills as a manager

2 Describe the value chain and value web concepts

3 Define *supply chain management* and explain its strategic importance

4 Highlight the differences between quality control and quality assurance

5 Identify four major ways that businesses use information

6 Differentiate between operational information systems and professional and managerial systems and give several examples of each

7 Identify seven important information systems issues that managers must be aware of in today's business environment

Fulfilling Customized Dreams at Carvin Guitars

www.carvin.com

Once beginning guitarists have mastered the nuances of "Mary Had a Little Lamb" and set their sights on making serious music, they often encounter a serious equipment dilemma. Low-cost, beginner guitars lack the materials and workmanship needed to produce top-quality sounds. Some are difficult to keep in tune, and some cannot produce true notes all the way up and down the neck. Plus, they just aren't very cool. Nobody wants to jump on stage in front of 50,000 adoring fans with a guitar purchased at the local discount store.

And so the shopping begins, as the aspiring guitarist looks to find a better "axe." As with just about every product category these days, the array of choices is dizzying. For a few hundred dollars, budding musicians can choose from several imports that offer improved quality. Jumping up toward $1,000 to $2,000, they can enter the world of such classic American brands as Fender, Gibson, and Martin—a world that reaches up to

Carvin offers personalized guitars at affordable prices through a combination of sophisticated production systems and old-world handicraft.

$10,000 and beyond for limited-edition models. Musicians with that much to spend and several months to wait can also hire skilled instrument builders known as *luthiers* to create custom guitars that reflect their individual personalities and playing styles. Luthiers can custom-craft just about any attribute a guitarist might want, from the types of wood used in the body to the radius of the fingerboard.

But what if a future superstar wants it all: world-class quality, the personalized touch of a custom guitar, and a mid-range price tag, without the long delays associated with hand-crafted instruments?

That "sweet spot" in the guitar market is the territory staked out by Carvin, a San Diego company that has been in the instrument business for over 60 years. How could Carvin profitably do business in this seemingly impossible market segment? How could they quickly customize guitars and sell them in the $750 to $1,500 range without compromising quality?[1] ■

An Introduction to Systems Thinking

Carvin (profiled in the chapter opener) faced a classic systems challenge: how to design and operate business processes that would enable the company to deliver its unique value to customers. One of the most important skills you can develop as a manager is the ability to view business from a systems perspective. This chapter offers an overview of systems concepts, followed by a look at some of the key systems within a business.

What Is a System?

A **system** is an interconnected and coordinated set of *elements* and *processes* that converts *inputs* to desired *outputs*. A company is made up of numerous individual systems in the various functional areas—marketing, accounting, manufacturing, and so

system
An interconnected and coordinated set of *elements* and *processes* that converts *inputs* to desired *outputs*

EXHIBIT 4.1

From Point to Line to Circle: The Systems View

The systems view considers all the steps in a process and "closes the loop" by providing feedback from the output of one cycle back to the input of the next cycle.

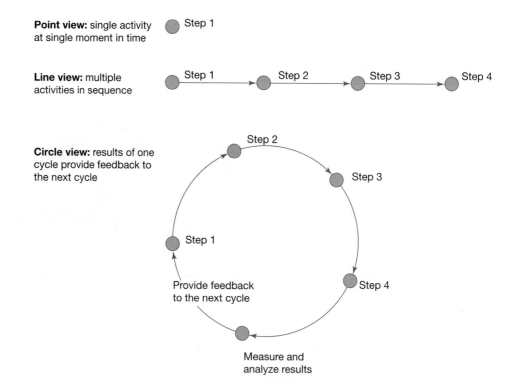

Point view: single activity at single moment in time   Step 1

Line view: multiple activities in sequence   Step 1 → Step 2 → Step 3 → Step 4

Circle view: results of one cycle provide feedback to the next cycle

Step 2
Step 3
Step 1
Provide feedback to the next cycle
Step 4
Measure and analyze results

on—that together constitute the overall system that is the company itself. Each of these individual systems can also be thought of as a *subsystem* of the overall business.

To grasp the power of systems thinking, consider a point, a line, and a circle (see Exhibit 4.1). If you poked your head into a nearby office building, what would this snapshot tell you? You could see only one part of the entire operation—and only at this one point in time. You might see people in the advertising department working on plans for a new ad campaign or people in the accounting department juggling numbers in spreadsheets, but neither view would tell you much about what it takes to complete these tasks or how that department interacts with the rest of the company.

If you stood and observed for several days, though, you could start to get a sense of how people do their jobs in this department. In the advertising department, for instance, you could watch as the staff transforms ideas, information, and goals into a plan that leads to the creation of a new magazine advertisement. Your "point" view would thereby extend into a "line" view, with multiple points connected in sequence. However, you still wouldn't have a complete picture of the entire process in action. Was the ad campaign successful? Did it generate enough revenue to finance another campaign? What did the advertising department learn from the campaign that could help it do even better next time? To see the process operate over and over, you need to connect the end of the line (the completion of this ad campaign) back to the beginning of the line (the start of the next ad campaign) to create a circle. Now you're beginning to form a systems view of what this department does and how its performance can be improved.

This circular view helps you understand the advertising system better, but it still isn't complete, because it doesn't show you how the advertising system affects the rest of the company, and vice versa. For instance, did the finance department provide enough money to run the ad? Was the manufacturing department ready with enough materials to build the product after customers started placing orders? Were the sales and customer service departments ready to handle the increase in their workloads? Each of these departments has its own system (its own "circle"), and all the subsystems connect to form the overall business system. Only by looking at the interconnected business system can you judge whether the ad campaign was a success for the company as a whole.

Principles of Systems Thinking

Professionals who specialize in systems analysis use a special language, complete with symbols that represent various elements and processes within a system. By simulating systems on computers, they can also predict the impact of business decisions before making any resource decisions (see Exhibit 4.2). These computer simulations, the basis of the related field of *systems dynamics*, allow decision makers to evaluate scenarios far more complicated than the human mind can grasp by looking at diagrams on paper.[2] However, even without learning the formal terminology, you can benefit from systems thinking by keeping these basic principles in mind:[3]

- *Help everyone see the big picture.* It's only human nature for individual employees and departments to focus on their own goals and lose sight of what the company as a whole is trying to accomplish. Showing people how they contribute to the overall goal—and rewarding them for doing so—helps ensure that the entire system works efficiently.

- *Understand how individual systems really work and how they interact.* Let's say you've just been put in charge of setting prices for a company that sells complex products to other companies. This industry has a long tradition in which suppliers set prices high but customers then negotiate down before purchasing. You conclude that all this negotiating is a waste of time since the prices usually end up at a lower level anyway. To make things efficient, you decide to lower the price to begin with and tell customers these new low prices aren't negotiable. Your prices are effectively the same as before, but sales drop off quickly. Why? You failed to realize that with the long history of price negotiations in this industry, purchasing agents in the customer organizations are rewarded for negotiating steep discounts. Buying from you makes the purchasing agents look bad because they can no longer negotiate big discounts. In other words, the change you made to your system made it incompatible with their systems.

- *Understand problems before you try to fix them.* The rapid pace of business makes it tempting to apply quick-fix solutions without taking the time to fully understand the underlying problems. The most obvious answer is not always the right answer, and poorly conceived solutions often end up causing more harm than good. When you analyze system behavior and malfunctions, make sure you focus on things that are *meaningful*, not merely things that are *measurable*. For instance, it's easy to measure how many reports employees write every month, but that might not be the most meaningful gauge of how well a process is working.

- *Understand the potential impact of solutions before you implement them.* Let's say you manage the customer support department, and one of the factors you are graded on is productivity—how many phone calls your staff can handle in a given amount of time. To encourage high productivity, you run a weekly contest to see who can handle the most calls. Trouble is, you're essentially rewarding people based on how quickly they can get the customer off the phone, not on how quickly they actually solve customer problems. Customers who aren't happy keep calling back—which adds to the department's workload and *decreases* overall productivity.

- *Don't just move problems around—solve them.* When one subsystem in a company is malfunctioning, its problems are sometimes just moved around the company, from one subsystem to the next, without ever getting solved. For instance, if the market research department does a poor job of understanding customers, this problem will get shifted to the engineering department, which is likely to design a product that doesn't meet customer needs. The problem will then get shifted to the advertising and sales departments, which will struggle to promote and sell the product. The engineering, advertising, and sales departments will all underperform, but the real problem is back in the market research department. Market research in this case is a *leverage point*, where a relatively small correction could make the entire company perform better.

EXHIBIT 4.2 System Diagram and Simulation

This example of a formal systems diagram models the flow of people at a ski resort, from arriving at the chairlift to taking the lift up to skiing down the hill, then returning to the lift line. The resort is anticipating a boom in business and needs to figure out how to handle the additional skiers. By mathematically modeling the number of skiers at each point in the system, the resort can simulate several options: doing nothing, getting a faster chairlift, switching to triple chairs, or switching to quadruple chairs. Doing nothing would result in a long line waiting to get on the lift, while getting a faster lift (shown in the graph) would solve that problem but result in overcrowding on the slope. The optimum solution turned out to be switching to quad chairs.

Ski Resort Dynamics
Core Model Structure

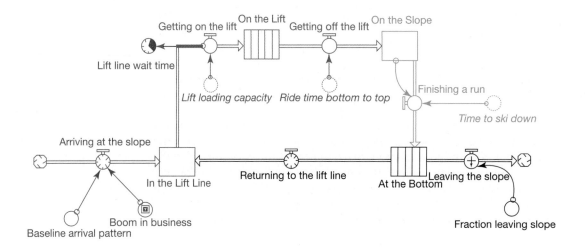

Ski Resort Dynamics
Simulate

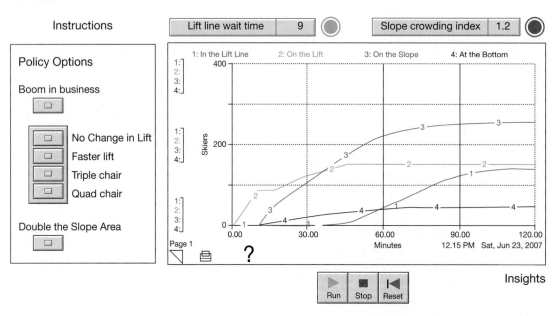

■ *Avoid the "bigger hammer" syndrome.* There's an old saying in business that when the only solution you have is a hammer, every problem looks like a nail. When you then "hammer" on a problem that isn't a "nail" and things don't get any better, you're tempted to think, "OK, I just need a bigger hammer." Don't automatically reach for the solutions you're most comfortable with; figure out what the system really needs.

■ *Understand how feedback works in the system.* Systems respond to *feedback*, which is information from the output applied back to the input. In the case of an ad campaign, the response from target customers is a form of feedback that helps the department understand whether the campaign is working. Feedback can work in unanticipated ways, too. A good example is when managers send mixed signals to their employees, such as telling them that customer satisfaction is the top priority but then criticizing anyone who spends too much time helping customers. Employees will respond to this feedback by spending less time with customers, leading to a decline in customer satisfaction.

■ *Use mistakes as opportunities to learn and improve.* When mistakes occur, resist the temptation to just criticize or complain and then move on. Pull the team together and find out why the mistake occurred, then identify ways to fix the system to eliminate mistakes in the future.

The Business Model

The **business model**, which is a company's plan to generate sales revenue and earn a profit based on that revenue, represents the firm's highest-level system and defines the major elements that make the company what it is—and isn't. For example, compare the search-engine giant Google with Hoovers (www.hoovers.com), which sells a variety of business information products such as in-depth company profiles and data about specific industries and markets. Both are online businesses that provide information, but their business models have a critical difference. Google provides a variety of information retrieval services but doesn't charge people for using its search engines. Google's business model is based on selling advertising that is linked to those searches, and those advertising fees make up nearly all of the company's revenue stream.[4] In other words, while millions of web surfers use Google every day, the company's paying customers are its advertisers. In contrast, Hoovers's business model is based on selling information directly. You can imagine how different Google's business model would be if it tried to sell search-engine results instead of ads associated with those results.

business model
A company's plan to generate sales revenue and earn a profit based on that revenue

Business models are sometimes articulated with a brief description, such as "Our business model involves providing flexible in-home nursing care tailored to each patient's medical and financial needs." This statement sounds compelling, but it doesn't explain how the business is actually going to operate in a way likely to generate a profit. Before anyone can have confidence in a business model, it needs to be defined and validated at a deeper level, and that's where a systems perspective is valuable. For example, to launch this in-home nursing service, you would need to understand how you're going to acquire customers, how you'll provide the specific services they need, how you'll balance variable customer demand with your capacity to deliver services, and so on—and how all these subsystems will work together to create a profitable business enterprise.

If the business model is fundamentally flawed, no amount of fine-tuning of all the various subsystems within the company will save it. For example, during the *dot-com boom* of the late 1990s, many business models were based on the idea of attracting lots of visitors to a website, then charging companies to advertise on the site (and thereby reach all those visitors). Many of these models—and the companies behind them—failed because they couldn't generate enough site traffic to attract sufficient advertising revenue to cover their costs and leave anything for profit. The models failed in a number of specific ways, including misjudging how hard it would be to build repeatable and measurable traffic levels, how expensive it was to build and maintain websites that large numbers of visitors would want to visit regularly, and how reluctant many major companies were to shift their advertising budgets from proven media such as magazines and television to the then-unproven medium of the Internet. Google stands out as one of the few companies that offered something compelling enough to keep millions of web surfers coming back day after day.

The hundreds of companies that collapsed after the dot-com boom went bust are a stark reminder of how important it is to understand and rationally evaluate business models. Understanding the model as a real-life, functioning system and not just as a vague concept that looks good on a PowerPoint slide is essential for everyone associated with the company. For example, before you buy stock in a company or accept a job offer there, make sure you can describe its business model in your own words. If you can't, you either don't understand the model, which is dangerous, or the model doesn't make sense, which is even more dangerous. If the model doesn't make sense, take your money, talents, or whatever else the company wants and run like the wind.

Production Systems

production
The creation of goods and services

All companies that create something of value, whether it's a bulldozer, a magazine, or the design for a new building, are involved in **production**. The *production system*, therefore, is made up of the elements and processes that enable the company to create those goods and services. This section explores the major aspects of production, from value chains to quality assurance.

Value Chains and Value Webs

value chain
All the elements and processes that add value as raw materials are transformed into the final products made available to the ultimate customer

The notion of creating or adding value is central to the production process, and production can be thought of as a series of steps that continually increase value. For instance, consider the chain from iron ore to steel to a car door to a completed car to a car delivered to a neighborhood car dealer. Each step, from digging the iron ore out of the ground to trucking the finished car to a convenient retail location, adds value. The **value chain** is a helpful way to view all the elements and processes that add value as raw materials are transformed into the final products made available to the ultimate customer (see Exhibit 4.3).[5]

core competencies
Functions in which a company has a distinct advantage over its competitors

In the several decades since Michael Porter introduced the value chain concept, many companies have come to realize that doing everything themselves is not always the most efficient or most successful way to run a business. Many now opt to focus on their **core competencies**, those functions for which they have a distinct advantage over their competitors, and let other companies handle the remaining business functions—a

EXHIBIT 4.3

The Value Chain

The value chain represents the major activities involved in producing a company's goods and services. With the advent of Internet-enabled networks of multiple business partners and outsourcing arrangements, some companies now think in terms of *value webs* instead.

	Buy		Add value	Sell		
Primary activities	Sourcing & procurement — sourcing, supply planning, materials procurement	Inbound logistics — receiving, incoming material storage	Operations — assembly, component fabrication, branch operations	Outbound logistics — warehousing, fulfillment, shipping	Sales & customer service — sales, order processing, customer support	
Support activities	Financial management — financing, planning, investor relations	Research & development — product design, testing, process design, material research	Facilities management — physical plant, office equipment, IT services, supplies, MRO procurement	Human resource management — recruiting, training, compensation	Marketing & advertising — market research, promotion, advertising, trade shows	Value

strategy known as **outsourcing**. The combination of extensive globalization in many industries and the development of electronic networking (including both the Internet and telecommunication networks) has made it easy for companies to connect with partners around the world. Instead of the linear value chain, some businesses now think in terms of **value webs**, multidimensional networks of suppliers and outsourcing partners.[6]

outsourcing
Contracting out certain business functions or operations to other companies

value webs
Multidimensional networks of suppliers and outsourcing partners

The outsourced, value-web approach has several key advantages, including speed, flexibility, and the opportunity to access a wide range of talents and technologies that might be expensive or impossible to acquire otherwise. Established companies can narrow their focus to excel at their core competencies; entrepreneurs with product ideas can quickly assemble a team of designers, manufacturing plants, and distributors in far less time than it would take to build an entire company from scratch. When Jim Van Dine wanted to launch a sports shoe company to go up against the likes of Nike, Trek, and other established brands, he and his partners created a value web of freelance product designers, manufacturing consultants, and other independent specialists. Shoe companies normally take ten months or more to design new models and get samples ready for retailers. Using a web of partners, Van Dine's team had 16 new shoe models ready in only two months. Their company, Keen Footwear (www.keenfootwear.com), took off like a rocket, registering $30 million in sales the first year. By comparison, Teva needed three years to hit $1 million in sales.[7]

Supply Chain Management

The lifeblood of every production operation is the **supply chain**, a set of connected systems that coordinates the flow of goods and materials from suppliers all the way through to final customers. **Supply chain management (SCM)** combines business procedures and policies with computer systems that integrate the various elements of the supply chain into a cohesive system, even if the supply chain involves a wide variety of outside suppliers and distribution partners. As companies rely more on outsourcing partners, SCM has grown far beyond the simple procurement of supplies to become a strategic management function that means the difference between success and failure. Successful implementation of SCM can have a profound strategic impact on companies, in three important ways:[8]

supply chain
A set of connected systems that coordinates the flow of goods and materials from suppliers all the way through to final customers

supply chain management (SCM)
The business procedures, policies, and computer systems that integrate the various elements of the supply chain into a cohesive system

- *Managing risks.* SCM can help companies manage the complex risks involved in a supply chain, risks that include everything from cost and availability to health and safety issues. For example, Southwest Airlines continues to enjoy a fuel cost advantage over its rivals because it locked in purchase contracts before prices jumped dramatically in recent years.[9]

- *Managing relationships.* SCM can also coordinate the numerous relationships in the supply chain and help managers focus their attention on the most important company-to-company relationships. For instance, General Motors buys massive quantities of both steel and aluminum, but the nature of the two markets puts a higher priority on GM's relationship with its aluminum supplier, Alcan. GM uses SCM to forge a close relationship with Alcan, including stabilizing prices in ways that help both companies.

- *Managing trade-offs.* Finally, SCM helps managers address the many trade-offs in the supply chain. These trade-offs can be a source of conflict within the company, and SCM helps balance the competing interests of the various functional areas. This holistic view helps managers balance both capacity and capability along the entire chain.

Just as each company has its own supply chain, all the companies in a given industry make up that industry's overall supply chain. For example, Spirit AeroSystems, a manufacturing company based in Wichita, Kansas, is part of the aircraft-industry supply chain. Spirit buys metal, carbon fiber, and other materials from its suppliers and transforms those into wings, fuselages, and other airplane parts that it then sells to Boeing, Airbus, and other aircraft manufacturers.[10]

Offshoring: Profits, Yes, But at What Cost?

Few business issues in recent years have generated the emotional intensity that outsourcing has. The use of outsourcing has been going on for about as long as businesses have existed, but it has become a hot topic as it expands from mostly lower-paying assembly positions to higher-paying technical and professional positions.

When companies outsource any function in the value chain, they often eliminate the jobs associated with that function as well. And, increasingly, those jobs aren't going across the street to another local company but rather around the world, a variation on outsourcing known as *offshoring*. (Offshoring can shift jobs to either another company or to an overseas division of the same company.) Dell, HP, IBM, Microsoft, and Accenture are among the many U.S. technology firms that have already moved thousands of technical jobs to India, which has a large pool of educated workers willing to work for far less than U.S. workers are typically paid. Offshoring is a possibility whenever firms can find less-expensive labor in another country, whether it's Japanese manufacturers moving work to China or U.S. firms moving work to Thailand.

Proponents say that offshoring is crucial to the survival of many U.S. companies and that it saves other U.S. jobs. Plus, offshoring helps raise the standard of living in other countries and thereby expands opportunities for U.S. companies to export their products. And some observers say that offshoring is going to continue for generations, so everyone might as well start adapting to the idea. In fact, some U.S. firms don't really consider themselves as "American" companies anymore, at least not in the sense that employees and local communities would define it, but rather as global corporations.

Opponents of offshoring say that companies are selling out the U.S. middle class in pursuit of profits and starting a trend that can only harm the country. When jobs in engineering, medicine, finance, scientific research, architecture, journalism, and law can move overseas, they ask, what jobs are going to be left in the United States? Offshoring that involves crucial health and safety issues is a big concern, too—for instance, half of all the "heavy" maintenance performed on U.S. commercial aircraft is now offshored to places such as Hong Kong and El Salvador as U.S. airlines struggle mightily to control costs.

Uncertainty is fueling the controversy, because measuring the impact of offshoring on the U.S. economy is proving to be difficult. Moreover, economists often struggle to identify the specific reasons one country gains jobs or another loses jobs. The emergence of new technology, phasing out of old technology, shifts in consumer tastes, changes in business strategies, and other factors can all create and destroy jobs.

Traditional economic theory suggests that outsourcing lower-level jobs to countries with lower wages is good for U.S. companies because it frees up money and employees to work on more valuable activities. However, now that those higher-value activities are starting to move overseas, quite a few people are questioning the theory.

With companies trying to reduce costs wherever possible but workers trying to protect as many jobs as possible, offshoring promises to be a hot topic for years to come—not only for businesses and employees but for governments and society as a whole.

Questions for Critical Thinking

1. Do U.S. companies have an obligation to keep jobs in the United States? Why or why not?
2. Will global labor markets eventually balance out, with workers in comparable positions all over the world making roughly the same wages? Explain your answer.

The best supply chains function as true partnerships, with buyers and sellers coordinating their efforts in a win-win approach. For instance, both Toyota and Honda have developed close, cooperative relationships with U.S. parts suppliers as these Japanese firms have expanded their manufacturing presence in North America (60 percent of all Toyotas and 80 percent of all Hondas sold in North America are built in North America). In the Japanese tradition of *keiretsu*, the two companies have spent years "growing" a close-knit supply network that meets their needs and helps their suppliers run their businesses more successfully as well. By developing their supplier network, Toyota and Honda have been able to design new cars in half the time it takes Ford, GM, and Chrysler—all of which have a reputation for more adversarial relationships with their suppliers.[11]

Supply Chains Versus Value Chains

The terms *supply chain* and *value chain* are sometimes used interchangeably, and the distinction between them isn't always clear in everyday usage. One helpful way to distinguish between the two is to view the supply chain as the part of the overall value chain that acquires and manages the goods and services needed to produce whatever it is the company produces and then deliver it to the final customer. Everyone in the company is part of the value chain, but not everyone is involved in the supply chain.[12] Another way to distinguish the two is that the supply chain focuses on the "upstream" part of the process, collecting the necessary materials and supplies with an emphasis on reducing waste and inefficiency. The value chain focuses on the "downstream" part of the process and on adding value in the eyes of customers.[13] Because of the overlap between the two ideas, both conceptually and in terms of the processes and systems used, it's possible that they will increasingly merge in the coming years.

Today's supply chains often span the globe, pulling in parts and materials from multiple countries.

Supply Chain Systems and Techniques

SCM is all about getting the right materials at the right price in the right place at the right time for successful production. Unfortunately, you can't just pile up huge quantities of everything you might eventually need, because **inventory**, the goods and materials kept in stock for production or sale, costs money to purchase and store. On the other hand, not having an adequate supply of inventory can result in expensive delays. This balancing act is the job of **inventory control**, which tries to determine the right quantities of supplies and products to have on hand, then tracks where those items are. One of the most important technologies to emerge in inventory control in recent years is **radio frequency identification (RFID)**. RFID uses small antenna tags attached to products or shipping containers; special sensors detect the presence of the tags.

Purchasing, or *procurement*, is the acquisition of the raw materials, parts, components, supplies, and finished products required to produce goods and services. The goal of purchasing is to make sure that the company has all the materials it needs, when it needs them, at the lowest possible cost. A company must always have enough supplies on hand to cover a product's *lead time*—the period that elapses between placing the supply order and receiving materials.

To accomplish these goals, operations specialists have developed a variety of systems and techniques over the years:

- **Material requirements planning (MRP)** helps a manufacturer get the correct materials where they are needed, when they are needed, without unnecessary stockpiling. Managers use MRP software to calculate when certain materials will be required, when they should be ordered, and when they should be delivered so that storage costs will be minimal. These systems are so effective at reducing inventory levels that they are used almost universally in both large and small manufacturing firms.

- **Manufacturing resource planning (MRP II)** expands the MRP with links to the company's financial systems and other processes. For instance, in addition to managing inventory levels successfully, an MRP II system can help ensure that material costs adhere to target budgets.[14] Because it draws together all departments, an MRP II system produces a companywide game plan that allows everyone to work with the same numbers. Moreover, the system can track each step of production, allowing managers throughout the company to consult other managers' inventories, schedules, and plans.

- **Enterprise resource planning (ERP)** extends the scope of research planning even further to encompass the entire organization. ERP systems are typically made up of software modules that address the needs of the various functional areas, from manufacturing to sales to human resources. Some companies deploy ERP on a global scale, with a single centralized system connecting all their operations worldwide.[15]

---

inventory
Goods and materials kept in stock for production or sale

inventory control
Determining the right quantities of supplies and products to have on hand and tracking where those items are

radio frequency identification (RFID)
Inventory tracking system that uses small antenna tags attached to products or shipping containers and special sensors to detect the presence of the tags

purchasing
The acquisition of the raw materials, parts, components, supplies, and finished products required to produce goods and services

material requirements planning (MRP)
Computer system that helps manufacturers get the correct materials where they are needed, when they are needed, without unnecessary stockpiling

manufacturing resource planning (MRP II)
An expansion of MRP that links to a company's financial systems and other processes

enterprise resource planning (ERP)
Materials and resource planning systems that encompass the entire organization

Production and Operations Management

The term *production* suggests factories, machines, and assembly lines staffed with employees making automobiles, computers, furniture, motorcycles, or other tangible goods. That's because in the past people used the terms *production* and *manufacturing* interchangeably. With the growth in the number of service-based businesses and their increasing importance to the economy, however, the term *production* is now used to describe the transformation of resources into both goods and services. The broader term **production and operations management**, or simply *operations management*, refers to overseeing all the activities involved in producing goods and services. Operations managers are responsible for a wide range of strategies and decisions, from locating production facilities to managing the supply chain.

production and operations management
Overseeing all the activities involved in producing goods and services

Facilities Location and Design

Choosing the location of production facilities is a complex decision that must consider such factors as land, construction, labor, local taxes, energy, local living standards, and transportation for both raw materials and finished products. The locations of manufacturing plants and service operations that don't require face-to-face contact with customers are chosen primarily on the basis of proximity to suppliers, labor costs, energy costs, and transportation options. In contrast, service businesses that require in-person contact with customers obviously need to be located wherever they can attract sufficient numbers of target customers. Support from local communities and governments often plays a key role in location decisions as well. To provide jobs and expand their income and sales tax bases, many local, state, and national governments often compete to attract companies by offering generous financial incentives such as tax reductions.

Once a site has been selected, managers must turn their attention to *facility layout*, the arrangement of production work centers and other elements (such as materials, equipment, and support departments) needed to process goods and services. Layout planning includes such decisions as how many steps are needed in the process, the amount and type of equipment and workers needed for each step, how each step should be configured, and where the steps should be located relative to one another.[16]

Well-designed facilities help companies operate more productively by reducing wasted time and wasted materials, but that is far from the only benefit. Smart layouts support close communication and collaboration among employees and help ensure their safety, both of which are important for employee satisfaction and motivation. In the delivery of services, facility layout can be a major influence on customer satisfaction in such important aspects as the amount of time that customers are forced to wait to be served.[17]

Forecasting and Capacity Planning

A smooth-running supply chain can provide the inputs a company needs, but managers need to figure out how much to buy. And to make that decision, they need to forecast demand for the goods they'll be manufacturing or the services they'll be delivering. Using customer feedback, sales orders, market research, past sales figures, industry analyses, and educated guesses about the future behavior of customers and competitors, operations managers prepare **production forecasts**—estimates of future demand for the company's products.

production forecasts
Estimates of future demand for a company's products

capacity planning
Establish the overall level of resources needed to meet customer demand

Once product demand has been estimated, management must balance that with the company's capacity to produce the goods or services. The term *capacity* refers to the volume of manufacturing or service capability that an organization can handle. **Capacity planning** is the collection of long-term strategic decisions that establish the overall level of resources needed to meet customer demand. When managers at Boeing plan for the production of an airliner, they have to consider not only the staffing of thousands of people but also massive factory spaces, material flows from hundreds of suppliers around the world, internal deliveries, cash flow, tools and equipment, and dozens of other factors. Because of the potential impact on finances, customers, and employees—and the difficulty of reversing major decisions—capacity choices are among the most important decisions that top-level managers make.[18]

Scheduling

In any production process, managers must do *scheduling*—determining how long each operation takes and deciding which tasks are done in which order. Manufacturing facilities often use a *master production schedule (MPS)* to coordinate production of all the goods the company makes. Services businesses use a variety of scheduling techniques as well, from simple appointment calendars for a small business to the comprehensive computer-based systems that airlines and other large service providers use.

Managers can use a variety of scheduling techniques. When a job has relatively few activities and relationships, many production managers keep the process on schedule with a **Gantt chart**, a special type of bar chart that shows the amount of time required to accomplish each part of a process. It allows managers to see at a glance whether the process is in line with the schedule they had planned (see Exhibit 4.4).

For more complex jobs, the **program evaluation and review technique (PERT)** is helpful. PERT helps managers identify the optimal sequencing of activities, the expected time for project completion, and the best use of resources within a complex project. To use PERT, managers map out all the activities in a network diagram (see Exhibit 4.5). The longest path through the network is known as the **critical path** because it represents the minimum amount of time needed to complete the project. Tasks in the critical path usually receive special attention because they determine when the project can be completed. Exhibit 4.5 shows a simplified PERT chart that outlines some of the tasks involved in opening a new retail store. In practice, most PERT charts are considerably more complicated than this example, but computerized scheduling tools can take much of the work out of creating and maintaining a PERT schedule.[19]

Lean Systems

Throughout all the activities in the production process, operations managers pay close attention to **productivity**, or the efficiency with which they can convert inputs to outputs. (Put another way, productivity is equal to the value of the outputs divided by the value of the inputs.) Productivity is one of the most vital responsibilities in operations management because it is a key factor in determining the company's competitiveness

Gantt chart
A type of bar chart used for project or process scheduling

program evaluation and review technique (PERT)
A planning tool that managers of complex projects use to determine the optimal order of activities, the expected time for project completion, and the best use of resources

critical path
In a PERT network diagram, the sequence of operations that requires the longest time to complete

productivity
The efficiency with which an organization can convert inputs to outputs

EXHIBIT 4.4 A Gantt Chart

A chart like this one enables a production manager to immediately see the dates on which production steps must be started and completed if goods are to be delivered on schedule. Some steps may overlap to save time. For instance, after three weeks of cutting table legs, cutting tabletops begins. This overlap ensures that the necessary legs and tops are completed at the same time and can move on together to the next stage in the manufacturing process.

ID	Task Name	Start Date	End Date	Duration	2008
1	Make legs	8/1/08	8/28/08	20d	
2	Cut tops	8/22/08	8/28/08	5d	
3	Drill	8/29/08	9/4/08	5d	
4	Sand	9/5/08	9/11/08	5d	
5	Assemble	9/12/08	9/25/08	10d	
6	Paint	9/19/08	9/25/08	5d	

EXHIBIT 4.5 Simplified PERT Diagram for Store Opening

This PERT diagram shows a subset of the many tasks involved in opening a new retail store. The tasks involved in staffing are on the critical path because they take the longest time to complete (51 days), whereas the promotion tasks can be completed in 38 days, and the merchandise tasks can be completed in 39 days. In other words, some delay can be tolerated in the promotion or merchandise tasks, but any delay in any of the staffing tasks will delay the store's opening day.

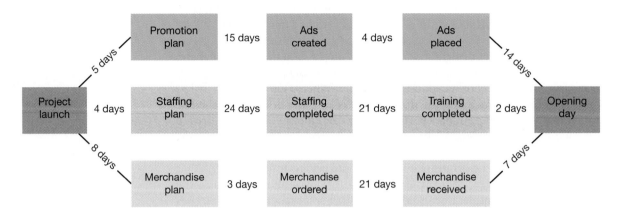

Advanced Technology on the Factory Floor

If you enjoy working with technology, then product design or manufacturing might be the place for you. Today's companies use a mind-boggling array of technologies to create quality products quickly, from automated testers that can simulate years of customer use in a few hours to programmable smart cameras that can sort fish by species or wood by grain patterns to a variety of industrial robots. Here are a few of the other important technologies you might encounter in product design and manufacturing:

■ *Computer-aided design (CAD)* applies advanced computer graphics and mathematical modeling to the design of products, helping designers create better products in less time. *Virtual reality* allows designers to see how finished products will look and operate before physical prototypes are built.

■ *Computer-aided engineering (CAE)*, a related technology, analyzes designs using a variety of engineering methods. For instance, engineers at BMW subject new designs to as many as 50 different crash scenarios to maximize occupant safety.

■ *Computer-aided manufacturing (CAM)* involves the use of computers to control production equipment. CAM is often linked with CAD; in a CAD/CAM system, computer-aided design data are converted automatically into processing instructions for production equipment to manufacture the part or product.

■ *Computer-integrated manufacturing (CIM)* is a strategy that links all the related functions of manufacturing—

design, engineering, testing, production, inspection, and materials handling. CIM is not a specific technology but rather a strategy that uses technology for organizing and controlling a factory.

■ *Product life-cycle management (PLM)* software integrates information flow through every part of the value chain, from the time products are first dreamed up in the design lab to the time the company stops making them. Boeing's 787 Dreamliner was designed with PLM in mind, since the company sells and supports each airplane model for as long as 20 or 30 years. As one benefit of this long-term approach, when Boeing customers want to make interior design choices, they can use the same software models that the plane's designers originally used.

■ *Flexible manufacturing systems (FMS)* link numerous programmable machine tools with automated materials-handling devices, creating the ability to quickly retool the production line from one product to the next. For instance, an FMS at Porsche's plant in Stuttgart, Germany, allows it to build 13 different versions of the 911 and Boxster models on the same line.

Questions for Critical Thinking

1. What does the pervasive use of information technology in product manufacturing imply for tomorrow's workforce?
2. Instead of investing money in flexible manufacturing systems, why wouldn't companies just reduce the number of product variations they offer?

and profitability. Companies that can produce similar goods or services with fewer resources have a distinct advantage over their competitors.

Lean systems, which maximize productivity by reducing waste and delays, are at the heart of many productivity improvement efforts. Many lean systems borrow techniques from Toyota; the *Toyota Production System* is world-renowned for its ability to continually improve both productivity and quality (see page 94 for more on quality).[20] Central to the notion of lean systems is **just-in-time (JIT)** inventory management, in which goods and materials are delivered throughout the production process right before they are needed, rather than being stockpiled in inventories. Reducing stocks to practically nothing reduces waste and forces factories to keep production flowing smoothly. Although JIT seems like a simple enough concept, it requires constant attention to quality and teamwork, because there is no room for delays or errors.[21] Without stockpiles of parts and materials waiting in inventory, each stage in the production process goes idle if the stages before it have not delivered on time.

lean systems
Manufacturing systems that maximize productivity by reducing waste and delays

just-in-time (JIT)
Inventory management in which goods and materials are delivered throughout the production process right before they are needed

mass production
The creation of identical goods or services, usually in large quantities

Mass Production, Customized Production, and Mass Customization

Both goods and services can be created through *mass production*, *customized production*, or *mass customization*, depending on the nature of the product and the desires of target customers. In **mass production**, identical goods or services are created, usually in large quantities, such as when Apple churns out a million identical iPhones. Although not normally associated with services, mass production is also what American Airlines is doing when it offers hundreds of opportunities for passengers to fly from, say, Dallas to Chicago every day—every customer on these flights gets the same service at the same time.

At the other extreme is **customized production**, sometimes called *batch-of-one production* in manufacturing, in which the producer creates a unique good or service for each customer. If you order a piece of furniture from a local craftsperson, for instance, you can specify everything from the size and shape to the types of wood and fabric used. Or you can hire a charter pilot to fly you wherever you want, whenever you want. Both products are customized to your unique requirements.

Mass production has the advantage of economies of scale, but it can't deliver many of the unique goods and services that today's customers demand. On the other hand, fully customized production can offer uniqueness but usually at a much higher price. An attractive compromise in many cases is **mass customization**, in which part of the product is mass produced, then the remaining features are customized for each buyer. As you'll read at the end of the chapter, this is the approach Carvin took; customers get the same basic guitar bodies but their own individual combinations of woods, fingerboard styles, finishes, and electronic components.

customized production
The creation of a unique good or service for each customer

Individual craftspeople often engage in customized production, creating a unique product for each customer.

mass customization
Manufacturing approach in which part of the product is mass produced and the remaining features are customized for each buyer

The Unique Challenges of Service Delivery

Many of the concepts of goods manufacturing apply to the delivery of services as well, since every business is engaged in the task of transforming inputs into outputs that customers will want to buy (see Exhibit 4.6). However, the intangible nature of services creates some unique issues:[22]

- *Customers are often involved in—and can affect the quality of—the service delivery.* For instance, personal trainers can instruct clients in the proper way to work out, but if the clients don't follow directions, the result will be unsatisfactory.

EXHIBIT 4.6 Input-Transformation-Output Relationships for Typical Production Systems

Both goods and services undergo a conversion process, but the components of the process vary to accommodate the differences between tangible and intangible outputs.

SYSTEM	REPRESENTATIVE INPUTS	TRANSFORMATION COMPONENTS	TRANSFORMATION FUNCTION	TYPICAL DESIRED OUTPUT
Hospital	Patients, medical supplies	Physicians, nurses, equipment	Perform medical services	Healthy individuals
Restaurant	Hungry customers, food	Chef, wait staff, environment	Prepare and serve food	Satisfied customers
Automobile factory	Sheet steel, engine parts	Tools, equipment, workers	Fabricate and assemble cars	High-quality cars
College or university	High school graduates, books	Teachers, classrooms	Impart knowledge and skills	Educated individuals
Department store	Shoppers, stock of goods	Displays, salesclerks	Attract shoppers, promote products, fill orders	Sales to satisfied customers
Online business information service	Company reports, interviews, research services	Researchers, writers, web producers, website servers	Research business topics, analyze research, write content, produce web pages	Helpful web content for paid subscribers

- *Many services are consumed at the same time they are produced.* If a 200-seat airliner takes off half empty, those 100 sales opportunities are lost forever. The airline can't create these products ahead of time and store them in inventory until somebody is ready to buy. This attribute can have a dramatic impact on the way service businesses are managed, from staffing (making sure enough people are on hand to help with peak demands) to pricing (using discounts to encourage people to buy services when they are available).

- *Customers often dictate when and where services are performed.* The equipment and food ingredients used in a restaurant can be produced just about anywhere, but the restaurant itself needs to be located close to customers and be open when customers want to eat. One of the most significant commercial advantages of the Internet is the way it has enabled many businesses to get around this constraint. For instance, online retailers and information providers can locate virtually anywhere on the planet.

- *Quality can be more subjective with services.* If you create a pair of scissors, both you and the customer can measure and agree on the hardness of the steel, the sharpness of the blades, the smoothness of the action, and so on. If you create a haircut using those scissors, however, you and the customer might disagree on the attractiveness of the style or the quality of the salon experience.

With the majority of workers in the United States now involved in the service sector, managers in thousands of companies need to pay close attention to these factors when designing service-delivery systems.

Product and Process Quality

None of these efforts to improve productivity will do a company much good unless it also focuses on quality. Fortunately, many of the efforts aimed at improving quality also improve productivity, and vice versa. Eliminating mistakes not only raises product quality but also eliminates the time required to fix the mistakes.

Quality has become a global imperative in practically every industry. To survive, companies today must produce high-quality goods and services as efficiently as possible. In some industries, quality is literally a matter of life and death. Nearly 100,000 deaths in the United States every year are attributed to medical errors; in Canada, a quarter of all patients who seek medical care wind up getting another illness as a result of medical mistakes.[23]

The traditional means of maintaining quality is called **quality control**—measuring quality against established standards after the good or service has been produced and weeding out any defects. A more comprehensive approach is **quality assurance**, a system of companywide policies, practices, and procedures to ensure that every product meets preset quality standards. Quality assurance includes quality control as well as doing the job right the first time by designing tools and machinery properly, demanding quality parts from suppliers, encouraging customer feedback, training employees, empowering them, and encouraging them to take pride in their work.

Statistical Quality Control and Continuous Improvement

Quality assurance also includes the widely used concept of **statistical quality control (SQC)**, in which all aspects of the production process are monitored so that managers can see whether the process is operating as it should. The primary tool of SQC is **statistical process control (SPC)**, which involves taking samples from the process periodically and plotting observations of the samples on a *control chart*. A large enough sample provides a reasonable estimate of the entire process. By observing the random fluctuations graphed on the chart, managers can identify whether such changes are normal or whether they indicate that some corrective action is required in the process.[24]

In addition to using SQC, companies can empower each employee to continuously improve the quality of goods production or service delivery. The Japanese word for continuous improvement is *kaizen*. Japanese manufacturers learned long before many U.S. manufacturers that continuous improvement is not something that can be delegated to one or a few people. Instead, it requires the full participation of every employee. This approach means encouraging all workers to spot quality problems, halt production when necessary, generate ideas for improvement, and adjust work routines as needed.[25]

Sometimes, however, the sure and steady pace of kaizen isn't enough. Toyota president Katsuaki Watanabe now encourages his employees to explore *kakushin*, meaning revolutionary change. Toyota's newest facility in Takaoka, Japan, represents such a radical departure. Rather than just being lean, the manufacturing process is "simple, slim, and speedy." By reducing complexity, Toyota hopes to dramatically reduce mistakes. For instance, one goal is to physically move parts as little as possible, since every move is an opportunity for a part to be damaged.[26]

Total Quality Management and Six Sigma

One of the most comprehensive approaches to quality is known as **total quality management (TQM)**, which is both a management philosophy and a strategic management process that focuses on delivering the optimal level of quality to customers by building quality into every organizational activity. Implementing TQM requires six elements:[27]

- Management commitment to supporting TQM at every level in the organization
- Clear focus on customers and their needs
- Employee involvement throughout the organization
- Commitment to continuous improvement
- Willingness to treat suppliers as partners
- Meaningful performance measurements

TQM was one of the hot management topics in the 1980s and 1990s, and some businesses that tried to establish TQM failed, for reasons ranging from an inability to change

quality control
Measuring quality against established standards after the good or service has been produced and weeding out any defective products

quality assurance
A more comprehensive approach of companywide policies, practices, and procedures to ensure that every product meets quality standards

statistical quality control (SQC)
Monitoring all aspects of the production process to see whether the process is operating as it should

statistical process control (SPC)
Use of random sampling and control charts to monitor the production process

total quality management (TQM)
A management philosophy and strategic management process that focuses on delivering the optimal level of quality to customers by building quality into every organizational activity

the corporate culture to ineffective measurement techniques.[28] TQM doesn't receive the attention that it once did in the business media, either, and some observers now dismiss it as another management fad that came and went. However, the principles of TQM infuse much of today's managerial practice, even if managers don't always use the TQM label.[29]

An alternative approach to focusing an organization on quality processes and products is **Six Sigma**, which began as a statistical approach to eliminating defects but has evolved into a "fully integrated management system" that "aligns business strategy with improvement efforts," in the words of Motorola, where the concept was first formalized. (*Six Sigma* is a statistical term that indicates 3.4 defects per million opportunities—near perfection, in other words.) Six Sigma is a highly disciplined, systematic approach to reducing the deviation from desired goals in virtually any business process, whether it's eliminating defects in the creation of a product or improving a company's cash flow.[30] Six Sigma efforts typically follow a five-step approach, known as DMAIC for short:[31]

Six Sigma
A quality management program that strives to eliminate deviations between the actual and desired performance of a business system

1. **D**efine the problem that needs to be solved
2. **M**easure current performance to see how far it deviates from desired performance
3. **A**nalyze the root causes of this deviation from the ideal
4. **I**mprove the process by brainstorming, selecting, and implementing changes
5. **C**ontrol the process long-term to make sure performance continues to meet expectations

Six Sigma shares the same focus on the customer and emphasis on employee involvement as TQM, but provides a simpler and widely accepted set of methods for business teams to follow. More than 80 percent of the largest companies in the United States now have Six Sigma programs, but like TQM, Six Sigma doesn't work when it is applied poorly or applied to the wrong problem. For instance, some experts argue that the rigid DMAIC framework can hamper the open-ended creative thinking that is required for new product design.[32]

Global Quality Standards

In addition to meeting the quality expectations of their customers, many companies now face the need to meet international quality standards as well. For instance, many companies in Europe require that suppliers comply with standards set by the International Organization for Standardization (ISO), a nongovernment entity based in Geneva, Switzerland. The ISO oversees a vast array of product standards, but the two of most general concern to businesses are the *ISO 9000* family, which concerns quality and customer satisfaction, and *ISO 14000*, which concerns environmental issues. Hundreds of thousands of organizations around the world have implemented ISO standards, making it a universally recognized indicator of compliance. The ISO 9000 and ISO 14000 families both focus on management systems, the processes and policies that companies use to create their goods and services, rather than on the goods and services themselves. Achieving ISO certification sends a reassuring signal to other companies that your internal processes meet these widely accepted international standards.[33]

How This Affects You

1. How could a systems approach to thinking help you get up to speed quickly in your first job after graduation?
2. How would you describe the business model of your last employer?
3. Is the business class you are currently taking an example of mass production, customization, or mass customization?

Information Systems

Information represents one of the most intriguing challenges you'll face as both an employee and a manager. Many companies now find themselves drowning in an ocean of data—but struggling to find real insights that can mean the difference between success and failure.

EXHIBIT 4.7 From Data to Information to Insight

Businesses generate massive amounts of data, but a key challenge is transforming all those individual data points into useful information, then applying creative thinking (sometimes with the additional help of computers) to extract deeper insights from the information.

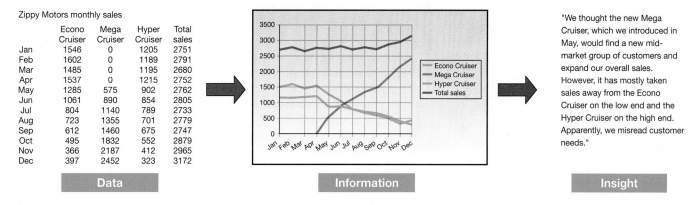

Zippy Motors monthly sales

	Econo Cruiser	Mega Cruiser	Hyper Cruiser	Total sales
Jan	1546	0	1205	2751
Feb	1602	0	1189	2791
Mar	1485	0	1195	2680
Apr	1537	0	1215	2752
May	1285	575	902	2762
Jun	1061	890	854	2805
Jul	804	1140	789	2733
Aug	723	1355	701	2779
Sep	612	1460	675	2747
Oct	495	1832	552	2879
Nov	366	2187	412	2965
Dec	397	2452	323	3172

Data

Information

Insight

"We thought the new Mega Cruiser, which we introduced in May, would find a new mid-market group of customers and expand our overall sales. However, it has mostly taken sales away from the Econo Cruiser on the low end and the Hyper Cruiser on the high end. Apparently, we misread customer needs."

The first step in turning information into a competitive advantage is understanding the difference between **data** (recorded facts and statistics), **information** (useful knowledge, often extracted from data), and **insight** (a deep level of understanding about a particular situation). The transformation from data to insight requires a combination of technology, information-management strategies, creative thinking, and business experience—and companies that excel at this transformation have a huge advantage over their competitors. In fact, entire industries can be created when a single person looks at the same data and information everyone else is looking at but sees things in a new way, yielding insights that no one has ever had before (see Exhibit 4.7).

Businesses collect data from a wide array of sources, from checkout scanners and website clicks to research projects and electronic sensors. A single customer order can generate hundreds of data points, from a credit card number to production statistics to accounting totals that end up on a tax form. Even a small business can quickly amass thousand or millions of individual data points; large companies generate billions and even trillions of data points.[34]

To keep all these data points under control and to extract useful information from them, companies rely on **databases**, computerized files that collect, sort, and cross-reference data. In addition to the daily chores of sending out bills, ordering new parts, and everything else that keeps the company running, databases can also be used for **data mining**, a powerful computerized analysis technique that identifies previously unknown relations among individual data points.[35]

Most large organizations employ a top-level manager, often called a **chief information officer (CIO)**, whose job is to understand the company's information needs and to create systems and procedures to deliver that information to the right people at the right time. This manager is expected to deliver quality information, which can be defined as *relevant* (the information delivered to each person relates directly to his or her needs), *accurate* (it's both current and free from errors), *timely* (delivered in time to make a difference), and *cost-effective* (costs a reasonable amount of money compared to the value it offers).

How Businesses Use Information

Companies invest heavily in information for the simple reason that they can't live without it. Here's a small sample of the ways managers rely on information:

- *Research and development.* In a sense, the cycle of information usage starts with understanding customer needs, then developing new goods and services to meet those needs. Information is vital at every step, from researching markets to analyzing competitors to testing new products.

data
Facts, numbers, statistics, and other individual bits and pieces that by themselves don't necessarily constitute useful information

information
Useful knowledge, often extracted from data

insight
A deep level of understanding about a particular subject or situation

databases
Computerized files that collect, sort, and cross-reference data

data mining
A method of extracting previously unknown relationships among individual data points in a database

chief information officer (CIO)
A high-level executive responsible for understanding the company's information needs and creating systems and procedures to deliver that information to the right people at the right time

Vital business information comes in many forms; here forecasters at FedEx's Memphis control center monitor the weather around the globe to ensure the safe and timely arrival of hundreds of flights every day.

Planning and control. Two of the most important functions of management are planning and control—deciding what to do, then making sure it gets done. Accounting managers need accurate financial information, sales managers need to know if their teams are meeting their sales goals, human resource managers need to make sure the company has enough of the right kind of employees, and so on.

Marketing and sales. Thanks to technology, marketing and sales have evolved from "gut feel" activities to scientific, information-driven functions. The convenience store chain 7-Eleven recently pulled itself up from bankruptcy to solid financial health, thanks in large part to one of the most sophisticated information systems in the industry. For instance, store managers can instantly tap into information on hot sales trends around the country and change the merchandise offerings in their stores overnight.[36]

Communication and collaboration. Throughout the organization, employees, managers, and teams of every size and shape rely on information to communicate and collaborate. In fact, information technology is changing the very definition of what an organization means, thanks to the Internet's ability to connect people from every corner of the globe.

Types of Business Information Systems

information systems (IS)
A collective label for all technologies and processes used to manage business information

information technology (IT)
A generally accepted synonym for information systems; many companies use *IT* to refer to the department that manages information systems

Over the years, the collective label for the technologies used to manage information has changed; what used to be called *data processing* is now called either **information systems (IS)** or **information technology (IT)**, depending on the context. The types of information systems used by a company generally fall into two major categories: (1) operational systems and (2) professional and managerial systems. (The specific systems you'll encounter in your career are likely to have their own names, often arcane acronyms that make no sense to outsiders.) Most systems meet the information needs of people at specific levels in the organization. In contrast, *enterprise systems* are designed to connect everyone in the organization, giving each person the information he or she needs to meet specific job responsibilities.

Operational Systems

Operational systems are the "front line" workhorses of information technology, collecting and processing the data and information that represent the day-to-day work of the business enterprise. These systems typically support daily operations and decision making for lower-level managers and supervisors:

Transaction processing systems. Much of the daily flow of data into and out of the typical business organization, particularly regarding sales, is handled by a *transaction processing system (TPS)*, which captures and organizes raw data and converts these data into information. Common transaction processing systems take care of customer orders, billing, employee payroll, inventory changes, and other essential transactions. Such systems are a vital part of supply chain management.

Process and production control systems. Operational systems are also used to make routine decisions that control operational processes. *Process control systems* monitor conditions such as temperature or pressure change in physical processes. *Production control systems* are used to manage the production of goods and services by controlling production lines, robots, and other machinery and equipment.

Office automation systems. *Office automation systems* address a wide variety of typical office tasks. Office automation systems range from a single personal computer with word-processing software to *content management systems* that help companies organize the content on their websites.

■ *Customer relationship management (CRM) systems. Customer relationship management systems* capture, organize, and capitalize on all the interactions that a company has with its customers, from marketing surveys and advertising through sales orders and customer support.

Professional and Managerial Systems

In contrast to operational systems, *professional and managerial systems* help with such higher-level tasks as designing new products, analyzing financial data, identifying industry trends, and planning long-term business needs. These systems are used by professionals such as engineers and marketing specialists and by managers up to the top executive and board of directors. An important advance for many professionals is the idea of a *knowledge management (KM) system*, which collects the expertise of employees across the organization. For instance, Roche Laboratories's Global Healthcare Intelligence Platform collects information from internal information systems, recommended websites, and other sources to give researchers access to materials that colleagues have already found.[37]

A **management information system (MIS)** provides managers with information and support for making routine decisions. (Note that *MIS* is sometimes used synonymously with both *IS* and *IT* to describe the entire information technology effort.) An MIS takes data from a database and summarizes or restates the data into useful information such as monthly sales summaries, daily inventory levels, product manufacturing schedules, employee earnings, and so on.

Whereas a management information system typically provides structured, routine information for managerial decision making, a *decision support system (DSS)* assists managers in solving highly unstructured and nonroutine problems through the use of decision models and specialized databases. Compared with an MIS, a DSS is more interactive (allowing the user to interact with the system instead of simply receiving information), and it usually relies on both internal and external information. Similar in concept to a DSS is an *executive support system (ESS)*, which helps top executives make strategic decisions.

Employee performance management systems help managers set employee performance goals, develop improvement plans, and reward employees based on measurable performance. By making performance evaluation more transparent and objective, such systems can help companies improve employee retention and job satisfaction.[38]

One of the more intriguing applications for computers in decision making and problem solving is the development of **artificial intelligence**—the ability of computers to solve problems through reasoning and learning and to simulate human sensory perceptions. For instance, an *expert system* mimics the thought processes of a human expert to help less-experienced individuals make decisions.

management information system (MIS)
Computer system that provides managers with information and support for making routine decisions

artificial intelligence
Ability of computers to solve problems through reasoning and learning and to simulate human sensory perceptions

The Internet Revolution

No single technology in recent decades has reshaped the business world as much as the Internet has—and continues to do. The Internet has helped many companies reach wider markets but has also exposed them to more competitors. It has created new business capabilities, such as online meetings and automated shopping, but has also raised the constant threat of viruses, network intrusions, and other malicious technology. It has even helped shift the balance of commercial power from sellers to buyers by giving buyers more information and more choices than they ever had before. You'll find the Internet being put to use all over the place, in virtually every part of many companies:

■ *Accelerating commerce.* E-commerce and online advertising are two of the most visible ways companies take advantage of the Internet. You'll read more about both topics in Chapter 11.

■ *Controlling costs.* Generating revenue through e-commerce is only one side of the Internet's financial story. Companies are also finding creative ways to reduce costs through online technologies. Sometimes the savings are dramatic, as when companies can forgo entire facilities or accomplish far more with fewer people. In other cases, the savings might not sound like much but can add up quickly. Boeing saves millions of dollars a year by giving its airline customers online access to technical manuals, parts lists, and other maintenance information, rather than printing, shipping, and constantly updating paper documents.[39]

- *Erasing borders.* One of the Internet's most profound changes has been its ability to erase borders—borders between departments, between companies, and even between countries. Thanks to *virtual meeting* technologies that let groups conduct meetings online, people across town or across the country can work together more efficiently. Nearly 30,000 companies now conduct online meetings every month using WebEx (www.webex.com), the leading provider of virtual meeting services.[40] Not only does this ability offer more flexibility in employment, since employees have more freedom to live where they want to live and companies can hire people who may not want to move, but it helps companies address the costs, security concerns, and productivity losses that are a part of air travel these days.

- *Collaborating and communicating.* Just about every web-based communication tool you can think of, including instant messaging, blogging, wikis, social networking, file sharing, and Internet phone services such as Skype (www.skype.com), is used in business today. The Internet also enables online collaboration via *virtual workspaces* or *groupware*. For instance, the toy and apparel company Kidrobot (www.kidrobot.com) uses an online project collaboration tool called Basecamp (www.37signals.com) to coordinate the work of its New York design team and its manufacturing partners in China.[41] Many of these tools are integrated with both *intranets* (restricted websites accessible only by people within the company) and *extranets* (external websites with access restricted to business partners or customers).

- *Simplifying research.* In much the same way that you now use the Internet to research school assignments, you'll use the Internet for business research as well—studying competitors, learning about new products, uncovering business opportunities, and so on. Newsfeed technologies such as *Really Simple Syndication (RSS)* help researchers automatically collect new material. Web-based surveys are commonly used in place of more expensive and time-consuming phone and mail surveys. You may also encounter specialized research tools. For instance, *reputation analysts* such as Evolve24 (www.evolve24.com) have developed ways to automatically monitor blogs and other online sources to see what people are saying about their corporate clients.[42] Of course, all the cautions that you apply (or at least should be applying!) to online research are still important in the business world. Experienced researchers know that the Internet can be a tremendous source of both data and information—and it can waste hours and hours of precious time and deliver inaccurate or biased information, exaggerated claims, and unsubstantiated rumors.

electronic business (e-business) Organization in which all major business functions take full advantage of the capabilities and efficiencies of information technology

From commerce to communication, various Internet capabilities help an organization move toward becoming an **electronic business (e-business)**, in which all major business functions take full advantage of the capabilities and efficiencies of information technology. Note that *e-commerce* and *e-business* are sometimes used interchangeably, but e-commerce generally refers specifically to buying and selling online, whereas e-business is a much broader term that encompasses every facet of the business operation. (For the latest information on e-business innovations, visit www.prenhall.com/bovée and click on "Real-Time Updates.")

Information Systems Management Issues

As you already know from your experiences as a student and a consumer, technology can deliver some amazing benefits, and every year seems to bring new technical miracles. As a business manager or entrepreneur, you can capitalize on all these benefits as well, but you'll also be responsible for a variety of legal, ethical, and administrative issues, starting with the challenge of ensuring privacy and security.

Ensuring Security and Privacy

Linking computers via networking technology creates enormous benefits for businesses and consumers, but there's a dark side to connecting everyone everywhere. Managers need constant vigilance these days to make sure their computer systems remain secure and that data on them remain private. In recent years, millions of employee and customer records have been stolen or exposed, and billions of dollars have been lost to damage from computer viruses. The financial damage from computer-based crime is climbing toward $100 billion a year.[43] Moreover, the collection, storage, and use of private information raises a host of legal and ethical issues that managers must consider.

The sources of potential trouble seem to multiply with every passing year and each new technological breakthrough:

- *Malicious software.* **Malware**, short for *malicious software*, is the term often applied to the diverse and growing collection of computer programs designed to disrupt websites, destroy information, or enable criminal activity. **Viruses** are invasive programs that reproduce by infecting legitimate programs; *worms* are a type of virus that can reproduce by themselves. *Trojan horses* allow outsiders to hijack infected computers and use them for purposes such as retransmitting spam e-mail. *Spyware* sneaks onto computers with the intent of capturing passwords, credit card numbers, and other valuable information. Chances are you've also met spyware's less-malicious cousin, *adware*, which creates pop-up ads on your computer screen.

- *Security breaches.* Anytime a computer is connected to any network, it becomes vulnerable to security breaches. Given the enormous value of information stored on business information systems, particularly credit card numbers and other personal data that can be used for identity theft, there is financial motivation for outsiders to break in and insiders to sell out.

- *Unauthorized software and services.* IT departments in many companies face a constant battle with employee use of unauthorized software and online services. Employees not only expose their companies to security risks but also legal risks if they download or transmit inappropriate content on company networks.

- *Web 2.0 technologies.* Web 2.0 technologies such as wikis, social-networking sites, and video-sharing sites help companies create a more open communication environment for employees, customers, and other communities. Unfortunately, these technologies also create new system vulnerabilities, such as virus-infected MySpace pages and employee blogs that divulge company secrets.[44]

- *Misuse of information systems.* More than a quarter of U.S. employers have terminated employees for misuse of company e-mail systems, according to one recent survey.[45] In addition, roughly the same percentage of employers now monitor internal e-mail, and half of them monitor external e-mail. This monitoring can involve both automated scans using software programmed to look for sensitive content and manual scans in which selected e-mail messages are actually read by security staff.[46]

- *Poor security planning and management.* Many viruses and worms are

malware
Short for *malicious software*; computer programs that are designed to disrupt websites, destroy information, or enable criminal activity

viruses
Invasive programs that reproduce by infecting legitimate programs

---

Learning from Business Blunders

Oops: Ten thousand lucky McDonald's customers in Japan recently received free MP3 digital music players. The devices even came preloaded with ten free songs. Unfortunately, some also came preloaded with the QQPass Trojan horse. As soon as the devices were connected to a PC, QQPass went about its nefarious business of stealing passwords and user names and sending them back to waiting hackers.

What You Can Learn: Computer crime has become a major global enterprise, with crooks constantly looking for ways to steal information that helps them steal money. Don't make their work any easier than it already is by being careless. Even if you're not downloading songs to 10,000 music players, make sure you use antivirus software on your computer and keep it updated.

able to wreak their havoc and intruders can gain access because computer owners haven't bothered to install available security patches in their software or haven't installed *firewalls*, hardware or software devices that block access to intruders. As larger companies with more resources and expertise work to improve their security, many criminals are now going after small businesses.[47] And as the networking options multiply, so do the areas of risk; new areas of concern include viruses sent through Internet phone service, viruses on mobile phones (including viruses downloaded from ringtone websites and viruses transmitted from phone to phone over Bluetooth wireless), and nasty things lurking on public wireless networks.[48]

- *Lack of physical control.* Software and network security isn't enough. Some of the most egregious security lapses involve the loss or theft of laptops that contain sensitive data such as employee records. Also, in a recent survey, IT professionals said portable storage devices (such as *USB flash drives*, which can be quickly connected to a computer and loaded with sensitive data, then slipped into a pocket) have replaced malware as their top security concern. On a worrisome note, most of those in the survey also said their firms lack effective policies for managing this risk.[49]

Whether it's human issues such as background checks on new hires and ongoing security training or technical issues such as firewalls, encryption, or disaster recovery plans, all managers need to devote time and energy to potentially harmful side effects of information technology. Sadly, as long as criminals can profit from digital theft and malware writers can amuse themselves by destroying the hard work of others, the problems are likely to only get worse. (For the latest information on security and privacy issues, visit www.prenhall.com/bovée and click on "Real-Time Updates.")

Protecting Property Rights

intellectual property
Creative outputs with commercial value, such as design ideas, manufacturing processes, brands, and chemical formulas

Digital technology has also increased concerns over the protection of both digital products (including software and entertainment products available in digital format) and **intellectual property**, a term that covers a wide range of creative outputs with commercial value, such as design ideas, manufacturing processes, brands, and chemical formulas. One of the most controversial issues in this area is *digital rights management (DRM)*, the protection of owners' rights in products that are in digital format. DRM limits the ways consumers can use music files, movies, and other digital purchases, and critics worry that major corporations are using DRM to stifle creativity and control popular culture. Intellectual property protection remains a contentious and complex issue, as copyright owners, privacy advocates, and consumer groups battle over how digital products can or can't be used. (For the latest information on DRM, visit www.prenhall.com/bovée and click on "Real-Time Updates.")

Guarding Against Information Overload

From simple RSS newreaders to enterprise-wide sales reporting systems, it's not uncommon for businesspeople to be stunned by how quickly their computerized systems start piling up data and information. Once you open the floodgates, it's difficult to stem the tide, so think carefully before you start collecting any data. Work backward from your most important decisions and separate the information you really need from the information that is merely interesting or potentially useful. Then analyze the needs of each decision maker to identify what information each person must have and the best way to present it. Managers can take advantage of new tools such as *data visualization*, which presents complex sets of data in simple visual formats, and *executive dashboards*, which show summaries of important operating variables (see Exhibit 4.8).

EXHIBIT 4.8 Executive Dashboard

Executive dashboards give top-level managers quick access to key operating variables. For instance, the following screen shows key performance variables for the operation of a hotel chain. By clicking on each hotel location on the left, a manager can display up-to-the-minute data on customer satisfaction, bookings, new income, and other important measures.

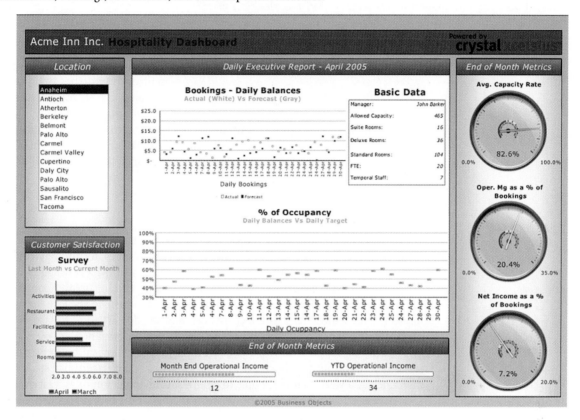

Monitoring Productivity

E-mail, IM, web surfing, and other technologies are key parts of what has been called the "information technology paradox," in which tools designed to save time can waste as much time as they save. For instance, many employers are so concerned about productivity losses from personal use of the Internet and e-mail at work that they are placing restrictions on how employees can use them, such as installing software that limits Internet access to business-related sites during working hours.[50]

Managers also need to guide their employees in productive use of information tools. The speed and simplicity of these tools is also one of their greatest weaknesses: It's simply too easy to send too many messages and to subscribe to too many blog feeds, Twitter groups, and other information sources. The flood of messages from an expanding array of electronic sources can significantly affect employees' ability to focus on their work. In one recent study, workers exposed to a constant barrage of e-mail, IM, and phone calls experienced an average ten-point drop in their functioning IQ.[51]

Managing Total Cost of Ownership

The true costs of information technology are a concern for every company. The *total cost of ownership (TCO)* of IT systems, which includes the purchase costs of hardware, software, and networking plus expenses for installation, customization, training, upgrades, and maintenance, can be three to five times higher than the purchase price.[52] And that's for IT that companies really need and actively use. Managers also need to

How This Affects You

1. Does this course provide you with data, information, or insight? Explain you answer.

2. How might you use information technology to find the ideal job after college?

3. Do you suffer from information overload? If so, what steps can you take to reduce the amount of noise, data, and information you currently receive?

guard against the all-too-common problems of buying technology they don't need or building poorly planned systems that are redesigned or even scrapped before being completed.

Developing Employee Skills

With the pervasiveness of information technology, virtually everyone from the mailroom to the executive suite is expected to have some level of skills with information technology. Not only will you need to keep your own skills up to date so that you can manage yourself and others efficiently, you'll need to make sure your employees have the skills they need. And don't overlook the fundamentals, either—with the importance that e-mail and IM have taken on in recent years, the ability to write well is more vital than ever.[53]

Maintaining the Human Touch

Technology can do wonderful things for business, but it can also get in the way of communication and collaboration. Even in the best circumstances, technology can't match the rich experience of person-to-person contact. Let's say you IM a colleague asking how she did with her sales presentation to an important client, and her answer comes back simply as "Fine." What does *fine* mean? Is an order expected soon? Did she lose the sale and doesn't want to talk about it? Was the client rude and she doesn't want to talk about it? If you communicate in person, she might provide additional information or you might be able to offer advice or support during a difficult time. As technological options increase, people seem to need the human touch even more. Some firms have taken such steps as banning e-mail one day a week to force people to communicate in person or at least over the phone.

Moreover, in-person communication is important to your career. You can create amazing documents and presentations without ever leaving your desk or meeting anyone in person. But if you stay hidden behind technology, people won't get to know the real you.

Summary of Learning Objectives

1 Identify eight principles of systems thinking that can improve your skills as a manager.

The eight principles identified in the chapter are (1) helping everyone see the big picture, including how individual employees and departments contribute to the company's overall goals; (2) understanding how individual systems really work and how they interact so that any changes you make are helpful rather than harmful; (3) understanding problems before you try to fix them, thereby avoiding the temptation of the quick-fix solution that only causes more problems in the long run; (4) understanding the potential impact of solutions before you implement them in order to avoid unintended consequences; (5) avoiding the temptation to just move problems from one subsystem to the next without fixing them; (6) avoiding the "bigger hammer" syndrome, in which you keep applying an inappropriate solution with ever-increasing energy; (7) understanding how feedback works in a system so that you can improve each

process by learning from experience; and (8) using mistakes as opportunities to learn and improve.

2 Describe the value chain and value web concepts.

The value chain is a helpful way to view all the elements and processes that add value as raw materials are transformed into the final products made available to the ultimate customer. The linear value chain concept tends to make the most sense when companies do most or all of the major business functions themselves. As more companies rely on business partners and outsourcing relationships, the multidimensional value web has become a more realistic model for many.

3 Define *supply chain management* and explain its strategic importance.

Supply chain management (SCM) combines business procedures and policies with computer systems that integrate the various elements of the supply chain into a cohesive system, encompassing all the company's outside suppliers and distribution partners. SCM continues to grow in strategic importance because it helps firms manage risks, manage relationships, and manage the many trade-offs that must be made in the supply chain.

4 Highlight the differences between quality control and quality assurance.

Quality control involves measuring product quality against established standards *after* the good or service has been produced and weeding out any defects. Quality assurance takes a more comprehensive and proactive approach with companywide policies, practices, and procedures to ensure quality is built into products from the beginning.

5 Identify four major ways that businesses use information.

Businesses use information in every decision and every facet of operations, but the four areas highlighted in the chapter are research and development (from understanding customer needs to developing new products), planning and control (assembling plans then monitoring how well the business executes them), marketing and sales (connecting with customers), and communication and collaboration (sharing information and working together throughout the organization).

6 Differentiate between operational information systems and professional and managerial systems, and give several examples of each.

Operational systems collect and process the data and information that represent the daily business of the enterprise, from sales receipts to production data to accounting records. The most common types are transaction processing systems, process and production control systems, office automation systems, and customer relationship management systems. In contrast, professional and managerial systems assist with analysis and decision making in both the professional and managerial ranks of the organization. Among the many varieties of these systems are knowledge management systems, management information systems, decision support systems, and executive support systems.

7 Identify seven important information systems issues that managers must be aware of in today's business environment.

Managers in virtually all industries need to address these seven technology-related challenges: ensuring privacy and security, protecting property rights, guarding against information overload, monitoring productivity, managing total cost of ownership, helping employees develop the necessary technical skills, and maintaining the human touch in interactions with both employees and customers.

Behind the Scenes

Carvin's Production System Satisfies Demanding Guitarists

Carvin has made a name for itself among serious guitarists by filling the gap between mass-produced and fully custom guitars. The company's secret has been perfecting the art and science of *mass customization*, the ability to adapt standardized products to the tastes of individual customers. In two to six weeks, and for roughly $700 to $1,500, Carvin can customize one of several dozen models of guitars and basses. All are available in a wide variety of woods, paints, stains, finishes, electronics, even the slight curvature in the fingerboard—so many choices that the discussion boards on Carvin's website buzz with debates about which combinations are "best" for specific styles of music.

Carvin's factory combines old-world craftsmanship with new-world technologies. Because the custom guitars are built on a standard set of body shapes and styles, Carvin can use computer-controlled cutting and milling

machines that cut and shape the bodies and necks quickly and precisely. A diamond-surface finishing machine mills fingerboards to tolerances of a thousandth of an inch. A dehumidification chamber removes internal stresses from the wood used in the guitar necks to minimize the chance of warping years down the road. Experienced craftspeople with sensitive eyes and ears take over from there, performing such tasks as matching veneer pieces on guitar tops (veneers are thin sheets of wood, usually exotic or expensive species), adjusting the action (the feel of the strings against the frets), and listening to the tone quality of finished instruments.

As with any customized offering, the buyer's involvement in the production process is a vital step in ensuring customer satisfaction. Carvin has several retail stores, but all are located in California, so most buyers interact with the company online. The company's website presents each guitar on a page that lists standard features, provides an interactive list of customization options, and computes the total price for the desired configuration. A pop-up window called the "virtual custom shop" lets online shoppers preview the many woods, paints, and stains. Buyers can quickly see what their dream instruments would look like in every shade from natural maple to translucent blue.

With this blend of automation and human touch, Carvin produces instruments that win rave reviews from appreciative customers. "Nothing can touch it in terms of sound quality and workmanship" and "I haven't seen anything close to this price that can outperform it" are typical of the comments that Carvin customers post online. Upon hearing a salesperson in another music store speak disparagingly of the brand, one indignant Carvin owner retrieved his guitar from his car and put on an impromptu concert for the store's sales staff to demonstrate just how good the Carvin product sounded. With a proven manufacturing approach and customer loyalty like that, Carvin will be fulfilling the musical dreams of guitarists for years to come.[54]

Critical Thinking Questions

1. If Carvin experienced an increase in orders from its website over a period of two weeks, should it expand its production capacity to make sure it can handle increased demand in the future? Why or why not?
2. Read about Carvin's GuitarTraq system at www.carvin.com/guitartraq/about. Other than allowing customers to track the progress of their orders through the factory, what other uses can you envision for this technology?
3. Wooden musical instruments have been carved by hand for hundreds of years. Why wouldn't Carvin want to continue this tradition?

LEARN MORE ONLINE

Visit the Carvin website at www.carvin.com. How does the company promote its customized products? Step through the process of customizing a guitar or bass; would you feel comfortable purchasing a musical instrument in this manner? Take the virtual factory tour to see both computer-controlled machinery and guitar builders in action. Visit the discussion boards; what are Carvin customers talking about these days? ■

Key Terms

artificial intelligence (99)
business model (85)
capacity planning (90)
chief information officer (CIO) (97)
core competencies (86)
critical path (91)
customized production (93)
data (97)
data mining (97)
databases (97)
electronic business (e-business) (100)
enterprise resource
    planning(ERP) (89)
Gantt chart (91)
information (97)
information systems (IS) (98)
information technology (IT) (98)
insight (97)
intellectual property (102)

inventory (89)
inventory control (89)
just-in-time (JIT) (93)
lean systems (93)
malware (101)
management information system
    (MIS) (99)
manufacturing resource planning
    (MRP II) (89)
mass customization (93)
mass production (93)
material requirements planning
    (MRP) (89)
outsourcing (87)
production (86)
production and operations
    management (90)
production forecasts (90)
productivity (91)

program evaluation and review
    technique (PERT) (91)
purchasing (89)
quality assurance (95)
quality control (95)
radio frequency identification
    (RFID) (89)
Six Sigma (96)
statistical process control (SPC) (95)
statistical quality control (SQC) (95)
supply chain (87)
supply chain management
    (SCM) (87)
system (81)
total quality management
    (TQM) (95)
value chain (86)
value webs (87)
viruses (101)

Test Your Knowledge

Questions for Review

1. What is a business model?
2. What is mass customization?
3. What role does feedback play in a system?
4. What are the purposes of data warehousing and data mining?
5. How do operational information systems differ from managerial systems?

Questions for Analysis

6. Why is it important to understand a company's business model before you accept a job offer there?

7. Why do some firms now think in terms of value webs instead of value chains?

8. How can supply chain management (SCM) help a company establish a competitive advantage?

9. Why is new information technology sometimes considered both a benefit and a curse?

10. **Ethical Considerations.** How does society's concern for the environment affect a company's decisions about facility location and layout?

Questions for Application

11. Business is booming. Sales last month were 50 percent higher than the month before, and so far this month is looking even better than last month. Should you hire more people to accommodate the increase? Explain your answer.

12. **How This Affects You.** Assume the city in which you currently live has announced it will offer free wireless Internet throughout the entire city. How will this affect your job? If you're not currently working, how will it affect your college experience?

13. **Integrated.** How might quality standards affect the efforts of a company that wants to begin expanding internationally?

14. **Integrated.** Does growth in online retailing mean that overall demand for products is increasing? Why or why not?

Practice Your Knowledge

Sharpening Your Communication Skills

As the newly hired manager of Campus Athletics—a shop featuring athletic wear bearing logos of colleges and universities—you are responsible for selecting the store's suppliers. Merchandise with team logos and brands can be very trendy. When a college team is hot, you've got to have merchandise. You know that selecting the right supplier is a task that requires careful consideration, so you have decided to host a series of selection interviews. Think about all the qualities you would want in a supplier, and develop a list of interview questions that will help you assess whether that supplier possesses those qualities.

Building Your Team Skills

A virus shut down the computer system of your major competitor last month, and you heard from a friend that they are still experiencing serious problems. So you decide to learn from their experience. As manager of the IT department you have assembled your team of top thinkers to brainstorm a list of precautions and steps your department should take to protect the company's data against computer viruses. Generate this list of recommendations and then group the recommendations into logical categories. Compare your team's recommendations with those generated by the other teams in your class.

Improving Your Tech Insights: Nanotechnology

Think small. Really small. Think about manufacturing products a molecule or even a single atom at a time. That's the scale of nanotechnology, a rather vague term that covers research and engineering done at nanoscale, or roughly 1/100,000 the width of a human hair.

The potential uses of nanotechnology range from the practical—smart materials that can change shape and heal themselves, more efficient energy generation and transmission, superstrong and superlight materials for airplanes, better cosmetics, smart medical implants, and ultrasmall computers—to the somewhat wilder—food-growing machines and microscopic robots that could travel through your body to cure diseases and fix injuries. (Like any new technology with lots of promise, nanotechnology also suffers from lots of hype.)

Nanotechnology products have begun to hit the market in a number of industries, from automotive materials to medicine to consumer products. According to the Project on Emerging Nanotechnologies, the most common nanotech consumer products are cosmetics and clothing.

Also, although they're slightly larger than the generally accepted scale of nanotechnology, *microelectromechanical systems (MEMS)* are already having a major impact in some industries. These tiny machines (pumps, valves, and so on), some no bigger than a grain of pollen, are used in the nozzles of ink-jet printers, air bag sensors, and ultraprecise miniature laboratory devices.

Conduct research to identify a product currently on the market that uses nanotechnology in some fashion. In an e-mail message to your instructor, describe the product, its target market, the role nanotechnology plays in the product's design, and any known safety concerns regarding the use of nanotechnology in this or similar products.[55]

Expand Your Knowledge

Discovering Career Opportunities

After learning about the many ways businesses use computers, you decide you'd like to pursue a career in this field. Search the *Occupational Outlook Handbook* at www.bls.gov/oco for professional and managerial jobs in information technology.

1. What sort of managerial possibilities do you see? Can you have a career in this field without being a computer programmer?

2. What is the outlook for careers in this profession? Does the site say anything about the trend of IT moving jobs overseas?

3. If you decide you want to work in an IT-related job, what additional classes should you consider taking before you graduate?

Developing Your Research Skills

Seeking increased efficiency and productivity, a growing number of producers of goods and services are applying technology to improve the production process. Find an article in a business journal or newspaper that discusses how one company used CAD, CAE, robots, or other technological innovations to refit or reorganize its production operations.

1. What problems led the company to rethink its production process? What kind of technology did it choose to address these problems? What goals did the company set for applying technology in this way?

2. Before adding the new technology, what did the company do to analyze its existing production process? What changes, if any, were made as a result of this analysis?

3. How did technology-enhanced production help the company achieve its goals for financial performance? For customer service? For growth or expansion?

See It on the Web

Visit these websites and answer the following questions for each one. (Up-to-date links for all websites mentioned in this chapter can be found on the Textbook Resources page for Chapter 4 at www.mybusinesslab.com. Please note that links to sites that become inactive after publication of the book will be removed from the Featured Websites section.)

1. What is the purpose of this website?

2. What kinds of information does this website contain? Please be specific.

3. How is the information provided at this website useful for businesspeople? Consumers?

4. How did you expand your knowledge of systems in business by reviewing the material at this website? What new things did you learn about this topic?

Make Quality Count

In today's competitive business environment, companies have to be concerned about the quality of their goods and services. For information and advice, many turn to the American Society for Quality (ASQ). You can learn about the basic concepts of quality and the measurement and analysis techniques that quality specialists use on the job. Read up on how quality concepts are applied in both manufacturing and service organizations. And while you're there, check out the many benefits of joining the ASQ. www.asq.org

Follow This Path to Continuous Improvement

The business of manufacturing is more complex than ever before. Today's operations managers must address the conflicting needs of customers, suppliers, employees, and shareholders. Discover why many operations managers turn to *IndustryWeek* magazine to stay on top of trends, technologies, and strategies to help drive continuous improvement throughout their organization. Log on to this magazine's website and read about the world's best-managed companies. Check out Manufacturing 101 to learn more about this vital part of business. Plus, you can subscribe to e-newsletters and read the publication's blogs to get the latest scoop on manufacturing topics. www.industryweek.com

Stay Informed with *CIO*

CIOs make smart business decisions by staying current in the field of information technology. Read articles that offer insight into what it's like to be a CIO in today's challenging business environment. Check out the blogs, webcasts, and podcasts offered on the site and subscribe to e-newsletters. And don't miss the copious career advice. www.cio.com

Companion Website

Learning Interactively

Log onto www.prenhall.com/bovée, locate your text, and then click on its Companion Website. For Chapter 4, take advantage of the interactive Chapter Quiz to test your knowledge of the chapter. Get instant feedback on whether you need additional studying. Also, you'll find an abundance of valuable resources that will help you succeed in this course, including PowerPoint presentations and Web Links.

Video Case

Managing Production Around the World: Body Glove

LEARNING OBJECTIVES

The purpose of this video is to help you:

1. Recognize the production challenges faced by a growing company

2. Understand the importance of quality in the production process

3. Discuss how and why a company may shift production operations to other countries and other companies

SYNOPSIS

Riding the wave of public interest in water sports, Body Glove began manufacturing wet suits in the 1950s. The founders, dedicated surfers and divers, came up with the idea of making the wet suits from neoprene, offering more comfortable insulation than the rubber wet suits of the time. The high costs of neoprene and labor were major considerations in Body Glove's eventual decision to have its wet suits made in Thailand. The company's constant drive for higher quality was also a factor. Now company management can focus on building Body Glove's image as a California-lifestyle brand without worrying about inventory and other production issues. In licensing its brand for a wide range of goods and services—from mobile phone cases to flotation devices, footwear, resorts, and more—Body Glove has created a network of partners around the world.

Discussion Questions

1. *For analysis:* Even though Body Glove makes its wet suits in Thailand, why must its managers continually research how U.S. customers use its products?

2. *For analysis:* Which aspects of product quality would wet suit buyers be most concerned about?

3. *For application:* When deciding whether to license its name for a new product, what production issues might Body Glove's managers research in advance?

4. *For application:* How might Body Glove's Thailand facility use forecasts of seasonal demand to plan production?

5. *For debate:* Should the products that Body Glove does not manufacture be labeled to alert buyers that they are produced under license? Support your chosen position.

ONLINE EXPLORATION

Visit the Body Glove website www.bodyglove.com and follow the links to read the Body Glove story and see the variety of products sold under the Body Glove brand. Also look at the electronics products, including the technology and music accessories. Then browse the contacts listing to find out which U.S. and international companies have licensed the Body Glove brand for various products. How do these licensed products fit with the Body Glove brand image? What challenges might Body Glove face in coordinating its work with so many different companies and licensed products?

PART 2

Organizing the Business Enterprise

CHAPTER 5
Business Structures

CHAPTER 6
Small Business and Entrepreneurship

CHAPTER 5

Business Structures

LEARNING OBJECTIVES

After studying this chapter, you will be able to

1 List five advantages and four disadvantages of sole proprietorships

2 List five advantages and two disadvantages of partnerships

3 Explain the differences between common and preferred stock from a shareholder's perspective

4 Highlight the advantages and disadvantages of public stock ownership

5 Cite four advantages and three disadvantages of corporations

6 Delineate the three groups that govern a corporation and describe the role of each

7 Identify six main synergies companies hope to achieve by combining their operations

Behind the Scenes

Google Searches for a Solution to the Display Advertising Business

www.google.com

At times, Google must seem like the company that has everything. The Mountain View, California, search-engine giant has thousands of the top creative and technical minds in the Internet industry. Its vaunted search engine attracts the lion's share of the search market and continues to dominate Yahoo!, Microsoft, and other competitors. Its stock price headed for the stratosphere as soon as the company went public and doesn't show signs of coming back to earth any time soon. And it has so much cash that it's a wonder the company's banks don't call to complain that they can't get the vault door closed.

But Google didn't have everything, at least not when CEO Eric Schmidt surveyed the Internet landscape in the spring of 2007. The primary source of Google's revenue is *search advertising*, which works in two basic ways. First, on Google's search engine page, advertisers can pay (through an online auction) to display small ads whenever the keywords they select are used in a search. These are the "Sponsored Results" that can appear above and to the right of the actual search results. For instance, a real estate agent in Tulsa might bid on the keywords "Tulsa real estate." Whenever anyone enters that phrase in Google's search field, the agent's ad will then appear next to the search results. Second, ads can also appear on the many websites that are in Google's advertising network.

Google (cofounders Larry Page and Sergey Brin are shown here) has expanded through a combination of organic growth, creating and marketing its own products, and the acquisition of other companies.

Rather than being triggered by search results, these ads are triggered by content on a webpage. For example, while reading an article on CNN.com about hiking in Hawaii, you might see a "Sponsored by Google" ad about Hawaiian vacation packages.

While search advertising has made billions of dollars for Google, it is only part of the picture. The other important part of online advertising is called *display* advertising and includes the larger graphical ads and video ads you see on many websites. As major consumer advertisers began to move more of their marketing budgets to the web, they wanted more than basic text ads. They wanted to run a variety of multimedia ads—and they wanted to target web surfers precisely.

Google had done some work in this area, but it wasn't nearly as far along as companies that specialized in display ads, such as DoubleClick, Specific Media, and Right Media. Moreover, the online display ad business is as much about relationships (with advertising agencies and website publishers) as it is about Internet technology. If you were Eric Schmidt, would you try to build your way into this business or buy your way in? Would you have Google's world-renowned technical experts develop the technology or just use some of the company's billions to buy a company that already has it?[1] ∎

Choosing a Form of Business Ownership

The decision Google (profiled in the chapter opener) faced regarding its online display advertising business is closely tied to a decision it made some years earlier to become a publicly traded corporation. Without the capital raised by selling shares to the public, Google would have far fewer opportunities for acquiring other companies.

One of the most fundamental decisions you must make when starting a business is selecting a form of business ownership. This decision can be complex and have far-reaching consequences for owners, employees, and customers. Picking the right ownership structure involves knowing your long-term goals and how you plan to achieve them. Your choice also depends on your desire for ownership and your tolerance for risk. Furthermore, as your business grows, chances are you may change the original form you selected.

The three most common forms of business ownership are sole proprietorship, partnership, and corporation. Each form has its own characteristic internal structure, legal status, size, and fields to which it is best suited. Each has key advantages and disadvantages for the owners (see Exhibit 5.1).

EXHIBIT 5.1 Characteristics of the Forms of Business Ownership

The best form of ownership for a given company depends on the objectives of the people involved in the business.

STRUCTURE	OWNERSHIP RULES AND CONTROL	TAX CONSIDERATIONS	LIABILITY EXPOSURE	EASE OF ESTABLISHMENT AND TERMINATION
Sole proprietorship	One owner has complete control.	Profits and losses flow directly to the owners and are taxed at individual rates.	Owner has unlimited personal liability for business debts.	Easy to set up but leaves owner's personal finances at risk. Owner must generally sell the business to get his or her investment out.
General partnership	Two or more owners; each partner is entitled to equal control unless agreement specifies otherwise.	Profits and losses flow directly to the partners and are taxed at individual rates. Partners share income and losses equally unless the partnership agreement specifies otherwise.	Personal assets of any operating partner are at risk from business creditors.	Easy to set up. Partnership agreement recommended but not required. Partners must generally sell their share in the business to recoup their investment.
Limited partnership	Two or more owners; the general partner controls the business; limited partners don't participate in the management.	Same as for general partnership.	Limited partners are liable only for the amount of their investment.	Same as for general partnership.
Corporation	Unlimited number of shareholders; no limits on stock classes or voting arrangements. Ownership and management of the business are separate. Shareholders in public corporations are not involved in daily management decisions; in private or closely held corporations, owners are more likely to participate in managing the business.	Profits and losses are taxed at corporate rates. Profits are taxed again at individual rates when they are distributed to the investors as dividends.	Investor's liability is limited to the amount of his or her investment.	Expense and complexity of incorporation vary from state to state; can be costly from a tax perspective. In a public corporation, shareholders may trade their shares on the open market; in a private corporation shareholders must find a buyer for their shares to recoup their investment.

Sole Proprietorships

A **sole proprietorship** is a business owned by one person (although it may have many employees), and it is the easiest and least expensive form of business to start. Many farms, retail establishments, and small service businesses are sole proprietorships, as are many home-based businesses (such as caterers, consultants, and computer programmers). Many of the local businesses you frequent around your college campus are likely to be sole proprietorships.

sole proprietorship
Business owned by a single individual

Advantages of Sole Proprietorships

A sole proprietorship has many advantages, starting with ease of establishment. About the only legal requirement is obtaining the necessary business licenses. Another advantage is the satisfaction of working for yourself. As a sole proprietor, you can make your own decisions, such as which hours to work (beware the old joke that working for yourself means you get to choose which 80 hours you work every week), whom to hire, what prices to charge, whether to expand, and whether to shut down. You also get to keep all the after-tax profits, and, depending on your filing status and taxable income, you may be obligated to pay less as a sole proprietor compared to what you would pay as a corporation (although you are also obligated to pay self-employment tax as a sole proprietor).

As a sole proprietor, you also have the advantage of privacy; you do not have to reveal your performance or plans to anyone. Although you may need to provide financial information to a banker if you need a loan, and you must provide certain financial information when you file tax returns, you do not have to prepare any reports for outsiders as you would if the company were a public corporation.

Disadvantages of Sole Proprietorships

One major drawback of a sole proprietorship is the proprietor's **unlimited liability**. From a legal standpoint, the owner and the business are one and the same. Any legal damages or debts incurred by the business are the owner's responsibility. As a sole proprietor, you might have to sell personal assets, such as your home, to satisfy a business debt. And if someone sues you over a business matter, from dissatisfaction with a product to slipping on ice in your parking lot, you might lose everything you own if you do not have the proper business insurance.

unlimited liability
Legal condition under which any damages or debts attributable to the business can also be attached to the owner because the two have no separate legal existence

partnership
Unincorporated business owned and operated by two or more persons under a voluntary legal association

In some cases, the sole proprietor's independence can also be a drawback because it means that the business depends on the talents and managerial skills of one person. If problems crop up, the sole proprietor may not recognize them or may be too proud to seek help, especially given the high cost of hiring experienced managers and professional consultants. Other disadvantages include the difficulty of a single-person operation obtaining large sums of capital and the limited life of a sole proprietorship. Although some sole proprietors pass their businesses on to their heirs as part of their estate, the owner's death may mean the demise of the business. And even if the business does transfer to an heir, the founder's unique skills may have been crucial to the successful operation of the business.

Partnerships

If starting a business on your own seems a little intimidating, you might decide to share the risks and rewards of going into business with a partner. In that case, you would form a **partnership**—a legal association of two or more people as co-owners of a business for profit. You and your partners would share the profits and losses of the business and perhaps the management responsibilities. Your partnership might remain a small, two-person operation or it might have multiple partners, and many professional service firms do.

Sole proprietorship offers some compelling benefits, but they must be weighed against the financial risks and limitations.

general partnership
Partnership in which all partners have the right to participate as co-owners and are individually liable for the business's debts

limited partnership
Partnership composed of one or more general partners and one or more partners whose liability is usually limited to the amount of their capital investment

Partnerships are of two basic types. In a **general partnership**, all partners are considered equal by law, and all are liable for the business's debts. If the business goes bankrupt, all the partners have to dig into their own pockets to satisfy creditors. To guard against personal liability exposure, some organizations choose to form a **limited partnership**. Under this type of partnership, one or more persons act as *general partners* who run the business, while the remaining partners are passive investors (that is, they are not involved in managing the business). These partners are called *limited partners* because their liability (the amount of money they can lose) is limited to the amount of their capital contribution. Many states now recognize *limited liability partnerships* (LLPs) in which all partners in the business are limited partners and have only limited liability for the debts and obligations of the partnership. The LLP was invented to protect members of partnerships from being wiped out by claims against their firms. Most states restrict LLPs to certain types of professionals such as attorneys, physicians, dentists, and accountants.[2] Of the three forms of business ownership, partnerships are the least common (see Exhibit 5.2).

Advantages of Partnerships

Proprietorships and partnerships have some of the same advantages. Like proprietorships, partnerships are easy to form. Partnerships also provide the same potential tax advantages as proprietorships.

However, in a couple of respects, partnerships are superior to sole proprietorships, largely because there's strength in numbers. When you have several people putting up their money, you can start a more ambitious enterprise. In addition, the diversity of skills that good partners bring to an organization leads to innovation in products, services, and processes, which improves your chances of success.[3] The partnership form of ownership also broadens the pool of capital available to the business. Not only do the partners' personal assets support a larger borrowing capacity but the ability to obtain financing increases because general partners are legally responsible for paying off the debts of the group. Finally, by forming a partnership you increase the chances that the organization will endure, because new partners can be drawn into the business to replace those who die or retire. For example, even though the original partners in the several accounting firms that eventually became industry giant KPMG (the roots of which stretch back to 1870) died many years ago, the company continues.

Disadvantages of Partnerships

Except in limited liability partnerships, at least one member of every partnership must be a general partner. All general partners have unlimited liability. Thus, if one of the firm's partners makes a serious mistake and is sued by a disgruntled client, all general

EXHIBIT 5.2

Forms of Business Ownership in the United States

The most popular form of business ownership is sole proprietorship, followed by corporations, then partnerships.

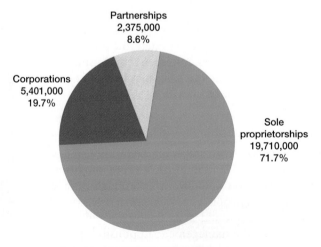

Partnerships
2,375,000
8.6%

Corporations
5,401,000
19.7%

Sole proprietorships
19,710,000
71.7%

Approximate number and percentages of existing firms in the United States

partners are financially accountable. General partners are also responsible for any debts incurred by the partnership.

Another disadvantage of partnerships is the potential for interpersonal problems. Difficulties can arise when each partner wants to be responsible for managing the organization. Electing a managing partner to lead the organization may diminish the conflicts, but disagreements are still possible. Moreover, the partnership may have to face the question of what to do with unproductive partners. And if a partner wants to leave the firm, conflicts can arise over claims on the firm's profits and on capital the partner invested. Provisions for handling the departure and addition of partners are usually covered in the partnership agreement.

Keeping It Together: The Partnership Agreement

A *partnership agreement* is a written document that states all the terms of operating the partnership by spelling out the partners' rights and responsibilities. Although the law does not require a written partnership agreement, it is wise to work with a lawyer to develop one. One of the most important features of such an agreement is to address sources of conflict that could result in battles between partners. The agreement spells out such details as the division of profits, decision-making authority, expected contributions, and dispute resolution. Moreover, a key element of this document is the buy/sell agreement, which defines the steps a partner must take to sell his or her partnership interest or what will happen if one of the partners dies.

Corporations

A **corporation** is a legal entity, distinct from any individual persons, with the power to own property and conduct business. Regardless of how many owners a corporation has (some have thousands of owners), the law generally treats the corporation the same way it treats an individual person. The modern corporation evolved in the nineteenth century when large sums of capital were needed to build railroads, steel mills, and manufacturing plants. Such endeavors required so much money that no single individual or group of partners could hope to raise it all. The solution was to sell *shares* in the business to numerous investors, who would get a cut of the profits in exchange for their money. These investors got a chance to vote on certain issues that might affect the value of their investment, but they were not involved in managing day-to-day operations. The investors were protected from the risks associated with such large undertakings by having their liability limited to the amount of their investment.

It was a good solution, and the corporation quickly became a vital force in the nation's economy. As rules and regulations developed to define what corporations could and could not do, they acquired the legal attributes of people. Like you, a corporation can receive, own, and transfer property; make contracts; sue; and be sued. Unlike the case with sole proprietorships and partnerships, a corporation's legal status and obligations exist independently of its owners.

Ownership

The corporation is owned by its **shareholders**, who are issued shares of stock in return for their investments. These shares are represented by a **stock certificate**, and they may be sold or bequeathed (given to upon death of the owner) to someone else. As a result, the company's ownership may change drastically over time while the company and its management remain intact (as long as the company is economically sound). The corporation's unlimited life span, combined with its ability to raise capital, gives it the potential for significant growth.

Common Stock   Most stock issued by corporations is **common stock**. Owners of common stock have voting rights and get one vote for each share of stock they own. Depending on the corporation, they can elect the company's board of directors in

corporation
Legally chartered enterprise having most of the legal rights of a person, including the right to conduct business, to own and sell property, to borrow money, and to sue or be sued; owners of the corporation enjoy limited liability

shareholders
Owners of a corporation

stock certificate
Document that proves stock ownership

common stock
Shares whose owners have voting rights and have the last claim on distributed profits and assets

addition to voting on major policies that will affect ownership—such as mergers and acquisitions. Besides conferring voting privileges, common stock frequently pays **dividends**, payments to shareholders from the company's profits. Dividends can be paid in cash or stock (called *stock dividends*). They are declared by the board of directors, but their payment is not mandatory. For example, some companies, especially young or rapidly growing ones, pay no dividends. Instead, they reinvest their profits in new product research and development, equipment, buildings, and other assets so they can grow and earn future profits.

dividends
Distributions of corporate assets to shareholders in the form of cash or other assets

Although dividends can be an attractive benefit of investing in common stock, the reason many investors buy stock is the opportunity to eventually sell their shares for more than they paid for them. Although both the overall stock market and individual stocks rise and fall over time, stocks have historically been a solid investment. However, investors have no guarantee that stocks will appreciate in value, so this risk must always be considered.

preferred stock
Shares that give their owners first claim on a company's dividends and assets after paying all debts

Preferred Stock   In contrast to common stock, **preferred stock** does not usually carry voting rights. It does, however, give preferred shareholders the right of first claim on the corporation's assets (in the form of dividends) after all the company's debts have been paid. This right is especially important if the company ever goes out of business. Moreover, preferred shareholders get their dividends before common shareholders do. The amount of preferred dividend is usually set (or fixed) at the time the preferred stock is issued and can provide investors with a source of steady income. Like common stock, however, dividends on preferred stock may be omitted in times of financial hardship. Still, most preferred stock is *cumulative preferred stock,* which means that any unpaid dividends must be paid before dividends are paid to common shareholders.

Public Versus Private Ownership   The ownership of corporations can be arranged in several ways, which occasionally leads to some confusion about terminology. The stock of a **private corporation** is held by only a few individuals or companies and is not publicly traded. By withholding their stock from public sale, the owners retain complete control over their operations and ownership. Such well-known companies as Hallmark Cards and Global Hyatt (owners of the Hyatt brand of hotel chains) have opted to remain private corporations (also referred to as *closed corporations* or *closely held companies*). These companies finance their operating costs and growth from either company

private corporation
Company owned by private individuals or companies

public corporation
Corporation that actively sells stock on the open market

earnings or other sources, such as bank loans. Doctors, lawyers, and some other professionals often join forces in a special type of private corporation called a *professional corporation*. As with other private corporations, shares in these professional corporations are not available to the public.

Although the Hyatt family of upscale hotel chains is one of the largest hospitality companies in the world, the company's owners, the Pritzker family of Chicago, have opted to retain private control.

In contrast, the stock of a **public corporation** such as Google is held by and available for sale to the general public—including not only individual investors but also mutual funds, nonprofit organizations, and other companies. These companies are said to be *publicly held* or *publicly traded*. Whenever you hear discussions about "corporations," people are nearly always talking about public corporations. These are the stocks you see listed in the newspaper stock tables and on various websites that offer investing information.

The primary reason for "going public" is to help finance the enterprise. In addition to providing a ready supply of capital, public ownership has other advantages and disadvantages. Among the advantages are increased *liquidity*, enhanced visibility, and the establishment of an independent market value for the company. Moreover, having a publicly traded stock gives companies the option of using their stock to acquire other firms.

Nevertheless, selling stock to the public also has distinct disadvantages: (1) The cost of going public is high (up to hundreds of thousands of dollars or more), (2) the filing requirements with the Securities and Exchange Commission (SEC) are burdensome, (3) ownership control is reduced, (4) management must be ready to handle the administrative and legal demands of heightened public exposure, and (5) the company is subjected to the stock market's incessant demand for quarterly results. Some companies find it just isn't worth the trouble. Kohler, a highly regarded maker of kitchen and bath fixtures based in Kohler, Wisconsin, has been in family hands for more than a hundred years—and plans to stay that way so it can develop strategies over decades without quarterly stock market pressures.[4]

Advantages of Corporations

No other form of business ownership can match the success of the corporation in bringing together money, resources, and talent; in accumulating assets; and in creating wealth. As it grows, a corporation gains from a diverse labor pool, greater financing options, and expanded research-and-development capabilities. The corporation has certain inherent qualities that make it the best vehicle for reaching those objectives, including limited liability. Although a corporate entity can assume tremendous liabilities, it is the corporation that is liable and not the various shareholders.

In addition to limited liability, corporations that sell stock to the general public have the advantage of **liquidity**, which means that investors can easily convert their stock into cash by selling it on the open market. This option makes buying stock in a corporation attractive to many investors. In contrast, liquidating the assets of a sole proprietorship or a partnership can be difficult. Moreover, shareholders of public corporations can easily transfer their ownership by selling their shares to someone else. Thus, corporations tend to be in a better position than proprietorships and partnerships to make long-term plans, with their unlimited life span and funding available through the sale of stock. As they grow, corporations can benefit from the diverse talents and experience of a large pool of employees and managers.

liquidity
The level of ease with which an asset can be converted to cash

Keep in mind that a company need not be large to incorporate. Most corporations, like most businesses, are relatively small, and most small corporations are privately held. The big ones, however, are *really* big (see Exhibit 5.3). At least ten corporations in the United States now generate more than $100 billion in annual revenue.[5] The workforce at Wal-Mart, the biggest U.S. corporation, is larger than the population of more than a dozen U.S. states.[6]

Disadvantages of Corporations

Corporations are not without some disadvantages. The administrative time and costs can be burdensome. Moreover, top executives must devote considerable time and energy to meeting with shareholders, financial analysts, and the news media. By one estimate, CEOs of large publicly held corporations can spend as much as 40 percent of their time on these externally focused activities.[7] In addition, corporations are taxed twice. They must pay federal and state corporate income tax on the company's profits, and individual shareholders must pay income taxes on their share of the company's profits received as dividends.

Another drawback pertains to publicly owned corporations. As mentioned earlier, such corporations are required by the government to publish information about their finances and operations. Disclosing financial information increases the company's vulnerability to competitors and to those who might want to take over control of the company against the wishes of the existing management. Entrepreneurs who've spent years building companies can even be kicked out of the company if enough other shareholders think it's time for a leadership change. Disclosure also increases the pressure on corporate managers to achieve short-term growth and earnings targets in order to satisfy shareholders and to attract potential investors.

EXHIBIT 5.3

U.S. Corporate Titans

Here are the 25 largest public corporations in the United States, as ranked by *Fortune* magazine.

RANK	COMPANY	REVENUE ($ MILLIONS)
1	Wal-Mart Stores	351,139
2	ExxonMobil	347,254
3	General Motors	207,349
4	Chevron	200,567
5	ConocoPhillips	172,451
6	General Electric	168,307
7	Ford Motor	160,126
8	Citigroup	146,777
9	Bank of America Corp.	117,017
10	American Intl. Group	113,194
11	J.P. Morgan Chase & Co.	99,973
12	Berkshire Hathaway	98,539
13	Verizon Communications	93,221
14	Hewlett-Packard	91,658
15	IBM	91,424
16	Valero Energy	91,051
17	Home Depot	90,837
18	McKesson	88,050
19	Cardinal Health	81,895
20	Morgan Stanley	76,688
21	UnitedHealth Group	71,542
22	Merrill Lynch	70,591
23	Altria Group	70,324
24	Goldman Sachs Group	69,353
25	Procter & Gamble	68,222

Special Types of Corporations

S corporation
Corporation with no more than 75 shareholders that may be taxed as a partnership; also known as a subchapter S corporation

Certain types of corporations enjoy special privileges provided they adhere to strict guidelines and rules. An **S corporation**, or *subchapter S corporation*, essentially combines the tax advantages of a partnership with the fund-raising options of a corporation. (The S corporation distinction is made only for federal income tax purposes; otherwise, in terms of legal characteristics, it is no different from any other corporation.) In addition, income and tax deductions from the business flow directly to the owners, who are taxed at individual income tax rates, just as they are in a partnership. Corporations seeking "S" status must meet certain criteria: (1) They must have no more than 75 investors, none of whom may be nonresident aliens; (2) they must be a domestic (U.S.) corporation; and (3) they can issue only one class of common stock, which means that all stock must share the same dividend and liquidation rights (but may have different voting rights).[8]

limited liability companies (LLCs)
Organizations that combine the benefits of S corporations and limited partnerships without the drawbacks of either

Limited liability companies (LLCs) are flexible business entities that combine the tax advantages of a partnership with the personal liability protection of a corporation. Furthermore, LLCs are not restricted in the number of shareholders they can have, and members' participation in management is not restricted as it is in limited partnerships.

Members of an LLC normally adopt an operating agreement (similar to a partnership agreement) to govern the entity's operation and management. These agreements generally are flexible and permit owners to structure the allocation of income and losses any way they desire, as long as certain tax rules are followed. In addition, the agreements can be designed to meet the special needs of owners, such as special voting rights, management controls, and buyout options. The only limit to what can be done is the owners' imagination.[9] The advantages of LLCs over other forms have made them quite popular in recent years. Although LLCs are favored by many small companies, they are by no means limited to small firms. Some fair-sized and well-known firms have gone the LLC route, including BMW of North America, the Albertsons's grocery store chain, and GMAC, a $2 billion finance company.[10]

Some corporations are not independent entities; that is, they are owned by a single entity. **Subsidiary corporations**, for instance, are partially or wholly owned by another corporation known as a **parent company**, which supervises the operations of the subsidiary. A **holding company** is a special type of parent company that owns other companies for investment reasons and usually exercises little operating control over those subsidiaries.

To further complicate matters, corporations can also be classified according to where they do business. An *alien corporation* operates in the United States but is incorporated in another country. A *foreign corporation,* sometimes called an *out-of-state corporation,* is incorporated in one state (frequently the state of Delaware, where incorporation laws are more lenient) but does business in several other states where it is registered. And a *domestic corporation* does business only in the state where it is chartered (incorporated).

Corporate Governance

Although a corporation's common shareholders own the business, they are rarely involved in managing it, particularly if the corporation is publicly traded. Instead, the common shareholders elect a *board of directors* to represent them, and the directors, in turn, select the corporation's top officers, who actually run the company (see Exhibit 5.4). The term **corporate governance** can be used in a broad sense to describe all the policies, procedures, relationships, and systems in place to oversee the successful and legal operation of the enterprise; media coverage tends to define governance in a more narrow sense: as the responsibilities and performance of the board of directors specifically.

The center of power in a corporation usually lies with the **chief executive officer (CEO)**. Together with the chief financial officer (CFO) and other "c-level" executives, such as the chief technology officer (CTO), chief information officer (CIO), and the chief operating officer (COO)—titles vary from one corporation to the next—the CEO is responsible for establishing company policies, managing corporate direction, and making the big decisions that will affect the company's growth and competitive position. The CEO may also be the chairman of the board, the president of the corporation, or sometimes all three.

Shareholders   Shareholders of a corporation can be individuals, other companies, nonprofit organizations, pension funds, and mutual funds. All shareholders who own voting shares are invited to an annual meeting where top executives present the previous

---

subsidiary corporations
Corporations whose stock is owned entirely or almost entirely by another corporation

parent company
Company that owns most, if not all, of another company's stock and that takes an active part in managing that other company

holding company
Company that owns most, if not all, of another company's stock but does not actively participate in the management of that other company

corporate governance
In a broad sense, describes the policies, procedures, relationships, and systems in place to oversee the successful and legal operation of the enterprise; in a narrow sense, describes the responsibilities and performance of the board of directors

chief executive officer (CEO)
Person appointed by a corporation's board of directors to carry out the board's policies and supervise the activities of the corporation

---

EXHIBIT 5.4 Corporate Governance

In theory the shareholders of a corporation own the business, but in practice they elect others to run it.

Shareholders → Elect → Board of directors → Appoints → Officers → Hire → Employees

Volkswagen executives address shareholders at the company's annual meeting.

proxy
Document authorizing another person to vote on behalf of a shareholder in a corporation

shareholder activism
Advocacy by individual or institutional shareholders, using their status as shareholders to influence management policies and decisions

board of directors
Group of people, elected by the shareholders, who have the ultimate authority in guiding the affairs of a corporation

Every Home Depot director must make formal visits to at least 20 stores each year to gain hands-on knowledge of the company's operation.

year's results and plans for the coming year and shareholders vote on various resolutions that may be before the board. Those who cannot attend the annual meeting in person vote by **proxy**, signing and returning a slip of paper that authorizes management to vote on their behalf. Because shareholders elect the directors, in theory they are the ultimate governing body of the corporation. In practice, however, most individual shareholders in large corporations—where the shareholders may number in the millions—usually accept the recommendations of management.

The more shareholders a company has, the less tangible the influence each shareholder has on the corporation. However, *institutional investors* (such as pension funds, insurance companies, mutual funds, religious organizations, and college endowment funds) with large holdings of stock can have considerable influence over management. For example, the 275 institutions that make up the Interfaith Center on Corporate Responsibility (ICCR) collectively control more than $100 billion in corporate stock.[11]

Shareholder activism, in which shareholders press management on matters ranging from executive pay to many of the corporate social responsibility issues discussed in Chapter 4, has become an increasingly visible factor in corporate governance. Activist shareholders are becoming better organized and more sophisticated in proposals they present, forcing boards to pay more attention to the concerns they raise.[12] Not everyone is happy with this development. Those who lean toward the minimalist view of CSR (see page 38) worry that such activism is beginning to undermine the ability of corporate boards to do their work effectively.[13]

Board of Directors   The **board of directors** in a corporation represents the shareholders and is responsible for declaring dividends, guiding corporate affairs, reviewing long-term strategic plans, selecting corporate officers, and overseeing financial performance. Depending on the size of the company, the board might have anywhere from 3 to 35 directors, although 15 to 25 is the typical range for traditional corporations and perhaps 5 to 10 for smaller or newer corporations. Directors are usually paid a combination of an annual fee and stock options, the right to buy company shares at a specified price.

The board's actual involvement in running the business varies from one company to another, from passive boards that contribute little to the management of the organization to extremely involved boards that participate in strategic decision making.[14] At Intel, for instance, the board's role has shifted in the past few years from passive oversight to active involvement. The job is demanding: Directors are expected to understand the company's complex technologies and to be able to analyze the management of Intel facilities worldwide. Directors spend an average of 300 hours a year on Intel business, a significant amount of time for people who often have companies of their own to run.[15]

In sharp contrast, some of the biggest corporate scandals of the past decade involved passive boards that failed in their oversight responsibilities. The board at failed telecom giant WorldCom once approved a $6 billion acquisition of another company during a 35-minute conference call—with no documents to review. And without even knowing it had done so, the board gave two top executives the authority to borrow unlimited amounts of money from the company. Investigators assert that if the board had questioned WorldCom's growing debt load, it could've stopped or at least slowed the company's descent into bankruptcy.[16]

Much of the attention focused on corporate reform in recent years has zeroed in on boards, but the challenge is not a simple one.

In response to both outside pressure and management's recognition of how important an effective board is, corporations are wrestling with a variety of board-related issues:

- *Composition.* Simply identifying the type of people who should be on the board can be a major challenge. The ideal board is a balanced group of seasoned executives, each of whom can "bring something to the table" that helps the corporation, such as extensive contacts in the industry, manufacturing experience, insight into global issues, and so on. The ratio of insiders (executives) to outsiders (independent directors) is another hot topic. The Sarbanes-Oxley legislation passed in the aftermath of the Enron and WorldCom collapses requires that the majority of directors be independent so they can provide an objective counterbalance to the CEO and other executives. However, in order to be effective, these outsiders must also have enough knowledge about the inner workings of the organization to make informed decisions. Diversity is also important, to ensure that adequate attention is paid to issues that affect stakeholders who have been historically underrepresented on corporate boards.[17]

- *Education.* Overseeing the modern corporation is an almost unimaginably complex task. Board members are expected to understand everything from government regulations to financial management to executive compensation strategies—in addition to the inner workings of the corporation itself. A key area of concern is the number of directors who aren't well versed enough in finance to understand their companies' financial statements; this problem has led a number of companies to start educational programs for directors.[18]

- *Liability.* One of the more controversial reform issues has been the potential for directors to be held legally and financially liable for misdeeds of the companies they oversee. In a few extreme cases, directors have even been forced to pay fines out of their own pockets, although this is quite rare.[19]

- *Recruiting challenges.* By now, you've probably gathered that being an effective director in today's business environment is a tough job—so tough that good candidates may start to think twice about accepting directorships. Good board members are more vital than ever, though, so corporate and government leaders have no choice but to solve these challenges.

Understanding Mergers, Acquisitions, and Alliances

As Google realized when it assessed the market for online display advertising, companies occasionally discover they don't have the right mix of resources and capabilities to achieve their goals. If managers decide that developing needed resources and capabilities internally isn't the right answer, they then have a choice of purchasing or partnering with a firm that has what they need.

Mergers and Acquisitions

Businesses can combine permanently through either *mergers* or *acquisitions*. The two terms are often discussed together, usually with the shorthand phrase "M&A," or used interchangeably (although they are technically different). In fact, sometimes an acquisition will be announced to the public and to employees as a merger to help the acquired company save face.[20] The business intentions and outcomes of a merger or an acquisition are usually the same, although the legal and tax ramifications can be quite different, depending on the details of the transaction.

In a **merger**, two companies join to form a single entity. Traditionally, mergers took place between companies of roughly equal size and stature, but mergers between companies of vastly difference sizes is common today. Companies can merge either by pooling their resources or by one company purchasing the assets of the other.[21] Although not strictly a merger, a **consolidation**, in which two companies create a new, third entity that then purchases the two original companies, is often lumped together with the other two merger approaches.[22] (Note that businesspeople and the media often use the term *consolidation* in two general senses: to describe any combination of two companies, merger or acquisition, and to describe situations in which a wave of mergers and acquisitions sweeps across an entire industry, reducing the number of competitors.)

In an **acquisition**, one company simply buys a controlling interest in the voting stock of another company. Unlike the real or presumed marriage of equals in a merger, the buyer is definitely the dominant player in an acquisition. In most acquisitions, the selling parties agree to be purchased; management is in favor of the deal and encourages shareholders to vote in favor of it as well. Since buyers frequently offer shareholders more than their shares are currently worth, sellers often have a motivation to sell. However, in a minority of situations, a buyer attempts to acquire a company against the wishes of management. In these **hostile takeovers**, the buyer tries to convince enough shareholders to go against management and vote to sell.

Buyers can offer sellers cash, stock in the acquiring company, or a combination of the two. Another option involves debt. A **leveraged buyout (LBO)** occurs when one or more individuals purchase a company's publicly traded stock by using borrowed funds. The debt is expected to be repaid with funds generated by the company's operations and, often, by the sale of some of its assets. For an LBO to be successful, the acquired company must have a reasonably priced stock, and the acquirer must have easy access to borrowed funds. Unfortunately, in many cases, the buyer must make huge interest and principle payments on the debt, which then depletes the amount of cash that the company has for operations and growth.

Whether it's technically a merger or an acquisition, the combination can take one of several forms (usually all referred to as "mergers" for simplicity's sake):

- A *vertical merger* occurs when a company purchases a complementary company at a different level in the value chain, such as when a company purchases one of its suppliers or one of its customers. For instance, a car manufacturer acquiring a windshield manufacturer would be a vertical merger since the two companies complement each other in the creation of automobiles.

- A *horizontal merger* involves two similar companies at the same level, such as a combination of two car manufacturers, two windshield manufacturers, two banks, or two retail chains. Because these mergers are often between two competitors, regulators review them closely to make sure the combined firm won't have monopoly power.

- In a *conglomerate merger*, the two firms offer dissimilar products or services, often in widely different industries.[23] Conglomeration was a popular strategy in the 1950s and 1960s, based on the hope that by diversifying into a variety of industries at once, the company could survive market downturns in one or a few of them. The stock prices of conglomerates often didn't live up to the hope, and the strategy's popularity declined in the 1970s.[24] Conglomerates didn't disappear, of course; the current list includes a number of large and successful companies, such as United Technologies and General Electric. In addition, a new twist on the conglomerate model has appeared in recent years, in which a company that is good in a particular area of business acquires underperforming companies that can benefit from that

merger
Combination of two companies in which one company purchases the other and assumes control of its property and liabilities

consolidation
Combination of two or more companies in which the old companies cease to exist and a new enterprise is created

acquisition
Form of business combination in which one company buys another company's voting stock

hostile takeovers
Situations in which an outside party buys enough stock in a corporation to take control against the wishes of the board of directors and corporate officers

leveraged buyout (LBO)
Situation in which individuals or groups of investors purchase companies primarily with debt secured by the company's assets

skill set. For instance, Danaher, an industrial company based in Washington, D.C., has acquired multiple companies that now take advantage of Danaher's ability to improve operating efficiency. By imposing the "Danaher Business System," modeled after the Toyota Production System (see page 93), on acquired companies, Danaher continues to post impressive financial results year after year.[25]

- A *market extension merger* combines firms that offer similar products and services in different geographic markets. Bank of America, which already had a strong presence in the West and Southeast, gained an instant presence in the Northeast when it acquired FleetBoston.[26]

- Companies pursue a *product extension merger* when they need to expand their offerings of goods or services and lack the time or resources to develop those products internally. This is the sort of merger Google was considering when it explored options for expanding its display advertising business. Such mergers are particularly common in the technology sector, as companies try to add missing pieces to their skill sets and product portfolios. For instance, in one recent period, information technology giant IBM acquired more than 60 companies. As the company's chief financial officer, Mark Loughridge, said, "In today's rapidly changing marketplace, one must look at all sources of innovation to sustain one's value proposition to the customer."[27]

CEO Dick Heckmann led K2 Sports on an acquisition binge to expand beyond winter skis into a sporting goods company for all seasons.

Advantages of Mergers and Acquisitions

Companies pursue mergers and acquisitions for a wide variety of reasons: They might hope to reduce costs by eliminating redundant resources, increase their buying power as a result of their larger size, increase revenue by cross-selling products to each other's customers, increase market share by combining product lines to provide more comprehensive offerings, eliminate overcapacity, or gain access to new expertise, systems, and teams of employees who already know how to work together. Bringing a company under new ownership can also be an opportunity to replace or improve inept management and thereby help a company improve its performance.[28]

Often these advantages are grouped under umbrella terms such as *economies of scale, efficiencies,* or *synergies,* which generally mean that the benefits of working together will be greater than if each company continued to operate independently. For example, when the giant Italian optics firm Luxottica acquired Oakley, the specialty maker of sports sunglasses based in Foothill Ranch, California, the stated reasons for the deal included synergies in both materials sourcing and product distribution. The goal of the acquisition is to grow the Oakley brand by taking advantage of Luxottica's worldwide network of materials suppliers and retail outlets.[29]

Learning from Business Blunders

Oops: US Airways's acquisition of America West was supposed to yield millions of dollars of synergistic cost savings and millions of dollars of new revenue as the airlines combined their complementary regional market coverage. Initially, US Airways's management received high marks from some observers for its careful approach to combining the two firms. However, two years later, their operations still hadn't been merged, so the hoped-for cost savings were still that—just hopes. Why the huge delay? The airlines continued to operate as two parallel companies because they were unable to get the two separate union groups to agree on new contracts. Key issues included resolving seniority ranking among employees of the combined firm and melding two corporate cultures. These aren't uncommon problems in a merger, but in the words of one industry analyst, US Airways's management team "took its eye off the ball" by launching a hostile and ultimately unsuccessful takeover bid of yet another airline (Delta), when it should've stayed focused on resolving the problems of the America West acquisition.

What You Can Learn: Merging two companies is an enormous task that requires sustained, hands-on attention from upper management. Completing the deal is only the beginning of the process, not the end. Executives need to stay engaged to make sure everything from computer systems to leadership philosophies are harmonized and integrated—particularly in the airline industry, with its long history of contentious labor-management relationships.

Disadvantages of Mergers and Acquisitions

While the advantages can be compelling, joining two companies is a complex process because it involves virtually every aspect of both organizations. For instance, executives have to agree on how the combination will be financed and how the power will be transferred and shared. Marketing departments need to figure out how to blend advertising campaigns and sales forces. Incompatible information systems often need to be rebuilt or replaced in order to operate together seamlessly. Companies often must deal with layoffs, transfers, and changes in job titles and work assignments. And through it all, the enterprise needs to keep its eye on customer service, accounting, and every other function.

Because of these risks and difficulties, two-thirds of mergers fail to meet their stated goals.[30] Some of the worst deals can destroy billions of dollars of market valuation (the total value of a company's stock). The AOL-Time Warner merger in 2001, widely regarded as one of the worst ever, wiped out $200 billion of shareholder wealth.[31] Every situation is unique, of course, but there are recurring themes. For instance, companies often borrow immense amounts of money to acquire a firm, and the loan payments on this corporate debt gobble up cash needed to run the business. Moreover, managers must help combine the operations of the two entities, pulling them away from their normal day-to-day responsibilities.

Another major obstacle companies face when combining forces is merging two corporate cultures. As you'll read in Chapter 12, a company's *culture* is a general term that describes the way people in a given organization approach the day-to-day business of running a company. Culture includes not only management style and practices but even the way people dress and how they communicate. *Culture clash* occurs when two joining companies have different beliefs about what is really important, how to make decisions, how to supervise people, how to communicate, and other fundamental aspects of running the business. Experts note that in too many deals the acquiring company imposes its values and management systems on the acquired company without any regard to what worked well there.

Without question, some mergers and acquisitions are beneficial to companies and shareholders in both the short term and the long term. However, managers need to approach mergers and acquisitions with caution by answering these questions: Will the regulatory environment change? How will competitors respond? Do the expected gains justify the up-front costs and disruption to business operations? Will the cultures, systems, processes, and product lines of the two companies blend well? Executives will continue to believe they can beat the odds and craft successful deals, but without seeking honest answers to these questions first, they're likely to only find themselves adding to the depressing statistics about mergers and acquisitions.

Trends in Mergers and Acquisitions

Each year, a few megadeals catch everyone's attention, but in reality, thousands of mergers and acquisitions occur every year. Chances are fairly good that at least one of the companies you will work for during your career will be involved in a merger or acquisition at some point.

The number of deals can vary widely from year to year, both within individual industries and across the economy as a whole. For instance, when a new industry or business model emerges, the market often fills up quickly with more suppliers than the number of customers can support. The stronger players then frequently acquire smaller, weaker players, reducing the number of suppliers left in the market (this is the *industry consolidation* referred to earlier).

Mergers and acquisitions can also occur in waves across the economy, based mainly on the amount of money companies have to spend and the availability of low-cost financing. Merger activity tapered off through the 1970s, during the waning years of the conglomeration age. The 1980s saw a brief surge in activity but nothing like the boom of the late 1990s, which was fueled by rapid price increases in technology stocks. Tens of thousands of mergers and acquisitions took place during this period, including a number of huge deals in media, automobiles, oil, and banking.[32]

However, when the stocks that financed so much of this activity cooled or collapsed, the number of mergers and acquisitions fell off rapidly as well. Then as the stock market began to show signs of recovery in 2003 and 2004, deal activity began to pick up again. By the time Google faced its build-or-buy decision regarding display advertising in 2007, the pace of buying and selling companies was at an all-time high. This surge was partly fueled by billions of dollars from pooled investment funds known as *private equity*. Peaks in M&A activity can feel like feeding frenzies, with companies being bought and sold at a dizzying rate as buyers try to keep their competitors from snatching up valuable finds. At the time of Google's decision, deals were flying so thick and fast that one investment manager said, "Your head is constantly spinning. Every single industry is being restructured."[33]

Merger-and-Acquisition Defenses

Every corporation that sells stock to the general public is potentially vulnerable to takeover by any individual or company that buys enough shares to gain a controlling interest, although as mentioned earlier, most takeovers are friendly acquisitions welcomed by the acquired company. A hostile takeover can be launched in one of two ways: by tender offer or by proxy fight. In a *tender offer,* the buyer, or *raider,* as this party is sometimes called, offers to buy a certain number of shares of stock in the corporation at a specific price. The price offered is generally more, sometimes considerably more, than the current stock price so that shareholders are motivated to sell. The raider hopes to get enough shares to take control of the corporation and to replace the existing board of directors and management. In a *proxy fight,* the raider launches a public relations battle for shareholder votes, hoping to enlist enough votes to oust the board and management. Proxy fights usually favor insiders, however; corporate boards and executives have devised a number of schemes to defend themselves against unwanted takeovers:

- *The poison pill.* This plan, triggered by a takeover attempt, makes the company less valuable in some way to the potential raider; the idea is to discourage the takeover from actually happening. A good example is a special sale of newly issued stock to current stockholders at prices below the market value of the company's existing stock. Such action increases the number of shares the raider has to buy, making the takeover more expensive. Many shareholders believe that poison pills are bad for a company because they can entrench weak management and discourage takeover attempts that would improve company value. Southwest Airlines and Yahoo! are among the companies whose shareholders have been trying to convince management to drop poison pills in recent years.[34]

- *The shark repellent.* This tactic is more direct; it is simply a requirement that stockholders representing a large majority of shares approve of any takeover attempt. Such a plan is viable only if the management team has the support of the majority of shareholders.

- *The white knight.* A white night is a third company that steps in to acquire a company that is in danger of being swallowed up in a hostile takeover. The takeover target is still purchased, but at least it happens on more positive terms.

Companies that don't want to be acquired can be quite aggressive when they need to be. To fight off a takeover attempt by a private investor, the British retail chain Marks & Spencer convinced shareholders not to sell out by demonstrating that it was serious about improving performance: The company quickly fired its CEO and other senior executives, abandoned costly plans to launch a chain of home furniture stores, and sold a credit card company it owned and gave the proceeds to shareholders as dividends.[35]

Strategic Alliances and Joint Ventures

Chapter 3 discussed strategic alliances and joint ventures from the perspective of international expansion, defining a *strategic alliance* as a long-term partnership between companies to jointly develop, produce, or sell products and a *joint venture* as a separate legal entity

Hey, Wanna Lose a Few Billion? Do We Have a Deal for You

If you were about to make a multibillion-dollar deal with the financial well-being of thousands of people on the line, but statistics suggested you had an 80 percent chance of failure, would you go for it? Sure you would, if you work in the slightly wacky world of corporate mergers and acquisitions.

Studies consistently show that the vast majority of mergers and acquisitions fail to meet their primary goal of increasing shareholder value—and half actually decrease value. During the deal-crazy period from 1995 to 2000, for instance, businesses around the world bought and sold each other to the tune of more than $12 trillion. Guess how much all that deal making increased shareholder value? It *decreased* net value by at least $1 trillion—that's more financial destruction than even the dot-com crash managed to generate. In many cases, the only people who win in these deals are the shareholders in acquired companies, when eager buyers shell out more for shares than they're really worth. It's no surprise that lots of investors are starting to wonder whose interests these boards have at stake.

Ethical concerns aside, how can so many otherwise talented people keep making so many mistakes? Although no one answer applies to every situation, experts cite these common mistakes:

- Companies often rush into deals in search of synergies but then fail to develop them.
- Mergers can drive customers away if they feel neglected while the two companies are busy with all the internal chores of stitching themselves together.
- Companies pay excessively high premiums for the companies they acquire.

- Managers are unable to reconcile differences in corporate cultures.

Why do companies keep merging and acquiring if the record of success is so disappointing? No doubt many managers believe they can beat the odds; others believe they have no choice but to acquire companies with resources they need. Samuel Thompson, director of the UCLA Law Center for the Study of Mergers and Acquisitions, offers a ray a hope, saying that mergers in the last few years have been more successful than deals in the past. IBM, for instance, has developed a comprehensive process for evaluating and implementing acquisitions. According to the company, its average acquisition doubles revenue within two years. Toro, a maker of lawn care equipment, also acknowledges the risks of deal making. One of its strategies is a "contra team" of senior executives, tasked with looking for weaknesses in any deal the company is considering. Such safeguards can keep companies from getting caught up in the sense of urgency and enthusiasm that often accompanies deal making.

Critical Thinking Questions

1. If you were on the board of directors at a company and the CEO announced plans to merge with a competitor, what types of questions would you want answered before you gave your approval? How would you view your ethical responsibilities in this situation?
2. If a CEO has the opportunity to merge with or acquire another company and is reasonably certain that the transaction will benefit shareholders, is the CEO obligated to pursue the deal? Why or why not?

established by the strategic partners. Strategic alliances can accomplish many of the same goals as a merger, consolidation, or acquisition without requiring a painstaking process of permanently integrating two companies.[36] They can help a company gain credibility in a new field, expand its market presence, gain access to technology, diversify offerings, and share best practices without forcing the partners to become permanently entangled. For example, Taser International, the maker of "stun guns" that allow police and other security personnel to incapacitate dangerous subjects, recently teamed up with iRobot to add taser capability to small robots.[37] Note that while strategic alliances may be simpler than full-scale mergers and acquisitions, they need to be entered into with equal care: Roughly half of all alliances fail to meet their objectives.[38]

How This Affects You

1. Have you (or someone you know) ever experienced a merger or acquisition as an employee? Was your job affected?
2. Have you ever experienced a merger or acquisition as a customer? In other words, has a company that you regularly do business with changed owners? Did customer service suffer during the transition of ownership?

Summary of Learning Objectives

1 List five advantages and four disadvantages of sole proprietorships.

Sole proprietorships have five advantages: (1) They are easy to establish, (2) they provide the owner with control and independence, (3) the owner reaps all the profits, (4) profits are taxed at individual rates, and (5) the company's plans and financial performance remain private. The four main disadvantages of a sole proprietorship are (1) the company's financial resources are usually limited, (2) management talent may be thin, (3) the owner is liable for the debts and damages incurred by the business, and (4) the business may cease when the owner dies.

2 List five advantages and two disadvantages of partnerships.

In addition to being easy to establish and having profits taxed at individual rates, partnerships offer a greater ability to obtain financing, longevity, and a broader base of skills. The two main disadvantages of partnerships are unlimited liability for general partners and the potential for personality and authority conflicts.

3 Explain the differences between common and preferred stock from a shareholder's perspective.

Common shareholders can vote and can share in the company's profits through discretionary dividends and adjustments in the market value of their stock. In other words, they can profit from their investment if the value of the stock rises above the price they paid for it, or they can lose money if the value of the stock falls below the price they paid for it. In contrast, preferred shareholders cannot vote, but they can get a fixed return (dividend) on their investment and a priority claim on assets after creditors.

4 Highlight the advantages and disadvantages of public stock ownership.

Public stock ownership offers a company increased liquidity, enhanced visibility, financial flexibility, and an independently established market value for the stock. The disadvantages of public stock ownership are high costs, burdensome filing requirements, loss of ownership control, heightened public exposure, and loss of direct control over the market value of the company's stock.

5 Cite four advantages and three disadvantages of corporations.

Because corporations are a separate legal entity, they have the power to raise large sums of capital, they offer the shareholders protection from liability, they provide liquidity for investors, and they have an unlimited life span. In exchange for these advantages, businesses pay large fees to incorporate, and they are taxed twice on company profits—corporations pay tax on profits and individuals pay tax on dividends (distributed corporate profits). Finally, if publicly owned, corporations must adhere to strict government reporting requirements.

6 Delineate the three groups that govern a corporation and describe the role of each.

Shareholders are the basis of the corporate structure. They elect the board of directors, who in turn hire the officers of the corporation. The corporate officers carry out the policies and decisions of the board. In practice, the shareholders and board members have often followed the lead of the chief executive officer.

7 Identify six main synergies companies hope to achieve by combining their operations.

By combining their operations, companies hope to eliminate redundant costs, increase their buying power, increase their revenue, improve their market share, eliminate manufacturing overcapacity, and gain access to new expertise and personnel.

Behind the Scenes

Google Buys a Major Stake in the Online Display Ad Business

By the beginning of 2007, Google was making billions as the leading supplier of search-related advertising. However, the company had made little progress in the other important part of online advertising: graphical and multimedia display ads. The display ad business was heating up as major advertisers grew more interested in reaching consumers online. In addition to the option of using display ads, these advertisers wanted to be able to run entire ad campaigns across carefully selected websites while targeting viewers based on their online behavior. To compete in this booming market, Google CEO Eric Schmidt knew his firm needed to boost its resources and capabilities, and fast.

With more money than time on its hands, Google opted to buy rather than build. In April 2007, the company purchased DoubleClick, a pioneer in online advertising. For $3.1 billion in cash, Google acquired an experienced engineering and sales team and DoubleClick's extensive ad serving and tracking technologies. These systems allow advertisers to target ads to specific types of web surfers, controlling where, when—and to an increasing degree—who sees their ads. The systems also let advertisers monitor the effectiveness of their ads by tallying *click-through* rates and other key data.

The acquisition brought more than just talent and technology, however. In the words of one industry executive, DoubleClick had "relationships with virtually every major online publisher and more than half of the online ad agencies." With advertising at the core of its business model and major advertisers clamoring for sophisticated display advertising capabilities, Google helped secure its future with one swift move.

Speaking of swift moves, competitive urgency also played a significant role in the purchase decision. The online advertising industry was quickly consolidating during that time frame, with the three major companies—Google, Yahoo!, and Microsoft—each trying to assemble the most compelling one-stop solution to entice big-name advertisers. A few months earlier, Yahoo! had purchased a minority stake in Right Media, a company with capabilities similar to DoubleClick's, and Microsoft was competing with Google to buy DoubleClick. Then soon after Google snagged DoubleClick, Yahoo! bought the rest of Right Media, and Microsoft turned around and shelled out $6 billion in cash for aQuantive, another major player in display advertising. Within the course of a few months, the entire industry was reshaped.

Of course, as with all mergers and acquisitions, the deal is only the beginning, not the end. Google still needs to integrate DoubleClick's people, technologies, and business relationships into its existing operations. The company also faces some criticism and government review of the deal. Privacy advocates weren't happy that Google could now analyze the search, browsing, and even buying habits of online consumers (although DoubleClick stressed at the time of the acquisition that data on web-surfing habits belongs to its clients and was therefore off-limits to Google). The Federal Trade Commission (FTC) also stepped in to review the deal. Although few people expect the FTC to prohibit Google from finalizing the acquisition, it could eventually require the company to sell off some parts of its newly combined operations to avoid giving it too much competitive dominance in the market.

Critical Thinking Questions

1. Why wouldn't Google take the simpler and cheaper route of creating a strategic alliance with DoubleClick, rather than purchasing the company outright?
2. The FTC doesn't have the authority to stop the Google acquisition on the basis of privacy concerns, but should it? Why or why not?
3. What are the risks of buying a company simply to keep it out of a competitor's hands? What is likely to happen to the acquired firm when this happens?

LEARN MORE ONLINE

Visit Google's website at www.google.com and click on "Advertising Programs." If you were a sole proprietor, how could you use these services to promote your business? If you were the advertising manager of a major corporation, how might you use Google's advertising services?

(For the latest information on Google's acquisition of DoubleClick and other strategic mergers, visit www.prenhall.com/bovée and click on "Real-Time Updates.") ∎

Key Terms

acquisition (122)	hostile takeovers (122)	private corporation (116)
board of directors (120)	leveraged buyout (LBO) (122)	proxy (120)
chief executive officer (CEO) (119)	limited liability companies	public corporation (116)
common stock (115)	(LLCs) (118)	S corporation (118)
consolidation (122)	limited partnership (114)	shareholder activism (120)
corporate governance (119)	liquidity (117)	shareholders (115)
corporation (115)	merger (122)	sole proprietorship (113)
dividends (116)	parent company (119)	stock certificate (115)
general partnership (114)	partnership (113)	subsidiary corporations (119)
holding company (119)	preferred stock (116)	unlimited liability (113)

Test Your Knowledge

Questions for Review

1. What are the three basic forms of business ownership?
2. What is the difference between a general and a limited partnership?
3. What is a closely held corporation, and why do some companies choose this form of ownership?
4. What is the role of a company's board of directors?
5. What is culture clash?

Questions for Analysis

6. Why is it advisable for partners to enter into a formal partnership agreement?
7. To what extent do shareholders control the activities of a corporation?
8. How might a company benefit from having a diverse board of directors that includes representatives of several industries, countries, and cultures?
9. Why do so many mergers fail?
10. **Ethical Considerations.** Your father sits on the board of directors of a large, well-admired public company. Yesterday, while looking for an envelope in his home office, you stumbled on a confidential memorandum. Unable to resist the temptation to read the memo, you discovered that your father's company is talking with another publicly traded company about the possibility of a merger, with Dad's company being the survivor. Dollar signs flashed in your mind. Should the merger occur, the value of the other company's stock is likely to soar. You're tempted to log onto your E*TRADE account in the morning and place an order for 1,000 shares of that company's stock. Better still, maybe you'll give a hot tip to your best friend in exchange for the four Dave Matthews Band tickets your friend has been flashing in your face all week. Would either of those actions be unethical? Explain your answer.

Questions for Application

11. Suppose you and some friends want to start a business to take tourists on wilderness backpacking expeditions. None of you has much extra money, so your plan is to start small. However, if you are successful, you would like to expand into other types of outdoor tours and perhaps even open up branches in other locations. What form of ownership should your new enterprise take, and why?
12. **How This Affects You.** Do you own or have you ever considered owning stock? If so, what steps have you taken to ensure that company management has shareholder interests in mind?
13. **Integrated.** Chapter 3 discussed international strategic alliances and joint ventures. Why might a U.S. company want to enter into those types of arrangements instead of merging with a foreign concern?
14. **Integrated.** You've developed considerable expertise in setting up new manufacturing plants, and now you'd like to strike out on your own as a consultant who advises other companies. However, you recognize that manufacturing activity tends to expand and contract at various times during the business cycle (see Chapter 1). Do you think a single-consultant sole proprietorship or a small corporation with a half dozen or more consultants would be better able to ride out tough times at the bottom of a business cycle?

Practice Your Knowledge

Sharpening Your Communication Skills

You have just been informed that your employer is going to merge with a firm in Germany. Because you know very little about German culture and business practices, you think it might be a good idea to do some preliminary research—just in case you have to make a quick trip overseas. Using the Internet or library sources, find information on German culture and customs and prepare a short report discussing such cultural differences as social values, decision-making customs, concepts of time, use of body language, social behavior and manners, and legal and ethical behavior.

Building Your Team Skills

Directors often have to ask tough questions and make difficult decisions, as you will see in this exercise. Imagine that the president of your college or university has just announced plans to retire. Your team, playing the role of the school's board of directors, must decide how to choose a new president to fill this vacancy next semester.

First, generate a list of the qualities and qualifications you think the school should seek in a new president. What background and experience would prepare someone for this key position? What personal characteristics should the new president have? What questions would you ask to find out how each candidate measures up against the list of credentials you have prepared?

Now list all the stakeholders that your team, as directors, must consider before deciding on a replacement for the retiring president. Of these stakeholders, whose opinions do you think are most important? Whose are least important? Who will be directly and indirectly affected by the choice of a new president? Of these stakeholders, which should be represented as participants in the decision-making process?

Select a spokesperson to deliver a brief presentation to the class summarizing your team's ideas and the reasoning behind your suggestions. After all the teams have completed their presentations, discuss the differences and similarities among credentials proposed by all the teams for evaluating candidates for the presidency. Then compare the teams' conclusions about stakeholders. Do all teams agree on the stakeholders who should participate in the decision-making process? Lead a classroom discussion on a board's responsibility to its stakeholders.

Improving Your Tech Insights: Groupware

Groupware is an umbrella term for systems that let people communicate, share files, present materials, and work on documents simultaneously. Groupware is changing the way employees interact with one another—and even the way businesses work together. In fact, groupware is changing the way some companies are structured. *Shared workspaces* are "virtual offices" that give everyone on a team access to the same set of resources and information: databases, calendars, project plans, archived instant messages and e-mails, reference materials, and team documents. These workspaces (which are typically accessible through a web browser) let you and your team organize your work files into a collection of electronic folders, making it easy for geographically dispersed team members to access shared files anytime, anywhere. Employees no longer need to be in the same office or even in the same time zone. They don't even need to be employees. Groupware makes it easy for companies to pull together partners and temporary contractors on a project-by-project basis. Groupware is often integrated with web-based meeting systems that combine instant messaging, shared workspaces, videoconferencing, and other tools such as *virtual whiteboards* that let teams collaborate in real time. Newer web-based systems offer cost-effective solutions for even the smallest companies, too.

Conduct research to identify a currently available groupware system. (Groupware systems aren't always identified as such, so you might want to search for "project collaboration systems" or similar terms.) Pick a company you might like to work for someday and in a brief e-mail message to your instructor, explain how this particular groupware system could help the employees and managers in this company be more productive.[39]

Expand Your Knowledge

Discovering Career Opportunities

Are you best suited to working as a sole proprietor, as a partner in a business, or in a different role within a corporation? For this exercise, select three businesses with which you are familiar: one run by a single person, such as a dentist's practice or a local landscaping firm; one run by two or three partners, such as a small accounting firm; and one that operates as a corporation, such as Target or Wal-Mart.

1. Write down what you think you would like about being the sole proprietor, one of the partners, and the corporate manager or an employee in the businesses you have selected. For example, would you like having full responsibility for the sole proprietorship? Would you like being able to consult with other partners in the partnership before making decisions? Would you like having limited responsibility when you work for other people in the corporation?

2. Now write down what you might dislike about each form of business. For example, would you dislike the risk of bearing all legal responsibility in a sole proprietorship? Would you dislike having to talk with your partners before spending the partnership's money? Would you dislike having to write reports for top managers and shareholders of the corporation?

3. Weigh the pluses and minuses you have identified in this exercise. In comparison, which form of business most appeals to you?

Developing Your Research Skills

Review recent issues of business newspapers or periodicals (print or online editions) to find an article or series of articles illustrating one of the following business developments: merger, acquisition, consolidation, hostile takeover, or leveraged buyout.

1. Explain in your own words what steps or events led to this development.

2. What results do you expect this development to have on (a) the company itself, (b) consumers, (c) the industry the company is part of? Write down and date your answers.

3. Follow your story in the business news over the next month (or longer, as your instructor requests). What problems, opportunities, or other results are reported? Were these developments anticipated at the time of the initial story, or did they seem to catch industry analysts by surprise? How well did your answers to question 2 predict the results?

See It on the Web

Visit these websites and answer the following questions for each one. (Up-to-date links for all websites mentioned in this chapter can be found on the Textbook Resources page for Chapter 5 at www.mybusinesslab.com. Please note that links to sites that become inactive after publication of the book will be removed from the Featured Websites section.)

1. What is the purpose of this website?

2. What kinds of information does this website contain? Please be specific.

3. How is the information provided at this website useful for businesspeople? Consumers?

4. How did you expand your knowledge of business structures and corporate governance by reviewing the material at this website? What new things did you learn about this topic?

Choose a Form of Ownership

Which legal form of ownership is best suited for a new business? Answering this question can be a challenge—especially if you're not familiar with the attributes of sole proprietorships, partnerships, and corporations. That's where Nolo can help. Because there's no right or wrong choice for everyone, your job is to understand how each legal structure works and then pick the one that best meets your needs. Start your research by browsing the "Business and Human Resources" section at Nolo. Browse "Main Topics" for important

information on starting a business and ownership structures, and check out the pages in the "Tools & Resources" section. www.nolo.com

Follow the Fortunes of the *Fortune* 500

Quick! Name the largest corporation in the United States, as measured by annual revenues. Give up? Just check *Fortune* magazine's yearly ranking of the 500 largest U.S. companies. The *Fortune* 500 not only ranks corporations by size but also offers brief company descriptions along with industry statistics and additional measures of corporate performance. You can search the list by ranking, by industry, by company name, or by CEO. And to help you identify the largest international corporations, there's a special Global 500 list as well. www.fortune.com

Build a Great Board

Want a great board of directors? This Inc.com guide contains the best resources for entrepreneurs who are ready to recruit outside directors for their boards. Find out how to recruit board members and how to persuade top-notch people to come on board. Once you've selected your members, learn how to maximize your board's impact and resolve conflicts among board members. Check out one expert's five practical tips for good nuts-and-bolts boardsmanship. www.inc.com/guides/growth/20672.html

Companion Website

Learning Interactively

Log onto www.prenhall.com/bovée, locate your text, and then click on its Companion Website. For Chapter 5, take advantage of the interactive Chapter Quiz to test your

knowledge of the chapter. Get instant feedback on whether you need additional studying. Also, you'll find an abundance of valuable resources that will help you succeed in this course, including PowerPoint presentations and Web Links.

Video Case

Doing Business Privately: Amy's Ice Creams

LEARNING OBJECTIVES

The purpose of this video is to help you:

1. Distinguish among the types of corporations

2. Consider the advantages and the disadvantages of incorporation

3. Understand the role that shareholders play in a privately held corporation

SYNOPSIS

Amy's Ice Creams, based in Austin, Texas, is a privately held corporation formed in 1984 by Amy Miller and owned by Miller and a small group of family members and friends. At the outset, one of the most important decisions Miller faced was choosing an appropriate legal ownership structure for the new business. Fueled by the founder's dedication to creating happy ice cream memories for customers, Amy's has continued to evolve and grow. The company now operates 11 stores and rings up close to $3.5 million in annual sales. Applying for a job is an adventure in creativity, and Miller welcomes employees' suggestions for new flavors and new promotions to keep sales growing.

Discussion Questions

1. *For analysis:* How does Amy's Ice Creams differ from a publicly held corporation?
2. *For analysis:* What are some of the particular advantages of corporate ownership for a firm such as Amy's Ice Creams?
3. *For application:* How well do you think Amy's Ice Creams is working to ensure its continued survival and success? Looking ahead to future growth, what marketing, financial, or other suggestions would you make?

4. *For application:* What are some of the issues that Amy Miller may have to confront because her 22 investors are family members and friends?
5. *For debate:* Should Amy's Ice Creams become a publicly held corporation? Support your chosen position.

ONLINE EXPLORATION

Find out what is required to incorporate a business in your state. You might begin by searching the CCH Business Owner's Toolkit site at www.toolkit.cch.com. If you were going to start a small business, would you choose to incorporate or choose a different form of legal organization? List the pros and cons that incorporation presents for the type of business you would consider.

CHAPTER 6

Small Business and Entrepreneurship

LEARNING OBJECTIVES

After studying this chapter, you will be able to

1 Highlight the major contributions small businesses make to the U.S. economy

2 Identify the key characteristics (other than size) that differentiate small businesses from larger ones

3 Discuss three factors contributing to the increase in the number of small businesses

4 Cite the key characteristics common to most entrepreneurs

5 List three ways of going into business for yourself

6 Identify six sources of small-business assistance

7 Discuss the principal sources of small-business private financing

GeniusBabies.com Builds a Smart Business

www.geniusbabies.com

As with many entrepreneurs, Michelle Donahue-Arpas based her idea for a new business on career experience and personal passions. In her case, working with emotionally disturbed children sparked an interest in music and toys that stimulate mental development in newborns and infants. The birth of her first child then provided the motivation to find a way to work from her North Carolina home.

Donahue-Arpas's first step was to identify an existing product that she figured needed improvement. She chose the gift baskets that families and friends often send to new parents. Donahue-Arpas thought these products offered little real value in relation to their high price tags, and she saw an opportunity to meet the same gift-giving need but with beneficial learning products instead of baby lotion and talcum powder. She wanted to design gift baskets

Michelle Donahue-Arpas founded GeniusBabies.com as a way to balance her family life, her ambitions as an entrepreneur, and her desire to promote beneficial products in the marketplace.

that contain a selection of puzzles and other toys that stimulate a baby's cognitive and physical development. Not only would such products meet a real market need, she surmised, but she could simultaneously fulfill her interest in quality learning products for infants. She even had a name for her new company: Genius Babies.

Donahue-Arpas had solved the *why* and the *what* questions of being a business owner, but she still faced the question of *how*: How could she realize her dream of selling educational baby products from home? To create a sustainable and profitable business, she would surely have to reach a much wider market than just her hometown. Moreover, she had very little cash to invest in her start-up operation, so an expensive retail storefront and other investments were out of the question. If you were pursuing her dream, how would you make it come true?[1] ■

Understanding the World of Small Business

Since you're studying business, chances are you've already had an idea or two for a new business. Is your objective to create a company that fits your lifestyle, as Michelle Donahue-Arpas of GeniusBabies.com (profiled in the chapter opener) has done, or do you have dreams of creating a major enterprise? Are you ready to wear a half dozen hats at once and do whatever it takes to get your company off the ground? Should you start something from scratch or buy an existing business? If you plan to join the millions of small-business owners around the United States, be prepared to answer all these questions and many more.

Most businesses start out like GeniusBabies.com: with an entrepreneur, an idea, and a drive to succeed. Since the founding of the United States, small businesses have been a vital part of the national economy. They play a role in virtually every sector of the economy, from e-commerce companies such as GeniusBabies.com to the independent contractors who drive routes for FedEx Ground, the freight arm of FedEx.[2] Many well-known entertainers, from singer Ani DiFranco to comedian/actor Bernie Mac, became small-business owners as a way to take control of their careers.[3] The opportunities for small business ownership are as diverse as the U.S. economy.

Defining just what constitutes a small business is surprisingly tricky because *small* is a relative term. While the definition of *small* is not simple, it is vitally important because billions of dollars are at stake in such areas as employment regulations, from which the smallest companies are often exempt, and government contracts reserved for small businesses.[4]

The U.S. Small Business Administration (SBA) starts by defining a **small business** as "one that is independently owned and operated and which is not dominant in its field of operation." Beyond that general starting point, the SBA defines the maximum size of "small" through either annual revenue or number of employees. For instance, in many agricultural categories a company can make up to $750,000 and still be considered small, but Internet service providers can make up to $23 million a year and still be considered small. Similarly, in some industries, 100 employees is the limit; in others, it's 500, 750, 1,000, or even 1,500 people.[5] Under the SBA's guidelines, the United States is home to more than 25 million small businesses—compared to only 17,000 large businesses.[6]

small business
Company that is independently owned and operated, is not dominant in its field, and meets certain criteria for the number of employees or annual sales revenue

Economic Roles of Small Businesses

Small businesses are the cornerstone of the U.S. economy. They bring new ideas, processes, and vigor to the marketplace. They generate about half of private sector output,[7] and they fill niche markets that often are not served by large businesses. Here are just some of the important roles small businesses play in the economy:

- *They provide jobs.* Small businesses employ about half of the private-sector workforce in this country and create somewhere between two-thirds and three-quarters of new jobs. However, it's important to recognize that most of this job growth comes from that subset of small businesses whose goal is to grow into midsize or large businesses; the overwhelming majority of small businesses have no employees at all.[8]

- *They introduce new products.* The freedom to innovate that is characteristic of many small firms continues to yield countless advances in both technologies and marketable goods and services. Google, now a multibillion-dollar company, was started by two college students who wanted a better way to find information.

- *They supply the needs of larger organizations.* Many small businesses act as distributors, servicing agents, and suppliers to large corporations. In addition, government agencies often reserve a certain percentage of their purchasing contracts for small businesses.

- *They inject a considerable amount of money into the economy.* If U.S. small businesses were a separate country, they would constitute the third-largest economy in the world.[9]

- *They take risks that larger companies sometimes avoid.* Entrepreneurs play a significant role in the economy as risk takers, the people willing to try new and unproven ideas. U.S. Rubber Recycling had experimented with rubber sidewalk pavers but didn't want to commercialize the product. Lindsay Smith was upset at seeing mature trees get cut down in her Gardena, California, neighborhood because their roots were cracking city sidewalks. She found out about the prototype pavers and knew they would save trees, keep tires out of landfills, and reduce municipal maintenance costs. Her company, Rubbersidewalks (www.rubbersidewalks.com) has now sold pavers to cities all over North America.[10]

- *They provide specialized goods and services.* Small businesses frequently spring up to fill niches that aren't being served by existing companies. For instance, Seattle entrepreneur Michael Eastman founded the online music service Chondo.Net (www.chondo.net) to give customers access to the incredible array of African-influenced music from independent artists all over the world. From Brazilian reggae to the *soukous* pop music of Congo to obscure acoustic blues from the American South, Chondo offers music that is difficult or impossible to find elsewhere.[11]

Japanese clothing designer and entrepreneur Risa Koyanagi has built a multimillion-dollar business on the strength of her unique fashions.

Characteristics of Small Businesses

The majority of small businesses are modest operations with little growth potential, although some have attractive income potential for the solo businessperson. The self-employed consultant, the corner florist, the family-owned neighborhood pizza parlor, and many e-commerce ventures (including GeniusBabies.com) are sometimes called *lifestyle businesses* because they are built around the personal and financial needs of an individual or a family. In contrast, other firms are small simply because they are young, but they have ambitious plans to grow. These *high-growth ventures* are usually run by a team rather than by one individual, and they expand rapidly by obtaining a sizable supply of investment capital and by introducing new products or services to a large market.

Regardless of their primary objectives, small companies tend to differ from large enterprises in a variety of important ways. First, most small firms have a narrower focus, offering fewer goods and services to fewer market segments. This can be both a blessing and a curse—a narrow focus can help you out-compete companies that serve multiple market needs, but it can also limit you in ways such as getting attention from distributors and retailers. Second, unless they are launched with generous financial backing, which is rare, small businesses get by with limited resources, which can mean anything from getting comfortable with used furniture and equipment to juggling a half-dozen different jobs at once. Professionals who've spent their careers working for large companies can be shocked to discover how many tasks someone else used to take care of that are now in their laps.

The third major difference between small and large companies is also one of the most common—and exciting—reasons people go into business for themselves: having the freedom to innovate and move quickly. As they grow in size, companies also tend to grow in both complexity and bureaucracy. Decision making becomes slower and more difficult as more departments get involved and various groups compete internally for resources and recognition. In contrast, entrepreneurial firms usually find it easier to operate "on the fly," making decisions quickly and reacting to changes in the marketplace. The entrepreneur's innovative spirit is so compelling, in fact, that many large companies and individuals within companies now try to duplicate it through *intrapreneurship*, a term coined by business consultant Gifford Pinchot (www.intrapreneur.com) to designate the entrepreneurial efforts within a larger corporation.[12]

Factors Contributing to the Increase in the Number of Small Businesses

Three factors are contributing to the increase in the number of small businesses today: e-commerce and other technological advances, the growing diversity in entrepreneurship, and corporate downsizing and outsourcing.

E-Commerce and Other Technologies

E-commerce and other technologies have spawned thousands of new business ventures in recent years—both firms that create the technology and firms that use it. GeniusBabies.com is a perfect example of a small business enabled by the Internet (see Exhibit 6.1). Consider the difference it has made in Michelle Donahue-Arpas's life after she opted to launch her company as an online-only retail operation. Without the Internet, she would have to either sacrifice family time and run her business out of a traditional retail store or find a considerable source of money to finance the catalog operations of a traditional mail-order company.

Growing Diversity in Entrepreneurship

Small-business growth is also being fueled by women, minorities, immigrants, and young people who want alternatives to traditional employment. For instance, women now own more than 10 million U.S. businesses.[13] This trend isn't limited to the United States, either, as women around the world seek a greater degree of financial independence and security through entrepreneurship, sometimes against considerable odds.

EXHIBIT 6.1 Country Heritage Farms

E-commerce has enabled the creation of many new businesses and expansion possibilities for thousands of existing companies, such as Country Heritage Farms of Dayton, Oregon.

When Kiran Mazumdar-Shaw started the biotechnology company Biocon in Bangalore, India, she struggled to find employees, office space, and raw materials—all because she was a woman. After nearly three decades of hard work, her company now employs hundreds of research scientists, and she's the richest woman in India.[14]

Minority business ownership is also on the rise across the United States. Minorities now own 15 percent of all U.S. businesses.[15] Part of this growth is attributed to firms that do a better job of marketing to specific segments of the population. For example, Hispanic-owned businesses have been doing better than the economy as a whole in recent years, thanks in large part to their success at marketing to the growing Hispanic American population.[16]

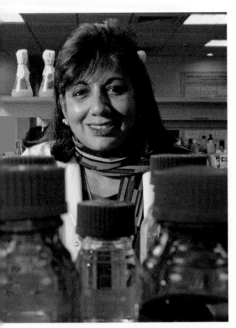

Kiran Mazumdar-Shaw worked for years to overcome biases against women in business and is now one of India's most successful entrepreneurs.

The tradition of immigrants starting small companies stretches back to the first days of the United States and continues strong today. With help from programs such as StartSmart, run by Coastal Enterprises in Wicasset, Maine, immigrants and political refugees get coaching and assistance on achieving financial independence through business ownership.[17]

Finally, young people are one of the strongest forces in entrepreneurship today and launch the majority of all new businesses.[18] It's never too early to start; Google, Microsoft, Dell, and plenty of other high-flying companies were started by college students. If you'd like to network with other aspiring entrepreneurs, see whether your college has a chapter of the College Entrepreneurs Organization (www.c-e-o.org). In the words of Joseph Keeley, who formed College Nannies and Tutors (www.collegenannies.com) when he was a freshman at the University of St. Thomas, "As a young entrepreneur, the risk is relatively low. If you have a well-thought-out plan, don't be afraid to execute it. The risk only gets higher as you get older."[19]

Downsizing and Outsourcing

Contrary to popular wisdom, business start-ups often soar when the economy sours. During hard times, many companies downsize or lay off talented employees, who then have little to lose by pursuing self-employment. In fact, several well-known companies were started during recessions. Tech titans William Hewlett and David Packard joined forces in Silicon Valley in 1938 during the Great Depression. Bill Gates started Microsoft during the 1975 recession. And the founders of Sun Microsystems, Compaq Computer, Adobe Systems, Silicon Graphics, and Lotus Development started their companies in 1982—in the midst of a recession and high unemployment.[20]

The outsourcing and value web phenomena discussed in Chapter 4 (page 87) create numerous opportunities for small businesses and entrepreneurs. Some companies subcontract special projects and secondary business functions to experts outside the organization, while others turn to outsourcing as a way to permanently eliminate entire departments. In fact, some entrepreneurs turn around and provide services to former employers. Regardless of the reason, the increased use of outsourcing provides opportunities for smaller businesses to service the needs of larger enterprises. (For the latest information on small business and entrepreneurship, visit www.prenhall.com/bovée and click on "Real-Time Updates.")

Starting a Small Business

Are you ready to join the hundreds of thousands of people who start businesses in the United States every year? A good place to start is by exploring the most common characteristics of others who've taken the entrepreneurial plunge.

Characteristics of Entrepreneurs

Entrepreneurs are sometimes portrayed in popular media as charismatic, slightly larger than life characters, people such as Sir Richard Branson, head of the Virgin business empire—people who have some secret success gene that protects them from failure. Or more darkly, entrepreneurs are occasionally portrayed as a greedy, predatory lot who're out to take more than their share. Neither characterization accurately reflects the multifaceted world of entrepreneurship, and the entrepreneurial myth is just that, a myth.[21] In any event, it's impossible to lump millions of people into a single category; successful entrepreneurs are as diverse as the rest of the population, although they do tend to share a number of characteristics:[22]

- They are highly disciplined.
- They have a high degree of confidence.
- They have plenty of physical energy and emotional stamina.
- They like to control their destiny.
- They relate well to others and have a talent for organizing team efforts in pursuit of a common goal.

- They are eager to learn whatever skills are necessary to reach their goals.
- They learn from their mistakes.
- They stay abreast of market changes.
- They are willing to exploit new opportunities.
- They are driven by a passion to succeed—but they often don't measure success in strictly financial terms.
- They think positively and are able to overcome failure and adversity; they are tenacious in pursuit of their goals.
- Contrary to popular stereotype, they are not compulsive gamblers who thrive on high-risk situations; rather, they embrace moderate risk when it is coupled with the potential for significant rewards.

The story of Craig Tanner illustrates the range of personal characteristics that a successful entrepreneur must have. After working as a stock broker and sales manager, Tanner recognized his real opportunity when he watched Tiger Woods win yet another amateur golf title early in his career. Woods hadn't yet become the global superstar he is today, but Tanner saw the future: "I knew that people of color and kids would get into golf." He founded Urban Golf Gear (www.urbangolfgear.com) in Oakland, California, with the goal of producing golf attire that combined the technical performance of athletic wear with the contemporary style of urban culture. Initial financing, all $1,500 of it, came from selling a car he had refurbished; he eventually took on more than $50,000 in credit card debt to grow the business. The products were attractive, and the market seemed to be there, but Tanner immediately ran into two obstacles. First, his products fell somewhere between the traditional golf apparel market and the urban apparel market, so working his way into retail outlets proved almost impossible. Second, no one would invest in a new company chasing an as-yet unproven opportunity. As tenacious as all successful entrepreneurs, Tanner created his own distribution channels, selling products to associates who would then resell them to consumers, displaying his wares at golf tournaments and events held by a variety of African American organizations, and working with promoters to get UGG gear featured in a variety of TV shows and movies. Gradually, satisfied customers began to spread the word, and sales took off.[23]

Entrepreneurs and small-business owners go into business for a variety of reasons (see Exhibit 6.2). Most have diverse backgrounds in terms of education and business experience. Some come from companies unlike the ones they start; others use their prior knowledge and skills—such as editing, telemarketing, public relations, or selling—to start their own businesses. Still others have less experience but an innovative idea or a better way of doing something. They find an overlooked corner of the market, exploit a demographic trend unnoticed by others, or meet an unsatisfied consumer need through better service or a higher-quality product.

EXHIBIT 6.2 Why Entrepreneurs Go into Business

Entrepreneurs seldom cite "making more money" as a primary reason for going into business.

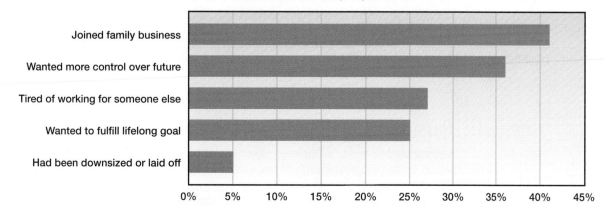

EXHIBIT 6.3 Business Start-Up Checklist

You have many tasks to perform before you start your business. Here are just a few.

✓ Choose a business name, verify the right to use it, and register it.

✓ Reserve a corporate name if you will be incorporating.

✓ Register a domain name for your website.

✓ Register or reserve state or federal trademarks.

✓ Apply for a patent if you will be marketing an invention.

✓ Write a business plan.

✓ Choose a location for the business.

✓ Identify and understand all the costs you're likely to encounter, both at start-up and over time.

✓ File partnership or corporate papers.

✓ Get any required business licenses or permits.

✓ Check local zoning laws.

✓ Identify any health, safety, or other special regulations that will apply to your business.

✓ Have business phone lines installed.

✓ Check into business insurance needs.

✓ Apply for a sales tax number.

✓ Apply for a federal employer identification number if you will have employees.

✓ Open business bank account(s).

✓ Have business cards and stationery printed.

✓ Purchase equipment and supplies.

✓ Order inventory, if needed.

✓ Order signs for the business, if needed.

✓ Produce your promotional materials (a website, brochures, etc., as needed).

✓ Send out publicity releases.

✓ Call everyone you know and tell them you are in business.

Importance of Preparing a Business Plan

Getting started in a new business requires a lot of work (see Exhibit 6.3), not the least of which is planning. Although many successful entrepreneurs claim to have done little formal planning, they all have at least *some* intuitive idea of what they're trying to accomplish and how they hope to do it. In other words, even if they haven't produced a formal printed document, chances are they've thought through the big questions, which is just as important. As FedEx founder Fred Smith put it, "Being entrepreneurial doesn't mean [you] jump off a ledge and figure out how to make a parachute on the way down."[24]

Planning forces you to think ahead. Before you rush in to supply a product, you need to be sure that a market exists. You must also try to foresee some of the problems that might arise and figure out how you will cope with them. For instance, what will you do if one of your suppliers suddenly goes out of business? Can you locate another supplier quickly? What if the neighborhood starts to change—even for the better? An influx of wealthier neighbors may lead to such a steep increase in rent that your business must move. Also, tough competition may move into the neighborhood along with the fatter pocketbooks. Do you have an alternative location staked out? What if styles suddenly change? Can you switch products quickly if consumer demand changes?

One of the first steps you should take toward starting a new business is to develop a **business plan**, a written document that summarizes the proposed business venture, communicates the company's goals, highlights how management intends to achieve those goals, and shows how customers will benefit from the company's products or services. Writing the business plan can be a daunting task, but you can get help from a wide variety of websites, books, classes, and software products that guide you through the process.[25] Also, keep an eye out for business plan competitions sponsored by colleges or business organizations. They're a popular way for entrepreneurs to get feedback from professionals—and win some start-up capital to boot.

Preparing a business plan serves two important functions: First, it guides the company operations and outlines a strategy for turning an idea into reality; second, it helps persuade lenders and investors to finance your business. In fact, if you don't have a business plan, many investors won't even grant you an interview. Keep in mind that sometimes the greatest service a business plan can provide an entrepreneur is the realization that "the concept just won't work." Discovering this reality on paper can save you considerable time and money.

As important as planning is, it's equally important to monitor the market and be ready to adjust once you start moving. You don't want to be so locked into your plan that you fail to see changes in the market or new opportunities along the way.

business plan
A written document that provides an orderly statement of a company's goals and a plan for achieving those goals

Small-Business Ownership Options

Once you've done your research and planning, if you decide to take the risk, you can get into business for yourself in three ways: Start from scratch, buy an existing business, or obtain a franchise. Roughly two-thirds of business founders begin **start-up companies**; that is, they start from scratch rather than buying an existing operation or inheriting a family business. Starting a business from scratch has many advantages and disadvantages (see Exhibit 6.4, page 143); in many cases it can be the most difficult option.

start-up companies
New business ventures

Another way to go into business for yourself is to buy an existing business. This approach tends to reduce the risks— provided, of course, that you check out the company carefully. When you buy a healthy business, you generally purchase an established customer base, functioning business systems, a proven product or service, and a known location. You don't have to go through the challenging period of building a reputation, establishing a clientele, finding suppliers, and hiring and training employees. In addition, financing an existing business is often

> ### *How This Affects You*
>
> 1. Think of several of the most innovative or unusual products you currently own or have recently used (don't forget about services as well). Were these products created by small companies or large ones?
>
> 2. Think about your current job if you have one or any previous job if you aren't currently working. How could you transform the skills used on that job into a small business?
>
> 3. Optimism and perseverance are two of the most important qualities for entrepreneurs. On a scale of 1 (lowest) to 10 (highest), how would you rate yourself on these two qualities? How would your best friend rate you?

Blueprint for an Effective Business Plan

Even for a small firm, the business plan still requires a great deal of thought. For example, before you open your doors (or open your virtual doors online), you have to make important decisions about personnel, marketing, facilities, suppliers, and distribution. A written business plan forces you to think about those issues and develop programs that will help you succeed. If you are starting out on a small scale and using your own money, your business plan may be relatively informal. But at a minimum, you should describe the basic concept of the business and outline its specific goals, objectives, and resource requirements. A formal plan, suitable for use with banks or investors, should cover these points:

- *Summary.* In one or two pages, summarize your business concept. Clearly articulate your business model and strategy for success—astute investors know what makes a business work, and they want to know that you do, too. Describe your product's market potential. Highlight some things about your company and its owners that will distinguish your firm from the competition. Summarize your financial projections and the amount of money investors can expect to make on their investment. Be sure to indicate how much money you will need and for what purpose.

- *Mission and objectives.* Explain the purpose of your business and what you hope to accomplish—and before you take another step, make sure that this is a mission you can pursue with passion, through thick and thin, with every ounce of commitment and energy you can muster.

- *Company and industry.* Give full background information on the origins and structure of your venture and the characteristics of its industry.

- *Products or services.* Give a complete but concise description of your product or service, focusing on its unique attributes. Explain how customers will benefit from using your product or service instead of those of your competitors.

- *Market and competition.* Provide data that will persuade the investor that you understand your target market and can achieve your sales goals. Be sure to identify the strengths and weaknesses of your competitors.

- *Management.* Summarize the background and qualifications of the principals, directors, and key management personnel in your company. Include résumés in the appendix.

- *Marketing strategy.* Provide projections of sales and market share, and outline a strategy for identifying and contacting customers, setting prices, providing customer services, advertising, and so forth. Whenever possible, include evidence of customer acceptance, such as advance product orders.

- *Design and development plans.* If your product requires design or development, describe the nature and extent of what needs to be done, including costs and possible problems.

- *Operations plan.* Provide information on the facilities, equipment, and labor needed.

- *Overall schedule.* Forecast development of the company in terms of completion dates for major aspects of the business plan.

- *Critical risks and problems.* Identify all negative factors and discuss them honestly.

- *Financial projections and requirements.* Include a detailed budget of start-up and operating costs, as well as projections for income, expenses, and cash flow for the first three years of business. Identify the company's financing needs and potential sources.

- *Exit strategy.* Explain how investors will be able to cash out or sell their investment, such as through a public stock offering, sale of the company, or a buyback of the investors' interest.

When covering these points, keep in mind that your audience wants short, concise information with realistic cost and revenue projections. Pay attention to quality, too; if your business plan is sloppy and unprofessional, readers will think you are too.

Questions for Critical Thinking

1. Why is it important to identify critical risks and problems in a business plan?
2. Many experts suggest that you write the business plan yourself, rather than hiring a consultant to write it for you. Why is this a good idea?

much easier than financing a new one; lenders are reassured by the company's history and existing assets and customer base. With these major details already settled, you can concentrate on making improvements.

Still, buying an existing business is not without disadvantages and risks. For starters, you may need a considerable amount of financing to buy a fully functioning company. You also inherit any problems the company has, from unhappy employees to obsolete

EXHIBIT 6.4 Weighing the Advantages and Disadvantages of Starting a New Business

Owning a business has many advantages, but you must also consider the potential drawbacks.

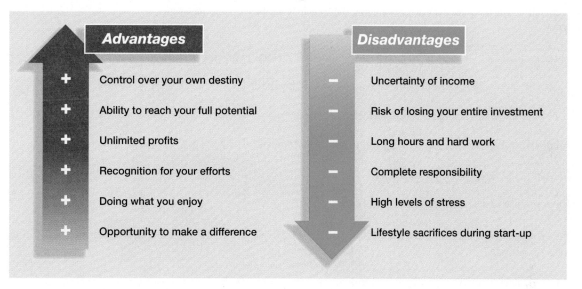

Advantages	Disadvantages
+ Control over your own destiny	− Uncertainty of income
+ Ability to reach your full potential	− Risk of losing your entire investment
+ Unlimited profits	− Long hours and hard work
+ Recognition for your efforts	− Complete responsibility
+ Doing what you enjoy	− High levels of stress
+ Opportunity to make a difference	− Lifestyle sacrifices during start-up

equipment to customers with overdue accounts, and you may not discover some of these problems until you've signed the deal. Thorough research is a must.[26]

The Franchise Alternative

An alternative to buying an existing business is to buy a **franchise** in somebody else's business. This approach enables the buyer to use a larger company's trade name and sell its products or services in a specific territory. In exchange for this right, the **franchisee** (the small-business owner who contracts to sell the goods or services) pays the **franchisor** (the supplier) an initial start-up fee then monthly royalties based on sales volume. Franchises are a rapidly growing presence in the U.S. economy: More than 2,500 franchise systems with an estimated 760,000 outlets ring up more than $1.5 trillion in sales every year.[27]

Types of Franchises

Franchises are of three basic types. A *product franchise* gives you the right to sell trademarked goods, which are purchased from the franchisor and resold. Car dealers and gasoline stations fall into this category. A *manufacturing franchise,* such as a soft-drink bottling plant, gives you the right to produce and distribute the manufacturer's products, using supplies purchased from the franchisor. A *business-format franchise* gives you the right to open a business using a franchisor's name and format for doing business. This format includes many well-known chains, including Taco Bell, Pizza Hut, UPS Stores, and Curves fitness centers.

How to Evaluate a Franchise

How do you protect yourself from a poor franchise investment? The best way is to study the opportunity carefully before you commit. Since 1978 the Federal Trade Commission (FTC) has required franchisors to disclose information about their operations to prospective franchisees. By studying this information, you can determine the financial condition of the franchisor and ascertain whether the

franchise
Business arrangement in which one business obtains rights to sell the goods or services of the supplier (franchisor)

franchisee
Small-business owner who contracts for the right to sell goods or services of the supplier (franchisor) in exchange for some payment

franchisor
Supplier that grants a franchise to an individual or group (franchisee) in exchange for payments

Prospective Subway franchisees must attend company training classes and pass a final exam before they can own a Subway sandwich shop.

EXHIBIT 6.5　Ten Questions to Ask Before Signing a Franchise Agreement

A franchise agreement is a legally binding contract that defines the relationship between the franchisee and the franchisor. Because the agreement is drawn up by the franchisor, the terms and conditions generally favor the franchisor. Before signing the franchise agreement, be sure to consult an attorney.

1. What does the initial franchise fee cover? Does it include a starting inventory of supplies and products?

2. How are the periodic royalties calculated and when are they paid?

3. Are all trademarks and names legally protected?

4. Who provides and pays for advertising and promotional items?

5. Who selects the location of the business?

6. Is the franchise assigned an exclusive territory?

7. If the territory is not exclusive, does the franchisee have the right of first refusal on additional franchises established in nearby locations?

8. Is the franchisee required to purchase equipment and supplies from the franchisor or other suppliers?

9. Under what conditions can the franchisor and/or the franchisee terminate the franchise agreement?

10. Can the franchise be assigned to heirs?

company has been involved in lawsuits with franchisees. Before signing a franchise agreement, it's also wise to consult an attorney. Buying a franchise is much like buying any other business: It requires analyzing the market, finding capital, choosing a site, hiring employees, buying equipment—and most important of all, evaluating the franchisor. One key tip: If the initial franchise fee is extremely high, this could be a sign that the franchisor makes most of its money from selling franchises, rather than sharing in the ongoing profits from those franchises.[28] In addition to the questions in Exhibit 6.5, consult *Consumer Guide to Buying a Franchise*, a free publication from the FTC (www.ftc.gov).

Some people find out too late that franchising isn't the best choice for them. They make a mistake common among prospective franchisees—buying without really understanding the day-to-day business. Often, prospects simply don't get beyond the allure of the successful name or concept or the mistaken notion that a franchise brings instant success. Experts caution that you need to have cash set aside for both personal and business expenses so that you can survive until your new franchise begins to turn a profit.[29]

Advantages of Franchising

Why is franchising so popular? For one thing, when you invest in a franchise—at least if you do your research and invest in a successful franchise—you know you are getting a viable business model, one that has worked many times before. If the franchise is well established, you get the added benefit of instant name recognition, national advertising programs, standardized quality of goods and services, and a proven formula for success. Buying a franchise also gives you access to a support network and in many cases a ready-made blueprint for building a business. For an initial investment (from a few thousand dollars to upward of a million, depending on the franchise), you get services such as site-location studies, market research, training, and technical assistance, as well as assistance with building or leasing your structure, decorating the building, purchasing supplies, and operating the business during your initial ownership phase. Some franchisors also assist franchisees in financing the initial investment.

Disadvantages of Franchising

Although franchising offers many advantages, it is not the ideal vehicle for everyone. The biggest disadvantage is the lack of control relative to other ownership options. This lack of control can affect a franchise at multiple levels. First, when you buy into a franchise system, you agree to follow the business format, and franchisors can prescribe virtually every aspect of the business, from the color of the walls to the products you can carry. In fact, if your primary purpose in owning a business is the freedom to be your own boss, franchising probably isn't the best choice because you don't have a great deal of freedom in many systems. Second, as a franchisors, you usually have little control over decisions the franchisor makes that affect the entire system. Disagreements and even lawsuits have erupted in recent years over actions taken by franchisors regarding product supplies, advertising, and pricing.[30] Third, if the fundamental business model of the franchise system no longer works—or never worked in the first place—or if customer demand for the goods and services you sell declines, you don't have the option of changing your business in response.

Why New Businesses Fail

Even if you carefully evaluate a prospective franchise or write a winning business plan, you have no guarantee of success. You may have heard some depressing statistics about the number of new businesses that fail. Some reports say your chances of succeeding are only one in three; others claim that the odds are even worse, stating that 85 or 90 percent of all new business ventures fail within ten years. Actual statistics, however, show otherwise. Among all companies that close their doors, only about one in seven actually fails—that is, goes out of business leaving behind unpaid debts. In fact, in one study of business closures conducted by the SBA, one-third of the businesses that closed were still financially successful; the owners had sold out according to a planned exit strategy or simply retired.[31] And even in the ultra-competitive restaurant business, the failure rate is much less than the often-quoted 90 percent; one carefully conducted study says it's more along the lines of 60 percent.[32] Moreover, the true failure rate is much lower if you remove those operations that business analysts say aren't really genuine businesses. For instance, a freelance writer who writes one article for a magazine and then stops writing would be counted as a failed business under the traditional measurement (which is based on tax returns).[33]

Whatever the real failure rate, the reality is that businesses do fail, and they can fail for a variety of reasons as Exhibit 6.6 suggests. Lack of management skills, experience,

EXHIBIT 6.6 Why New Businesses Fail

Experts have identified these ten reasons as the most likely causes of new business failure.

- Managerial incompetence
- Lack of relevant experience
- Inadequate financing
- Poor cash management
- Lack of strategic planning
- Ineffective marketing
- Uncontrolled growth
- Poor location
- Poor inventory control
- Inability to make the transition from corporate employee to entrepreneur

Learning from Business Blunders

Oops: Amp'd Mobile, a Los Angeles mobile phone company that targeted teens and young adults with several dozen video and music channels, managed to grow itself right into bankruptcy. After the young company blitzed MTV with an ad campaign, its subscriber base climbed to 175,000. There was a slight hitch, however: The company was struggling to expand its service to support all those customers. Actually, there was another slight hitch: Nearly *half* of those customers the company was struggling to support weren't paying their bills. It wasn't long before Amp'd couldn't pay its bills, either. By the time it filed for bankruptcy, Amp'd owed Verizon $33 million in back payments for use of Verizon's wireless network.

What You Can Learn: Growth can put a tremendous strain on any company, particularly when the company has to invest in equipment and support systems to provide service to customers who aren't paying their bills. Unfortunately, Amp'd isn't the first company to lose a bundle after targeting young consumers who find out they can't pay for all the goods and services they'd like to have.

and proper financing are among the top ten reasons for failure. Jumping on a hot trend without considering the long-term picture is another way to risk everything. Although it sounds counterintuitive, growing *too* quickly is also a significant source of business failures, for several reasons. Growth puts tremendous pressure on companies, in every area from finding enough qualified employees to financing new equipment or facilities. Plus, the entrepreneurial skills needed to get a business off the ground are not the same skills required to transform a hot start-up into a stable business organization. Inventive minds who are stimulated by the joy of discovery and the puzzle-solving aspects of assembling a company can grow bored with the day-to-day work of managing a maturing business.

In some cases, entrepreneurs have been able to reinvent themselves along the way and become successful executives. In others, they recognize their limitations and hire seasoned executives to take over, as eBay founder Pierre Omidyar did when he replaced himself with Meg Whitman—who has since led the company to dominance in online auctions.[34]

Also, as small companies begin to grow, they often find themselves butting heads with much larger competitors—without having the resources of these larger companies. Consultant Doug Tatum describes this dilemma as "being too big to be small and too small to be big."[35] For instance, customers start to miss the personal attention and flexible response they enjoyed when the company was small, but the company isn't yet able to compensate with the comprehensive customer support systems that larger competitors can afford.

If you go into business for yourself, you'll probably make mistakes. But they don't have to be fatal; plenty of entrepreneurs make mistakes, learn from them, and go on to succeed. Also, the number of resources now available to entrepreneurs means you can learn from other people's experiences (including their mistakes).

Sources of Small-Business Assistance

Today's entrepreneurs and small-business owners can turn to a huge variety of sources for advice and assistance, from government agencies to online social networks.

Government Agencies and Nonprofit Organizations

A number of city, state, and federal government agencies offer business owners advice, assistance, and even financing in some cases. For instance, many cities and states have an office of economic development (or similarly named agency) chartered with helping companies prosper so that they might contribute to the local or regional economy. At the federal level, small businesses can apply for loans backed by the Small Business Administration (www.sba.gov) and learn more about selling to the federal government—including bidding on the many contracts reserved for small or minority-owned companies—at www.business.gov. Many government agencies also have special offices (check their websites) to help small firms compete.

Some of the best advice available to small businesses is delivered by thousands of volunteers from Service Corps of Retired Executives (SCORE), a resource partner of the Small Business Administration. These experienced business professionals offer advice and one-to-one counseling sessions on topics such as developing a business plan, securing financing, and managing business growth. Every year, SCORE counselors help some 400,000 U.S. businesses, such as *Virginia Horse Journal*, a magazine published by the husband-and-wife team of Dean and Darlene Jacobsen in Charlottesville, Virginia. Two SCORE counselors, both seasoned publishing industry professionals, helped the Jacobsens turn their struggling magazine into a thriving business.[36] You can contact a local SCORE counselor or learn more about available programs at www.score.org.

Many colleges and universities also offer entrepreneurship and small business programs. Check with your college's business school to see if resources are available to help you launch or expand a company. The U.S. Chamber of Commerce (www.chamberofcommerce.com) and its many local chambers offer advice and special programs for small business as well.

With help from SCORE, Wayne Erbsen turned his passion for preserving and performing traditional music into a business that reaches customers all over the world from his home in Asheville, North Carolina. Native Ground Books & Music (www.nativeground.com) offers books and recordings of songs and folklore from the Civil War, the Old West, Appalachia, railroading, gospel, and many other elements of America's heritage.

Business Partners

The companies you do business with can also be a source of advice and support. For example, Bank of America's (www.bankofamerica.com) Small Business Resource Center offers a variety of articles, online tutorials, and financial calculators. Similarly, Microsoft (www.microsoft.com/smallbusiness) offers free seminars, podcasts, and webcasts with information of interest to small business. As you might expect, the free resources these companies offer are part of their marketing strategies, so a certain amount of self-promotion is to be expected, but don't let that stop you from taking advantage of all the free advice you can get.

Mentors and Advisory Boards

Many entrepreneurs and business owners take advantage of individual mentors and advisory boards. Mentoring can happen through both formal programs such as SCORE and informal relationships. In either case, the advice of a mentor who has been down the road before can be priceless.

Advisory boards are a form of "group mentoring," in which you assemble a team of people with subject-area expertise or vital contacts to help review plans and decisions. Danielle Ayotte and Julie Dix, co-founders of the baby-goods company Taggies (www.taggies.com), found that the advice they were getting from individual experts was too fragmented to help. "We needed everyone in the room," Ayotte explained. They asked seven experts in areas such as law and marketing to sit on their advisory board so that the entire group could address the company's business challenges together. Taggies's sales have been growing by leaps and bounds ever since.[37]

Unlike a corporate board of directors, an advisory board does not have legal responsibilities, and you don't have to incorporate to establish an advisory board. In some cases, advisors will agree to help for no financial compensation. In other cases, particularly for growth companies who want high-profile experts, advisors agree to serve in exchange for either a fee or a small portion of the company's stock (up to 3 percent is standard).[38]

Print and Online Media

Your local library and the Internet offer enough information to help any small-business owner face just about every challenge imaginable. For instance, blogs written by business owners, investors, and functional specialists such as marketing consultants can offer valuable insights. Websites such as Kauffman eVenturing (www.eventuring.org) provide free advice on every aspect of managing an entrepreneurial organization. Also, the websites affiliated with these well-known business magazines should be on every small-business owner's regular reading list:

- *Inc.* (www.inc.com). Be sure to check out the many "Resource Centers," addressing such topics as women in business, finance and capital, marketing, and law and taxation.
- *Business 2.0* (www.business2.com). Focused on technology-oriented businesses, this site offers lots of real-life success stories that profile entrepreneurs in action.
- *BusinessWeek* (www.businessweek.com/smallbiz). The small business section of this widely read business magazine's website offers advice on every aspect of running a business.
- *Fortune Small Business* (http://money.cnn.com/magazines/fsb). Similar to *BusinessWeek*'s small-business coverage, this publication is affiliated with the highly regarded *Fortune* magazine.

Networks

No matter what industry you're in or what stage your business is in, you can probably find a local or online network of people with similar interests. For instance, some entrepreneurs meet regularly in small groups to analyze each other's progress month by month. Being forced to articulate your plans and decisions to peers—and to be held accountable for results—can be an invaluable "reality check." In addition to local in-person groups, you can find an endless array of entrepreneurial networks online. For example, Ryze, one of the leading professional networking websites, has a special section that helps entrepreneurs connect (http://entrepreneurs-network.ryze.com). You might want to look into both Young Entrepreneur (www.youngentrepreneur.com) and the Young Entrepreneurs Organization (www.yeo.org). You can find many others by searching online for "entrepreneurs network" or "small business network."

Business Incubators and Accelerators

business incubator
Facility that houses small businesses and provides support services during a company's early growth phases

A **business incubator** is a center that provides "newborn" businesses with just about everything a company needs to get started, from office space to information technology to management coaching, usually at sharply reduced costs. Many incubators are nonprofit organizations (often partnerships between local governments, universities, and established businesses), although a number of for-profit incubators now exist as well, and some companies have internal incubators to nurture new ventures. Incubators have spread rapidly in the past two decades; there are about 1,000 in North America and another 4,000 around the world. The objectives of specific incubators vary, such as facilitating the transfer of new technologies from universities to the commercial sector or developing local economies. For example, the Louisiana Technology Park in Baton Rouge, Louisiana, helps Internet, e-commerce, and biotechnology start-ups that show promise of making substantial contributions to the state economy. Like most incubators, the Louisiana Technology Park wants to help companies that are close to launching their products, so it sets time limits of 12 to 24 months for companies in the program. Nationwide, the success rate of incubators is extremely high—nearly 90 percent of companies that "graduated" from incubators are still in business.[39] To learn more about incubators or to find one in your area, visit the National Business Incubation Association website at www.nbia.org.

business accelerators
Similar in concept to an incubator but focused more on advisory services and (in some cases) financing

A **business accelerator** is similar to an incubator, and the terms are often used interchangeably. Generally speaking, accelerators focus more on providing advice and financing (in some cases) and less on providing office space and other infrastructure. To find an incubator or accelerator in your area, search online or contact your city or state economic development office.

Financing a New Business

Even the simplest home-based businesses require some start-up capital. The costs for a retail shop or small manufacturing facility can run to several hundred thousand dollars, and a more complex business might require millions of dollars of invested cash before it can begin to generate sales revenue. Of all the mistakes that first-time business owners make, underestimating the amount of money it takes to get rolling is one of the most common. This mistake can happen in several areas: overestimating sales, overestimating how quickly money will come in from those sales (corporate customers often take 30 to 60 days or longer to pay, for instance), and underestimating expenses. Entrepreneurs are optimists by nature, but experts strongly recommend against using best-case scenarios when estimating your financing needs. Lower your sales expectations, raise your expense estimates, and run your numbers past an experienced professional (such as a SCORE advisor) to make sure you've identified all the potential costs. And even when things work as planned, you might have to survive for several months before you can start putting money in the bank. Follow the example of Ross McDowell, who borrowed enough money to keep his new running-shoe store in Oshkosh, Wisconsin, going for three months without a single sale. Fortunately, he began to generate revenue sooner, so he banked the leftover start-up cash for emergency expenses down the road.[40]

Figuring out *how much* you'll need requires good insights into the particular industry you plan to enter. Figuring out *where* to get the money is a creative challenge no matter which industry you're in. As you can imagine, financing a business enterprise is a complex undertaking, and chances are you'll need to piece together funds from multiple sources, possibly using a combination of *equity* (in which you give investors a share of the business in exchange for their money) and *debt* (in which you borrow money that must be repaid). You'll read more about equity and debt financing in Chapter 7. Again, use the resources available today for advice; they can point you in the right direction for seeking both *private financing* and *public financing*.

Seeking Private Financing

Private financing covers every source of funding except selling stock to the public via a stock market. Virtually every company starts with private financing, even companies that eventually go public. The range of private financing options is diverse, from personal savings to investment funds set up by large corporations looking for entrepreneurial innovations. Many firms get *seed money*, their very first infusion of capital, through family loans. If you go this route, be sure to make the process as formal as a bank loan would be, complete with a specified repayment plan. Otherwise, problems with the loan can cause problems in the family.[41]

Four common categories of private financing, each of which requires its own special approach in order to be successful, are banks and microlenders, venture capitalists, angel investors, and that old standby of the entrepreneur—credit cards.

Banks and Microlenders

Bank loans are one of the most important sources of financing for small business—but there's an important catch: In most cases, banks won't lend money to a start-up that hasn't established a successful track record.[42] As your company grows, a bank will nearly always be a good long-term partner, helping you finance expansions and other major expenses. However, as a start-up, about your only chance of getting a bank loan is by putting up marketable collateral, such as buildings or equipment, to back the loan.[43] You'll learn more about working with banks in Chapter 8.

In response to the needs of entrepreneurs who don't qualify for standard bank loans or who don't need the amount of a regular loan, a number of organizations now serve as *microlenders*, offering loans or grants ranging from several hundred dollars up to several thousand or more to help very small operations get started. For instance, the worldwide Trickle Up program, www.trickleup.org, helps low-income people with grants to start businesses. When Renee Turning Heart, a member of the Cheyenne River Sioux Lakota Nation in South Dakota, was injured and lost her job, Trickle Up provided a small grant to help her start a business selling quilts. Two years later, Turning Heart's business was doing well enough that she qualified for a bank loan to expand.[44] Similarly, the Association for Enterprise Opportunity, www.microenterpriseworks.org, provides links to microlenders throughout the United States. While the companies that use microlenders may never grow up to be corporate giants, microlending is proving to be an effective way to help people move out of poverty and off public assistance.[45]

Venture Capitalists

venture capitalists (VCs)
Investors who provide money to finance new businesses or turnarounds in exchange for a portion of ownership, with the objective of reselling the business at a profit

Venture capitalists (VCs) are investment specialists who raise pools of capital from large private and institutional sources (such as pension funds) to fund ventures that have high growth potential and a need for large amounts of capital. VC funding often makes the headlines in the business media, such as when a high-flying start-up gets an injection of $10 million or $20 million. However, VCs are extremely selective; in a typical year, they finance only a few thousand companies in the United States with an average investment of around $7 million.[46]

Given the amounts of money involved and the expectations of sizable returns, VCs typically invest in high-potential areas such as information technology, biotechnology, and digital media. Unlike banks or most other financing sources, VCs do more than simply provide money. They also provide management expertise in return for a sizable ownership interest in the business. Once the business becomes profitable, VCs reap the reward by selling their interest to long-term investors, usually after the company goes public.

Because they risk considerable amounts of money, VCs are quite demanding of the management teams in the companies in which they do invest—and even more so after the dot-com, telecom, and biotech boom-and-bust years of the late 1990s. Unlike in those crazy days, VCs today are no longer willing to hand millions of dollars over to unproven firms led by recent college grads (sorry!); they now insist on experienced management running the company. Moreover, they want to invest in companies that are already profitable or that can show a strong possibility of becoming profitable if they receive funding. For instance, VCs investing in biotechnology are no longer content to fund years of unfocused research; they want their money going into specific products that show near-term potential.[47]

Angel Investors

Start-up companies that can't attract VC investment often look for *angel investors*, private individuals who put their own money into start-ups with the goal of eventually selling their interest for a large profit. These wealthy individuals are willing to invest smaller amounts than VCs usually invest and to stay involved with the company for a longer period of time. Many of these investors join *angel networks* or *angel groups* that invest together in chosen companies. Angel investing tends to have a more local focus than venture capitalism, so you can search for angels through local business contacts and organizations. You can also find many angel networks online or through *Inc.* magazine's *Directory of Angel-Investor Networks* at www.inc.com.[48]

A little creativity can always help, too. After Peter Cooper, an English entrepreneur, got his web-based newsfeed service FeedDigest (www.feeddigest.com) up and running, he asked early users to donate via PayPal to help cover his expenses. After enthusiastic users contributed $5,000, two angel investors from Seattle were intrigued enough by the burgeoning business to invest around $100,000 to help Cooper continue to grow.[49]

Credit Cards

Just like U.S. consumers, U.S. small-business owners are crazy about credit cards; roughly half of all small businesses are now financed with them. It's an easy way to get money for your business, particularly with credit card companies pitching you new cards all the time. It's also an incredibly easy way to get into trouble if things don't work out. Unfortunately, there is no simple answer about using credit cards; some entrepreneurs have used them to launch successful, multimillion-dollar businesses, while others have destroyed their credit ratings and racked up debts that will take years to pay off. Lindsay Smith of Rubbersidewalks (see page 135) financed her new company with $250,000 in credit card loans to match a grant from a California state agency. "I am not encouraging people to use that model," she explains, "but without it I wouldn't have been able to use the grant."[50] Her company has been a wonderful success story, but not all credit card financing plans work out, so entrepreneurs must approach this option with great caution.

Small Business Administration Assistance

If your business doesn't fit the profile of high-powered venture-capital start-ups, or you can't find an angel, you might be able to qualify for a bank loan backed by the Small Business Administration (SBA). SBA financing has helped launch some of the best-known companies in the United States, including FedEx, Intel, and Apple Computer. To get an SBA-backed loan, you apply to a regular bank, which actually provides the money; the SBA guarantees to repay between 50 to 85 percent of the loan (depending on the program) if you fail to do so. The upper limit on SBA-backed loans is currently $2 million.[51] In addition to operating its primary loan guarantee program, known as the 7(a) program, the SBA also manages a microloan program, known as 7(m), in conjunction with nonprofit, community-based lenders. The limit on these loans is currently $35,000.[52] Another option for raising money is one of the investment firms created by the SBA. These Small Business Investment Companies (SBICs) offer loans, venture capital, and management assistance, although they tend to make smaller investments and are willing to consider businesses that VCs or angel investors may not want to finance.[53]

Going Public

Companies with solid growth potential may also seek funding from the public at large, although only a small fraction of the companies in the United States are publicly traded. Whenever a corporation offers its shares of ownership to the public for the first time, the company is said to be *going public*. The initial shares offered for sale are the company's **initial public offering (IPO)**. Going public is an effective method of raising needed capital, but it can be an expensive and time-consuming process with no guarantee you'll get the amount of money you need. Public companies must meet a variety of regulatory requirements, as you'll explore in more detail in Chapter 7.

initial public offering (IPO)
A corporation's first offering of shares to the public

How This Affects You

1. Are you a good candidate for owning and operating a franchise? Why or not?

2. Think about a small business idea you've had or one of the small businesses you patronize frequently. Could this business be expanded into a national or international chain? Why or why not?

3. Would you be willing to take on $250,000 of credit card debt as Lindsay Smith did in order to start a company? If not, how much would you be willing to borrow against your credit cards?

Summary of Learning Objectives

1   Highlight the major contributions small businesses make to the U.S. economy.

Small businesses bring new ideas, processes, and vigor to the marketplace. They generate about half of private sector output and create between two-thirds and three-quarters of all new jobs. Small businesses introduce new goods and services, provide specialized products, and supply the needs of large corporations. Additionally, they spend almost as much as big businesses in the economy each year.

2   Identify the key characteristics (other than size) that differentiate small businesses from larger ones.

In general, small businesses tend to sell fewer products and services to a more targeted group of customers. They have closer contact with their customers and many tend to be more open-minded and innovative because they have less to lose than established companies. Small-business owners generally make decisions faster and give employees more opportunities for individual expression and authority. Because they have limited resources, however, small-business owners often must work harder and perform a variety of job functions.

3   Discuss three factors contributing to the increase in the number of small businesses.

One factor is the advancement of e-commerce and other technologies, which make it easier to start a small business, compete with larger firms, or work from home. A second factor is the increase in the number of women and minorities who are interested in becoming entrepreneurs. Third, corporate downsizing and outsourcing have pushed more professionals into self-employment and created more markets for their goods and services.

4   Cite the key characteristics common to most entrepreneurs.

Successful entrepreneurs are highly disciplined, intuitive, innovative, ambitious individuals who are eager to learn and like to set trends. They prefer excitement and are willing to take risks to reap the rewards. Few start businesses for the sole purpose of making money.

5   List three ways of going into business for yourself.

You can start a new company from scratch, you can buy an existing company, or you can invest in a franchise. Each option has its advantages and disadvantages when it comes to cost, control, certainty, support, and independence.

6   Identify six sources of small-business assistance.

First, government agencies and nonprofit organizations (including colleges and universities) can provide a variety of support services, advice, and even financing help. Second, business partners sometimes offer training or advice. Third, mentors and advisory boards can give business owners valuable advice and feedback on plans and decisions. Fourth, a wealth of information is available through print and online media, including business publications, blogs, and a variety of websites. Fifth, networks composed of other entrepreneurs and small-business owners can provide advice, encouragement, and contacts. Sixth, business incubators and accelerators can provide the support and infrastructure that emerging businesses need to get through the early growth stage.

7   Discuss the principal sources of small-business private financing.

Bank loans are a principal source of private financing, although they are difficult for many small businesses to obtain. Microlenders fill the need for smaller loans and grants in many cases. Family and friends are another source. Other alternatives include big businesses, venture capitalists, angel investors, and credit cards. Finally, the Small Business Administration, though not an actual source, can assist entrepreneurs by partially guaranteeing small bank loans.

Behind the Scenes

Another Web-Based Dream Becomes Reality at GeniusBabies.com

Michelle Donahue-Arpas dreamed of creating a company that would fulfill her twin goals of helping people find educational products for infants and young children and working from home to stay with her family. Establishing GeniusBabies.com as an Internet-only retailer met her need to run the business from home. However, unlike so many dot-com businesses that piled up investor cash then went looking for sales under the pressure to generate unachievable growth rates, Donahue-Arpas emphasized sensible, sustainable growth from the start. In fact, she started with less than $5,000 and coaxed the business along for $300 or so a month in the beginning. She managed her finances carefully and stayed focused on her target market—parents of newborns—both to avoid speculative investments in unproven markets and to concentrate her limited advertising budget for maximum impact.

Her career as a social worker gave plenty of insight into children, parents, and the products she was offering at GeniusBabies.com, but Donahue-Arpas knew she lacked experience in both business management and the technology needed for a successful Internet operation. So she turned to more experienced business owners for help. She teamed up with fellow "mompreneurs" with similar business goals to share advice, ideas, and even marketing support through a cooperative website called MyBabyShops.com. This advice and lots of trial-and-error learning have expanded Donahue-Arpas's business and technical skills and improved the operation along the way. For example, she redesigned her website to make it easier to find through Internet search engines and discontinued international sales when she realized the company couldn't satisfy overseas customers to the standard she wanted. Dropping international sales also meant she and her family could scale back their hours a bit, approaching something like a normal life at times.

Without a huge marketing budget, GeniusBabies.com emphasizes positive word of mouth, cooperative online marketing with similar companies, and a personal touch that keeps customers happy. Donahue-Arpas knows that simple moves such as personal notes and thank-you messages with orders can pay back big time in customer satisfaction and positive referrals. She says that consumers are so used to impersonal treatment from large corporations that they're pleasantly shocked when her small company communicates in such an intimate way.

Success naturally leads to growth, but Donahue-Arpas has kept it a mom-friendly, family affair. The staff now includes four other moms and the newest addition to the GeniusBabies.com family: her husband George. Her mother and grandmother even pitch in, along with a small army of temporary help during the holiday season.

Managing with limited resources, learning on the fly, digging deep for inspiration—these are all classic elements of the entrepreneurial experience. And so is hard work. Donahue-Arpas routinely works nights and weekends to keep customers satisfied and to manage the many facets of a growing business. Like most entrepreneurs, she has to put more into her work than the average job, but she wouldn't have it any other way. From staying at home to being her own boss to doing work she truly believes in, Michelle Donahue-Arpas has made her personal dream of entrepreneurship come true.[54]

Critical Thinking Questions

1. Why would Donahue-Arpas want to build her business slowly, rather than trying to achieve maximum market penetration as quickly as possible?
2. GeniusBabies.com proudly displays the Yahoo! Shopping five-star award for customer service (the site is hosted by Yahoo!'s Small Business e-commerce services). Visit Yahoo! Small Business at http://smallbusiness.yahoo.com; why would Donahue-Arpas choose Yahoo! to host her online business, rather than creating her own e-commerce website?
3. One of the risks that every small e-commerce retailer faces is that popular products are likely to be picked up by giants such as Amazon.com, which can probably offer lower prices. How can Donahue-Arpas ensure that her customers will keep buying from her if the products she carries start appearing on Amazon.com?

LEARN MORE ONLINE

Visit GeniusBabies.com at www.geniusbabies.com and explore the site, starting at the home page. How does it compare to the major online retailing sites? Imagine you're shopping for a gift for a family with a newborn daughter. Does GeniusBabies.com make it easy to find appropriate gift possibilities? Does the site's "homegrown," hands-on feel make you more or less inclined to purchase from the company? ■

▎Key Terms

business accelerator (148)	franchisee (143)	small business (135)
business incubator (148)	franchisor (143)	start-up companies (141)
business plan (141)	initial public offering	venture capitalists
franchise (143)	(IPO) (151)	(VCs) (150)

Test Your Knowledge

Questions for Review

1. What are two essential functions of a business plan?
2. What are the advantages of buying a business rather than starting one from scratch?
3. What are the advantages and disadvantages of owning a franchise?
4. What are the key reasons for most small-business failures?
5. What is a business incubator?

Questions for Analysis

6. Why is writing a business plan an important step in starting a new business?
7. Why is it important to establish a time limit for a new business to generate a profit?
8. What things should you consider when evaluating a franchise agreement?
9. What factors should you consider before selecting financing alternatives for a new business?
10. **Ethical Considerations.** You're thinking about starting your own hot dog and burger stand. You've got the perfect site in mind, and you've analyzed the industry and all the important statistics. It looks as if all systems are go. Uncle Pete is even going to back you on this one. You really understand the fast-food market. In fact, you've become a regular at a competitor's operation (down the road) for over a month. The owner thinks you're his best customer. He even wants to name a sandwich creation after you. But you're not there because you love Frannie's fancy fries. No, you're actually spying. You're learning everything you can about the competition so you can outsmart them. Is this behavior ethical? Explain your answer.

Questions for Application

11. Briefly describe an incident in your life in which you failed to achieve a goal you set for yourself. What did you learn from this experience? How could you apply this lesson to a future experience as an entrepreneur?
12. **How This Affects You.** Based on your total life experience up to this point—as a student, consumer, employee, parent, and any other role you might've played—what sort of business would you be best at running? Why?
13. **Integrated.** Entrepreneurs are one of the five factors of production as discussed in Chapter 1. Review that material plus Exhibit 1.2 ("Entrepreneurial Success Stories") on page 7 and explain why entrepreneurs are an important factor for economic success.
14. **Integrated.** Pick a local small business or franchise that you visit frequently and discuss whether that business competes on price, speed, innovation, convenience, quality, or any combination of those factors. Be sure to provide some examples.

Practice Your Knowledge

Sharpening Your Communication Skills

Effective communication begins with identifying your primary audience and adapting your message to your audience's needs. This is true even for business plans. One of the primary reasons for writing a business plan is to obtain financing. With that in mind, what do you think are the most important things investors will want to know? How can you convince them that the information you are providing is accurate? What should you assume investors know about your specific business or industry?

Building Your Team Skills

The ten questions shown in Exhibit 6.5 cover major legal issues you should explore before plunking down money for a franchise. In addition, however, there are many more questions you should ask in the process of deciding whether to buy a particular franchise.

With your team, think about how to investigate the possibility of buying a Papa John's franchise (www.papajohns.com, then click on "Franchise Opportunities"). First, brainstorm with your team to draw up a list of sources (such as printed sources, Internet sources, and any other suitable sources) where you can locate basic background information about the franchisor. Also list at least two sources you might consult for detailed information about buying and operating a Papa John's franchise. Next, generate a list of at least ten questions any interested buyer should ask about this potential business opportunity.

Choose a spokesperson to present your team's ideas to the class. After all the teams have reported, hold a class discussion to analyze the lists of questions generated by all the teams. Which questions were on most teams' lists? Why do you think those questions are so important? Can your class think of any additional questions that were not on any team's list but seem important?

Improving Your Tech Insights: Social Networking Technology

If you've used Friendster, Facebook, or MySpace, you're already familiar with social networking. Business versions of this technology are changing the way many professionals communicate. Social network applications, which can be either stand-alone software products or websites, help identify potential business connections by indexing e-mail and instant messaging address books, calendars, and message archives. For instance, you might find that the sales lead you've been struggling to contact at a large customer is a golf buddy of one of your suppliers or a relative of your child's soccer coach.

One of the biggest challenges small-business owners face is finding the right people and making those connections, whether you're looking for a new employee, an investor, a potential customer, or anyone else who might

be important to the future of your business. With social network applications, businesspeople can reach more people than they could ever hope to reach via traditional, in-person networking.

Visit LinkedIn (www.linkedin.com), Ryze (www.ryze.com), or Spoke (www.spoke.com) and read about that company's networking service. In a brief e-mail to your instructor, describe how you could use this service to locate potential candidates to serve on the advisory board of your small business (make up any details you need about your company).[55]

Expand Your Knowledge

Discovering Career Opportunities

Would you like to own and operate your own business? Whether you plan to start a new business from scratch or buy an existing business or a franchise, you will need certain qualities to be successful. Start your journey to entrepreneurship by reviewing this chapter's section on entrepreneurs.

1. Which of the entrepreneurial characteristics mentioned in the chapter describe you? Which of those characteristics can you develop more fully in advance of running your own business?

2. Visit the Small Business Planner at www.sba.gov and review "Is Entrepreneurship for You?" and "Do You Have What It Takes?" Which of the characteristics discussed in this chapter are mentioned or suggested by these two planning tools?

3. Study all the questions and points made in the two documents mentioned in the previous step. Which points seem the most critical for entrepreneurial success?

Which characteristics do you believe you already have? Before you go into business for yourself, which characteristics will you need to work on?

Developing Your Research Skills

Scan issues of print or online editions of business journals or newspapers for articles describing problems or successes faced by small businesses in the United States. Clip or copy three or more articles that interest you and then answer the following questions.

1. What problem or opportunity does each article present? Is it an issue faced by many businesses, or is it specific to one industry or region?

2. What could a potential small-business owner learn about the risks and rewards of business ownership from reading these articles?

3. How might these articles affect someone who is thinking about starting a small business?

See It on the Web

Visit these websites and answer the following questions for each one. (Up-to-date links for all websites mentioned in this chapter can be found on the Textbook Resources page for Chapter 6 at www.mybusinesslab.com. Please note that links to sites that become inactive after publication of the book will be removed from the Featured Websites section.)

1. What is the purpose of this website?

2. What kinds of information does this website contain? Please be specific.

3. How is the information provided at this website useful for businesspeople? Consumers?

4. How did you expand your knowledge of entrepreneurship and small-business ownership by reviewing the

material at this website? What new things did you learn about this topic?

Guide Your Way to Small-Business Success

Inc.com has an outstanding selection of articles and advice on buying, owning, and running a small business that you won't want to miss. If you're considering a franchise, the tools and tips at this site will help you find your ideal business. Concerned about financing? Check out the articles on raising start-up capital, finding an angel, or attracting venture capital. You can also find information on how to create or spruce up a website, set up your first office, develop entrepreneurial savvy, and overcome burnout. Running a small business is no easy feat, so get a head start by reading the Inc.com guides online. www.inc.com/guides

neurship is for you. Then do your research and discover some of the secrets of success. www.sba.gov

Start a Small Business

Thinking about starting your own business? The U.S. Small Business Administration (SBA) website puts you in touch with a wealth of resources to assist you in your start-up. Perhaps you would like some professional business counseling, financial assistance, or advice on developing a business plan. Starting a new business or buying an existing one can be an overwhelming process. But you can increase your chances of success by taking your first steps with the SBA's Small Business Planner. So log on to find out if entrepre-

Learn the ABCs of IPOs

Taking a company public is not for the faint of heart. But like a Broadway opening, a successful debut can launch a relatively unknown company into stardom—or allow it to quietly disappear from the public eye. Even today's largest corporations were at some point small start-ups looking for public financing. Find out who is going public this week at Hoovers's IPO Central, and see which recent IPO fared the best and worst in the stock market. www.hoovers.com (click on "IPO Central")

Companion Website

Learning Interactively

Log onto www.prenhall.com/bovée, locate your text, and then click on its Companion Website. For Chapter 6, take advantage of the interactive Chapter Quiz to test your

knowledge of the chapter. Get instant feedback on whether you need additional studying. Also, you'll find an abundance of valuable resources that will help you succeed in this course, including PowerPoint presentations and Web Links.

Video Case

Managing Growth at Student Advantage

LEARNING OBJECTIVES

The purpose of this video is to help you:

1. See how a company is successfully making the transition away from being a small business
2. Understand some of the pitfalls of growing beyond a small, entrepreneurial organization
3. Recognize how important partnerships with established companies can be for many small businesses

SYNOPSIS

Many students are familiar with the Student Advantage discount card, saving them up to 50 percent on everyday purchases on and off campus, including air and ground transportation. Keeping pace with the growing consumer base among high school and college students, Student Advantage, Inc., has successfully implemented an aggressive growth strategy. Working with hundreds of colleges, universities and campus organizations, and more than 15,000 merchant locations, the company reaches customers offline through the Student Advantage Membership and online through its website. Eleven acquisitions in its first ten years of existence have taught this company and its young CEO, Ray Sozzi, that communication is the key to growing beyond

a small business without losing the original entrepreneurial vision.

Discussion Questions

1. *For analysis:* Even though Student Advantage may have started as a small company, it was clearly created with an eye on growth, rather than as a lifestyle business designed to support one family. In a company that must partner with dozens of other companies and provide services to more than a million customers, what are the risks of growing quickly?
2. *For analysis:* Based on what you learned in the video, what steps did Student Advantage take to avoid the potential problems of a high-growth strategy based on frequent acquisitions?
3. *For analysis:* How does the "buddy system" help Student Advantage integrate employees from acquired companies?
4. *For application:* Student Advantage's corporate lawyer made a strong case for a go-slow approach to growing internationally. Given the millions of students in other countries who might want to use the company's services—and who might find other alternatives before Student Advantage becomes available in their respective countries—why would it be wise to grow slowly and

carefully, rather than jumping into new markets quickly, before competitors can spring up?

5. *For debate:* One of the Student Advantage executives describes the challenge of growing into the job without the benefit of previous managerial or executive experience. What are the pros and cons of bringing in experienced outside managers to help a small company, versus giving existing employees the opportunity to grow into managerial jobs?

ONLINE EXPLORATION

Visit Student Advantage's website at www.studentadvantage.com. Based on the types of services you see, what sort of companies does Student Advantage seek out as partners? How does the company promote its services to students? How does the website try to appeal to student lifestyle concerns, such as summer vacation or spring break?

PART 3

Managing for Profitability

CHAPTER 7
Accounting and Financial Management

CHAPTER 8
Banking and Securities

CHAPTER 7

Accounting and Financial Management

LEARNING OBJECTIVES
After studying this chapter, you will be able to

1. Discuss how managers and outsiders use financial information

2. Describe what accountants do

3. Summarize the impact of the Sarbanes-Oxley Act

4. State the basic accounting equation and explain the purpose of double-entry bookkeeping and the matching principle

5. Differentiate between cash basis and accrual basis accounting

6. Explain the purpose of the balance sheet and identify its three main sections

7. Explain the purpose of the income statement and statement of cash flows

8. Explain the purpose of ratio analysis and list the four main categories of financial ratios

9. Identify the responsibilities of a financial manager

Microsoft Looks for Ways to Unload a Mountain of Cash

www.microsoft.com

On the list of nice problems to have, this one has to rank near the top: After more than two decades of growing sales and careful management of its finances, Microsoft found itself sitting on $60 billion—and couldn't figure out what to do with it. (This amount included both cash and *cash equivalents*, assets the company could quickly convert to cash if needed.)

Microsoft Chairman Bill Gates and CEO Steve Ballmer faced an extraordinary dilemma: what to do with $60 billion in cash.

The company's second option, reinvesting internally, makes sense in principle, but spending $60 billion is not as easy as you might think. Even if executives wanted to dramatically expand the workforce, it would be virtually impossible to hire fast enough to consume that kind of money. Acquisitions are another possibility, and Microsoft has purchased a number of companies over the years. However, it has always done so for strategic reasons only, such as acquiring emerging technologies or filling in gaps in its product mix. Spending money for the sake of spending money has never been a viable alternative.

Publicly owned companies such as Microsoft have three basic choices for using cash the business generates above and beyond its day-to-day operational needs: (1) save it for emergencies and unexpected cash shortages; (2) invest it in the company's future; or (3) distribute it to stockholders in the form of *dividends*, which are regular payments at a designated amount per share.

Microsoft is known for its fiscally conservative management, which includes the habit of keeping enough cash on hand to deal with emergencies and unexpected expenses. However, it's hard to imagine any emergency dire enough to soak up $60 billion, so the rainy day savings plan option wasn't realistic.

Investors in Microsoft stock had been clamoring for option three, distributing a big chunk of that cash to shareholders. Microsoft was no longer the hot growth stock it had once been, but it wasn't paying the sizable cash dividends that mature companies often pay, either.

If you were advising Microsoft Chairman Bill Gates and CEO Steve Ballmer, which option would you choose?[1] ∎

Understanding Accounting

As Microsoft's Bill Gates and Steve Ballmer (profiled in the chapter opener) know, it's impossible to manage a business without accurate and up-to-date financial information. **Accounting** is the system a business uses to identify, measure, and communicate financial information to others, inside and outside the organization. Financial information is important to businesses for two reasons: First, it helps managers and owners plan and control a company's operations and make informed business decisions. Second, it helps outsiders evaluate a business. Suppliers, banks, and other lenders want to know whether a business is creditworthy; investors and shareholders are concerned with a

accounting
Measuring, interpreting, and communicating financial information to support internal and external decision making

company's profit potential; government agencies are interested in a business's tax accounting.

Because insiders and outsiders use accounting information for different purposes, accounting has two distinct facets. **Management accounting** involves the preparation of cost analyses, profitability reports, budgets, and other information for internal use by company managers. **Financial accounting** involves the preparation of financial statements and other information for outsiders such as stockholders and *creditors* (people or organizations that have lent a company money or have extended it credit). To be useful, all accounting information must be accurate, objective, consistent over time, and comparable to information supplied by other companies. As you'll see in this chapter, the accounting function is highly regimented and regulated in order to ensure quality financial information.

management accounting
Preparing data for use by managers within the organization

financial accounting
Preparing financial information for users outside the organization

What Accountants Do

Even if you don't enter the accounting and financial profession, knowing the fundamental principles of various accounting activities will make you a more effective manager. Accounting is sometimes confused with **bookkeeping**, which is the clerical function of recording the economic activities of a business. Although some accountants do perform bookkeeping functions, their work generally goes well beyond the scope of this activity. Accountants design accounting systems, prepare financial statements, analyze and interpret financial information, prepare financial forecasts and budgets, and prepare tax returns. Some accountants specialize in certain areas of accounting, such as *cost accounting* (computing and analyzing production and operating costs), *tax accounting* (preparing tax returns and interpreting tax law), *financial analysis* (evaluating a company's performance and the financial implications of strategic decisions such as product pricing, employee benefits, and business acquisitions), or *forensic accounting* (combining accounting and investigating skills to assist in legal and criminal matters).

bookkeeping
Recordkeeping, clerical aspect of accounting

controller
Highest-ranking accountant in a company, responsible for overseeing all accounting functions

certified public accountants (CPAs)
Professionally licensed accountants who meet certain requirements for education and experience and who pass a comprehensive examination

In addition to traditional accounting tasks, accountants may also help clients improve business processes, plan for the future, evaluate product performance, analyze profitability by customer and product groups, design and install new computer systems, assist companies with decision making, and provide a variety of other management consulting services. Performing these functions requires a strong business background and a variety of business skills beyond accounting.

Many accountants are *private accountants* (sometimes called *corporate accountants*), working for businesses, government agencies, or nonprofit organizations.[2] Private accountants generally work together as a team under the supervision of the organization's **controller**, who reports to the vice president of finance or the chief financial officer (CFO). Exhibit 7.1 shows the typical finance department of a large company. In smaller organizations, the controller may be in charge of the company's entire finance operation and report directly to the president.

Although certification is not required of private accountants, many are licensed **certified public accountants (CPAs)**. Specific requirements vary by state, but to receive a CPA license, an

Learning from Business Blunders

Oops: When you're in the business of preparing other peoples' taxes, making a $32 million mistake on your own taxes is not a way to build public confidence. Unfortunately, that's precisely the public embarrassment that H&R Block recently endured. The Kansas City, Missouri, tax-preparation giant handles the annual tax chores for more than 20 million customers but discovered it had miscalculated state tax rates when preparing its own taxes.

What You Can Learn: Obviously, making a giant blunder in your area of core competency is not a recommended strategy for encouraging current customers to keep using your services or enticing potential customers to give you a try. However, revising financial statements and tax filings is not all that uncommon, particularly for a company with as many moving parts as H&R Block, which serves customers through more than 11,000 company-owned and franchised offices throughout the country. The firm was quick to point out that its mistake was a result of bookkeeping errors, not fraud. Moreover, it emphasized that this type of error can occur only with corporate taxes, not the individual tax returns that it prepares for its customers. Fortunately, the blunder doesn't appear to have had a negative impact; the company served a record number of clients during the following tax season.

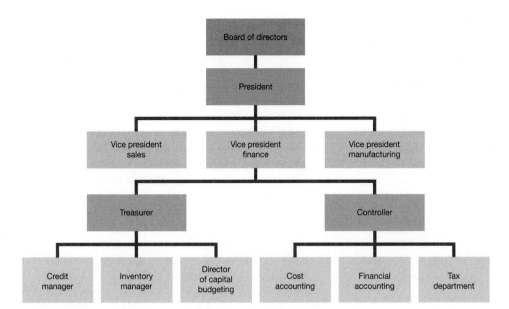

EXHIBIT 7.1

Typical Finance Department
Here is a typical finance department of a large company. In smaller companies, the controller may be the highest-ranking accountant and report directly to the president. The vice president in charge of finance is often called the chief financial officer (CFO).

individual must complete a certain number of hours of college-level coursework, have a minimum number of years of work experience in the accounting field, and pass a rigorous state-certified licensing exam.[3] A growing number of private accountants are becoming **certified management accountants (CMAs)**; to do so they must pass a two-day exam (given by the Institute of Management Accountants) that is comparable in difficulty to the CPA exam.[4]

In contrast to private accountants, **public accountants** are independent of the businesses, organizations, and individuals they serve. Most public accountants are employed by public accounting firms that provide a variety of accounting and consulting services to their clients. The largest of these firms, commonly known as the "Big Four," are Deloitte & Touche (www.deloitte.com), Ernst & Young (www.ey.com), KPMG (www.kpmg.com), and PricewaterhouseCoopers (www.pwcglobal.com). Whether they belong to one of these giant firms or a smaller regional or local firm, public accountants generally are CPAs and must obtain CPA and state licensing certifications before they are eligible to conduct an **audit**—a formal evaluation of a company's accounting records and processes to ensure the integrity and reliability of a company's financial statements. Whether they work for major public accounting firms, for corporations, or as independent CPAs, accountants play an increasingly vital role in the national and global economy.

certified management accountants (CMAs)
Accountants who have fulfilled the requirements for certification as specialists in management accounting

public accountants
Professionals who provide accounting services to other businesses and individuals for a fee

audit
Formal evaluation of the fairness and reliability of a client's financial statements

The Rules of Accounting

To make informed decisions, investors, bankers, suppliers, and other parties need some means to verify the quality of the financial information that companies release to the public. They also need some way to compare information from one company to the next. To accommodate these needs, financial accountants are expected to follow a number of rules, some of which are voluntary and some of which are required by law. The two most significant sets of rules are known as *GAAP*, which has evolved over decades, and *Sarbanes-Oxley*, major legislation affecting public corporations that was passed in the wake of several major accounting scandals in the past decade.

GAAP

Companies whose stock is publicly traded in the United States are required to file audited financial statements with the Securities and Exchange Commission (SEC). During an audit, CPAs who work for an independent accounting firm, also known as *external auditors*, review a client's financial records to determine whether the statements

Putting Accountability Back into Public Accounting

For a profession that is supposed to be all about trust and financial responsibility, public accounting seems to be lurching from one scandal to another: Billions of dollars in accounting fraud that slipped past auditors, multimillion-dollar fines for selling shady tax shelters, accountants arrested for destroying documents, accusations of overbilling, an endless parade of lawsuits from investors and clients—and the biggest black eye of them all, the collapse of the once-mighty accounting firm Arthur Andersen after it was convicted of obstruction of justice in the aftermath of the Enron scandal. (That conviction was later overturned, but not before the company—and 85,000 jobs—virtually disappeared.) How did all this happen, and how can the profession restore public confidence?

No situation this complex will surrender to a simple explanation, but observers point out several issues that have contributed to many of the recent problems:

■ *Deliberate deception by corporate clients.* Auditors maintain that in many cases it's impossible to detect deliberately misleading bookkeeping, and it's unfair to hold them accountable when they don't. An auditor "cannot provide 100 percent guarantee against fraud," says Chuck Landes, director of auditing for the American Institute of Certified Public Accountants (AICPA).

■ *Changes in accounting practices.* Some claim that auditors aren't looking in the right places. In the past, auditors used a labor-intensive process of sifting through thousands of transactions to determine whether bookkeeping entries were correct. Now they focus on analyzing the computerized bookkeeping programs and internal controls. While this approach prevents low-level employees from swiping petty cash, it can't always catch executives who shift millions or billions around using creative accounting schemes.

■ *Conflict of interest.* Others blame the conflict of interest that exists when an accounting firm earns millions performing consulting work for an audit client. "If you are

auditing your own creations, it is very difficult to criticize them," says one accounting expert. Critics say these cozy relationships and lucrative consulting contracts discouraged some auditors from examining corporate books closely enough or challenging CEOs when potential irregularities did surface.

■ *Overly aggressive business practices.* In 1991, the AICPA changed its code of conduct to allow tax accountants to charge performance-based fees, meaning that firms could charge a percentage of the money they saved clients by lowering their taxes. The IRS and industry insiders say this spawned a rash of overly aggressive tax shelters throughout the 1990s. After the IRS finally got its arms around the problem, it started banning these shelters, fining accountants who sold them, and recovering back taxes from clients who used them. Some of these clients are suing their accountants, claiming they were misled.

With billions of dollars and the financial health of millions of people on the line, the three-way tension among shareholders, auditors, and corporate managers is likely to go on for years. After PricewaterhouseCoopers paid $225 million to settle a shareholder lawsuit that claimed it should've detected the criminal financial fraud going on at one of its clients, attorneys said the large payout "sends a message to accounting firms." How well auditors pay attention to that message in coming years remains to be seen, but another message has come through loud and clear in the past few years: Auditing is a vital function upon which free enterprise and the health of the global economy depend.

Questions for Critical Thinking

1. Should accounting firms be allowed to perform management consulting functions for their audit clients? Why or why not?

2. Why is the auditing function of such vital importance to the global economy?

---

generally accepted accounting principles (GAAP)
Professionally approved U.S. standards and practices used by accountants in the preparation of financial statements

that summarize these records have been prepared in accordance with **generally accepted accounting principles (GAAP)**, basic accounting standards and procedures that have been agreed on by regulators, auditors, and companies. GAAP aims to give a fair and true picture of a company's financial position.

Once the auditors have completed an audit, they summarize their findings in a report attached to the client's published financial statements. Sometimes these reports disclose information that might materially affect the client's financial position, such as the bankruptcy of a major supplier, a large obsolete inventory, costly environmental problems, or questionable accounting practices. Most companies, however, receive a clean audit report, which means that to the best of the auditors' knowledge the company's financial statements are accurate.

To assist with the auditing process, many large organizations use *internal auditors*—employees who investigate and evaluate the organization's internal operations and data to determine whether they are accurate and whether they comply with GAAP, federal laws, and industry regulations. Although this self-checking process is vital to an organization's financial health, an internal audit is not a substitute for having an independent auditor look things over and render an unbiased opinion.

All U.S. public companies must publish their financial statements in accordance with GAAP. This requirement makes it possible for external parties to compare the financial results of one company with those of another and to gain a general idea of a firm's relative effectiveness and its standing within a particular industry. From time to time, companies experience special situations, such as incurring a significant onetime loss, which managers believe may distort the overall financial picture. In the recent past, it was common for companies in these situations to publish *pro forma* or *non-GAAP* numbers that removed the effect of these deviations from the financial results. Some companies claimed their investors wanted to see these numbers, but critics say that too often the technique was used to hide losses that would depress stock prices. The SEC now requires companies that publish pro forma results to also publish GAAP-equivalent results so that investors can compare the difference.[5]

In the United States, the Financial Accounting Standards Board (FASB) is responsible for overseeing GAAP. FASB tries to balance the interests of three groups: corporate managers, auditors, and investors. Over the years, the board has been criticized for allowing managers and auditors to exert too much influence, resulting in GAAP guidelines that obscured information of interest to investors. One possible reform in the future could be appointing more representatives of the investment community to the board.[6]

Other countries have similar governing boards with accounting rules that don't always match GAAP conventions, which means that foreign companies such as Nissan or Toyota may report accounting data using rules that are different from those used by U.S. companies such as Ford or General Motors. Foreign companies that list their securities on a U.S. stock exchange must, however, convert financial statements prepared under foreign accounting rules to GAAP. This requirement ensures that all companies listed on U.S. stock exchanges are on even ground.

The International Accounting Standards Board (IASB) has been working for years to develop a uniform set of global accounting rules known to help eliminate such differences. The IASB's proposed guidelines would simplify accounting for multinational companies, give foreign companies easier access to U.S. stock markets, and help investors select stocks from companies around the world.[7]

Sarbanes-Oxley

GAAP sets forth the principles and guidelines for companies and accountants to follow when preparing financial reports or recording accounting transactions, but high-profile scandals involving Enron, WorldCom, and other big corporations damaged investor confidence in corporate accounting practices. In response, Congress passed the Public Company Accounting Reform and Investor Protection Act of 2002, usually referred to as **Sarbanes-Oxley** (or informally as *Sarbox* or simply *Sox*). The legislation aims to stop abuses and errors in several important areas. The act[8]

Sarbanes-Oxley
Comprehensive legislation, passed in the wake of Enron and other scandals, designed to improve integrity and accountability of financial information

- Outlaws most loans by corporations to their own directors and executives
- Creates the Public Company Accounting Oversight Board (PCAOB) to oversee external auditors
- Requires corporate lawyers to report evidence of financial wrongdoing
- Prohibits external auditors from providing some nonaudit services
- Requires that audit committees on the board of directors have at least one financial expert and that the majority of board members be independent (not employed by the company in an executive position)

U.S. corporations continue to struggle with the complex requirements of Sarbanes-Oxley, a point underscored by SEC Chairman Christopher Cox when he held up a copy of Sarbanes-Oxley for Dummies while testifying before Congress.

▪ Prohibits investment bankers from influencing stock analysts

▪ Requires CEOs and CFOs to sign statements attesting to the accuracy of their financial statements

▪ Requires companies to document and test their internal financial controls and processes

The last item in particular, the result of the brief "Section 404" of the legislation, generated considerable controversy in the business community. Representative Michael Oxley, co-sponsor of the legislation, says that "99.9 percent of the complaints you hear are about 404." Oxley adds that it's not the two paragraphs in this section of the legislation that caused so much grief but rather the several hundred pages of regulations the PCAOB generated to enforce it.[9]

Critics complain that the cost of meeting the detailed documentation and test requirements far outweighs the benefits to investors. Some go so far as to assert that Sarbanes-Oxley has damaged American competitiveness.[10] One particular area of concern was that companies from other countries would stop listing on U.S. stock exchanges because the regulatory burdens were too extreme. For instance, the London Stock Exchange's AIM—a specialized stock market that caters to smaller and newer companies—has attracted many new listings in recent years thanks to its more relaxed financial reporting standards. However, while some of the biggest global IPOs in recent years were launched outside the United States, the number of non-U.S. IPOs on U.S. stock exchanges has been climbing. In fact, some companies view U.S. regulatory requirements as a benefit, not a deterrent. RRSat Global Communications Network, an Israeli company, chose the United States for its IPO *because* of the strict reporting regulations, not in spite of them. Following U.S. regulations "supports the confidence of the shareholder in the reporting by the company, and it improves [our] internal processes," says RRSat's chief financial officer.[11]

To address concerns about compliance costs for smaller companies, the PCAOB has recommended that these firms be allowed to focus only on high-risk aspects of their financial reporting processes, rather than worrying about every little detail. Nonetheless, the controversy over Sarbanes-Oxley is not going to die down anytime soon, with investors claiming that it is necessary to maintain public trust in the stock markets and management and auditors claiming that it is onerous and overreaching.[12] (For the latest information on Sarbanes-Oxley and other financial compliance and reporting matters, visit www.prenhall.com/bovée and click on "Real-Time Updates.")

Fundamental Accounting Concepts

All businesspeople—not just accountants and not just managers in publicly traded corporations—need to understand basic accounting concepts. The following sections discuss the fundamental accounting concepts, explore the key elements of financial statements, and explain how managers and investors analyze a company's financial statements to make decisions.

In their work with financial data, accountants are guided by three basic concepts: the *fundamental accounting equation, double-entry bookkeeping,* and the *matching principle.*

The Accounting Equation

assets
Any things of value owned or leased by a business

Assets are valuable items a company owns or leases, such as equipment, cash, land, buildings, inventory, investments, patents, and copyrights.

Liabilities are amounts the business owes to its creditors, such as banks and suppliers. What remains after liabilities have been deducted from assets is **owners' equity**:

$$\text{Assets} - \text{Liabilities} = \text{Owners' equity}$$

As a simple example, if your company has $1,000,000 in assets and $800,000 in liabilities, your equity would be $200,000:

$$\$1,000,000 - \$800,000 = \$200,000$$

This equation can be restated in a variety of formats. The most common is the simple **accounting equation**, which serves as the framework for the entire accounting process:

$$\text{Assets} = \text{Liabilities} + \text{Owners' equity}$$
$$\$1,000,000 = \$800,000 + \$200,000$$

This equation suggests that either creditors or owners provide all the assets in a corporation. Think of it this way: If you were starting a new business, you could contribute cash to the company to buy the assets you needed to run your business, you could borrow money from a bank (the creditor), or you could do both. The company's liabilities are placed before owners' equity in the accounting equation because creditors get paid first. After liabilities have been paid, anything left over belongs to the owners or, in the case of a corporation, to the shareholders. As a business engages in economic activity, the dollar amounts and composition of its assets, liabilities, and owners' equity change. However, the equation must always be in balance; in other words, one side of the equation must always equal the other side.

Double-Entry Bookkeeping and the Matching Principle

To keep the accounting equation in balance, most companies use a **double-entry bookkeeping** system that requires two entries for every transaction affecting assets, liabilities, or owners' equity. Each transaction is entered as both a **debit**, an increase in liabilities, and as a **credit**, an increase in assets. (This method predates computers by hundreds of years, and was originally created to minimize errors caused by entering and adding figures by hand.)

For example, if your company purchases a $5,000 computer on credit, your assets would increase by $5,000 (the value of the computer) and your liabilities would also increase by $5,000 (the amount you owe the company.) Your equity remains the same, and the double entries keep the accounting equation in balance:

$$\text{Assets} = \text{Liabilities} + \text{Owners' equity}$$
$$\$1,005,000 = \$805,000 + \$200,000$$

Similarly, if you paid cash, your assets would increase by the $5,000 value of the computer but simultaneously decrease by the $5,000 reduction in your cash holdings, so your equity would remain the same and the equation would stay in balance.

The **matching principle** requires that expenses incurred in generating revenues be deducted from the revenue they generated during the same accounting period. This matching of expenses and revenue enables financial statements to present an accurate picture of the profitability of a business. Accountants match revenue to expenses by adopting the **accrual basis** of accounting, which states that revenue is recognized when you make a sale, not when you get paid. Similarly, your expenses are recorded when you receive the benefit of any purchases you make—not when you pay for them. Accrual accounting focuses on the economic substance of the event instead of on the movement of cash. It's a way of recognizing that revenue can be earned either before or after cash is received and that expenses can be incurred when you receive a benefit (such as a shipment of supplies) whether before or after you pay for it.

---

liabilities
Claims against a firm's assets by creditors

owners' equity
Portion of a company's assets that belongs to the owners after obligations to all creditors have been met; called shareholders' or stockholders' equity in publicly traded companies

accounting equation
Basic accounting equation that assets equal liabilities plus owners' equity

double-entry bookkeeping
Way of recording financial transactions that requires two entries for every transaction so that the accounting equation is always kept in balance

debit
An increase in liabilities

credit
In bookkeeping, an increase in assets

matching principle
Fundamental principle requiring that expenses incurred in producing revenue be deducted from the revenues they generate during an accounting period

accrual basis
Accounting method in which revenue is recorded when a sale is made and expense is recorded when it is incurred

cash basis
Accounting method in which revenue is recorded when payment is received and expense is recorded when cash is paid

In contrast to the accrual basis, many smaller businesses run on a **cash basis**, in which the company records revenue only when money from the sale is actually received. Your checking account is a simple cash-based accounting system: You record checks at the time of purchase and deposits at the time of receipt. Revenue thus equals cash received, and expenses equal cash paid. Cash-based accounting can be misleading, however, because expenses and income can be misrepresented by the way payments are timed. It's easy to inflate income, for example, by delaying the payment of bills. For that reason, public companies are required to keep their books on an accrual basis.

During the normal course of business, a company enters into many transactions that benefit more than one accounting period—such as the purchase of buildings, inventory, and equipment. That new computer you purchased for $5,000, for instance, will help you generate revenue for several years even though you might have paid for it in just one month. **Depreciation**, the allocation of the cost of a tangible long-term asset over a period of time, helps companies match expenses with revenue. When you buy a piece of real estate or equipment, instead of deducting the entire cost of the item at the time of purchase, you *depreciate* it, or spread its cost over the asset's useful life. For tax purposes, the Internal Revenue Service requires companies to depreciate various types of assets over specific numbers of years. If a company were to expense long-term assets at the time of purchase, its financial performance would look artificially worse in the year of purchase and artificially better in all future years when these assets continue to generate revenue.

depreciation
Accounting procedure for systematically spreading the cost of a tangible asset over its estimated useful life

Using Financial Statements

close the books
The act of transferring net revenue and expense account balances to retained earnings for the period

As part of the accounting process, sales, purchases, and other transactions are recorded and classified into individual accounts. Once these individual transactions are recorded and summarized, accountants must review the resulting transaction summaries and adjust or correct all errors or discrepancies before they can **close the books**, or transfer net revenue and expense items for a specific time period to *retained earnings*. Exhibit 7.2 presents

EXHIBIT 7.2 The Accounting Process

The accounting process involves numerous steps between recording the sales and other transactions to the internal and external reporting of summarized financial results. (The paper forms illustrated here are classic accounting forms; today, nearly all companies record this information on computers.)

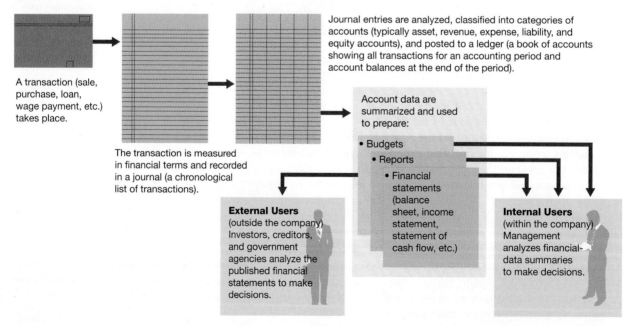

A transaction (sale, purchase, loan, wage payment, etc.) takes place.

The transaction is measured in financial terms and recorded in a journal (a chronological list of transactions).

Journal entries are analyzed, classified into categories of accounts (typically asset, revenue, expense, liability, and equity accounts), and posted to a ledger (a book of accounts showing all transactions for an accounting period and account balances at the end of the period).

Account data are summarized and used to prepare:

- Budgets
  - Reports
    - Financial statements (balance sheet, income statement, statement of cash flow, etc.)

External Users
(outside the company) Investors, creditors, and government agencies analyze the published financial statements to make decisions.

Internal Users
(within the company) Management analyzes financial-data summaries to make decisions.

the process for putting all of a company's financial data into standardized formats that can be used for decision making, analysis, and planning. To make sense of these individual transactions, accountants summarize them by preparing *financial statements.*

Understanding Financial Statements

The three primary financial statements are the *balance sheet,* the *income statement,* and the *statement of cash flows.* These statements are required by law for all publicly traded companies, but they are vital management tools for every company, no matter how large or small. Together the three statements provide information about an organization's financial strength and ability to meet current obligations, the effectiveness of its sales and collection efforts, and its effectiveness in managing its assets. Organizations and individuals use financial statements to spot opportunities and problems, to make business decisions, and to evaluate a company's past performance, present condition, and future prospects. The following sections examine simplified financial statements of Computer Central Services, a mid-size corporation that sells personal computers and related products.

Balance Sheet

The **balance sheet**, also known as the *statement of financial position,* is a snapshot of a company's financial position on a particular date (see Exhibit 7.3). In effect, it freezes all business actions and provides a baseline from which a company can measure change. This statement is called a balance sheet because it includes all elements in the accounting equation and shows the balance between assets on one side of the equation and liabilities and owners' equity on the other side. In other words, as in the accounting equation, a change on one side of the balance sheet means changes elsewhere.

Every company prepares a balance sheet at least once a year, most often at the end of the **calendar year**, covering from January 1 to December 31. However, many business and government bodies use a **fiscal year**, which may be any 12 consecutive months. For example, a company may use a fiscal year of June 1 to May 31 because its peak selling season ends in May. Its fiscal year would then correspond to its full annual cycle of operations. Some companies prepare a balance sheet more often than once a year, perhaps at the end of each month or quarter. Every balance sheet is dated to show the exact date when the financial snapshot was taken.

By reading a company's balance sheet you should be able to determine the size of the company, the extent of its assets, any asset changes that occurred in recent periods, how the company's assets are financed, and any major changes that have occurred in the company's debt and equity in recent periods.

Assets   As discussed earlier in the chapter, an asset is something of value owned by a company that will be used to generate income directly or indirectly. Assets can consist of cash, things that can be converted into cash (such as investments), and equipment needed to produce goods or services for sale. For example, Computer Central Services needs a warehouse and office facility and a sizable inventory to sell computer products to its customers. Assets can also be *intangible*; these include intellectual property, such as patents and business methods, and *goodwill*, which includes reputation and brand recognition. As you might expect, assigning value to intangible assets is not an easy task, and some companies do not list intangibles on their balance sheets.

Most often, the asset section of the balance sheet is divided into *current assets* and *fixed assets.* **Current assets** include cash and other items that will or can become cash within the following year. **Fixed assets** (sometimes referred to as *property, plant, and equipment*) are long-term investments in buildings, equipment, furniture and fixtures, transportation equipment, land, and other tangible property used in running the business. Fixed

balance sheet
Statement of a firm's financial position on a particular date; also known as a *statement of financial position*

calendar year
Twelve-month accounting period that begins on January 1 and ends on December 31

fiscal year
Any 12 consecutive months used as an accounting period

current assets
Cash and items that can be turned into cash within one year

fixed assets
Assets retained for long-term use, such as land, buildings, machinery, and equipment; also referred to as *property, plant, and equipment*

The goodwill that a highly regarded brand name such as Mercedes-Benz enjoys is an important intangible asset.

EXHIBIT 7.3 Balance Sheet for Computer Central Services

Here is a simplified version of the balance sheet for Computer Central Services. (The numbers have been rounded off to make it easy for you to see how the various entries add up.)

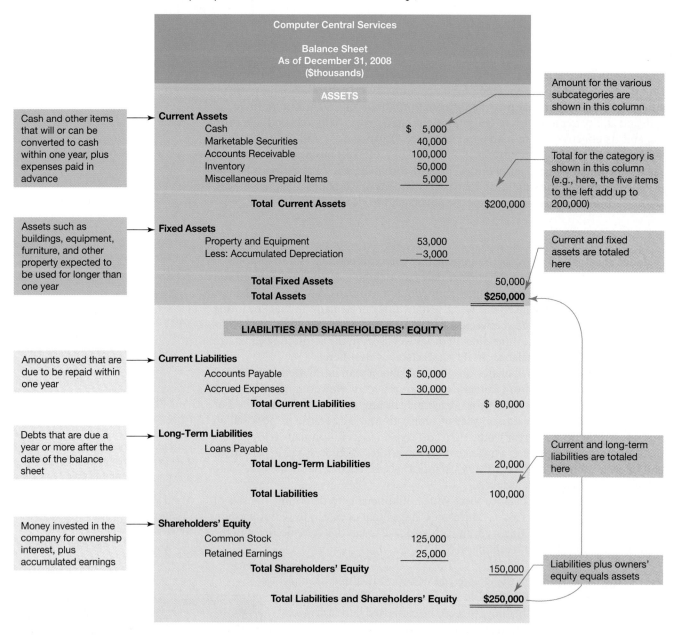

Cash and other items that will or can be converted to cash within one year, plus expenses paid in advance

Assets such as buildings, equipment, furniture, and other property expected to be used for longer than one year

Amounts owed that are due to be repaid within one year

Debts that are due a year or more after the date of the balance sheet

Money invested in the company for ownership interest, plus accumulated earnings

Amount for the various subcategories are shown in this column

Total for the category is shown in this column (e.g., here, the five items to the left add up to 200,000)

Current and fixed assets are totaled here

Current and long-term liabilities are totaled here

Liabilities plus owners' equity equals assets

Computer Central Services

Balance Sheet
As of December 31, 2008
($thousands)

ASSETS

Current Assets		
Cash	$ 5,000	
Marketable Securities	40,000	
Accounts Receivable	100,000	
Inventory	50,000	
Miscellaneous Prepaid Items	5,000	
Total Current Assets		$200,000
Fixed Assets		
Property and Equipment	53,000	
Less: Accumulated Depreciation	−3,000	
Total Fixed Assets		50,000
Total Assets		**$250,000**

LIABILITIES AND SHAREHOLDERS' EQUITY

Current Liabilities		
Accounts Payable	$ 50,000	
Accrued Expenses	30,000	
Total Current Liabilities		$ 80,000
Long-Term Liabilities		
Loans Payable	20,000	
Total Long-Term Liabilities		20,000
Total Liabilities		100,000
Shareholders' Equity		
Common Stock	125,000	
Retained Earnings	25,000	
Total Shareholders' Equity		150,000
Total Liabilities and Shareholders' Equity		**$250,000**

assets have a useful life of more than one year. Computer Central Services's principal fixed asset is the company's warehouse and office facility.

Assets are listed in descending order by *liquidity*, or the ease with which they can be converted into cash. Thus, current assets are listed before fixed assets. The balance sheet gives a subtotal for each type of asset and then a grand total for all assets. Computer Central Services's current assets consist primarily of cash, investments in short-term **marketable securities** such as money-market funds, **accounts receivable** (amounts due from customers), and inventory (such as computers, software, and other items the company sells to customers).

Liabilities Liabilities come after assets because they represent claims against the company's assets, as shown in the basic accounting equation: Assets = Liabilities + Owners' equity. Liabilities may be current or long-term, and they are listed in the order in which

marketable securities
Stocks, bonds, and other investments that can be turned into cash quickly

accounts receivable
Amounts that are currently due to a company

they will come due. The balance sheet gives subtotals for **current liabilities** (obligations that have to be met within one year of the date of the balance sheet) and **long-term liabilities** (obligations that are due one year or more after the date of the balance sheet), and then it gives a grand total for all liabilities.

Current liabilities include accounts payable, short-term financing, and accrued expenses. **Accounts payable** are amounts a company owes its suppliers—its "bills," in other words. *Short-term financing* consists of *trade credit*—the amount owed to suppliers for products purchased but not yet paid for—and *commercial paper*—short-term promissory notes of major corporations sold in denominations of $100,000 or more, with maturities of up to 270 days (the maximum allowed by the SEC without registration).

Accrued expenses are expenses that have been incurred but for which bills have not yet been received. For example, because Computer Central Services's account executives earn commissions on computer sales to customers, the company has a liability to its account executives once the sale is made—regardless of when a check is issued to the employee. Thus, the company must record this liability because it represents a claim against company assets. If such expenses and their associated liabilities were not recorded, the company's financial statements would be misleading and would violate the matching principle (because the commission expenses that were earned at the time of sale would not be matched to the revenue generated from the sale).

Long-term liabilities include loans, leases, and bonds. The borrowing company makes principal and interest payments to the bank over the term of the loan, and its obligation is limited to these payments (see "Debt Versus Equity Financing" on page 178). Leases are an alternative to loans. Rather than borrowing money to buy a piece of equipment, a firm may enter into a long-term *lease*, under which the owner of an item allows another party to use it in exchange for regular payments. Bonds are certificates that obligate the company to repay a certain sum, plus interest, to the bondholder on a specific date. Bonds are traded on organized securities exchanges and are discussed in detail in Chapter 8.

Owners' Equity   The owners' investment in a business is listed on the balance sheet under owners' equity (or *shareholders'* or *stockholders' equity* for corporations). Sole proprietorships list owner's equity under the owner's name with the amount (assets minus liabilities). Small partnerships list each partner's share of the business separately, and large partnerships list the total of all partners' shares. In a corporation, the shareholders' total investment value is the sum of two amounts: the total value of the all the shares currently held, plus **retained earnings**—cash that is kept by the company rather than distributed to shareholders in the form of *dividends* (see page 116 in Chapter 5). As Exhibit 7.3 shows, Computer Central Services's retained earnings amount to $25 million. Hardly the $60 billion Microsoft had piled up, but an impressive amount nonetheless. The company doesn't pay dividends—many small and growing corporations don't—but rather builds its cash reserves to fund expansion in the future. (Shareholders' equity can be slightly more complicated than this, depending on how the company's shares were first created, but this gives you the basic idea of how the assets portion of the balance sheet works.)

Income Statement

If the balance sheet is a snapshot, the income statement is a movie. The **income statement** shows an organization's profit performance over a specific period of time, such as a month or a year (see Exhibit 7.4). It summarizes all **revenues** (or sales), the amounts that have been or are to be received from customers for goods or services delivered to them, and all **expenses**, the costs that have arisen in generating revenues. Expenses and income taxes are then subtracted from revenues to show the actual profit or loss of a company, a figure known as **net income**—profit, or the *bottom line*. By briefly reviewing a company's income statements you should have a general sense of the company's size,

current liabilities
Obligations that must be met within a year

long-term liabilities
Obligations that fall due more than a year from the date of the balance sheet

accounts payable
Short-term credit or debt amounts that a company owes its suppliers; the company's "bills" in other words

retained earnings
The portion of shareholders' equity earned by the company but not distributed to its owners in the form of dividends

income statement
Financial record of a company's revenues, expenses, and profits over a given period of time

revenues
Amount earned from sales of goods or services and inflow from miscellaneous sources such as interest, rent, and royalties

expenses
Costs created in the process of generating revenues

net income
Profit earned or loss incurred by a firm, determined by subtracting expenses from revenues; also called the *bottom line*

EXHIBIT 7.4 Income Statement for Computer Central Services

An income statement summarizes the company's financial operations over a particular accounting period, usually a year.

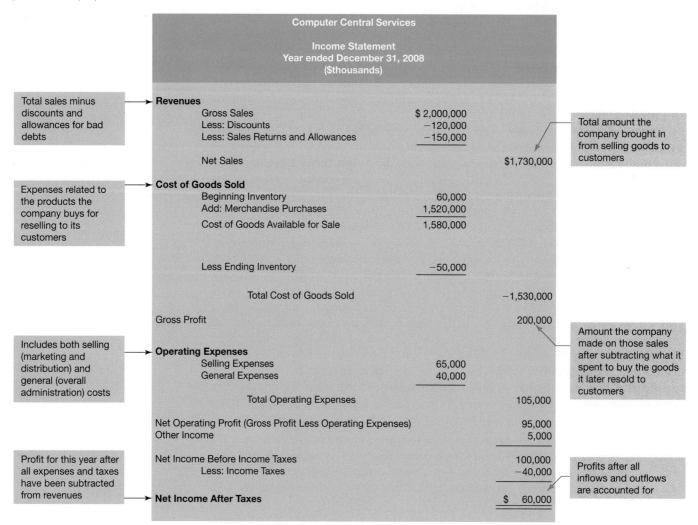

Total sales minus discounts and allowances for bad debts

Expenses related to the products the company buys for reselling to its customers

Includes both selling (marketing and distribution) and general (overall administration) costs

Profit for this year after all expenses and taxes have been subtracted from revenues

Total amount the company brought in from selling goods to customers

Amount the company made on those sales after subtracting what it spent to buy the goods it later resold to customers

Profits after all inflows and outflows are accounted for

Computer Central Services

Income Statement
Year ended December 31, 2008
($thousands)

Revenues		
Gross Sales	$ 2,000,000	
Less: Discounts	−120,000	
Less: Sales Returns and Allowances	−150,000	
Net Sales		$1,730,000
Cost of Goods Sold		
Beginning Inventory	60,000	
Add: Merchandise Purchases	1,520,000	
Cost of Goods Available for Sale	1,580,000	
Less Ending Inventory	−50,000	
Total Cost of Goods Sold		−1,530,000
Gross Profit		200,000
Operating Expenses		
Selling Expenses	65,000	
General Expenses	40,000	
Total Operating Expenses		105,000
Net Operating Profit (Gross Profit Less Operating Expenses)		95,000
Other Income		5,000
Net Income Before Income Taxes		100,000
Less: Income Taxes		−40,000
Net Income After Taxes		$ 60,000

its sales trends, its major expenses, and the resulting net income or loss. Owners, creditors, and investors can evaluate the company's past performance and future prospects by comparing net income for one year with net income for previous years.

Expenses include both the direct costs associated with creating or purchasing products for sale and the indirect costs associated with operating the business. Whether a company manufactures or purchases its inventory, the cost of storing the product for sale (such as heating the warehouse, paying the rent, and buying insurance on the storage facility) is added to the difference between the cost of the beginning inventory and the cost of the ending inventory in order to compute the actual cost of items that were sold during a period—or the **cost of goods sold**. The computation can be summarized as follows:

Cost of goods sold = Beginning inventory + Net purchases − Ending inventory

As shown in Exhibit 7.4, cost of goods sold is deducted from sales to obtain a company's **gross profit**—a key figure used in financial analysis. In addition to the costs directly associated with producing goods, companies deduct **operating expenses**, which include both *selling expenses* and *general expenses,* to compute a firm's *net operating income,* or the income that is generated from business operations. **Selling expenses** are

cost of goods sold
Cost of producing or acquiring a company's products for sale during a given period

gross profit
Amount remaining when the cost of goods sold is deducted from net sales; also known as *gross margin*

operating expenses
All costs of operation that are not included under cost of goods sold

selling expenses
All the operating expenses associated with marketing goods or services

operating expenses incurred through marketing and distributing the product (such as wages or salaries of salespeople, advertising, supplies, and other sales department expenses such as telephone charges and website-hosting fees). **General expenses** are operating expenses incurred in the overall administration of a business. They include professional services (accounting and legal fees), office salaries, depreciation of office equipment, insurance for office operations, and supplies.

    A firm's net operating income is then adjusted by the amount of any nonoperating income or expense items such as the gain or loss on the sale of a building. The result is the firm's net income or loss before income taxes, a key figure used in budgeting, cash-flow analysis, and a variety of other financial computations. Finally, income taxes are deducted to compute the company's net income or loss for the period.

general expenses
Operating expenses, such as office and administrative expenses, not directly associated with creating or marketing a good or a service

Statement of Cash Flows

In addition to preparing a balance sheet and an income statement, all public companies and many privately owned companies prepare a **statement of cash flows** to show how much cash the company generated over time and where it went (see Exhibit 7.5). The statement of cash flows tracks the cash coming into and flowing out of a company's bank accounts. It reveals the increase or decrease in the company's cash for the period and summarizes (by category) the sources of that change. From a brief review of this statement, you should have a general sense of the amount of cash created or consumed by daily operations, the amount of cash invested in fixed or other assets, the amount of debt borrowed or repaid, and the proceeds from the sale of stock or payments for dividends. In addition, an analysis of cash flows provides a good idea of a company's ability to pay its short-term obligations when they become due.

statement of cash flows
Statement of a firm's cash receipts and cash payments that presents information on its sources and uses of cash

EXHIBIT 7.5 **Statement of Cash Flows for Computer Central Services**

A statement of cash flows shows a firm's cash receipts and cash payments as a result of three main activities—operating, investing, and financing—for an identified period of time (such as the year indicated here).

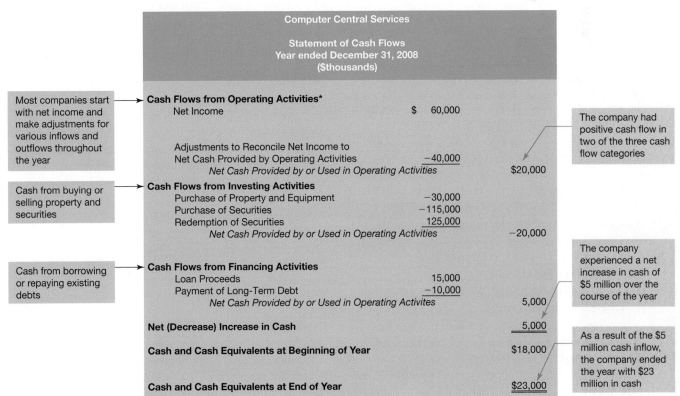

Computer Central Services

Statement of Cash Flows
Year ended December 31, 2008
($thousands)

Most companies start with net income and make adjustments for various inflows and outflows throughout the year	**Cash Flows from Operating Activities***		
	Net Income	$ 60,000	
	Adjustments to Reconcile Net Income to Net Cash Provided by Operating Activities	−40,000	
	Net Cash Provided by or Used in Operating Activities		$20,000

The company had positive cash flow in two of the three cash flow categories

Cash from buying or selling property and securities	**Cash Flows from Investing Activities**		
	Purchase of Property and Equipment	−30,000	
	Purchase of Securities	−115,000	
	Redemption of Securities	125,000	
	Net Cash Provided by or Used in Operating Activities		−20,000

Cash from borrowing or repaying existing debts	**Cash Flows from Financing Activities**		
	Loan Proceeds	15,000	
	Payment of Long-Term Debt	−10,000	
	Net Cash Provided by or Used in Operating Activites		5,000

The company experienced a net increase in cash of $5 million over the course of the year

Net (Decrease) Increase in Cash			5,000
Cash and Cash Equivalents at Beginning of Year			$18,000
Cash and Cash Equivalents at End of Year			$23,000

As a result of the $5 million cash inflow, the company ended the year with $23 million in cash

*Numbers preceded by minus sign indicate cash outflows

Analyzing Financial Statements

Once financial statements have been prepared, managers and other interested parties can use these documents to evaluate the financial health of the organization, make business decisions, and spot opportunities for improvements by looking at the company's performance in relation to its past performance, the economy as a whole, and the performance of its competitors.

Trend Analysis

The process of comparing financial data from year to year in order to identify changes is known as *trend analysis*. You can use trend analysis to uncover shifts in the nature of the business over time. Most large companies provide data for trend analysis in their annual reports. Their balance sheets and income statements typically show three to five years or more of data (making comparative statement analysis possible). Changes in other key items—such as revenues, income, earnings per share, and dividends per share—are usually presented in tables and graphs.

Of course, when you are comparing one period with another, it's important to take into account the effects of extraordinary or unusual items such as the sale of major assets, the purchase of a new line of products from another company, weather, or economic conditions that may have affected the company in one period but not the next.

How to Read an Annual Report

Whether you're thinking of investing, becoming a supplier, or applying for a job, knowing how to read a company's annual report will be an important skill throughout your career. Thus, it's worth your while to consider the advice of *Newsweek* columnist Jane Bryant Quinn, who provided these pointers.

READ THE LETTERS

First, turn to the report of the certified public accountant. This third-party auditor will tell you right off the bat if the report conforms with generally accepted accounting principles. Now turn to the letter from the board chair. This letter should tell you how the company fared this year, but more important, the letter should tell you why. Keep an eye out for sentences that start with "Except for . . ." and "Despite the. . ." They're clues to potential problems. The chair's letter should also give you insights into the company's future. For example, look for what's new in each line of business. Is management positioning the company for new market developments and changing competition?

DIG INTO THE NUMBERS

Check out the trend in the company's working capital (the difference between current assets and current liabilities). If working capital is shrinking, it could mean trouble. One possibility: The company may not be able to keep dividends growing rapidly.

Another important number to analyze is earnings per share. Management can boost earnings by selling off a plant or by cutting the budget for research or advertising. See the footnotes; they often tell the whole story. If earnings are down only because of a change in accounting, maybe that's good! The company owes less tax and has more money in its pocket. If earnings are up, maybe that's bad. They may be up because of a special windfall that won't happen again next year. One good indicator is the trend in net sales. If sales increases are starting to slow, the company may be in trouble.

GET OUT YOUR CALCULATOR AND COMPARE

High and rising debt, relative to equity, may be no problem for a growing business. But it shows weakness in a company that's leveling out. So get out your calculator and divide long-term liabilities by shareholders' equity. That's the debt-to-equity ratio. A high ratio means the company borrows a lot of money to fund its growth. That's okay—if sales grow too, and if there's enough cash on hand to meet the payments. But if sales fall, watch out. The whole enterprise may slowly sink.

Remember, one ratio, one annual report, one letter won't tell you much. You have to compare. Is the company's debt-to-equity ratio better or worse than it used to be? Better or worse than the industry norms? In company watching, comparisons tell all—especially if management is staying on top of things.

Questions for Critical Thinking

1. Why might a job seeker want to read a company's annual report before applying for a job with that company?
2. What types of valuable nonfinancial information might an annual report disclose to a potential supplier?

These extraordinary items are usually disclosed in the text portion of a company's annual report or in the notes to the financial statements.

Ratio Analysis

Managers and others compute *financial ratios* to facilitate the comparison of one company's financial results with those of competing firms and with industry averages. **Ratio analysis** compares two elements from the same year's financial figures. They are called *ratios* because they are computed by dividing one element of a financial statement by another. The advantage of using ratios is that it puts companies on the same footing; that is, it makes it possible to compare different-size companies and changing dollar amounts. For example, by using ratios, you can easily compare a large supermarket's ability to generate profit with a similar statistic for a small grocery store.

Financial ratios help companies understand their current operations and answer key questions: Is inventory too large? Are credit customers paying too slowly? Can the company pay its bills? Ratios also set standards and benchmarks for gauging future business by comparing a company's scores with industry averages that show the performance of competition. Every industry tends to have its own "normal" ratios, which act as yardsticks for individual companies. Dun & Bradstreet and Robert Morris Associates are among the firms that publish both average financial figures and ratios for a variety of industries and company sizes.

Before reviewing specific ratios, consider two rules of thumb: First, avoid drawing too strong a conclusion from any one ratio. Each company's circumstances are unique, and being "too high" or "too low" with a given ratio may not necessarily be a bad thing. Second, after ratios have presented a general indication, refer back to the specific data involved to see whether the numbers confirm what the ratios suggest. In other words, do a little investigating, because statistics can be misleading.

Types of Financial Ratios

Financial ratios can be organized into the following groups, as Exhibit 7.6 shows: profitability, liquidity, activity, and leverage (or debt).

Profitability Ratios **Profitability ratios** show the state of the company's financial performance by measuring its ability to generate profits. Three of the most common profitability ratios are **return on sales**, or profit margin (the net income a business makes per unit of sales); **return on investment (ROI)**, or return on equity (the income earned on the owner's investment); and **earnings per share** (the profit earned for each share of stock outstanding). Exhibit 7.6 shows how to compute these profitability ratios by using the financial information from Computer Central Services.

Liquidity Ratios **Liquidity ratios** measure the ability of the firm to pay its short-term obligations. As you might expect, lenders and creditors are keenly interested in liquidity measures. Liquidity can be judged on the basis of *working capital,* the *current ratio,* and the *quick ratio.* A company's **working capital**, current assets minus current liabilities, is an important indicator of liquidity. The dollar amount of working capital can be misleading, however. For example, it may include the value of slow-moving inventory items that cannot be used to help pay a company's short-term debts.

A different picture of the company's liquidity is provided by the **current ratio**—current assets divided by current liabilities. This figure compares the current debt owed with the current assets available to pay that debt. The **quick ratio**, also called the *acid-test ratio,* is computed by subtracting inventory from current assets and then dividing the result by current liabilities. This ratio is often a better indicator of a firm's ability to pay creditors than the current ratio because the quick ratio leaves out inventories—which may be difficult to sell quickly. Analysts generally consider a quick ratio of 1.0 to be reasonable, whereas a current ratio of 2.0 is considered a safe risk for short-term credit. Exhibit 7.6 shows that both the current and quick ratios of Computer Central Services are well above these benchmarks and industry averages.

---

ratio analysis
Use of quantitative measures to evaluate a firm's financial performance

profitability ratios
Ratios that measure the overall financial performance of a firm

return on sales
Ratio between net income after taxes and net sales; also known as *profit margin*

return on investment (ROI)
Ratio between net income after taxes and total owners' equity; also known as *return on equity*

earnings per share
Measure of profitability calculated by dividing net income after taxes by the average number of shares of common stock outstanding

liquidity ratios
Ratios that measure a firm's ability to meet its short-term obligations when they are due

working capital
Current assets minus current liabilities

current ratio
Measure of a firm's short-term liquidity, calculated by dividing current assets by current liabilities

quick ratio
Measure of a firm's short-term liquidity, calculated by adding cash, marketable securities, and receivables, then dividing that sum by current liabilities; also known as the *acid-test ratio*

EXHIBIT 7.6 How Well Does This Company Stack Up?

Nearly all companies use ratios to evaluate how well the company is performing in relation to prior performance, the economy as a whole, and the company's competitors. This chart shows how Computer Central Services stacks up against several competitors in its industry.

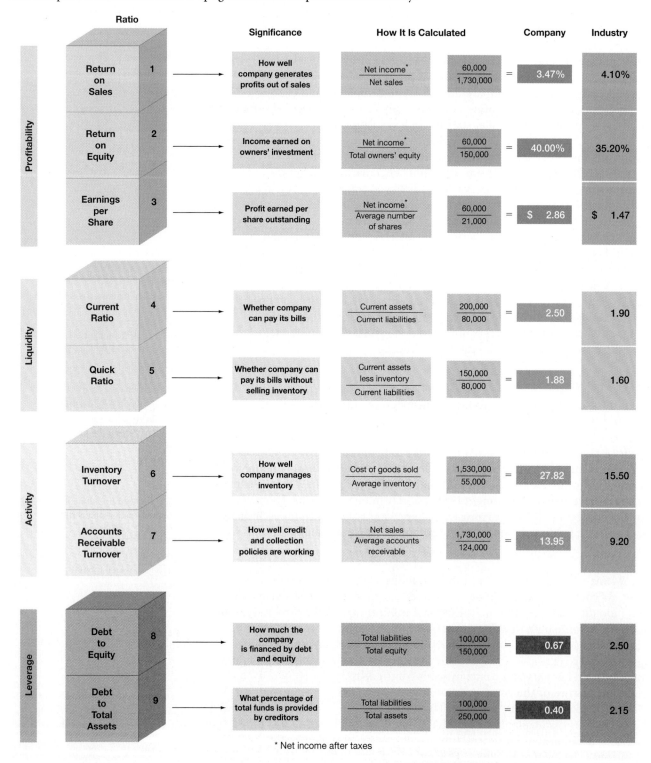

Ratio		Significance	How It Is Calculated		Company	Industry
Profitability						
Return on Sales	1	How well company generates profits out of sales	Net income* / Net sales	60,000 / 1,730,000	3.47%	4.10%
Return on Equity	2	Income earned on owners' investment	Net income* / Total owners' equity	60,000 / 150,000	40.00%	35.20%
Earnings per Share	3	Profit earned per share outstanding	Net income* / Average number of shares	60,000 / 21,000	$ 2.86	$ 1.47
Liquidity						
Current Ratio	4	Whether company can pay its bills	Current assets / Current liabilities	200,000 / 80,000	2.50	1.90
Quick Ratio	5	Whether company can pay its bills without selling inventory	Current assets less inventory / Current liabilities	150,000 / 80,000	1.88	1.60
Activity						
Inventory Turnover	6	How well company manages inventory	Cost of goods sold / Average inventory	1,530,000 / 55,000	27.82	15.50
Accounts Receivable Turnover	7	How well credit and collection policies are working	Net sales / Average accounts receivable	1,730,000 / 124,000	13.95	9.20
Leverage						
Debt to Equity	8	How much the company is financed by debt and equity	Total liabilities / Total equity	100,000 / 150,000	0.67	2.50
Debt to Total Assets	9	What percentage of total funds is provided by creditors	Total liabilities / Total assets	100,000 / 250,000	0.40	2.15

* Net income after taxes

activity ratios
Ratios that measure the effectiveness of the firm's use of its resources

Activity Ratios A number of **activity ratios** may be used to analyze how well a company is managing its assets. The most common is the **inventory turnover ratio**, which measures how fast a company's inventory is turned into sales; in general, the quicker the better, because holding excess inventory can be expensive. When inventory sits on the shelf, money is tied up without earning interest; furthermore, the company incurs expenses for its storage, handling, insurance, and taxes. In addition, there is always a risk that the inventory will become obsolete before it can be converted into finished goods and sold. The firm's goal is to maintain enough inventory to fill orders in a timely fashion at the lowest cost.

Keep in mind that it's difficult to judge a company by its inventory level. For example, lower inventories might mean one of many things: You're running an efficient operation, the right inventory is not being stocked, or sales are booming and you need to increase your orders. Likewise, higher inventories could signal a decline in sales, careless ordering, or stocking up because of favorable pricing. The "ideal" turnover ratio varies with the type of operation. As Exhibit 7.6 shows, Computer Central Services turned its inventory nearly 28 times a year, unusually high compared with industry averages.

Another popular activity ratio is the **accounts receivable turnover ratio**, which measures how well a company's credit and collection policies are working by indicating how frequently accounts receivable are converted to cash. The volume of receivables outstanding depends on the financial manager's decisions regarding several issues, such as who qualifies for credit and who does not, how long customers are given to pay their bills, and how aggressive the firm is in collecting its debts. Be careful here as well. If the ratio is going up, you need to determine whether the company is doing a better job of collecting or sales are rising. If the ratio is going down, it may be because sales are decreasing or because collection efforts are lagging. As Exhibit 7.6 shows, Computer Central Services turned its accounts receivable nearly 14 times a year—considerably higher than the industry average.

Leverage, or Debt, Ratios   You can measure a company's ability to pay its long-term debts by calculating its **debt ratios**, or leverage ratios. Lenders look at these ratios to determine whether the potential borrower has put enough money into the business to serve as a protective cushion for the loan. The **debt-to-equity ratio** (total liabilities divided by total equity) indicates the extent to which a business is financed by debt as opposed to invested capital (equity). From the lender's standpoint, the lower this ratio, the safer the company, because the company has less existing debt and may be able to repay additional money it wants to borrow. However, a company that is conservative in its long-term borrowing is not necessarily well managed; often a low level of debt is associated with a low growth rate. Computer Central Services's low debt-to-equity ratio reflects the company's practice of financing its growth by using excess cash flow from operations and by selling shares of common stock to the public.

The **debt-to-total-assets ratio** (total liabilities divided by total assets) also serves as a simple measure of a company's ability to carry long-term debt. As a rule of thumb, the amount of debt should not exceed 50 percent of the value of total assets. For Computer Central Services, this ratio is a fairly low 40 percent and again reflects the company's policy of using retained earnings to finance its growth. However, this ratio, too, is not a magic formula. Like grades on a report card, ratios are clues to performance. Managers, creditors, lenders, and investors can use them to get a fairly accurate idea of how a company is doing. But remember, one ratio by itself doesn't tell the whole story.

Understanding Financial Management

Financial management starts with the simple fact that all companies need to pay their bills and still have some money left over to improve the business and provide a cushion in case of emergencies. Furthermore, a key goal of any business is to increase the value to its owners by making it grow; most companies also try to keep growing and developing as a way to provide fresh opportunities for employees. Maximizing owner wealth sounds simple enough: Just sell a good product for more than it costs to make. Before you can earn any revenue, however, you need money to get started. Once the business is off the ground, your need for money continues—whether it's to buy parts, build a new warehouse, hire employees, or even acquire another company.

Planning for a firm's current and future money needs is the foundation of **financial management**, or finance. In most smaller companies, the owner is responsible for the

inventory turnover ratio
Measure of the time a company takes to turn its inventory into sales, calculated by dividing cost of goods sold by the average value of inventory for a period

accounts receivable turnover ratio
Measure of time a company takes to turn its accounts receivable into cash, calculated by dividing sales by the average value of accounts receivable for a period

debt ratios
Ratios that measure a firm's reliance on debt financing of its operations (sometimes called *leverage ratios*)

debt-to-equity ratio
Measure of the extent to which a business is financed by debt as opposed to invested capital, calculated by dividing the company's total liabilities by owners' equity

debt-to-total-assets ratio
Measure of a firm's ability to carry long-term debt, calculated by dividing total liabilities by total assets

financial management
Effective acquisition and use of money

firm's financial decisions, whereas in larger operations financial management is the responsibility of the finance department, which reports to a vice president of finance or a chief financial officer (CFO). This department also includes the accounting function. In fact, most financial managers are accountants.

Financial management involves making decisions about alternative sources and uses of funds, with the goal of maximizing a company's value (see Exhibit 7.7). To achieve this goal, financial managers develop and implement a financial plan, monitor and manage cash flow, establish and manage budgets, and raise capital to finance continued growth.

Developing and Implementing a Financial Plan

financial plan
A forecast of financial requirements and the financing sources to be used

Successful financial management starts with a **financial plan**, a document that shows the funds a firm will need for a period of time as well as the sources and uses of those funds. When you prepare a financial plan for a company, you have two objectives: achieving a positive cash flow and efficiently investing excess cash flow to help your company grow. Financial planning requires looking beyond the four walls of the company to answer questions such as: Is the company introducing a new product in the near future or expanding its market? Is the industry growing? Is the economy declining? Is inflation heating up? Would an investment in new technology improve productivity?[13]

Monitoring Cash Flow

The income statement indicates a firm's net income, but financial managers need to go a step beyond the income statement by monitoring cash flows. Overall income is important, of course, but knowing precisely how much cash is flowing into and out of the company—and when—is critical, since cash is necessary to purchase assets and supplies, pay employees, and distribute dividends to shareholders. Cash flows are generally related to net income; that is, companies with relatively high accounting profits generally have relatively high cash flows, but the relationship is not precise.

A vital step in maintaining positive cash flow is monitoring *working capital accounts:* accounts receivable, accounts payable, inventory, and cash. Financial managers use commonsense procedures such as shrinking accounts receivable collection periods, dispatching bills on a timely basis without paying bills earlier than necessary, controlling the level of inventory, and investing excess cash so the company can earn as much interest as possible.

budget
Planning and control tool that reflects expected revenues, operating expenses, and cash receipts and outlays

Developing a Budget

In addition to developing a financial plan and monitoring cash flow, financial managers are responsible for developing a **budget**, a financial blueprint for a given period (often one

EXHIBIT 7.7

Sources and Uses of a Company's Funds

Financial management involves finding suitable sources of funds and deciding on the most appropriate uses for those funds.

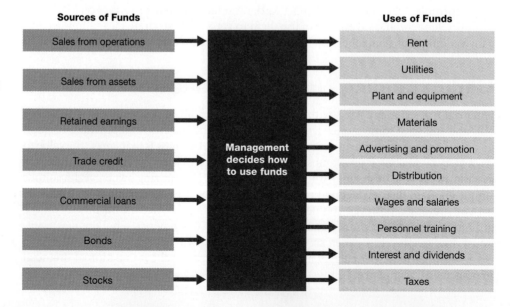

Sources of Funds		Uses of Funds
Sales from operations		Rent
Sales from assets		Utilities
Retained earnings		Plant and equipment
Trade credit	Management decides how to use funds	Materials
Commercial loans		Advertising and promotion
Bonds		Distribution
Stocks		Wages and salaries
		Personnel training
		Interest and dividends
		Taxes

year). *Master* (or *operating*) *budgets* help financial managers estimate the flow of money into and out of the business by structuring financial plans in a framework of a firm's total estimated revenues, expenses, and cash flows. Accountants provide much of the data required for budgets and are important members of the budget development team because they have a complete understanding of the company's operating costs.

The master operating budget sets a standard for expenditures, provides guidelines for controlling costs, and offers an integrated and detailed plan for the future. For example, by reviewing the budget of any airline you can determine whether the company plans on increasing its fleet of aircraft, adding more routes, hiring more employees, increasing employees' pay, or continuing or abandoning any discounts for travelers. (With information such as this, it should come as no surprise that companies like to keep their budgets confidential.) Once a budget has been developed, the finance manager compares actual results with projections to discover variances and recommends corrective action—a process known as **financial control**.

In addition to developing operating budgets, financial managers develop capital budgets to forecast and plan for a firm's **capital investments** such as major expenditures in buildings or equipment. Capital investments generally cover a period of several years and help the company grow. Before investments can be made, however, a firm must decide on which of the many possible capital investments to make, how to finance those that are undertaken, and even whether to make any capital investments at all. This process is called **capital budgeting**.

The process generally begins by having all divisions within a company submit their capital requests. Next, the financial manager decides which investments need evaluating and which don't. For example, the routine replacement of old equipment probably wouldn't need evaluating; however, the construction of a new manufacturing facility would. Finally, a financial evaluation is performed to determine whether a particular investment will increase revenues or decrease operating costs enough to justify the expenditure. On the basis of this analysis, the financial manager can determine which projects to recommend to senior management for purchase approval.

Companies plan for construction projects such as this one years in advance and reflect the costs of such long-term projects in their capital budgets.

financial control
The process of analyzing and adjusting the basic financial plan to correct for forecasted events that do not materialize

capital investments
Money paid to acquire something of permanent value in a business

capital budgeting
Process for evaluating proposed investments in select projects that provide the best long-term financial return

Securing Financing

Few businesses are able to reach their goals without receiving outside financial assistance somewhere along the way. As you can imagine, financing an enterprise is a complex undertaking. The process begins by assessing the firm's financing needs and determining whether funds are needed for the short or the long term. Managers must also assess the cost of obtaining financing and weigh the advantages and disadvantages of financing through debt or equity, taking into consideration the firm's special needs and circumstances. Choosing a company's *capital structure*—the mix of debt and equity—is one of the most important decisions top managers ever make.

Length of Term

Financing can be either short-term or long-term. *Short-term financing* is any financing that will be repaid within one year, whereas *long-term financing* is any financing that will be repaid in a period longer than one year. The primary purpose of short-term debt financing is to ensure that a company maintains its liquidity, or its ability to meet financial obligations (such as rent), as they become due. By contrast, long-term financing is used to acquire long-term assets such as buildings and equipment or to fund a start-up and expansion via any number of growth options.

Cost of Capital

In general, a company wants to obtain money at the lowest cost and least amount of risk. However, lenders and investors want to receive the highest possible return on their investment, also at the lowest risk. A company's *cost of capital*, the average rate of interest it must pay

How This Affects You

1. Have you ever created a personal balance sheet, showing your assets and liabilities? (It might not look too encouraging at this point, particularly if you have school loans, but apply what you learn in your business classes, and you can surely grow your personal owner's equity—your net worth—over time! See Appendix B for more information.)

2. In your personal balance sheet, how would you value an intangible asset such as your college education?

3. Have you ever established a personal budget? Have you at least tracked your spending for a period of time? If so, were you shocked to see where all the money goes?

on its financing, depends on three main factors: the risk associated with the company, the prevailing level of interest rates, and management's selection of funding vehicles. Just as a good credit rating lowers the interest rate you'll pay on a home mortgage, businesses with solid credit ratings also receive more favorable terms.

Time also plays a vital role in the cost of capital. Because a dollar will be worth less tomorrow than it is today, lenders need to be compensated for waiting to be repaid. As a result, long-term financing generally costs a company more than short-term financing.

Regardless of how financially solid a company is, the cost of money will vary over time because interest rates fluctuate. Companies must take such interest rate fluctuations into account when making financing decisions. For instance, a company planning to finance a short-term project when interest rates are 8.5 percent would want to reevaluate the project if interest rates rose to, say, 10 percent a few months later. Even though companies try to time their borrowing to take advantage of drops in interest rates, this option is not always possible. A firm's need for money doesn't always coincide with a period of favorable rates. At times, a company may be forced to borrow when rates are high and then renegotiate the loan when rates drop. Sometimes projects must be put on hold until interest rates become more affordable.

Debt Versus Equity Financing

debt financing
Acquiring funds through borrowing

Debt financing refers to acquiring funds through borrowing; that is, taking on debt. A creditor agrees to lend money to a debtor in exchange for repayment, with accumulated interest, at some future date. Loans can be secured or unsecured. *Secured loans* are those backed by something of value, known as *collateral*, which may be seized by the lender if the

EXHIBIT 7.8 Debt Versus Equity Financing

The two primary types of financing offer distinct advantages and disadvantages.

CHARACTERISTIC	DEBT	EQUITY
Maturity	**Specific** Specifies a date by which it must be repaid.	**Nonspecific** Specifies no maturity date.
Claim on income	**Fixed cost** Company must pay interest on debt held by bondholders and lenders before paying any dividends to shareholders. Interest payments must be met regardless of operating results.	**Discretionary cost** Shareholders may receive dividends after creditors have received interest payments; however, company is not required to pay dividends.
Claim on assets	**Priority** Lenders have prior claims on assets.	**Residual** Shareholders have claims only after the firm satisfies claims of lenders.
Influence over management	**Little** Lenders are creditors, not owners. They can impose limits on management only if interest payments are not received.	**Varies** As owners of the company, shareholders can vote on some aspects of corporate operations. Shareholder influence varies, depending on whether stock is widely distributed or closely held.

borrower fails to repay the loan. The most common types of collateral are accounts receivable, inventories, and property such as marketable securities, buildings, and other assets. *Unsecured loans* are loans that require no collateral. Instead, the lender relies on the general credit record and the earning power of the borrower.

Equity financing is achieved by selling shares of a company's stock. "Going public" is an effective method of raising needed capital, but as Chapter 5 noted, it can be an expensive and time-consuming process with no guarantee you'll get the amount of money you need.

When choosing between debt and equity financing, you should weigh the advantages and disadvantages of each (see Exhibit 7.8). In addition to considering whether the financing is for the short or the long term and assessing the cost of the financing, such as interest, fees, and other charges, you must also evaluate your desire for ownership control. Two of the biggest benefits of debt financing are (1) the lender does not gain an ownership interest in the business and (2) a firm's obligations are limited to repaying the loan. In contrast, equity financing involves an exchange of money for a share of business ownership: It allows firms to obtain funds without pledging to repay a specific amount of money at a particular time, but in exchange for this benefit the firm must give up some ownership control.

equity financing
Acquiring funds by selling shares of a company's stock

Summary of Learning Objectives

1 Discuss how managers and outsiders use financial information.

Managers use financial information to control a company's operation and to make informed business decisions. Outsiders use financial information to evaluate whether a business is creditworthy or a good investment. Specifically, banks want to know if a business is able to pay back a loan, investors want to know if the company is earning a profit, and governments want to be assured the company is paying the proper amount of taxes.

2 Describe what accountants do.

Accountants design and install accounting systems, prepare financial statements, analyze and interpret financial information, prepare financial forecasts and budgets, prepare tax returns, interpret tax law, compute and analyze production costs, evaluate a company's performance, and analyze the financial implications of business decisions. In addition to these functions, accountants help managers improve business procedures, plan for the future, evaluate product performance, analyze the firm's profitability, and design and install computer systems. Auditors are licensed certified public accountants who review accounting records and processes to assess whether they conform to GAAP and whether the company's financial statements fairly present the company's financial position and operating results.

3 Summarize the impact of the Sarbanes-Oxley Act.

Sarbanes-Oxley introduced a number of rules covering the way publicly traded companies manage and report their finances, including restricting loans to directors and executives, creating a new board to oversee public auditors, requiring corporate lawyers to report financial wrongdoing, requiring CEOs and CFOs to sign financial statements under oath, and requiring companies to document their financial systems.

4 State the basic accounting equation and explain the purpose of double-entry bookkeeping and the matching principle.

The basic accounting equation is Assets = Liabilities + Owners' equity. Double-entry bookkeeping is a system of recording financial transactions to keep the accounting equation in balance. The matching principle makes sure that expenses incurred in producing revenues are deducted from the revenue they generated during the same accounting period.

5 Differentiate between cash basis and accrual basis accounting.

Cash basis accounting recognizes revenue at the time payment is received, whereas accrual basis accounting recognizes revenue at the time of sale, even if payment is not made.

6 Explain the purpose of the balance sheet and identify its three main sections.

The balance sheet provides a snapshot of the business at a particular point in time. It shows the size of the company, the major assets owned, how the assets are financed, and the amount of owners' investment in the business. Its three main sections are assets, liabilities, and owners' equity.

7 Explain the purpose of the income statement and statement of cash flows.

The income statement reflects the results of operations over a period of time. It gives a general sense of a company's size and performance. The statement of cash flows shows how a company's cash was received and spent in three areas: operations, investments, and financing. It gives a general sense of the amount of cash created or consumed by daily operations, fixed assets, investments, and debt over a period of time.

8 Explain the purpose of ratio analysis and list the four main categories of financial ratios.

Financial ratios provide information for analyzing the health and future prospects of a business. Ratios facilitate financial comparisons among different-size companies and between a company and industry averages. Most of the important ratios fall into one of four categories: profitability ratios, which show how well the company generates profits; liquidity ratios, which measure the company's ability to pay its short-term obligations; activity ratios, which analyze how well a company is managing its assets; and debt ratios, which measure a company's ability to pay its long-term debt.

9 Identify the responsibilities of a financial manager.

The responsibilities of a financial manager include developing and implementing a firm's financial plan, monitoring a firm's cash flow and deciding how to create or use excess funds, budgeting for current and future expenditures, recommending specific investments, raising capital to finance the enterprise for future growth, and interacting with banks and capital markets.

Behind the Scenes

Microsoft Hands Out Cash to Happy Shareholders

Microsoft Chairman Bill Gates and CEO Steve Ballmer had the highly unusual task of deciding what to do with $60 billion in cash that had piled up over more than two decades as the company rose to dominate the personal computer industry. Gates and his fellow board members had three options: save the money for a rainy day, invest it in the company, or distribute it to shareholders.

The first option wasn't realistic. No company is likely to encounter an emergency that requires $60 billion in cash, particularly when it continues to generate billions of dollars of new cash every year. The second option wasn't terribly realistic, either. Although Microsoft does invest billions of dollars in developing the technologies and products it offers customers, it simply couldn't spend $60 billion in a rational manner. Hiring that many people was impossible, and even buying other companies wouldn't soak up that much. Microsoft isn't a conglomerate that's interested in building a diverse portfolio of businesses in a variety of unrelated industries. Any addition must complement its strategic focus, which severely limits the number of companies that would qualify as sensible acquisitions.

Microsoft went with option number three. In a move one analyst termed "breathtaking," the company initiated a plan to distribute the bulk of the money to its shareholders, who had been clamoring for some of that ever-expanding pile of cash. These investors have had good reason to clamor, too. Stocks fall into two general categories: *growth stocks*, which investors buy in the hope that the price of their shares will increase, and *income stocks*, which aren't expected to increase in value as much but that do pay regular cash dividends. By the early years of the twenty-first century, Microsoft's stock had wandered into a gray area between the two—it was no longer growing at the torrid pace of previous years, but it hadn't yet begun to pay serious dividends, either. The company had finally initiated a $0.08 per share annual dividend in 2003 and raised that to $0.16 per share a year later (meaning that if you

owned 1,000 shares, you received $160), but that was far below the best income stocks and also not enough to make a meaningful dent in the growing billions sitting in the bank.

A dramatic step was needed, and it came in the form of a special, one-time $3.00 per share dividend. With more than 10 billion shares to cover, the payout totaled $32.6 billion—a sum so large that it helped lift the national personal income total by 3.7 percent the month it was distributed. (Bill Gates donated his own $3 billion windfall to the Bill & Melinda Gates Foundation, which is one of the world's premiere charitable organizations.) Microsoft also doubled the annual dividend payment again and pegged another large pile of cash to buy back many of its own shares, which should also help shareholders by nudging the stock price up. In all, the company figures it will transfer $75 billion of value to shareholders over the course of several years.[14]

Critical Thinking Questions

1. Why wouldn't Microsoft just lower its prices in order to stop generating so much cash?
2. Would giving every employee a big raise be a smart thing to do with the extra cash? Why or why not?
3. Microsoft will always have some cash on hand, of course, which leaves the question of how to manage this reserve. Should the company put that money in riskier investments that might pay off more in the long run but could lose value, or leave it in safer investments that won't return as much? Why?

LEARN MORE ONLINE

Visit the Microsoft website at www.microsoft.com and navigate to the "Investor Relations" section. What does the company say about its stock dividend these days? What trends do you see in revenue and net income over the past several years (look for "Financial Highlights" in the latest annual reports)? How might those trends affect Microsoft's cash management issues in the near future? ■

Key Terms

accounting (159)
accounting equation (165)
accounts payable (169)
accounts receivable (168)
accounts receivable turnover
    ratio (175)
accrual basis (165)
activity ratios (174)
assets (164)
audit (161)
balance sheet (167)
bookkeeping (160)
budget (176)
calendar year (167)
capital budgeting (177)
capital investments (177)
cash basis (166)
certified management accountants
    (CMAs) (161)
certified public accountants
    (CPAs) (160)
close the books (166)
controller (160)
cost of goods sold (170)

credit (165)
current assets (167)
current liabilities (169)
current ratio (173)
debit (165)
debt financing (178)
debt ratios (175)
debt-to-equity ratio (175)
debt-to-total-assets ratio (175)
depreciation (166)
double-entry bookkeeping (165)
earnings per share (173)
equity financing (179)
expenses (169)
financial accounting (160)
financial control (177)
financial management (175)
financial plan (176)
fiscal year (167)
fixed assets (167)
general expenses (171)
generally accepted accounting
    principles (GAAP) (162)
gross profit (170)

income statement (169)
inventory turnover ratio (175)
liabilities (165)
liquidity ratios (173)
long-term liabilities (169)
management
    accounting (160)
marketable securities (168)
matching principle (165)
net income (169)
operating expenses (170)
owners' equity (165)
public accountants (161)
profitability ratios (173)
quick ratio (173)
ratio analysis (173)
retained earnings (169)
return on investment (ROI) (173)
return on sales (173)
revenues (169)
Sarbanes-Oxley (163)
selling expenses (170)
statement of cash flows (171)
working capital (173)

Test Your Knowledge

Questions for Review

1. What is GAAP?
2. What is an audit and why is it performed?
3. What is the matching principle?
4. What are the three main profitability ratios, and how is each calculated?
5. What is the primary goal of financial management?

Questions for Analysis

6. Why is accounting important to business?
7. Why are auditors, corporate managers, and investors sometimes at odds when it comes to financial reporting?
8. Why are the costs of fixed assets depreciated?
9. Why do companies prepare budgets?
10. **Ethical Considerations.** In the process of closing the company books, you encounter a problematic transaction. One of the company's customers was charged twice for the same project materials, resulting in a $1,000 overcharge. You immediately notify the controller, whose response is, "Let it go; we've probably undercharged them by that amount before." What should you do now?

Questions for Application

11. The senior partner of an accounting firm is looking for ways to increase the firm's business. What other services besides traditional accounting can the firm offer to its clients? What new challenges might this additional work create?
12. **How This Affects You.** From Hoovers, www.hoovers.com, or any other online source (including the companies' own websites) retrieve the latest balance sheets for Ford Motor Company and General Motors Corporation. Compute the working capital, current ratio, and quick ratio for each company. If you were planning to invest $1,000 in the stock of one of these two companies, which would you choose based on this brief analysis? Why?
13. **Integrated.** Review the discussion of corporate governance in Chapter 5. How is Sarbanes-Oxley likely to affect corporate boards and their relationship with CEOs?
14. **Integrated.** Your appliance manufacturing company recently implemented a just-in-time inventory system (see Chapter 4) for all parts used in the manufacturing process. How might you expect this move to affect the company's inventory turnover rate, current ratio, and quick ratio?

Practice Your Knowledge

Sharpening Your Communication Skills

Obtain a copy of the annual report of a business (visit the website of almost any public company) and examine what the report shows about finances and current operations. In addition to other chapter material, use the information in "How to Read an Annual Report" on page 172 as a guideline for understanding the annual report's content.

- Consider the statements made by the CEO regarding the past year: Did the company do well, or are changes in operations necessary to its future well-being? What are the projections for future growth in sales and profits?

- Examine the financial summaries for information about the fiscal condition of the company: Did the company show a profit?

- If possible, obtain a copy of the company's annual report from the previous year, and compare it with the current report to determine whether past projections were accurate.

- Prepare a brief written summary of your conclusions.

Building Your Team Skills

Divide into small groups and compute the following financial ratios for Alpine Manufacturing using the company's balance sheet and income statement. Compare your answers to those of your classmates:

- Profitability ratios: return on sales; return on equity; earnings per share

- Liquidity ratios: current ratio; quick ratio

- Activity ratios: inventory turnover; accounts receivable turnover

- Leverage ratios: debt to equity; debt to total assets

ALPINE MANUFACTURING
INCOME STATEMENT
YEAR ENDED DECEMBER 31, 2008
(in $thousands)

Sales	$ 1,800
Less: Cost of Goods Sold	1,000
Gross Profit	$ 800
Less: Total Operating Expenses	450
Net Operating Income Before Income Taxes	350
Less: Income Taxes	50
NET INCOME AFTER INCOME TAXES	$ 300

ALPINE MANUFACTURING
BALANCE SHEET
DECEMBER 31, 2008
(in $thousands)

ASSETS	
Cash	$ 100
Accounts Receivable (beginning balance $350)	300
Inventory (beginning balance $250)	300
Current Assets	$ 700
Fixed Assets	2,300
Total Assets	$ 3,000
LIABILITIES AND SHAREHOLDERS' EQUITY	
Current Liabilities (beginning balance $300)	$ 400
Long-Term Debts	1,600
Shareholders' Equity (100 common shares outstanding valued at $12 each)	1,000
Total Liabilities and Shareholders' Equity	$ 3,000

Improving Your Tech Insights: Compliance Management Software

The Sarbanes-Oxley Act requires publicly traded companies to regularly verify their internal accounting controls. To assist in this recurring task, a number of software companies now offer *compliance management software.*

Verifying accounting controls can be a considerable task for large or decentralized companies with multiple accounting systems. For instance, one recent study found that the average billion-dollar public company has 48 separate financial systems. Rather than creating their own software solutions to the problem or adapting existing accounting software, many companies now turn to ready-made compliance management software. The costs can be considerable (up to $100,000 or more just to purchase the software and possibly many times more than that to have it customized and installed); the companies buying these solutions say it's cheaper and faster than building their own, plus they can take advantage of the compliance knowledge programmed into the software. Whether they build or buy, a number of firms are also using the new reporting requirements as an opportunity to streamline and improve their business operations.

Conduct research to find out how a company has benefited from using compliance management software. Has the software helped the company beyond the compliance challenge? For instance, did tighter financial controls help the company decrease costs or accelerate accounts receivable, for instance? A very good place to start your research is with one of the business journals that cover the corporate software market, including *Computerworld* (www.computerworld.com), *CIO* (www.cio.com), *InformationWeek* (www.informationweek.com), *eWeek* (www.eweek.com), and *CFO* and *CFO IT* (www.cfo.com). Search their respective websites for "compliance software" to get the latest news.[15]

Expand Your Knowledge

Discovering Career Opportunities

People interested in entering the field of accounting can choose among a wide variety of careers with diverse responsibilities and challenges. Select one of the occupations mentioned in this chapter and conduct research to learn more about your chosen occupation. Searching online for "accounting careers" will point you to many websites that offer information about careers in this field.

1. What are the day-to-day duties of this occupation? How would these duties contribute to the financial success of a company?

2. What skills and educational qualifications would you need to enter this occupation? How do these qualifications fit with your current plans, skills, and interests?

3. What kinds of employers hire people for this position? According to your research, does the number of employers seem to be increasing or decreasing? How do you think this trend will affect your employment possibilities if you choose this career?

Developing Your Research Skills

Select an article from a business journal or newspaper (print or online editions) that discusses the quarterly or year-end performance of a company that industry analysts consider notable for either positive or negative reasons.

1. Did the company report a profit or a loss for this accounting period? What other performance indicators were reported? Is the company's performance improving or declining?

2. Did the company's performance match industry analysts' expectations, or was it a surprise? How did analysts or other experts respond to the firm's actual quarterly or year-end results?

3. What reasons were given for the company's improvement or decline in performance?

See It on the Web

Visit these websites and answer the following questions for each one. (Up-to-date links for all websites mentioned in this chapter can be found on the Textbook Resources page for Chapter 7 at www.mybusinesslab.com. Please note that links to sites that become inactive after publication of the book will be removed from the Featured Websites section.)

1. What is the purpose of this website?

2. What kinds of information does this website contain? Please be specific.

3. How is the information provided at this website useful for businesspeople? Consumers?

4. How did you expand your knowledge of accounting and financial management by reviewing the material at this website? What new things did you learn about this topic?

Link Your Way to the World of Accounting

Looking for one accounting supersite packed with information and links to financial resources? Check out the WebCPA, an online launching point for accountants. This is the place to find answers to all kinds of questions about accounting, financial analysis, taxes, and more. Participate in one of the many focused discussion groups. Visit the niche sites for information on financial planning, practice management, technology consulting, or CPA requirements. Read the latest issues of *Accounting Today, Accounting Technology, Practical Accountant, Wealth Provider*, and *SMB Finance.* Don't leave without checking out the CareerZone, where you'll find information on the latest accounting hot jobs and opportunities. www.webcpa.com

Sharpen Your Pencil

Take a virtual field trip to the Report Gallery, where you can click to view the annual reports of Allstate, Boeing, and many other U.S. and international firms. Select an annual report for any company and examine the financial statements, chairman's letter, and auditor's report. Was it a good or bad year for the company? Who are the company's auditors? Did they issue a clean audit report? www.reportgallery.com

Think Like an Accountant

Find out how the world of accounting is changing by exploring the valuable links at CPAnet. Learn about the many facets of accounting such as taxes, finance, auditing, and more. Follow the link to your state CPA society, and discover what it takes to become a CPA or how to prepare for the CPA exam. Learn how to read a financial report, and discover what financial statements say about your business. Check out the financial calculators. Increase your knowledge of accounting terms and accounting basics before participating in one of the site's discussion forums. CPAnet claims to be a complete resource for the accounting profession. www.cpanet.com

Companion Website

Learning Interactively

Log onto www.prenhall.com/bovée, locate your text, and then click on its Companion Website. For Chapter 7, take advantage of the interactive Chapter Quiz to test your knowledge of the chapter. Get instant feedback on whether you need additional studying. Also, you'll find an abundance of valuable resources that will help you succeed in this course, including PowerPoint presentations and Web Links.

Video Case

Accounting for Billions of Burgers: McDonald's

LEARNING OBJECTIVES

The purpose of this video is to help you:

1. Understand the challenges a company may face in managing financial information from operations in multiple countries

2. Consider how management and investors use the financial information reported by a public company

3. Recognize how different laws and monetary systems can affect the accounting activities of a global corporation

SYNOPSIS

Collecting, analyzing, and reporting financial data from 27,000 restaurants in more than 100 countries is no easy task, as the accounting experts at McDonald's know all too well. Every month, the individual restaurants send their sales figures to be consolidated with data from other restaurants at the local or country level. From there, the figures are sent to country-group offices and then to one of three major regional offices before going to their final destination at the McDonald's headquarters in Oak Brook, Illinois. In the past, financial information arrived in Illinois in bits and pieces, sent by courier, mail, or fax. Today, local and regional offices log onto a special secure website and enter their month-end figures, enabling the corporate controller to quickly produce financial statements and projections for internal and external use.

Discussion Questions

1. *For analysis:* Why does McDonald's use "constant currency" comparisons when reporting its financial results?

2. *For analysis:* What types of assets might McDonald's list for depreciation in its financial statements?

3. *For application:* What effect do the corporate income tax rates in the countries where McDonald's operates have on the income statements prepared in local offices?

4. *For application:* What problems might arise if individual McDonald's restaurants were required to enter sales data directly on the company's centralized accounting website, instead of following the current procedure of sending it through country and regional channels?

5. *For debate:* To help investors and analysts better assess the company's worldwide financial health, should McDonald's be required to disclose detailed financial results for every country and region? Support your chosen position.

ONLINE EXPLORATION

Visit the McDonald's corporate website at www.mcdonalds.com/corp.html, locate the most recent financial report (quarterly or annual), and examine both overall and regional results. What aspects of its results does McDonald's highlight in this report? What does McDonald's say about its use of constant currency reporting? Which regions are doing particularly well? Which are lagging? How does management explain any differences in performance?

CHAPTER 8

Banking and Securities

LEARNING OBJECTIVES

After studying this chapter, you will be able to

1 Highlight the functions, characteristics, and common forms of money

2 Discuss the responsibilities and insurance methods of the FDIC

3 Discuss how industry deregulation and the repeal of the Glass-Steagall Act are affecting the banking industry

4 Highlight the distinguishing features of common stock, preferred stock, bonds, and mutual funds

5 Explain the advantages of index funds

6 Discuss the importance of establishing investment objectives and identify five factors to consider when making investment choices

7 Explain how government regulation of securities trading tries to protect investors

Behind the
Scenes

Charles Schwab Takes on the Titans of Wall Street

www.schwab.com

Innovation has been a hallmark of Charles Schwab from its beginning more than three decades ago. When the Securities and Exchange Commission (SEC) ended fixed stock commissions in the 1970s, the company forged new ground by opening the discount brokerage house that bears the founder's name. When mutual funds became popular in the 1980s, Schwab revolutionized the industry by creating a low-cost mutual-fund supermarket where investors could buy and sell hundreds of mutual funds in a single account. When e-commerce took off in the mid-1990s, Schwab was an early leader there as well.

Through it all, Schwab developed a reputation for bold responses to market changes. That attitude was put to the test time and again during the first half-dozen years of the new millennium, through the dot-com collapse in 2000 and 2001, a persistent recession that followed, corporate financial scandals that scared investors away, and the market-depressing effects of terrorist attacks and global political uncertainty. Schwab responded in true character, redefining the company to meet changing conditions while taking

First, Charles Schwab grabbed huge chunks of market share from traditional brokers. Then, it cleaned up in the discount and online markets. Now it's going after the full-service brokers—again.

on old-school Wall Street at every step.

With its discount brokerage business in trouble, Schwab expanded from its discounter roots to recapture wealthier customers who had been migrating to Merrill Lynch and other full-service firms. Schwab purchased U.S. Trust Co., a money-management firm that focused on the needs of the wealthiest customers. With the addition of other services such as financial planning, Schwab was steadily moving away from its low-cost roots and moving toward becoming a full-service financial services provider. It also expanded beyond individual investors to institutional investing, acquiring firms that provided research and advice to pension funds and other big organizational investors.

Unfortunately, these changes were not terribly successful. Both the strategy and the executive who championed it, CEO David Pottruck, were jettisoned. The board of directors asked founder and company namesake Charles Schwab to come out of semiretirement to get the company back on track. If you were in Schwab's position, what actions would you take to return the company to profitability?[1] ∎

Money and Financial Institutions

As Charles Schwab (profiled in the chapter opener) knows, businesses and individuals have an abundance of options when it comes to investing money. They can deposit it in a bank account, purchase company stocks or bonds, or acquire real estate, artwork, or other assets that they hope will appreciate over time. This chapter discusses two investment options—banking and securities markets—that are likely to play important roles in your professional and personal financial success. Following that is a look at common types of financial institutions, the services they provide, and the changing nature of the U.S. banking environment. The second half of the chapter explores three principal types of securities investments—stocks, bonds, and mutual funds—and discusses the types of securities markets where such investments are traded. The chapter concludes by looking at securities-trading procedures, performance barometers, and regulations.

Characteristics and Types of Money

money
Anything generally accepted as a means of paying for goods and services

Money is anything generally accepted as a means of paying for goods and services. To be an effective medium of exchange, money must have these important characteristics: It must be divisible (easy to divide into smaller denominations), portable (easy to carry), durable, difficult to counterfeit, and relatively stable in its valuation. In addition, money must perform three basic functions: First, it must serve as a medium of exchange—a tool for simplifying transactions between buyers and sellers. Second, it must serve as a measure of value so that you don't have to negotiate the relative worth of dissimilar items every time you buy something. Finally, money must serve as a temporary store of value—a way of accumulating your wealth until you need it.

currency
Bills and coins that make up a country's cash money

demand deposit
Money that can be used by the customer at any time, such as checking accounts

Paper money and coins are the most visible types of money, but money exists in a variety of forms. **Currency** consists of coins, bills, traveler's checks, cashier's checks, and money orders. **Demand deposits** are money available immediately on demand, whereas **time deposits** restrict the owner's right to withdraw funds on short notice.

time deposits
Bank accounts that pay interest and require advance notice before money can be withdrawn

Checking and Savings Accounts

checks
Written orders that tell the user's bank to pay a specific amount to a particular individual or business

Businesses take advantage of the same two basic types of bank accounts that consumers can use: checking and savings. Money put into a checking account is a demand deposit, available immediately (on demand) through the use of **checks**, written orders that direct your bank to pay the stated amount of money to you or to someone else. Several types of checking accounts exist, each offering benefits in exchange for monthly fees, minimum account balances, or other requirements. For example, Negotiable Order of Withdrawal (NOW) checking accounts pay interest but may limit the number of checks customers can write and impose a fee if the account balance falls below a minimum level.

You can also earn interest on the money you put in savings accounts. Originally, these accounts were known as *passbook savings accounts* because customers received a small passbook in which the bank recorded all deposits, withdrawals, and interest. In general, money in savings accounts can be withdrawn at any time, but certain types of savings accounts may require advance notice or impose withdrawal limits. For example, money in a *money-market deposit account* earns more interest, but you are allowed only a limited number of monthly withdrawals. Money held in a *certificate of deposit (CD)* earns an even higher interest rate, but you cannot withdraw the funds for a stated period, such as six months or more. If you want to make an early withdrawal from a CD, you will lose some or all of the interest you've earned.

Credit Cards, Debit Cards, and Smart Cards

credit cards
Plastic cards that allow the user to buy now and repay the loaned amount at a future date

For everyday access to short-term credit, banks and other institutions issue **credit cards**, plastic cards that entitle customers to make purchases now and repay the amount later. Businesses make extensive use of credit cards, such as providing cards for all employees who incur travel expenses as part of their work. A major reason for using cards over cash is that spending done via cards is much easier to track and analyze. Many credit card issuers offer detailed spending breakdowns on a quarterly or yearly basis to help financial managers stay on top of employee spending. (For more information on consumer uses of credit cards, refer to Appendix B.)

Credit cards have become immensely popular because they are convenient and allow people to postpone payment on purchases they make. They also help people manage their finances by either choosing to repay the full amount when they are billed or making small payments month by month until the debt has been repaid. Credit card companies make money by charging customers interest on their unpaid account balances and by charging businesses a processing fee, which can range from 2 to 5 percent of the value of each sales transaction paid by credit card. Nearly every store accepts credit cards, and both mail-order and Internet retailers are especially dependent on credit cards to facilitate purchases.

In addition to credit cards, many banks offer **debit cards**, plastic cards that function like checks in that the amount of a purchase is electronically deducted from the user's checking account and transferred to the retailer's account at the time of the sale. Debit cards are ideal for customers who must control their spending or stick to a budget.

Smart cards are similar to debit cards; however, these plastic cards contain tiny computer chips that can store amounts of money (from the user's bank or other account) and selected data (such as shipping address, credit card information, frequent-flyer account numbers, health and insurance details, or other personal information). When a purchase is made, the store's equipment electronically deducts the amount from the value stored on the smart card and reads and verifies requisite customer information. Users reload money from their bank accounts to their smart cards as needed.

Although popular in Europe, smart cards have been slow to catch on in the United States for two reasons: Low U.S. telephone rates (compared to those of European countries) make it affordable to verify conventional credit card transactions over the phone, and it is not cost-effective for most U.S. businesses to replace current credit card infrastructures with smart-card readers and computer chip technology. American Express has offered smart cards in the United States for several years, but its promotions now tend to focus on product benefits that aren't directly related to the smart-card technology.[2] Smart cards are also used in a number of public transportation systems around the country, such as the CharlieCard offered by the Massachusetts Bay Transportation Authority and the Breeze card offered by the Metropolitan Atlanta Rapid Transit Authority.[3]

Financial Institutions and Services

Consumers and businesses can choose from a variety of financial institutions and services to help them manage cash flow and build financial assets.

Deposit and Nondeposit Financial Institutions

The types of services provided by a financial institution are generally governed by whether it is a *deposit institution* or *nondeposit institution.* Deposit institutions accept deposits from customers or members and offer checking and savings accounts, loans, and other banking services. Among the many deposit institutions are the following:

- *Commercial banks,* which are profit-oriented financial institutions that operate under state or national charters. Commercial banks make money by charging customers fees and higher interest rates on loans than the interest rates they pay on customers' deposits.

- *Thrifts, savings and loan associations,* which use most of their deposits to make home-mortgage loans; and *mutual savings banks,* which are owned by their depositors.

- *Credit unions,* which are nonprofit member-owned organizations that take deposits only from members, such as one company's employees or one union's members or another designated group. Credit unions generally pay favorable interest rates because they are tax-exempt institutions.

Nondeposit institutions offer specific financial services but do not accept deposits. Among the many nondeposit financial institutions are the following:

- *Insurance companies,* which provide insurance coverage for life, property, and other potential losses; they invest the payments they receive in real estate, in construction projects, and in other ways.

debit cards
Plastic cards that allow the bank to take money from the user's demand-deposit account and transfer it to a retailer's account

smart cards
Cards with embedded computer chips that store bank account amounts and personal data

- *Pension funds*, which are set up by companies to provide retirement benefits for employees; money contributed by the company and its employees is put into securities and other investments.

- *Finance companies*, which lend money to consumers and businesses for home improvements, expansion, purchases, and other purposes.

- *Brokerage firms*, which allow investors to buy and sell stocks, bonds, and other investments; many also offer checking accounts, high-paying savings accounts, and loans to buy securities.

- *Investment banks*, which offer a variety of services related to initial public stock offerings, mergers and acquisitions, and other investment matters.

In the past, each financial institution focused on offering a particular set of financial services for specific customer groups. However, the competitive situation changed dramatically after the passage of the Depository Institutions Deregulation and Monetary Control Act of 1980. This law deregulated banking and made it possible for all financial institutions to offer a wider range of services—thereby blurring the line between banks and other financial institutions and encouraging more competition between different types of institutions.

Loans

line of credit
Arrangement in which the financial institution makes money available for use at any time after the loan has been approved

Loans are one of the most important services financial institutions provide. Consumers look to banks and financial services firms for home mortgage loans, auto loans, home-improvement loans, student loans, and many other types of loans. Businesses rely on banks to provide loans for expansion, purchases of new equipment, construction or renovation of plants and facilities, or other large-scale projects. Some businesses obtain a working capital **line of credit**, which is an agreed-on maximum amount of money a bank is willing to lend to a business during a specific period of time, usually one year. Once a line of credit has been established, the business may obtain unsecured loans for any amount up to that limit.

Electronic Banking

automated teller machines (ATMs)
Electronic terminals that permit people to perform basic banking transactions 24 hours a day without a human teller

electronic funds transfer systems (EFTS)
Computerized systems for completing financial transactions

Most deposit institutions offer electronic banking services that may be conducted from sites other than the bank's physical location. The most visible form of electronic banking consists of the **automated teller machines (ATMs)** now located everywhere from street corners to shopping malls to airports. By linking with regional, national, and international ATM networks, banks let customers withdraw cash far from home, make deposits, and handle other transactions. Some bank ATMs also provide web access, allowing customers to perform a wide variety of online banking tasks, from paying bills to transferring funds between accounts.

Electronic funds transfer systems (EFTS) are computerized systems that allow users to conduct financial transactions efficiently from remote locations. Many employees take advantage of EFTS when their employers use *direct deposit* to transfer wages directly into employees' bank accounts. This procedure saves employers and employees the worry and headache of handling large amounts of cash. Banks sometimes provide discounted service fees for customers who use direct deposit, since handling payroll transactions electronically is less expensive.

In addition to ATMs and EFTS, most major banks and many smaller financial institutions now offer a variety of online banking services. Services typically offered include the ability to transfer money between accounts, check account balances, pay bills, and apply for loans. Some banks also offer personal financial management

Electronic banking options such as ATMs offer speed and convenience, but many banks find that customers still want the personal communication offered by branches.

services, such as the ability to establish household budgets and track spending by categories. Approaching the same challenge from the opposite direction, Intuit, maker of the popular Quicken and QuickBooks financial software, is beginning to integrate its product with online banking services as well.[4]

One of the newest areas of innovation in electronic banking is *mobile banking*, whereby customers can access their accounts with their mobile phones. For example, through special software downloaded to their phones, Citibank customers can view account information, pay bills, and transfer funds. Future possibilities include retail checkout systems that can detect the presence of suitably equipped mobile phones and deduct purchase amounts from the user's bank account.[5]

Bank Safety and Regulation

Banks are among the nation's most heavily regulated businesses. As many as 9,000 U.S. banks failed during the Depression years from 1929 to 1934. To restore public confidence in the banking system, the Glass-Steagall Act (also known as the Banking Act of 1933) established the Federal Deposit Insurance Corporation (FDIC). The FDIC insures money on deposit in U.S. banks up to a maximum of $100,000 per account by collecting insurance premiums from member banks and depositing the premiums into the U.S. Treasury's Savings Association Insurance Fund (for thrifts) and Bank Insurance Fund (for commercial banks). Similar to the FDIC, the National Credit Union Association protects deposits in credit unions by collecting premiums from members and depositing them into funds.

In addition to FDIC protection against bank failure, a number of government agencies supervise and regulate banks and conduct periodic examinations to ensure that the bank is complying with regulations. State-chartered banks come under the watchful eyes of each state's banking commission; nationally chartered banks are under the federal Office of the Comptroller of the Currency; and thrifts are under the federal Office of Thrift Supervision. The overall health of the country's banking system is, ultimately, the responsibility of the Federal Reserve Board, as Chapter 1 discussed.

Chapter 1 also noted that banks also play a vital role in government efforts to prevent terrorists and criminal organizations from transferring funds between accounts and geographic locations. For instance, banking is among several industries required to file *suspicious activity reports (SARs)* with government authorities whenever they detect types of financial transactions flagged by the USA PATRIOT Act and similar legislation. The number of SARs has skyrocketed in recent years, as have other reporting requirements, leading to complaints by some banking executives that they are required to report millions of routine and harmless transactions every year. One key regulatory reform banks would like to see is "seasoned customer exemption," by which banks would no longer be required to report on routine transactions involving known customers.[6]

The Evolving U.S. Banking Environment

Since the deregulation of the banking industry in 1980, the number of U.S. financial institutions has declined significantly. Today, there are fewer banking main offices in the United States than there were in the depths of the Great Depression of the 1930s.[7] The decline is due in part to an increase in bank combinations, competitive pressure, and financial problems.

During the 1980s and 1990s, some U.S. banks, especially savings and loans, searched for higher profits by investing heavily in real estate and oil-drilling activities, by lending money to foreign governments, and by financing company buyouts. But when real estate markets collapsed, oil prices plummeted, and real estate developers went bankrupt, borrowers could not make payments on their bank loans. As a result, lending institutions were forced to close up shop or were taken over by stronger banks.

Also during that era, some U.S. banks sought strength, efficiency, and access to more customers by undergoing a series of mergers, acquisitions, and takeovers. Then,

Community bankers excel at personal service. They will meet with small-business owners and work with them on their business plan, and they will lend them money to help them grow their business to the next level.

in 1999, Congress opened the floodgates for consolidation among banks, brokerage firms, and insurance companies by passing the 1999 Financial Services Modernization Act. This law repealed the Glass-Steagall Act of 1933 and portions of the 1956 Bank Holding Act, which for decades had kept banks out of the securities and insurance businesses. Originally enacted after the stock market crash of 1929 and the Great Depression, the Glass-Steagall Act was designed to restore confidence in U.S. financial houses by restricting investment banks and commercial banks from crossing into each others' businesses and potentially abusing their fiduciary duties at the expense of customers. Moreover, it helped ensure that a catastrophic failure in one part of the finance industry would not invade every other part, as it did in 1929. The 1956 Bank Holding Company Act restricted what banks could do in the insurance business.[8]

The repeal of the Glass-Steagall Act and the lifting of other bank restrictions made it possible for banks to combine with other banks and insurance companies to create financial supermarkets. These mega-institutions offer customers a full range of services—from traditional loans to investment banking services to public stock offerings to insurance—blurring the line between bankers, brokers, and insurers. Charles Schwab is one of many brokerage firms to expand into banking and other financial services. For example, E*TRADE Financial (www.etrade.com), which began as an online brokerage firm, has expanded its services to include consumer banking and home mortgages.[9]

While some banks are focusing on becoming financial supermarkets, others choose to remain comparatively smaller players. *Community banks* are smaller banks that concentrate on serving the needs of local consumers and businesses. Some community banks have multiple locations within a small, well-defined area. Others have expanded into new markets by opening branch operations or merging with banks across state lines. Such interstate operations were made possible by the Riegle-Neal Interstate Banking and Branching Efficiency Act of 1994, a landmark law that reversed legislation dating back to 1927.[10] As a result, customers can now make deposits, cash checks, or handle any banking transaction in any branch of their bank, regardless of location.

Like every industry, banking continues to evolve. One of the latest changes is the entry of mainstream retailers into banking-related services. For instance, Wal-Mart recently spent a year trying to obtain a federal banking charter, which would have allowed it to open bank branches in its retail stores across the country (the company says it wanted the charter only to get access to the less-expensive money transfer system of the Federal Reserve). Wal-Mart eventually withdrew its application in the face of vigorous protests from the banking industry. However, the giant retailer is rolling out its own ATM network and MoneyCenter departments in many of its stores. MoneyCenters offer check cashing, bill payment, money orders, and other functions, often serving people who don't have regular bank accounts.[11] (For the latest information on the banking industry, visit www.prenhall.com/bovée and click on "Real-Time Updates.")

How This Affects You

1. Roughly what percentage of your personal financial transactions are conducted using cash? Are you comfortable in the "cashless economy," where transactions involve credit cards, debit cards, and direct deductions from or deposits to your bank accounts, rather than cash?

2. If you have credit cards, do you carry any balances on them? If so, do you know what your total annual interest expenses are?

3. Do you do your banking at a traditional bank branch or through some other option, such as an online-only bank, a bank affiliated with a stock brokerage, or a limited-service retail facility such as Wal-Mart's MoneyCenters?

Types of Securities Investments

With the line between banks and brokerage houses such as Charles Schwab blurring, consumers now have more options as to where they can purchase **securities**—stocks, bonds, and other investments—to meet their investment goals. Securities are traded in organized markets. Corporations sell stocks or bonds to finance their operations or expansion, while governments and municipalities issue bonds to raise money for building or public expenses—from national defense to road improvements. Here's a closer look at these three principal types of securities investments.

securities
Investments such as stocks, bonds, options, futures, and commodities

Stocks

As discussed in Chapter 5, a share of stock represents ownership in a corporation and is evidenced by a stock certificate. The number of stock shares a company sells depends on the amount of equity capital the company will require and on the price of each share it sells. A corporation's board of directors sets a maximum number of shares into which the business can be divided. In theory, all these shares—called *authorized stock*—may be sold at once. In practice, however, the company sells only a part of its authorized stock. The part sold and held by shareholders is called *issued stock*; the unsold portion is called *unissued stock*. From time to time a company may announce a **stock split**, in which it increases the number of shares that each stock certificate represents while proportionately lowering the value of each share. Companies generally use a stock split to make the share price more affordable. For instance, if a company with 1 million shares outstanding and a stock price of $400 per share announces a two-for-one split, it is doubling the number of shares. After the split, the company will have 2 million shares outstanding, and each original share will become two shares worth $200 each.

stock split
Increase in the number of shares of ownership that each stock certificate represents, at a proportionate drop in each share's value

Common Stock

Most investors buy common stock, which represents an ownership interest in a publicly traded corporation. Shareholders of this class of stock vote to elect the company's board of directors, vote on other important corporate issues, and receive dividend payments from the company's profits. But they have no say in the day-to-day business activities. Still, common shareholders have the advantage of limited liability if the corporation gets into trouble, and as part owners, they share in the fortunes of the business and are eligible to receive dividends as long as they hold the stock. In addition, common shareholders stand to make a profit if the stock price goes up and they sell their shares for more than the purchase price. The reverse is also true: Shareholders of common stock can lose money if the market price drops and they sell the stock for less than they paid for it.

Preferred Stock

Investors who own preferred stock, the second major class of stock, enjoy higher dividends and a better claim (after creditors) on assets if the corporation fails. The amount of the dividend on preferred stock is printed on the stock certificate and set when the stock is first issued. If interest rates fluctuate, the market price of preferred stock will go up or down to adjust for the difference between the market interest rate and the stock's dividend. Preferred stock often comes with special privileges. *Convertible preferred stock* can be exchanged, if the shareholder chooses, for a certain number of shares of common stock issued by the company. *Cumulative preferred stock* has an additional advantage: If the issuing company stops paying dividends for any reason, the dividends on these shares will be held (accumulate) until preferred shareholders have been paid in full—before common stockholders are paid.

Bonds

Unlike stock, which gives the investor an ownership stake in the corporation, bonds are debt financing. A **bond** is a method of raising money in which the issuing organization

bond
Method of funding in which the issuer borrows from an investor and provides a written promise to make regular interest payments and repay the borrowed amount in the future

EXHIBIT 8.1 Corporate Bond Ratings

Standard & Poor's (S&P) and Moody's Investors Service are two companies that rate the safety of corporate bonds. When its bonds receive a low rating, a company must pay a higher interest rate to compensate investors for the higher risk.

	S&P	INTERPRETATION	MOODY'S	INTERPRETATION
Investment grade	AAA	Highest rating	Aaa	Prime quality
	AA	Very strong capacity to pay	Aa	High grade
	A	Strong capacity to pay; somewhat susceptible to changing business conditions	A	Upper-medium grade
	BBB	More susceptible than A-rated bonds	Baa	Medium grade
Not investment grade	BB	Somewhat speculative	Ba	Somewhat speculative
	B	Speculative	B	Speculative
	CCC	Vulnerable to nonpayment in default	Caa	Poor standing; may be in default
	CC	Highly vulnerable to nonpayment	Ca	Highly speculative; often in default
	C	Bankruptcy petition filed or similar action taken	C	Lowest rated; extremely poor chance of ever attaining real investment standing
	D	In default		

borrows from an investor and issues a written pledge to make regular interest payments and then repay the borrowed amount later. When you invest in this type of security, you are lending money to the company, municipality, or government agency that issued the bond. Bonds are usually issued in multiples of $1,000, such as $5,000, $10,000, and $50,000. Also like stocks, bonds are evidenced by a certificate, which shows the issuer's name, the amount borrowed (the **principal**), the date this principal amount will be repaid, and the annual interest rate investors receive.

The interest is stated in terms of an annual percentage rate but is usually paid at six-month intervals. For example, the holder of a $1,000 bond that pays 8 percent interest due January 15 and July 15 could expect to receive $40 on each of those dates. A look at the financial section of any newspaper will show that some corporations sell new bonds at an interest rate two or three percentage points higher than that offered by other companies. Yet the terms of the bonds seem similar. Why? Because bonds are not guaranteed investments. The variations in interest rates reflect the degree of risk associated with the bond, which is closely tied to the financial stability of the issuing company. Agencies such as Standard & Poor's (S&P) and Moody's rate bonds on the basis of the issuers' financial strength (see Exhibit 8.1). Low-rated bonds, known as *high-yield* or *junk bonds*, pay higher interest rates to compensate investors for the higher risk.

Corporate Bonds

Companies issue a variety of corporate bonds. **Secured bonds** are backed by company-owned property (such as airplanes or plant equipment) that will pass to the bondholders if the issuer does not repay the amount borrowed. *Mortgage bonds,* one type of secured bond, are backed by real property owned by the issuing corporation. **Debentures** are unsecured bonds, backed only by the corporation's promise to pay. Because debentures are riskier than other types of bonds, investors who buy these bonds receive higher interest rates. **Convertible bonds** can be exchanged at the investor's option for a certain number of shares of the corporation's common stock. Because of this feature, convertible bonds generally pay lower interest rates.

principal
Amount of money a corporation borrows from an investor through the sale of a bond

secured bonds
Bonds backed by specific assets that will be given to bondholders if the borrowed amount is not repaid

debentures
Corporate bonds backed only by the reputation of the issuer

convertible bonds
Corporate bonds that can be exchanged at the owner's discretion into common stock of the issuing company

U.S. Government Securities and Municipal Bonds

Just as corporations raise money by issuing bonds, so too do federal, state, city, and local governments and agencies. As an investor, you can buy a variety of U.S. government securities, including three types of bonds issued by the U.S. Treasury, U.S. savings bonds, and bonds issued by various U.S. municipalities.

Treasury bills (also referred to as *T-bills*) are short-term U.S. government bonds that are repaid in less than one year. Treasury bills are sold at a discount and redeemed at face value. The difference between the purchase price and the redemption price is, in effect, the interest earned for the time periods. **Treasury notes** are intermediate-term U.S. government bonds that are repaid from one to ten years after they were initially issued. **Treasury bonds** are long-term U.S. government bonds that are repaid more than ten years after they were initially issued. Both Treasury notes and Treasury bonds pay a fixed amount of interest twice a year. But in general, U.S. government securities pay lower interest than corporate bonds because they are considered safer: There is very little risk that the government will fail to repay bondholders as promised. Another benefit is that investors pay no state or local income tax on interest earned on these bonds. Also, these bonds can easily be bought or sold through the Treasury or in organized securities markets.

A traditional choice for many individual investors, **U.S. savings bonds** are issued by the U.S. government (www.treasurydirect.com). The U.S. Treasury currently sells two types of savings bonds: Series EE and Series I; the difference is primarily in how interest is calculated. Both series are available in paper format in amounts ranging from $50 to $10,000 and in electronic formats in any amount from $25 upward. Savings bonds can be redeemed after as little as one year, although an interest penalty applies if they are redeemed in less than five years. Interest on savings bonds, while fairly modest, is exempt from state and federal income tax.[12]

Municipal bonds (often called *munis*) are issued by states, cities, and special government agencies to raise money for public services such as building schools, highways, and airports. Investors can buy two types of municipal bonds: general obligation bonds and revenue bonds. A **general obligation bond** is a municipal bond backed by the taxing power of the issuing government. When interest payments come due, the issuer makes payments out of its tax receipts. In contrast, a **revenue bond** is a municipal bond backed by the money to be generated by the project being financed. As an example, revenue bonds issued by a city airport are paid from revenues raised by the airport's operation. To encourage investment, the federal government doesn't tax the interest that investors receive from municipal bonds. Also exempt from state income tax is the interest earned on municipal bonds that are issued by the governments within the taxpayer's home state. However, **capital gains**—the return investors get from selling a security for more than its purchase price—are taxed at both the federal and state levels.

Mutual Funds

Mutual funds are financial instruments in which money pooled from many investors is used to buy a diversified mix of stocks, bonds, or other securities. (The term *mutual fund* is sometimes applied to an investment company that offers such funds as well.) Mutual funds are particularly well suited for investors who wish to diversify their investment over a variety of securities and do not have the time or experience to search out and manage individual investment opportunities.

Mutual funds are classified in a variety of ways. *No-load funds* charge no fee to buy or sell shares, whereas *load funds* charge investors a commission to buy or sell. Funds can also be open or closed. Most funds are *open-ended*, meaning they issue additional shares as new investors ask to buy them. These shares aren't traded on stock exchanges. The number of shares outstanding changes daily as investors buy new shares or redeem old ones. In contrast, *closed-end funds* raise all their money at once by distributing a fixed number of shares that do trade on stock exchanges. A similar term, *closed fund*, applies to an open-ended mutual fund that closes to new investors at some point, either

Treasury bills
Short-term debt securities issued by the federal government; also referred to as *T-bills*

Treasury notes
Debt securities issued by the federal government that are repaid within one to ten years after issuance

Treasury bonds
Debt securities issued by the federal government that are repaid more than ten years after issuance

U.S. savings bonds
Debt instruments sold by the federal government in a variety of amounts

municipal bonds
Bonds issued by city, state, and government agencies to fund public services

general obligation bond
Municipal bond that is backed by the government's authority to collect taxes

revenue bond
Municipal bond backed by revenue generated from the projects it is financing

capital gains
Return that investors receive when they sell a security for a higher price than the purchase price

mutual funds
Financial organizations pooling money to invest in diversified blends of stocks, bonds, or other securities

Is an Index Fund Right for Your Financial Future?

Life doesn't present many opportunities in which the less work you do, the more successful you can be, but index funds offer just that promise. Index funds are mutual funds that replicate a broad swath of the stock market, such as the NASDAQ Composite or the 500 stocks in the Standard & Poor's 500 Index.

The appeal of index funds is based on evidence showing that many actively managed funds don't perform as well as the stock market as a whole, so why not skip all that picking and choosing and just ride the market as a whole. Proponents of index investing admit that the *best* active mutual funds will always outperform index funds, but identifying these high performers ahead of time is so difficult that the average investor is better off just sticking with an index. They argue that stocks have historically risen around 10 percent on average over the course of many decades, so an index fund that tracks the broader market should give the long-term investor a healthy 10 percent return. That's not a spectacular return, but it's enough to build a safe retirement if you start early and invest regularly.

The argument against index funds is also compelling: The best actively managed funds do beat the market, sometimes by a wide margin. Moreover, even though stocks have risen an average of 10 percent a year or so, there have been extended periods when the overall stock market went nowhere or declined for extended periods of time. In other words, riding an index is certainly no guarantee of success—particularly if you're investing for a short-term goal, such as saving for a house.

Aside from the long-term performance question, index funds have an advantage when it comes to cost. In any

mutual fund, you pay a portion of your balance every year to cover the company's cost of managing the fund. In an actively managed fund, you'll pay an average of 1.5 percent or so per year, whereas the cost of many index funds is 0.5 percent or less. Does a single percentage point matter? Assume you invest $500 a month starting at age 25 and continue until you're 55, and the fund gains an average of 10 percent a year. That extra percentage point in costs will lower your retirement nest egg by roughly $150,000. So, yes, small percentages do matter.

The arguments for and against indexing often devolve into statistical boxing matches in which either side can find numbers to support its case. However, the argument in favor of index investing is compelling enough that it warrants your attention. If you plan to invest for the long term but don't have the time or inclination for research, index funds make a lot of sense. Even if you do have the time and resources to actively pick stocks yourself or pick mutual funds that actively pick stocks, an index find still might be a sensible part of your overall portfolio.

Questions for Critical Thinking

1. Why do you suppose so many people continue to invest in actively managed mutual funds even though most don't do as well as the market overall (and hence don't do as well as index funds)?
2. Why are index funds recommended particularly for long-term, buy-and-hold investors?

temporarily or permanently. The most common reason for closing is that a fund has grown so large that its managers can no longer pursue their original strategies efficiently.[13]

Mutual funds are also classified by their investment priorities and strategies. A *money-market fund* invests in short-term debts such as government and corporate bonds. *Growth funds* invest in stocks of rapidly growing companies. *Income funds* invest in securities that pay high dividends and interest. *Balanced funds* invest in a carefully chosen mix of stocks and bonds. *Sector funds* (also known as *specialty* or *industry funds*) invest in companies within a particular industry. *Global funds* invest in foreign and U.S. securities, whereas *international funds* invest strictly in foreign securities.

Finally, funds can be classified by the degree of involvement that the fund managers have in investment decisions. Most funds are *actively managed*, meaning that a manager or team of managers chooses which securities to buy based on an established investment strategy. In contrast, index funds simply try to mimic a segment of the overall stock market by buying the stocks represented by a particular *stock market index*. For example, the Vanguard 500 index fund buys the stock of the 500 companies listed in the Standard & Poor's 500 Index, a widely followed measure of the U.S. stock market.[14] Index funds offer three potential advantages: lower cost (meaning less of your investment is eaten up by fees), simple diversification, and better performance than the majority of actively managed funds.

Securities Markets

Securities are bought and sold in two kinds of marketplaces: primary markets and secondary markets. Newly issued shares (IPOs) are sold in the **primary market** with the assistance of *investment banks*, financial institutions that specialize in raising capital for both corporations and government bodies. Once these shares have been issued, subsequent investors can buy and sell them from each other in the **secondary market**. This section offers a look at the recent changes in the secondary market and the efforts to protect investors through regulation of securities markets.

Evolution of Securities Markets

Investors and the news media sometimes refer to the "stock market" as if were a single entity or organization, but in reality, there are a number of different stock markets involved in the buying and selling of securities. An organization that facilities the buying and selling is known as a **stock exchange**. Some of these are actual physical facilities, whereas others are little more than computer networks. The most famous of the physical variety is the New York Stock Exchange (NYSE), also known as the "Big Board," which is located in the Wall Street area in New York City (leading to the frequent use of "Wall Street" as a metaphor for either the NYSE itself or the larger community of financial companies in the immediate area). The stocks of nearly 3,000 companies are currently sold on the NYSE, including such well-known firms as Campbell Soup, Coca-Cola, Ford Motor, Nike, and Walt Disney.[15] Stocks that sell on the NYSE or any other exchange are said to be *listed* on that exchange. Other major cities around the world, including Tokyo, London, Frankfurt, Paris, Toronto, and Montreal, also have stock exchanges with national or international importance. *Regional stock exchanges* also play a role in buying and selling many lesser-known stocks.

For much of its history, the NYSE operated as an **auction exchange**, in which all buy and sell orders were funneled onto an auction floor. There, *floor brokers* representing buyers and sellers were matched by *stock specialists* who occupied posts on the trading floor and conducted all the trades in specific stocks. These specialists not only helped match buyers and sellers but also helped minimize the *volatility* of a stock price by controlling buying and selling in a way that prevented prices from climbing or falling out of control.

Thousands of other stocks are sold outside of organized stock exchanges in what is known as the **over-the-counter (OTC) market** (the name dates from the time such stocks were literally sold over the counter in banks and other places).[16] In the United States, most such stocks are sold through the well-known **NASDAQ (National Association of Securities Dealers Automated Quotations)**. In contrast to auction exchanges such as the NYSE, NASDAQ is a **dealer exchange** that has no physical marketplace for making transactions. Instead, all buy and sell orders are executed through a computer network by *market makers*, registered stock and bond representatives who sell securities out of their own inventories. NASDAQ is a significant competitor to the NYSE and home to such high-profile stocks as Amazon.com, Apple Computer, Electronic Arts, Intel, and Microsoft.[17]

In addition to auction and dealer exchanges, a third major type of marketplace is involved in the buying and selling of securities. **Electronic communication networks (ECNs)** use computer networks to link buyers and sellers; they have no exchange floors, specialists, or market makers. In fact, they are nothing more than networks with software programs that match buy and sell orders directly, bypassing the once-dominant market makers and specialists.

The world's securities exchanges are in the midst of some dramatic changes, changes that involve vigorous international competition and the nature of the exchanges themselves. ECNs continue to revolutionize stock trading, and both the NYSE and NASDAQ have acquired or

primary market
Market where firms sell new securities issued publicly for the first time

secondary market
Market where subsequent owners trade previously issued shares of stocks and bonds

stock exchange
Location where traders buy and sell stocks and bonds

auction exchange
Centralized marketplace where securities are traded by specialists on behalf of investors

over-the-counter (OTC) market
Network of dealers who trade securities on computerized linkups rather than a trading floor

NASDAQ (National Association of Securities Dealers Automated Quotations)
National over-the-counter securities trading network

dealer exchange
Decentralized marketplace where securities are bought and sold by dealers out of their own inventories

electronic communication networks (ECNs)
Computer-based trading networks that connect buyers and sellers without market makers or other intermediaries

More than 3,000 companies trade their stock on the NASDAQ exchange, including such well-known firms as Merrill-Lynch, 1-800 Flowers, Microsoft, and Apple Computer.

merged with ECN operators in the past few years.[18] The venerable NYSE, long epitomized by the frenzied shouting of brokers and stock specialists on its auction floor, now bills itself as a *hybrid market* that combines the traditional auction floor with automated electronic trading.[19] Most of its trading volume is now handled electronically, and some observers speculate that it may only be a matter of time before the traditional stock specialists are replaced entirely by computer networks. In fact, most of the world's major stock exchanges, including the London Stock Exchange, have long operated as electronic exchanges.[20] In 2007, the NYSE took another step in this direction by merging with Euronext, a company that operates electronic exchanges in Paris and other European capitals.[21]

Regulation of Securities Markets

The buying and selling of securities is governed by a variety of state and federal laws; Exhibit 8.2 lists some of the most significant ones. Combined with industry self-regulation, these laws are designed to ensure that you and all investors receive accurate information and

EXHIBIT 8.2 Major Federal Legislation Governing the Securities Industry

Although you have no guarantee that you'll make money on your investments, you are protected by laws against unfair securities trading practices.

LEGISLATION	KEY PROVISIONS
Securities Act (1933)	Requires full disclosure of relevant financial information from companies that want to sell new stock or bond issues to the general public; also known as the Truth in Securities Act
Securities Exchange Act (1934)	Creates the Securities and Exchange Commission (SEC) to regulate the national stock exchanges and to establish trading rules
Maloney Act (1938)	Creates the National Association of Securities Dealers to regulate over-the-counter securities trading
Investment Company Act (1940)	Extends the SEC's authority to cover the regulation of mutual funds
Amendment to the Securities Exchange Act (1964)	Extends the SEC's authority to cover the over-the-counter market
Securities Investor Protection Act (1970)	Creates the Securities Investor Protection Corporation (SIPC) to insure individual investors against losses in the event of dealer fraud or insolvency
Commodity Futures Trading Commission Act (1974)	Creates the Commodity Futures Trading Commission (CFTC) to establish and enforce regulations governing futures trading
Insider Trading and Securities Fraud Act (1988)	Toughens penalties, authorizes bounties for information, requires brokerages to establish written policies to prevent employee violations, and makes it easier for investors to bring legal action against violators
Securities Market Reform Act (1990)	Increases SEC market control by granting additional authority to suspend trading in any security for ten days, to restore order in the event of a major disturbance, to establish a national system for settlement and clearance of securities transactions, to adapt rules for actions affecting market volatility, and to require more detailed record keeping and reporting of brokers and dealers
Private Securities Litigation Reform Act (1995)	Protects companies from frivolous lawsuits by investors: Limits how many class-action suits can be filed by the same person in a three-year period, and encourages judges to penalize plaintiffs who bring meritless cases
Public Company Accounting Reform and Investor Protection Act of 2002 (Sarbanes-Oxley)	Among its far-reaching efforts aimed at reforming corporate accounting and the securities industry, the act prohibits investment bankers from influencing stock analysts and requires CEOs and CFOs to sign statements attesting to the accuracy of their financial statements

EXHIBIT 8.3 Investment Information on EDGAR

Here are some of the key financial documents you can retrieve from the Securities and Exchange Commission's EDGAR database of corporate filings.

FORM	SIGNIFICANCE
10-K	Detailed annual financial report required by the SEC
10-Q	Abridged version of the 10-K; filed quarterly for the first three quarters each year
8-K	Report required whenever a company experiences events or changes significant enough to affect investors
12b-25	Notification that a required form such as the 10-K or 10-Q will not be filed on time; late filing is sometimes interpreted by investors as a possible sign of financial reporting difficulties
S-1	Registration statement required when a company wants to begin selling stock to the public
Schedule 14	Proxy statement to shareholders with information about director elections and issues to be discussed at a corporation's annual meeting
Forms 3, 4, and 5	Reports related to the buying and selling of stock by company insiders (officers and directors) or any investor who holds 10 percent or more of the company's stock

that no one artificially manipulates the market price of a given security. Trading in stocks and bonds is monitored by the SEC, which works closely with the stock exchanges and the NASD to police securities transactions and maintain the system's integrity.

SEC Filing and Disclosure Requirements

One of the most significant protections afforded by the SEC is the requirement that all companies wishing to sell securities to the public (including foreign companies that want to sell securities in the United States) must file a number of detailed financial reports with the SEC, which then makes all these reports available to the public at no charge. Exhibit 8.3 lists the major types of reports, but this is just a small sample of the various reports that the SEC requires. You can access the reports on any company or mutual fund through the SEC's Electronic Data Gathering, Analysis, and Retrieval (EDGAR) database: visit the SEC website at www.sec.gov, then click on "Filings & Forms (EDGAR)."

These filing requirements are part of the SEC's mission to ensure *full and fair disclosure*, which means that all investors get all the relevant information they need—and they can all get it at the same time. For instance, Regulation FD (Full Disclosure) was adopted to prohibit companies from "selectively disclosing" important information (such as earnings estimates) to big institutional shareholders and Wall Street analysts before giving the information to individual investors.[22]

Securities Fraud

In spite of constant efforts by the SEC, the NASD, and others to police the financial markets, fraud will be a problem as long as dishonest people can find a way to reach trusting targets. Securities fraud can take many forms, including insider trading, inaccurate or incomplete disclosure of information, market manipulation (buying or selling in ways designed to influence prices), and deceptive sales practices.[23] *Phishing*, the use of fraudulent e-mail messages that link to counterfeit websites, is one tactic used in securities fraud. In a typical phishing attack, an e-mail message that appears to be from a legitimate financial services company or organization prompts recipients to visit a website for some important reason, such as reactivating an account. However, like the message, the website is also fake, designed to capture confidential information such as credit card numbers or to provide misleading information about investment opportunities.[24] You

EXHIBIT 8.4 Ten Questions to Ask Before You Invest

You can avoid getting taken in an online stock scam by asking yourself these ten questions before you invest.

1. Is the investment registered with the SEC and your state's securities agency?

2. Have you read the company's audited financial statements?

3. Is the person recommending this investment a registered broker?

4. What does the person promoting the investment have to gain?

5. If the tip came from an online bulletin board or e-mail, is the author identifiable or using an alias? Is there any reason to trust that person?

6. Are you being pressured to act before you can evaluate the investment?

7. Does the investment promise you'll get rich quick, using words like "guaranteed," "high return," or "risk free"?

8. Does the investment match your objectives? Could you afford to lose all of the money you invest?

9. How easy would it be to sell the investment later? Remember, stocks with fewer shares are easy for promoters to manipulate and hard for investors to sell if the price starts falling.

10. Does the investment originate overseas? If yes, beware: It is tougher to track money sent abroad and harder for burned investors to have recourse to justice.

can learn more about protecting yourself from phishing at www.antiphishing.org. In any aspect of investing, your best defenses against fraud are to carefully research securities before you buy and to steer clear of any investment that seems too good to be true (see Exhibit 8.4). (For the latest information on the investment industry and investment regulations, visit http://introbusinessstudent.com and click on "Real-Time Updates.")

Investment Strategies and Techniques

Done wisely, investing in stocks and bonds can help you meet your financial goals, whether you're investing as an individual or on behalf of your company. But you must first make decisions about how much you want to invest and where to invest it. To choose well, you need to know what choices you have and what risks they entail. Before you start to trade, take time to think about your objectives, both long term and short term. Next, look at how various investment opportunities match your objectives and your attitude toward risk, because most investment choices involve potential losses.

Establishing Investment Objectives

Investment opportunities cover a wide spectrum, from safe to extremely risky. Given this range of options, it's absolutely critical to establish objectives before you invest any money. Are you saving up to buy a business, put your children

Learning from Business Blunders

Oops: In the space of four years, superinvestor Warren Buffett's $358 million investment in preferred stock of US Airways was nearly wiped out.

What You Can Learn: Thousands of investors learn from Buffett's stock market moves and his highly informative annual reports for Berkshire Hathaway, the holding company that serves as his investment vehicle. And they pay attention to Buffett for good reason: From 1964 to 2006, the value of Berkshire Hathaway stock increased 361,156%. (A single share of the stock costs more than $100,000 these days.) One of the reasons so many investors follow Buffett is his honest self-assessment. In the aftermath of the US Airways investment, he told shareholders his analysis of the airline's business "was both superficial and wrong." Three things to learn here: investigate investment opportunities thoroughly, be honest with yourself, and learn from mistakes—yours and those of other investors. Fortunately for Buffett and his shareholders, he was unable to unload his US Airways stock when he tried—and it eventually recovered.

through college, care for your parents, prepare for your own retirement, or several of these reasons at once? After identifying your goals, you can start to select investments based on five factors: *income* (regular cash payments that an investment provides, such as quarterly dividends from a stock), *growth* (gains in the market value of the investment), *safety* (the risk that the value of the investment might decline, even below the amount that you paid for it), *liquidity* (the ease and speed with which you can sell the investment when you need to), and *tax consequences* (investments have markedly different tax ramifications, and some are designed specifically to minimize taxes). As with all well-crafted goals, you need to establish a timeframe for your investment objectives, too. Real estate is usually a good long-term investment but generally not a good short-term investment because of its poor liquidity (real estate can take a long time to sell and the transaction costs are significant).

Both income and growth investors care about safety, of course. Generally, the higher the potential for income or growth, the greater the risk of the investment. Government bonds are safer than corporate bonds, which are safer than common stocks, which are safer than futures contracts, which are safer than commodities. **Speculators** operate at the extreme end of the safety spectrum; they are willing to take the highest risks in the hopes of achieving the highest returns. *Long-term* or *buy-and-hold investors*, in contrast, stick with their investments for years, riding out the inevitable ups and downs.

speculators
Investors who make risky investment decisions in anticipation of making large profits quickly

Creating an Investment Portfolio

Unfortunately, no single investment provides an ideal combination of income, growth potential, safety, liquidity, and tax consequences. For this reason, investors build **investment portfolios**, or collections of various types of investments. Managing a portfolio to gain the highest rates of return while reducing risk as much as possible is known as **asset allocation**. A portion of the portfolio might be devoted to cash instruments such as money-market mutual funds, a portion to income instruments such as government and corporate bonds, and a portion to equities (mainly common stock). Investors then determine how much each portion should be, on the basis of both his or her objectives and prevailing economic and market conditions—not an easy task. For instance, someone who believes that the stock market is heading for a sharp decline might shift a major portion of assets out of stock (before share prices drop) and into cash.

investment portfolios
Assortment of investment instruments

asset allocation
Method of shifting investments within a portfolio to adapt them to the current investment environment and investor objectives

Asset allocation is related to another major portfolio concern, which is **diversification**—reducing the risk of overall loss by investing in several areas in the hope that a loss in one area will be balanced by gains or at least stability in others. One way to diversify is by investing in securities from unrelated industries and a variety of countries. Another way is by allocating your assets among different investment types. The rapid growth of mutual funds in recent years is partly attributable to diversification concerns; even individuals with small amounts to invest can diversify their holdings by buying mutual funds that own dozens or hundreds of stocks.

diversification
Assembling investment portfolios in such a way that a loss in one investment won't cripple the value of the entire portfolio

Buying and Selling Securities

Once you've set your goals and decided which types of investments to purchase, you're ready to enter the market. How you make these purchases depends on what you're buying. For instance, you can purchase mutual funds directly from the mutual fund company, or you can buy them through a broker such as Charles Schwab. However, to purchase specific stocks or bonds, you must buy them through a broker.

Securities Brokers

A **broker** is an expert who has passed a series of formal examinations and is legally registered to buy and sell securities on behalf of individual and institutional investors. As an investor, you pay *transaction costs* for every buy or sell order, to cover the broker's commission, which varies with the type of broker and the size of your trade. (The term *broker* is applied to both individual professionals and the firms that employ them.) A

broker
An expert who has passed specific tests and is registered to trade securities for investors

full-service broker provides financial management services such as investment counseling and planning, whereas a *discount broker* provides fewer or limited services and generally charges lower commissions than a full-service broker. As you probably gathered from the Charles Schwab story at the beginning of the chapter, however, the brokerage market seems to be in a state of ongoing upheaval, so the once-clear line between full-service and discount is anything but clear these days.

Most brokers give you several ways to execute a trade: online, over the phone, or in person at their offices. The choice is a matter of cost, convenience, and personal preference. You should also consider whether access to customer service personnel is important to you, or if you're comfortable doing everything yourself online or on the phone—brokerages vary widely in the quality and availability of support personnel.

Orders to Buy and Sell Securities

market order
Authorization for a broker to buy or sell securities at the best price that can be negotiated at the moment

limit order
Market order that stipulates the highest or lowest price at which the customer is willing to trade securities

stop order
An order to sell a stock when its price falls to a particular point to limit an investor's losses

open order
Limit order that does not expire at the end of a trading day

day order
Any order to buy or sell a security that automatically expires if not executed on the day the order is placed

discretionary order
Market order that allows the broker to decide when to trade a security

margin trading
Borrowing money from brokers to buy stock, paying interest on the borrowed money, and leaving the stock with the broker as collateral

short selling
Selling stock borrowed from a broker with the intention of buying it back later at a lower price, repaying the broker, and keeping the profit

Regardless of which broker you use and how you access its services, you can place a variety of different types of buy and sell orders. A **market order** tells the broker to buy or sell at the best price that can be negotiated at the moment. A **limit order** specifies the highest price you are willing to pay when buying or the lowest price at which you are willing to sell. A **stop order**, or *stop-loss order*, tells the broker to sell if the price of your security drops to or below the price you set, protecting you from losing more money if prices are dropping. You can also place a time limit on your orders. An **open order** instructs the broker to leave the order open until you cancel it. A **day order** is valid only on the day you place it. All of these orders can have a significant effect on your finances, so make sure you understand the specific details of how your broker implements each type. If you have special confidence in your broker's ability, you may place a **discretionary order**, which gives the broker the right to buy or sell your securities at the broker's discretion.

Investors sometimes borrow cash to buy stocks, a practice known as **margin trading**. Instead of paying for the stock in full, you borrow some of the money from your stockbroker, paying interest on the borrowed money and leaving the stock with the broker as collateral. The Federal Reserve establishes limits on how much you can borrow on margin, and many brokers have their own limits.[25] Be aware, however, that margin trading increases risk. If the price of a stock you bought on margin goes down far enough to exceed those margin limits, you'll get a *margin call* notice from the broker, meaning you need to put more cash in your account or sell your stock if you don't have the cash—even if that means selling at a steep loss.

If you believe that a stock's price is about to drop, you may choose a trading procedure known as **short selling**. With this procedure, you essentially borrow stock from a broker, sell it, then buy it back later after the price drops to replace the shares you borrowed. For example, you might decide to borrow shares that are selling for $30 and sell them short because you think the price is going to plummet. When the stock's price declines to, say, $20, you buy the same number of shares on the open market, return them to your broker and pocket $10 per share (minus transaction costs). Be aware that selling short carries higher risks. If you buy that $30 stock outright, the most you can lose is $30 a share (if the price drops all the way to zero). However, with short selling, the losses are potentially unlimited. If instead of dropping, the stock you shorted climbs to $80, you could lose $50 on every share of that $30 stock.

Analyzing Financial News

Whether you are buying, holding, or selling securities, you need to keep current on the overall economy, the stock market, and the performance of specific companies and industries. Good sources of financial information include daily newspaper reports on securities markets, newspapers aimed specifically at investors (such as *Investor's Business Daily* and *Barron's*), and general-interest business publications that follow the corporate world and give advice about investing (such as the *Wall Street Journal, Forbes, Fortune,* and *BusinessWeek*). Standard & Poor's, Moody's Investor Service, and Value Line also

Put Your Money Where Your Mouse Is

The Internet has been hailed as the great equalizer between individual investors and Wall Street. Today's investors have access to a staggering amount of valuable information and investment tools—many of which are used by Wall Street professionals. But having access to information is one thing; using it wisely is another. So before you put money into any investment, learn as much as possible about the market, the security, its issuer, and its potential. Here are some of the many websites that can help you succeed.

For "how-to" advice, try the Motley Fool (www.fool.com), Investopedia (www.investopedia.com), or CNN/Money.com (http://money.cnn.com). For the latest online news and commentary about stocks, check out The Street (www.thestreet.com), MarketWatch (www.marketwatch.com), or Yahoo! Finance (http://finance.yahoo.com). Be sure to research individual companies using your favorite search engine; stop by each company's website to read its press releases and financial statements. Dig into specialty areas such as Morningstar's mutual fund reports (www.morningstar.com) or bond prices and market performance (www.investinginbonds.com).

Before you invest real money, construct a hypothetical portfolio on any of the sites that offer free portfolio tracking. By investing imaginary money first, you can learn from mistakes and figure out ways to make better choices with real money.

Now you're in a better position to buy securities, but your research shouldn't end here. Even after you start trading, you need to stay on top of the latest news and industry developments that can affect the securities in which you have invested. And if a potential investment seems too good to be true, point your web browser to the North American Securities Administrators Association (www.nasaa.org) and get some tips on investment fraud. Remember, when it comes to investments, your web surfing can really pay off.

Questions for Critical Thinking

1. Why is it important to learn about a company's financial results and background before buying its stock or bonds?
2. What are the risks involved in searching for investment information on the Internet?

---

publish newsletters and special reports on securities. Online sources include your brokerage firm's website, the websites of all the financial periodicals just listed, plus a growing number of excellent financial websites listed in "Put Your Money Where Your Mouse Is."

The list of specific types of information you might want to follow could fill a book and, in fact, has filled several thousand investing books and hundreds of websites. Don't be put off if it all seems confusing at first—it's confusing to everyone in the beginning. But you'll gradually pick up on the terminology and start to identify which topics you need to care about and which of the many arcane topics you can leave to the specialists. For instance, you'll soon get familiar with the general conditions of the stock market and learn the terms that define its ups and downs. If stock prices have been rising over a long period, the industry and the media will often describe this situation as a **bull market**. The reverse is a **bear market**, one characterized by a long-term trend of falling prices. You can see these broad market movements in Exhibit 8.5. You'll hear about stocks being *overvalued* and *corrections* that occur when enough people realize a stock is overpriced and sell, pushing the price down.

All beginners can learn from **institutional investors**—such as pension funds, insurance companies, investment companies, banks, and colleges and universities—that buy and sell securities in large quantities. Because these institutions have such large pools of money to work with, their investment decisions have a major impact on the marketability of a company's shares as well as the overall behavior of the securities market. If the stock market is down on heavy volume (that is, if prices are moving downward and a lot of trading is going on), institutional investors may be trying to sell before prices go down further—a bearish sign. At the same time, don't think that you should necessarily mimic institutional investors; they usually don't pay attention to smaller stocks that could fit nicely in a growth-oriented portfolio, for instance.

Watching Market Indexes and Averages

One way to determine whether the market is bullish or bearish is to watch **market indexes** and averages, which use the performance of a representative sampling of stocks,

bull market
Rising stock market

bear market
Falling stock market

institutional investors
Companies and other organizations that invest significant amounts of money, often funds entrusted to them by others

market indexes
Measures of market activity calculated from the prices of a selection of securities

EXHIBIT 8.5 The Stock Market's Ups and Downs

The peaks and valleys on this chart represent swings in the Dow Jones Industrial Average, a widely used indicator of U.S. stock prices.

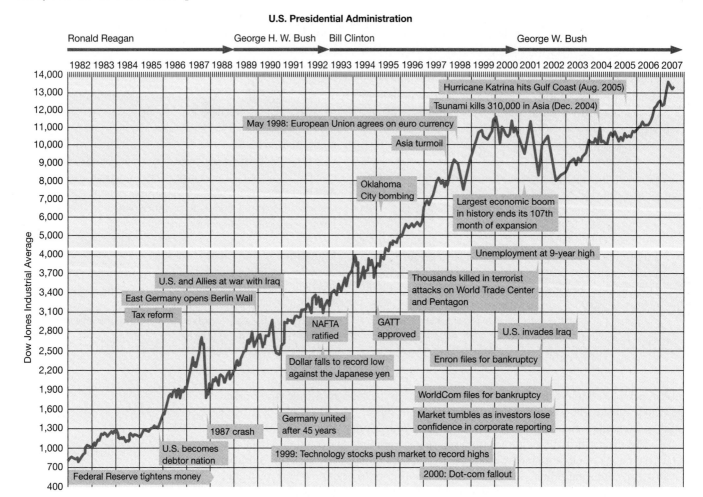

bonds, or commodities as a gauge of broader market activity. The most famous U.S. stock index is the Dow Jones Industrial Average (DJIA), which tracks the prices of 30 *blue-chip* or well-established stocks, each representing a particular sector of the U.S. economy. The DJIA currently contains such bedrock companies as Microsoft, Intel, Home Depot, and Wal-Mart, but the editors of the *Wall Street Journal*, who oversee the index, periodically replace companies to keep the index relevant.[26]

Many other indexes have developed over the years in attempts to better reflect either the overall stock market or specific sectors within it. The Standard & Poor's 500 Stock Average (S&P 500), for instance, tracks the performance of 500 stocks, many more than the DJIA. The S&P 500 is also weighted by market value (the total value of share price times the number of shares), not just by stock price, so large companies affect it far more than small companies. People are usually referring to the S&P 500 when they say such things as "the market is up today."[27] NASDAQ also publishes several indexes related to the stocks in its trading system, including the often-quoted NASDAQ Composite; because this group includes so many high-tech companies, it is sometimes used as a measure of how well the technology sector is doing. You can also look at indexes to learn about the performance of foreign markets, such as Japan's Nikkei 225 Index and the United Kingdom's FT-SE 100 Index.

Interpreting the Financial News

In addition to watching market trends, you will want to follow the securities you own and others that look like promising investments. You can follow the ups and downs of most stocks in either major daily newspapers or on one of the many websites that offer stock quotes (see Exhibit 8.6). At a minimum, a stock quote shows high and low prices for the past 52 weeks, the number of shares traded (volume), and the change from the previous day's closing price.

Included in the stock exchange report is the **price-earnings ratio**, or *p/e ratio* (also known as the price-earnings multiple), which is computed by dividing a stock's market price by its earnings per share (EPS). The p/e ratio is usually calculated using EPS over the previous 12 months, in which case it is known as *trailing p/e*. Some investors also calculate a *forward p/e* ratio using expected earnings for the next 12 months. The p/e ratio is an important relative measure of the value of a stock, and the ratio for a given stock is usually compared to its peers in the same industry or to all stocks in a broad swath of the market (such as the S&P 500). Growth stocks usually have higher than average p/e ratios, but investors also weigh the p/e of a stock to judge whether it is *overpriced*

price-earnings ratio
Ratio calculated by dividing a stock's market price by its earnings per share over a 12-month period (usually the previous 12 months)

EXHIBIT 8.6 How to Read a Stock Quotation

Whether you get quotes from a newspaper or website, you'll usually see some combination of the variables listed here. In addition, financial websites usually let you click through to additional data, such as charts of the stock's price going back several months or years. What can you surmise about these four stocks based on these data points? (On this particular day, stocks were down across the U.S. market, which is why all four dropped.)

(1)	(2)	(3)		(4)	(5)	(6)	(7)	(8)		(9)	(10)
STOCK	SYM	52-WEEK HIGH	52-WEEK LOW	DIV	YLD %	PE	VOL	HI	LOW	CLOSE	NET CHG
Apple	AAPL	148.92	62.58	-	-	38.55	24,230,234	135.95	131.50	131.85	−3.40%
Nordstrom	JWN	59.70	33.06	$0.54	1.12%	18.02	3,155,658	48.21	46.07	46.07	−4.36%
Starbucks	SBUX	40.01	25.22	-	-	32.22	16,806,057	26.95	26.30	26.31	−2.27%
Disney	DIS	36.09	27.99	$0.31	0.90%	15.96	12,642,400	34.62	33.84	33.90	−1.34%

1. **Stock:** The company's name may be abbreviated in newspaper listings.

2. **Symbol:** Symbol under which this stock is traded on stock exchanges.

3. **52-week high/low:** Indicates the highest and lowest trading price of the stock in the past 52 weeks plus the most recent week but not the most recent trading day (adjusted for splits). Stocks are quoted in dollars and cents. In most newspapers, bold-faced entries indicate stocks whose price changed by at least 4% but only if the change was at least $0.75 a share.

4. **Dividend:** Dividends are usually annual payments based on the last quarterly or semiannual declaration, although not all stocks pay dividends. Special or extra dividends or payments are identified in footnotes.

5. **Yield:** The percentage yield shows dividends as a percentage of the share price.

6. **PE:** Price-earnings ratio, calculated by dividing the stock's closing price by the earnings per share for the latest four quarters.

7. **Volume:** Daily total of shares traded. The format of the numbers varies by source; some show exact numbers (as above), but others show hundreds of shares.

8. **High/Low:** The stock's highest and lowest price for that day.

9. **Close:** Closing price of the stock that day.

10. **Net change:** Change in share price from the close of the previous trading day.

Typical common stock footnotes: d—new 52-week low; n—new; pf—preferred; s—stock split or stock dividend of 25 percent or more in previous 52 weeks; u—new 52-week high; v—trading halted on primary market; vi—in bankruptcy; x—ex dividend (the buyer won't receive a recently declared dividend, but the seller will)

EXHIBIT 8.7 How to Read a Bond Quotation

Bond quotations usually show some combination of these variables. Newspaper quotations typically show the company name, coupon, and maturity date in abbreviated form. For instance, the Time Warner bond would be listed as TimeWar 9 1/8 13 (where 9 1/8 is the coupon and 13 represents the year 2013). Some listings also provide such variables as daily volume, change in price from the previous day, and the months in which the bond pays outs dividends.

(1) ISSUER	(2) COUPON	(3) MATURITY	(4) CUR YLD	(5) RATINGS	(6) CLOSE	(7) CUSIP
Avnet	6.000	09-01-2015	6.071	Ba1/BBB-	98.836	053807AM5
General Electric	5.000	20-01-2013	4.981	Aaa/AAA	100.390	369604AY9
Morgan Stanley	4.000	01-15-2010	4.078	Aa3/AA-	98.082	61746SBC2
Time Warner	9.125	01-15-2013	7.850	Baa2/BBB+	116.239	887315AK5

1. **Issuer:** Name of company or organization that issued the bond.

2. **Coupon:** The rate of interest that the issuer promises to pay, expressed as an annual percentage of the bond's face value.

3. **Maturity:** Date on which the principle is due and payable to the bondholder.

4. **Current yield:** Annual interest divided by the closing price.

5. **Ratings:** Moody's and S&P ratings for each bond (ratings are provided on some websites).

6. **Close:** Price of the bond at the close of the last day's business; the value shown represents the price per $1,000 expressed in hundreds. The Morgan Stanley bond, for instance, has a price of $980.82 per $1,000.

7. **CUSIP:** A unique identifier for municipal, U.S. government, and corporate bonds assigned by the Committee on Uniform Security Identification Procedures (CUSIP).

(commanding a higher price than the company is really worth). A lower than average p/e also needs to be interpreted carefully; it can mean that a stock is headed downward because the price is falling, or it can signal an "undiscovered gem" that stands to go up as more investors learn about the stock.

To follow specific bonds, you can check the bond quotation tables in major newspapers or on financial websites (see Exhibit 8.7). When reading these tables, remember that the price is quoted as a percentage of the bond's value. For example, a $1,000 bond shown closing at 65 actually sold at $650.

Newspapers and websites also offer price quotations for investments such as mutual funds, commodities, options, and government securities (see Exhibit 8.8). These same publications also carry news about current challenges the securities industry is facing, securities regulations, reported frauds, and proposals to improve investor protection—all of which are important issues for investors.

How This Affects You

1. What is your level of comfort when it comes to potentially risky investments? Are you willing to accept some risk for the chance of higher returns, or do you prefer safe investments, even if they yield lower results?

2. If you have purchased a stock, bond, or mutual fund, what type of research did you do beforehand?

3. If you unexpectedly came into $10,000, where would you spend or invest it? Why?

EXHIBIT 8.8 How to Read a Mutual Fund Quotation

Mutual fund quotations typically show such variables as the *net asset value* (NAV) of one share, the change in NAV from the previous day, expense ratio, and returns over various time spans. Some listings (particularly those offered online) also show fund objective or investing style, asset allocation, minimum investment amount, and risk/reward assessments.

(1) FUND NAME	(2) SYMBOL	(3) NAV	(4) CHANGE	YTD	(5) 3 YR	5 YR	(6) FRONT LOAD	(7) EXPENSE RATIO	(8) YIELD
Lord Abbett CA Tax-Free Income	LCFIX	$10.62	−$0.03	−0.51	3.92	3.76	3.25	0.93	4.00
FBR Small Cap	FBRVX	$55.38	−$0.86	2.84	18.00	25.39	None	1.38	-
Janus Contrarian	JSVAX	$19.00	−$0.29	12.89	26.32	24.65	None	1.69	-
Vanguard Mid Cap Index	VIMSX	$20.60	−$0.59	4.17	17.39	17.49	None	0.22	-

1. **Fund name:** Name of mutual fund.

2. **Symbol:** Fund's symbol.

3. **NAV:** Net asset value, the per-share value of the fund.

4. **Change:** Decrease or increase in NAV from previous day.

5. **YTD, 3 yr, 5 yr:** Performance year-to-date, over the past 3 years, over the past 5 years (expressed as a percentage increase or decrease).

6. **Front load:** Percentage of a new investment charged as a sales fee; no-load funds do not charge a front load.

7. **Expense ratio:** Annual cost of owning the mutual fund.

8. **Yield:** Annual yield of income-producing funds, expressed as a percentage.

Summary of Learning Objectives

1 Highlight the functions, characteristics, and common forms of money.

Money functions as a medium of exchange, a measure of value, and a store of value. It must be divisible, portable, durable, stable, and difficult to counterfeit. Common forms of money include currency, such as coins, bills, traveler's checks, cashier's checks, and money orders; demand deposits, such as checking accounts; and time deposits, such as savings accounts, certificates of deposit, and money-market deposit accounts.

2 Discuss the responsibilities and insurance methods of the FDIC.

The Federal Deposit Insurance Corporation is a federal insurance program that protects deposits in member banks. Banks pay premiums to the FDIC, which insures funds on deposit with a particular bank for up to $100,000 in case of bank failure. The FDIC supervises the Bank Insurance Fund, which covers deposits in commercial banks and savings banks, and the Savings Association Insurance Fund, which covers deposits in savings and loan associations.

3 Discuss how industry deregulation and the repeal of the Glass-Steagall Act are affecting the banking industry.

Deregulation and the repeal of the Glass-Steagall Act are fueling a raft of megamergers among banks, insurance companies, and brokerage firms and increasing the competition among these institutions. As a result, the line between the types of financial services offered by banks, securities brokers, and insurance companies is blurring. Meanwhile, community banks are stepping in to fill a void created by bank consolidations by focusing on the needs of local customers (generally, small businesses).

4 Highlight the distinguishing features of common stock, preferred stock, bonds, and mutual funds.

Common stock gives shareholders an ownership interest in the company, the right to elect directors and vote on important issues, and the chance to earn dividends and share in the fortunes of the company—while limiting the shareholder's liability to the price paid for the shares. Preferred stock gives shareholders a higher dividend than common stock and a preferred claim over creditors if the corporation fails. Special types of preferred stock have certain privileges. Bonds are long-term loans investors make to the issuing entity in return for a stated interest amount. The loan or principal is paid back to the bondholder over the life of the bond. Bonds may be secured, unsecured, or convertible. They may be issued by corporations or federal, state, city, and local agencies. Mutual funds are pools of money drawn from many investors to buy a variety of stocks, bonds, and other marketable securities. The primary benefit of this investment is diversification.

5 Explain the advantages of index funds.

Index mutual funds offer three potential advantages: lower cost (less of the investor's money is consumed by fees), simple diversification (with even a small investment, the investor's money is spread across many stocks and often multiple industries and geographic regions), and better performance than the majority of actively managed funds.

6 Discuss the importance of establishing investment objectives and identify five factors to consider when making investment choices.

Adding up all the stocks, bonds, mutual funds, real estate possibilities, and other vehicles, investors face literally millions of competing investment opportunities spread across a wide range of potential risk and reward levels. Some investment options are appropriate for some investing objectives, but completely inappropriate for others. Therefore, establishing objectives first is essential to making smart investment choices. The five factors investors should always consider are income, growth, safety, liquidity, and tax consequences.

7 Explain how government regulation of securities trading tries to protect investors.

The government tries to prevent fraud in the securities markets by requiring companies to file registration papers, fulfill certain requirements, and file periodic information reports so that investors receive accurate information. Government regulations also control the listing of companies on stock exchanges and prohibit such fraudulent acts as improper release of information, insider trading, stock scams, and other acts designed to deceive investors.

Behind the Scenes

Schwab Innovates All the Way Back to Its Roots

If it were presented as an adventure novel, the history of Charles Schwab Corporation would certainly make for a fast-paced read. From innovation to market tumult to more innovations and more tumult, the financial services firm never seems to have a dull day.

As the stock market struggled to recover in the aftermath of the dot-com collapse and the September 11 terrorist attacks, then-CEO David Pottruck took Schwab in several new directions: money management for wealthier investors, advice for institutional investors, and a variety of other financial services. These initiatives failed to return the company to consistent profitability, however.

Meanwhile, additional competitive forces emerged from two other directions. The first involved brokers that operate exclusively or almost entirely online, such as E*TRADE and TD Ameritrade. With lower operating costs, these new players quickly put downward pressure on the brokerage fees that were central to Schwab's revenue stream.

The second involved Fidelity Investments, the nation's largest mutual fund company. For years, Fidelity had been viewed as a "sleeping giant" in the brokerage business, emphasizing its own mutual funds business more than the business of helping customers buy and sell. About 2003, however, the giant woke up. After having quietly expanded its online systems and customer service capabilities, Fidelity unleashed an aggressive marketing campaign and quickly began adding new clients. Schwab lost 10 percent of its clients, and E*TRADE lost 20 percent of its clients during the onslaught. Moreover, half of Fidelity's brokerage clients' assets are in the company's own mutual funds, which helped make Fidelity "ragingly more profitable than Schwab," in the creative words of one industry analyst.

Schwab's board of directors decided it was time for a change. The board asked company founder, namesake, and former CEO Charles Schwab (then serving as chairman), to come out of semiretirement and retake the reins. Schwab admits that he had been assuming the company's ongoing troubles were caused mainly by external forces. After taking over day-to-day operations, however, he realized the company had created some of the problems itself. Its cost structure had gotten out of control, its brokerage fees were too high, employee morale was "about as low as I could have imagined," and customer satisfaction was slipping. "We lost our emotional connection with our clients. We did a long series of things that antagonized them."

He moved quickly to restructure the company and refocus its attention on the firm's original target market of individual investors. He lowered brokerage fees to counter the low-priced Internet-only competition, and lowered or eliminated a variety of other fees. He launched a major national advertising campaign, using a variety of media to invite investors to "Talk to Chuck." And he sold U.S. Trust, the high-end money management firm the company had purchased several years earlier.

In his second stint as CEO, more than 30 years after founding the company, Charles Schwab is enjoying newfound success. The changes he made after taking over quickly put the firm back on solid financial ground, with continually increasing revenue and record profits. As Schwab looks toward handing the controls over to a new CEO once again, maybe this time around he can really retire and enjoy a dull day or two.[28]

Critical Thinking Questions

1. Why did Schwab sell U.S. Trust?
2. Even though clients can access essentially all its services via the company's website, Schwab maintains several hundred local offices around the United States. Why would the company spend the money to keep these offices?
3. Novice investors sometimes fail to understand that full-service stock brokers often function as commissioned salespeople in addition to providing financial advice. Schwab believes it is important for clients to know exactly how its employees are compensated. The company provides extensive and detailed information on its website (www.aboutschwab.com/about/overview/compensation.html) regarding the compensation of every class of employee who deals with clients. Why would the company divulge this information to the public?

LEARN MORE ONLINE

Visit Charles Schwab's customer website at www.schwab.com. What types of information and advice does the company provide the public and its clients on this site? How does the firm help new investors get started? How does the firm help customers facing significant financial challenges such as saving for college or planning for retirement? (For the latest information on Charles Schwab, visit www.prenhall.com/bovée and click on "Real-Time Updates.") ∎

▌Key Terms

asset allocation (201)
auction exchange (197)
automated teller machines (ATMs) (190)
bear market (203)
bond (193)
broker (201)
bull market (203)
capital gains (195)
checks (188)
convertible bonds (194)
credit cards (188)
currency (188)
day order (202)
dealer exchange (197)
debentures (194)
debit cards (189)
demand deposit (188)
discretionary order (202)
diversification (201)

electronic communication networks (ENCs) 197
electronic funds transfer systems (EFTS) (190)
general obligation bond (195)
institutional investors (203)
investment portfolios (201)
limit order (202)
line of credit (190)
margin trading (202)
market indexes (203)
market order (202)
money (188)
municipal bonds (195)
mutual funds (195)
NASDAQ (National Association of Securities Dealers Automated Quotations) (197)
open order (202)

over-the-counter (OTC) market (197)
price-earnings ratio (205)
primary market (197)
principal (194)
revenue bond (195)
secondary market (197)
secured bonds (194)
securities (192)
short selling (202)
smart cards (189)
speculators (201)
stock exchange (197)
stock split (193)
stop order (202)
time deposits (188)
Treasury bills (195)
Treasury bonds (195)
Treasury notes (195)
U.S. savings bonds (195)

Test Your Knowledge

Questions for Review

1. How do credit cards, debit cards, and smart cards work?
2. What are examples of deposit and nondeposit financial institutions?
3. What are the differences between a Treasury bill, a Treasury note, a U.S. savings bond, a general bond, and a revenue bond?
4. What happens during a 2-for-1 stock split?
5. What is the function of the Securities and Exchange Commission?

Questions for Analysis

6. How can smaller community banks compete with large commercial banks?
7. What are some of the advantages of mutual funds?
8. When might an investor sell a stock short? What risks are involved in selling short?
9. How are the Internet and e-commerce redefining the banking and investment industry?
10. Ethical Considerations. You work in the research-and-development department of a large corporation and have been involved in a discovery that could lead to a new, profitable product. News of the discovery has not been made public. Is it legal for you to buy stock in the company? Now assume the same scenario but you talk to your friend about your discovery while dining at a restaurant. The person at the next table overhears the conversation. Is it legal for the eavesdropper to buy the company's stock before the public announcement of the news?

Questions for Application

11. What are the advantages and disadvantages of using cash, checks, credit cards, and debit cards to pay for goods and services?
12. How This Affects You. If you unexpectedly came into $10,000 next week, what would you do with the money? Compare the benefits of (a) spending all the money on the best vacation you've ever had, (b) socking the money away in a savings account for ten years, and (c) investing it in an index mutual fund for ten years. (You can easily find savings calculators online.) For the savings account, assume you'll earn 3 percent per year, risk-free. For the index fund, assume you'll earn 8 percent per year *on average*—but with more risk. For instance, if you encounter an extended bear market, the fund's value could decline over a period of several years. Which of the three options will you choose? Why?
13. Integrated. Besides watching market indexes, which economic statistics discussed in Chapter 1 might investors want to monitor? Why?
14. Integrated. Look ahead to discussion of mission statements in Chapter 12. Suppose you were thinking about purchasing 100 shares of common stock in General Electric. Why might you want to first review the company's mission statement? What would you be looking for in the company's mission statement that could help you decide whether or not to invest?

Practice Your Knowledge

Sharpening Your Communication Skills

Interviewing a broker is one of the most important steps you can take before hiring that broker to execute your trades or manage your funds and investment portfolio. Practice your communication skills by developing two sets of questions:

1. Questions you might ask a stockbroker to help you decide whether you would use his or her services.
2. Questions you might pose to that broker to help you evaluate the merits of purchasing a specific security.

Building Your Team Skills

You and your team are going to pool your money and invest $5,000. Before you plunge into any investments, how can you prepare yourselves to be good investors? First, consider your group's goals. What will you and your teammates do with any profits generated by your investments? Once you have agreed on a goal for your team's profits, think about how much money you will need to achieve this goal and how soon you want to achieve it.

Next, think about how much risk you personally are willing to take to achieve the goal. Bear in mind that safer investments generally offer lower returns than riskier investments—and certain investments, such as stocks, can lose money. Now hold a group discussion to find a level of risk that feels comfortable for everyone on your team.

Once your team has decided how much risk to take, consider which investments are best suited to your group's goals and chosen risk level. Will you choose stocks, bonds, a combination of both, or other securities? What are the advantages and disadvantages of each type of investment for your team's situation? Then, come to a decision about specific investment opportunities—particular stocks, for example—that your group would like to investigate further.

Compare your group's goal, risk level, and investment possibilities with those of the other teams in your class and discuss the differences and similarities you see.

Improving Your Tech Insights: Online Investing

Online investing has turned much of the securities industry on its head, giving individual investors information and control they never had before and introducing price competition that continues to help investors and hurt brokerage firms. At the same time, online investing has exposed individual investors to greater risk than they might've experienced when going through traditional brokers. When you invest online, no one is there to ask, "Are you *sure* about that?" before you buy or sell a security. Moreover, in the vast proliferation of chat rooms, blogs, and websites that discuss investing, plenty of misinformation (both confused and downright dishonest) is floating around. In other cases, investors simply misuse the tools,

such as trying to use online brokerage sites to conduct *day trading*, a risky technique that requires ultrafast processing available only through specialized terminals connected directly to exchanges. Online investing gives individual investors more power, but to keep from hurting themselves, they need to use that power wisely.

Research several of the leading online brokers. You can start with three popular personal finance magazines, *Kiplinger's* (www.kiplinger.com), *Money* (http://money.cnn.com), and *SmartMoney* (www.smartmoney.com), which regularly run articles about choosing brokers. Select an online brokerage that seems like the right choice for you, and in a brief e-mail message to your instructor, explain why you chose that particular company.[29]

Expand Your Knowledge

Discovering Career Opportunities

Think you might be interested in a job in the securities and commodities industry? This industry has one of the most highly educated and skilled workforces of any industry. And the requirements for entry are high—most brokerage clerks have a college degree. Log on to the Bureau of Labor Statistics, Career Guide to Industries, at www.bls.gov/oco/cg/home.htm, and click on "Finance Activities" followed by "Securities, commodities, and other investments." Read the article, then answer these questions:

1. What are the licensing and continuing education requirements for securities brokers?

2. What is the typical starting position for many people in the securities industry?

3. What factors are expected to contribute to the projected long-term growth of this industry?

Developing Your Research Skills

Identify a company whose recent disclosure of negative information dramatically affected its stock price or bond rating. Then perform some research on that company so you can answer the following questions:

1. On what exchanges do the company's shares trade and under what ticker symbol?

2. What negative information did the company disclose? When? Did the company commit a fraudulent act? How did the information affect the company as a whole?

3. How did the negative information impact the company's securities? What was the company's stock price prior to the release of the negative information? Following the release of the information? What was the stock's 52-week high and low during the year the disclosure was made?

4. How did the DJIA and NASDAQ perform on the day the negative information was made public?

See It on the Web

Visit these websites and answer the following questions for each one. (Up-to-date links for all websites mentioned in this chapter can be found on the Textbook Resources page for Chapter 8 at www.prenhall.com/bovée. Please note that links to sites that become inactive after publication of the book will be removed from the Featured Websites section.)

1. What is the purpose of this website?

2. What kinds of information does this website contain? Please be specific.

3. How is the information provided at this website useful for businesspeople? Consumers?

4. How did you expand your knowledge of banking and securities by reviewing the material at this website? What new things did you learn about this topic?

Tour the U.S. Treasury

Take a virtual tour of the U.S. Treasury at www.ustreas.gov and click on "Education." Read about the duties and functions of the U.S. Treasury, explore the fact sheets, and discover how money gets into circulation. Take the link to the Bureau of Engraving and Printing (BEP) and read the "Fun Facts." Do you know how long $10 billion would last if you spent $1 every second of every day? To find out how, follow the link to BEP and brush up on your money facts. www.ustreas.gov

Stock Up at the NYSE

Tour the New York Stock Exchange at www.nyse.com. Read about NYSE's recent merger with Euronext. Visit the trading floor and learn about the hectic pace of trading. Find out why having a seat doesn't necessarily mean you'll have a chance to sit down. Listen in on a stock transaction and discover how a stock is bought and sold. Learn how investors are protected and how unusual stock transactions are spotted. Get the latest market information as well as a historical perspective of the exchange. www.nyse.com

Invest Wisely—Like a Fool

Here's a fun securities website you can fool around at for a while. Visit the Motley Fool and don't be afraid to ask a foolish investment question or two. (The idea of an investing Fool is somebody who's not afraid to ask tough questions of the rich and powerful.) Roll up your sleeves and do a little work on your own. Discover the strategies, ideas, and information needed to make investment decisions at Fool's School. Learn the steps to investing foolishly. Read the investing basics and learn how to value stocks, analyze stocks, or pick a stockbroker. Expand your knowledge of stocks, bonds, and mutual funds. Finally, discover the keys to successful investing. www.fool.com

Companion Website

Learning Interactively

Log onto www.prenhall.com/bovée, locate your text, and then click on its Companion Website. For Chapter 8, take advantage of the interactive Chapter Quiz to test your knowledge of the chapter. Get instant feedback on whether you need additional studying. Also, you'll find an abundance of valuable resources that will help you succeed in this course, including PowerPoint presentations and Web Links.

Video Case

Learn More to Earn More with Motley Fool

LEARNING OBJECTIVES

The purpose of this video is to help you:

1. Identify the wide variety of investments available to individuals
2. Describe the process by which securities are bought and sold
3. Recognize the risks involved in commodities and other investments

SYNOPSIS

Despite news reports about lottery winners and others who have become millionaires overnight, individuals have a better chance of getting rich if they learn to select investments that are appropriate for their long-term financial goals. Experts advise looking for investments that will beat inflation and keep up with or—ideally—beat general market returns. Individuals can invest in preferred or common stock, newly issued stock from initial public offerings (IPOs), managed or index mutual funds, bonds, or commodities. These investments are far from risk-free, however; commodities and IPOs can be particularly risky. Therefore, individuals should become educated about securities and investment strategies by surfing websites such as the Motley Fool (www.fool.com).

Discussion Questions

1. *For analysis:* Why is the Securities and Exchange Commission concerned about stock rumors that circulate on the Internet?

2. *For analysis:* Why do Motley Fool's experts advise individuals to invest in index funds rather than in actively managed mutual funds?
3. *For application:* What should you consider when deciding whether to buy and sell stock through a broker, through a web-based brokerage, or directly through the company issuing the stock?
4. *For application:* If you were about to retire, why might you invest in preferred stock rather than common stock?
5. *For debate:* Should stock rumors that circulate on the Internet be covered by the individual's constitutional right to freedom of speech rather than being regulated by the SEC? Support your chosen position.

ONLINE EXPLORATION

Mutual funds that seek out environmentally and socially conscious firms in which to invest are becoming more popular because they offer investors a way to earn returns that don't offend their principles. Investigate the following websites: www.socialfunds.com, www.ethicalfunds.com, and www.domini.com. What types of firms does each fund avoid? What type does each prefer to invest in? Would you choose one of these funds if you wanted to invest in a mutual fund? Explain your answer.

PART 4

Creating and Satisfying Customers

CHAPTER 9
Marketing Concepts and Strategies

CHAPTER 10
Products and Pricing

CHAPTER 11
Distribution and Customer Communication

CHAPTER 9

Marketing Concepts and Strategies

LEARNING OBJECTIVES
After studying this chapter, you will be able to

1 Explain what marketing is

2 Describe the four utilities created by marketing

3 Explain how techniques such as social commerce and permission-based marketing help companies nurture positive customer relationships

4 Explain why and how companies learn about their customers

5 Discuss how marketing research helps the marketing effort and highlight its limitations

6 Outline the three steps in the strategic marketing planning process

7 Define *market segmentation* and name three fundamental factors used to identify segments

8 Identify the four elements of a company's marketing mix

Behind the Scenes

Toyota Scion: Connecting with a New Generation of Car Buyers

www.scion.com

If you are in your twenties and in the market for your first new car, are you likely to rush out and buy the same car your parents have? You know—that sensible, conventional car such as the Toyota they drive to the grocery store and to your little sister's soccer practice?

Toyota's marketing experts know you probably won't, and they know this because they have already tried selling conventional cars to younger buyers using conventional advertising messages. Over the past few decades, Toyota grew to a position of prominence in the

Everything from the shape of the cars to the accessories available at dealerships to the style of promotional activities is designed to establish Scion as a unique brand in the automotive marketplace.

United States by offering your parents refreshing alternatives to the cars that *their* parents drove; now the company wants to continue that cycle of success with the next generation of drivers.

Scion Vice President Mark Templin and his colleagues knew the conventional Toyota approach wouldn't work with this new audience, but what approach would? The search for an answer started with research, research, and more research. And that approach to research had to be unconventional—for example, hiring 50 young Californians to record video diaries with their friends. The company even went so far as to learn how core groups of trendsetters discover new ideas and products before spreading them through the larger population.

The research yielded a wide range of insights, including the fact that Japan has emerged as a new center of cool and the realizations that young adults strongly resist being sold to and put a high priority on individualism, self-expression, and authenticity.

The research results helped Toyota create a new line of cars called Scion, the most unconventional of which is the aggressively boxy xB model. The cars benefit from the Toyota heritage of top-notch quality at low prices, and Toyota and after-market suppliers created a wide range of accessories to let buyers personalize their cars—from illuminated cup holders to colored steering wheels. A small number of "Release Series" limited-edition vehicles help create buzz each year, too.

If you had Mark Templin's assignment to market an entirely new line of cars to a generation of drivers who are skeptical about advertising and leery of buying products that "old people" buy, what kind of marketing strategy would you put in place? How would you shape the design of the products to make sure they're different enough to attract the target audience but not so different as to become oddities that no one would buy? What steps would you take to make Scion part of the cultural landscape? How would you get the Scion message out to an audience that doesn't like to be advertised to or sold to?[1] ∎

Marketing in a Changing World

Toyota's strategy for introducing the Scion product line (profiled in the chapter opener) demonstrates both the careful analysis and the extensive effort required to launch new products in today's hotly competitive markets. Your experiences as a consumer may not have given you lots of insights into accounting, production, and other business functions, but you already know a lot about marketing. Companies have been targeting you as a customer since you were a child, and if you're now a young adult about to enter your professional career, thousands of companies would like to get a piece of your future paycheck. You've been on the receiving end of plenty of marketing tactics—contests, advertisements, merchandise displays, discounts, and product giveaways, to name just a few. However, marketing involves much more than displays, commercials, and contests. Successfully marketing a product line such as the Toyota Scion requires a wide range of skills, from research and analysis to strategic planning to persuasive communication.

The American Marketing Association (AMA) defines **marketing** as planning and executing the conception, pricing, promotion, and distribution of ideas, goods, and services to create exchanges that satisfy individual and organizational objectives.[2] With respect to products, marketing involves all the decisions related to a product's characteristics, price, production specifications, market-entry date, distribution, promotion, and sales. With respect to customers, marketing involves understanding customers' needs and their buying behavior, creating consumer awareness, providing **customer service**—which is everything a company does to satisfy its customers—and maintaining relationships with customers long after the sales transaction is complete (see Exhibit 9.1).

In addition to goods and services, marketing applies to nonprofit organizations, people, places, and causes. Politicians constantly market themselves. So do places that

marketing
Process of planning and executing the conception, pricing, promotion, and distribution of ideas, goods, and services to create and maintain relationships

customer service
Efforts a company makes to satisfy its customers to help them realize the greatest possible value from the products they are purchasing

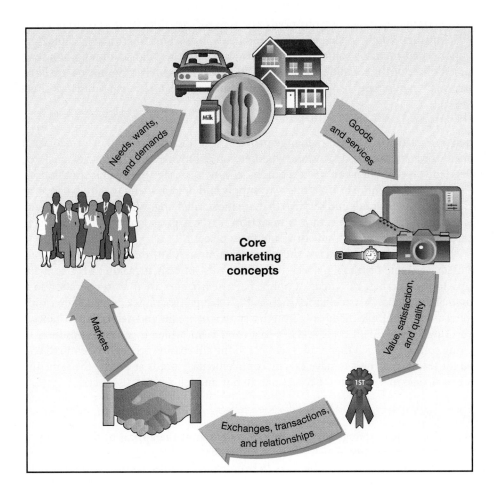

EXHIBIT 9.1
What Is Marketing?

Each of the core marketing concepts—needs, wants, demands, products, services, value, satisfaction, quality, exchanges, transactions, relationships, and markets—builds on the ones before it.

Avon has made breast cancer awareness and research funding a focus of its cause-related marketing.

want to attract residents, tourists, and business investments. **Place marketing** describes efforts to market geographical areas ranging from neighborhoods to entire countries. **Cause-related marketing** promotes a cause or a social issue—such as physical fitness, cancer awareness, recycling, or highway safety—while also promoting a company and its products. For instance, Avon has for many years raised money and awareness for breast cancer screening and research through such activities as the Avon Walk for Breast Cancer.[3]

The Role of Marketing in Society

Take another look at the AMA definition of marketing. Notice that marketing involves an exchange between two parties, both of whom seek some level of satisfaction from the transaction. This definition suggests that marketing plays an important role in society by helping people satisfy their needs and wants and by helping organizations determine what to produce.

Needs and Wants

place marketing
Marketing efforts to attract people and organizations to a particular geographical area

cause-related marketing
Identification and marketing of a social issue, cause, or idea to selected target markets

need
Difference between a person's actual state and his or her ideal state; provides the basic motivation to make a purchase

wants
Specific goods, services, experiences, or other entities that are desirable in light of a person's experiences, culture, and personality

exchange process
Act of obtaining a desired object or service from another party by offering something of value in return

transaction
Exchange of value between parties

Both individual human beings and organizations have a wide variety of needs, from food and water necessary for survival to transaction processing systems that make sure a retail store gets paid for all the credit card purchases it records. As a consumer, you experience a **need** anytime there is a difference or a gap between your actual state and your ideal state. You're hungry and you don't want to be hungry: You need to eat. Needs create the motivation to buy products and are, therefore, at the core of any discussion of marketing.

Your **wants** are based on your needs but are more specific. Producers do not create needs, but they do try to shape your wants by exposing you to attractive choices. For instance, when you need some food, you may want a Snickers bar, an orange, or a seven-course dinner at the swankiest restaurant in town. If you have the means, or *buying power*, to then purchase the product that you want, you create *demand* for that product.[4]

Exchanges and Transactions

When you participate in the **exchange process**, you trade something of value (usually money) for something else of value, whether you're buying an airline ticket, a car, or a college education. When you make a purchase, you encourage the producer of that item to create or supply more of it. In this way, supply and demand tend toward balance, and society obtains the goods and services that are most satisfying. When the exchange actually occurs, it takes the form of a **transaction**. Party A gives Party B $1.29 and gets a medium Coke in return. A trade of values takes place.

Most transactions in today's society involve money, but money is not necessarily required. Bartering or trading, which predates the use of cash, is making a big comeback thanks to the Internet. Hundreds of online barter exchanges are now in operation in the United States alone. Intermediaries such as BizXchange (www.bizx.bz) facilitate cashless trading among multiple members through a system of credits and debits. For instance, an advertising agency might trade services to a dairy farm, which then trades products to a catering company, which then trades services to the advertising agency. By eliminating the need for trading partners to have exactly complementary needs at exactly the same time, these exchanges make it easy for companies to buy and sell without using cash.[5]

The Four Utilities

utility
Power of a good or service to satisfy a human need

To encourage the exchange process, marketers enhance the appeal of their goods and services by adding **utility**, which is any attribute that increases the value that customers place on the product (see Exhibit 9.2). When organizations change raw materials into

EXHIBIT 9.2 Examples of the Four Utilities

The utility of a good or service has four aspects, each of which enhances the product's value to the consumer.

UTILITY	EXAMPLE
Form utility	Kettle Valley's Fruit Snack (www.kettlevalley.net) bars provide the nutritional value of real fruit in a form that offers greater convenience and longer storage life.
Time utility	LensCrafters (www.lenscrafters.com) has captured a big chunk of the market for eyeglasses by providing on-the-spot, one-hour service.
Place utility	By offering convenient home delivery of the latest fashion apparel and accessories, dELiA*s (www.delias.com) catalog and website have become favorites of teenaged girls.
Possession utility	RealNetworks's Rhapsody music streaming service (www.rhapsody.com) gives customers the option of buying individual songs.

finished goods, they are creating **form utility** desired by consumers. For example, when Nokia combines plastic, computer chips, and other materials to make mobile phones, the company is providing form utility. In other cases, marketers try to make their products available when and where customers want to buy them, creating **time utility** and **place utility**. Overnight couriers such as FedEx create time utility, whereas coffee carts in office buildings and ATMs in shopping malls create place utility. Services such as Apple's iTunes create both time and place utility: You can purchase music almost instantly, without leaving your computer. The final form of utility is **possession utility**—the satisfaction that buyers get when they actually possess a product, both legally and physically. Mortgage companies, for example, create possession utility by offering loans that allow people to buy homes they could otherwise not afford.

The Marketing Concept

In earlier business eras, companies typically focused more on their own production or sales functions and less on long-term relationships with markets and customers. In contrast, many of today's companies try to embrace the **marketing concept**, the idea that companies should respond to customers' needs and wants while seeking long-term profitability and coordinating their own marketing efforts to achieve the company's long-term goals. These *customer-focused* companies build their marketing strategies around the goal of long-term relationships with satisfied customers.[6] The term **relationship marketing** is often applied to these efforts to distinguish them from efforts that emphasize production or sales transactions. One of the most significant goals of relationship marketing is **customer loyalty**, the degree to which customers continue to buy from a particular retailer or buy the products offered by a particular manufacturer. The payoff from becoming customer-focused can be considerable, but the process of transforming a product- or sales-driven company into one that embraces the marketing concept can take years and involve changes to major systems and processes throughout the company, as well as the basic culture of the company itself.[7]

Focusing on product features and quality, rather than working backwards from customers to create solutions that meet their needs and wants, is a risky strategy. If history were any guide, Sony should be the top dog in portable music players, not Apple—after all, Sony invented the entire product category and revolutionized the way people listen to music with its Walkman tape player and Discman CD player. However, critics claim that Sony's insistence on using its own digital file format, rather than the formats that the market has already accepted, has kept it a minor player in the new world of digital music players.[8]

form utility
Customer value created by converting raw materials and other inputs into finished goods and services

time utility
Customer value added by making a product available at a convenient time

place utility
Customer value added by making a product available in a convenient location

possession utility
Customer value created when someone takes ownership of a product

marketing concept
Approach to business management that stresses customer needs and wants, seeks long-term profitability, and integrates marketing with other functional units within the organization

relationship marketing
A focus on developing and maintaining long-term relationships with customers, suppliers, and distribution partners for mutual benefit

customer loyalty
Degree to which customers continue to buy from a particular retailer or buy the products of a particular manufacturer or service provider

EXHIBIT 9.3

The Selling Concept Versus the Marketing Concept

Firms that practice the selling concept sell what they make rather than make what the market wants. In contrast, firms that practice the marketing concept determine the needs and wants of a market and deliver the desired product or service more effectively and efficiently than competitors do.

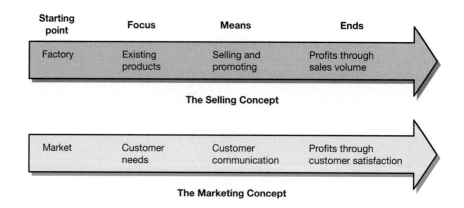

Sony's approach is an example of pursuing the *product concept* instead of the marketing concept. Another limiting mind-set is the *sales concept*, in which the emphasis is on building a business by generating as many sales transactions as possible, rather than on creating lasting relationships with customers (see Exhibit 9.3).[9]

Why all the emphasis on customer service and customer satisfaction in the marketing concept, by the way? It's not just about being nice and helpful, although many firms are certainly motivated by those factors as well—satisfying customers is simply good business. The most successful companies often push to get a step beyond satisfaction with the goal of *delighting* their customers by exceeding expectations. Among the many positive results of satisfying and delighting your customers: (1) greater customer loyalty, which can sharply reduce marketing costs; (2) positive *word of mouth*, in which happy customers help promote your products to friends, family, and colleagues; (3) the opportunity to sell more different types of products to customers who are satisfied with the purchases they've made from you already; and (4) reduced sensitivity to price.[10] When Dave Meisburger of Mobile, Alabama, experienced the fast, reassuring service from Progressive Insurance after his wife had been in an automobile accident, he said that "they could double their rate, and I wouldn't care. Their customer service means more to me than anything." Even though its prices remain competitive, delighted customers have helped Progressive enjoy annual profit gains of as much as 75 percent in recent years.[11]

In contrast, negative customer experiences can quickly damage a company's reputation and business prospects, particularly when competitors may be only a few mouse clicks away. One recent survey suggests that customers generally give a company one more chance after a bad experience, but after two mistakes, they're ready to take their business elsewhere. Moreover, the majority of customers share their bad experiences with friends, family, and colleagues, spreading the damage even further.[12]

Marketing on the Leading Edge

As business has progressed from the product concept to the sales concept to the marketing concept, the role of marketing has become increasingly complicated. You'll read about some specific challenges in the next two chapters, but here are four issues that many successful, responsible marketing organizations are wrestling with today: involving the customer in the marketing process, making marketing more accountable, using technology without losing the human touch, and conducting marketing with greater concern for ethics and etiquette.

Involving the Customer in the Marketing Process

The Internet has changed business in many ways, but perhaps none is as intriguing and potentially far-reaching as the way it brings customers into the marketing process. In the past, buyers and potential buyers had limited ability to connect with one another or to

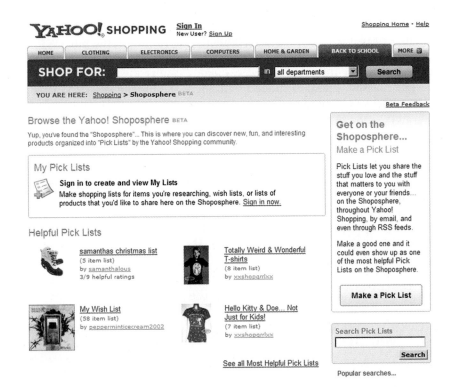

EXHIBIT 9.4

Social Commerce

Websites such as Yahoo!'s Shoposphere give customers and potential customers the opportunity to participate in the marketing process by sharing information about products.

exert much influence on companies beyond their purchase decisions. Marketing communication was a one-way, mass-communication broadcast controlled by sellers, not buyers.

Thanks to a variety of capabilities enabled by the Internet, however, customers have the power of information on their side. Marketers can encourage this **social commerce**, in which customers create and share information about products, by facilitating the exchange of information in ways that promote positive buying responses (see Exhibit 9.4).[13] For example, Amazon.com and many other online retailers let consumers write product reviews, post product photos, create lists of products that other enthusiasts might like, and show products that other shoppers purchased after considering a particular product. Of course, these networked communities of customers and enthusiasts can make or break products. Products that fail to satisfy customers can quickly get a bad reputation in the online world.

social commerce
The creation and sharing of product-related information among customers and potential customers

Making Marketing More Accountable

The marketing function has always been haunted by a lack of measurability and accountability; many decisions and activities are difficult if not impossible to measure, and even some that can be measured won't yield definitive answers for months after the fact. For instance, if you introduce a new product and it fails, is the reason the price, the advertising, the sales training, the product itself, the wrong market, or some other factor? And what about that expensive website or those millions you spent on advertising? How can you tell if those investments paid off in increased sales? Today's CEOs and CFOs are demanding that marketing find some way to justify these expenses and decisions.[14] Internet-based advertising has proven to be helpful in this quest, since it's much easier to track response patterns by following people's click trails and analyzing their online behavior, but measuring the effectiveness of many other marketing efforts remains a considerable challenge.

Balancing Technology and the Human Touch

For all the amazing technologies that marketers now have at their disposal, from virtual reality websites to mobile commerce that can put electronic coupons in customers' hands as they walk past a storefront, marketing has always been and will always be about the choices, beliefs, and emotions of human beings. When commerce first reached the Internet, many predicted that online technology would change the way people think, feel, and behave, and indeed change the very nature of business. As revolutionary as it has been, however, the Internet didn't and couldn't change the fact that people are still people—and marketers need to connect with them at a human level, no matter which technologies they might be using.[15]

Marketing with Greater Concern for Ethics and Etiquette

Let's face it: Advertising, sales, public relations, and other activities within the marketing function don't always have a shining reputation with the general public—and often for good reason. Under pressure to reach and persuade buyers in a business environment that gets more fragmented and noisier all the time, marketers occasionally step over the line and engage in practices that are rude, manipulative, or even downright deceptive. The result is an increasing degree of skepticism of and hostility toward advertising and other marketing activities.[16]

Mining Your Deepest Secrets

They know more about you than some of your closet friends and relatives might know, and you've probably never heard of them. Knowing where you live, where you work, how much you earn—yawn; that's all basic stuff. These organizations keep track of the deeper secrets: your medication, your online shopping habits, your religious and political affiliations, whether or not you gamble, and maybe even your sexual orientation.

Who are these organizations? They are companies such as ChoicePoint, Acxiom, Equifax, HNC Software, and LexisNexis that compile data files on consumers and resell the information to marketers, landlords, banks, government agencies, and others with the legal right to purchase it.

And how do they know all this about you? Every time you make a purchase using a credit card, a gift card, or a frequent-shopper card, the information about your transaction goes into databases. Unless you pay with cash, virtually every commercial transaction you make is recorded somewhere by somebody. Not buying anything today? No problem, just send in a warranty registration card, get married, buy a house, get arrested—every major and minor decision you make probably gets recorded. And whenever you venture online, from search engines to shopping sites, you leave electronic footprints all over the place. Sign up for news articles at a car-related website? Bingo—you've just been tagged as a potential car buyer. Reading up on some interesting stocks you might want to invest in? Don't be surprised if your web browser starts spitting out ads for mutual funds and stockbrokers.

Companies have been collecting information like this for years, but recent advances in web tracking and data mining make it easier than ever to cross-index multiple databases and to uncover relationships between your data points. In

fact, most consumers would be stunned to discover (a) how much information various companies know about them, (b) how easy it is for companies to buy and sell this information, and (c) how little privacy protection they really have under current laws. By one recent tally, 100 million confidential consumer and employee records were lost or stolen in more than 500 reported incidences in the two-year period from 2005 to 2006. In Europe, strict privacy regulations prevent companies from using data about individuals without asking permission and explaining how the data will be used. But in the United States and many other countries, marketers have few restrictions about using such information.

Things may change in the coming years, however, thanks to several recent high-profile instances involving theft or misappropriation of consumer data. Identity theft experts warn that database owners aren't doing enough to protect data. Expect a loud and long fight over database privacy, however. Companies claim that constitutionally protected freedom of speech gives them the right to market to consumers using publicly available information. Security experts say that the global fight against terrorism makes it imperative to give government agencies access to personal records. Meanwhile, if you don't want anybody to know what you're buying, you better pay cash.

Questions for Critical Thinking

1. Should a marketer selling long-distance telephone service be allowed to see your telephone records without your knowledge or permission?
2. Should web marketers be required to conspicuously post their privacy policies and ask consent before collecting and using visitors' personal data?

To avoid intensifying the vicious circle in which marketers keep doing the same old things, only louder and longer—leading customers to get more angry and defensive—some marketers are looking for a better way. Social commerce shows a lot of promise for redefining marketing communication from one-way promotion to two-way conversation. Another hopeful sign is **permission-based marketing**, in which marketers invite potential or current customers to receive information in areas that genuinely interest them. Many websites now take this approach, letting visitors sign up for specific e-mail newsletters with the promise that they won't be bombarded with information they don't care about. Some go a step further with *reciprocation*, giving customers something of value in exchange for the opportunity to present promotional information.[17] Business-to-business technology marketers frequently do so through *white papers* and other materials that give readers valuable information they can use in running their businesses.

At the same time, the emergence of **stealth marketing**, in which customers don't know they're being marketed to, has raised an entirely new set of concerns about ethics and intrusion. One stealth marketing technique is sending people into public places to use particular products in a conspicuous manner and then discuss them with strangers—as though they were just regular people on the street, when in fact they are employed by a marketing firm. Another is to pay consumers (or reward them with insider information and other perks) to promote products to their friends without telling them it's a form of advertising. Critics complain that such techniques are deceptive because they don't give their targets the opportunity to raise their instinctive defenses against the persuasive powers of marketing messages.[18] Stealth marketing may be successful in many cases, but it's likely to generate yet another backlash from parents, privacy watchdogs, and the general public.

In addition, the rapidly multiplying options in electronic commerce create tremendous concerns over privacy and data security. Marketers will continue to face scrutiny from the public and government regulators as they try to balance their own commercial interests with the rights and wishes of consumers. (For the latest information on marketing and its role in society, visit www.prenhall.com/bovée and click on "Real-Time Updates.")

Is this a group of boys just talking, or is one of these boys a stealth marketing agent pitching a product to his unsuspecting buddies?

permission-based marketing
Marketing approach in which firms first ask permission to deliver messages to an audience and then promise to restrict their communication efforts to those subject areas in which audience members have expressed interest

stealth marketing
The delivery of marketing messages to people who are not aware that they are being marketed to; these messages can be delivered by either acquaintances or strangers, depending on the technique

Understanding Today's Customers

To implement the marketing concept, companies must have good information about what customers want. This is a challenge because today's customers, both individual consumers and organizational buyers, are a diverse and demanding group, with little patience for marketers who do not understand them or will not adapt business practices to meet their needs. They expect goods and services to be delivered faster and more conveniently. And most have no qualms about switching to competitors if their demands are not met—and the Internet makes switching as easy as a few mouse clicks in many cases. For instance, consumers faced with complex purchase decisions such as cars or homes can now find extensive information online about products, prices, competitors, customer service rankings, safety issues, and other factors. They no longer have to put their fate entirely in the hands of companies that once had the upper hand by hoarding all the information.

This phenomenon isn't limited to technical purchases, either. The fashion industry is experiencing an upheaval of its own as more customers no longer wait for a select few design houses to tell everyone what's "in" or "out" for the coming season. Hemlines, necklines, necktie widths, lapel widths, fabrics, colors, and other design elements used to ebb and flow with remarkable similarity across the industry. However, with visual images reaching around the globe through innumerable print, broadcast, cable, satellite, and

consumer market
Individuals or households that buy goods and services for personal use

organizational market
Businesses, nonprofit organizations, and government agencies that purchase goods and services for use in their operations

customer buying behavior
Behavior exhibited by consumers as they consider, select, and purchase goods and services

cognitive dissonance
Tension that exists when a person's beliefs don't match his or her behaviors; a common example is *buyer's remorse*, when someone regrets a purchase immediately after making it

online media, many shoppers follow the mix-and-match creativity of Susannah Brunings of Mission Viejo, California: "I'm interested in becoming my own trendsetter."[19]

The first step toward understanding customers is recognizing the different purchase and ownership habits of the **consumer market**, made up of individuals and families who buy for personal or household use, and the **organizational market**, composed of both companies and a variety of noncommercial institutions, from local school districts to the federal government.

The Consumer Decision Process

Think about several purchase decisions you've made recently. Classical economics suggests that your **customer buying behavior** would follow the rational process in Exhibit 9.5, first recognizing a need, gathering information, identifying alternative solutions, then making your choice from those alternatives. But how often do you really make decisions like that? Researchers now understand that consumer behavior tends to be far less logical and far more complicated—and more interesting—than this model suggests. In fact, some research suggests that as much as 95 percent of the decision-making process is subconscious and that sensory cues can play a much larger role than objective information.[20]

Even in situations in which consumers gather lots of information and appear to be making a well-thought-out, rational decision, they often are acting more on gut feelings and emotional responses. For instance, you might see one of the latest Scion models drive past on the street, and in that split second—before you even start "thinking" about it—you've already decided to buy one just like it. Sure, you'll gather brochures, do research on the Internet, test-drive other models, and so on, but chances are you're not really evaluating alternatives. Instead, your rational, conscious brain is just looking for evidence to support the decision that your emotional, semiconscious brain has already made.

Moreover, we consumers make all kinds of decisions that are hard to explain by any rational means. We might spend two weeks gathering data on $200 music players, then choose a college with $20,000 annual tuition simply because our best friend is going there. Sometimes we buy things for no apparent reason other than the fact that we have money in our pockets. As a result, at one time or another, all consumers suffer from **cognitive dissonance**, which occurs when our beliefs and behaviors don't match. A common form of this situation is *buyer's remorse*, when we make a purchase then regret doing so—sometimes immediately after the purchase.

You can start to understand why so many decisions seem mysterious from a rational point of view if you consider all the influences that affect purchases:

- *Culture.* The cultures (and subgroups within cultures) that people belong to shape their values, attitudes, and beliefs and influence the way they respond to the world around them.

EXHIBIT 9.5 The Rational Model of Buyer Decisions

In the classic, rational model of buyer behavior, customers work through several steps in logical order before making a purchase decision. However, newer research shows that most consumer decisions are less rational and more subconscious than the classical model suggests.

■ *Social class.* In addition to being members of a particular culture, people also perceive themselves as members of a certain social class—be it upper, middle, lower, or somewhere in between. In general, members of various classes pursue different activities, buy different goods, shop in different places, and react to different media—or at least like to believe they do.

■ *Reference groups.* Consumers are also influenced by *reference groups* that provide information about product choices and establish values that individual consumers perceive as important. Reference groups can be either *membership* or *aspirational*. As the name suggests, membership groups are those to which consumers actually belong; families, networks of friends, sports teams, clubs, and work groups are common examples. In contrast, consumers don't belong to aspirational reference groups but use them as role models for style, speech, opinions, and various other behaviors.[21] For instance, millions of consumers buy products that help them identify with popular musicians or professional athletes.

> ### *Learning from Business Blunders*
>
> **Oops:** On the surface, it looked like Hallmark Cards did everything you're supposed to do. Its researchers, monitoring the demographic bulge of the baby boom generation, created the Time of Your Life product line to appeal specifically to people reaching the 50-year milestone in life. Their careful customer research showed that while boomers might be aging, they don't want to think of themselves as old. In response, the product line featured youthful, healthy images of people in the prime of life. The products were displayed in a special Time of Your Life section in Hallmark stores. Hallmark had succeeded with other product lines aimed at specific groups of customers, such as Mahogany (African-American themes) and Tree of Life (Jewish themes). Time of Your Life sounded like another winner, but the product line was a flop.
>
> **What You Can Learn:** While the products themselves may have been right on the mark in terms of customer wants and needs, the final piece of the puzzle—the retail presentation—put people off. Boomers who didn't want to think of themselves as old weren't about to shop in the "old people's" section of the card store. Marketers need to consider the entire consumer experience; a mistake at any stage can doom the entire effort.

■ *Situational factors.* These factors include events or circumstances in people's lives that are more circumstantial but that can influence buying patterns. Such factors might include having a coupon, being in a hurry, celebrating a holiday, being in a bad mood, and so on. If you've ever indulged in "retail therapy" to cheer yourself up, you know all about situational factors—and the buyer's remorse that often comes with it.

■ *Self-image.* Many consumers tend to believe that "you are what you buy," so they make or avoid choices that support their desired self-images. Marketers capitalize on people's need to express their identity through their purchases by emphasizing the image value of goods and services.

The Organizational Customer Decision Process

The purchasing behavior of organizations is easier to understand because it's more clearly driven by economics and influenced less by subconscious, emotional factors. Here are some of the significant ways in which organizational purchasing differs from consumer purchasing:[22]

■ *An emphasis on economic payback and other rational factors.* Most organizational purchases are carefully evaluated for financial impact, technical compatibility, reliability, and other objective factors. Organizations don't always make the best choices, of course, but their choices are usually based on a more rational analysis of needs and alternatives. However, some business-to-business marketers make the mistake of assuming that customer emotions play little or no role in the purchase decision, forgetting that organizations don't make decisions, people do. Fear of change, fear of failure, excitement over new technologies, and the pride of being associated with world-class suppliers are just a few of the emotions that can influence organizational purchases.

■ *A formal buying process.* From office supplies to new factories, most organizational purchases follow a formal buying process, particularly in government agencies and in mid- to large-size companies. In fact, the model in Exhibit 9.5 is a better representation of organizational purchasing than it is of consumer purchasing, although organizational purchasing often includes additional steps such as establishing budgets, analyzing potential suppliers, and requesting proposals.

■ *The participation and influence of multiple people.* Except in the very smallest businesses, where the owner may make all the purchasing decisions, the purchase process usually involves a group of people. This team can include end users, technical experts, the manager with ultimate purchasing authority, and a professional purchasing agent whose job includes researching suppliers, negotiating prices, and evaluating supplier performance.

■ *Closer relationships between buyers and sellers.* Close and long-lasting relationships between buyers and sellers are common in organizational purchasing. In some cases, employees from the seller even have offices inside the buyer's facility to promote close interaction.

Marketing Research and Market Intelligence

marketing research
The collection and analysis of information for making marketing decisions

Understanding customer purchase behavior is one of the many goals of **marketing research**—the process of gathering and analyzing *market intelligence* about customers, markets, and related marketing issues. As markets grow increasingly dynamic and open to competition from all corners of the globe, today's companies realize that information is the key to successful action. Without it, they're forced to use guesswork, analogies from other markets that may or may not apply, or experience from the past that may not correspond to the future.[23] At the same time, however, marketing research can't provide the answer to every strategic or tactical question. As a manager or entrepreneur, you'll find yourself in situations that require creative thinking and careful judgment to make the leap beyond what the data alone can tell you.

Research techniques range from the basic to the exotic, from simple surveys to advanced statistical techniques to neurological scanning that tries to discover how and why customers' brains respond to visual and verbal cues about products. You can see a sample of techniques in Exhibit 9.6. As with other aspects of marketing, some research techniques raise ethical concerns over the invasion of consumer privacy. For instance, *video mining*, the visual counterpart of data mining, involves videotaping shoppers so that researchers can study their movements and behaviors throughout a store. Most consumers understand the need for security cameras in stores, but few are aware that these cameras are often used for marketing research, too.[24]

database marketing
Process of building, maintaining, and using customer databases for the purpose of contacting customers and transacting business

Another way to learn about customer preferences is to gather and analyze all kinds of customer-related data. **Database marketing** is the process of recording and analyzing customer interactions, preferences, and buying behavior for the purpose of contacting and transacting with customers. Capital One, for example, has become a leading credit card company by collecting extensive records on millions of consumers and using that information to plan its marketing strategies. Every credit card use, online transaction, and frequent-buyer purchase leaves behind a trail of information that retailers can use to their advantage. Frequent-shopper card programs, good for a wealth of discounts at checkout, have convinced customers to share some of the most intimate details about their lives. For instance, customer grocery purchases reveal preferences for everything from hygiene products to

How This Affects You

1. What is your reaction when you feel as though you're being "sold to" by a company that is clearly more interested in selling products than in meeting your needs as an individual consumer? Have you ever decided against buying something you really wanted just because you didn't like the way you were being treated?

2. Do you read product reviews and advice online before making important purchases? Why or why not? Have you ever contributed to social commerce by posting your own reviews or product advice?

3. Why did you buy the clothes you are wearing at this very moment?

EXHIBIT 9.6 Marketing Research Techniques

Marketers can use a wide variety of techniques to learn more about customers, competitors, and threats and opportunities in the marketplace.

TECHNIQUE	EXAMPLES
Observation	Any in-person, mechanical, or electronic technique that monitors and records behavior, including video mining, website usage tracking, and monitoring of blogs and social tagging websites.
Surveys	Data collection efforts that measure responses from a representative subset of a larger group of people; can be conducted in person (when people with clipboards stop you in a mall, that's called a *mall intercept*), over the phone, by mail or e-mail, or online. Designing and conducting a meaningful survey requires thorough knowledge of statistical techniques such as *sampling to* ensure valid results that truly represent the larger group. For this reason, many of the simple surveys that you see online these days do not produce statistically valid results.
Interviews and focus groups	One-on-one or group discussions that try to probe deeper into issues than a survey typically does. *Focus groups* involve a small number of people guided by a facilitator while being observed or recorded by researchers. Unlike surveys, interviews and focus groups are not designed to collect statistics that represent a larger group; their real value is in uncovering issues that might require further study.
Process data collection	Any method of collecting data during the course of other business tasks, including warranty registration cards, sales transaction records, gift and loyalty program card usage, and customer service interactions.
Experiments	Controlled scenarios in which researchers adjust one or more variables to measure the effect these changes have on customer behavior. For instance, separate groups of consumers can be exposed to different ads to see which ad is most effective. *Test marketing*, the launch of a product under real-world conditions but on a limited scale (such as in a single city), is a form of experimental research.

junk food to magazines. The proliferation of gift cards in recent years has given marketers yet another source of electronic data.[25]

Planning Your Marketing Strategies

By now you can see why successful marketing rarely happens without carefully analyzing and understanding your customers. Once you have learned about your customers, you're ready to begin planning your marketing strategies. **Strategic marketing planning** is a process that involves three steps: (1) examining your current marketing situation, (2) assessing your opportunities and setting your objectives, and (3) developing a marketing strategy to reach those objectives (see Exhibit 9.7). Companies often record the results of their planning efforts in a formal *marketing plan.*

A solid marketing strategy both flows from and supports the overall business strategy; it is also closely coordinated with other functional strategies. For instance, in order to reach out to younger drivers with the high-quality, low-cost Scion, Toyota not only needs an effective marketing strategy, but a manufacturing strategy that can create the necessary products, a financial strategy that supports the price levels required by the marketing strategy, a human resource strategy that makes sure the right workers are in place across all the functions, and so on. Here's a closer look at the three steps in the process.

strategic marketing planning
The process of examining an organization's current marketing situation, assessing opportunities and setting objectives, then developing a marketing strategy to reach those objectives

Step 1: Examining Your Current Marketing Situation

Examining your current marketing situation includes reviewing your past performance (how well each product is doing in each market where you sell it), evaluating your competition, examining your internal strengths and weaknesses, and analyzing the external environment.

EXHIBIT 9.7 The Strategic Marketing Planning Process

Strategic marketing planning comprises three steps: (1) examining your current marketing situation, (2) assessing your opportunities and setting objectives, and (3) developing your marketing strategy.

Examine current marketing situation

✓ Review past/current performance

✓ Evaluate competition

✓ Examine internal strengths and weaknesses

✓ Analyze external environment

Assess opportunities and set objectives

✓ Assess product and market opportunities

✓ Set specific and measurable objectives

Develop marketing strategy

✓ Segment market

✓ Choose target market

✓ Position product

✓ Develop marketing mix

Reviewing Performance

Unless you're starting a new business, your company has a history of marketing performance. Maybe sales have slowed in the past year; maybe you've had to cut prices so much that you're barely earning a profit; or maybe sales are going quite well and you have money to invest in new marketing activities. Reviewing where you are and how you got there is critical, because you will want to repeat your successes and learn from your past mistakes.

Evaluating Competition

In addition to reviewing past performance, you must also evaluate your competition. If you own a Burger King franchise, for example, you need to watch what McDonald's and Wendy's are doing. You also have to keep an eye on Taco Bell, KFC, Pizza Hut, and other restaurants in addition to paying attention to any number of other ways your customers might satisfy their hunger—including fixing a sandwich at home. Furthermore, you need to watch the horizon trends that could affect your business, such as consumer interest in organic foods or locally produced ingredients.

Examining Internal Strengths and Weaknesses

Successful marketers try to identify both sources of competitive advantage and areas that need improvement. They look at such factors as financial resources, production capabilities, distribution networks, business partnerships, managerial expertise, and promotional capabilities. This step is important because you can't develop a successful marketing strategy if you don't know your strengths as well as your limitations. On the basis of your internal analysis, you will be able to decide whether your business should (1) limit itself to those opportunities for which it possesses the required strengths or (2) challenge itself to reach higher goals by acquiring and developing new strengths.

Understanding your strengths and weaknesses is especially important when evaluating the merits of global expansion. Selling products overseas requires not only managerial expertise and financial resources but also the ability to adjust your operation to different cultures, customs, legal requirements, and product specifications.

Analyzing the External Environment

Marketers must also analyze a number of external environment factors when planning their marketing strategies. These factors include:

■ *Economic conditions.* Marketing activities are greatly affected by trends in interest rates, inflation, unemployment, personal income, and savings rates. In tough times, consumers put off buying expensive items such as major appliances, cars, and homes. They cut back on travel, entertainment, and luxury goods. Conversely, when the economy is good, consumers open their wallets and satisfy their pent-up demand for higher-priced goods and services.

■ *Natural environment.* Changes in the natural environment can affect marketers, both positively and negatively. Interruptions in the supply of raw materials can upset even the most carefully conceived marketing plans. Floods, droughts, and cold weather can affect the price and availability of many products as well as the behavior of target customers.

In recent years, many homebuilders misread a surge in housing demand, resulting in excess inventory—and desperate attempts to lure buyers.

■ *Social and cultural trends.* Planners also need to study the social and cultural environment to determine shifts in customer needs, values, and behaviors. For example, in recent years, U.S. homebuilders were in a frenzy, building new homes at a rapid pace as demand surged. However, the increase wasn't driven entirely by the formation of new households (through marriage, divorce, immigration, and other social changes), which is the primary force behind sustainable housing demand. Much of the apparent demand surge came from real estate speculators who were buying new houses and condos with the intent to "flip" them quickly for a profit rather than living in them. When overheated real estate markets around the country began to cool off, the flippers quickly disappeared—and so did the artificial surge in demand. By misreading a social trend, homebuilders made the expensive mistake of creating more housing inventory than the market really needed. As the chief economist for the National Association of Home Builders later admitted, "The influx of investors and speculators was much, much bigger than anybody appreciated at the time."[26]

■ *Laws and regulations.* Like every other function in business, marketing is controlled by laws at the local, state, national, and international levels. From product design to pricing to advertising, virtually every task you'll encounter in marketing is affected in some way by laws and regulations.

■ *Technology.* When technology changes, so must your marketing approaches. Technological innovations can help a company in some instances and hurt it in others. For example, online retailing has helped numerous companies reach customers around the world, but it has exposed them to competition from around the world, too. *Disruptive technologies*, those that fundamentally change the nature of an industry, can be powerful enough to create or destroy entire companies. Forward-thinking managers try to cause these disruptions themselves or at least spot these shifts early so they can capitalize on them if possible or minimize the damage the changes might bring.

Step 2: Assessing Your Opportunities and Setting Your Objectives

Once you've examined your current marketing situation, you're ready to assess your marketing opportunities and set your objectives. Successful companies are always on the lookout for new marketing opportunities, which can be classified into four options:[27]

■ *Market penetration:* Selling more of your existing products in current markets

■ *Product development:* Creating new products for your current markets

■ *Market development:* Selling your existing products to new markets

■ *Diversification:* Creating new products for new markets

These four options are listed in order of increasing risk; creating new products for unfamiliar markets is usually the riskiest choice of all because you encounter uncertainties in both dimensions (you may fail to create the product you need, and the market might not be interested in it). Once you've framed the opportunity you want to pursue, you are ready to set your marketing objectives. A common marketing objective is to achieve a certain level of **market share**, which is a firm's portion of the total sales within a market (market share can be defined by either number of units sold or by sales revenue).

market share
A firm's portion of the total sales in a market

Step 3: Developing Your Marketing Strategy

Using your current marketing situation and your objectives as your guide, you're ready to move to the third step. This is where you develop your **marketing strategy**, which consists of dividing your market into *segments,* choosing your *target markets* and the *position* you'd like to establish in those markets, and then developing a *marketing mix* to help you get there.

Dividing Markets into Segments

A **market** contains all the customers who might be interested in a product and can pay for it. However, most markets contain subgroups of potential customers with different interests, values, and behaviors. To maximize their effectiveness in reaching these subgroups, many companies subdivide the total market by identifying *market segments,* homogeneous groups of customers that are significantly different from each other. This process is called **market segmentation**; its objective is to group customers with similar characteristics, behavior, and needs. Each of these market segments can then be targeted by offering products that are priced, distributed, and promoted differently. For instance, Toyota knows that a 25-year-old whose primary interests are clubbing, mountain biking, and launching a career won't respond to the same marketing messages as a 50-year-old whose primary concerns are getting the kids through college and saving for retirement—even though these two consumers might end up buying the exact same vehicle.

The overall goal of market segmentation is to understand why and how certain customers buy what they buy so that you use your finite resources to create and market products in the most efficient manner possible.[28] The three fundamental factors marketers use to identify market segments are demographics, psychographics, and geographics:

- *Demographics.* When you segment a market using **demographics**, the statistical analysis of a population, you subdivide your customers according to characteristics such as age, gender, income, race, occupation, and ethnic group. Be aware, however, that demographic variables are poor predictors of behavior. For instance, even though they may fit a particular demographic profile, not all consumers aged 35 to 44 making $200,000 per year buy luxury cars. And those who do may not purchase such cars for the same reasons.[29]

- *Psychographics.* Whereas demographic segmentation is the study of people from the outside, **psychographics** is the analysis of people from the inside, focusing on their psychological makeup, including attitudes, interests, opinions, and lifestyles. Psychographic analysis focuses on why people behave the way they do by examining such issues as brand preferences, media preferences, reading habits, values, and self-concept. Markets can also be segmented according to customers' knowledge of, attitude toward, use of, or response to products or product characteristics, an approach known as **behavioral segmentation**. Segmenting by degree of customer loyalty can also be an effective step toward planning the best way to interact with each type of customer. For instance, if you know that certain customers buy from you some of the time but from your competitors at other times, you can study their needs more carefully to figure out how to capture a greater share of their business.[30]

- *Geographics.* When differences in buying behavior are influenced by where people live, it makes sense to use **geographic segmentation**. Segmenting the market into different geographical units such as regions, cities, counties, or neighborhoods allows companies to customize and sell products that meet the needs of specific markets. Of course, geographic segments change as population patterns shift. For instance, responding to changes in small towns across the country, the U.S. Census Bureau created the "micropolis" designation for boom towns such as Silverthorne, Colorado, and Palm Coast, Florida, that are near major metropolitan centers but so self-contained that many residents no longer need to travel into the city for shopping and employment.[31]

Starting with these three sets of variables, researchers can also combine different types of data to identify target segments with even greater precision. **Geodemographics**

---

marketing strategy
Overall plan for marketing a product; includes the identification of target market segments, a positioning strategy, and a marketing mix

market
A group of customers who need or want a particular product and have the money to buy it

market segmentation
Division of a diverse market into smaller, relatively homogeneous groups with similar needs, wants, and purchase behaviors

demographics
Study of statistical characteristics of a population

psychographics
Classification of customers on the basis of their psychological makeup, interests, and lifestyles

behavioral segmentation
Categorization of customers according to their relationship with products or response to product characteristics

geographic segmentation
Categorization of customers according to their geographical location

geodemographics
Method of combining geographical data with demographic data to develop profiles of neighborhood segments

combines demographic and geographic data to identify both *how* and *where* consumers live. Even more advanced segmentation approaches combine all three types of analysis. For example, one of the better known of these approaches is the PRIZM NE system developed by Claritas Corporation (www.claritas.com). Using geographic, demographic, and behavioral data, PRIZM NE divides the U.S. consumer market into dozens of "neighborhood" types such as "Bright Lites, Li'l City" (childless professional couples living in upscale communities near big cities) and "Young Digerati" (ethnically diverse and technically sophisticated young urbanites).[32]

Choosing Your Target Markets

After you have segmented your market, the next step is to find appropriate target segments or **target markets** on which to focus your efforts. Deciding exactly which segments to target—and when—is not an easy task. Sometimes the answer will be obvious, such as when you lack the necessary technological skills or financial power to enter a particular market segment. At other times, you'll have the resources to compete in several segments but not enough resources to compete in all of them at the same time.

Marketers use a variety of criteria to narrow their focus to a few suitable market segments, including the magnitude of potential sales within each segment, the cost of reaching those customers, fit with existing core competencies, and any risks in the business environment. Identifying which customers you *do* want also implies identifying those you *don't* want. For instance, the retailer Best Buy identified a segment of customers who were costing the company money through their relentless bargain hunting, a high rate of product returns, and frequent calls for technical support. By reducing sales promotions and charging a small fee for restocking returned products, the company is effectively excluding this group of shoppers from its stores.[33]

Exhibit 9.8 diagrams three popular strategies for reaching target markets. Companies that practice *undifferentiated marketing* (or mass marketing) ignore differences among buyers and offer only one product or product line to satisfy the entire market. This strategy, which concludes that all buyers have similar needs that can be served with the same standardized product, was more popular in the past than it is today. Henry Ford, began by selling only one car type (the Model T) and in one color (black) to the entire market.

By contrast, companies that manufacture or sell a variety of products to several target customer groups practice *differentiated marketing*. This is Toyota's approach, with the Scion brand aimed at young buyers, the Toyota brand for its core audience, and the Lexus brand for those wanting a luxury car. Differentiated marketing is a popular strategy, but it requires substantial resources because you have to tailor products, prices, promotional efforts, and distribution arrangements for each customer group.

Concentrated marketing is the narrowest approach, focusing on only a single market segment. With this approach, you acknowledge that various other market segments may exist but you choose to target just one. For instance, NetJets (www.netjets.com) targets travelers whose needs and resources put them above first class in commercial airlines but below full ownership of a private jet. By offering fractional ownership (rather like a time-share condo arrangement), the company offers nearly all the advantages of private jet ownership without all the expense.[34] The biggest advantage of concentrated marketing is that it allows you to focus all your time and resources on a single type of customer (which is why this approach is usually the best option for start-up companies, by the way). The strategy can be risky, however, because you've staked your fortunes on just one segment.

Moreover, it's important to understand whether you're going after a niche that will always be a niche or simply gaining a foothold in a small segment as part of a carefully sequenced plan to expand into other segments. For instance, Southwest Airlines started out as a regional carrier but is now the nation's busiest airline in terms of number of passenger flights.[35]

target markets
Specific customer groups or segments to whom a company wants to sell a particular product

EXHIBIT 9.8

Market-Coverage Strategies

Three alternative market-coverage strategies are undifferentiated marketing, differentiated marketing, and concentrated marketing.

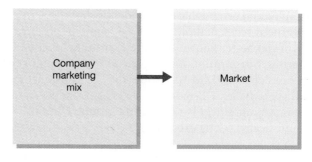

1. Undifferentiated marketing

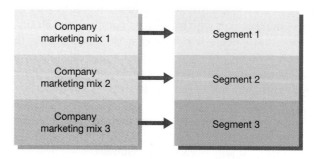

2. Differentiated marketing

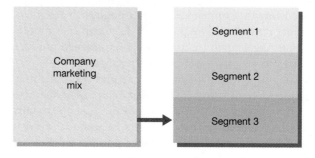

3. Concentrated marketing

Positioning Your Product

positioning
Using promotion, product, distribution, and price to differentiate a good or service from those of competitors in the mind of the prospective buyer

Once you have decided which segments of the market to enter, your next step is to decide what position you want to occupy in those segments. **Positioning** your product is the process of designing your company's offerings, messages, and operating policies so that both the company and its products occupy distinct and desirable competitive positions in your target customers' minds. For instance, for every product category that you care about as a consumer, you have some ranking of desirability in your mind—you believe that certain colleges are more prestigious than others, that certain brands of shoes are more fashionable than others, that one video game system is better than the others, and so on. Successful marketers are careful to choose the position they'd like to occupy in buyers' minds. One of Toyota's original goals in positioning the Scion brand was to make sure buyers *didn't* think it was a Toyota, and, therefore, the parent company name is rarely seen in Scion promotions (you'll have to look hard to see it on the Scion website, for instance).

A product can also be *repositioned* if the position it occupies is no longer favorable in some respect or new uses or qualities of the product make a different position more attractive to the marketer. For instance, you've probably seen Mountain Dew's commercials featuring skateboarders, snowboarders, and other extreme-sports figures who encourage you to "do the Dew." You might be surprised to learn that the soft drink was positioned quite differently a few decades ago, when the tagline was "It'll tickle your innards" and the spokesperson was a cartoon hillbilly who was usually pictured firing a shotgun at a government agent who had come to bust up his moonshine operation. The hillbilly disappeared after PepsiCo bought the brand in 1964.[36]

A vital and often overlooked aspect of positioning is that although marketers take all kinds of steps to position their products, it is the customers who ultimately decide on the positioning—they're the ones who interpret the many different messages they encounter in the marketplace and decide what they think and feel about each product. For example, you can advertise that you have a luxury product, but if consumers aren't convinced, it's not really positioned as a luxury product. As with everything else in marketing, the only result that matters is what the customer believes, not what the marketer believes. Scion's Mark Templin puts it this way: "Everyone works so hard to control and define what their brand stands for, when they ought to just let the consumer do it."[37]

In their attempts to secure favorable positions, marketers seek out positions that are both unique (no one else occupies that position in the customer's mind) and achievable (the firm can deliver the bundle of value needed to achieve that position).[38] They can position their products on specific product features or attributes (such as size, ease of use, style, performance, quality, durability, or design), on the services that accompany the product (such as convenient delivery, lifetime customer support, or installation methods), on the product's image (such as reliability or sophistication), on price (such as low cost or premium), on category leadership (such as the leading online bookseller), and so forth. For example, BMW and Porsche associate their products with performance, Mercedes Benz with luxury, and Volvo with safety. Organizing products and services into categories based on the perceived position helps consumers simplify the buying process. Instead of test-driving all cars, for instance, they may focus on those they perceive to be high-performance vehicles.

Developing Your Marketing Mix

After you've segmented your market, selected your target market, and taken steps to position your product, your next task is to develop a marketing mix. A firm's **marketing mix** consists of product, price, distribution, and customer communication (see Exhibit 9.9).

marketing mix
The four key elements of marketing strategy: product, price, distribution, and promotion

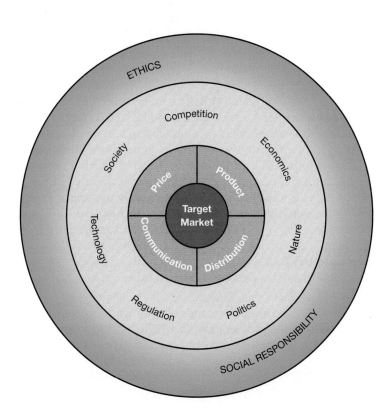

EXHIBIT 9.9

Positioning and the Marketing Environment

When positioning products for target markets, you need to consider the four marketing-mix elements plus the external environment.

(You might also hear references to "the four Ps" of the marketing mix, which is short for products, pricing, place or physical distribution, and promotion. However, with the advent of digital goods and services, distribution is no longer exclusively a physical concern. And many companies now view customer communication as a broader and more interactive activity than the functions implied by *promotion*.)

Products   The most basic marketing-mix element is *product*, which covers the product itself plus brand name, design, packaging, services, quality, and warranty. From a marketing standpoint, a **product** is anything offered for the purpose of satisfying a want or a need in a marketing exchange. If you were asked to name three popular products off the top of your head, you might think of Doritos tortilla chips, the Mini Cooper, and Gatorade drinks. You might not think of the Boston Celtics, Disney World, and the latest massively multiplayer online game. That's because we tend to think of products as *tangible* objects, or things that we can actually touch and possess. Basketball teams, amusement parks, and online gaming provide an *intangible* service for your use or enjoyment, not for your ownership; nevertheless, these and other services are products just the same. In fact, broadly defined, products can be persons, places, physical objects, ideas, services, and organizations. No matter what it is, every product possesses a number of *features* or *attributes* (what the product is or does) that create *benefits* (how it helps the customer).

You can read more about products in Chapter 10, but here is a quick overview of three essential product concepts:

- *Product life cycle.* Most products and product categories progress through a *product life cycle* consisting of four stages: introduction, growth, maturity, and decline. Personal music players illustrate this cycle nicely. Mobile phones with music capability are in the introduction phase, dedicated digital music players such as Apple's iPod family are in the growth phase, CD players are in the maturity phase, and cassette players are in the decline phase (and 8-track players are long gone, if you're old enough to remember those). As you can imagine, marketing strategies and tactics need to change as a product moves through the cycle. Companies often plan the introduction of new products months or even years in advance and spend considerable effort and resources on activities to launch the product. The growth phase is usually all about maximizing sales opportunities and expanding distribution. In the maturity phase, sales level off, and companies usually reduce investments in marketing and attempt to squeeze as much profit out of the product as they can. In the decline phase, sales drop as buyers switch to newer alternatives.

- *Product identity.* In all but the most basic commodities, companies work hard to establish unique identities for their goods and services. The essential element of product identity is the *brand*, which is a unique name, symbol, or design that sets a product (or an entire company) apart from its competitors. Brand names and symbols can be given protected legal status as *trademarks*, which prevent other companies from using them. Above and beyond the functional value of the product, the brand itself has value as well, a concept known as *brand equity*. Over time, every brand takes on a particular meaning—positive or negative—in the eyes of customers. For instance, if you currently own a Scion and are having a positive experience with the car, the Scion brand is building positive associations in your mind. When it's time to buy your next car, you will already be biased toward Scion, which obviously makes Toyota's marketing task much easier.

- *Product lines and product mixes.* Most companies have more than one product, and some large companies produce thousands of products. A *product line* is a group of similar products from a single company, such as Toyota's sport utility vehicles. Some companies have just one product line, but some have a *product mix*, a collection of multiple product lines. Honda's product mix, for example, includes several lines of automobiles, a line of motorcycles, a line of all-terrain vehicles, a line of personal watercraft, and a line of lawn mowers. As companies seek to expand revenue by

product
Good or service used as the basis of commerce

offering more products, they have to make product line and product mix decisions carefully. Adding a similar product to an existing product line might be a safe choice, for instance, but it might do little to expand total sales. Conversely, venturing into new product lines could expand sales considerably but doing so usually involves more risk and expense.

Pricing   **Price**, the amount of money customers pay for the product (including any discounts), is the second major component of a firm's marketing mix. Setting and managing a product's price is one of the most critical decisions a company must make, because price is the only element in a company's marketing mix that produces revenue—all other elements represent cost. Moreover, setting a product's price not only determines income but also can differentiate the product from competition. As you can imagine, determining the right price is not an easy task, and marketers constantly worry whether they've turned away profitable customers by charging too much or "left money on the table" by charging too little.

A number of factors influence pricing decisions, including marketing objectives, government regulations, production costs, customer perceptions, competition, and customer demand. In pricing decisions, the company's costs establish the minimum amount it can charge, and the various external forces establish the maximum. Somewhere in between those extremes lies an optimum price point. Products also exhibit different levels of *price elasticity*, which is a measure of how sensitive customers are to changes in price. If you don't have a digital camera yet, and the price of these products drops by 25 percent, you might well be tempted to buy one. In contrast, if the price of broccoli drops by 25 percent, chances are you won't eat more veggies as a result.

As you learned in Chapter 1, supply and demand interact according to price. This interaction is what makes pricing decisions so complicated. Marketers need to consider both the *fixed costs* of production (which do not fluctuate no matter how many units are produced or sold) and the *variable costs* (which do fluctuate by volume). They have to be able to sell enough products to hit the *break-even point*, the sales volume at which a product can cover its fixed costs and begin to turn a profit.

Marketers can choose from a number of pricing strategies to help meet their business objectives for each product. *Cost-plus pricing* simply adds a given profit margin to the company's cost of creating or buying the product to yield a sales price. This is indeed a simple method, but by ignoring external forces it can generate price points that are too high (making the product less competitive) or too low (forgoing some profits by charging less than customers would be willing to pay). Alternatives to cost-plus pricing take cost into consideration, of course, but start with external market forces and customer behavior to narrow down a range of potential prices. These strategies include *skim pricing* (pricing a hot new product at a temporarily high level to capture demand from the first wave of buyers), *penetration pricing* (setting the price low in order to penetrate a market), and *premium pricing* (setting the price high to convey the notion of quality and exclusivity). Computers are now used extensively in pricing as companies search for just the right price for each product. In air travel and some other industries, prices fluctuate constantly as marketers try to match supply and demand. You can read more about pricing in Chapter 10.

Distribution   *Distribution* is the third marketing-mix element. It covers the organized network of firms and systems that move goods and services from the producer to the customer. This network is also known as *marketing channels, marketing intermediaries,* or **distribution channels**. As you can imagine, channel decisions are interdependent with virtually everything else in the marketing mix. Key factors in distribution planning include customer needs and expectations, product support requirements, market coverage, distribution costs, competition, and positioning. For example, to lower the risk for dealers with the new Scion brand, Toyota allows existing Toyota dealers to co-locate Scion's retail facilities on the same sites where they sell the Toyota brand. However, to protect the exclusive image of its Lexus brand, the company requires any dealer that

price
The amount of money charged for a product or service

distribution channels
Systems for moving goods and services from producers to customers; also known as marketing channels

wants to carry Lexus to build and staff an entirely separate dealership that carries only Lexus.[39]

Marketing intermediaries perform a variety of essential marketing functions, including providing information to customers, providing feedback to manufacturers, providing sales support, gathering assortments of goods from multiple producers to make shopping easier for customers, and transporting and storing goods. These intermediaries fall into two general categories: *wholesalers* and *retailers*. The basic distinction between them is that wholesalers sell to other companies whereas retailers sell to individual consumers. Across industries, you can find tremendous variety in the types of wholesalers and retailers, from independent representatives who sell products from several manufacturers to huge distribution companies with national or international scope to purely digital retailers such as Apple's iTunes service. You can read more about distribution in Chapter 11.

promotion
Wide variety of persuasive techniques used by companies to communicate with their target markets and the general public

Customer Communication   In traditional marketing thought, the fourth element of the marketing mix is **promotion**, all the activities a firm undertakes to promote its products to target customers. The goals of promotion include *informing*, *persuading*, and *reminding*. Among these activities are advertising in a variety of media, personal selling, public relations, and sales promotion. Promotion may take the form of direct, face-to-face communication or indirect communication through such media as television, radio, magazines, newspapers, direct mail, billboards, bus ads, the Internet, and other channels.

Questionable Marketing Tactics on Campus

Alarmed by how quickly college students can bury themselves in debt and fed up with aggressive sales tactics, a growing number of universities are banning or restricting credit card marketing on campus.

College administrators complain that students are bombarded with credit card offers from the moment they step on campus as freshmen. Marketers have shown up on campuses unannounced and without permission to hawk cards in dorms and other areas. They stuff applications into bags at college bookstores. They entice students to apply for cards and take on debt with free gifts and promises of an easy way to pay for spring break vacations. Some yell at students to get their attention and follow them through hallways to make a sale. And they even get student organizations to work for them so that friends pressure friends.

College students are, of course, a prized target for the credit card industry because consumers tend to be loyal to their first credit card. And even though college students often have little or no income, they are not considered high-risk borrowers because parents often bail them out if they get into trouble. As a result, at least 80 percent of full-time college students now have a credit card in their own name. But only about half of those students pay their bills in full each month, and the number who usually make just the minimum payment is rising. The average balance carried is now in the neighborhood of $3,000, and 10 percent of students carry balances of $8,000 or more.

Many young people can't even keep up with the minimum payment. In fact, it is estimated that in one year 150,000 people younger than 25 will declare personal bankruptcy. That means for 150,000 young people, their first significant financial event as an adult will be to declare themselves a failure—a failure that will complicate their lives for years. And for each one who goes into bankruptcy, there are dozens just behind them, struggling with credit card bills—like Katy Spivak, for instance. Within her first three years at college, Spivak ran up $9,000 in credit card debt—forcing her to work two part-time jobs just to pay off her credit card bills.

While some universities have banned credit card marketers from campus to protect students from their own potentially destructive credit practices, many students say it's paternalistic for schools to do so. Plus, the marketers don't give up easily. Many just move across the street or to other locations frequented by students, such as spring break vacation hot spots. Moreover, credit cards have almost become a necessity in modern consumer life in recent years, since so many businesses require them as security or identification even when you don't use them for purchasing.

Questions for Critical Thinking
1. Should credit card companies be prohibited from soliciting on college campuses? Why or why not?
2. Why do credit card companies target students even though most have little or no income?

However, as "Involving the Customer in the Marketing Process" on page 218 points out, today's progressive companies have moved beyond the unidirectional approach of promotion to interactive customer communication. By talking *with* their customers instead of *at* their customers, marketers get immediate feedback on everything from customer service problems to new product ideas. Promotion is still a vital part of customer communication, but by encouraging two-way conversations, marketers can also learn while they are informing, persuading, and reminding. Moreover, by replacing "sales pitches" with conversations and giving customers some control over the dialog, marketers can also help break down some of the walls and filters that audiences have erected after years of conventional marketing promotion.[40]

In many cases, the Internet enables these two-way conversations, such as when customers are invited to write online product reviews or respond to company blogs. However, the shift from promotion to conversation is vitally important in such areas as personal selling. When salespeople are trained to listen to customers and use that information to propose solutions to customer needs, rather than delivering canned sales pitches, they also break down those audience barriers.

You can read more about customer communication in Chapter 11, but here are brief summaries of the major communication vehicles in the *promotional mix*:

- *Personal selling.* Personal selling can take place in person, over the phone, or through e-mail or instant messaging. The most effective personal selling efforts are usually problem-solving conversations in which the salesperson asks questions to uncover customer wants and needs, and then responds by describing goods and services that will meet those needs.

- *Advertising.* Advertising is no doubt the most visible element of customer communication. Virtually any medium that can carry human communication has been put to use as an advertising vehicle, from magazines and newspapers to video games and search engine results. Today's advertisers have the advantage of having many options from which to choose but the simultaneous disadvantage of a fragmented audience that can no longer be reached through a handful of national television networks and major newspapers. Regardless of the medium chosen, marketers can choose a variety of appeals, including logic, emotion, celebrity, and sex.

- *Direct marketing.* Unlike advertising, in which marketers buy space or time from various content publishers, direct marketing involves the distribution of promotional materials directly to target audiences. Direct mail and marketing e-mail are the most commonly used vehicles in direct marketing.

- *Public relations.* Public relations includes a wide range of communication efforts with various company stakeholders, including community relations, government affairs ("lobbying"), investor relations, and media relations with print, broadcast, and online media.

- *Sales promotion.* Sales promotion consists of short-term incentives to build the reputation of a brand or to encourage the purchase of a product or service. These incentives range from coupons to free samples to cross-promotions between products, such as fast-food and toy tie-ins with movies.

- *Social media. Social media* include any communication vehicles in which customers and other members of the public can play an active role, including blogs, wikis, *user-contributed content* websites such as YouTube (www.youtube.com), and *social bookmarking* sites such as Digg (www.digg.com) and del.icio.us

How This Affects You

1. Who were the primary competitors when you chose the college you now attend? Why did you choose this particular school?

2. How would you describe yourself as a target market? Summarize your demographic, psychographic, and geographic profile.

3. Think of three car brands or specific models. How are these products positioned in your mind? What terms do you use to describe them? Given your transportation needs in the near future (assuming you will need a car), which model is the most desirable? The least desirable?

(http://del.icio.us). Businesses need to approach social media in a completely different way than they approach advertising and other traditional marketing. Rather than carefully preparing a message and disseminating it through channels over which they have a high degree of control, they need to enable and participate in conversations in the social media landscape.

- *Post-sales communication.* Although not often considered part of the promotional mix, communication after the sale can be as important as any promotional activity before the sale. Providing helpful information about using products and responding positively to customer service issues improves the ownership experience for customers—and increases the likelihood that they'll buy from you again and tell their friends, families, and colleagues about you.

Summary of Learning Objectives

1 Explain what marketing is.

Marketing is the process of planning and executing the conception, pricing, promotion, and distribution of ideas, goods, and services to create exchanges that satisfy individual and organizational objectives. It involves all decisions related to a product's characteristics, price, production specifications, market-entry date, distribution, promotion, and sale. It involves understanding and satisfying customers' needs and buying behavior to encourage consumer purchases, in addition to maintaining long-term relationships with customers after the sale.

2 Describe the four utilities created by marketing.

Marketers enhance the appeal of their products and services by adding utility. Form utility is created when companies turn raw materials into finished goods desired by consumers. Time utility is created by making the product available when the consumer wants to buy it. Place utility is created when a product is made available at a location that is convenient for the consumer. Possession utility is created by facilitating the transfer of ownership from seller to buyer.

3 Explain how techniques such as social commerce and permission-based marketing help companies nurture positive customer relationships.

Social commerce is an important new way for customers to participate in the marketing process, which helps shift the relationship power from sellers to buyers. Permission-based marketing helps in the effort to build long-term relationships by demonstrating not only respect for customers but a willingness to meet *their* needs, as opposed to the marketer's need.

4 Explain why and how companies learn about their customers.

Today's customers generally are sophisticated, price sensitive, demanding, more impatient, more informed, and difficult to satisfy. Companies learn about their customers so they can stay in touch with their current needs and wants, deliver quality products, and provide effective customer service. Such attention tends to keep customers satisfied and helps retain their long-term loyalty. Moreover, studies show that sales to repeat customers are more profitable. Most companies learn about their customers by studying consumer buying behavior, conducting marketing research, and capturing and analyzing customer data.

5 Discuss how marketing research helps the marketing effort, and highlight its limitations.

Marketing research can help companies set goals, develop new products, segment markets, plan future marketing programs, evaluate the effectiveness of a marketing program, keep an eye on competition, and measure customer satisfaction. On the other hand, marketing research is a poor predictor of what will excite consumers in the future. It is sometimes ineffective because it is conducted in an artificial setting. And, it is not a substitute for good judgment.

6 Outline the three steps in the strategic marketing planning process.

The three steps in the strategic marketing planning process are (1) examining your current marketing situation, which includes reviewing your past performance, evaluating your competition, examining your internal strengths and weaknesses, and analyzing the external environment; (2) assessing your opportunities and setting your objectives; and (3) developing your marketing strategy, which covers segmenting your market, choosing your target markets, positioning your product, and creating a marketing mix to satisfy the target market.

7 Define *market segmentation* and name three fundamental factors commonly used to identify segments.

Market segmentation is the process of subdividing a market into homogeneous groups to identify potential customers and to devise marketing approaches geared to their needs and interests. The three primary factors used to identify segments are demographics (external statistical descriptors such as age, income, gender, and profession), psychographics (internal descriptors such as attitudes, interests, and values, as well as behaviors and habits), and geographics (location).

8 Identify the four elements of a company's marketing mix.

The four elements are product, price, distribution, and customer communication. Products are goods, services, persons, places, ideas, organizations, or anything else offered for the purpose of satisfying a want or need in a marketing exchange. Price is the amount of money customers pay for the product. Distribution is the organized network of firms that move the goods and services from the producer to the customer. Customer communication involves the activities used to communicate with and promote products to target markets.

Behind the Scenes

Scion's New-Generation Marketing Strategy Pays Off

Toyota's research discoveries have shaped virtually every aspect of its efforts in marketing the new Scion line. The company downplays the Toyota name, even though it has a worldwide reputation for value and quality, and shuns most traditional mass-market advertising. Instead it favors small-scale, neighborhood-centered promotions that allow trendsetters to "discover" the Scion product line and share the word with other young adults (for example, putting posters near popular hangouts, bearing phrases such as "Ban Normality" and "No Clone Zone").

As part of the quest to reach younger buyers, Toyota even started a music label, Scion A/V, to help promote such groups as the DaKAH hip-hop orchestra from Los Angeles and to work with a variety of DJs in cities around the country whose Scion-sponsored concerts, in turn, present Scion as a cutting-edge brand for a new generation. Scion marketers also work with emerging fashion designers and artists to further align the brand with cultural forces that shape the buying influences of younger drivers. Scion owners can show off their cars at Scion VIP nights, gatherings designed, of course, to attract even more potential owners.

By virtue of these media and event choices, much of Scion marketing is hidden from older buyers, although that hasn't stopped many of them from buying. In fact, the number of buyers in their 50s and 60s has pushed the average age of Scion owners to 39 years—although that is the lowest among all auto brands and significantly below Toyota's average age of 54.

By combing an appealing product, competitive pricing, and promotional efforts that tell the world Scion is not your average automobile, the Scion launch exceeded Toyota's expectations, even during a time when the economy was still sputtering and most of the automotive world's attention was focused on SUVs and pickups. The company continues to add to a loyal base of customers who are happy to buy a Toyota product even though buying a "Toyota" might be about the last thing they'd like to do with their hard-earned money.

With Scion, Toyota has also accomplished a financial feat of some note. Unlike Saturn, for example, General Motors's initiative to create a separate car brand, Scion is already profitable. In fact, even though Scions cost about $10,000 less than the average passenger vehicle now on the market, each one generates as much profit as the average Toyota model.[41]

Critical Thinking Questions

1. What other product categories would you apply the Scion marketing approach to?
2. Why would younger buyers possibly shun a brand that their parents remain loyal to?
3. As Scion sales grow, the newness wears off, and more owners come to grips with the fact that they're really driving Toyotas, do you think the allure of the Scion brand will diminish?

LEARN MORE ONLINE

Visit the Scion website at www.scion.com. What is your first impression of Scion's online presence? How is the presentation of cars balanced with information about culture and community? What do you think of the ability to customize a Scion product online? Do you find any discussion of price? Overall, does Scion's marketing mix make you intrigued enough to learn more about the cars? (For the latest information on Scion, visit http://introbusinessstudent.com and click on "Real-Time Updates.") ∎

Key Terms

behavioral segmentation (228)
cause-related marketing (216)
cognitive dissonance (222)
consumer market (222)
customer buying behavior (222)
customer loyalty (217)
customer service (215)
database marketing (224)
demographics (228)
distribution channels (233)
exchange process (216)
form utility (217)
geodemographics (229)
geographic segmentation (228)

market (228)
market segmentation (228)
market share (227)
marketing (215)
marketing concept (217)
marketing mix (231)
marketing research (224)
marketing strategy (228)
need (216)
organizational market (222)
permission-based marketing (221)
place marketing (216)
place utility (217)
positioning (230)

possession utility (217)
price (233)
product (232)
promotion (234)
psychographics (228)
relationship marketing (217)
social commerce (219)
stealth marketing (221)
strategic marketing planning (225)
target markets (229)
time utility (217)
transaction (216)
utility (216)
wants (216)

Test Your Knowledge

Questions for Review

1. What are some of the characteristics of today's customers?
2. How does the organizational market differ from the consumer market?
3. What is strategic marketing planning, and what is its purpose?
4. What external environmental factors affect strategic marketing decisions?
5. What are the four basic components of the marketing mix?

Questions for Analysis

6. If relationship marketing is such a good idea, why don't more businesses do it?
7. How can marketing research and database marketing help companies improve their marketing efforts?
8. Why does a marketer need to consider its current marketing situation, including competitive trends, when setting objectives for market share?
9. Why do companies segment markets?
10. **Ethical Considerations.** Thanks to the Internet you can contact a company for product information with a click of a mouse. But while lots of companies promote a variety of online customer service features, many fail to respond in a timely manner to customers' questions, and some don't respond at all. Companies claim that they simply can't keep up with the number of customer e-mail queries they receive and they can't afford to increase their customer service staff. Website promises

such as "Click here to talk to customer service," or "Got a question, let us help" look good, but the reality is too many companies promote a service they can't support. Is this unethical? Review a few of your favorite retail websites and analyze the different online customer service options these companies offer. Do they provide a projected response time? Do they send an autoreply message for e-mail queries? Do they offer a self-service help page for frequently asked questions. In your opinion, how could companies better handle online customer support when they are short of resources?

Questions for Application

11. How might a retailer use relationship and database marketing to improve customer loyalty?
12. **How This Affects You.** Think of a product you recently purchased and review your decision process. Why did you need or want that product? How did the product's marketing influence your purchase decision? How did you investigate the product before making your purchase decision? Did you experience cognitive dissonance after your decision?
13. **Integrated.** Why is it important to analyze a firm's marketing plan before designing the production process for a service or a good? What kinds of information are generally included in a marketing plan that might affect the design of the production process as discussed in Chapter 4?
14. **Integrated.** How might these economic indicators, discussed in Chapter 1, affect a company's marketing decisions: consumer price index, inflation, unemployment?

Practice Your Knowledge

Sharpening Your Communication Skills

In small groups as assigned by your instructor, take turns interviewing each person in the group about a product that each person absolutely loves or detests. Try to probe for the real reasons behind the emotions, touching on all the issues you read about in this chapter, from self-image to reference groups. Do you see any trends in the group's collective answers? Do people learn anything about themselves when answering the group's questions? Does anyone get defensive about his or her reasons for loving or hating a product? Be prepared to share with the class at least two marketing insights you learned through this exercise.

Building Your Team Skills

In the course of planning a marketing strategy, marketers need to analyze the external environment to consider how forces outside the firm may create new opportunities and challenges. One important environmental factor for merchandise buyers at Sears is weather conditions. For example, when merchandise buyers for lawn and garden products think about the assortment and number of products to purchase for the chain's stores, they don't place any orders without first poring over long-range weather forecasts for each market. In particular, temperature and precipitation predictions for the coming 12 months are critical to the company's marketing plan, because they offer clues to consumer demand for barbecues, lawn furniture, gardening tools, and other merchandise.

What other products would benefit from examining weather forecasts? With your team, brainstorm to identify at least three types of products (in addition to lawn and garden items) for which Sears should examine the weather as part of its analysis of the external environment. Share your recommendations with the entire class. How many teams identified the same products your team did?

Improving Your Tech Insights: Data Mining

To find a few ounces of precious gold, you dig through a mountain of earth. To find a few ounces of precious information, you dig through mountains of data using data mining, a combination of technologies and techniques that extract important customer insights buried within thousands or millions of transaction records.

As you read in Chapter 4, data mining is an essential part of business intelligence because it helps transform millions of pieces of individual data (including demographics, purchase histories, customer service record, and research results) accumulating in supersized databases known as *data warehouses* or department-specific subsections known as *data marts*. Data mining helps marketers identify who their most profitable customers are, which goods and services are in highest demand in specific markets, how to structure promotional campaigns, where to target upcoming sales efforts, and which customers are likely to be high credit risks, among many other benefits (see also "Mining Your Deepest Secrets" on page 220). You may hear the term *analytics* used in this context as well, describing efforts to extract insights from databases.

Research one of the commercially available data mining systems. You might start with *Intelligent Enterprise* magazine, www.intelligententerprise.com, which offers numerous articles and news updates on data mining, data warehousing, and other business intelligence topics. You can also learn about specific solutions from the companies that either offer stand-alone data mining products or incorporate the technology into databases and other products, including Angoss (www.angoss.com), Business Objects (www.businessobjects.com), Insightful (www.insightful.com), Megaputer Intelligence (www.megaputer.com), SAS (www.sas.com), SPSS (www.spss.com), IBM (www.ibm.com), Microsoft (www.microsoft.com), and Oracle (www.oracle.com). In a brief e-mail message to your instructor, describe how the system you've chosen can help companies market more efficiently and more effectively.[42]

Expand Your Knowledge

Discovering Career Opportunities

Jobs in marketing cover a wide range of activities, including a variety of jobs such as personal selling, advertising, marketing research, product management, and public relations. You can get more information about various marketing positions by consulting the *Occupational Outlook Handbook* (www.bls.gov/oco), job-search websites such as CareerBuilder.com (www.careerbuilder.com) and Monster.com (www.monster.com), and other online resources.

1. Select a specific marketing job that interests you and use the sites mentioned above to find out more about this career path. What specific duties and responsibilities do people in this position typically handle?

2. Search through help-wanted ads in newspapers, specialized magazines, or websites to find two openings in the field you are researching. What educational background and work experience are employers seeking in

candidates for this position? What kind of work assignments are mentioned in these ads?

3. Now think about your talents, interests, and goals. How do your strengths fit with the requirements, duties, and responsibilities of this job? Do you think you would find this field enjoyable and rewarding? Why?

Developing Your Research Skills

From recent issues of business journals and newspapers (print or online editions), select an article that describes in some detail a particular company's attempt to build relationships with its customers (either in general or for a particular product or product line).

1. Describe the company's market. What geographic, demographic, behavioral, or psychographic segments of the market is the company targeting?

2. How does the company hold a dialogue with its customers? Does the company maintain a customer database? If so, what kinds of information does it gather?

3. According to the article, how successful has the company been in understanding its customers?

See It on the Web

Visit these websites and answer the following questions for each one. (Up-to-date links for all websites mentioned in this chapter can be found on the Textbook Resources page for Chapter 9 at www.mybusinesslab.com. Please note that links to sites that become inactive after publication of the book will be removed from the Featured Websites section.)

1. What is the purpose of this website?

2. What kinds of information does this website contain? Please be specific.

3. How is the information provided at this website useful for businesspeople? Consumers?

4. How did you expand your knowledge of marketing by reviewing the material at this website? What new things did you learn about this topic?

Join the Conversation on Social Media

Learn from marketing veteran Jennifer Jones's weekly insights on social media on her blog, Marketing Voices. You'll discover how social media are changing the marketing profession and even the basic concepts of marketing. www.marketingvoices.com

Get Some Marketing Power

Rub shoulders with marketing pros at MarketingPower.com, published by the American Marketing Association (AMA). Get information about marketing trends, careers and professional development, online and in-person events, and AMA membership, publications, and blogs. www.marketingpower.com

Learn to Think Like Your Customers

You can't truly connect with target customers until you know how they think and what they feel. The Buyer Persona blog published by Adele Revella explains the concept of using *archetypes* based on real customer characteristics to represent target customers. With a clear picture of a buyer persona in mind, you can shape marketing programs much more effectively. www.buyerpersona.com

---

Companion Website

Learning Interactively

Log onto www.prenhall.com/bovée, locate your text, and then click on its Companion Website. For Chapter 9, take advantage of the interactive Chapter Quiz to test your knowledge of the chapter. Get instant feedback on whether you need additional studying. Also, you'll find an abundance of valuable resources that will help you succeed in this course, including PowerPoint presentations and Web Links.

Video Case

In Consumers' Shoes: Skechers USA

LEARNING OBJECTIVES

The purpose of this video is to help you:

1. Describe the role of the four Ps in a company's marketing mix

2. Explain how a company shapes its market research to fit its marketing goals

3. Discuss the effectiveness of target marketing and segmentation in analyzing consumers

SYNOPSIS

Skechers USA enjoys a reputation for producing footwear that combines comfort with innovative design, and the company has built its product line into a globally recognized brand distributed in more than 110 countries and territories throughout the world. From its corporate headquarters in Manhattan Beach, California, Skechers has engineered steady growth in market share while competing against some powerful players in the high-ticket, branded athletic shoe industry.

Since its start in 1992, Skechers has solidified its image as a maker of hip footwear through a savvy marketing strategy that calls for catering to a closely targeted consumer base. Maintaining brand integrity and its reputation for innovation is a crucial goal in all of Skechers's product development and marketing activities.

Director of Public Relations Kelly O'Connor discusses her work and the marketing activities that are critical to maintaining Skechers's edge in the highly competitive footwear marketplace. She describes the company's goal of creating a megabrand with an image, personality, and "feel" that can be translated and marketed globally. Skechers has been successful in brand building by means of an "Ask, Don't Tell" approach to product development and marketing—that is, it aims to find out what the market wants and then appeal to customers' wants rather than trying to influence the market with the products that it makes available.

Discussion Questions

1. *For analysis:* Which of the four Ps of the marketing mix seems to govern Skechers' marketing strategy? Why?

2. *For analysis:* How do you suppose Skechers alters elements of its American marketing mix to attract consumers in international markets?

3. *For application:* Skechers collects a lot of *primary* data in its market research. What kinds of primary data does the company prefer to gather? Why do these kinds of data suit the company's marketing goals? How do the data suit its consumer base? Given Skechers's fairly limited consumer base, are there other types of research data that you would recommend to company marketers?

4. *For application:* Describe Skechers's target market and explain how company marketers segment it. How effective is this strategy in analyzing customers? How successful are Skechers's marketing efforts among 12- to 24-year-olds (and consumers wishing they were in that demographic segment)?

5. *For debate:* Building brand loyalty is a major effort that presents both opportunities and challenges to marketers and product developers. How might Skechers increase loyalty for its brand? Do you think Skechers should expand its current product lines to include other new products such as clothing or accessories? How could the company go about investigating the market potential for such products?

ONLINE EXPLORATION

Go online to find out about the product lines and target markets of such companies as Nike (www.nike.com), Reebok (www.reebok.com), Lady Foot Locker (www.ladyfootlocker.com), and FUBU (www.fubu.com). How does the approach to segmentation at these companies compare with that of Skechers?

CHAPTER 10

Products and Pricing

LEARNING OBJECTIVES

After studying this chapter, you will be able to

1 Describe the four stages in the life cycle of a product

2 Describe six stages of product development

3 Cite three levels of brand loyalty

4 Discuss the functions of packaging and labeling

5 Identify four ways of expanding a product line and discuss two risks that product-line extensions pose

6 List the factors that influence pricing decisions and identify seven common pricing strategies

7 Explain why cost-based pricing can be a flawed strategy

Behind the Scenes

Allergan Stumbles onto a Billion-Dollar Product

www.botoxcosmetic.com

Some companies spend million of dollars following rigorous processes to develop new product ideas, only to have them crash land in the marketplace, generating little or no revenue. Allergan took the opposite approach: It more or less stumbled onto a new market for an obscure medical treatment and within a few years had a billion-dollar hit on its hands.

That hit product was Botox Cosmetic, a temporary treatment for facial wrinkles that revolutionized cosmetic care. Botox was developed in the 1970s by a San Francisco doctor looking for ways to correct crossed eyes, or strabismus. He found that injections of small amounts of purified botulinum toxin (from the same bacterium that causes botulism, a life-threatening paralytic illness) paralyzed the overactive muscles that cause strabismus, allowing other eye muscles to operate normally. The injections also improved uncontrollable eye blinking and uncontrollable neck spasms. Allergan, an Irvine, California, company, purchased the rights to the doctor's discovery in 1987 and started marketing Botox after receiving

Botox Cosmetic has grown into a billion-dollar product for Allergan.

FDA approval for these uses in 1989.

Then in the mid-1990s, doctors noticed something intriguing: Botox's paralyzing properties seemed to greatly reduce frown lines and wrinkles in patients using it for eye problems. As word of the Botox effect spread, more and more doctors began using it to relax the facial muscles that create eyebrow furrows, crow's feet, and horizontal forehead lines. Allergan conducted clinical trials and received FDA regulatory approval to use a version of Botox for cosmetic procedures. (This version is formally known by its trademarked name, Botox Cosmetic.)

If you were faced with the challenge of bringing Botox to market, what decisions would you make? What would you call the product? What steps would you take to encourage people to continue using the product and thereby prevent it from becoming just a fad? How would you encourage trial use from people who might be leery of using such a radically different product? Would you set a high price to make a lot of money from a small number of sales, or set a lower price to reach a broad market?[1] ∎

Characteristics of Products

Allergan's experience with Botox (profiled in the chapter opener) illustrates the challenges involved in defining a combination of product and price that will appeal to target markets—and the rewards that come to companies that make the right decisions. As the central element in every company's exchanges with its customers, products naturally command considerable attention from managers planning new offerings and coordinating the marketing mixes for their existing offerings. To understand the nature of these decisions, it's important to recognize the various types of products and the stages that products go through during their "lifetime" in the marketplace.

Types of Products

Think about Botox, Doritos tortilla chips, Intel computer chips, and your favorite musical artist. You wouldn't market all these products in the same way because buyer behavior, product characteristics, market expectations, competition, and other elements of the equation are entirely different.

Marketers frequently classify products on the basis of tangibility and use. Some products are predominantly tangible; others are mostly intangible. Most products, however, fall somewhere between those two extremes. The *product continuum* indicates the relative amounts of tangible and intangible components in a product (see Exhibit 10.1). Education is a product at the intangible extreme, whereas salt and shoes are at the tangible extreme. The complete Botox product includes both the tangible medication and the intangible services of the medical professionals who administer it.

Deciding how much or how little to expand on the core product is one of the most important product strategy decisions that managers need to make. In many markets, competitors offer a wide range of possibilities, from "bare-bones" offerings to products with all the "bells and whistles," as marketers like to say. For example, with most of today's mobile phones increasingly laden with everything from video recording to GPS navigation features, a few manufacturers are going in the opposite direction. The Samsung Jitterbug mobile phone does nothing but make phone calls; it's aimed at older consumers who aren't interested in or comfortable with today's typical mobile phone.[2] Exhibit 10.2 shows some of the ways marketers can *augment*, or enhance, a basic product with additional services and accessories.

Service Products

As Chapter 4 points out, the unique characteristics of services require special consideration in every part of the business, and that's particularly true for marketing. For instance, the intangibility of services makes them more difficult to demonstrate in advertisements (particularly in print ads). Services marketers often compensate for intangibility by using tangible symbols or by adding tangible components to their products. Prudential Financial (www.prudential.com), for example, uses the Rock of Gibraltar as a symbol of stability. Similarly, companies that deliver services often give clients tangible representations of the service, both to add to its value and to remind customers of the value they've received. Business consultants usually give their clients printed reports in addition to in-person presentations, for instance. Testimonials from satisfied customers are another important tactic marketers can use to compensate for the inability to demonstrate services.

Consumer Products

Marketers also classify products by use as a way to channel marketing strategies toward specific market segments. Both organizations and consumers use many of the same products, but they use them for different reasons and in different ways. Individual consumers or households generally purchase smaller quantities of goods and services for personal use. Products that are primarily sold to individuals for personal consumption

EXHIBIT 10.1

The Product Continuum

Products contain both tangible and intangible components; predominantly tangible products are categorized as goods, whereas predominantly intangible products are categorized as services.

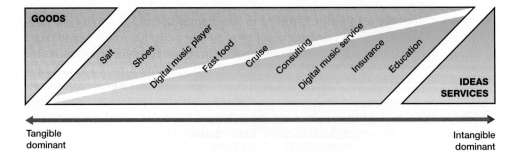

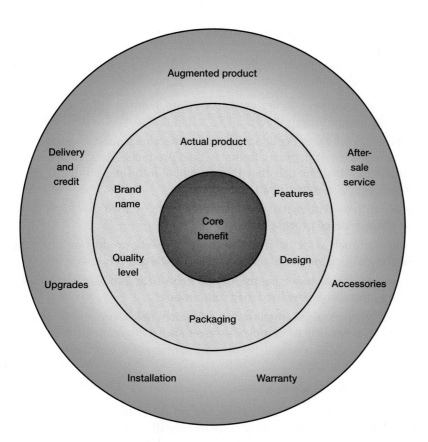

are known as *consumer products*. Consumer products can be classified into four subgroups, depending on how people shop for them:

- *Convenience products* are the goods and services that people buy frequently, usually without much conscious planning, such as toothpaste, dry cleaning, and gasoline.

- *Shopping products* are fairly important goods and services that people buy less frequently, such as music players, computers, refrigerators, and college educations. Such purchases require more thought and comparison shopping to check on price, features, quality, and reputation.

- *Specialty products* are particular brands that the buyer especially wants and will seek out, regardless of location or price, such as Prada clothing and accessories or Suzuki violin lessons. The Danish firm Bang & Olufsen (www.bang-olufsen.com) fares well selling its world-renowned home entertainment gear, which includes $5,000 CD players and $20,000 speakers.[3] Specialty products are not necessarily expensive, but they are products that customers go out of their way to buy and for which they rarely accept substitutes.

- *Unsought products* are things that many people do not normally think of buying, such as life insurance, cemetery plots, and new products. Part of the marketing challenge in these cases is simply making people aware of the product.

Industrial and Commercial Products

In contrast to consumer products, *industrial and commercial products* are generally purchased by firms in large quantities and are used for further processing or in conducting a business. Two categories of industrial products are *expense items* and *capital items*. Expense items are relatively inexpensive goods and services that organizations generally use within a year of purchase. Examples are pencils and printer cartridges. Capital items are more expensive organizational products and have a longer useful life. Examples include computers, vehicles, production machinery, and even entire factories.

Aside from dividing products into expense and capital items, industrial buyers and sellers often classify products according to their intended use:

- *Raw materials* such as iron ore, crude petroleum, lumber, and chemicals are used in the production of final products.

- *Components* such as semiconductors and fasteners are similar to raw materials; they also become part of the manufacturers' final products. Many companies also buy completed subsystems that they then assemble into final products; Boeing buys complete engines for its aircraft, for instance.

- *Supplies* such as pencils, nails, and lightbulbs that are used in a firm's daily operations are considered expense items.

- *Installations* such as factories, power plants, airports, production lines, and semiconductor fabrication machinery are major capital projects.

- *Equipment* includes less-expensive capital items such as desks, telephones, and fax machines that are shorter lived than installations.

- *Business services* range from simple and fairly risk-free services such as landscaping and cleaning to complex services such as management consulting and auditing.

The Product Life Cycle

product life cycle
Four basic stages through which a product progresses: introduction, growth, maturity, and decline

Regardless of a product's classification, few products last forever. Most products undergo a **product life cycle**, passing through four distinct stages in sales and profits: introduction, growth, maturity, and decline (see Exhibit 10.3). As the product passes from stage to stage, various marketing approaches become appropriate.

The product life cycle can describe a product class (gasoline-powered automobiles), a product form (sport utility vehicles), or a brand or model (Ford Explorer). Product classes and forms tend to have the longest life cycles, whereas specific brands tend to have shorter life cycles. The amount of time that a product remains in any one stage depends on customer needs and preferences, economic conditions, the nature of the product, and the marketer's strategy. Still, the proliferation of new products, changing technology, globalization, and the ability to quickly imitate competitors is hurtling many product forms and brands through their life cycles much faster today than in the past.

EXHIBIT 10.3

The Product Life Cycle

Most products and product categories move through a life cycle similar to the one represented by the curve in this diagram. However, the duration of each stage varies widely from product to product. Automobiles, crayons, and telephone service have been selling well in the maturity stage for decades, but faxing services barely made it into the introduction stage before being knocked out of the market by low-cost fax machines that every business and home office could afford.

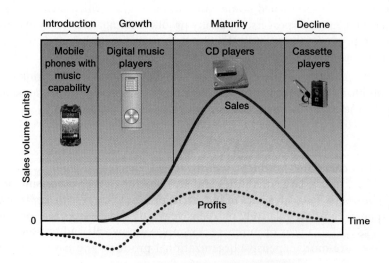

Designing Safer Products

Drivers of ordinary cars and trucks can die in 30 or 40 mph crashes, but race car drivers routinely walk away from 150 or 200 mph crashes. Clearly, the technology exists to protect vehicle occupants better than the average automobile does, but few consumers are in a position to shell out millions of dollars for cars with carbon-fiber *safety cells* (a super-strong "pod" that encloses the driver and fuel tank). And few people would consent to wearing the harnesses, helmets, and head-and-neck restraint systems that protect racers.

Although most situations aren't this dramatic, product safety frequently involves *trade-offs* between costs and benefits. Moreover, this trade-off is just one of many judgment calls and decisions that designers must address during the product-development process:

- *Safety margins.* How far beyond normal conditions should your product be able to operate safely? For instance, airplanes are designed to withstand stresses and strains far beyond anything they're likely to encounter in everyday operation, but designing in such safety margins adds to the cost of the product.
- *Predictable use, abuse, and misuse.* How will customers use the product after it leaves your control? Used responsibly, *pocket bikes*, those miniature motorcycles that teenagers like to zip around on these days, can be safe enough, but they become extremely dangerous when riders dart in and out of traffic (which is why many local governments are starting to ban or restrict them).
- *Maintenance and repair issues.* What are the customer's responsibilities in terms of keeping the product in safe working condition—and what might happen if the customer ignores these responsibilities? If you tell car owners to get the brakes serviced every 30,000 miles but they don't, what will happen and whose fault will it be?

- *Unintended consequences.* Some admirable efforts to increase product safety in some areas can create hazards of their own. Asbestos is an effective insulating material that is resistant to heat and flame, making buildings safer in that respect—but asbestos particles also cause a variety of serious illnesses if inhaled. Similarly, flame-retardant chemicals applied to bedding and children's clothing can make them safer but also present health risks themselves.

Thanks to a combination of government regulations, market pressures, engineering pride, and technological advances in design and testing, most of today's products have an admirable record of safety. For instance, with everything from antilock brakes to airbags, automobiles are safer today than they have ever been.

Autos are also a good example of how an entire industry sometimes has to change its attitude about product safety, from auto executive Lee Iacocca's remark in the 1970s that "safety doesn't sell" to today's market, where companies constantly promote safety features. As one example, General Motors announced that its StabiliTrak stability control system will become a standard feature on all GM cars. As Bob Austin of Rolls Royce recently put it, "Making safety a hallmark of all its brands is probably a good corporate strategy."

Questions for Critical Thinking

1. Think about Lee Iacocca's remark that "safety doesn't sell." Do manufacturers have a responsibility to create safe products even if customers don't care and don't want to pay for safety features? Why or why not?
2. What role do customers have in ensuring product safety?

Introduction

The first stage in the product life cycle is the *introductory stage*, which extends from the research-and-development (R&D) phase through the product's first commercial availability. The introductory stage is a crucial phase that requires careful planning and often considerable investment. Marketing staffs often work long hours for weeks or months before a product launch, preparing promotional materials, training sales staff, completing packaging, finalizing the price, and wrapping up countless other tasks. In many markets, a vital activity in the prelaunch phase is generating buzz for the product by discussing it with journalists, demonstrating it to user groups, and other activities. Some markets offer the luxury of building demand over time if the introduction isn't a blockbuster, but in others, a weak introduction can doom a product. The opening weekend for a movie, for instance, often determines its success or failure—a tremendously stressful scenario for people who have invested years and many millions of dollars making it.

Learning from Business Blunders

Oops: For years, Kryptonite locks, produced by a company of the same name headquartered in Canton, Massachusetts, have had a reputation for near invincibility. The company's tubular U-shaped locks are particularly popular with bicycle owners. That reputation took a hit when an online bike forum posted videos showing how certain models of the locks could be opened with a simple Bic ballpoint pen.

What You Can Learn: Sometimes vulnerabilities pop up when and where you least expect them. Kryptonite's designers took great care to use special high-strength steel, for instance, since the presumed enemies were hacksaws and bolt cutters, not the flimsy plastic barrels of Bic pens. In any area of business, look beyond the obvious when you're trying to identify risks and threats. Not only did this oversight hurt Kryptonite's reputation, but it also cost the company millions of dollars to replace 400,000 locks in 21 countries at no charge to customers.

Growth

After the introductory stage comes the *growth stage*, marked by a rapid jump in sales—assuming the product is successful—and, usually, an increase in the number of competitors and distribution outlets. As competition increases, so does the struggle for market share. This situation creates pressure to introduce new product features and to maintain large promotional budgets and competitive prices. In fact, marketing in this stage is so expensive that it can drive out smaller, weaker firms. With enough growth, however, a firm can often produce and deliver its products more economically than in the introduction phase. Thus, the growth stage can reap handsome profits for those who survive.

Maturity

During the *maturity stage*, usually the longest in the product life cycle, total sales begin to level off or show a slight decline. Markets tend to get saturated with all the supply that buyers demand, so the only way a firm can expand its sales in this phase is to win sales away from other suppliers. Because the costs of introduction and growth have diminished in this stage, most companies try to keep mature products alive so they can use the resulting profits to fund the development of new products (which is often referred to as "milking a cash cow").

Decline

Although maturity can be extended for many years, most products eventually enter the *decline stage*, when sales and profits slip and then fade away. Declines occur for several reasons: changing demographics, shifts in popular taste, product competition, and advances in technology. When a product reaches this point in the life cycle, the company must decide whether to keep it and reduce the product's costs to compensate for declining sales or discontinue it and focus on developing newer products. Sometimes an entire product category begins to decline, which is currently happening to film-based cameras as digital cameras gain widespread acceptance. Nikon, a long-time leader in film cameras, recently decided to stop making all its consumer-grade film cameras and all but a handful of its professional-class film cameras in order to focus on digital products.[4]

Product Enhancements and Makeovers

Of course, companies can continue to make their products more compelling and competitive at any stage from growth through decline. For example, software products are often upgraded every few years as developers add new features and take advantage of more powerful computer hardware. Car models are typically refreshed every few years as well. Recent enhancements include in-dash navigation systems and audio connections for iPods, but sometimes the changes are more subtle. Ford recently improved the way its car doors sound when opening and closing, for instance; a new latch in the Taurus model makes a sound like a bank vault door.[5] In an attempt to stay one step ahead of its surging competitors, Singapore Airlines recently spent $1 million on a machine that can simulate environmental conditions inside a flying aircraft—so that it could improve the taste of its onboard meals. The company learned that taste buds sense flavors differently in the pressure and humidity conditions in flight, so it took such steps as making dishes less spicy to compensate.[6] From subtle refinements to complete makeovers, product improvements can be a great way to maintain competitiveness and maximize the returns on the money and effort invested in new-product development.

The New-Product Development Process

Mad scientists and basement inventors still create new products, but many of today's products appear on the market as a result of a rigorous, formal *product development process*—a series of stages through which a product idea passes (see Exhibit 10.4). Here are the six stages of the process:

- *Idea generation.* The first step is to come up with ideas that will satisfy unmet needs. Customers, competitors, and employees are often the best source of new-product ideas. Like Botox Cosmetic, some ideas are more or less sheer luck: The microwave oven was invented after a Raytheon engineer in the 1940s noticed that a chocolate bar in his pocket melted when he stood close to a radar component known as a magnetron.[7] The popular photo-sharing website Flickr (www.flickr.com) started as a feature in a massively multiplayer online game; developers soon realized the photo-sharing tool was a better business opportunity than the game they were creating.[8] Some consumer products companies employ thousands of teenagers to report back on what's hot and what's not all over the world.[9] Of course, many "new" product ideas are simply improvements to or variations on existing products, but even those slight alterations can generate big revenues.

- *Idea screening.* From the mass of ideas suggested, the company culls a few that appear to be worthy of further development, applying broad criteria such as whether the product can use existing production facilities and how much technical and marketing risk is involved. Research suggests that sharply narrowing the possibilities at this stage is better than keeping a large number of ideas alive, since each idea competes for attention or resources until it is abandoned or implemented as a real product.[10] In the case of industrial or technical products, this phase is often referred to as a *feasibility study*, in which the product's features are defined and its workability is tested. In the case of consumer products, marketing consultants and advertising agencies are often called in to help evaluate new ideas. In some cases, potential customers are asked what they think of a new product idea—a process known as *concept testing*. Some companies involve customers early in the design process to make sure new products truly meet customer needs instead of the design team's perception of customer needs. Xerox's Chief Technology Officer Sophie Vandebroek refers to her company's approach as "customer-led innovation" and says that "dreaming with the customer" is essential to creating the right products.[11]

- *Business analysis.* A product idea that survives the screening stage is subjected to a business analysis. During this stage, the company reviews the sales, costs, and profit projections to see if they meet the company's objectives. To answer these questions, the company forecasts the probable sales of the product, assuming various pricing strategies. In addition, it estimates the costs associated with various levels of production. Given these projections, analysts calculate the potential profit that will

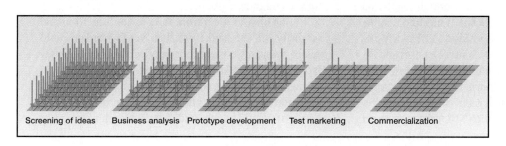

Screening of ideas   Business analysis   Prototype development   Test marketing   Commercialization

EXHIBIT 10.4

The Product Development Process

For every hundred ideas generated, only one or two salable products may emerge from the lengthy and expensive process of product development.

be achieved if the product is introduced. If the product meets the company's objectives, it can then move to the product-development stage.

- *Prototype development.* At this stage, the firm actually develops the product concept into a physical product. The firm creates and tests a few samples, or *prototypes*, of the product, including its packaging. These units are rigorously analyzed for durability, manufacturability, customer appeal, and other vital criteria. In addition, the company begins to plan for large-scale production and identifies the resources required to bring the product to market.

test marketing
Product-development stage in which a product is sold on a limited basis—a trial introduction

- *Test marketing.* During **test marketing**, the firm introduces the product in selected areas of the country and monitors consumer reactions. Test marketing gives the marketer experience with marketing the product before going to the expense of a full introduction. Fisher-Price's Play Lab (www.fisher-price.com) is the centerpiece of the company's success. There, marketers observe as children and infants play with dozens of new toy concepts. "Kids are pretty humbling," notes one product designer. "You can have what you think is a great idea, and they shoot it down in minutes." Infants are even harsher critics. Show babies something that they don't like, and they'll cry, push it away, or throw it on the floor. Drool, however, is the highest praise.[12] Test marketing can be expensive and time-consuming, however, so not all companies choose to take this step with every new product.

commercialization
Large-scale production and distribution of a product

- *Commercialization.* The final stage of development is **commercialization**, the large-scale production and distribution of products that have survived the testing process. This phase (also referred to as a *product launch*) requires the coordination of many activities—manufacturing, packaging, distribution, pricing, and promotion. For example, a classic mistake is letting marketing get out of phase with production by promoting the product before the company can supply it in adequate quantity. Many companies roll out their new products gradually, going from one geographic area to the next. This plan enables them to spread the costs of launching the product over a longer period and to refine their strategy as the rollout proceeds.

Ringing Up Business in Creative New Ways

When engineers at Motorola introduced the first mobile phone back in the 1980s, the two-pound, $4,000 brick-size unit was a technological marvel, but the designers probably couldn't imagine all the uses that their innovation would be put to one day. Ringtones alone have become a billion-dollar business, as mobile phone owners announce their musical tastes to the world with song snippets that can cost up to several dollars each. The music world is paying close attention, too; ringtones sold through websites such as Zingy (www.zingy.com) have become a new source of income for many musicians.

Ringtones are only part of the industry growing up around mobile phone services—these days, talking seems like about the last thing some people do on their mobile phones. From offering games to mobile blogs that let you share the sights and sounds of your latest vacation or business meeting, mobile phones are morphing into multipurpose gadgets that defy categorization. Hands-On Mobile (www.handson.com) and EA Mobile (www.eamobile.com) are just two of the many companies that offer games, music, video, and news to mobile handsets. The National Basketball Association (www.nba.com) is betting heavily that consumers will feel a need to get

scores and highlights on their phones. Other companies are racing to expand handheld travel guides so you'll never be lost, hungry, or out of places to shop.

These mobile phone services are great examples of how a product developed for one purpose (giving business executives a way to stay in touch while they were on the move) can spawn countless other ideas in the hands of creative entrepreneurs. Next time you're playing around with your phone (you know, like, when you should be studying), maybe you'll dream up a new product idea of your own.

Questions for Critical Thinking

1. What other services can you think of that could be offered on mobile phones?
2. Pick one of your ideas from the previous question and identify the infrastructure that would need to be in place in order to make that service a reality. Let's say your idea is a pet-tracking service, through which pet owners could keep track of the location of their pets. In addition to the mobile phone itself, what other product elements would be required to launch such a service?

Product Identities

Creating an identity for products is one of the most important decisions marketers make. That identity is encompassed in the **brand**, which can have meaning at three levels: (1) a unique name, symbol, or design that sets the product apart from those offered by competitors, (2) the legal protections afforded by a trademark and any relevant intellectual property, and (3) the overall company or organizational brand.[13] For instance, the Nike "swoosh" symbol is a unique identifier on every Nike product, a legally protected piece of intellectual property, and a symbol that represents the entire company.

Branding helps a product in many ways. It provides customers with a way of recognizing and specifying a particular product so that they can choose it again or recommend it to others. It provides consumers with information about the product. It facilitates the marketing of the product. And it creates value for the product. This notion of the value of a brand is also called **brand equity**. In fact, a brand name can be an organization's most valuable asset. According to Interbrand, a leading global branding consultancy, the world's most valuable brands—including Coca-Cola, Microsoft, IBM, and General Electric—are each worth more than $50 billion—and that's just the intangible value of the brand name.[14] Strong brands simplify marketing efforts because the target audience tends to associate positive qualities with any product that carries a respected brand name, and vice versa. For instance, the quality of General Motors, Ford, and Chrysler automobiles has climbed steadily in recent years, but the "Big 3" U.S. automakers still fight perceptions that Toyota and Honda offer higher quality. "Actual quality is so close, but reputation for quality is another issue," explains one researcher.[15]

Customers who buy the same brand again and again are evidence of the strength of **brand loyalty**, or commitment to a particular brand. Brand loyalty can be measured in degrees. The first level is *brand awareness*, which means that people are likely to buy a product because they are familiar with it. The next level is *brand preference*, which means people will purchase the product if it is available, although they may still be willing to experiment with alternatives if they cannot find the preferred brand. The third and ultimate level of brand loyalty is *brand insistence*, the stage at which buyers will accept no substitute.

Brands help consumers make confident choices from the thousands of products available in today's supermarkets.

brand
A name, term, sign, symbol, design, or combination of those used to identify the products of a firm and to differentiate them from competing products

brand equity
The value that a company has built up in a brand

brand loyalty
The degree to which customers continue to purchase a specific brand

Brand Name Selection

Botox Cosmetic, Jeep, Levi's 501, and iPod are **brand names**, the portion of a brand that can be spoken, including letters, words, or numbers. McDonald's golden arches and the Nike "swoosh" symbols are examples of a **brand mark**, the portion of a brand that cannot be expressed verbally. The choice of a brand name and any associated brand marks can be a critical success factor.

Brand names and brand symbols may be registered with the U.S. Patent and Trademark Office as **trademarks**, brands that have been given legal protection so that their owners have exclusive rights to their use. The Lanham Trademark Act, a federal law, prohibits the unauthorized use of a trademark on goods or services when the use would likely confuse consumers as to the origin of those goods and services. For trademark infringement, the evidence must show that an appreciable number of ordinary prudent purchasers are likely to be confused as to the source, sponsorship, affiliation, or connection of the goods or services.[16] Companies zealously protect their brand names because if a name becomes too widely used in a general sense, it no longer qualifies for protection under trademark laws. Cellophane, kerosene, linoleum, escalator, zipper, shredded wheat, and raisin bran are just a few of the many brand names that have passed into the public domain, much to their creators' dismay.

brand names
Portion of a brand that can be expressed orally, including letters, words, or numbers

brand mark
Portion of a brand that cannot be expressed verbally

trademarks
Brands that have been given legal protection so that their owners have exclusive rights to their use

Brand Sponsorship

national brands
Brands owned by the manufacturers and distributed nationally

private brands
Brands that carry the label of a retailer or a wholesaler rather than a manufacturer

generic products
Products characterized by a plain label, with no advertising and no brand name

co-branding
Partnership between two or more companies to closely link their brand names together for a single product

license
Agreement to produce and market another company's product in exchange for a royalty or fee

Brand names may be associated with a manufacturer, a retailer, a wholesaler, or a combination of business types. Brands offered and promoted by a national manufacturer, such as Procter & Gamble's Tide detergent and Pampers disposable diapers, are called **national brands**. **Private brands** are not linked to a manufacturer but instead carry a wholesaler's or a retailer's brand. DieHard batteries and Kenmore appliances are private brands sold by Sears. As an alternative to branded products, some retailers also offer **generic products**, which are packaged in plain containers that bear only the name of the product. Note that "generics" is also a term used in the pharmaceutical industry to describe products that are copies of an original drug (other companies are allowed to make these copies after the patent on the original drug expires).

Co-branding occurs when two or more companies team up to closely link their names in a single product. For example, Lenovo sells laptop computers co-branded with Disney's Power Rangers brand. The co-branding arrangement is aimed at families in which young children can influence the PC purchase decision.[17]

Sometimes companies, such as Warner Brothers, **license** or sell the rights to specific well-known names and symbols—such as Looney Tunes cartoon characters—and then manufacturers use these licensed labels to help sell products. Licensing is an especially hot growth area for automotive marketers, where sales of licensed goods amount to over $6 billion annually. For instance, children can ride around in Jeep and Land Rover strollers, and their parents can drive around in special Harley-Davidson edition Ford trucks.[18]

Packaging

Another way that marketers create an identity for their products is through packaging. Most products need some form of packaging to protect them from damage or tampering. Packaging can also make it convenient for customers to purchase or use a product, such as Nabisco's 100-calorie snack packs and Hidden Valley Ranch's "easy squeeze" upside-down salad dressing bottles.

In some cases, packaging is an essential part of the product itself, such as microwave popcorn or toothpaste in pump dispensers. Besides function, however, packaging plays an important role in a product's marketing strategy. Packaging makes products easier to display, facilitates the sale of smaller products, serves as a means of product differentiation, and enhances the product's overall appeal and convenience. In addition, in an effort to reduce shoplifting, retailers have put a lot of pressure on manufacturers to adopt packages that are difficult to conceal or to open in the store. Those stiff plastic packages known as "clamshells" that consumers love to hate—and that account for hundreds of injuries every year as people attempt to slice them open—are one such response to shoplifting. Many manufacturers know that consumers despise the clamshell concept (some even refer to it privately as "rage wrap"), so package designers are working on alternatives.[19] Packaging is also a major environmental concern, in both the resources used and waste generated, so expect innovations and new regulations in this area in the coming years.

Labeling

Labeling is an integral part of packaging. Whether the label is a separate element attached to the package or a printed part of the container, it serves to identify a brand. Labels also provide grading information about the product and information about ingredients, operating procedures, shelf life, and risks. The labeling of foods, drugs, cosmetics, and many health products is regulated under various federal laws, which often require disclosures about potential

Product packaging usually has a number of functions, from promoting and protecting the product to displaying legally required health and safety information to providing cinstructions for use.

dangers, benefits, and other issues consumers need to consider when making a buying decision.

Labels do more than communicate with consumers. They are also used by manufacturers and retailers as a tool for monitoring product performance and inventory. **Universal Product Codes (UPCs)**, those black scanner stripes you see on packages everywhere, have saved countless billions of dollars by improving efficiency throughout the supply chain.[20] In the future, RFID tags (see page 53) may supplant UPCs in some applications, but UPCs are so widely entrenched and cost-effective that they're bound to stay in use for years.

Universal Product Codes (UPCs)
Bar codes on product packages that provide information read by optical scanners

Product-Line and Product-Mix Strategies

Why does General Motors offer a product in nearly every category from economy cars to giant SUVs, whereas Aston Martin offers only a handful of models, all of which are ultraexpensive sports cars? Why does L.L.Bean sell casual and outdoor clothing from head to toe but not tuxedos or evening gowns? Why is Nokia now an electronics company and not the paper and tire company it used to be? Why can't you buy a burger and fries at Starbucks or fettuccine Alfredo at McDonald's? The answers to some of these questions might seem obvious, but every company needs to address these product strategy questions at some point—and sometimes over and over again as managers try to increase sales and maintain competitiveness.

In addition to developing product identities, a company must decide how many and what kinds of products it will offer. To stay competitive, most companies continually add and drop products to ensure that declining items will be replaced by growth products. Companies that offer more than one product also need to pay close attention to how those products are positioned in the marketplace relative to one another. The responsibility for managing individual products, product lines, and product mixes is usually assigned to one or more managers in the marketing department. In a smaller company, the *marketing manager* tackles this effort; in larger companies with more products to manage, individual products or groups of products are usually assigned to **brand managers**, known in some companies as *product managers* or *product line managers*.

brand managers
Managers who develop and implement a complete strategy and marketing program for specific products or brands

Product Lines

A **product line** is a group of products from a single manufacturer that is similar in terms of use or characteristics. The General Mills (www.generalmills.com) snack-food product line, for example, includes Bugles, Fruit Roll-Ups, Nature Valley Granola Bars, and Pop Secret Popcorn. Within each product line, a company confronts decisions about the number of goods and services to offer. On the one hand, offering additional products can help a manufacturer boost revenues and increase its visibility in retail stores. On the other hand, creating too many products and product variations can be expensive for everyone in the supply chain and confusing to consumers.

product line
A series of related products offered by a firm

Product Mix

An organization with several product lines has a **product mix**—a collection of diverse goods or services offered for sale. The General Mills product mix consists of cereals, baking products, desserts, snack foods, main meals, and so on (see Exhibit 10.5). Three important dimensions of a company's product mix are *width*, *length*, and *depth*, and each dimension presents its own set of challenges and opportunities. A product mix is *wide* if it has several different product lines. General Mills's product mix, for instance, is fairly wide, with a half dozen or more product lines. A company's product mix is *long* if it carries several items in its product lines, as General Mills does. For instance, General Mills carries a number of different cereal brands within the ready-to-eat cereal line.

product mix
Complete list of all products that a company offers for sale

EXHIBIT 10.5 The Product Mix at General Mills

These selected products from General Mills illustrate the various dimensions of its product mix. The mix is *wide* because it contains multiple product lines (cereals, fruit snacks, pasta, soup, yogurt, and more). The cereal product line is *long* because it contains many individual brands (only four of which are shown here). And these four cereal brands show different depths. The Trix brand is a shallow line with no subbrands, whereas the Cheerios brand is *deep* with nine subbrands.

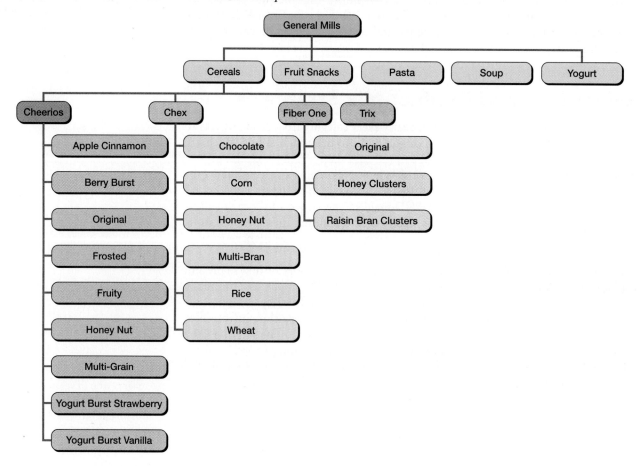

A product mix is *deep* if it has a number of versions of *each* product in a product line. The Cheerios brand, for example, currently has nine different varieties. The same is true for many other products in the company's other product lines.[21]

When deciding on the dimensions of a product mix, a company must weigh the risks and rewards associated with various approaches. Some companies limit the number of product offerings and focus on selling a few items in higher quantities. Doing so keeps the production costs per unit down and limits selling expenses. However, counting too heavily on a narrow group of products leaves a company vulnerable to competitive threats and market shifts. Other companies diversify their product offerings as a protection against shifts in consumer tastes, economic conditions, and technology. For example, like many newspapers, the *Washington Post* is diversifying into a variety of web-based multimedia offerings. In the face of declining advertising revenues from the print medium, the "website simply has to come through," says CEO Donald Graham.[22]

Retailers often have considerable influence on manufacturers' product line decisions as well, particularly in the store-based retail channel. In general, the more revenue a manufacturer represents, the better chance it has of getting all-important shelf space. Consequently, retail store aisles tend to be dominated by a few large brands, and manufacturers look for ways to build portfolios of best sellers that can command attention at the retail level.

In contrast to store-based retailing and its frequent focus on a small number of best sellers, online retailing presents much better opportunities for very large numbers of specialized and low-volume products. Without the physical limitations of a "bricks and mortar" facility, online retailers can offer a much greater variety of products. For example, the average physical bookstore might offer 40,000 volumes, whereas the major online book retailers offer several million.[23] While these products may individually sell at lower volumes, collectively they represent a substantial business opportunity that has been termed the *long tail* (referring to a sales volume graph in which a vast number of low-volume products stretches out toward infinity).[24]

Product Expansion Strategies

As Exhibit 10.6 shows, you can expand your product line and mix in a number of ways. One approach is to introduce additional items in a given product category under the same brand name—such as new flavors, forms, colors, ingredients, or package sizes. Another approach is to expand a product line to add new and similar products with the same product name—a strategy known as **family branding**. For instance, the ESPN family includes not only the original ESPN cable sports channel, but the ESPN2, ESPN Classics, and ESPN Deportes TV channels, as well as ESPN Radio, *ESPN the Magazine*, and other sports media.

Conversely, in a **brand extension**, a company applies a successful brand name to a new product category in the hopes that the recognition and reputation of the brand will give it a head start in the new category. Building on the name recognition of an existing brand cuts the costs and risks of introducing new products. However, there are limits to how far a brand name can be stretched to accommodate new products and still fit the buyer's perception of what the brand stands for. ESPN tried to launch a sports-themed mobile phone service but abandoned the effort because of lower-than-expected consumer interest.[25]

Product-line extensions present two important risks that marketers need to consider carefully. First, stretching a brand to cover too many categories or types of products can dilute the brand's meaning in the minds of target customers. For instance, if ESPN were to branch out into business and financial news, its original sports audience might wonder if the company was still committed to being a leader in sports journalism. Second, additional products do not automatically guarantee increased sales revenue. Marketers need to make sure that new products don't simply *cannibalize*, or take sales away from, their existing products.

family branding
Using a brand name on a variety of related products

brand extension
Applying a successful brand name to a new product category

EXHIBIT 10.6 Expanding the Product Line

Knowing that no product or category has an unlimited life cycle, companies use one or more of these product-line expansion methods to keep sales strong.

METHOD OF EXPANSION	HOW IT WORKS	EXAMPLE
Line filling	Developing items to fill gaps in the market that have been overlooked by competitors or have emerged as consumer tastes and needs shift	Alka-Seltzer Plus cold medicine
Line extension	Creating a new variation of a basic product	Tartar Control Crest toothpaste
Brand extension	Putting the brand for an existing product category into a new category	Virgin Cola
Line stretching	Adding higher- or lower-priced items at either end of the product line to extend its appeal to new economic groups	Marriott Marquis hotel

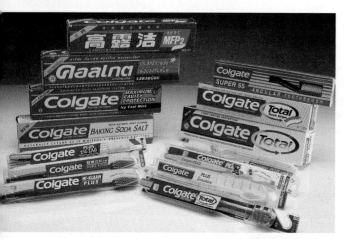

Notice how these localized versions of the Colgate toothpaste package maintain key brand identifiers such as color and type style.

Product Strategies for International Markets

As Chapter 3 notes, product adaptation is one of the key changes that companies need to consider when moving into other countries. First, they must decide on which products and services to introduce in which countries. When selecting a country, they must take into consideration the type of government, market-entry requirements, tariffs and other trade barriers, cultural and language differences, consumer preferences, foreign-exchange rates, and differing business customs. Then, they must decide whether to standardize the product, selling the same product everywhere, or to customize the product to accommodate the lifestyles and habits of local target markets. Keep in mind that the degree of customization can vary. A company may change only the product's name or packaging, or it can modify the product's components, size, and functions.

For example, French consumers have been eating McDonald's (www.mcdonalds.com) food from the moment the company first arrived in 1972, and France is now the company's third largest market in Europe. However, the burger giant has a unique look in that country. To accommodate a culture known for its cuisine and dining experience, many McDonald's outlets in France have upgraded their decor to a level that would make them almost unrecognizable in the United States. Gone are the Golden Arches, utilitarian chairs and tables, and other plastic fixtures. Instead the restaurants have hardwood floors, brick architecture, armchairs, and extras such as music videos that entice customers to linger over their meals. And while the basic burger offerings remain the same, menus at the upscale restaurants include a premiere line of sandwiches, espresso, and brioche (a soft bread common in France).[26]

(For a look at the latest innovations in product strategy, visit http://introbusiness student.com and click on "Real-Time Updates.")

Pricing Strategies

The second key factor in the marketing mix is pricing. The pricing decisions for a product are determined by manufacturing and selling costs, competition, and the needs of wholesalers and retailers who distribute the product to the final customer. In addition, pricing is influenced by a firm's marketing objectives, government regulations, consumer perceptions, and consumer demand:

■ *Marketing objectives.* The first step in setting a price is to match it to the objectives you set in your strategic marketing plan. Is your goal to increase market share, increase sales, improve profits, project a particular image, or combat competition? For instance, in order to compete with cut-rate credit cards, many banks and card issuers now offer low interest rates (a form of price) but make up for it with higher fees for late payments and other consumer mistakes.[27]

■ *Government regulations.* Government plays a big role in pricing in many countries. To protect consumers and encourage fair competition, governments around the world have enacted various price-related laws over the years. These regulations are particularly important in three areas: (1) *price fixing*—an agreement among two or more companies supplying the same type of products as to the prices they will charge, (2) *price discrimination*—the practice of unfairly offering attractive discounts to some customers but not to others, and (3) *deceptive pricing*—pricing schemes that are considered misleading. For example, British Airways was fined roughly $500 million by the British government after competitor Virgin Airways blew the whistle on a price-fixing scheme involving fuel surcharges.[28]

■ *Quality perceptions.* Another consideration is the perception of quality that your price will elicit from your customers. When people shop, they usually have a rough price range in mind. An unexpectedly low price triggers fear that the item is of low quality. On the other hand, an unexpectedly high price makes buyers question whether the product is worth the money. Of course, in some consumer markets, high price is part of the appeal because it connotes exclusivity.

■ *Customer demand.* Whereas a company's costs establish a floor for prices, demand for a product establishes a ceiling. Theoretically, if the price for an item is too high, demand falls and the producers reduce their prices to stimulate demand. Conversely, if the price for an item is too low, demand increases and the producers are motivated to raise prices. As prices climb and profits improve, producers boost their output until supply and demand are in balance and prices stabilize. Nonetheless, the relationship between price and demand isn't always this perfect. Some goods and services are relatively insensitive to changes in price; others are highly responsive. Marketers refer to this sensitivity as **price elasticity**—how responsive demand will be to a change in price. SanDisk (www.sandisk.com), which makes electronic memory cards for digital cameras and other devices, largely attributes a recent 40 percent increase in revenue to lower prices, which spurred demand from consumers.[29]

Buyers often believe that prices ending in "9" are a bargain, which is why these fast-food products are priced at 99 cents and not an even dollar.

Marketers often take other financial and psychological factors into account, such as the "9 effect." You've probably noticed that many prices end in a 9, such as $9.99 or $5,999. Your conscious mind says, "Gimme a break; we all know that's really $10 or $6,000." However, research suggests that our minds equate that 9 with a bargain—even when it isn't. In one experiment, for example, a dress sold more when priced at $39 than when it was priced at $34.[30]

price elasticity
A measure of the sensitivity of demand to changes in price

When companies set their prices, they take these factors—among others—into account before choosing a general pricing approach. Common pricing approaches include cost-based, price-based, optimal, skimming, penetration pricing, loss-leader pricing, and a variety of price adjustment methods.

Cost-Based Pricing

Many companies simplify the pricing task by using *cost-based pricing*, also known as *cost-plus pricing*. (As you'll see in a moment, however, cost-based pricing is not as simple as it seems.) Companies using this approach start with the cost of producing a good or a service and then add a markup to the cost of the product to produce a profit. How does a company determine the amount of profit it will earn by selling a certain product? **Break-even analysis** is a tool companies use to determine the number of units of a product they must sell at a given price to cover all manufacturing and selling costs, or to break even.

break-even analysis
Method of calculating the minimum volume of sales needed at a given price to cover all costs

In break-even analysis, you consider two types of costs. **Variable costs** change with the level of production. These include raw materials, shipping costs, and supplies consumed during production. **Fixed costs**, by contrast, remain stable regardless of the number of products produced. These costs include rent payments, insurance premiums, and real estate taxes. The total cost of operating the business is the sum of a firm's variable and fixed costs. The **break-even point** is the minimum sales volume the company must achieve to avoid losing money. Sales volume beyond the break-even point will generate profits; sales volume below the break-even amount will result in losses.

variable costs
Business costs that increase with the number of units produced

fixed costs
Business costs that remain constant regardless of the number of units produced

break-even point
Sales volume at a given price that will cover all of a company's costs

You can determine the break-even point in number of units with this simple calculation:

$$\text{Break-even point} = \frac{\text{Fixed costs}}{\text{Selling price} - \text{Variable costs per unit}}$$

For example, if you wanted to price haircuts at $20 and you had fixed costs of $60,000 and variable costs per haircut of $5, you would need to sell 4,000 haircuts to break even:

$$\text{Break-even point} = \frac{\$60,000}{\$20 - \$5} = 4,000 \text{ units}$$

Of course, $20 isn't your only pricing option. Why not charge $30 instead? When you charge the higher price, you need to give only 2,400 haircuts to break even (see Exhibit 10.7). However, before you raise your haircut prices to $30, bear in mind that a lower price may attract more customers and enable you to make more money in the long run.

Break-even analysis doesn't dictate what price you should charge; rather, it provides some insight into the number of units you have to sell at a given price to start making a profit. This analysis is especially useful when you are trying to calculate the amount to mark up a price to earn a profit.

By this point you might've picked up on the two major weaknesses in cost-based pricing. First, in many industries, variable costs are often affected by volume, so your break-even equation could have two variables going in opposite directions at once, making it difficult to arrive at a stable answer.[31] As a simple example, the $30 haircut price might seem to lower your break-even point to 2,400, but at that lower level of sales, you might lose the volume purchasing discounts you'd been getting from your suppliers on shampoo, conditioner, and other materials. In other words, your break-even point is no longer what you thought it was because your variable costs changed. Second, cost-based pricing doesn't factor in either customers or competitors. What if customers think a $20 haircut is so inexpensive that it must be of poor quality? Or what if they're willing to pay $60 or $80? For these reasons, cost-based pricing is a risky approach, even if it is simple.

Price-Based Pricing

Most manufacturers design a product, then try to figure out how to make it for a price. But recent thinking holds that cost should be the last item analyzed in the pricing formula, not the first. Companies that use *priced-based pricing* can maximize their profit by first establishing a target price. This figure is based on the product's competitive advantages, the users' perception of the item, and the target market. Once the desired price has been established, the firm focuses its energies on keeping costs at a level that will allow a healthy profit.

At IKEA (www.ikea.com), the price literally comes first. IKEA's corporate mantra is "Low price with meaning." The goal is to make products less expensive without making customers feel that the products are cheap. New products are born at IKEA by first establishing a price point. The company surveys competition to figure out how much the new product should cost and then targets a price 30 to 50 percent below that of rivals. After settling on a target price for a product, IKEA determines what materials will be used and which manufacturer will do the assembly work—even before the new item is actually designed. IKEA's price-driven manufacturing process is a key factor in its success. While the price of other companies' products tends to rise over time, IKEA has reduced its retail prices by about 20 percent during the past four decades.[32]

Another popular price-based approach is *value pricing*, charging a fairly affordable price for a high-quality offering. Many restaurants offer value menus for certain times of

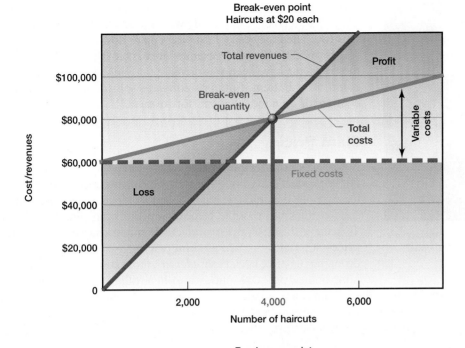

Break-even point
Haircuts at $20 each

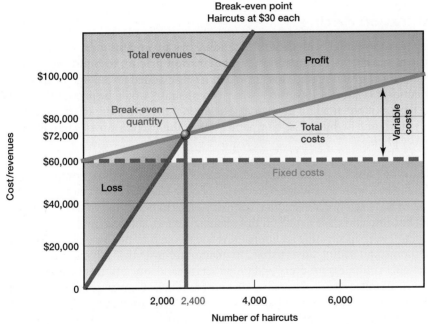

Break-even point
Haircuts at $30 each

EXHIBIT 10.7

Break-Even Analysis

The break-even point is the point at which revenues just cover costs. After fixed costs and variable costs have been met, any additional income represents profit. The graphs show that at $20 per haircut, the break-even point is 4,000 haircuts; charging $30 yields a break-even point at only 2,400 haircuts.

the day or certain customer segments, such as seniors. This strategy builds loyalty among price-conscious customers without damaging a product's quality image.

Optimal Pricing

Research shows that many retailers routinely underprice or overprice the merchandise on their shelves. They generally set a price by marking up from cost, by benchmarking against the competition's prices, or simply by hunch. *Optimal pricing* can minimize both errors by using computer software to generate the ideal price for every item, at each individual store, at any given time.

A price-optimization program feeds reams of data from checkout scanners, seasonal sales figures, competitors, and other sources into probability algorithms to come

Customers who need to have the latest and greatest products are often willing to pay higher prices than those who wait until later in the product life cycle.

skim pricing
Charging a high price for a new product during the introductory stage and lowering the price later

penetration pricing
Introducing a new product at a low price in hopes of building sales volume quickly

loss-leader pricing
Selling one product at a loss as a way to entice customers to consider other products

up with an individual demand curve for each product in each store. From that, retailers can identify which products are the most price sensitive. Then they can adjust prices up or down according to each store's priorities—profit, revenue, or market share. Until recently, these systems have been so expensive that only the largest retailers could afford them, but new software solutions are affordable enough for even independent store owners.[33]

Skim Pricing

A product's price seldom remains constant and will vary depending on the product's stage in its life cycle. During the introductory phase, for example, the objective might be to recover product development costs as quickly as possible, before competitors can enter the market. To achieve this goal, the manufacturer might charge a high initial price—a practice known as **skim pricing**—with the intention of dropping the price later. *Early adopters*, those customers who tend to jump on new products quickly, are often willing to pay a premium to get their hands on the new products as soon as possible. In consumer markets, some people simply want to have the latest and greatest before anyone else; in organizational markets, new types of equipment can give companies a short-term competitive advantage.

Penetration Pricing

Skim prices are set high with the understanding that many customers won't be willing to pay them. In contrast, companies use **penetration pricing** to build sales volume by charging a low initial price. This approach has the added advantage of discouraging competition, because the low price—which competitors would be pressured to match— limits the profit potential for everyone. (However, if the intent of penetration is to drive competitors out of business, companies open themselves up to charges of illegal *predatory pricing*.)

Ireland's Ryanair offers a startling example of how effective penetration pricing can be. To capture a share of the European air travel market, the young company's fares are shockingly low, with an average ticket price of only $53. And that's not all. Twenty-five percent of all tickets are *free*, and the company plans to boost that to half of all tickets by 2010. The company is able to pull off this seemingly impossible feat by (1) keepings its costs extremely low, (2) generating additional revenue through related services such as booking hotel rooms and selling advertising (its planes are essentially flying billboards), and (3) charging customers for every additional service and amenity, from baggage to coffee. The unusual strategy works: Ryanair is the most profitable company in the airline industry.

However, penetration pricing doesn't work if the company can't sustain the low price levels profitably, if prices for a particular product are inelastic, or if customers weigh other factors more heavily than price. Moreover, as mentioned earlier, prices that are far below the market's expectations can raise concerns about quality, reliability, and safety. Everyone would like to pay less for medical care, but few people would be willing to go to cut-rate clinics if they thought their health might be jeopardized.[34]

Loss-Leader Pricing

As part of a larger marketing plan, some companies occasionally resort to **loss-leader pricing**, setting a price on one product so low that they lose money on every sale (or earn very little profit in some cases) but recoup that loss by enticing customers to try a new product or buy other products. For instance, grocery stores can use milk and other staples as loss leaders to encourage shoppers to visit.

Of course, loss-leader pricing can cause considerable pain for competitors if they can't match the low prices. If you were ever a fan of the Harry Potter novels, you might have assumed that every retailer who carried the hit series made a healthy profit on the books. While the young wizard had the potential to work some magic for perpetually beleaguered independent bookstores, loss-leader pricing by giant competitors such as Amazon.com and Wal-Mart was too strong for even his powers. "It's sad that what little profit the industry can make off Harry Potter is being stripped away," lamented Bonnie Stuppin of Alexander Book Company in San Francisco.[35]

Auction Pricing

In an **auction**, the seller doesn't set a firm price but allows buyers to competitively bid on the products being sold. Auctions used to be confined to a few market sectors such as fine art, agricultural products, and government bonds, but that all changed when eBay turned selling and buying via auctions into a new national pastime. Consumers selling off old stuff from the basement aren't the only ones using eBay, either. Many companies now use eBay and other auction sites to sell everything from modular buildings to tractors to industrial equipment. *Procurement auctions* or *reverse auctions* are another twist on dynamic pricing, in which potential buyers post the goods or services they need and the prices they're willing to pay, then suppliers respond with offers at the prices they're willing to charge. In other words, in a regular auction, the price starts low and increases until only one buyer is left willing to buy at that price, while in a reverse auction, the price starts high and drops until there is only one seller left willing to sell at that price. A variation on the reverse auction is the name-your-price method, such as that used on the travel website Priceline.com. On Priceline, buyers can name a price for a desired travel service, then see if any sellers are willing to match it.[36]

auction
Selling method in which the price is set by customers bidding against each other

Price Adjustment Strategies

After a company has set a product's price, it may choose to adjust that price from time to time to account for changing market situations or changing customer preferences. Three common price adjustment strategies are price discounts, bundling, and dynamic pricing.

Price Discounts

When you use **discount pricing**, you offer various types of temporary price reductions, depending on the customer being targeted and the item being offered. You may decide to offer a trade discount to wholesalers or retailers as a way of encouraging orders, or you may offer cash discounts to reward customers who pay cash or pay promptly. You may offer a quantity discount to buyers who buy large volumes, or you may offer a seasonal discount to buyers who buy merchandise or services out of season.

discount pricing
Offering a temporary reduction in price

Although discounts are a popular way to boost sales of a product, the down side is that they can touch off *price wars* between competitors. Price wars can occur whenever (a) one supplier believes that underpricing the competition is the best way—or perhaps the only way—for it to increase sales volume and (b) customers believe that price is the only meaningful differentiator among the various suppliers. This situation occurs frequently in the air travel industry, which is why it has been wracked with price wars ever since it was deregulated years ago. Price wars present two significant dangers: that customers will begin to believe that price is the only factor to care about in the market and that desperate competitors will cut prices so far that they'll damage their finances—perhaps beyond repair.

Bundling

Sometimes sellers combine several of their products and sell them at one reduced price. This practice, called **bundling**, can also promote sales of products consumers might not otherwise buy—especially when the combined price is low enough to entice them to purchase the bundle. Examples of bundled products are season tickets, vacation

bundling
Offering several products for a single price that is presumably lower than the total of the products' individual prices

How This Affects You

1. Have you ever purchased a hot new product as soon as it hit the market, only to see the price drop a few months later? If so, did you resolve never to buy so quickly again?

2. Have you ever bid on anything on eBay, another online auction site, or an in-person auction? If so, how did you decide which price to bid? Did you set a maximum price you'd allow yourself to spend? Did you get caught up in the competitive emotions of bidding against someone else?

3. Do you generally wait for items to go on sale before you buy them?

packages, computer software with hardware, and wrapped packages of shampoo and conditioner. A key disadvantage from the buyer's perspective is that bundling can make price comparisons difficult.

Dynamic Pricing

dynamic pricing
Continually adjusting prices to reflect changes in supply and demand

In **dynamic pricing**, companies continually reprice their products and services to meet supply and demand. Dynamic pricing not only enables companies to move slow-selling merchandise instantly but also allows companies to experiment with different pricing levels. Because price changes are immediately distributed via computer networks, customers always have the most current price information. Airlines and hotels have used this type of continually adjusted pricing for years, a technique often known as *yield management*.

(For a look at the latest innovations in pricing strategy, visit http://introbusiness student.com and click on "Real-Time Updates.")

Summary of Learning Objectives

1 Describe the four stages in the life cycle of a product.

Products start in the introductory stage, during which marketers focus on stimulating demand for the new product. As the product progresses through the growth stage, marketers focus on increasing the product's market share. During the maturity stage, marketers try to extend the life of the product by highlighting improvements or by repackaging the product in different sizes. Eventually, products move to a decline stage, where the marketer must decide whether to keep the product and reduce its costs to compensate for declining sales or to discontinue it.

2 Describe six stages of product development.

The first two stages of product development involve generating and screening ideas to isolate those with the most potential. In the third stage, promising ideas are analyzed to determine their likely profitability. Those that appear worthwhile enter the fourth, or prototype development stage, in which a limited number of the products are created. In the fifth stage, the product is test marketed to determine buyer response. Products that survive the testing process are then commercialized, the final stage.

3 Cite three levels of brand loyalty.

The first level of brand loyalty is brand awareness, in which the buyer is familiar with the product. The next level is

brand preference, in which the buyer will select the product if it is available. The final level is brand insistence, in which the buyer will accept no substitute.

4 Discuss the functions of packaging and labeling.

Packaging provides protection for the product, makes products easier to display, and attracts attention. In addition, packaging enhances the convenience of the product and communicates its attributes to the buyer. Labels help identify and distinguish the brand and product. They provide information about the product—including ingredients, risks, shelf life, and operating procedures. And they contain UPC codes, which are used for scanning sales information and monitoring inventory and pricing.

5 Identify four ways of expanding a product line and discuss two risks that product-line extensions pose.

A product line can be expanded by filling gaps in the market, extending the line to include new varieties of existing products, extending the brand to new product categories, and stretching the line to include lower- or higher-priced items. Two of the biggest risks with product-line extensions include a loss of brand identity (weakening of the brand's meaning) and cannibalization of sales of other products in the product line.

6 **List the factors that influence pricing decisions and identify seven common pricing strategies.**

Pricing decisions are influenced by manufacturing and selling costs, competition, the needs of wholesalers and retailers who distribute the product to the final customer, a firm's marketing objectives, government regulations, quality perceptions, and customer demand. Common pricing methods include cost-based pricing, price-based pricing, optimal pricing, skim pricing, penetration pricing, loss-leader pricing, and auction pricing.

7 **Explain why cost-based pricing can be a flawed strategy.**

Cost-based pricing suffers from two major weaknesses. First, determining variable costs can be difficult since they often depend on production and sales volume. As the projected volume goes up or down, variable costs (necessary to compute the break-even point or profit margin) might be going down or up in response. Second, cost-based pricing doesn't take into account the influences of competitors or customers, both of which can dramatically affect the ability to sell at a given price point.

Behind the Scenes

Allergan Puts a New Face on Cosmetic Medicine

Nothing in Allergan's history could have prepared it for the transformation of one of its oddest products into a profitable sensation. Prior to the Botox Cosmetic phenomenon, Allergan was a small firm selling little-known eye and skin drugs, some surgical devices, and a line of over-the-counter lens cleaners. Then doctors noticed that the form of Botox they were using to treat strabismus (crossed eyes) and other muscle disorders also relaxed the muscles that generate frown lines and wrinkles. With only a few minor injections, patients could reverse some of the visual effects of aging for up to four months at a time.

The early buzz and media attention boosted Botox sales in a few major urban areas. But Allergan recognized that selling the general public on Botox would require more than word-of-mouth promotion. The company would have to overcome several negative attributes: The treatment is not permanent, it's not covered by health insurance, and it does involve injecting a toxic substance into the face (although to be fair, most medicines are toxic in the wrong dosages). On the plus side, Botox is far less expensive and less invasive than cosmetic surgery, and it has proven to be a safe and fairly painless procedure.

To get the word out, Allergan decided to promote the entire Botox experience. It began training doctors on how to inject Botox. And the company showed doctors how to design and decorate their offices to appeal to patients who want to be pampered.

The timing was perfect. A goodly number of baby boomers aren't inclined to grow old without a fight and are turning to Botox and other cosmetic treatments that help in that struggle. Several million people a year now get Botox treatments, spending about a billion dollars on them.

With a safe, simple, and fairly inexpensive way to diminish the visible effects of aging, Allergan is ideally positioned to profit as the Baby Boom generation advances in years. Of course, a huge market invites lots of competition. A Scottish company called Pure Logicol is among those bringing Botox alternatives to the market. Consumers can also turn to collagen injections, chemical peels, laser treatments, and a variety of other wrinkle-battling methods. However, Allergan clearly has a head start with its product and the enormous brand equity built up in the Botox name. Not bad for a product that started by accident.

Critical Thinking Questions

1. Was it a good idea for Allergan to include the word *Botox* in the Botox Cosmetic brand name? Why or why not?
2. Would it be a good idea for Allergan to extend the Botox Cosmetic brand name to medical products outside of the cosmetics market, such as cold and flu medications?
3. A number of patients were recently injured when doctors around the country purchased and administered an unsafe product that its maker claimed was just like Botox Cosmetic. Even though Allergan's product remains safe and it had nothing to do with the deceptive product, what steps, if any, should it take to protect the Botox brand name?

LEARN MORE ONLINE

Visit the Botox Cosmetic website at www.botoxcosmetic.com. How is the product presented to potential customers? How does the website attempt to segment customers according to usage or loyalty patterns? Does Allergan promote Botox Cosmetic the same way to both women and men? What information is given about potential side effects and other safety issues? In what ways does Allergan promote the benefits of a product that is largely intangible?

Key Terms

auction (261)	co-branding (252)	price elasticity (257)
brand (251)	commercialization (250)	private brands (252)
brand equity (251)	discount pricing (261)	product life cycle (246)
brand extension (255)	dynamic pricing (262)	product line (253)
brand loyalty (251)	family branding (255)	product mix (253)
brand managers (253)	fixed costs (257)	skim pricing (260)
brand mark (251)	generic products (252)	test marketing (250)
brand names (251)	license (252)	trademarks (251)
break-even analysis (257)	loss-leader pricing (260)	Universal Product Codes
break-even point (257)	national brands (252)	(UPCs) (253)
bundling (261)	penetration pricing (260)	variable costs (257)

Test Your Knowledge

Questions for Review

1. What are the four main subgroups of consumer products?
2. Why are most services perishable?
3. What are the functions of packaging?
4. How many books will a publisher have to sell to break even if fixed costs are $100,000, the selling price per book is $60, and the variable costs per book are $40?
5. How does cost-based pricing differ from price-based pricing?

Questions for Analysis

6. Why do businesses continually introduce new products, given the high costs of the introduction stage of the product life cycle?
7. How could a marketer confuse a consumer when developing a product's positioning strategies?
8. Why are brand names important?
9. Why is it important to review the objectives of a strategic marketing plan before setting a product's price?
10. **Ethical Considerations.** If your college neighborhood is typical, many companies in the area adorn themselves in your school colors and otherwise seek to identify their names with your school name and thereby encourage business from students. Some of these firms probably have brand licensing agreements with your college or are involved in sponsoring various groups on campus. However, chances are some of them are using school colors and other branding elements without having any formal arrangement with the college. In other words, they may be getting commercial benefit from the association without paying for it.[37] Is this ethical? Why or why not?

Questions for Application

11. In what ways might Mattel modify its pricing strategies during the life cycle of a toy product?
12. **How This Affects You.** Do you consider yourself an *early adopter* when it comes to trying out new products or new fashions, or do you tend to take a wait-and-see attitude? How does your attitude toward new products and new ideas influence your decision making as a consumer?
13. **Integrated.** Review the theory of supply and demand in Chapter 1 (see pages 9–12). How do skimming and penetration pricing strategies influence a product's supply and demand?
14. **Integrated.** Review the discussion of cultural differences in international business in Chapter 3 (see pages 66–67). Which cultural differences do you think Disney had to consider when planning its product strategies for Disneyland Paris? Originally the company offered a standardized product but was later forced to customize many of the park's operations. What might have been some of the cultural challenges Disney experienced under a standardized product strategy?

Practice Your Knowledge

Sharpening Your Communication Skills

Now's your chance to play the role of a marketing specialist trying to convince a group of customers that your product concept is better than the competition's. You're going to wade into the industry battle over digital photo printing. Choose a side: either the photo printer manufacturers, who want consumers to buy printers to print their own digital photos (visit HP at www.hp.com for a good overview of photo-quality printers), or the service providers, who claim their way is better (visit one of the many retailers that offer a service-based approach, such as www.cvs.com or www.walmart.com). Prepare a short presentation on why the approach you've chosen is better for consumers. Feel free to segment the consumer market and choose a particular target segment if that bolsters your argument.

Building Your Team Skills

Select a high-profile product with which you and your teammates are familiar. Do some online research to learn more about that brand. Then answer these questions and prepare a short group presentation to your classmates summarizing your findings.

- Is the product a consumer product, an industrial product, or both?
- At what stage in its life cycle is this product?
- Is the product a national brand or a private brand?
- How do the product's packaging and labeling help boost consumer appeal?
- How is this product promoted?
- Is the product mix to which this product belongs wide? Long? Deep?
- Is the product sold in international markets? If so, does the company use a standardized or a customized strategy?
- How is the product priced in relation to competing products?

Improving Your Tech Insights: Digital Products

The category of digital products encompasses an extremely broad range of product types, from e-books to music and movie files to software and instruction sets for automated machinery. Digital products are commonplace these days, but the ability to remotely deliver product value is quite a staggering concept when you think about it. (If you remember the pre-iPod days, try to imagine how much work it would take to collect 10,000 songs and carry them around with you!)

Supplying music over the Internet is amazing enough, but nowadays even *tangible* products can be delivered electronically: The technology that deposits layers of ink in inkjet printers is being adapted to deposit layers of other liquefied materials, including plastics and metals. Called *3D printing*, *inkjet fabrication*, or *additive fabrication*, this technology is already being used to "print" product prototypes and simple electronic components such as RFID antennas. As the price of the technology continues to drop, it's not too far-fetched to imagine a day when you'll be able to download product description files from the Internet and fabricate physical items right on your own home "printer." For more about this technology, visit Desktop Factory (www.desktopfactory.com), Dimension 3D Printing (www.dimensionprinting.com), Stratasys (www.stratasys.com), or Z Corporation (www.zcorp.com).

Choose a category of products that has been changed dramatically by the ability to deliver value digitally. In a brief e-mail message to your instructor, explain how digital technology revolutionized this market segment.[38]

Expand Your Knowledge

Discovering Career Opportunities

Being a marketing manager is a big responsibility, but it can be a lot of fun at the same time. Read what the U.S. Department of Labor has to say about the nature of the work, working conditions, qualifications, and job outlook for marketing managers by accessing the Bureau of Labor Statistics's *Occupational Outlook Handbook* at www.bls.gov/oco.

1. What does a marketing manager do?
2. What are some key questions you might want to ask when interviewing for a job in marketing?
3. What training and qualifications should a marketing manager have?

Developing Your Research Skills

Scan recent business journals and newspapers (print or online editions) for an article related to one of the following:

- New-product development
- The product life cycle
- Pricing strategies
- Packaging

1. Does this article report on a development in a particular company, several companies, or an entire industry? Which companies or industries are specifically mentioned?
2. If you were a marketing manager in this industry, what concerns would you have as a result of reading the article? What questions do you think companies in this industry (or related ones) should be asking? What would you want to know?
3. In what ways do you think this industry, other industries, or the public might be affected by this trend or development in the next five years? Why?

See It on the Web

Visit these websites and answer the following questions for each one. (Up-to-date links for all websites mentioned in this chapter can be found on the Textbook Resources page for Chapter 10 at www.mybusinesslab.com. Please note that links to sites that become inactive after publication of the book will be removed from the Featured Websites section.)

1. What is the purpose of this website?

2. What kinds of information does this website contain? Please be specific.

3. How is the information provided at this website useful for businesspeople? Consumers?

4. How did you expand your knowledge of products and pricing in business by reviewing the material at this website? What new things did you learn about this topic?

Be a Sharp Shopper

Put your marketing knowledge to practice. Visit the Sharper Image website and think like a marketer. Evaluate the company's product mix. Is the product mix wide? Deep? What types of consumer products does this company sell? Who is its target market? Do the products have recognizable brand names? Which other stores carry this type of product? Be sure to read about the company's mission. And don't leave without checking out the new products. www.sharperimage.com

Protect Your Trademark

Do you have a winning idea for a new product? Don't forget to protect your trademark by registering it with the U.S. Patent and Trademark Office. Visit this government agency's website and learn the basic facts about registering a trademark, such as who is allowed to use the TM symbol and how a trademark differs from a service mark. Find out how the process works and how much it costs. In fact, why not search its database now to see whether anyone has already registered your trademark? www.uspto.gov

Uncover Hidden Costs

When you buy something online, the selling price is usually only part of your total cost. Factor in extra costs such as shipping and sales tax, and the total cost can vary dramatically from one website to another. Using comparison-shopping sites can help you ferret out hidden costs. Take a look at Best Book Buys, which compares the total cost of buying a book from a variety of Internet sources. Check out one of the best-selling books or search for your favorite book. Click to see a table comparing the item price, shipping cost, and total cost at different retail websites. Then simply click to buy. www.bestbookbuys.com

Companion Website

Learning Interactively

Log onto www.prenhall.com/bovée, locate your text, and then click on its Companion Website. For Chapter 10, take advantage of the interactive Chapter Quiz to test your knowledge of the chapter. Get instant feedback on whether you need additional studying. Also, you'll find an abundance of valuable resources that will help you succeed in this course, including PowerPoint presentations and Web Links.

Video Case

Sending Products into Space: MCCI

LEARNING OBJECTIVES

The purpose of this video is to help you:

1. Recognize how and why a company develops specialized products for organizational customers

2. Describe some of the decisions a company faces in pricing specialized products under long-term contracts for organizational customers

3. Understand how a company can use quality to differentiate its products

SYNOPSIS

MCCI designs and produces highly specialized products that are customized to the detailed specifications of its organizational customers. When a telecommunications company or government agency needs a radio frequency filter for a new satellite, it calls on MCCI to design one especially for that situation. Custom-made from tiny components and precious materials, this filter must be top quality to withstand powerful vibration and temperature extremes in space—and continue to perform exactly as promised for 20 years. Because some contracts cover products purchased over a decade or more, MCCI must carefully assess the risks of designing a product and pricing it for long-term profit. Yet speed is also a factor: MCCI once created a new product during a single weekend to win a contract from an important customer.

Discussion Questions

1. *For analysis:* Are MCCI's products capital or expense items? How do you know?
2. *For analysis:* Given its in-depth knowledge of the market, why does MCCI develop new products for individual customers rather than creating new products to meet general industry needs?
3. *For application:* The price of gold can fluctuate widely, depending on market conditions. How might this affect MCCI's pricing decisions for products that incorporate components made from gold?
4. *For application:* What factors must MCCI analyze as it prices a custom-designed product?

5. *For debate:* At the start of a long-term contract, should MCCI price a product to return little or no profit in the hope that it will be able to generate more profit from other products sold to this customer later in the contract period? Support your chosen position.

ONLINE EXPLORATION

One of MCCI's products went to Mars on the Sojourner Rover sent by NASA. What other kinds of goods and services does NASA buy? Visit its procurement website, http://acquisition.jpl.nasa.gov, and follow the link to see some of the requests for proposals on this site. Do any contain a document with questions and answers? Why would MCCI need to read such a document before preparing a proposal to develop a product for NASA? Now examine the listing of other links. How could MCCI use information from the sites on this listing in planning a product for NASA?

CHAPTER 11

Distribution and Customer Communication

LEARNING OBJECTIVES
After studying this chapter, you will be able to

1 Explain what marketing intermediaries do and list their seven primary functions

2 Explain how wholesalers and retailers function as intermediaries

3 Discuss the key factors that influence channel design and selection

4 Differentiate intensive, selective, and exclusive distribution strategies

5 Identify the seven categories of customer communication

6 Discuss the importance of integrated marketing communications

7 Explain the purpose of defining a core marketing message

8 Describe the use of social media in marketing communications

Behind the Scenes

Costco Makes the Good Life More Affordable

www.costco.com

With an unusual mix of low prices and quality goods, Costco Wholesale has become the country's largest and most profitable warehouse club chain. The company knows that low prices on high-quality, high-end merchandise can transcend the common notion of "discount." And, in what amounts to a treasure hunt played out along Costco's cement-floor aisles, the high/low shopping experience is a powerful elixir for middle-class shoppers.

Once new members get the hang of the treasure hunt mentality, they get hooked on Costco because even though they don't know what will be on display, they're sure it will be something at a price that will make the good life more affordable. It's not unusual, for instance, for a 1,000-piece lot of Ralph

Costco shoppers have learned to look for great buys on both everyday items and an ever-changing mix of luxury and specialty goods.

Lauren golf jackets, selling 75 percent below retail at $19.99 each, to vanish in an afternoon. Like other warehouse clubs, Costco Wholesale sells a mix of everything from giant boxes of cereal to patio furniture. In fact, Costco often asks vendors to change their factory runs to produce specially built packages that are bigger and cheaper. Unlike other warehouse clubs, Costco shoppers can occasionally find $10,000 diamond rings and grand pianos, too.

If you were Costco president and CEO Jim Sinegal, how would you keep Costco on the leading edge of retailing? How would you integrate your physical retail stores with your online e-commerce operation? What can you do to keep your bargain-conscious but demanding customers coming back for more?[1] ∎

Developing Distribution Strategies

Costco (profiled in the chapter opener) is just one example of how producers use intermediaries to get their products to market. *Distribution channels*, also known as *marketing channels*, are organized networks of systems and firms that work together to get goods and services from producer to customer. A company's **distribution strategy**, which is its overall plan for moving products to buyers, plays a major role in the firm's success.

Think of all the products you buy. How many of them do you purchase directly from the producer? For most people, the answer is not many. Instead, producers in many industries work with **marketing intermediaries** (previously known as *middlemen*) to bring their products to market.

distribution strategy
Firm's overall plan for moving products to intermediaries and final customers

marketing intermediaries
Businesspeople and organizations that channel goods and services from producers to customers

Understanding the Role of Marketing Intermediaries

The two main types of marketing intermediaries are wholesalers and retailers. **Wholesalers** sell primarily to retailers, to other wholesalers, and to organizational users such as government agencies, institutions, and commercial operations. In turn, the customers of wholesalers either resell the products or use them to make products of their own. Ingram Book Group, for example, the world's largest wholesaler of books and related products, supplies thousands of retail outlets from an inventory of more than 1 million items.[2] By contrast, **retailers** sell products to consumers for personal use. (Note that the terminology surrounding wholesalers and retailers can get a bit confusing. For instance, some retail firms use *warehouse* or *wholesale* in their names to convey low prices to consumers. Just remember the simple rule: When a marketing intermediary is selling to individual consumers, it's functioning as a retailer; when an intermediary sells to any type of organization, from a mom-and-pop store to the Pentagon, it's functioning as a wholesaler.)

Wholesalers and retailers are instrumental in creating place, time, and possession utility. They provide an efficient process for transferring products from the producer to the customer, they reduce the number of transactions, and they ensure that goods and services are available at a convenient time and place for customers. To accomplish these goals, wholesalers and retailers perform a number of specific distribution functions that make life easier for both producers and customers:

- *Match buyers and sellers.* By making sellers' products available to multiple buyers, intermediaries such as Costco reduce the number of transactions between producers and customers. In the business-to-business market, giant online trading hubs such as Covisint (automotive and healthcare products, www.covisint.com) and ChemConnect (chemicals and plastics, www.chemconnect.com) bring together thousands of buyers and sellers.[3]
- *Provide market information.* Intermediaries collect valuable data about customer purchases: who buys, how often, and how much. Collecting such data allows them to spot buying patterns and to share marketplace information with producers.
- *Provide promotional and sales support.* Many intermediaries assist with marketing activities, such as creating in-store displays or advising shoppers on product choices.
- *Gather assortments of goods.* Intermediaries receive bulk shipments from producers and break them into more convenient units by sorting, standardizing, and dividing bulk quantities into smaller packages.
- *Transport and store products.* Intermediaries frequently maintain an inventory of merchandise that they acquire from producers so they can quickly fill customers' orders.
- *Assume risks.* When intermediaries accept goods from manufacturers, they often take on the risks associated with damage, theft, product perishability, and obsolescence.
- *Provide financing.* Large intermediaries sometimes provide loans to smaller producers.

Although "cutting out the middleman" is often used as a promotional phrase, in most cases intermediaries actually lower costs and save time for buyers (see Exhibit 11.1). For instance, imagine how expensive groceries would be—and how limited the selection would be—if your local market had to go out to hundreds of individual farms and factories to fill its shelves, rather than letting high-volume wholesalers do the work.

Wholesalers

Most consumers rarely come in contact with wholesaling operations, but these intermediaries can truly lay claim to being the backbone of the economy. The majority of wholesalers are **merchant wholesalers**, independently owned businesses that buy from

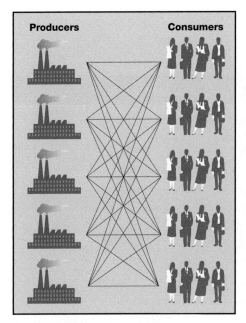

Number of transactions required when consumers buy directly from manufacturers

Number of transactions required when buying is conducted via intermediary

EXHIBIT 11.1

How Intermediaries Simplify Commerce

Intermediaries actually reduce the price customers pay for many goods and services, because they reduce the number of contacts between producers and customers that would otherwise be necessary. They also create place, time, and possession utility.

producers, take legal title to the goods, then resell them to retailers or to organizational buyers. For instance, Supervalu's (www.supervalu.com) grocery wholesaling operation is the intermediary between hundreds of producers and more than 5,000 retailers.[4] Merchant wholesalers offer various levels of service, from full-service firms that provide storage, sales, order processing, delivery, and promotional support, to limited-service wholesalers such as *drop shippers*, who take ownership but not physical possession of the goods they handle.

Merchant wholesalers can also be distinguished by their customers. Supervalu and others that sell primarily to other intermediaries are usually known in the trade simply as *wholesalers*. In contrast, firms that sell goods to companies for use in their own products and operations are usually called *distributors*.

Unlike merchant wholesalers, *agents* and *brokers* (the terms are sometimes used interchangeably, but there are distinctions in some industries) never take title to the products they handle, and they perform fewer services. Their primary role is to bring buyers and sellers together; they are generally paid a commission for arranging sales. For example, manufacturers that aren't large enough to support their own in-house sales forces often use *manufacturers' representatives*, agents who sell various noncompeting product lines to business customers.

Retailers

As any shopper knows, retailers come in an almost endless variety of formats and sizes, and creative retailers keep thinking up innovative ways to connect with customers. The major types of retailers are described in Exhibit 11.2.

Two particular forces have helped create this wide variety of retail formats. The first is known as the **wheel of retailing**, whereby a retailer with low operating costs attracts customers by offering low prices but still turns a profit by providing limited service and selection. As this store adds more services and new product lines to broaden its appeal, its prices creep upward, opening the door for lower-priced competitors. Eventually, these competitors also upgrade their operations and are replaced by still other lower-priced stores that later follow the same upward pattern.

wheel of retailing
Evolutionary process by which stores that feature low prices gradually upgrade until they no longer appeal to price-sensitive shoppers and are replaced by new low-price competitors

EXHIBIT 11.2 Types of Retail Stores

The definition of retailer covers many types of outlets. This table shows some of the most common types.

TYPE OF RETAILER	DESCRIPTION	EXAMPLES
Online retailer	Web-based store offering anything from a single product line to comprehensive selections in multiple product areas; can be web-only (e.g., Amazon.com) or integrated with physical stores (e.g., REI.com)	REI.com Amazon.com
Category killer	Type of specialty store focusing on specific products on a giant scale and dominating retail sales in respective product categories	Office Depot Bed Bath & Beyond
Convenience store	Offers staple convenience goods, long service hours, quick checkouts	7-Eleven
Department store	Offers a wide variety of merchandise under one roof in departmentalized sections and many customer services	Sears JCPenney Nordstrom
Discount store	Offers a wide variety of merchandise at low prices and few services	Wal-Mart Target
Factory/retail outlet	Large outlet store selling discontinued items, overruns, and factory seconds	Nordstrom Rack Nike outlet store
Hypermarket	Giant store offering food and general merchandise at discount prices	Wal-Mart Supercenters Carrefour
Off-price store	Offers designer and brand-name merchandise at low prices and few services	T.J. Maxx Marshall's
Specialty store	Offers a complete selection in a narrow range of merchandise	Payless Shoes
Supermarket	Large, self-service store offering a wide selection of food and nonfood merchandise	Kroger Safeway
Warehouse club	Large, warehouse-style store that sells food and general merchandise at discount prices; some require club membership	Sam's Club Costco

For example, Wal-Mart revolutionized retailing and much of the business world with low prices made possible by its extraordinary abilities at cost control and efficiency. Far less attention was paid to the visual presentation within its stores and other merchandising nuances. In fact, the company characterized its approach as "stack it high and watch it fly." In recent years, though, Wal-Mart has shifted upward slightly from its original bare-bones approach, improving the presentation of merchandise and offering higher-priced goods. Meanwhile, it faces low-price competition from the likes of Dollar General and other so-called "dollar stores" that are multiplying across the retail landscape.[5]

The second concept that continues to reshape retailing is **scrambled merchandising**, in which a store attempts to draw in more shoppers and increase the average revenue per customer by adding products unrelated to its original product mix. For example, you can now buy just about everything from stationery and automotive supplies to cameras and toys at Walgreens drugstores.[6] Some stores even add mini stores-within-stores, such as the limited-service medical clinics inside Target retail stores.[7] As they diversify their

scrambled merchandising
Strategy of adding products unrelated to a store's original product mix

product mixes in this way, companies blur the lines between traditional retailing types and create new hybrid forms along the way.

Store-Based Retailing Formats   Store-based retailing includes everything from newsstands to malls, but the most significant forms to study from a marketing perspective are *specialty stores*, *department stores*, *category killers*, and *discount stores*. When you shop in a pet store, a shoe store, or a stationery store, for instance, you are in a **specialty store**—a store that carries only particular types of goods. The basic merchandising strategy of a specialty shop is to offer a limited number of product lines but an extensive selection of brands, styles, sizes, models, colors, materials, and prices within each line. The range and variety of specialty stores are practically endless, from florists and bridal shops to antique dealers and party-supply stores.

Category killers are supersized specialty stores that dominate a particular product category by stocking every conceivable variety of merchandise in every important product line in that category—often at prices that smaller specialty stores can't match. The Home Depot (tools and home improvement), Staples (office supplies), and Bed Bath & Beyond (home products) are well-known category killers.

Department stores are the classic major retailers in the United States, with the likes of Bloomingdale's, Macy's, Nordstrom, Dillard's, Kohl's, Sears, and JCPenney. These stores can have a local, regional, or national presence and different price and quality offerings, but most tend to carry clothing, housewares, bedding, furniture in some cases, and similar items. Shopping malls often feature them as *anchors*, stores with wide appeal that mall developers can count on to bring in business for all the shops in the mall.

Wal-Mart and Target are good examples of **discount stores**, stores that tend to be fairly large with a wide variety of aggressively priced merchandise. Some offer few services at all, whereas others offer a range of services from film processing to banking. Larger discount stores such as Wal-Mart are often called *mass merchandisers*. The largest are sometimes called *supercenters*, which combine discount stores with grocery stores.

E-Commerce and Other Nonstore Formats   Nonstore retailing can trace its origin back to such classics as the mail-order catalogs sent out by Sears Roebuck and Montgomery Ward during the late 1800s, selling everything from household goods to ready-to-assemble houses. Today, Amazon.com, Apple iTunes, and thousands of other online retailers carry on that tradition through **e-commerce**, short for *electronic commerce*. Even venerable old Sears has a busy website (www.sears.com), and Montgomery Ward, which went bankrupt several years ago, has been reborn as an e-commerce store, www.wards.com.[8]

For products that can be created in or converted to purely digital formats, including software, information, music, and movies, the Internet is a natural fit. Products that don't require physical evaluation, such as concert tickets and insurance policies, are also a good choice for online distribution. In other categories, the choice between e-commerce and a traditional retail store often comes down to the specific product and the individual consumer. For instance, some people are comfortable buying clothes online, but others want to try clothes on in a store. Consequently, in the decade or so that e-commerce has been a viable retail alternative, its impact has varied widely from industry to industry. For instance, more than 40 percent of computer-related products are now purchased online, but overall, e-commerce's share of the retail marketplace is still below 10 percent.[9]

Not surprisingly, 24-hour access and the ability to shop from home are among the top reasons people shop online.[10] However, store-based retailing offers numerous advantages as well. Beyond the obvious advantages of allowing customers to evaluate products in person, take them home immediately after purchase, and avoid shipping charges, store shopping offers entertainment and socialization aspects that are largely missing in e-commerce. Some store retailers now use **retail theater**, offering entertainment and

specialty store
Store that carries only a particular type of goods

category killers
Discount chains that sell only one category of product

department stores
Full-price retailers that sell clothing, housewares, furniture, and related items

discount stores
Retailers that sell a variety of goods below the market price by keeping their overhead low

e-commerce
Short for *electronic commerce*; retailing through the Internet and other electronic channels such as mobile phone services

retail theater
Offering entertainment and education opportunities in addition to shopping

No, this isn't some trendy new restaurant—it's a grocery store. Whole Foods Markets aims to make food shopping more enjoyable by making the retail environment more interesting and pleasant.

multichannel retailing
Coordinated efforts to reach customers through more than one retail channel

mail-order firms
Companies that sell products through catalogs and ship them directly to customers

education opportunities (such as cooking and home improvement classes) in addition to shopping. Moreover, some shoppers simply consider in-store shopping to be easier, particularly when they compare it to e-commerce websites that are poorly designed or that lack such features as instant messaging chat with a salesperson.

For many retailers, physical stores and e-commerce are becoming complementary elements of **multichannel retailing**, coordinated efforts to reach customers through more than one retail channel. For instance, even when they purchase in physical stores, many consumers research their choices first online.[11] Retailers often use the term *clicks and mortar* (a play on *bricks and mortar*) to indicate retailing that integrates stores and e-commerce. Saks Fifth Avenue (www. saksfifthavenue.com) reports that people who shop through multiple channels spend five times as much as those who shop through only one channel.[12] "This synchronization of multiple sales channels is absolutely the future of retail," says one industry consultant.[13]

In the coming years, e-commerce will continue to grow, but at a more moderate rate than in the past decade.[14] Expect to see innovations in such areas as *mobile commerce*, or *m-commerce*, as mobile phones become increasingly central to the lives of many consumers. *Comparison shopping engines* continue to evolve as tools to let consumers find the lowest prices. *Recommendation engines* suggest products that might be of interest to shoppers, based on past purchasing behavior. Online retailers also continue to innovate in terms of the overall shopping experience, with *virtual reality* simulations that give shoppers a better feel for products (see Exhibit 11.3) and *avatars*, talking animated figures that interact with shoppers.

Meanwhile, the **mail-order firms** that inspired e-commerce are still going strong in many industries, as a look inside any mailbox in the country will verify. Attractive catalogs are a powerful marketing tool, but printing and mailing them is expensive, so many mail-order firms are working to integrate their catalog efforts with e-commerce. Some do so in innovative ways, such as reproducing catalog pages on-screen so that customers who've selected a product from the catalog don't have to learn how the website works and repeat the shopping process online; instead, they simply type in the catalog page number and it pops up.

Another common form of nonstore retailing is *automatic vending,* in which machines dispense everything from gasoline to candy bars to hot meals to train tickets. Vending machines are quite common in countries such as Japan, which boasts 1 vending machine for every 23 residents.[15] Interactive *kiosks,* freestanding electronic displays that combine elements of vending machines and e-commerce, also play a role in retailing.

EXHIBIT 11.3

E-Commerce Innovations

Want to try on a thousand pairs of eyeglasses without leaving home? You can, thanks to e-commerce websites such as FramesDirect.com, which lets you upload a photo of yourself, then see how you look in a variety of eyeglass styles. Flexible media technologies make it easy to adapt promotional messages to the interests of individual audience members.

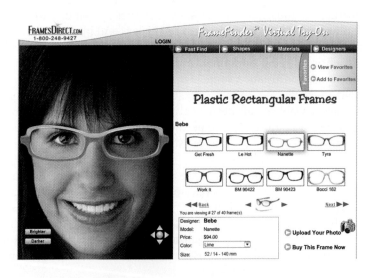

Located in showrooms or shopping areas, kiosks can inform customers about new products, availability, products, and store promotions; take and process orders; help people fill out applications; sell small items such as entertainment and transportation tickets; and even provide virtual product demonstrations. For instance, at Dell's Direct Store shopping mall kiosks, buyers can inspect a limited selection of computers, printers, and other products and get information on the company's entire product line.[16] (For more on the latest innovations in e-commerce, visit www.prenhall.com/bovée and click on "Real-Time Updates.")

Selecting Your Marketing Channels

With so many types of distribution channels available, a company's decision about the number and type of intermediaries to use—its **distribution mix**—depends on a variety of factors (see Exhibit 11.4). Five in particular warrant a closer look: *channel length*, *market coverage*, *cost*, *control*, and *channel conflict*.

distribution mix
Combination of intermediaries and channels a producer uses to get a product to final customers

EXHIBIT 11.4 Factors That Influence Distribution Channel Choices

Designing a distribution mix is rarely a simple task; here are some of the most important factors to consider.

FACTOR	ISSUES TO CONSIDER
Customer needs and expectations	Where are customers likely to look for your products? How much customer service do they expect from the channel? Can you make your offering more attractive by choosing an unconventional channel?
Product support requirements	How much training do salespeople need to present your products successfully? How much after-sale support is required? Who will answer questions when things go wrong?
Positioning and targeting	Which intermediaries—if any—can present your products to target customers while maintaining your positioning strategy?
Competitors' channels	Which channels do your competitors use? Do you need to use the same channels in order to reach your target customers or can you use different channels to distinguish yourself?
Established channel structure	Which intermediaries are already in place? Can you take advantage of them or do you need to find or create alternatives? Will retailers demand that you use specific wholesalers or distributors?
Channel length	Do you want to deal directly with customers? Can you? Do you need to engage other intermediaries to perform vital functions?
Market coverage	Are you going for intensive, selective, or exclusive distribution? Are the right intermediaries available in your target markets? Can they handle the volumes at which you hope to sell?
Cost	How much will intermediaries add to the price that final customers will eventually pay? Put another way, how much of a discount from the retail price will intermediaries expect from you?
Control	How much control do you need to maintain as products move through the channel—and how much can you expect to maintain with each potential intermediary? What happens if you lose control?
Channel conflict	What are the potential sources of channel conflict, both now and in the future? If such conflict can't be avoided, how will you minimize its effect?

Channel Length

Some channels are short and simple; others are long and complex. Many businesses purchase goods they use in their operations directly from producers, so those distribution channels are short. In contrast, the channels for consumer goods are usually longer and more complex (see Exhibit 11.5). The four primary channels for consumer goods are

- *Producer to consumer.* Producers who sell directly to consumers through catalogs, telemarketing, infomercials, and e-commerce are using the shortest, simplest distribution channel. Although this approach eliminates payments to intermediaries, it can also force producers to handle distribution functions such as storing inventory and selling to consumers.

- *Producer to retailer to consumer.* To reach more customers without taking on the selling function, some producers sell their products to retailers, who then sell to consumers.

- *Producer to wholesaler to retailer to consumer.* Most manufacturers of supermarket and drugstore items rely on even longer channels. They sell their products to wholesalers, who in turn sell to the retailers.

- *Producer to agent/broker to wholesaler to retailer to consumer.* Additional channel levels are common in certain industries, such as agriculture, where specialists are required to negotiate transactions or to perform other functions.

Market Coverage

The appropriate market coverage—the number of wholesalers or retailers that will carry a product—depends on a number of factors in the marketing strategy. Inexpensive convenience goods or organizational supplies such as computer paper and pens sell best if they are available in as many outlets as possible. Such **intensive distribution** requires wholesalers and retailers of many types. In contrast, shopping goods (goods that require some thought before being purchased such as Sub-Zero refrigerators) require different market coverage because customers shop for such products by comparing features and prices. For these items, the best strategy is usually **selective distribution**, selling through a limited number of outlets that can give the product adequate sales and service support. If producers of expensive specialty, luxury, or technical products do not sell directly to customers, they may choose **exclusive distribution**, offering products in only one outlet in each market area.

intensive distribution
Market coverage strategy that tries to place a product in as many outlets as possible

selective distribution
Market coverage strategy that uses a limited number of outlets to distribute products

exclusive distribution
Market coverage strategy that gives intermediaries exclusive rights to sell a product in a specific geographical area

EXHIBIT 11.5

Common Distribution Channel Models

Producers of consumer and business goods and services must analyze the available channels of distribution for their products so they can select the channels that best meet their marketing objectives and their customers' needs.

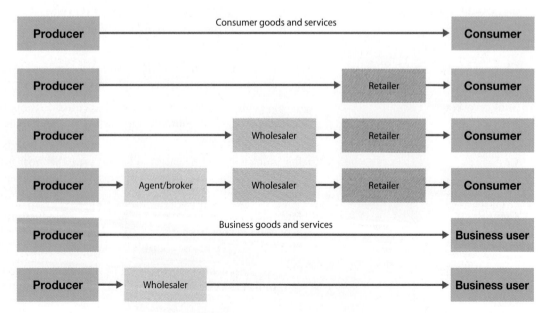

| Producer | | | | Consumer goods and services | Consumer |

Cost

Cost plays a major role in determining a firm's channel selection (and it is one of the major reasons that so many small companies have come to life on the Internet). Small or new producers often cannot afford to perform many of the functions required to sell to either retailers or consumers, so they need the help of intermediaries. Of course, those intermediaries don't work for free, so the producers need to compensate them either by selling products to intermediaries at a discount or paying commissions when intermediaries sell products to the final customer.

Control

A third issue to consider when selecting distribution channels is control of how, where, when, and for how much your product is sold. Longer distribution channels mean less control for producers, who become increasingly distant from sellers and buyers as the number of intermediaries multiplies. On the other hand, companies may not want to concentrate too many distribution functions in the hands of too few intermediaries.

Marketers of luxury products often use exclusive distribution through carefully selected stores to ensure an optimum shopping experience for their customers.

Control is important because a brand's reputation is closely linked to the performance and market perceptions of the channel partners it selects. For instance, a designer of high-priced purses, such as Kate Spade or Louis Vuitton, generally limits distribution to exclusive boutiques or high-end retail stores such as Neiman Marcus. Otherwise, the brand could lose some of its appeal. Similarly, producers of complex technical products such as X-ray machines don't want their products handled by unqualified intermediaries that can't provide adequate customer service.

Channel Conflict

Because the success of individual channel members depends on the success of the entire channel system, ideally all channel members work together smoothly. However, individual channel members must also run their own businesses profitably, which means they can disagree on the roles each member should play. Such disagreements create **channel conflict**.[17]

A common source of channel conflict is the decision by manufacturers to sell products directly to the same target market as its existing channel partners. The advent of e-commerce created quite a few of these conflicts, with manufacturers selling directly from their websites, in competition with the retailers in their distribution mix. Conflict can also occur when a manufacturer establishes or expands its own retail stores and thereby begins to compete with the retailers that carry its products. As Apple continues to expand its retail presence with nearly 200 retail stores across the United States, some of the independent retailers that carry its products are getting uncomfortable. "It's adversarial. Apple would like to sell everything themselves," says the owner of MacHeads in Lancaster, Pennsylvania.[18]

channel conflict
Disagreements between channel partners over pricing, product availability, and other distribution matters

Managing Physical Distribution

Physical distribution encompasses all the activities required to move finished products from the producer to the customer, including order processing, inventory control, warehousing, materials handling, and outbound transportation (see Exhibit 11.6). For many companies, **logistics**—the planning and movement of goods and information throughout the supply chain—has become a strategic priority.

In any industry, the key to success in managing physical distribution is to achieve a competitive level of customer service at the lowest total cost. Doing so requires trade-offs because as the level of service improves, the cost of distribution usually increases. For instance, if you reduce the level of inventory to cut your storage costs, you run the risk of being unable to fill orders in a timely fashion. Or, if you use slower forms of transportation, you can reduce your shipping costs, but you might aggravate customers.

physical distribution
All the activities required to move finished products from the producer to the customer

logistics
The planning, movement, and flow of goods and related information throughout the supply chain

EXHIBIT 11.6

Steps in the Physical Distribution Process

The phases of a distribution system should mesh as smoothly as the cogs in a machine. Because the steps are interrelated, a change in one phase can affect the other phases. The objective of the process is to provide a target level of customer service at the lowest overall cost.

Forecasting → Inventory control → Warehousing → Materials handling → Outbound transportation

Order processing

The trick is to optimize the *total* cost of achieving the desired level of service. This optimization requires a careful analysis of each step in the distribution process in relation to every other step in the physical distribution process:

- *Order processing.* Order processing involves preparing orders for shipment and receiving orders when shipments arrive. It includes a number of activities, such as checking the customer's credit, recording the sale, making the appropriate accounting entries, arranging for the item to be shipped, adjusting the inventory records, and billing the customer.

- *Inventory control.* Trying to balance supply and demand throughout the distribution chain is an ongoing challenge, particularly for long channels that involve multiple companies. Supply chain management software can play a vital role in ensuring the smooth flow of goods.

warehouse
Facility for storing inventory

distribution centers
Warehouse facilities that specialize in collecting and shipping merchandise

- *Warehousing.* Products held in inventory are physically stored in a **warehouse**, which may be owned by the manufacturer, by an intermediary, or by a private company that leases space to others. **Distribution centers** serve as command posts for moving products to customers. In a typical distribution center, goods produced at a company's various locations are collected, sorted, coded, and redistributed to fill customer orders. Shipping firms such as FedEx and UPS and major retailers such as Wal-Mart and Amazon.com have invested millions of dollars in state-of-the-art automated distribution centers.

materials handling
Movement of goods within a firm's warehouse terminal, factory, or store

- *Materials handling.* An important part of warehousing activities is **materials handling**, the movement of goods within and between physical distribution facilities. Materials handling also involves keeping track of inventory so that the company knows where in the distribution process its goods are located and when they need to be moved.

- *Outbound transportation.* The cost of transportation is often the largest single item in the overall cost of physical distribution. Five common types of outbound transportation are railways, trucks, ships, airplanes, and pipelines. When choosing among these five modes of transportation, managers consider such factors as storage, financing, sales, inventory size, speed, product perishability, dependability, and flexibility.

Moving goods quickly, accurately, and safely is a strategic priority for every company that depends on physical distribution.

Developing Customer Communication Strategies

Customer communication, including promotion, is the fourth major element in the marketing mix. As Chapter 9 explains, *promotion* is the traditional term for these activities, but *customer communication* is a more comprehensive term that includes both nontraditional social media and post-sales communication activities—both of which are vital to marketing these days. Promotion is still at the center of all these efforts, but be sure to approach these activities with the notion of talking *with* your customers, not *at* them. With so many communication channels at your disposal, it's vital to develop a **promotional strategy** or *communication strategy* that identifies your communication goals, your core message, your market approach, and your communication mix.

Setting Your Communication Goals

You can use communication to achieve four basic goals: to inform, to persuade, to remind, and to support. *Informing* is the first promotional priority, because people cannot buy something until they are aware of it and know what it can do for them. Potential customers need to know where the item can be purchased, how much it costs, and how to use it. *Persuading* is also an important priority, because most people need to be encouraged to purchase something new or to switch brands. Advertising that meets this goal is classified as **persuasive advertising**. *Reminding* the customer of the product's availability and benefits is also important, because such reminders stimulate additional purchases. The term for such promotional efforts is **reminder advertising**. *Supporting* customers may not strike you as a marketing function, but it is essential to ensuring customer satisfaction—which increases opportunities for repeat business from existing customers and referrals to new customers.

Beyond these general objectives, your communication strategy should accomplish specific objectives. Examples include attracting new customers, increasing product usage among existing customers, helping distributors, stabilizing sales, boosting brand-name recognition, generating sales leads, differentiating the product, and influencing decision makers.

Defining Your Message

After establishing communication goals, your next step is to define your *message*. This is the single most important idea you hope to convey to the target audience about your product or your company. Ideally, the message can be expressed in a single sentence, such as "The Caterpillar 330D Ultra High Demolition Excavator can increase productivity at every stage of the most demanding demolition projects."[19] From this foundation, the marketing team can then develop advertisements, sales presentations, website content, webcasts—you name it, all based on the core message. Each communication effort can expand on the core message as appropriate. For instance, advertisements try to communicate a few key points quickly, without going into great detail. A sales presentation could go into more detail, and a technical brochure or a website can provide extensive detail.

All promotional messages fall on a spectrum from purely logical to purely emotional; most combine both types of appeals (see Exhibit 11.7). The basic approach with a logical appeal is to make a claim based on a rational argument supported by solid evidence. In the case of the Caterpillar excavator (a 200,000-pound behemoth designed to knock down buildings), the logical appeal would provide evidence to back up the claims of increased productivity.

promotional strategy
Statement or document that defines the direction and scope of the promotional activities that a company will use to meet its marketing objectives

persuasive advertising
Advertising designed to encourage customers to try new products or to switch brands

reminder advertising
Advertising intended to remind existing customers of a product's availability and benefits

Learning from Business Blunders

Oops: In one of the e-newsletters that it regularly sends out to suggest party ideas and thereby encourage use of its web-based event planning services, Evite suggested that the Yom Kippur holiday would be a good "reason to party." Not a move likely to foster a positive response from Jewish members of their audience, for whom Yom Kippur is a day of solemn atonement for one's sins. The company responded with an apology the following day.

What You Can Learn: Whether Evite staffers failed to recognize the nature of the Yom Kippur holiday or simply made a mistake when compiling their newsletter, the result was an embarrassing promotional blunder. When writing promotional messages, you must take great care with references to any aspect of people's culture, whether it's adhering to a particular religious faith, being a single parent, being young, being old—or any of the dozens of other variables that define the human experience.

EXHIBIT 11.7

The Spectrum of Emotional and Logical Appeals

All marketing messages strike a balance between logical and emotional appeals. Premier Building Systems, a maker of building materials, relies primarily on logical appeals. At the other extreme, the Diamond Trading Company relies almost entirely on emotional appeals on its website. Gladiator® GarageWorks lies somewhere between these two, emphasizing both the logical and emotional advantages of its garage organizers.

To help convince home builders to use its innovative panel system instead of traditional frame construction, Premier Building Systems focuses on logical factors such as cost, efficiency, and quality.

Gladiator® GarageWorks uses a combination of logical and emotional appeals by promising to make your garage "a place to work, entertain and show off to your friends and neighbors."

Gladiator® GarageWorks website photograph used with permission of Whirlpool Corporation

The Diamond Trading Company uses an appeal that is entirely emotional (for instance, it doesn't attempt to promote the investment value of a diamond).

In contrast, an emotional appeal calls on audience feelings and sympathies rather than facts, figures, and rational arguments. For instance, you can make use of the emotion surrounding certain words. The word *freedom* evokes strong feelings, as do words such as *success, prestige, passion, security,* and *comfort.*

Deciding on Your Market Approach

The selection of your communication mix also depends on whether you plan to focus your marketing effort on intermediaries or on final customers. With a **push strategy**, a producer focuses on intermediaries, trying to persuade wholesalers or retailers to carry its products and promote them to their customers. Conversely, with a **pull strategy**, the producer appeals directly to end customers. Customers learn of the product through these communication efforts and request it from retailers, in the case of consumers, or wholesalers, in the case of business customers (see Exhibit 11.8). If you hear a TV commercial telling you to "ask your pharmacist about" a specific product, the company is using a pull strategy. Many companies use both push and pull strategies to increase the impact of their promotional efforts.

Selecting Your Communication Mix

With clear goals, a compelling message, and a push/pull strategy in place, the next step is to implement the various communication tools that make up the **communication mix**, or *promotional mix*. The tools available include personal selling, advertising, direct marketing, sales promotion, public relations, social media, and postsales communication.

As the number of communication vehicles continues to increase, the need for companies to "speak with one voice" becomes even greater as well. Coordinating promotional and communication efforts across all channels is vital if a company is to send a consistent message and boost that message's effectiveness. In the customer's mind, messages from various sources blur into one single message about the company. Thus, conflicting messages from different sources can result in confused company images and brand positions.[20] **Integrated marketing communications (IMC)** is a strategy of coordinating and integrating all one's communication and promotional efforts to ensure clarity, consistency, and maximum communication impact.[21]

Personal Selling

Personal selling is the interpersonal aspect of the communication mix. It involves person-to-person presentation—face-to-face, by phone, or by interactive media such as instant messaging and webcasting—for the purpose of making sales and building customer

push strategy
Promotional approach designed to motivate wholesalers and retailers to push a producer's products to end users

pull strategy
Promotional strategy that stimulates consumer demand, which then exerts pressure on wholesalers and retailers to carry a product

communication mix
Particular blend of personal selling, advertising, direct marketing, sales promotion, and public relations that a company uses to reach potential customers

integrated marketing communications (IMC)
Strategy of coordinating and integrating all communications and promotional efforts with customers to ensure greater efficiency and effectiveness

personal selling
Personal communication between a seller and one or more potential buyers

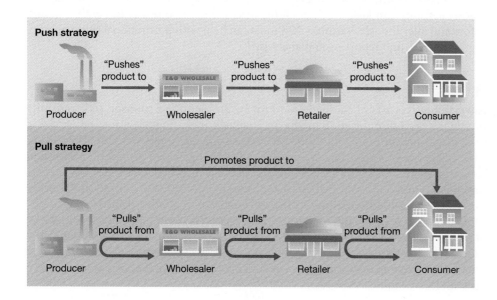

Push strategy

"Pushes" product to — Producer → Wholesaler → Retailer → Consumer

Pull strategy

Promotes product to

"Pulls" product from — Producer / Wholesaler / Retailer / Consumer

EXHIBIT 11.8

Push and Pull Strategies

In a push strategy, the manufacturer "pushes" products through the distribution channel, first promoting and distributing them to wholesalers, who then push them to retailers, who then push them to consumers. In a pull strategy, the manufacturer promotes its products directly to consumers who then "pull" the products through the distribution channel by requesting them from retailers, who then request them from wholesalers, who then request them from the manufacturer. Many companies use a combination of push and pull strategies.

EXHIBIT 11.9 The Personal Selling Process

The personal selling process can involve up to seven steps, starting with prospecting for sales leads and ending with following up after the sale has been closed.

1	2	3	4	5	6	7
Prospecting →	Preparing →	Interviewing →	Presenting →	Handling objections →	Closing →	Following up

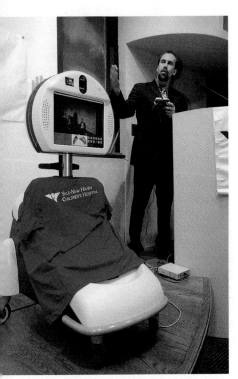

Personal selling is an important promotional element for many business-to-business marketers.

advertising
Paid, nonpersonal communication to a target market from an identified sponsor using mass communications channels

media
Communications channels, such as newspapers, radio, and television

product advertising
Advertising that tries to sell specific goods or services, generally by describing features, benefits, and, occasionally, price

institutional advertising
Advertising that seeks to create goodwill and to build a desired image for a company rather than to sell specific products

relationships. Personal selling allows for immediate interaction between the buyer and seller. It also enables the seller to adjust the message to the specific needs, interests, and reactions of the individual customer. The chief disadvantages are potentially high cost (particularly if travel is required) and the finite number of prospects who can be reached with a given number of salespeople.

Sales situations vary widely, of course; some retail sales happen in a matter of minutes, but complex business-to-business sales can take weeks or months to complete. To make the most of their time, professional salespeople usually follow a fairly structured process that is built around discovering the potential customer's needs and suggesting compelling solutions to those needs (see Exhibit 11.9):

- *Prospecting.* Finding and qualifying potential buyers of the product or service.
- *Preparing.* Considering various options for approaching the prospect and preparing for the sales call.
- *Interviewing.* Learning more about the customer's needs and expectations so they can present relevant and attractive solutions (the best salespeople spend as much time listening as they do talking).
- *Presenting.* Describing a proposed solution to the buyer's needs and possibly demonstrating products.
- *Handling objections.* Seeking to understand any questions or concerns the buyer might raise and providing information to address those issues.
- *Closing.* Asking the prospect to buy the product.
- *Following up.* Checking with the customer after to sale to make sure everything is satisfactory and to build goodwill in anticipation of future sales opportunities.

In addition to careful planning, many companies now take advantage of software tools to manage the sales process. For example, *customer relationship management (CRM)* software can keep track of all the interactions a company has with customers, before and after the sale. Various CRM tools can help with promotional campaigns, customer support, and reporting and analysis.[22]

Advertising

Advertising consists of messages paid for by an identified sponsor and transmitted through mass communication **media**, or channels, including television, radio, newspapers, magazines, or online media (other than a company's own website). The two most basic categories of advertising are **product advertising**, which promotes specific goods and services, and **institutional advertising**, which is intended to create goodwill among stakeholders and build a desired image for a company or other organization. Advertising can also be classified according to the sponsor. *National advertising* is sponsored by companies that sell products on a nationwide basis. The term *national* refers to the level of the advertiser, not the geographic coverage of the ad. *Local advertising* is sponsored by a local merchant. *Cooperative advertising* is a cross between national and local; in such arrangements, companies with products sold nationally share the costs of local advertising with local wholesalers or retailers.

Depending on the medium, advertising can be a cost-effective way to reach thousands or even millions of potential buyers at once. However, to be effective, your messages must be persuasive, stand out from the competition's messages, and motivate your target audience to respond—a lofty goal considering that the average "plugged-in" U.S. resident (someone with regular mobile phone and web usage habits) sees an estimated 3,000 to 5,000 promotional messages every day.[23] As Exhibit 11.10 shows, each major advertising medium has distinct advantages and disadvantages that marketers weigh as they assemble their *media mixes.*

Although its share of advertising budgets in the United States has been slipping in recent years, television continues to attract the largest share of ad spending (roughly half, depending on how it's measured). This is particularly true among major consumer goods companies, automobile manufacturers, and mobile phone service providers—companies that are perennially among the biggest ad spenders in the country. Magazines are the second most popular medium in terms of dollars spent, consistently attracting around 15 percent of ad budgets. Newspapers continue to lose both readership and advertising spending as more and more people look online for the latest breaking news.[24]

The big news in advertising media these days, not surprisingly, is happening online. After a few shaky starts, online advertising has grown rapidly, taking ad budget share away from traditional media. While online advertising still lags behind the other major media in terms of overall ad spending, it is the only medium experiencing meaningful growth and could surpass newspapers in the next few years.[25] The principal advantages of online marketing are audience tracking and targeting, timeliness, global reach,

EXHIBIT 11.10 Comparison of Major Advertising Media

Each of the major advertising media has distinct advantages and disadvantages.

MEDIUM	ADVANTAGES	DISADVANTAGES
Newspapers	Extensive market coverage; low cost; short lead time for placing ads; good local market coverage; geographic selectivity	Poor graphic quality; short life span; cluttered pages; visual competition from other ads
Television	Great impact; broad reach; appealing to senses of sight, sound, and motion; creative opportunities for demonstration; high attention; entertainment carryover	High cost for production and air time; less audience selectivity; long preparation time; commercial clutter; short life for message; vulnerability to remote controls; losing ground to new media options
Radio	Low cost; high frequency; immediacy; highly portable; high geographic and demographic selectivity	No visual possibilities; short life for message; commercial clutter; lower attention than television; lower level of engagement makes it easier to switch stations
Magazines	Good production quality; long life; local and regional market selectivity; authority and credibility; multiple readers	Limited demonstration possibilities; long lead time between placing and publishing ads; high cost; less compelling than other major media
Internet	Rich media options and creative flexibility can make ads more compelling and more effective; changes and additions can be made quickly and easily in most cases; webpages can provide an almost unlimited amount of information; can be personalized more than any other medium through tracking and targeting capabilities	Extreme degree of audience fragmentation (millions of websites); increasing clutter (such as pop-up ads); technical glitches can interrupt ad display; not as portable as magazines or newspapers

relatively low cost, and interactivity—such a compelling blend of communication power that even many advertisers that initially shunned the Internet now embrace it.

Online advertising falls into two basic categories. The first is **search advertising**, also called *search-related* or *search-engine advertising*, which works in conjunction with search engines such as those offered by Google, Yahoo!, and MSN. Search advertising works in two basic ways. First, advertisers can pay to display small ads whenever the keywords they select are used in a search. These are the "sponsored results" that can appear above and to the right of the actual search results. In Google's model, for example, advertisers bid on keywords through an online auction; the more an advertiser is willing to pay for particular keywords, the more prominently its ad is displayed. Second, these ads can also appear on the many websites that are in the search engine's *advertising exchange* or *advertising network*, a collection of websites that sell space on their pages for such ads.[26] These ads are triggered by content on a webpage and can appear anywhere on the page, even inserted between sections of an online article.

The second category is **online display advertising**, which includes the larger visual and multimedia ads you see on many websites. Roughly speaking, search ads are more like the simple classified ads in a newspaper, whereas display ads are more akin to the full-color visual ads in magazines or television commercials. Of course, online display ads can include everything from music video clips to interactive games, which is one of the reasons they are so attractive to companies hoping to break through today's advertising clutter.

The technologies and techniques behind online advertising continue to develop rapidly, so you can expect to see continuous innovation in the coming years. For example, with increasing accuracy, web-tracking technologies will be able to piece together your online habits and display the types of advertising you're most likely to respond to as you surf. Before long, that web-surfing data will be combined with location data (based on where you travel with your mobile phone) and information on television watching habits to target you just about anywhere you go. As you can imagine, this development will yield some powerful advertising techniques—and serious questions about consumer privacy.[27]

In the field of search advertising, the auctioning of keywords is becoming much more scientific, with the use of sophisticated math algorithms similar to those used to make investment decisions in financial markets. New companies have sprung up to help advertisers select the best keywords and make financially prudent bids for them based on expected advertising returns. For instance, one of the leaders in this area, Efficient Frontier (www.efrontier.com), manages over 30 million keyword combinations for its advertising clients and uses a proprietary computer model to help identify the most productive mix of keywords for every search advertising campaign.[28]

Direct Marketing

Direct marketing is defined by the Direct Marketing Association as "an interactive process of addressable communication that uses one or more advertising media to effect, at any location, a measurable sale, lead, retail purchase, or charitable donation, with this activity analyzed on a database for the development of ongoing mutually beneficial relationships between marketers and customers, prospects, or donors."[29] The key distinction between advertising and direct marketing is that advertising involves the purchase of time (in radio and television) or space (in print and online media) from a broadcaster or publisher that then carries the message to the target audience. With direct marketing, companies bypass those media owners and speak directly to their audiences through *addressable* communication vehicles such as direct mail.

Direct marketing is an effective promotional tool for many companies because it enables them to more precisely target and personalize messages to specific consumer and business segments and build long-term customer relationships.[30] The most popular direct-marketing vehicles are direct mail, targeted e-mail, and telemarketing:

- *Direct mail.* The principal vehicle for direct marketing is **direct mail**, which includes catalogs, brochures, videotapes, CDs, and other promotional materials delivered through the postal service or private carriers such as FedEx.

search advertising
Online ads that are linked to search engine results or website content

online display advertising
Larger visual and multimedia ads that appear on websites

direct marketing
Direct communication other than personal sales contacts designed to effect a measurable response

direct mail
Advertising sent directly to potential customers, usually through the mail

Hey! Where Did Everybody Go?

Looking around at today's media-saturated world, it's hard to imagine a time when "mass media" consisted of three nationwide television networks, radio, local newspapers, and a handful of popular magazines. If you wanted to launch a new product nationwide, you simply bought commercial time on ABC, CBS, or NBC, and you would've had a pretty good chance of reaching your target market. Advertisers didn't have to look very far to find consumers because consumers didn't have anywhere else to turn (and they didn't even have remote controls to mute commercials or change the channel).

Fast-forward to the twenty-first century, when advertisers wonder where everybody went. Consumers are still around, of course, but now they're scattered in smaller, isolated pockets all over the media landscape, from blogs to social networking sites to digital cable systems with hundreds of channels. And many people, particularly younger consumers, are spending less time watching TV and more time living online.

How can advertisers reach audiences that won't sit still and won't pay attention when they are sitting still? Nobody has the answer for every situation, but advertisers are trying plenty of possibilities. *Product placement,* in which advertisers put their products right into a TV show or movie, is more common than ever. Did you notice those Coke-logo beverage cups the judges drink from on *American Idol*? Coca-Cola paid $20 million to put them there. Another common move is taking the ads to wherever the customers are, from posters in restrooms to TV screens positioned near checkout lines, gas pumps, and other places people are forced to wait. Highway billboards have gone high tech, too, with flashy electronic displays that can be altered by remote control to catch the eye of drivers stuck in traffic. One company pays college students to wear company logos on their foreheads. Tremor, a promotions company started by consumer giant Procter & Gamble, has recruited several hundred thousand teenagers to help promote its products—without pay. These boys and girls are treated to sneak previews and inside information about various products, and they're only too happy to share the news with their friends.

Television commercials aren't going away, of course, but advertisers are working harder to make them more entertaining and more memorable, if sometimes more risqué or even disgusting in some eyes. If you don't like these new ads, don't think you can get away by switching off the TV to play a video game instead; a number of games now have ads built right into them (and if you play networked games over the Internet, somebody's probably measuring your response to these ads, too).

Of course, every new solution seems to create another round of problems. With ads everywhere, consumers are now complaining that there's nowhere to hide. Until somebody dreams up a better way to reach consumers, though, chances are that wherever you go, you'll find an ad waiting for you—and it might be delivered by your best friend.

Questions for Critical Thinking

1. Do fragmented media make it easier or harder for marketers to engage in segmented or concentrated marketing? Explain your answer.
2. Is it ethical to engage consumers to help promote your products without explicitly telling them you're doing so? Explain your answer.

- *Targeted e-mail.* As millions of consumers and business employees got connected to e-mail in recent years, e-mail looked to be a promising medium for advertising. The ability to reach millions of people inexpensively and direct them to an e-commerce website was a compelling combination. As anyone with an e-mail account knows, however, legitimate e-mail campaigns are now getting buried in a deluge of spam campaigns that vary from the suspicious to the downright illegal. To avoid being tarred with the "spam" label, some legitimate, big-name advertisers, such as Microsoft and T-Mobile, have abandoned mass e-mailing.[31] To avoid the spam problem and to help potential customers get the information they really do want, many companies now emphasize **permission marketing**, in which they first ask for permission before sending e-mail messages (usually through "opt-in" choices that are displayed on their websites). Permission-based efforts also let recipients select the specific information they want, which benefits both recipients and marketers by making the communication more efficient. In fact, many consumers don't mind getting e-mail from companies they do business with, as long as the companies respect their privacy and don't overload them with messages.[32]

- *Telemarketing.* For years, **telemarketing**, or selling over the phone, was popular with direct marketers because of its relative low costs and high efficiency. However,

permission marketing
Promotional campaigns that send information only to those people who've specifically asked to receive it

telemarketing
Selling or supporting the sales process over the telephone

sales promotion
Wide range of events and activities (including coupons, rebates, contests, in-store demonstrations, free samples, trade shows, and point-of-purchase displays) designed to stimulate interest in a product

consumer promotion
Sales promotion aimed at final consumers

coupons
Certificates that offer discounts on particular items and are redeemed at the time of purchase

rebates
Postsales reductions in price; must be applied for by the purchaser

point-of-purchase (POP) display
Advertising or other display materials set up at retail locations to promote products to potential customers as they are making their purchase decisions

premiums
Free or bargain-priced items offered to encourage customers to buy a product

specialty advertising
Advertising that appears on various items such as coffee mugs, pens, and calendars, designed to help keep a company's name in front of customers

trade promotions
Sales-promotion efforts aimed at inducing distributors or retailers to push a producer's products

consumer complaints about interruptions led to the creation of the National Do Not Call Registry in 2003, partially blocking telemarketing access to millions of U.S. homes. (Telemarketers are required to compare their call lists against the registry every 31 days to make sure they remove any newly registered numbers.[33]) The registry does not affect nonprofit organizations or several specific industries, including, ironically enough, the telephone companies themselves. Also, telemarketers are still allowed to call their existing customers, homes not registered on the do-not-call list, and other businesses—which is leading some telemarketers to target consumers at work.[34]

Mobile phones are still an unresolved factor in the field of direct marketing. Telemarketing to mobile phones has been limited so far, partly out of fear that such moves will alienate consumers and partly because using automated dialers to call mobile phones is illegal. However, mobile telemarketing is likely to increase as more consumers get web-enabled phones.[35] Direct marketing via text messaging is beginning to take off, particularly with campaigns that target younger consumers; Generation Y is more comfortable texting and more willing to opt-in to text-messaging advertising.[36]

Sales Promotion

Sales promotion includes a wide range of events and activities designed to stimulate immediate interest in and encourage the purchase of your product or service. The impact of sales promotion activities is often short-term; thus, sales promotions are not as effective as advertising or personal selling in building long-term brand preference.[37] Sales promotion consists of two basic categories: consumer promotion and trade promotion.

Consumer promotion is aimed directly at final users of the product. Companies use a variety of promotional tools and incentives to stimulate repeat purchases and to entice new users. Two of the most common are **coupons**, certificates that give buyers a discount when they purchase, and **rebates**, which let buyers apply for a partial reimbursement of the purchase price. A third widely used consumer promotion technique are **point-of-purchase (POP) displays**, strategically placed presentations in retail stores designed to stimulate spontaneous purchases. *Samples* are an effective way to introduce new products and encourage nonusers to try an existing product, whether it's free food from a grocery store or short-term trial versions of software. Note that many sales promotion activities involve *cross-promotion*, using one brand to advertise another, noncompeting brand. Movies have become a regular vehicle for cross-promotion, for instance, with tie-ins to automobiles, soft drinks, fast food, toys, and other product categories. Finally, sponsoring special events has become one of the most popular sales-promotion tactics. In fact, it's becoming increasingly difficult to find a major sporting, entertainment, or cultural event that isn't sponsored by one or more corporations.

Other popular consumer sales-promotion techniques include in-store demonstrations, loyalty and frequency programs such as frequent-flyer miles, and **premiums**, which are free or bargain-priced items offered to encourage the consumer to buy a product. Contests, sweepstakes, and games are also quite popular in some industries and can generate a great deal of public attention, particularly when valuable or unusual prizes are offered. **Specialty advertising** (on pens, calendars, T-shirts, mouse pads, and so on) helps keep a company's name in front of customers for a long period of time.

Trade promotions are aimed at inducing distributors or retailers to sell a company's products by offering them a discount on the product's price, or a **trade allowance**. The distributor or

Point-of-purchase displays are a widely used sales promotion tactic.

retailer can pocket the savings and increase company profits or can pass the savings on to the consumer to generate additional sales. Besides discounts, other popular trade-allowance forms are display premiums, dealer contests or sweepstakes, and travel bonus programs. All are designed to motivate distributors or retailers to push particular merchandise.

Public Relations

Public relations encompasses a wide variety of nonsales communications that businesses have with their many stakeholders—communities, investors, industry analysts, government agencies and officials, and the news media. Companies rely on public relations to build a favorable corporate image and foster positive relations with these groups.

In fact, successful companies recognize that a good reputation is one of a business's most important assets. A recent study shows that companies with a good public image have a big edge over less-respected companies. Customers are more than twice as likely to buy new products from companies they admire, which is why smart companies work hard to build and protect their reputations. Smart executives not only work to build a positive public image but also prepare a *crisis communication plan* to make sure they're ready to communicate in the event of accidents, financial stumbles, product tampering, or any disaster.

Two standard public relations tools are the news release and the news conference. A traditional **news release** is a short message sent to the media covering topics that are of potential news interest; a *video news release* is a brief video clip sent to television stations. Companies use news releases in the hope of getting favorable news coverage about themselves and their products. When a business has significant news to announce, it will often arrange a **news conference**. Both tools are used when the company's news is of widespread interest, when products need to be demonstrated, or when company officials want to be available to answer questions from the media.

Until recently, news releases were intended only for members of the news media and crafted in a way to provide information to reporters who would then write their own articles if the subject matter was interesting to their readers. Thanks to the Internet, however, the nature of the news release is changing. Many companies now view it as a general-purpose tool for communicating directly with customers and other audiences, writing *direct-to-consumer news releases*. As new-media expert David Meerman Scott puts it, "Millions of people read press releases directly, unfiltered by the media. You need to be speaking directly to them."[38] Similarly, the traditional news conference is being replaced in many cases with *webcasts*, online presentations that can reach thousands of viewers at once and be archived for later retrieval.

Social Media

Customers and other stakeholders are no longer content to be passive listeners in a one-way process controlled by business. They now expect to be active participants in a real conversation—and not only with companies but with other customers. *Blogs*, *podcasts*, *wikis*, *social bookmarking* and *tagging* sites such as del.icio.us (http://del.icio.us) and Digg (www.digg.com), photo- and video-sharing sites such as Flickr (www.flickr.com) and YouTube (www.youtube.com), *social networking* sites such as MySpace (www.myspace.com) and Facebook (www.facebook.com), and other electronic tools that invite participation are known as **social media**.[39]

Today's smart companies are learning to adapt their communication efforts to this new media landscape and to welcome customers' participation. With social media, the vital concepts are enabling, influencing, and responding—not controlling. Unlike with advertising and direct mail, marketers cannot control what is being said about their companies and their products. And unethical attempts at doing so, such as writing fake blogs, or *flogs*, in which a company insider masquerades as an adoring customer, for example, quickly bring the wrath of the online community as soon as they are unmasked.

---

trade allowance
Discount offered by producers to wholesalers and retailers

public relations
Nonsales communication that businesses have with their various audiences (includes both communication with the general public and press relations)

news release
Brief statement or video program released to the press announcing new products, management changes, sales performance, and other potential news items

news conference
Gathering of media representatives at which companies announce new information; also called a press conference or press briefing

social media
Electronic media that invite participation by the general public

Instead, marketers should focus on *enabling* online conversations among customers and product enthusiasts (such as by supporting social commerce efforts that let customers submit product reviews); *influencing* the conversation by offering useful, interesting, and entertaining information; and *responding* whenever people have questions or criticisms. For example, after Michael Arrington, an influential blogger in the high-tech industry, criticized a start-up company called Ning (www.ning.com), the company responded quickly by providing additional information and even inviting him to their offices. By the time Ning went public with its new social networking software, Arrington had learned enough to change his mind and posted a widely read retraction of his initial criticism.[40]

word of mouth
Informal communication between customers and potential customers

Although the technologies of social media are fairly new, the underlying communication mechanism has been around for as long as human beings have been complimenting or criticizing products and product suppliers. **Word of mouth** describes any type of communication between customers and potential customers, and it is vitally important to all companies. Negative product reviews, rumors, and other information can spread across the globe in a matter of hours, and managers need to know what the online community is saying—whether it's positive or negative. *Reputation analysts* such as Evolve24 (www.evolve24.com) have developed ways to automatically monitor blogs and other online sources to see what people are saying about their corporate clients.[41]

widgets
Small software programs that provide part of the functionality of a website

As with online advertising, the field of social media continues to develop rapidly. For example, **widgets** are small software modules that people can drop onto their webpages to add an endless variety of functions and links, from weather forecasts to video clips to movie logos. (Note that the term *widget* is also used to refer generally to products, as in, "building a thousand widgets a month requires careful supply chain management.")

Widgets appear to be simple little webpage features or even just decorations, but they are having a dramatic impact on online marketing communication, for two reasons. The first is technological: Widgets let website publishers replicate parts of their websites all over the Internet. Instead of visiting a dozen websites every morning to get your daily dose of news, sports, and celebrity gossip, you can add widgets from your favorite sites to your personal home page and get everything you need in one place—and you can offer all your widgets to anyone who visits your page. When the music discovery site iLike (www.ilike.com) created a widget that lets Facebook users share music recommendations, the number of visitors to iLike's website jumped so quickly that staffers had to race around in a rented truck, begging other companies to sell spare computer servers to help handle the surge. "We are completely reorienting our entire company to focus on it," founder Ali Partovi says of the widget concept.[42]

The second reason is behavioral: Many people who don't want conventional ads on their blogs or social networking pages are willing to put company-sponsored widgets on their pages as long as the widgets are entertaining or useful.[43] Whether it's widgets or the next online sensation, innovations will continue to reshape social media—which will in turn reshape marketing communication.

Postsales Communication

In many markets, communicating with customers after the sale is every bit as important as communicating with them before the sale. Satisfied customers can be the best sales force a company could hope for, and dissatisfied customers can be a company's worst nightmare. The Internet makes it easy for unhappy customers to find alternatives—and tell thousands of people to avoid doing business with you. Plus, acquiring new customers is usually much more expensive than taking the steps necessary to keep your existing customers. In other words, the failure to keep existing customers satisfied is a very expensive mistake.

Fortunately, many of these mistakes can be avoided with thoughtful, customer-focused communication after the sale. Giving your customers the ability to communicate with someone in your firm is the first step. This sounds obvious, but according to the U.S. Department of Commerce's Office of Consumer Affairs, consumers' number one complaint is not being able to talk to the companies from which they buy goods and services.[44] Beyond that, look for ways to cement the relationship with your customers through communication, such as tips and techniques for using the products they've purchased from you. Even simple steps such as calling customers after they've made a purchase to make sure their expectations were met can have a lasting impact on their perceptions.[45]

Respecting Ethics, Etiquette, and Regulations

Marketing communication in all its forms is a powerful and pervasive force in modern life and, as such, it continues to generate concerns about ethics and etiquette. In response to these concerns, government bodies the world over have enacted a wide variety of regulations affecting both the content and delivery of advertising messages.

In spite of the negative image some consumers have of the advertising business, responsible companies and advertising agencies recognize the vital importance of ethical communication. Professional associations such as the American Association of Advertising Agencies (www.aaaa.org), the Direct Marketing Association (www.the-dma.org), the American Marketing Association (www.marketingpower.com), and the Word of Mouth Marketing Association (www.womma.org) devote considerable time and energy to ethical issues in marketing, including ongoing education for practitioners and self-regulation efforts aimed at avoiding or correcting ethical lapses. For instance, the National Advertising Review Council (www.narcpartners.org), whose members include advertisers, agencies, and the general public, works with the Better Business Bureau to investigate and resolve complaints of deceptive advertising in order to foster public trust.[46]

In addition to ethical concerns, advertisers should also consider the issue of simple etiquette, whether it's the decades-old problem of interrupting consumers at dinnertime with telemarketing calls or newer problems such as respecting privacy in light of increasingly powerful consumer tracking tools. This is a tough balancing act with no easy solution, however. Ads that don't get anyone's attention clearly have no value, but the techniques often used to get attention, from ultra-loud TV commercials to flashing electronic billboards that distract drivers on busy streets, are a frequent source of complaints about advertising's intrusive reach into people's lives. To protect the long-term value of their brands, advertisers need to seek a balance between effectiveness and sensitivity to their audiences.

Not all companies maintain high ethical standards in their advertising, and even those that do can't always agree on where to draw the line, so government regulators have enacted a variety of laws designed to prohibit deceptive and abusive promotion. In the United States, the Federal Trade Commission (www.ftc.gov) has regulations regarding such areas as misleading claims, supporting evidence, fairness in comparative ads, the use of expert endorsements, and the manner in which products are demonstrated in ads. Other agencies address concerns in specific industries, such as the Food and Drug Administration (www.fda.gov), whose concerns include packaging and labeling; the Federal Communications Commission (www.fcc.gov), which oversees radio and television; and the U.S. Postal Service (www.usps.gov), which has authority in areas of direct mail advertising.[47]

For the latest information on customer communication technologies and trends, visit www.prenhall.com/bovée and click on "Real-Time Updates."

How This Affects You

1. Roughly what percentage of all your purchases do you make online? What could store-based retailers do to attract a greater portion of your business?

2. What is your "core message" as a future business professional? How would you summarize, in one sentence, what you can offer a company?

3. Does knowing that advertisers are trying to track your online behavior in order to target you with personalized ads make you want to limit or change your web surfing? Do you think advertisers have the right to do this? Why or why not?

Summary of Learning Objectives

1 Explain what marketing intermediaries do, and list their seven primary functions.

Marketing intermediaries, or middlemen, bring producers' products to market and help ensure that the goods and services are available in the right time, place, and amount. More specifically, intermediaries match buyers and sellers; provide market information; provide promotional and sales support; sort, standardize, and divide merchandise; transport and store the product; assume risks; and provide financing.

2 Explain how wholesalers and retailers function as intermediaries.

Wholesalers buy from producers and sell to retailers, to other wholesalers, and to organizational customers such as businesses, government agencies, and institutions. Retailers buy from producers or wholesalers and sell the products to the final consumers.

3 Discuss the key factors that influence channel design and selection.

Channel design and selection are influenced by the type of product and industry practices. They are also influenced by a firm's desired market coverage (intense, selective, or exclusive), financial ability, desire for control, and potential for channel conflict.

4 Differentiate intensive, selective, and exclusive distribution strategies.

With an intensive distribution strategy, a company attempts to saturate the market with its products by offering them in every available outlet. Companies that use a more selective approach to distribution choose a limited number of retailers that can adequately support the product. Firms that use exclusive distribution grant a single wholesaler or retailer the exclusive right to sell the product within a given geographic area.

5 Identify the seven categories of customer communication.

The seven basic categories of promotion are (1) personal selling, which involves contacting customers by phone, interactive media, or in person to make a sale; (2) advertising, which is a paid sponsored message transmitted by mass communication media; (3) direct marketing, which is the distribution of promotional material to customers via direct mail, e-mail, telemarketing, or the Internet to generate an order or other customer response; (4) sales promotion, which includes a number of tools designed to stimulate customer interest in a product and encourage a purchase; (5) public relations, which includes nonsales communications between businesses and their stakeholders to foster positive relationships; (6) social media, which involves efforts to influence and support the interaction of customers and product enthusiasts; and (7) postsales communication, which helps ensure high levels of customer satisfaction and repeat business.

6 Discuss the importance of integrated marketing communications.

When companies use a greater variety of marketing communications, the likelihood of sending conflicting marketing messages to consumers increases. Integrated marketing communications (IMC) is a process of coordinating all of a company's communications and promotional efforts so that they present only one consistent message to the marketplace. Properly implemented, IMC increases marketing and promotional effectiveness.

7 Explain the purpose of defining a core marketing message.

The core marketing message is the single most important idea you hope to convey to the target audience about your product or your company. Ideally, the message can be expressed in a single sentence. All communication effort can then expand on the core message as appropriate.

8 Describe the use of social media in marketing communications.

With social media, the vital concepts are *enabling*, *influencing*, and *responding*—not *controlling*. Unlike advertising and direct mail, with social media marketers cannot control what is being said about their companies and their products. Instead, marketers should focus on *enabling* online conversations among customers and product enthusiasts; *influencing* the conversation by offering useful, interesting, and entertaining information; and *responding* whenever people have questions or criticisms.

Behind the Scenes

Costco Pushes Its Supply Chain to Satisfy Customers

The merchandise sold at Costco may be similar to that of its two main competitors—Sam's Club and BJ's—but Costco aims to be a cut above by offering many unique or unusual items. Its stores also look slightly more upscale than other club stores, the brands it carries have more cachet, and the products are often a bit more expensive, but they still offer extremely good value. And unlike some discounters, Costco does not offer everything under the sun. The stores actually carry only about 4,000 products, which is a small fraction of the more than 100,000 items stocked by conventional discounters such as Target or Wal-Mart. About 3,000 of Costco's carefully chosen products are a consistent array of everyday basics, from canned tuna to laundry detergent to printer cartridges. The other 1,000 items are a fast-moving assortment of luxury goods such as designer-label clothing, big-name watches, and premium wines. These items change week to week, reinforcing the idea of buying something when you see it because it'll probably be gone next week.

Costco prefers to offer name-brand products and has successfully introduced some branded luxury items such as Kate Spade and Coach purses. However, high-end suppliers such as Cartier and Cannondale flinch at the idea of their goods being sold in a warehouse setting, so carrying those brands isn't always possible. Some suppliers, hoping to protect their higher-end retail customers, have been known to spurn Costco's offers "officially," only to call back later to quietly cut a deal. In other cases, Costco goes on its own treasure hunts, using third-party distributors to track down hot products, even though these "gray market" channels can be unpredictable. And if that doesn't work, Costco can commission another manufacturer to create a lookalike product—leather handbags are one example—with its own Kirkland Signatures label.

To give its millions of members the best prices on everything, Costco negotiates directly—and fiercely—with suppliers. Aiming to be known as the toughest negotiators in the business, Costco's buyers won't let up until they get their target price on the merchandise. Often, the "right" price is determined by how much cheaper Costco can make a product itself. Using this approach, the company has managed to drive down price points in several categories, including photo film and over-the-counter drugs. Costco then passes on the savings to customers, who never pay more than 14 percent above cost.

Costco is rolling through its third decade with strong financial health, a dominant market position, and millions of consumers and business customers that rely on Costco bargains. International expansion is one of the items on Costco's strategic menu for the next few years, although the company will maintain a sensible pace of adding only a few new international stores per year, including additional stores in Asia and expansion into Australia and across Europe. For instance, the company thinks Taiwan could support 20 Costco stores and Japan could support 50, but finding enough land for the giant footprint of a warehouse store—typically 15 acres—that is near population centers but not in areas with zoning regulations that prohibit big-box retailers is a particular challenge in some of these countries.[48]

Critical Thinking Questions

1. If customers repeatedly ask Costco to carry certain items that the company thinks are outside its price/quality "comfort zone" (because they're too expensive or not of high enough quality), should it give in and carry the items? Why or why not?
2. Most of the items on Costco's website are available only through Costco. Should it expand its online product selection to include more commonly available products, since an online store doesn't have the physical constraints of a brick-and-mortar location? Why or why not?
3. If Costco can't find enough land in, say, Japan, to build its usual store format, should it leverage the Costco brand name anyway and build something such as conventional department stores or grocery stores in these areas? Why or why not?

LEARN MORE ONLINE

Visit the Costco website at www.costco.com. What evidence do you see of clicks-and-bricks integration? Are nonmembers allowed to make purchases online? How does the online shopping experience compare to retailers such as eToys (www.etoys.com) or Apple iTunes (www.itunes.com), which sell exclusively online? ∎

Key Terms

advertising (282)
category killers (273)
channel conflict (277)
communication mix (281)
consumer promotion (286)
coupons (286)
department stores (273)
direct mail (284)
direct marketing (284)
discount stores (273)
distribution centers (278)
distribution mix (275)
distribution strategy (269)
e-commerce (273)
exclusive distribution (276)
institutional advertising (282)
integrated marketing communications (IMC) (281)
intensive distribution (276)
logistics (277)

mail-order firms (274)
marketing intermediaries (269)
materials handling (278)
media (282)
merchant wholesalers (270)
multichannel retailing (274)
news conference (287)
news release (287)
online display advertising (284)
permission marketing (285)
personal selling (281)
persuasive advertising (279)
physical distribution (277)
point-of-purchase (POP) display (286)
premiums (286)
product advertising (282)
promotional strategy (279)
public relations (287)
pull strategy (281)
push strategy (281)

rebates (286)
reminder advertising (279)
retail theater (273)
retailers (270)
sales promotion (286)
scrambled merchandising (272)
search advertising (284)
selective distribution (276)
social media (287)
specialty advertising (286)
specialty store (273)
telemarketing (285)
trade allowance (287)
trade promotions (286)
warehouse (278)
wheel of retailing (271)
wholesalers (270)
widgets (288)
word of mouth (288)

Test Your Knowledge

Questions for Review

1. What is a distribution channel?
2. What forms of utility do intermediaries create?
3. What are the two main types of intermediaries, and how do they differ?
4. What are the three basic goals of promotion?
5. What are some common types of consumer promotion?

Questions for Analysis

6. How does the presence of intermediaries in the distribution channel affect the price of products?
7. What trade-offs must you consider when adopting a physical distribution system?
8. Why is public relations an important element of a firm's promotional mix?
9. Do marketers have any control over social media? Why or why not?
10. **Ethical Considerations.** Is your privacy being violated when a website you visit displays ads that are personalized in any way, even if it's just geographically targeted to the local area (based on your computer's Internet address)? Why or why not?

Questions for Application

11. Local Better Business Bureaus monitor thousands of small-business ads each year. If the agency determines

an advertiser is using false or misleading ads and refuses to change the ads, the case is referred to the FTC. Scan your local papers and highlight or clip ads that could possibly mislead the public. What do you find misleading about the ad? How would you improve the ad?
12. **How This Affects You.** Think about an advertisement (in any medium) that had either a strongly positive or strongly negative effect on your attitude toward the product being advertised or the advertiser itself. Why did the ad have this effect? If you responded positively to the ad, do you think you were being manipulated in any way? If you responded negatively—and you are a potential buyer of the product that was advertised—what changes would you make to the ad to make it more successful?
13. **Integrated.** Chapter 4 discusses the fact that supply-chain management integrates all the activities involved in the production of goods and services from suppliers to customers. What are the benefits of involving distributors in the design, manufacturing, or sale of a company's product or service?
14. **Integrated.** Does integrated marketing communications reflect the *systems thinking* approach described in Chapter 4? Why or why not?

Practice Your Knowledge

Sharpening Your Communication Skills

Select a product you're familiar with, and examine the strategies used to advertise and promote that product. Identify the media (website, print, television, radio, billboards, and so on) used to advertise the product. Consider the following:

- Where do the ads appear?
- Who is the target audience? Does the company attempt to appeal to a wide variety of people with differing ads?
- What creative theme or appeal is being used?
- Is the company taking advantage of any Internet technologies for promotion?

Prepare a brief summary of your findings as directed by your instructor. Compare your findings with those of other students, and note any differences or similarities in the promotion of your selected products.

Building Your Team Skills

In small groups, discuss three or four recent ads or consumer promotions that you think were particularly effective. Using the knowledge you've gained from this chapter, try to come to consensus on what attributes contributed to the success of each ad or promotion. For instance, was it persuasive? Informative? Competitive? Creative? Did it stimulate you to buy the product? Why? Compare your results with those of other teams. Did you mention the same ads? Did you list the same attributes?

Improving Your Tech Insights: Individualized Advertising

Don't be surprised if you look out the window one morning to see clouds in the sky arranged in letters that spell out your name and invite you to try a refreshing bottle of Coke or remind you to get your oil changed at Jiffy Lube. Maybe it won't get quite that far, but advertisers are perfecting a variety of technologies that allow them to pinpoint individual audience members with customized messages. Given the continuing fragmentation of mainstream media and advertisers' growing disappointment in mass advertising that no longer brings in the results it used to, individualized advertising promises to be the next big thing in promotional strategies. A few examples: personalized magazine covers (including one that showed an aerial photograph of each subscriber's neighborhood with his or her home or office circled in red), commercials on digital cable systems that can be targeted to viewers in an individual neighborhood or even an individual household (with messages shaped by the demographics of the residents of the house), narrowly focused audio messages that can be aimed at a single shopper in a retail store, and web-tracking technologies that piece together your online habits and display the types of advertising you're most likely to respond to as you surf. In the near future, expect to see web surfing data combined with location data (based on where you travel with your mobile) and digital television watching habits.

Individualized advertising is still a young technology, so you might find a variety of terminology in use. Start by searching for "personalized advertising," "customized advertising," "individualized advertising," "behavioral targeting," and similar terms. Check out the Yahoo! SmartAds program and similar innovations that are likely to appear. Identify one technology or service and in a brief e-mail to your instructor, explain how the system works and how it could make advertising more effective.[49]

Expand Your Knowledge

Discovering Career Opportunities

Retailing is a dynamic, fast-paced field with many career opportunities in both store and nonstore settings. In addition to hiring full-time employees when needed, retailers of all types often hire extra employees on a temporary basis for peak selling periods, such as the year-end holidays. You can find out about seasonal and year-round job openings by checking newspaper classified ads, looking for signs in store windows, and browsing the websites of online retailers.

1. Select a major retailer, such as a chain store in your area or a retailer on the Internet. Is this a specialty store, discount store, department store, or another type of retailer?

2. Visit the website of the retailer you selected. Does the site discuss the company's hiring procedures? If so, what are they? What qualifications are required for a position with the company?

3. Research your chosen retailer using library sources or online resources. Is this retailer expanding? Is it profitable? Has it recently acquired or been acquired by another firm? What are the implications of this acquisition for job opportunities?

Developing Your Resarch Skills

Find an article in a business journal or newspaper (online or print editions) discussing changes a company is making to its distribution strategy or channels. For example, is a manufacturer selling products direct to consumers? Is a physical retailer offering goods via a company website? Is a company eliminating an intermediary? Has a nonstore retailer decided to open a physical store? Is a category killer opening smaller stores? Has a major retail tenant closed its stores in a mall?

1. What changes in the company's distribution structure or strategy have taken place? What additional changes, if any, are planned?

2. What were the reasons for the changes? What role, if any, did electronic commerce play in the changes?

3. If you were a stockholder in this company, would you view these changes as positive or negative? What, if anything, might you do differently?

See It on the Web

Visit these websites and answer the following questions for each one. (Up-to-date links for all websites mentioned in this chapter can be found on the Textbook Resources page for Chapter 11 at www.mybusinesslab.com. Please note that links to sites that become inactive after publication of the book will be removed from the Featured Websites section.)

1. What is the purpose of this website?

2. What kinds of information does this website contain? Please be specific.

3. How is the information provided at this website useful for businesspeople? Consumers?

4. How did you expand your knowledge of distribution and customer communication by reviewing the material at this website? What new things did you learn about this topic?

Explore the World of Wholesaling

Thinking about a career as a wholesale sales representative? The *Occupational Outlook Handbook* is a great source for learning about careers in business. Read the online material discussing the functions wholesale sales reps perform, the skills and experience manufacturers look for in candidates, and how to acquire any necessary training. Find out what a typical day on the job involves. How will you be compensated? Will travel be required? Will you be required to work long hours? What types of reports will you be expected to submit? A career in wholesale sales may be just the thing for you. http://stats.bls.gov/oco/ ocos119.htm

Learn the Consumer Marketing Laws

Thinking about advertising or marketing your product? There are some laws you'll need to obey. Visit the Federal Trade Commission (FTC) website to learn how this agency protects consumers against unfair and deceptive marketing practices. Do you know what the FTC's policies are on deceptive pricing, use of the word *free,* or use of endorsements and testimonials? Find out what it means to substantiate product claims such as "tests prove," or "studies show." Learn what the rules are for unsolicited telephone calls and telephone slamming before you telemarket your product. Tune in to the FTC now and avoid making some serious mistakes later. www.ftc.gov

See How the Pros Put Marketing to Work

MarketingSherpa offers a compelling mix of articles, advice, and on-the-job interviews with marketing experts. The site's valuable content archives require nominal fees, but you can view the material for no charge for seven days after it's first published, so visit frequently to get free insights into real-world marketing challenges. Plus, sign up for free e-newsletters in B2B and B2C marketing, e-mail marketing, marketing careers, and media relations. Check out SherpaBlog for late-breaking news and ideas. www.marketingsherpa.com

Companion Website

Learning Interactively

Log onto www.prenhall.com/bovée, locate your text, and then click on its Companion Website. For Chapter 11, take advantage of the interactive Chapter Quiz to test your knowledge of the chapter. Get instant feedback on whether you need additional studying. Also, you'll find an abundance of valuable resources that will help you succeed in this course, including PowerPoint presentations and Web Links.

Video Case

Revving Up Promotion: BMW Motorcycles

LEARNING OBJECTIVES

The purpose of this video is to help you:

1. Describe the purpose of product promotion
2. Understand how and why a company must coordinate all the elements in its promotional mix
3. Discuss how the message and the media work together in an effective advertising campaign

SYNOPSIS

Although U.S. car buyers are extremely familiar with the BMW brand, the brand has a lower awareness among motorcycle buyers. This is a major challenge for BMW Motorcycles, which has been producing high-end motorcycles for more than 80 years. The company's promotional goal is to attract serious riders who are looking for an exceptional riding experience. To do so, its marketers carefully coordinate every promotional detail to convey a unified brand message positioning the BMW motorcycle as "the ultimate riding machine," as its advertising slogan states. Using print and television advertising, personal selling in dealerships, sales promotion, and a virtual showroom on the web, BMW is driving its brand message home to motorcycle enthusiasts across the United States.

Discussion Questions

1. *For analysis:* What are the advantages of using personal advertising copy and encouraging customers to become missionaries for BMW motorcycles?
2. *For analysis:* Why would BMW use its website as a virtual showroom rather than also selling online directly to consumers?
3. *For application:* What are some ways that BMW might use public relations to build brand awareness?
4. *For application:* How might BMW use direct mail to bring potential buyers into its motorcycle dealerships?
5. *For debate:* Should BMW develop and promote a new brand to differentiate its motorcycles from competing motorcycle brands as well as from BMW cars? Support your chosen position.

ONLINE EXPLORATION

Visit the BMW Motorcycles site, www.bmwmotorcycles.com, and notice the links on the home page. Which elements of the promotional mix are in evidence on this site? How does this site support the company's "ultimate riding machine" brand message? How does the site make it easy for customers to obtain more information and ask questions about BMW motorcycles and dealer services? Do you find the site easy to navigate?

PART 5
Leading and Supporting Employees

CHAPTER 12
Management Functions and Skills

CHAPTER 13
Organization, Teamwork, and Motivation

CHAPTER 14
Human Resources

CHAPTER 12
Management Functions and Skills

LEARNING OBJECTIVES
After studying this chapter, you will be able to

1 Define the four basic management functions

2 Outline the strategic planning process

3 Explain the purpose of a mission statement

4 Discuss the benefits of SWOT analysis

5 Explain the importance of setting long-term goals and objectives

6 Cite three common leadership styles and explain why no one style is best

7 Identify and explain four important types of managerial skills

8 Summarize the six steps involved in the decision-making process

Behind the Scenes

Wegmans Satisfies Customers by Putting Employees First

www.wegmans.com

Thousands of companies repeat "the customer is king" and similar slogans, proclaiming in various ways that customers are their number one priority. Not Wegmans, a regional grocery store based in Rochester, New York. Wegmans makes a clear statement of its priorities: employees first, customers second.

What do customers think about this, you ask? They love it. Customers routinely drive miles out of their way, past other grocery stores, to shop at Wegmans. The company receives thousand of letters of praise every year from current customers—and several thousand more letters from consumers in cities where it doesn't have stores, begging the chain to open a Wegmans nearby.

Such enthusiasm has helped the company post a solid record of success since its founding back in 1915. As a private company, Wegmans isn't required to report its financial results to the public, but the numbers that are available are impressive. Its operating margin (a measure of profitability) is twice as high as national chains such as Safeway and Kroger. Sales per square foot, a key measure of selling efficiency, are estimated to be 50 percent higher than the industry average. The *Wall*

Wegmans CEO Danny Wegman carries on the family tradition of satisfying customers by paying attention to employees and their needs.

Street Journal once called Wegmans the "best chain in the country, maybe in the world."

Such results would be impressive in any industry, but they're almost unfathomable in the grocery retailing business, one of the toughest industries on earth. Most grocery retailers struggle with constant price wars that guarantee paper-thin profit margins (making one or two cents on every dollar of revenue is typical), frequent labor troubles, high employee turnover, and a customer base that views most grocery stores as virtually indistinguishable. And as if those problems weren't enough, grocers across the country face the steamrolling cost efficiencies of Wal-Mart and other discount mass merchandisers, which have already captured a third of the grocery business in the United States.

If you were Danny Wegman, the company's third-generation CEO, how would you sustain the Wegmans way of doing business in the face of relentless competitive pressures? How would you hold your own against the giant discounters that have rampaged through the grocery industry? How would you make sure that Wegmans attracts the best employees in the business and keeps them satisfied and productive?[1] ■

The Four Basic Functions of Management

Whether they are front-line supervisors or top executives like Danny Wegman (profiled in the chapter opener), managers play a vital role in every organization. The job is far from simple. According to one recent survey, more than a third of the people who take on new managerial positions fail within the first 18 months.[2] If you aspire to become a manager, you can take steps to avoid this unpleasant fate by gaining a thorough understanding of what being a manager really entails, starting with the four basic functions of **management**: planning, organizing, leading, and controlling resources (such as land, labor, capital, and information) to efficiently reach a company's goals (see Exhibit 12.1).[3]

management
Process of coordinating resources to meet organizational goals

EXHIBIT 12.1 The Four Basic Functions of Management

To varying degrees at different times, all managers engage in the four primary functions of planning, organizing, leading, and controlling. Although these functions tend to occur in a somewhat progressive order, they often occur simultaneously, and the process is often ongoing.

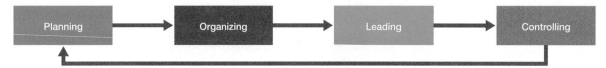

Planning → Organizing → Leading → Controlling

managerial roles
Behavioral patterns and activities involved in carrying out the functions of management; they include interpersonal, informational, and decisional roles

In the course of performing the four management functions, managers play a number of **managerial roles** that fall into three main categories:

- *Interpersonal roles.* Management is largely a question of getting work accomplished through the efforts of other people, so managers must play a number of interpersonal roles, including providing leadership to employees, building relationships, and acting as a liaison between groups and individuals both inside and outside the company (such as suppliers, competitors, government agencies, consumers, special-interest groups, and interrelated work groups).

- *Informational roles.* Managers spend a fair amount of time gathering information from sources both inside and outside the organization. They also distribute information to employees, other managers, and other stakeholders.

- *Decisional roles.* From deciding how to respond to a customer complaint to deciding whether to acquire another company or develop a new product line, managers up and down the organizational ladder face an endless stream of decisions. Many of these decisions are fairly routine, such as deciding which of several job candidates to hire or setting the prices of new products. Other decisions, however, might occur only once or twice in a manager's career, such as responding to a product-tampering crisis or the threat of a hostile takeover.

planning
Establishing objectives and goals for an organization and determining the best ways to accomplish them

strategic plans
Plans that establish the actions and the resource allocation required to accomplish strategic goals; they're usually defined for periods of two to five years and developed by top managers

Being able to move among these roles comfortably while performing the four basic management functions is just one of the many skills that managers must have. The following sections provide a closer look.

The Planning Function

Managers engage in **planning** when they develop strategies for success, establish goals and objectives for the organization, and translate their strategies and goals into action plans. Planning can be considered the primary management function because it drives all the other functions. To develop long-term strategies and goals, managers must be well informed on a number of key issues and topics that could influence their decisions. A closer look at the strategic planning process will give you a clearer idea of the types of information managers need to help them plan for the company's future.

Understanding the Strategic Planning Process

When Wendelin Wiedeking took over as CEO of Porsche, the company was racing toward record losses of $150 million. Few people believed that Wiedeking could get Porsche back on track. But Wiedeking had a clear vision for the company—one that adopted lean and efficient Japanese production systems at Porsche. Thanks to Wiedeking's vision and leadership, Porsche is back in the fast lane.

Strategic plans outline the firm's long-range (often two to five years) organizational goals and set a course of action the firm will pursue to reach its goals. One of the most important questions at this stage is the company's business model—a clear, simple outline of how the business intends to generate revenue. For instance, Marvel Enterprises, which owns the rights to Spider-Man, the X-Men, Daredevil, the Fantastic Four, and more than 5,000 other characters, started as a comic book publisher back in 1939. Today, however, comic books contribute just 15 percent of the company's revenue. Marvel's business model now emphasizes licensing deals with toymakers, movie producers, video-game creators, and other companies that purchase the right to use Marvel characters.[4]

Beyond the fundamental business model, a good strategic plan answers such important questions as: Where are we going? How do we get there? What is the business environment going to be like?[5] The answers to these questions involve every aspect of the company, including product research and design, production, customer communication, distribution, financial management, human resources, and all the company's responsibilities to its various stakeholders. Not only are these questions often difficult to resolve, but many top executives struggle to find enough time to ponder and discuss them. In one survey of large companies, top executives spent an average of only three hours a month discussing vital strategic questions, so simply finding the time and mental energy to do it is one of the key challenges of strategic planning.[6]

To define the long-range plan, managers need extensive amounts of information. For instance, they must formulate budgets, review production schedules, study industry and economic data, research customer preferences and competitive data, and so on. Managers use this information to set a firm's long-term course of direction during the *strategic planning process*, which consists of seven interrelated steps: developing a clear vision, creating a mission statement, performing a SWOT analysis, developing forecasts, analyzing the competition, establishing goals and objectives, and developing action plans (see Exhibit 12.2).

The circular arrangement of Exhibit 12.2 is no coincidence, by the way. Strategic planning should be a never-ending process, as you establish strategies, measure outcomes, monitor changes in the business environment, and make adjustments as needed. The history of business is full of companies that no longer exist because they were unwilling or unable to redirect their strategies as the world changed around them.

Develop a Clear Vision   Most organizations are formed in order to realize a **vision**, a realistic and achievable view of the future that grows out of and improves on the present.[7] For instance, Seattle-based Hydrogen Power sees "the world on the threshold of a

vision
A viable view of the future that is rooted in but improves on the present

EXHIBIT 12.2

Seven Steps in the Strategic Planning Process

For most firms, strategic planning in today's nonstop business environment is an ongoing process involving these seven steps.

new economy—one based on hydrogen fuel, eventually replacing fossil fuel."[8] Such visions can be startling to people whose views of the world—and revenue streams—are locked in the present, but many industries that everyone takes for granted today, from air travel to computers, were also viewed with skepticism and even derision in their formative days. In fact, business visionaries who've been able to see beyond the way things are to the way things could be can rightly take much of the credit for the standard of living that developed countries now enjoy. (Of course, visionaries do miss the mark from time to time; we don't yet have the flying cars and personal robots that some bold thinkers predicted a few decades ago.)

Translate the Vision into a Meaningful Mission Statement   A well-crafted vision statement gives the company a clear target, but to translate that vision into reality, managers must define specific organizational goals, objectives, and philosophies. A good starting point is to write a **mission statement**, a brief articulation of why your organization exists, what it seeks to accomplish, and the principles that the company will adhere to as it tries to reach its goals (see Exhibit 12.3). Typical components of a mission statement include the company's product or service; primary market; fundamental concern for survival, growth, and profitability; managerial philosophy; and commitment to quality and social responsibility.

Note that some organizations use the terms *vision* and *mission statement* rather loosely and even interchangeably at times. One easy way to distinguish them is to think of vision as your view of the future and mission as the role you intend to play in that future.

A well-written mission statement is a powerful call to action. Consider this from Translink, a consortium of public transportation companies in Belfast, Northern Ireland: "To provide a transformed network of coordinated bus and rail services which attracts a growing number of passengers, enjoys public confidence and is recognized for its quality and innovation."[9] Virtually every word in this statement is packed with importance and challenge, from transforming the existing transportation infrastructure to building public confidence through safety and dependability. The collective effort of

mission statement
A statement of the organization's purpose, basic goals, and philosophies

EXHIBIT 12.3 Mission Statement

Kodak defines its mission statement in the context of clearly stated corporate values.

> **Kodak's corporate values:**
>
> - We show respect for the dignity of the individual.
> - We uphold uncompromising integrity.
> - We give and receive unquestionable trust.
> - We prove and maintain constant credibility.
> - We support continual improvement and personal renewal.
> - We recognize and celebrate achievement.
>
> **Kodak's mission:**
>
> With the above mentioned values in mind, we plan to grow more rapidly than our competitors by providing customers with the solutions they need to capture, store, process, output and communicate images—anywhere, anytime. We will derive our competitive advantage by delivering differentiated, cost-effective solutions—including consumables, hardware, software, systems and services—quickly and with flawless quality. All this is thanks to our diverse team of energetic, results-oriented employees with the world-class talent and skills necessary to sustain Kodak as the world leader in imaging.

an entire organization springs forth from this single sentence. Translink employees can use the mission statement to align their own work with the organization's mission, and executives can use it to make sure the decisions they make stay true to the stated mission. For instance, a proposal to open a theme park might have the compelling argument of increasing passenger traffic for Translink, but such a business venture would be outside the company's stated mission.

Assess the Company's Strengths, Weaknesses, Opportunities, and Threats Before establishing long-term goals, you need to have a clear assessment of your firm's strengths and weaknesses compared with the opportunities and threats it faces. Such analysis is commonly referred to as *SWOT*, which stands for strengths, weaknesses, opportunities, and threats.

Strengths are positive internal factors that contribute to a company's success, which can be anything from a team of expert employees to financial resources to unique technologies. For instance, brand loyalty and a comprehensive global infrastructure are among Coca-Cola's strengths.[10] *Weaknesses* are negative internal factors that inhibit the company's success, such as obsolete facilities, inadequate financial resources to fund the company's growth, or lack of managerial depth and talent. Identifying a firm's internal strengths and weaknesses helps management understand its current abilities so it can set proper goals. When Alan Mulally took over as CEO of a seriously ailing Ford Motor Company, he was blunt in his assessment: "We're not competitive and it's been getting worse year after year. The most important thing we can do is recognize our reality and deal with it."[11]

Once you've taken inventory of your company's internal strengths and weaknesses, your next step is to identify the external opportunities and threats that might significantly affect your ability to attain desired goals. *Opportunities* are positive external situations that represent the possibility of generating new revenue. Shrewd managers and entrepreneurs recognize opportunities before others do and then promptly act on their ideas (see Exhibit 12.4). Some opportunities are found in existing markets, going against established competitors by offering more attractive products. In other instances, an innovator creates something so radically different that it redefines a market, as Cirque du Soleil did with its inventive reinterpretation of the circus. Cirque du Soleil is now a multimillion-dollar enterprise in an industry that had been in serious, long-term decline.[12]

Threats are negative forces that could inhibit a firm's ability to achieve its objectives. Most threats are external and include new competitors, new government regulations, economic recession, changes in interest rates, disruptions in supply, technological advances that render products obsolete, theft of intellectual property, product liability lawsuits, and even the weather. Other threats are internal, such as workplace violence. Some companies even view success as something of a threat because it can breed complacency. Toyota, one of the most successful companies in history and now the world's largest automaker, fears it could succumb to "big-company disease" and lose its fierce commitment to continual improvement in every facet of the business.[13]

Develop Forecasts By its very nature, planning requires managers to predict the future, even if it's only to make the assumption that all the employees currently working on a project will still be working on it next week or next month. Forecasting is a notoriously difficult and error-prone part of strategic planning. You need to predict not only *what* will (or will not) occur, but *when* it will occur and *how* it will affect your business. Moreover, the range of variables that must be predicted is immense—everything from product demand to the appearance of new competitors to changes in government regulations. At the same time, forecasting is crucial to every company's success because it influences the decisions managers make regarding virtually every business activity. As Bernardo Huberman, a manager at HP who is involved in the company's efforts to improve forecasting, puts it, "A company that can predict the future is a company that is going to win."[14]

EXHIBIT 12.4 Some of the Greatest Management Decisions Ever Made

Great business decisions can change the world. Here are some of the greatest management decisions made in the last 100 years.

Coca-Cola

- During World War II, Robert Woodruff, president of Coca-Cola, committed to selling bottles of Coke to members of the armed services for a nickel a bottle. Customer loyalty never came cheaper.

Diners Club

- In 1950, when Frank McNamara found himself in a restaurant with no cash, he came up with the idea of the Diners Club Card. The first credit card changed the nature of buying and selling throughout the world.

Holiday Inn

- When the Wilson family of Memphis went on a motoring vacation, they discovered it was not much fun staying in motels that were either too expensive or too slovenly. So Kemmons Wilson built his own. The first Holiday Inn opened in Memphis in 1952.

Honda

- When Honda arrived in America in 1959 to launch its big motorbikes, customers weren't keen on their problematic performance. However, they did admire the little Supercub bikes Honda's managers used. So Honda bravely changed direction and transformed the motorbike business overnight.

Weight Watchers

- After Jean Nidetch was put on a diet by the Obesity Clinic at New York Department of Health, she invited six dieting friends to meet in her apartment every week. In 1961 she started Weight Watchers and helped create the diet industry.

CNN

- Ted Turner launched the Cable News Network in 1980. Few thought a 24-hour news network would work, but CNN has become a fixture in global news media.

Sony

- Sony chief Akito Morita noticed that young people liked listening to music wherever they went. So in 1980 he and the company developed what became the Walkman, the forerunner of all portable music players.

Tylenol

- When Johnson & Johnson pulled Tylenol from store shelves in 1982 after capsules were found to be poisoned, the company put customer safety before corporate profit. And it provided a lesson in media openness.

Dell

- In 1984 Michael Dell decided to sell PCs direct and built to order. By driving costs down, Dell helped make personal computers widespread, which in turn helped spread e-commerce and web-based life in general.

Amazon.com

- With relentless focus on the mundane, behind-the-scenes details, such as warehousing, packaging, and shipping, Jeff Bezos proved that large-scale e-commerce can work.

Managerial forecasts fall under two broad categories: *quantitative forecasts,* which are typically based on historical data or tests and often involve complex statistical computations, and *qualitative forecasts,* which are based more on intuitive judgments. Statistically analyzing the cycles of economic growth and recession over several decades to predict when the economy will take a downward turn is an example of quantitative forecasting. Making predictions about sales of a new product on the basis of experience or on the likely response of competitors to the new product is an example of qualitative forecasting. Neither method is foolproof, but both are valuable tools, helping managers to fill in the unknown variables that inevitably crop up in the planning process.

Regardless of the type of forecast or the variables being predicted, reliable inputs are key. Forecasters collect pertinent data and information in a wide variety of ways, such as reviewing internal data, conducting surveys and other research, purchasing industry forecasts from research companies that specialize in particular industries, and reviewing projections from the many periodicals, industry organizations, and government agencies that publish forecasts on business and economic issues. In the past few years, several companies have been experimenting with an intriguing addition to the forecasting toolkit: a *prediction market*. With this method, which is based on stock market futures trading, a group of people who have insights into the question at hand are given a small sum of money and asked to bet on the likelihood of various outcomes. The theory here is that such markets can be an efficient way to distill the separate pieces of insight and wisdom of a group, rather than relying on a single manager or planner. Prediction markets have improved the accuracy of sales forecasts at HP, new-product idea screening at Eli Lilly, and project management scheduling at Microsoft.[15]

You won't find cheap frying pans at Williams-Sonoma. This retailer competes by focusing on a narrow market: top-of-the-line cookware for gourmet cooks.

Analyze the Competition Every effort to implement strategy takes place in a competitive context, even if it's competing against totally unrelated companies for a share of the customer's budget. With insight into its own capabilities and those of its competitors, a company can then work to gain a competitive edge through at least one of three basic strategies:

- *Differentiation.* A company using differentiation develops a level of service, a product image, unique product features (including quality), or new technologies that distinguish its product from competitors' products. Even though it nearly always matches Wal-Mart on prices of most products, for instance, archrival Target works hard to differentiate itself through a more stylish brand image, lines of new products resurrected from famous designers who've lost some of their luster (such as Isaac Mizrahi and Mossimo Giannulli), and a generally more perceptive finger on the pulse of what consumers consider hip at any given moment.[16]

- *Cost leadership.* Businesses that pursue this strategy aim to become the low-cost leader in an industry by producing or selling products more efficiently and economically than competitors. Cost leaders have a competitive advantage by reaching buyers whose primary purchase criterion is price. Wal-Mart is perhaps the best-known cost leader in the world, keeping prices low by continually squeezing inefficiencies out of its operations and those of its suppliers.

- *Focus.* When using a focus strategy, companies concentrate on a specific segment of the market, seeking to develop a better understanding of those customers and to tailor products specifically to their needs. For instance, Nike competes in a variety of sporting goods segments, but Calloway, TaylorMade, and Tommy Armour focus solely on the golf segment of the sports market.

Many firms gain a competitive advantage by excelling in two of these areas at once, such as Toyota's efforts to excel at both quality (a differentiation strategy) and lower cost. However, pursuing more than one strategic focus at a time can be risky if it leads to mediocre efforts across the board.[17]

Establish Company Goals and Objectives As mentioned earlier, establishing goals and objectives is the key task in the planning process. Although these terms are often used interchangeably, a **goal** is a broad, long-range accomplishment that the organization wants to attain in typically five or more years, whereas an **objective** is a specific, short-range target designed to help reach that goal. For Wegmans, a *goal* might be to capture 15 percent of the grocery market in the mid-Atlantic region over the next five years, and

goal
Broad, long-range target or aim

objective
Specific, short-range target or aim

an *objective* might be to open four new stores in Virginia in the next two years. To be effective, organizational goals and objectives should be specific, measurable, relevant, challenging, attainable, and time limited. For example, "substantially increase our sales" is a poorly worded statement because it doesn't define what *substantial* means or when it should be measured.

Setting appropriate goals has many benefits: It increases employee motivation, establishes standards for measuring individual and group performance, guides employee activity, and clarifies management's expectations. By establishing organizational goals, managers set the stage for the actions needed to achieve those goals. If actions aren't planned, the chances of reaching company goals are slim.

tactical plans
Plans that define the actions and the resource allocation necessary to achieve tactical objectives and to support strategic plans

operational plans
Plans that lay out the actions and the resource allocation needed to achieve operational objectives and to support tactical plans

Develop Action Plans Once you've established long-term strategic goals and objectives, your next step is to develop a plan of execution. **Tactical plans** lay out the actions and the allocation of resources necessary to achieve specific, short-term objectives that support the company's broader strategic plan. Tactical plans typically focus on departmental goals and cover a period of one to three years. Their limited scope permits them to be changed more easily than strategic plans. **Operational plans** designate the actions and resources required to achieve the objectives of tactical plans. Operational plans usually define actions for less than one year and focus on accomplishing specific objectives, such as securing additional financing or opening a new retail channel.

Keep in mind that many highly admired entrepreneurs and executives have stumbled not because they didn't have strategies for success, but because they didn't execute their strategies or deliver on their commitments. Coming up with a brilliant strategy is only a small part of the equation of success; executing is what counts. Wegmans's strategy of supporting its employees and delighting its customers is easy to observe but difficult to copy day in and day out.

Planning for a Crisis

crisis management
Procedures and systems for minimizing the harm that might result from some unusually threatening situations

No matter how well a company plans for its future, any number of problems can arise to threaten its existence. An ugly fight for control of a company, a product failure, a breakdown in routine operations, or an environmental accident could develop into a serious and crippling crisis. Managers can help a company survive these setbacks through **crisis management**, a plan for handling such unusual and serious problems. The goal of crisis management is to keep the company functioning smoothly both during and after a crisis. Successful crisis management requires both comprehensive contingency plans to help managers make important decisions and communication plans to reach affected parties quickly. During a crisis, employees, their families, the surrounding community, and others will demand information. Moreover, rumors can spread unpredictably and uncontrollably, particularly online. You can expect the news media to descend instantly as well, asking questions of anyone they can find.

Companies that respond quickly with the information people need tend to fare much better in these circumstances than those that go into hiding or release bits and pieces of uncoordinated or inconsistent information. The crisis management plan should outline communication tasks and responsibilities, which can include everything from media contacts to news release templates. The plan should clearly specify the people who are authorized to speak for the company, contact information for all key executives, and the media outlets and technologies that will be used to disseminate information. Many companies now go one step further by regularly testing crisis communications in realistic practice drills lasting a full day or more.[18]

The Organizing Function

organizing
Process of arranging resources to carry out the organization's plans

Organizing, the process of arranging resources to carry out the organization's plans, is the second major function of managers. During the organizing stage, managers think through all the activities that employees perform (from programming computers to mailing letters), as well as all the facilities and equipment employees need in order to complete those activities. Managers also give people the ability to work toward organizational goals by determining who will have the authority to make decisions, to perform or supervise activities, and to distribute resources.

Chapter 13 discusses the organizing function in more detail; for now, it's sufficient to recognize the three levels of a typical corporate hierarchy—top, middle, bottom—commonly known as the **management pyramid** (see Exhibit 12.5). In general, **top managers** are the upper-level managers who have the most power and who take overall responsibility for the organization. An example is the chief executive officer (CEO). Top managers establish the structure for the organization as a whole, and they select the people who fill the upper-level positions. Top managers also make long-range plans, establish major policies, and represent the company to the outside world at official functions and fund-raisers. The term *executive* applies to top managers.

Middle managers have similar responsibilities but on a smaller scale, such as for an individual department or facility. The term *middle management* is somewhat vague, but in general, managers at this level report upward to top executives, while first-line managers report to them. In other words, they usually manage other managers, not workers. A smaller company might have a single layer of middle management (or none at all, in many cases), whereas a large corporation could have as many as a half dozen or more layers of middle managers. Many companies today are *flattening* their organizational structures, largely by removing layers of middle management.

At the bottom of the management pyramid are **first-line managers** (or *supervisory managers*). They oversee the work of operating employees, and they put into action the plans developed at higher levels. Positions at this level include supervisor, department head, and office manager.[19] Reducing the number of first-line managers is another step companies are taking to flatten their organizational pyramids. For instance, a company might remove a department supervisor and have the employees manage themselves as a team or may have the employees report up to someone who was previously considered a middle manager.

The Leading Function

Leading—the process of influencing and motivating people to work willingly and effectively toward common goals—is the third basic function of management. Managers with good leadership skills have greater success in influencing the attitudes and actions of others and motivating employees to put forth their best performance.

All managers have to be effective leaders to be successful, but management and leadership are not the same thing. The easiest way to distinguish the two is to view

management pyramid
Organizational structure comprising top, middle, and lower management

top managers
Those at the highest level of the organization's management hierarchy; they are responsible for setting strategic goals, and they have the most power and responsibility in the organization

middle managers
Those in the middle of the management hierarchy; they develop plans to implement the goals of top managers and coordinate the work of first-line managers

first-line managers
Those at the lowest level of the management hierarchy; they supervise the operating employees and implement the plans set at the higher management levels; also called supervisory managers

leading
Process of guiding and motivating people to work toward organizational goals

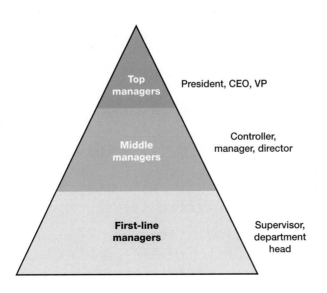

EXHIBIT 12.5

The Management Pyramid

Different job titles designate the three basic levels in the management pyramid.

management as the rational, intellectual, and practical side of guiding an organization and to view leadership as the inspirational, visionary, and emotional side. Both management and leadership involve the use of power, but management involves *position power* (so called since it stems from the individual's position in the organization), whereas leadership involves *personal power* (which stems from a person's own unique attributes, such as expertise or charisma).[20]

Researchers have been studying effective leaders for years, trying to figure out (a) what makes them effective, (b) how to identify potential leaders who possess the same traits as successful leaders, and (c) how to train or develop leadership skills in both current and future leaders. Successful leaders tend to share many of the same traits, but no magic set of personal qualities automatically destines someone for leadership. Nevertheless, in general, good leaders possess a balance of several types of intelligence. IQ, the widely known but often misunderstood *intelligence quotient*, measures a fairly narrow set of human capabilities, such as problem-solving logic. Although IQ is often touted as the standard of intelligence, it is an incomplete measure of human intelligence and a poor predictor of success in leadership.[21]

Do You Have What It Takes to Be a Leader?

The fact that thousands upon thousands of books and articles have been written on the subject of leadership and hundreds more appear every year suggests a couple of things: (1) it's an important and popular topic, and (2) nobody has quite figured it out yet. Recent research suggests that effective leaders are as diverse as the organizations and people they lead; there is no single set of traits that define the ideal leader. Moreover, the media image of the all-seeing, all-knowing CEO who has movie star charisma (and movie star pals) and superhuman powers of persuasion is just that—a media image. All that really matters is whether you can help an organization achieve the right goals in the right way.

While there is no standard set of traits that define great leaders, successful leaders do tend to share a number of skills. Assess your leadership readiness by pondering these questions:

- *Can you listen?* Can you truly listen to what people mean to say, not just what they actually say or what you want to hear?
- *Can you communicate?* If you find yourself frequently being misunderstood, for whatever reason, consider this a warning that you need to improve your communication skills.
- *Can you lead by example?* Are you a living, breathing example of what you want the organization to be?
- *Are you dedicated to the organization's success above your own?* Leaders who put personal power or wealth ahead of the organization's success may shine brightly, but they usually shine briefly.
- *Do you know what makes other people tick?* Knowing what motivates the diverse people around you is crucial to leading them all in the same direction.

- *Do you manage yourself well?* If you can't get your own work done, whether it's meeting deadlines or developing the skills that you lack, your shortcomings will be amplified throughout the organization. For instance, if you're constantly late when making major decisions, you'll slow down every employee affected by those decisions.
- *Are you willing to accept responsibility?* Business leaders sometimes need to make tough decisions that affect the lives of hundreds or thousands of people; will you be ready when it's time to make the tough call or to accept blame for company mistakes?
- *Can you face reality?* Whether they're blinded by their own egos or just simple optimism, leaders who refuse to see the world the way it really exists usually set their companies up for failure.
- *Can you solve problems but stay focused on opportunities?* Leaders who get mired in problems miss opportunities; those who look only at opportunities can get bitten by problems that they should've solved.
- *Are you willing to trust your employees?* If you can't delegate responsibility, you'll swamp yourself with too much work and hinder the growth of your employees.

Questions for Critical Thinking

1. Would it be wise to start a company right out of college, without having gained any experience as an employee in another company? Why or why not?
2. Does leadership experience in school activities (such as student government and athletics) help prepare you for business leadership? Why or why not?

Research pioneered by Daniel Goleman has highlighted the importance of *emotional intelligence*, or *emotional quotient (EQ)*, in both leadership and life in general. The characteristics of a high EQ include[22]

- *Self-awareness.* Self-aware managers have the ability to recognize their own feelings and the effect those feelings have on their own job performance and on the people around them.

- *Self-regulation.* Self-regulated managers have the ability to control or reduce disruptive impulses and moods. They can suspend judgment, think before acting, and utilize the appropriate emotion at the right time and in the right amount.

- *Motivation.* Motivated managers are driven to achieve beyond expectations, both their own and everyone else's.

- *Empathy.* Empathetic managers thoughtfully consider employees' feelings, along with other factors, in the process of making intelligent decisions.

- *Social skill.* Socially skilled managers tend to have a wide circle of acquaintances, and they have a knack for finding common ground with people of all kinds.

In addition to IQ and EQ, successful managers also possess good *social intelligence*. This *social quotient (SQ)* goes beyond the social skills that are part of EQ by looking outward to understand the dynamics of social situations and the emotions of other people, in addition to your own.[23] Finally, researcher James Clawson has identified a fourth key leadership intelligence, which he calls *change quotient (CQ)*, and defines it as the ability to recognize the need for change and to manage that change in an efficient, effective way.[24]

Looking at these four types of intelligence, you can easily see how people who might be logically brilliant (high IQ) could fail as leaders if, for instance, they don't respond well to frustrating circumstances (low emotional quotient), can't understand what makes other people "tick" and therefore can't motivate them (low social quotient), or fear change so much that they disrupt the organization's efforts to grow and adapt (low change quotient).

autocratic leaders
Leaders who do not involve others in decision making

democratic leaders
Leaders who delegate authority and involve employees in decision making

participative management
Philosophy of allowing employees to take part in planning and decision making

laissez-faire leaders
Leaders who leave the most instances of decision making up to employees, particularly concerning day-to-day matters

Developing an Effective Leadership Style

These leadership traits can manifest themselves in a variety of *leadership styles*. Every manager has a definite style, although an individual's style might vary over time and from situation to situation. **Autocratic leaders** control the decision-making process in their organizations, often reserving the right to make all major decisions by themselves and restricting the decision-making freedom of subordinates. Autocratic leadership has a bad reputation, and when it's overused or used inappropriately, it can certainly produce bad results or stunt an organization's growth. However, companies can find themselves in situations where autocratic leadership is needed to stave off collapse.

In contrast, **democratic leaders** delegate authority and involve employees in decision making. Even though their approach can lead to slower decisions, soliciting input from people familiar with particular situations or issues can result in better decisions. As more companies adopt the principles of teamwork, democratic leadership continues to gain in popularity. Meg Whitman, CEO of eBay, is a great example of a democratic leader. Even though she is considered one of the most influential executives in business today, she is well known for delegating decision-making authority and claims that she doesn't consider herself to be powerful.[25] By spreading power around, Whitman is also practicing **participative management**.

The third leadership style, laissez-faire, is sometimes referred to as free-rein leadership. The French term *laissez-faire* can be translated as "leave it alone," or more roughly as "hands off." **Laissez-faire leaders** such as Danny Wegman take the role of consultants, encouraging employees' ideas and offering insights or opinions when asked, and they

Meg Whitman, CEO of eBay, is a great example of a democratic leader. She attributes much of eBay's success to involvement of employees and managers in decision making. "I'm really proud of what we've created at eBay, but I haven't done it alone."

empowerment
Granting decision-making and problem-solving authority to employees so they can act without getting approval from management

emphasize employee **empowerment**—giving employees the power to make decisions that apply to their specific aspects of work.

More and more businesses are adopting democratic and laissez-faire leadership as they reduce the number of management layers in their corporate hierarchies and increase the use of teamwork and technology. However, experienced managers know that no one leadership style works every time. In fact, new research shows that leaders with the best results adapt their approach to match the requirements of the particular situation.[26] Adapting leadership style to current business circumstances is called *contingency leadership*. One of the more important contingency styles is *situational leadership*, in which leaders adapt their style based on the readiness of employees to accept the changes or responsibilities the manager wants them to accept.[27] You can think of leadership styles as existing along a continuum of possible leadership behaviors, as suggested by Exhibit 12.6.

Aside from these styles, leaders also differ in the degree to which they try (or need) to reshape their organizations. *Transactional leaders* tend to focus on meeting established goals, making sure employees understand their roles in the organization, making sure the correct resources are in place, and so on. In contrast, some leaders can "take it up a notch," inspiring their employees to perform above and beyond the everyday, expected responsibilities of their jobs. These *transformational leaders* can reshape the destinies of their organizations by inspiring employees to see the world in new ways, to find creative solutions to business challenges, to rise above self-interest, and to create new levels of success for the company as a whole.[28]

Coaching and Mentoring

coaching
Helping employees reach their highest potential by meeting with them, discussing problems that hinder their ability to work effectively, and offering suggestions and encouragement to overcome these problems

Leadership also carries an important responsibility for education and encouragement, resulting in the roles of coaching and mentoring. **Coaching** involves taking the time to meet with employees, discussing any problems that may hinder their ability to work effectively, and offering suggestions and encouragement to help them find their own solutions to work-related challenges. Aisha Mootry, a supervisor at Chicago's Tapestry Partners media agency, says that coaching benefits both employees and managers. "It says a lot about you as a manager if your direct reports are promotable."[29] (Be aware that

EXHIBIT 12.6 Continuum of Leadership Behavior

Leadership style occurs along a continuum, ranging from boss centered to employee centered. Situations that require managers to exercise greater authority fall toward the boss-centered end of the continuum. Other situations call for a manager to give workers leeway to function more independently.

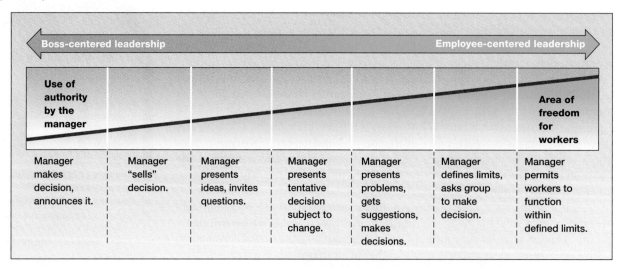

the term *executive coaching* usually refers to hiring an outside management expert to help senior managers.)

Mentoring is similar to coaching but is based on long-term relationships between senior and junior members of an organization. The mentor is usually an experienced manager or employee who can help guide other managers and employees through the corporate maze. Mentors have a deep knowledge of the business and can explain office politics, serve as a role model for appropriate business behavior, and provide valuable advice about how to succeed within the organization. Mentoring programs are used in a variety of ways, such as helping newly promoted managers make the transition to leadership roles and helping women and minorities prepare for advancement. Cigna, a large insurance company headquartered in Philadelphia, emphasizes bringing more women and minorities into its managerial and executive ranks, and mentoring is a vital part of that effort.[30]

Aisha Mootry, shown here with employee Ross Grimes, is a supervisor at Tapestry, a media agency in Chicago. She believes that coaching her employees not only helps them develop but helps her career as a manager as well.

Managing Change

Another important function of leaders is managing the process of change. The stimulus for change can come from any direction, both inside and outside the organization. Internally, a shift in strategy might require changes to the structure of the organization and to the jobs of many people within the company. In other cases managers might identify a need to improve performance or fix organizational weaknesses. For instance, to address the competitive weaknesses he identified after taking over at Ford, Alan Mulally instituted changes in the organization structure the product mix, and even the way executives are developed and promoted.[31]

mentoring
Experienced managers guiding less-experienced colleagues in nuances of office politics, serving as role models for appropriate business behavior, and helping to negotiate the corporate structure

Outside the organization, changes can come from many directions, in many flavors. Some develop over time and are relatively easy to prepare for, such as shifts in demographics. For instance, if your company markets exclusively to teenagers and you observe that birth rates have been declining, you know it won't be too many years before your market will start to shrink. Other times, you know that change is heading your way but you can't reliably predict the effects it will have on your organization. This is often the case with new competitors, new technologies, new regulations, and shifts in political influence. Still other changes come without warning, such as natural disasters and terrorist attacks. Leaders in these situations often need to institute decisive and dramatic changes.

Change presents a major leadership challenge for one simple reason: Most people don't like it. They may fear the unknown, they may be unwilling to give up current habits or benefits, they may believe that the change is bad for the organization, or they may not trust the motives of the people advocating change.[32] As a result, many—perhaps most—change initiatives fail, according to one study.[33] To improve the chances of success when the organization needs to change, managers can follow these steps:[34]

1. *Identify what needs to change.* Changes can involve the structure of the organization, technologies and systems, or people's attitudes, beliefs, skills, or behaviors.[35]

2. *Identify the forces acting for and against the change.* By understanding these forces, managers can work to amplify the forces that will facilitate the change and remove or diminish the negative forces. For instance, if uncertainty is one of the forces working against the change, education and communication may help reduce these forces and thereby reduce resistance to the change.

3. *Choose the approach, or combination of approaches, best suited to the situation.* Managers can institute change through a variety of techniques, including communication, education, participation in the decision making, negotiation with groups opposed to the change, visible support from top managers or other opinion leaders, or coercive use of authority (usually recommended only for crisis situations).

Helping people understand the need for change is often called *unfreezing* existing behaviors.

4. *Reinforce changed behavior and monitor continued progress.* Once the change has been made, managers need to reinforce new behaviors and make sure old behaviors don't creep back in. This effort is commonly called *refreezing* new behaviors.

In many industries and markets, change now appears to be a constant aspect of business, making change management a vital skill for leaders at all levels of the organization.

Building a Positive Organizational Culture

Strong leadership is a key element in establishing a productive *organizational culture*—the set of underlying values, norms, and practices shared by members of an organization. When you visit an organization, observe how the employees work, dress, communicate, address each other, and conduct business. Each organization has a special way of doing things. In corporations, these influences are often referred to as **corporate culture**.

Just as your social culture influences the way you think, what you believe, and how you behave, so too do company cultures influence the way people treat and react to each other

corporate culture
A set of shared values and norms that support the management system and that guide management and employee behavior

---

Creating the Ideal Culture in Your Company

You can't create a culture directly, but you can establish the behaviors and values that in turn do create a culture. Use this list of questions to explore the many ways you can foster a positive culture—and avoid the growth of a negative culture.

COMPANY VALUES

- Have you articulated a compelling vision for the company?
- Have you defined a mission statement, based on that vision, that employees understand and can implement?
- Do employees know how their work relates to this vision?
- Is there a common set of values that bind the organization together?
- Do you and other executives or owners demonstrate these values day in and day out?

PEOPLE

- How are people treated?
- Do you foster an atmosphere of civility and respect?
- Do you value and encourage teamwork, with all ideas welcomed?
- Do you acknowledge, encourage, and act upon (when appropriate) ideas from employees?
- Do you give employees credit for their ideas?
- Have you shown a positive commitment to a balance between work and life?

COMMUNITY

- Have you clarified how the company views its relationship with the communities it affects?
- Do your actions support that commitment to community?

COMMUNICATION

- Do you practice and encourage open communication?
- Do you share operating information throughout the company so that people know how the company is doing?
- Do you regularly survey employees on workplace issues and ask for their input on solutions?
- Is there an open-door policy for access to management?

EMPLOYEE PERFORMANCE

- Do you handle personnel issues with fairness and respect?
- Do employees receive feedback regularly?
- Are employee evaluations based on agreed-upon objectives that have been clearly communicated?

Questions for Critical Thinking

1. How might a job candidate find the answers to these questions?
2. Why is it important to learn about the company's culture before accepting a job?

and to customers and suppliers. Culture shapes the way employees feel about the company and the work they do; the way they interpret and perceive the actions taken by others; the expectations they have regarding changes in their work or in the business; and their ability to lead, be productive, and choose the best course of action. For example, in a meeting at *Consumer Reports*'s auto testing facility, a group of Ford engineers became increasingly defensive as the magazine's editors pointed out some design flaws in the company's cars. Alan Mulally stopped the meeting and handed the engineers notepads with the advice, "You know what? Let's just listen and take notes." He was sending a message that Ford's culture of rationalizing mistakes, rather than facing them and fixing them, needed to change.[36]

Positive cultures create an environment that encourages employees to make ethical decisions for the good of the company and its customers. At companies with legendary corporate cultures, such as Nordstrom and Southwest Airlines, employees routinely go the extra mile to make sure customers are treated well. In contrast, negative, dysfunctional cultures can lead employees to make decisions that are bad for customers, bad for the company—and even unethical or illegal.

The Controlling Function

Controlling is the fourth managerial function. In management, **controlling** means monitoring a firm's progress toward meeting its organizational goals and objectives, resetting the course if goals or objectives change in response to shifting conditions, and correcting deviations if goals or objectives are not being attained. Rather than focus primarily on financial results, many companies now use a **balanced scorecard**, which monitors the performance from four perspectives: finances, operations, customer relationships, and the growth and development of employees and intellectual property.[37]

One of the most important performance variables that fall under managerial control is **quality**—a measure of how closely goods or services conform to predetermined standards and customer expectations. Many firms control for quality through a four-step cycle that involves all levels of management and all employees (see Exhibit 12.7). In the first step, top managers set **standards**, or criteria for measuring the performance of the organization as a whole. At the same time, middle and first-line managers set departmental quality standards so they can meet or exceed company standards. Establishing control standards is

controlling
Process of measuring progress against goals and objectives and correcting deviations if results are not as expected

balanced scorecard
Method of monitoring the performance from four perspectives: finances, operations, customer relationships, and the growth and development of employees and intellectual property

quality
A measure of how closely a product conforms to predetermined standards and customer expectations

standards
Criteria against which performance is measured

EXHIBIT 12.7 The Control Cycle

The control cycle has four basic steps: (1) On the basis of strategic goals, top managers set the standards by which the organization's overall performance will be measured. (2) Managers at all levels measure performance. (3) Actual performance is compared with the standards. (4) Appropriate corrective action is taken (if performance meets standards, nothing other than encouragement is needed; if performance falls below standards, corrective action may include improving performance, establishing new standards, changing plans, reorganizing, or redirecting efforts).

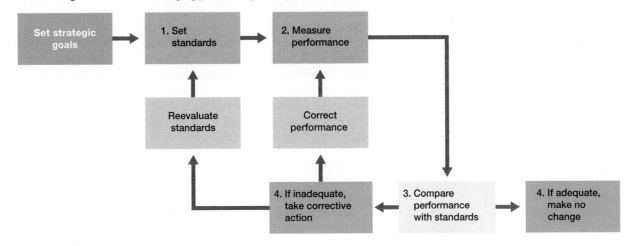

Learning from Business Blunders

Oops: When the worst blackout in North American history shut off electrical power to 50 million people in the eastern United States and Canada and drained up to $10 billion from the U.S. and Canadian economies in the summer of 2003, both countries discovered just what a complicated managerial challenge the power industry faces. Electrical suppliers and customers are connected via a complex grid of transmission lines that ensure continued power even as supply and demand ebb and flow in various parts of the grid. Every power station has automatic controls that prevent the grid from drawing too much power, which can happen when demand rises across the grid or when other stations reduce the power they make available to the grid. The system can usually respond to localized power shortages by managing availability, but power station operators need to know what's going on to make these decisions.

Believe it or not, this economic disaster was triggered by a few trees. Three high-voltage lines in Ohio owned by the power company FirstEnergy shorted out when they came into contact with trees that should have been trimmed but weren't. Then FirstEnergy's monitoring facility didn't detect the problem because its computer system wasn't operating properly and employees weren't trained adequately. Because the company didn't respond to its own problems or alert other power generators, a surge of unmet demand for electricity began to roll through the grid—which set off automatic protection systems at other stations across the grid and continued to compound the problem until it rolled all the way to the East Coast.

What You Can Learn: The events leading up to this massive blackout yielded several key business lessons: (1) Monitoring and control, based on reliable data, are essential to the operation of every business; (2) unless they are detected and dealt with quickly, relatively small mistakes can mushroom into huge problems—and complex systems need vigorous, constant scrutiny; (3) employee training and system maintenance are crucial—managers can't just assume that people or systems will work properly; (4) when various independent business entities are connected (either literally connected, as in the power industry, or financially connected, as in banking, for instance), problems can spread quickly. The bottom line: Know yourself—and your business partners.

closely tied to the planning function and depends on information supplied by employees, customers, and other external sources. Examples of specific standards might be "Produce 1,500 circuit boards monthly with less than 1 percent failures." A common approach to setting standards is **benchmarking**, or collecting and comparing data on business practices in other companies and other industries. The variables companies benchmark range from information systems and knowledge managing to human resource practices and financial returns.[38] HP, the computer and printer giant, benchmarks itself against competitors in multiple ways. "We want to be the best in class" in every business function says an executive.[39]

In the second step of the control cycle, managers assess performance, using both quantitative (specific, numerical) and qualitative (subjective) performance measures. In the third step, managers compare performance with the established standards and search for the cause of any discrepancies. If the performance falls short of standards, the fourth step is to take corrective action. If performance meets or exceeds standards, no corrective action is taken. As Exhibit 12.7 shows, if everything is operating smoothly, controls permit managers to repeat acceptable performance. If results are below expectations, controls help managers take any necessary action, which can range from a minor adjustment in the recipe on a food production line to a complete strategic shift.

benchmarking
Collecting and comparing process and performance data from other companies

Management Skills

Managers rely on a number of skills to perform their functions and maintain a high level of quality in their organizations. These skills can be classified into four basic categories: *interpersonal, technical, conceptual,* and *decision-making*. As managers rise through the organization's hierarchy, they may need to strengthen their abilities in one or more of these skills. Such managers may also need to de-emphasize skills that helped them in lower-level jobs and develop different skills. For instance, staying closely involved with project details is often a plus for first-line supervisors, but it can lead to serious performance issues for higher-level managers who should be spending time on more strategic issues.[40]

Interpersonal Skills

interpersonal skills
Skills required to understand other people and to interact effectively with them

The various skills required to communicate with other people, work effectively with them, motivate them, and lead them are **interpersonal skills**. Because managers mainly get things done through people at all levels of the organization, they need good interpersonal skills in countless situations. Encouraging employees to work together toward common goals, interacting with employees and other managers, negotiating with partners and suppliers, developing employee trust and loyalty, and fostering innovation—all these activities require interpersonal skills.

Communication, or exchanging information, is the most important and pervasive interpersonal skill that managers use. Effective communication not only increases the manager's and the organization's productivity but also shapes the impressions made on colleagues, employees, supervisors, investors, and customers. In your role as a manager, communication allows you to perceive the needs of these stakeholders (your first step toward satisfying them), and it helps you respond to those needs.[41] Moreover, as the workforce becomes more diverse—and as more companies recognize the value of embracing diversity in their workforces—managers need to adjust their interactions with others, communicating in a way that considers the different needs, backgrounds, experiences, and expectations of their workforces.

Technical Skills

A person who knows how to operate a machine, prepare a financial statement, program a computer, or pass a football has **technical skills**; that is, the individual has the knowledge and ability to perform the mechanics of a particular job. Technical skills are most important at lower organizational levels because managers at these levels work directly with employees who are using the tools and techniques of a particular specialty, such as automotive assembly or computer programming. Still, today's managers must have a strong technology background, not only to make good decisions about investments in their own facilities and systems but also to understand changes in the external environment.

technical skills
Ability and knowledge to perform the mechanics of a particular job

In today's increasingly technology-driven business environment, managers often need to have a solid understanding of the processes they oversee. One obvious reason is that they need to grasp the technical matters if they are to make smart decisions regarding planning, organizing, leading, and controlling. They don't necessarily need to be technical experts, but they do need to be able to understand the advice and input that technical experts give them. Another key reason for understanding technical matters is that demonstrating a level of technical aptitude gives managers credibility in the eyes of their employees. Maria Azua, vice president of technology and innovation at IBM, says her experience as a programmer earlier in her career helped her earn respect from the people she now leads. "They don't see me as a stodgy executive who doesn't understand, because I've done the same work they do."[42]

Managers at all levels use **administrative skills**, which are the technical skills necessary to manage an organization. Administrative skills include the abilities to make schedules, gather information, analyze data, plan, and organize. Managers often develop such skills through education and then improve them by working in one or more functional areas of an organization, such as accounting or marketing.[43] Project management is becoming an increasingly important administrative skill. Managers must know how to start a project or work assignment from scratch, map out each step in the process to its successful completion, develop project costs and timelines, and establish checkpoints at key project intervals.

administrative skills
Technical skills in information gathering, data analysis, planning, organizing, and other aspects of managerial work

Conceptual Skills

Managers need **conceptual skills** to see organizations, systems, and markets both as complete entities in the context of their environments and as interrelated pieces of a whole. Conceptual skills are especially important to top managers, since they are the strategists who develop the plans that guide the organization toward its goals. Managers use their conceptual skills to acquire and analyze information, identify both problems and opportunities, understand the competitive environment in which their companies operate, and develop strategies and plans. The ability to conceptualize solutions that don't yet exist, to see things as they could be rather than simply as they are, is a vital skill for executives.

conceptual skills
Ability to understand the relationship of parts to the whole

EXHIBIT 12.8

Steps in the Decision-Making Process

Following these six steps will help you make better decisions.

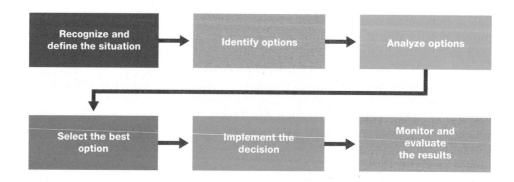

Decision-Making Skills

decision-making skills
Ability to identify a decision situation, analyze the problem, weigh the alternatives, choose an alternative, implement it, and evaluate the results

Decision-making skills involve the ability to define problems and select the best course of action. Most managers make decisions by following a formal process such as the six steps highlighted in Exhibit 12.8:

1. *Recognize and define the problem or opportunity.* Most companies look for problems or opportunities by gathering customer feedback, conducting studies, or monitoring such warning signals as declining sales or profits, excess inventory buildup, or high customer turnover.

2. *Identify and develop options.* The goal of this step is to develop a list of alternative courses of action. A problem that is easy to identify, such as a steady decline in sales revenue, might not have any easy answers. This step requires solid conceptual skills. Managers may need to break old thinking habits and throw away long-held assumptions in order to find promising solutions to tough problems.

3. *Analyze the options.* Once the ideas have been generated, most companies develop a list of decision-making criteria such as cost, feasibility, availability of existing resources, market acceptance, potential for revenue generation, and compatibility with the company's mission and vision, to evaluate the options. Some companies rank their criteria by importance, assigning a numerical value to criteria so that important criteria receive more weight in the process. This weighting is especially important in cases in which certain criteria, such as cost, labor, or implementation time, are scarce. As you can imagine, this step often involves a great deal of discussion and debate among managers.

4. *Select the best option.* After all options have been analyzed and debated, management selects the best one. For some decisions, the "numbers" can identify a clear choice from among the available options. In other decisions, however, managers might have to rely on intuition and experience to point the way. The systems thinking and systems dynamics methods discussed in Chapter 4 can be powerful tools for comparing options in an objective, clear-headed manner.

5. *Implement the decision.* Once a final option has been selected, it's time to implement the decision. This step generally requires the development of action plans.

6. *Monitor the results.* Finally, managers monitor the results of decisions over time to see whether the chosen alternative works, whether any new problems or opportunities arise because of the decision, and whether the decision should be modified to meet changing circumstances.

How This Affects You

1. What is your personal mission statement for your career and your life? Have you ever thought about your future in this way?

2. Consider a career path that you might pursue upon graduation and perform a quick SWOT analysis. What are some of your internal strengths and weaknesses and external opportunities and threats?

3. Regarding the three basic leadership styles—autocratic, democratic, and laissez-faire—what is your natural inclination? Think about times in school, at work, or in social situations in which you played a leadership role. How did you lead?

Summary of Learning Objectives

1 Define the four basic management functions.

The four management functions are (1) planning—establishing objectives and goals for the organization and translating them into action plans; (2) organizing—arranging resources to carry out the organization's plans; (3) leading—influencing and motivating people to work effectively and willingly toward company goals; and (4) controlling—monitoring progress toward organizational goals, resetting the course if goals or objectives change in response to shifting conditions, and correcting deviations if goals or objectives are not being attained.

2 Outline the strategic planning process.

The strategic planning process begins with a clear vision for the company's future. This vision is then translated into a mission statement so it can be shared with all members of the organization. Next, managers assess the company's strengths, weaknesses, opportunities, and threats; they develop forecasts about future trends that affect their industry and products; and they analyze the competition—paying close attention to their strengths and weaknesses so that they can use this information to gain a competitive edge. Managers use this information to establish company goals and objectives. Finally, they translate these goals and objectives into action plans.

3 Explain the purpose of a mission statement.

A mission statement defines why the organization exists, what it does, what it hopes to achieve, and the principles it will abide by to meet its goals. It is used to bring clarity of focus to members of the organization and to provide guidelines for the adoption of future projects.

4 Discuss the benefits of SWOT analysis.

An organization identifies its strengths, weaknesses, opportunities, and threats prior to establishing long-term goals. Identifying internal strengths and weaknesses gives the firm insight into its current abilities. The organization must then decide whether new abilities must be learned to meet current or more ambitious goals. Internal strengths become a firm's core competence if they are a bundle of skills and technologies that set the company apart from competitors.

Identifying a firm's external opportunities and threats helps prepare it for challenges that might interfere with its ability to reach its goals.

5 Explain the importance of setting long-term goals and objectives.

Goals and objectives establish long- and short-range targets that help managers fulfill the company's mission. Setting appropriate goals increases employee motivation, establishes standards by which individual and group performance can be measured, guides employee activity, and clarifies management's expectations.

6 Cite three common leadership styles, and explain why no one style is best.

Three common leadership styles are autocratic, democratic, and laissez-faire (also called free-rein). Each may work best in a given situation: autocratic when quick decisions are needed, democratic when employee participation in decision making is desirable, and laissez-faire when fostering creativity is a priority. Good leaders are flexible enough to respond with the best approach for the situation.

7 Identify and explain four important types of managerial skills.

Managers use interpersonal skills to communicate with other people, work effectively with them, and lead them; technical skills to perform the mechanics of a particular job; administrative skills to manage an organization efficiently; conceptual skills to see the organization as a whole, to see it in the context of its environment, and to understand how the various parts interrelate; and decision-making skills to ensure that the best decisions are made.

8 Summarize the six steps involved in the decision-making process.

The decision-making process begins by recognizing that a problem or opportunity exists. Next, managers identify and develop options using a variety of brainstorming techniques. Once the options have been put forth, they analyze the options using appropriate criteria. Then they select the best option, implement the decision, and monitor the results, making changes as needed.

Behind the Scenes

Customers Believe in Wegmans Because Wegmans Believes in Its Employees

The conventional response to all challenges in the retail grocery industry is to just keep squeezing everything—customer service, wages, employee benefits, training, and anything else—to keep prices low and still eke out a profit. However, CEO Danny Wegman and his colleagues are adamant that joining the discounters in a never-ending race to cut, cut, cut is not the Wegmans way. Instead, the company defines its mission as being "the very best at serving the needs of our customers." In pursuit of that mission, the company makes employees its number-one priority and counts on employees to then meet the needs of customers.

To compete successfully against both traditional grocers and Wal-Mart, Wegmans's strategy emphasizes a huge selection of products and employees who know food and love serving customers. The cheese department is a good example. Unlike the typical selection of two or three dozen varieties at most, Wegmans shoppers find four or five *hundred* varieties—and a knowledgeable staff that can help them select and serve the perfect cheese. In fact, chances are the department manager has been sent on a research tour of cheese-producing areas in Europe so that he or she has firsthand knowledge of the tastes and traditions of each region.

Such training is expensive, to be sure. Add in higher-than-average wages and employee benefits, and Wegmans's labor costs are higher than those of its competitors. Moreover, Wegmans managers exhibit a degree of personal concern for employees not often found in the hectic retail industry. As an example, when one manager whose job required frequent out-of-town travel learned that her mother had been diagnosed with cancer, Wegmans executives modified her responsibilities so that she could stay in town to care for her mother—before she even asked.

This investment in employees pays off in important ways. For starters, customers buy more when they understand how to use various products and are successful and satisfied with them. These positive experiences with Wegmans employees also help shoppers build emotional bonds with the store, further increasing customer loyalty. And employees who enjoy their work and feel they are treated with respect are more productive and less likely to leave in search of other jobs. Employee turnover (the percentage of the workforce that leaves and must be replaced every year) is a major expense for more retailers, but turnover at Wegmans is a fraction of the industry average.

The mission to be the best at serving consumers extends to the company's decision-making style as well. For day-to-day decisions, laissez-faire management is widespread; executives want front-line employees to make whatever choices are needed to keep customers happy. Employees have the authority to make whatever choices are needed to satisfy customers. As one Wegmans executive joked, "We're a $3 billion company run by 16-year-old cashiers."[44]

Critical Thinking Questions

1. Wegmans has always been managed by members of the Wegman family. Do you think the company could continue its winning ways if the next generation doesn't want to take over, forcing the company to hire someone from outside the family as CEO? Explain your answer.
2. Would the Wegmans approach work for a car dealer? A bookstore? A manufacturer of industrial goods? Explain you answers.
3. How does low employee turnover contribute to Wegmans's distinct and positive corporate culture?

LEARN MORE ONLINE

Visit the Wegmans website at www.wegmans.com and click on "Employment." On the "Who We Are" page, look for the link to a subpage that explains why Wegmans's employees are proud to work there (or go to www.wegmans.com/about/jobs/why_we_are_proud.asp). Read the quotations from employees and review the top ten reasons for working there. Imagine yourself as someone who wants to join the company. Does the information on this website increase your interest in the company? Could you see yourself launching a career at Wegmans? (For the latest information on Wegmans and managerial skills in general, visit www.prenhall.com/bovée and click on "Real-Time Updates.") ■

Key Terms

administrative skills (313)
autocratic leaders (307)
balanced scorecard (311)
benchmarking (312)
coaching (308)
conceptual skills (313)
controlling (311)
corporate culture (310)
crisis management (304)
decision-making skills (314)
democratic leaders (307)
empowerment (308)

first-line managers (305)
goal (303)
interpersonal skills (312)
laissez-faire leaders (307)
leading (305)
management (297)
management pyramid (305)
managerial roles (298)
mentoring (309)
middle managers (305)
mission statement (300)
objective (303)

operational plans (304)
organizing (304)
participative management (307)
planning (298)
quality (311)
standards (311)
strategic plans (298)
tactical plans (304)
technical skills (313)
top managers (305)
vision (299)

Test Your Knowledge

Questions for Review

1. What is management? Why is it so important?
2. What is forecasting, and how is it related to the planning function?
3. What is the goal of crisis management?
4. What are some common characteristics of effective leaders?
5. Why are interpersonal skills important to managers at all levels?

Questions for Analysis

6. Is the following statement an example of a strategic goal or an objective? "To become the number-one retailer of computers and computer accessories in terms of revenue, growth, and customer satisfaction." Explain your answer.
7. How do the three levels of management differ?
8. How do autocratic, democratic, and laissez-faire leadership differ?
9. Why are coaching and mentoring effective leadership techniques?
10. Ethical Considerations. When an organization learns about a threat that could place the safety of its workers or its customers at risk, is management obligated to immediately inform these parties of the threat? Explain your answer.

Questions for Application

11. What are your long-term goals? Develop a set of long-term career goals for yourself and several short-term objectives that will help you reach those goals. Make sure your goals are specific, measurable, and time limited.
12. How This Applies to You. What's your personality type? Find out by taking the free mini-version of the Keirsey Temperament Sorter II personality test at www. keirsey.com.
13. Integrated. Using Kodak's mission statement in Exhibit 12.3 as a model and the material you learned in Chapter 2, develop a mission statement that balances the pursuit of profit with responsibility to employees and community. Choose either a manufacturer of musical instruments or a retailer of children's clothing as the company.
14. Integrated. What is the principal difference between a business plan (as discussed in Chapter 6) and a strategic plan?

Practice Your Knowledge

Sharpening Your Communication Skills

As the manager of Richter's Restaurant Supply, you see a huge potential for selling company products on the Internet to customers around the world. Your company already has a website but it's geared to U.S. sales only. Before you propose your ideas to senior management, however, you're going to do your homework. Studies show that companies selling in the global marketplace benefit by modifying their websites to accommodate cultural differences. For instance, a mailbox with a raised flag has no meaning in many foreign countries.

Your task is to review the websites of several leading global companies and take notes on how they adapt their websites for global audiences. Once you've gathered your notes, write a short memo to management highlighting (via bullet points) some of the ways these leaders make their websites effective for a global audience.

Building Your Team Skills

A good mission statement should define the organization's purpose and ultimate goals and outline the principles that are to guide managers and employees in working toward those goals. Using library sources such as annual reports or Internet sources such as organizational websites, locate mission statements from one nonprofit organization, such as a school or a charity, and one company with which you are familiar.

Bring these statements to class and, with your team, select four mission statements to evaluate. How many of the mission statements contain all five of the typical components (product or service; primary market; concern for survival, growth, and profitability; managerial philosophy; commitment to quality and social responsibility)? Which components are most often absent from the mission statements you are evaluating? Which components are most often included? Of the mission statements your team is analyzing, which is the most inspiring? Why?

Now assume that you and your teammates are the top management team at each organization or company. How would you improve these mission statements? Rewrite the four mission statements so that they cover the five typical components, show all organization members how their roles are related to the vision, and inspire commitment among employees and managers.

Summarize your team's work in a written or oral report to the class. Compare the mission statement that your team found the most inspiring with the statements that other teams found the most inspiring. What do these mission statements have in common? How do they differ? Of all the inspiring mission statements reported to the class, which do you think is the best? Why? Does this mission statement inspire you to consider working for or doing business with this organization?

Improving Your Tech Insights: Business Intelligence Systems

One of the maddening ironies of contemporary business is that many decision makers are awash in data but starved for true information and insights. *Business intelligence* (BI) systems aim to harness all that data and turn it into the information and insights that managers need. BI systems are helping managers and professionals in many industries grapple with both strategic and tactical challenges.

The good news is that a number of companies now offer solutions to this problem. The bad news is there's a dizzying array of terminology in use today. The wide range of technologies that fall under the BI umbrella includes the executive information systems and decision support systems that you encountered in Chapter 4, and you'll also encounter such terms as *performance metrics* (systems that measure and report on progress toward organizational goals) and *online analytical processing (OLAP)* and *business analytics* (data analysis tools that help managers discover trends and relationships in operating data).

Because business intelligence is a broad term that describes a variety of approaches, technologies, and specific products, you can expect to find a wide range of information. Start with Business Intelligence.com, www. businessintelligence.com, then try several of the leading vendors, including Actuate (www.actuate.com), Cognos (www.cognos.com), Business Objects (www.businessobjects. com), Information Builders (www.informationbuilders. com), Microsoft (www.microsoft.com/bi), Oracle (www. oracle.com), SAP (www.sap.com), and SAS (www.sas.com). Research a BI system offered by one of these vendors, and in a brief e-mail to your instructor, summarize the system's benefits for managerial decision makers.[45]

Expand Your Knowledge

Discovering Career Opportunities

If you become a manager, how much of your day will be spent performing each of the four basic functions of management? This is your opportunity to find out. Arrange to shadow a manager (such as a department head, a store manager, or a shift supervisor) for a few hours. As you observe, categorize the manager's activities in terms of the four management functions and note how much time each activity takes. If observation is not possible, interview a manager in order to complete this exercise.

1. How much of the manager's time is spent on each of the four management functions? Is this the allocation you expected?

2. Ask whether this is a typical workday for this manager. If it isn't, what does the manager usually do differently?

During a typical day, does this manager tend to spend most of the time on one particular function?

3. Of the four management functions, which does the manager believe is most important for good organizational performance? Do you agree?

Developing Your Research Skills

Find two articles in business journals or newspapers (print or online editions) that profile two senior managers who lead a business or a nonprofit organization.

1. What experience, skills, and business background do the two leaders have? Do you see any striking similarities or differences in their backgrounds?

2. What kinds of business challenges have these two leaders faced? What actions did they take to deal with those

challenges? Did they establish any long-term goals or objectives for their company? Did the articles mention a new change initiative?

3. Describe the leadership strengths of each person as they are presented in the articles you selected. Is either leader known as a team builder? Long-term strategist? Shrewd negotiator? What are each leader's greatest areas of strength?

See It on the Web

Visit these websites and answer the following questions for each one. (Up-to-date links for all websites mentioned in this chapter can be found on the Textbook Resources page for Chapter 12 at www.mybusinesslab.com. Please note that links to sites that become inactive after publication of the book will be removed from the Featured Websites section.)

1. What is the purpose of this website?
2. What kinds of information does this website contain? Please be specific.
3. How is the information provided at this website useful for businesspeople? Consumers?
4. How did you expand your knowledge of management functions and skills by reviewing the material at this website? What new things did you learn about this topic?

Become a Better Manager

Emerald for Managers can help you become a better manager. Focused on management theory and practice, this website is a management portal that explores in-depth management issues including leadership, time management, training, strategy, knowledge management, personal development, customer relationship management, and more. Each channel provides lengthy articles, advice, and a collection of carefully annotated links. Log on today and join Emerald for Managers to become information rich and well organized. Learn why knowledge management is important. Discover what emotional intelligence is all about. And find out why companies form strategic alliances. http://managers.emeraldinsight.com

Linking to Organizational Change

Looking for more information on every aspect of organizational change management? You'll find a comprehensive collection of links on the website of the Management Assistance Program for Nonprofits. This is the place to access articles, discussion groups, and other resources related to organizational change in businesses and in not-for-profit organizations. Start with the overview, which sets the stage for browsing the many links devoted to exploring management and employee perspectives on the challenges and goals of managing change. www.managementhelp.org/org_chng/org_chng.htm

Learn from the Best

Learn how today's leaders are guiding their small companies to success. Check out Inc.com's Leadership Resource center for regular columns on leadership and management topics, how-to guides, and articles on everything from strategy to crisis management. www.inc.com/resources/leadership

Companion Website

Learning Interactively

Log onto www.prenhall.com/bovée, locate your text, and then click on its Companion Website. For Chapter 12, take advantage of the interactive Chapter Quiz to test your knowledge of the chapter. Get instant feedback on whether you need additional studying. Also, you'll find an abundance of valuable resources that will help you succeed in this course, including PowerPoint presentations and Web Links.

Video Case

Creative Management: Creative Age Publications

LEARNING OBJECTIVES

The purpose of this video is to help you:

1. Understand how and why managers set organizational goals
2. Identify the basic skills that managers need to be effective
3. Discuss how corporate culture can affect an organization

SYNOPSIS

Creative Age Publications uses creativity in managing its beauty-industry publications. With offices or franchised operations in Europe, Japan, Russia, and other countries, the company has expanded rapidly—thanks to sound management practices. One of the company's goals is to avoid overtaxing its management team by growing slowly in the near future. The CEO is working toward delegating most or all of the decisions to her management team rather than making these decisions herself. As Creative Age's managers moved up through the ranks, they honed their technical skills as well as their skills in working with others. "Having heart" is a major part of the company's culture—an important element that, in the CEO's opinion, many companies lack.

Discussion Questions

1. *For analysis:* How does global growth affect Creative Age's emphasis on the management skill of interacting well with other people?
2. *For analysis:* How does moving Creative Age's managers up through the ranks help them develop their conceptual skills?
3. *For application:* How would you suggest that the CEO spread Creative Age's culture throughout its global offices?
4. *For application:* How might the CEO manage Creative Age's growth through the process of controlling?
5. *For debate:* Do you agree with the CEO's policy of allowing managers and employees to work on any company magazine they choose? Support your position.

ONLINE EXPLORATION

Visit Creative Age's website www.creativeage.com and follow the link to *NailPro* magazine. Scan the magazine's home page and then click on the "About Us" link to read more about the magazine and its parent company. Why would Creative Age call attention to each magazine's goals and market rather than focusing on the parent company? How might Creative Age use a corporate website to communicate with other people and organizations that affect its ability to achieve its goals?

CHAPTER 13

Organization, Teamwork, and Motivation

LEARNING OBJECTIVES
After studying this chapter, you will be able to

1 Discuss the function of a company's organization structure

2 Explain the concepts of accountability, authority, and delegation

3 Define five major types of organization structure

4 Highlight the advantages and disadvantages of working in teams

5 List the characteristics of effective teams

6 Review the five stages of team development and highlight six causes of team conflict

7 Compare Maslow's hierarchy of needs and Herzberg's two-factor theory, then explain their application to employee motivation

8 Explain why expectancy theory is considered by some to be the best description of employee behavior

Reinventing the Retail Experience at The Container Store

www.containerstore.com

Let's face it: Frontline jobs in retail sometimes don't have the greatest reputation. From an employee's perspective, these sales positions often combine low pay with high stress, leading to rapid burnout and frequent turnover. From a customer's perspective, frontline retail employees in some stores seem to fall into two categories: poorly trained and poorly motivated rookies or aggressive staffers who seem more intent on getting their commissions than helping customers.

What if you wanted to put a new face on retailing? What if you wanted shopping to be a pleasant, welcome experience for both employees and customers? Too much to ask for, perhaps?

This is the challenge Garrett Boone and Kip Tindell set for themselves when they opened the first Container Store in Dallas, Texas. The chain, which has now expanded to several dozen locations across the country, carries a staggering

Effective team communication behind the scenes is key to creating positive customer experiences at The Container Store.

array of products that help customers organize their lives. Store employees are expected to help customers solve every storage problem imaginable, from sweaters to DVDs to rubber stamps to tax records, with a variety of boxes, baskets, hangers, hooks, closet organizers, and more. The Container Store, which certainly lives up to its motto, "Contain Yourself," offers some sort of storage solution for every room in the house, from the kitchen to the garage to the home office.

If you were in Boone and Tindell's shoes, what steps would you take to break out of the retail rut and create a company that is satisfying for both customers and employees? How would you attract the best and the brightest employees and pull off a minor miracle in retailing—hanging on to them year after year? How would you organize the staffs in your stores? How much information would you share with them, and how would you communicate it?[1] ∎

Designing an Effective Organization Structure

organization structure
Framework that enables managers to divide responsibilities, ensure employee accountability, and distribute decision-making authority

As Garrett Boone and Kip Tindell (profiled in the chapter opener) can tell you, a company's **organization structure** has a dramatic influence on the way employees and managers make decisions, communicate, and accomplish important tasks. A well-designed structure helps the company achieve its goals by providing a framework for managers to divide responsibilities, effectively distribute the authority to make decisions, coordinate and control the organization's work, and hold employees accountable for their work. In contrast, a poorly designed structure can create enormous waste, confusion, and frustration for employees, suppliers, and customers. No matter what your role in the company might be, understanding organization structures, teamwork, and motivation will make you a more productive employee and a more effective manager.

organization chart
Diagram showing how employees and tasks are grouped and where the lines of communication and authority flow

When managers design the organization's structure, they use an **organization chart** to provide a visual representation of how employees and tasks are grouped and how the lines of communication and authority flow (see Exhibit 13.1). An organization chart depicts the

EXHIBIT 13.1 Organization Chart for Grocery Store Chain

The traditional model of an organization is a pyramid in which numerous boxes form the base and lead up to fewer and fewer boxes on higher levels, ultimately arriving at one box at the top. A glance at this chart reveals who has authority over whom, who is responsible for which functional areas, and who is accountable to whom.

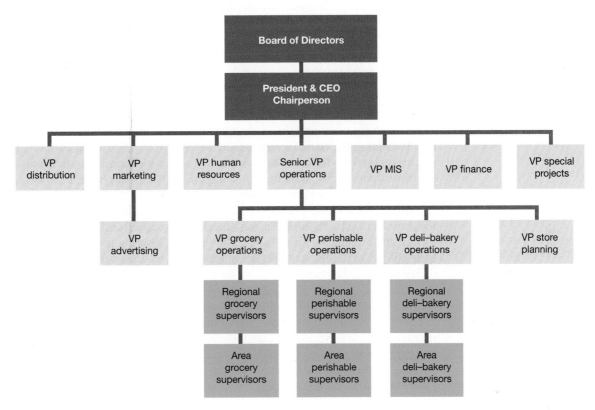

official design for accomplishing tasks that lead to achieving the organization's goals, a framework known as the **formal organization**. Every company also has an **informal organization**—the network of interactions that develop on a personal level among workers.

How do companies design an organization structure, and which organization structure is the most effective? As management guru Peter Drucker put it, "There is no such thing as one right organization. Each has distinct strengths, distinct limitations, and specific applications."[2] To identify the best structure for their organizations, managers need to identify job responsibilities, define the chain of command, and organize the workforce in a way that maximizes effectiveness and efficiency.

Identifying Job Responsibilities

The nature of the work employees are expected to do is a critical aspect of the organization decision. Management must first decide on the optimal level of **work specialization**, sometimes referred to as the *division of labor*—the degree to which organizational tasks are broken down into separate jobs.[3] Specialization can improve efficiency by enabling each worker to perform tasks that are well defined and that require specific skills. When employees concentrate on the same specialized tasks, they can perfect their skills and perform their tasks more quickly.

Work specialization continues to be a prominent feature in business organizations, from the various responsibilities along an automobile assembly line to an accounting firm in which various staff members specialize in different aspects of taxation. In addition to aligning skills with job tasks, specialization prevents overlapping responsibilities and communication breakdowns. For instance, in business-to-business markets, the ongoing relationship

formal organization
A framework officially established by managers for accomplishing the organization's tasks

informal organization
Networks of informal employee interactions that are not defined by the formal structure

work specialization
Specialization in or responsibility for some portion of an organization's overall work tasks; also called division of labor

between a supplier and a customer can sometimes involve dozens or even hundreds of employees. To ensure efficient communication, *relationship managers* (frequently senior salespeople and purchasing agents) are often put in charge of the relationship on both sides. Other employees will communicate back and forth, to be sure, but significant issues, such as contract negotiations and schedule updates, are usually left to these two people.

However, organizations can overdo specialization. If a task is defined too narrowly, employees may become bored and disengaged when performing the same limited, repetitious job. Moreover, an overemphasis on specialization can lead employees to focus so intently on their own responsibilities that it may reduce their contribution to the organization's overall success.

Defining the Chain of Command

Once the various jobs and their individual responsibilities have been identified, the next step is defining the **chain of command**, the lines of authority that connect the various groups and levels within the organization. The chain of command helps organizations function smoothly by making two things clear: who is responsible for each task, and who has the authority to make official decisions.

All employees have a certain amount of **responsibility**—the obligation to perform the duties and achieve the goals and objectives associated with their jobs. As they work toward the organization's goals, employees must also maintain their **accountability**, their obligation to report the results of their work to supervisors or team members and to justify any outcomes that fall below expectations. Managers ensure that tasks are accomplished by exercising **authority**, which is the power to make decisions, issue orders, carry out actions, and allocate resources to achieve the organization's goals. Authority is vested in the positions that managers hold, and it flows down through the management pyramid. **Delegation** is the assignment of work and the transfer of authority, responsibility, and accountability to complete that work.[4]

The simplest and most common chain-of-command system is known as **line organization** because it establishes a clear line of authority flowing from the top down, as Exhibit 13.1 depicts. However, line organization sometimes falls short because the technical complexity of a firm's activities may require specialized knowledge that individual managers don't have and can't easily acquire. A more elaborate system called **line-and-staff organization** was developed out of the need to combine specialization with management control. In such an organization, managers in the chain of command are supplemented by functional groupings of people known as *staff*, who provide advice and specialized services but who are not in the line organization's overall chain of command (see Exhibit 13.2).

chain of command
Pathway for the flow of authority from one management level to the next

responsibility
Obligation to perform the duties and achieve the goals and objectives associated with a position

accountability
Obligation to report results and to justify outcomes that fall below expectations

authority
Power granted by the organization to make decisions, take actions, and allocate resources

delegation
Assignment of work and the authority and responsibility required to complete it

line organization
Chain-of-command system that establishes a clear line of authority flowing from the top down

line-and-staff organization
Line organization that adds functional groups of people who provide advice and specialized services

EXHIBIT 13.2

Simplified Line-and-Staff Structure

A line-and-staff organization divides employees into those who are in the direct line of command (from the top level of the hierarchy to the bottom) and those who provide staff (or support) services to line managers at various levels. Staff report directly to top management.

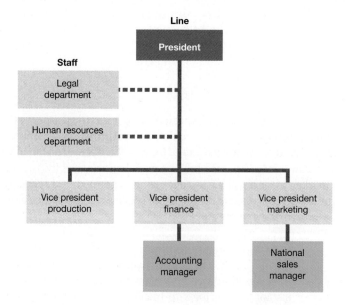

The number of people a manager directly supervises is called the **span of management**, or *span of control*. When a large number of people report directly to one person, that person has a wide span of management. This situation is common in **flat organizations** with relatively few levels in the management hierarchy. In contrast, **tall organizations** have many hierarchical levels, typically with fewer people reporting to each manager than is the case in a flat organization. In these organizations, the span of management is narrow (see Exhibit 13.3). Under tall organization structures, employees who want to institute a change or solve a problem often need to ask a supervisor, who in turn must ask a manager, who in turn must ask another manager at the next level up, and so on. To reduce the time it takes to make decisions, many companies are now flattening their organization structures by removing layers of management and pushing responsibilities and authority to lower levels. Such moves have the added benefit of putting senior executives in closer contact with customers and the daily action of the business.[5]

However, these changes must be considered with care, since flatter organizations can increase the demand on individual managers. Moreover, flat structures can make it harder for the organization to learn; with fewer managers overseeing more workers and with workers busier managing themselves, everyone has less time to observe, study, and find solutions to recurring problems. For instance, supervisors at Southwest Airlines, famous for its efficient, low-cost operations, actually have a narrower span of control than their counterparts at American Airlines, one of the classic, higher-cost major airlines. By having more managers overseeing maintenance work, Southwest is better able to address concerns and questions, a capability that plays an important role in its superior on-time flight performance.[6]

Organizations that focus decision-making authority near the top of the chain of command are said to be centralized. **Centralization** can benefit a company by utilizing top management's experience and broad perspective, by coordinating large undertakings more efficiently, and by accelerating decision making.

However, the trend in business today is toward decentralization. **Decentralization** pushes decision-making authority down to lower organizational levels—such as department heads—while control over essential companywide matters remains with top management. Implemented properly, decentralization can stimulate responsiveness because decisions don't have to be referred up the hierarchy.[7]

span of management
Number of people under one manager's control; also known as span of control

flat organizations
Organizations with a wide span of management and few hierarchical levels

tall organizations
Organizations with a narrow span of management and many hierarchical levels

centralization
Concentration of decision-making authority at the top of the organization

decentralization
Delegation of decision-making authority to employees in lower-level positions

EXHIBIT 13.3 Tall Versus Flat Organizations

A tall organization, such as the U.S. Army's, has many levels with a narrow span of management at each level so that relatively few people report to each manager on the level above. In contrast, a flat organization, such as the Catholic Church, has relatively few levels with a wide span of management so that more people report to each manager.

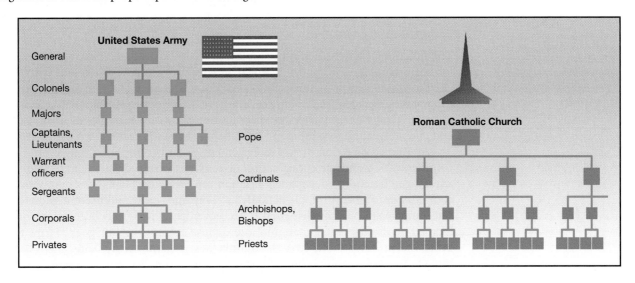

Learning from Business Blunders

Oops: In an attempt to accelerate innovation by decentralizing decision making, telecommunication equipment maker Lucent Technologies split its 3 operating divisions into 11 largely independent business units. Unfortunately, the move toward decentralization apparently made matters worse, slowing decision making, creating new communication and control issues, and adding another layer of cost and complexity to the organizational structure. Experts say the reorganization played a significant role in a decline that saw the company lose money every quarter for more than three years and shed more than 100,000 jobs. (To be fair, just about everybody in the telecommunication business at that time was getting hammered, but Lucent's losses were extraordinarily painful.)

What You Can Learn: Decentralization works only if the various units of a company can truly work independently. However, Lucent makes complex systems that require close coordination across many groups within the company to be successful. Since the failed experiment in decentralization, the company has become more efficient by becoming even more centralized than it was before.

However, decentralization does not work in every situation or in every company. At times, strong authority from the top of the chain of command may be needed to keep the organization focused on immediate goals. In other cases, a company may need strong central decision making to coordinate efforts on complex projects or to present a unified image to customers. Managers should select the level of decision making that will most effectively serve the organization's needs given the individual circumstances.[8] After its Saturn division accumulated thousands of adoring customers but not a dime of profit in 14 years of mostly autonomous operation, General Motors pulled the division closer to the corporate fold. Saturn now shares design and manufacturing with Chevrolet, Buick, and other GM brands.[9]

Organizing the Workforce

The decisions regarding job responsibilities, span of management, and centralization versus decentralization provide the insights managers need in order to choose the best organization structure. The arrangement of activities into logical groups that are then clustered into larger departments and units to form the total organization is known as **departmentalization**.[10] The choice must involve both the *vertical structure*—how many layers the chain of command is divided into from the top of the company to the bottom—and the *horizontal structure*—how the various business functions and work specialties are divided across the company.

Variations in the vertical and horizontal designs of the organization can produce an almost endless array of structures—some flat, some wide; some simple and clear; others convoluted and complex. Within this endless variety of structure possibilities, most designs fall into one of five types: functional, divisional, matrix, network, or hybrids that combine features of two or more types. Keep in mind that large companies often combine structure choices at different levels in the organization. For example, a company might first divide into divisions, then use a functional structure within each of those divisions.

Functional Structures

The **functional structure** groups employees according to their skills, resource use, and job requirements. Common functional subgroups include research and development (R&D), production or manufacturing, marketing and sales, and human resources.

Splitting the organization into separate functional departments offers several advantages: (1) Grouping employees by specialization allows for the efficient use of resources and encourages the development of in-depth skills, (2) centralized decision making enables unified direction by top management, and (3) centralized operations enhance communication and the coordination of activities within departments. Despite these advantages, functional departmentalization can create problems with communication, coordination, and control, particularly as companies grow and become more complicated and geographically dispersed.[11] Moreover, employees may become too narrowly focused on departmental goals and lose sight of larger company goals. Firms that use functional structures often try to counter these weaknesses by using *cross-functional teams* to coordinate efforts across functional boundaries, as you'll see later in the chapter.

departmentalization
Grouping people within an organization according to function, division, matrix, or network

functional structure
Grouping workers according to their similar skills, resource use, and expertise

Divisional Structures

The **divisional structure** establishes self-contained "mini" organizations that encompass all the major functional resources required to achieve their goals.[12] In some companies, these divisions operate with great autonomy, almost as multiple small companies within a larger company; such divisions are often called *business units*. Common divisional structure types are based on similarities in product, process, customer, or geography. For instance, Motorola is organized into three major divisions by customer type, whereas the semiconductor company Intel is organized around five product divisions.[13]

Divisional structures offer both advantages and disadvantages. First, because divisions are self-contained, they can react quickly to change, making the organization more flexible. In addition, because each division focuses on a limited number of products, processes, customers, or locations, divisions can offer better service to customers. Moreover, top managers within divisions can focus on problem areas more easily, and managers can gain valuable experience by dealing with the various functions in their divisions. However, divisional departmentalization can also increase costs by duplicating the use of resources such as facilities and personnel. Furthermore, poor coordination between divisions may cause them to focus too narrowly on divisional goals and neglect the organization's overall goals. Finally, divisions may compete with one another for resources and customers, causing rivalries that hurt the organization as a whole.[14]

divisional structure
Grouping departments according to similarities in product, process, customer, or geography

Matrix Structures

A **matrix structure** attempts to overcome drawbacks of both the functional and divisional structures by pooling and sharing resources across divisions and functional groups (see Exhibit 13.4). In Dell's case, for instance, sales regions and product groups are linked in a permanent matrix structure. Within that framework, *business councils* also focus on specific types of customers, such as small-business owners.[15]

The matrix structure can help big companies function like smaller ones by allowing teams to devote their attention to specific projects or customers without permanently reorganizing the company's structure. A matrix can also make it easier to deploy limited resources where they're needed the most and to bring a mix of skills to bear on important tasks. On the downside, people in a matrix structure have to get used to reporting to two bosses, more communication and coordination is usually required, and struggles over resources can foster unhealthy competition between the two sides of the matrix.[16]

matrix structure
Structure that uses functional and divisional patterns simultaneously

Network Structures

Chapter 4 describes value webs as multidimensional networks of suppliers and outsourcing partners. This **network structure** stretches beyond the boundaries of the company to connect a variety of partners and suppliers that perform selected tasks for a

network structure
Virtual organization in which a company relies on multiple external partners to complete its business model

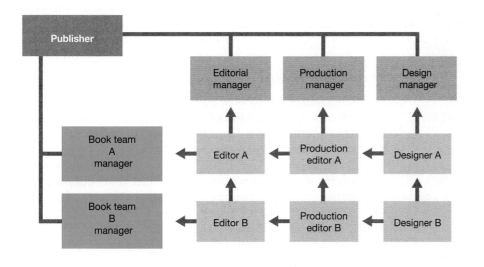

EXHIBIT 13.4

Matrix Structure

In a matrix structure, each employee is assigned to both a functional group (with a defined set of basic functions, such as production management) and a project team (which consists of members of various functional groups working together on a project, such as bringing out a new consumer product).

headquarters organization. Also called a *virtual organization,* the network organization can outsource engineering, marketing, research, accounting, production, distribution, or other functions. The design of a network structure stems from decisions about core competencies, with executives deciding which functions to focus on internally and which to outsource.

The network structure presents an intriguing blend of benefits and risks. A virtual structure can lower costs and increase flexibility, allowing you to react more quickly to market demands. It can also boost competitiveness by taking advantage of specific skills and technologies available in other companies. On the other hand, relying too heavily on outsiders can render you vulnerable to events beyond your control, such as key suppliers going out of business, offering the same goods and services to your competitors, or going into direct competition with you. Moreover, outsourcing too many fundamental tasks such as product design can leave a company without any real competitive distinctions to speak of.[17]

Hybrid Structures

hybrid structure
Structure that combines elements of functional, divisional, matrix, and network organizations

Some companies find it most effective to adopt a **hybrid structure**, combining various elements from the four standard types of structure. For example, Inergy Automotive Systems, a Paris-based manufacturer of fuel and energy subsystems for automobiles and other vehicles, has both functional groups (such as research and development) and geographic customer groups that give the firm a local presence in Japan, North America, and other major automotive assembly regions.[18]

Working in Teams

team
A unit of two or more people who share a mission and collective responsibility as they work together to achieve a common goal

While the vertical chain of command is a tried-and-true method of organizing for business, it is limited by the fact that decision-making authority is often located high up the management hierarchy while real-world feedback from customers is usually located at or near the bottom of the hierarchy. Companies that organize vertically may become slow to react to change, and high-level managers may overlook many great ideas for improvement that originate in the lower levels of the organization. In addition, many business tasks and challenges demand the expertise of people who work in many parts of the company, isolated by the formal chain of command. To combat these issues, organizations such as The Container Store work to involve employees from all levels and functions of the organization in the decision-making process, using a variety of *team formats* in day-to-day operations.

Even though the team approach has many advantages, shifting to a team structure often requires a fundamental shift in the organization's culture. Teams must also have clear goals that are tied to the company's strategic goals, and their outcomes need to be measured and compared with benchmarks. Moreover, employees must be motivated to work together in teams.

What Is a Team?

A **team** is a unit of two or more people who work together to achieve a shared goal. Teams differ from work groups in that work groups interact primarily to share information and to make decisions to help one another perform within each member's area of responsibility. In other words, the performance of a work group is merely the summation of all group members' individual contributions.[19] In contrast, the members of a team have a shared mission and are collectively responsible for their work. By coordinating their individual efforts, the members of successful teams accomplish more together than they could individually, a result known as *synergy.*[20]

Companies that emphasize teamwork often design office spaces to encourage casual interaction among team members.

Although the team's goals may be set by either the team itself or someone in the formal chain of command, it is the job of the team leader to make sure the team stays on track to achieve those goals. Team leaders are often appointed by senior managers, but sometimes they emerge naturally as the team develops. Some teams complete their work and disband in a matter of weeks or months, while those working on complex projects can stay together for years. In one of the more extreme examples of team longevity, pairs of advertising copywriters and art directors (the two creative halves of a typical ad-development team) in England are usually hired—and fired—as a team and often work together for many years.[21]

Types of Teams

Companies have developed a variety of team formats to address different business challenges. The five most common forms of teams are *problem-solving teams, self-managed teams, functional teams, cross-functional teams,* and *virtual teams.*

- **Problem-solving teams** are assembled to find ways of improving quality, efficiency, or other performance issues. For instance, to address concerns of U.S. car buyers, the German automaker Audi pulled together U.S. and German personnel to collaborate on a range of quality and reliability issues.[22]

- As the name implies, **self-managed teams** manage their own activities and require minimum supervision. Typically, they control the pace of work and determination of work assignments. As you might imagine, some managers are reluctant to embrace self-managed teams because it requires them to give up significant control.

- **Functional teams,** or *command teams,* are organized along the lines of the organization's vertical structure and thus may be referred to as *vertical teams.* They are composed of managers and employees within a single functional department, and the structure of a vertical team typically follows the formal chain of command.[23]

- In contrast to functional teams, **cross-functional teams,** or *horizontal teams,* draw together employees from various functional areas and expertise. For example, Boeing uses multiple "design-build" teams that include aircraft engineers, production workers, and suppliers.[24] Cross-functional teams can facilitate the exchange of information, improve coordination among departments, encourage new solutions for organizational problems, and aid the development of new organizational policies and procedures.[25] Cross-functional teams can take on a number of formats. A **task force** is a cross-functional team formed to work on a specific activity with a specific deadline. In contrast, a **committee** usually has a long life span and may become a permanent part of the organization structure.

- **Virtual teams** are groups of physically dispersed members who communicate electronically. One of the major benefits of virtual teams is the opportunity to assemble teams of experts wherever they may be, rather than rely on the people who happen to work in a given geographic location. To be successful, though, virtual teams need to take steps to overcome the disadvantages of not being able to communicate face to face. For instance, some virtual teams meet in person at least once to allow the members to get to know one another before diving into their work. Improvements in online meeting systems have helped virtual teams communicate by combining audio and video feeds with presentation software and other tools.

Note that these classifications are not exclusive. For example, a problem-solving team may also be self-managed and cross-functional.

Advantages and Disadvantages of Working in Teams

Even though teams can play a vital role in helping an organization reach its goals, they are not appropriate for every situation, nor do they automatically ensure higher performance. Managers must weigh both the advantages and the disadvantages of teams when deciding whether to use them. A well-run team can deliver a variety of advantages:[26]

problem-solving teams
Informal teams that meet to find ways of improving quality, efficiency, and the work environment

self-managed teams
Teams in which members are responsible for an entire process or operation

functional teams
Teams whose members come from a single functional department and that are based on the organization's vertical structure

cross-functional teams
Teams that draw together employees from different functional areas

task force
Team of people from several departments who are temporarily brought together to address a specific issue

committee
Team that may become a permanent part of the organization and is designed to deal with regularly recurring tasks

virtual teams
Teams that use communication technology to bring geographically distant employees together to achieve goals

By pulling together the diverse viewpoints and expertise of their various members, effective teams can accomplish far more than a collection of individuals working solo.

- *Higher-quality decisions.* Many business challenges require the input of people with diverse experiences and insights, and teams can be an effective way to bring these multiple perspectives together.

- *Increased commitment to solutions and changes.* Employees who feel they've had an active role in making a decision are more likely to support the decision and encourage others to accept it.

- *Lower levels of stress and destructive internal competition.* When people work together toward a common goal, rather than competing for individual recognition, their efforts and energies tend to focus on the common good.

- *Improved flexibility and responsiveness.* Because they don't have the same degree of permanence as formal departments and other structural elements, many teams are easier to reformulate in response to changing business needs.

While the advantages of teamwork help explain the widespread popularly of teams in today's business environment, teams also present a number of potential disadvantages, particularly if they are poorly structured or poorly managed:[27]

- *Inefficiency.* Potential sources of inefficiency include internal politics, too much emphasis on consensus, and excessive socialization among team members.

- *Groupthink.* Like all social structures, business teams can generate tremendous pressures to conform with accepted norms of behavior. *Groupthink* occurs when these peer pressures cause individual team members to withhold contrary or unpopular opinions. The result can be decisions that are worse—not better—than the team members might've made individually.

- *Diminished individual motivation.* Balancing the need for team harmony with individual motivation is a constant issue with teams. This can be a particularly strong concern in areas such as sales or software development, where the contributions of the best performers can far exceed the group average. Without the promise of individual recognition and reward, these high-performance individuals may feel less incentive to keep working at such high levels.

- *Structural disruption.* Teams can become so influential within an organization that they compete with the formal chain of command, in effect superimposing a matrix on the existing structure.

- *Excessive workloads.* The time and energy required to work on teams isn't free, and when team responsibilities are layered on top of individuals' regular job responsibilities, the result can be overload.

Characteristics of Effective Teams

To be successful, teams need to be designed as carefully as any other part of the organization structure. Establishing the size of the team is one of the most important decisions. While there is no "magic number" for the size of every team, four to six people is usually an effective size. Smaller teams might lack the diversity of skills and insights required. Conversely, as teams grow larger, communication becomes more difficult and may discourage some members from sharing their ideas. Larger groups are also prone to disagreements and factionalism because so many opinions must be considered, thus making the team leader's job more difficult. Moreover, people in larger teams can start to feel that their individual contribution is less valuable, so they give in to the temptation of skipping meetings and reducing their overall contribution.[28]

The makeup of types of individuals on the team is also vital. People who assume the *task-specialist role* focus on helping the team reach its goals. In contrast, members who take on the *socioemotional role* focus on supporting the team's emotional needs

EXHIBIT 13.5 Team Member Roles

Team members assume one of these four roles. Members who assume a dual role often make effective team leaders.

	Task-specialist role	**Dual role**
High	• Focuses on task accomplishment over human needs • Important role, but if adopted by everyone, team's social needs won't be met	• Focuses on task and people • May be a team leader • Important role, but not essential if members adopt task-specialist and socioemotional roles
Member task behavior	**Nonparticipator role**	**Socioemotional role**
Low	• Contributes little to either task or people needs of team • If adopted by too many members, team will disband or fail at its mission	• Focuses on people needs of team over task • Important role, but if adopted by everyone, team's tasks won't be accomplished
	Low **Member social behavior** High	

and strengthening the team's social unity. Some team members are able to assume dual roles, contributing to the task and still meeting members' emotional needs. These members often make effective team leaders. At the other end of the spectrum are members who contribute little to reaching the team's goals or to meeting members' emotional needs. These **free riders** are team members who don't contribute their fair share to the group's activities, often because they aren't being held individually accountable for their work. Obviously, a team staffed with too many free riders isn't going to accomplish anything. Exhibit 13.5 outlines the behavior patterns associated with each of these roles.

Beyond the right number of the right sort of people, effective teams share a number of other characteristics:[29]

free riders
Team members who do not contribute sufficiently to the group's activities because members are not being held individually accountable for their work

- *Clear sense of purpose.* Team members clearly understand the task at hand, what is expected of them, and their respective roles on the team.

- *Open and honest communication.* The team culture encourages discussion and debate. Team members speak openly and honestly, without the threat of anger, resentment, or retribution. They listen to and value feedback from others. As a result, all team members participate. Conversely, members who either don't share valuable information because they don't understand that it's valuable—or worse, withhold information as a way to maintain personal power—can undermine the team's efforts.[30]

- *Creative thinking.* Effective teams encourage original thinking, considering options beyond the usual.

- *Focus.* Team members get to the core issues of the problem and stay focused on key issues.

- *Decision by consensus.* All decisions are arrived at by consensus. But this point comes with a warning: Teams that worry too much about consensus can take forever to make decisions. In many cases, team members need to commit to the group's decision even though they may not all support it 100 percent.

Learning these team skills takes time and practice, so U.S. companies now teach teamwork more frequently than any other aspect of business.[31] For a brief review of characteristics of effective teams, see Exhibit 13.6.

EXHIBIT 13.6 Characteristics of Effective Teams

Effective teams follow these guidelines to ensure successful completion of their missions.

MAKE WORKING IN TEAMS A TOP MANAGEMENT PRIORITY

✓ Recognize and reward group performance where appropriate

✓ Provide ample training opportunities for employees to develop team skills

SELECT TEAM MEMBERS WISELY

✓ Involve key stakeholders and decision makers

✓ Limit team size to the minimum number of people needed to achieve team goals

✓ Select members with a diversity of views

✓ Select creative thinkers

BUILD A SENSE OF FAIRNESS IN DECISION MAKING

✓ Encourage debate and disagreement without fear of reprisal

✓ Allow members to communicate openly and honestly

✓ Consider all proposals

✓ Build consensus by allowing team members to examine, compare, and reconcile differences—but don't let a desire for 100 percent consensus bog the team down

✓ Avoid quick votes

✓ Keep everyone informed

✓ Present all the facts

MANAGE CONFLICT CONSTRUCTIVELY

✓ Share leadership

✓ Encourage equal participation

✓ Discuss disagreements openly and calmly

✓ Focus on the issues, not the people

✓ Don't let minor disagreements boil over into major conflicts

STAY ON TRACK

✓ Make sure everyone understands the team's purpose

✓ Communicate what is expected of team members

✓ Stay focused on the core assignment

✓ Develop and adhere to a schedule

✓ Develop rules and obey norms

Stages of Team Development

Developing an effective team is an ongoing process. Like the members who form them, teams grow and change as time goes by. Several models of team development have been proposed over the years; a model defined by researcher Bruce Tuckman identified five stages of development, nicknamed *forming, storming, norming, performing,* and *adjourning*:[32]

- *Forming.* The forming stage is a period of orientation and ice-breaking. Members get to know each other, determine what types of behaviors are appropriate within the group, identify what is expected of them, and become acquainted with each other's task orientation.

- *Storming.* In the storming stage, members show more of their personalities and become more assertive in establishing their roles. Conflict and disagreement often arise during the storming stage as members jockey for position or form coalitions to promote their own perceptions of the group's mission.

- *Norming.* During the norming stage, these conflicts are resolved, and team harmony develops. Members come to understand and accept one another, reach a consensus on who the leader is, and reach agreement on what each member's roles are.

- *Performing.* In the performing stage, members are really committed to the team's goals. Problems are solved, and disagreements are handled with maturity in the interest of task accomplishment.

- *Adjourning.* Finally, if the team has a specific task to perform, it goes through the adjourning stage after the task has been completed. In this stage, issues are wrapped up and the team is dissolved.

As the team moves through these various stages of development, two important developments occur. First, the team develops a certain level of **cohesiveness**, a measure of how committed the members are to the team's goals. Cohesiveness is influenced by many factors, although the two primary factors are competition with other teams and recognition by the rest of the organization.

The second development is the emergence of **norms**, informal but often powerful standards of conduct that members share and use to guide their behavior. By encouraging consistent behavior, norms boost efficiency and help ensure the group's survival. Individuals who deviate from these norms can find themselves ridiculed, isolated, or even removed from the group entirely (this fear is the leading cause of groupthink, by the way).[33]

cohesiveness
A measure of how committed the team members are to their team's goals

norms
Informal standards of conduct that guide team behavior

Team Conflict

Of all the skills needed to make a team successful, none is more important than the ability to handle *conflict*—which can range from simple creative differences to all-out battles—resulting from differences in ideas, opinions, goals, or methods of work. Conflict can be *constructive* if it generates creative solutions to problems or encourages team members to understand opposing viewpoints, but it can be *destructive* if it creates a poisonous emotional atmosphere or distracts the team's performance.[34]

Causes of Team Conflict

Team conflicts can arise for a number of reasons. First, individuals may feel they are in competition for resources. Second, team members may disagree about who is responsible for a specific task; this type of disagreement is usually the result of poorly defined responsibilities and job boundaries. Third, poor communication can lead to misunderstandings and misperceptions about other team members or other teams. In addition, intentionally withholding information can undermine trust among members. Fourth, basic differences in values, attitudes, and personalities may lead to clashes. Fifth, power struggles may result when one party questions the authority of another or when people or teams with limited authority attempt to increase their

Conflict is an inevitable part of working in teams, but effective teams know how to keep destructive conflict from disrupting the team's efforts to reach its goals.

power or exert more influence. Sixth, conflicts can arise because individuals or teams are pursuing different goals.[35] Keep in mind that while "conflict" sounds negative, in many cases it is simply the result of different perspectives. Teams always have some level of conflict; the question is how successfully they address it.

Solutions to Team Conflict

Teams handle conflict in a variety of ways. Depending on the strength of the team leadership and the urgency of the situation, a team may simply force a resolution to the conflict, bringing it out in the open and resolving it as quickly as possible. At the other extreme, the team leadership may choose to ignore the conflict and wait for it to subside naturally—which may only serve to quiet the arguments temporarily without actually solving the problem. Other alternatives include negotiating compromises or reminding the team to refocus on its shared goals.[36] In the worst cases, a team may need to be disbanded or reformed with different members.

Team members and team leaders can also take several steps to prevent conflicts. First, by establishing clear goals that engage every member, the team reduces the chance that members will battle over objectives or roles. Second, by developing well-defined tasks for each member, the team leader ensures that all parties are aware of their responsibilities and the limits of their authority. Third, by facilitating open communication, the team leader can ensure that all members understand their own tasks and objectives as well as those of their teammates. Communication builds respect and tolerance, and it provides a forum for bringing misunderstandings into the open before they turn into full-blown conflicts.

Productive Team Meetings

Too many meetings are unproductive because they are either poorly planned or poorly conducted. Companies can make better use of valuable meeting time by following these steps:

- *Clarify the purpose of the meeting.* Although many meetings combine purposes, most focus on one of two types: *Informational meetings* involve sharing information and perhaps coordinating action. *Decision-making meetings* involve persuasion, analysis, and problem solving.

- *Select participants carefully.* With a clear purpose in mind, it's easier to identify the right participants. If the session is purely informational and one person will do most of the talking, you can invite a large group. For problem-solving and decision-making meetings, invite only those people who are in a direct position to help the meeting reach its objective.

- *Establish a clear agenda.* The success of any meeting depends on the preparation of the participants. Distribute a carefully written agenda to participants, giving them enough time to prepare as needed. A productive agenda answers three key questions: (1) What do we need to do in this meeting to accomplish our goals? (2) What issues will be of greatest importance to all participants? (3) What information must be available in order to discuss these issues?[37]

- *Keep the meeting on track.* A good meeting draws out the best ideas and information the group has to offer. As a meeting leader, experience will help you recognize when to be dominant and press the group forward and when to step back and let people talk.

How This Affects You

1. Do you enjoy working or playing on teams, or do you prefer individual pursuits? If your inclination is toward solo activities, what adjustments can you make to become a valuable—and satisfied—team member when collaboration is required?

2. Think back to several team activities in which you were recently involved (in athletics, school, work, volunteering, or any other environment). Which of the four roles outlined in Exhibit 13.5 did you assume in each of these team settings? Did you adopt the same role on every team? How would you judge your performance as a team player?

3. What is your natural response when you encounter conflict in interpersonal relationships of any kind? Will this response help you or hurt you in your business career?

- *Follow agreed-upon rules.* Business meetings run the gamut from informal to extremely formal, complete with detailed rules for speaking, proposing new items to discuss, voting on proposals, and so on. The larger the meeting, the more formal you'll need to be to maintain order.

- *Encourage participation.* As the meeting gets under way, you'll discover that some participants are too quiet and others are too talkative. Draw out quiet participants by asking for their input on issues that particularly pertain to them. For the overly talkative, simply say that time is limited and others need to be heard from.

- *Close effectively.* At the conclusion of the meeting, verify that the objectives have been met; if not, arrange for follow-up work as needed. Make sure all participants agree on the outcome and give people a chance to clear up any misunderstandings.

Motivating Employees

In any organization, success stems directly from employees' sense of **engagement**, which is both a rational and an emotional commitment to their work. This commitment leads to higher-quality work and increased productivity while sharply reducing the likelihood that employees will leave the company in search of more satisfying opportunities.[38] Employees who are thoroughly engaged in their work generally exhibit high **morale**, a positive attitude toward both their jobs and their employers.

In your years as a student, you've surely experienced a few assignments that you just couldn't get excited about, for whatever reason. Without a strong intellectual or emotional connection to the work, chances are you didn't expend much more than the minimum amount of effort required. Conversely, let's hope you've had more than a few assignments in which the opposite was true: You poured your heart and soul into these projects because you made a commitment to excel, and at some level, you even enjoyed what you were doing. In other words, you were *engaged* with the work and *motivated* to do your best.

Making sure employees are engaged and motivated is one of the most important challenges you'll face as a manager. It's also one of the most complex; human beings are complicated creatures to begin with, and today's demanding business environment makes the challenge that much greater. You can start to appreciate the challenge by first learning more about what motivation is, then by considering some of the many theories proposed over the years to explain motivation in the workplace.

What Is Motivation?

Motivation is the combination of forces that moves individuals to take certain actions and avoid others in pursuit of individual objectives. Motivation is a complex psychological subject, and researchers have proposed a variety of theories to help explain why humans are driven to behave the way they do. For instance, some theories suggest a process in which people take action to fulfill perceived needs, then evaluate the outcomes of those actions to determine whether the effort was worthwhile:

1. *Need.* We are all born with certain needs but can acquire other needs as we grow up, such as a need for achievement, a need for power, or a need to affiliate with compatible friends and colleagues.[39]

2. *Action.* To fulfill the need, the individual takes actions or adopts behaviors that he or she believes will result in the need being satisfied. The *quality* of the action is a matter of choosing which action to take, deciding how much effort to put into the action, and deciding how long to sustain that effort.[40]

3. *Outcome.* The individual then observes the outcome of the action and determines whether the effort was worthwhile enough to repeat.

Even from this simple model you can start to grasp the challenges involved. For instance, what if two or more needs conflict, leading to incompatible actions? It's hard to

Satisfied, motivated employees tend to be more productive and more effective, leading to higher rates of customer satisfaction and repeat business.

engagement
An employee's rational and emotional commitment to his or her work

morale
Attitude an individual has toward his or her job and employer

motivation
The combination of forces that moves individuals to take certain actions and behaviors and avoid other actions or behaviors

balance the need to relax and have fun with the need to generate enough money to pay the rent. Or what if an employee's need for recognition motivates him or her to work hard in the hopes of getting a promotion, but thanks to a tough economy, the company isn't growing and can't offer the promotion? Or what if top management doesn't notice the hard work—or worse yet, credits it to someone else?

Theories of Motivation

Researchers have suggested a variety of theories of human motivation, some that describe *what* motivates people and others that describe *how* they go about fulfilling their needs. No single theory offers a complete and proven picture of motivation, but each can offer some perspective. As you read about these theories, bear in mind that motivational theory is a broad field in which researchers continue to piece together this complex puzzle. As a manager, don't settle on a single theory to the exclusion of all others, and pay attention to new developments and ideas.

One of the earliest motivational researchers, Frederick W. Taylor, a machinist and engineer from Philadelphia, studied employee efficiency and motivation in the late nineteenth and early twentieth centuries. He is credited with developing **scientific management**, an approach that sought to improve employee efficiency through the scientific study of work. In addition to analyzing work and business processes in order to develop better methods, Taylor also popularized compensation schemes that emphasized financial incentives for good performance. His work truly revolutionized business and had a direct influence on the rise of the United States as a global industrial power in the first half of the twentieth century.[41]

Although money proved to be a significant motivator for workers, scientific management didn't consider other motivational elements, such as opportunities for personal satisfaction. For instance, scientific management can't explain why someone still wants to work even though that person's spouse already makes a good living or why a successful executive will take a hefty pay cut to serve in government. Therefore, other researchers have looked beyond money to discover what else motivates people.

Maslow's Hierarchy of Needs

In 1943 psychologist Abraham Maslow proposed the theory that behavior is determined by a variety of needs, which he organized into categories arranged in a hierarchy. As Exhibit 13.7 shows, the most basic needs are at the bottom of this hierarchy and the more advanced needs are toward the top. In Maslow's hierarchy, all of the requirements for basic survival—food, clothing, shelter, and the like—fall into the category of

scientific management
Management approach designed to improve employees' efficiency by scientifically studying their work

EXHIBIT 13.7

Maslow's Hierarchy of Needs

According to Maslow, needs on the lower levels of the hierarchy must be satisfied before higher-level needs can be addressed.

- Self-actualization needs ← Leadership role
- Esteem needs ← Job title; recognition from CEO
- Social needs ← Friends at work
- Safety needs ← Health insurance; pension plan
- Physiological needs ← Salary

physiological needs. These basic needs must be satisfied before the person can consider higher-level needs such as *safety needs, social needs* (the need to give and receive love and to feel a sense of belonging), and *esteem needs* (the need for a sense of self-worth and integrity).[42]

At the top of Maslow's hierarchy is *self-actualization*—the need to become everything one can become. This need is also the most difficult to fulfill—and even to identify in many cases. Employees who reach this point work not just because they want to make money or impress others but because they feel their work is worthwhile and satisfying in itself. Self-actualization needs partially explain why some people make radical career changes or strike out on their own as entrepreneurs. Conversely, when faced with tough or unstable economic conditions, employees may temporarily downplay higher-order needs and focus on the physiological and safety needs—making a steady paycheck more important than personal fulfillment.

Although Maslow's hierarchy is a convenient way to classify human needs, it would be a mistake to view it as a rigid sequence. A person need not completely satisfy each level of needs before being motivated by a higher need. Indeed, at any one time, most people are motivated by a combination of needs.

Herzberg's Two-Factor Theory

In the 1960s Frederick Herzberg and his associates asked accountants and engineers to describe specific aspects of their jobs that made them feel satisfied or dissatisfied. The researchers found that two entirely different sets of factors were associated with dissatisfying and satisfying work experiences: *hygiene factors* and *motivators* (see Exhibit 13.8). What Herzberg called **hygiene factors** are associated with *dissatisfying* experiences. The potential sources of dissatisfaction include working conditions, company policies, pay, and job security. Management can decrease worker dissatisfaction by improving hygiene factors, but such improvements seldom increase satisfaction. On the other hand, managers can help employees feel more motivated and, ultimately, more satisfied by paying attention to **motivators** such as achievement, recognition, responsibility, and other personally rewarding factors.[43] "We believe money is always a factor, but if employees feel respected and valued, their personal satisfaction is far greater, and their performance is

hygiene factors
In Herzberg's two-factor model, aspects of the work environment that are associated with dissatisfaction

motivators
In Herzberg's two-factor model, factors that may increase motivation

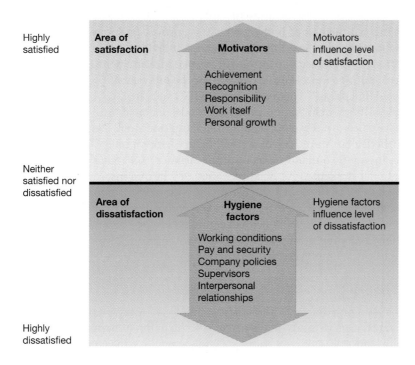

EXHIBIT 13.8

Two-Factor Theory

Hygiene factors such as working conditions and company policies can influence employee dissatisfaction. On the other hand, motivators such as opportunities for achievement and recognition can influence employee satisfaction.

positively affected," says Joel G. Crowell, CEO of Cape Cod Cooperative Bank in Yarmouth Port, Massachusetts.[44]

According to Herzberg's model, managers need to focus on removing dissatisfying elements (such as unpleasant working conditions or low pay) and adding satisfying elements (such as interesting work and professional recognition). The specific areas to address vary from one situation to the next. A skilled, well-paid, middle-aged employee may be motivated to perform better if motivators are supplied. However, a young, unskilled worker who earns low wages or an employee who is insecure will probably still need the support of strong hygiene factors to reduce dissatisfaction before the motivators can be effective.

Theory X, Theory Y, and Theory Z

In the 1960s psychologist Douglas McGregor identified two radically different sets of assumptions that underlie most management thinking, which he classified as *Theory X* and *Theory Y*. According to McGregor, **Theory X**-oriented managers believe that employees dislike work and can be motivated only by the fear of losing their jobs or by *extrinsic rewards*—those given by other people, such as money, promotions, and tenure. This management style emphasizes physiological and safety needs and tends to ignore the higher-level needs in Maslow's hierarchy. In contrast, **Theory Y**-oriented managers believe that employees like work and can be motivated by working for goals that promote creativity or for causes they believe in. Consequently, Theory Y-oriented managers seek to motivate employees through *intrinsic rewards*—which employees essentially give themselves.[45] For example, creating products known for high quality is a powerful intrinsic reward. At Cobalt Boats, a motorboat manufacturer based in Neodesha, Kansas, veteran boatbuilders take such pride in their work that they've been known to hound each other (and newer employees in particular) to make sure nothing is done to tarnish Cobalt's reputation for sterling quality. As employee Robert Allen puts it, "We have a job to do: To build the best boats in the world. Simple as that."[46]

The assumptions behind Theory X emphasize authority; the assumptions behind Theory Y emphasize growth and self-direction. However, it's a mistake to conclude that Theory X is necessarily a bad approach and that Theory Y is necessarily a good approach. Effective managers assess every situation and use their judgment and experience to apply the right methods.

In the 1980s, when U.S. businesses began to feel a strong competitive threat from Japanese companies, William Ouchi proposed another approach to motivation that was based on his comparative study of Japanese and U.S. management practices. His **Theory Z** merged the best of both systems, as expressed in seven principles: long-term employment, consensus-based decision making, individual responsibility, slow evaluation and promotion, informal control with formal measurements, a moderate degree of career specialization, and a holistic concern for the individual.[47]

Although the phrase "Theory Z" isn't used as much in current management discussions as it was after Ouchi first proposed the model, many of the principles embodied in Theory Z have been widely embraced by both large and small companies. Mark Cuban, owner of the Dallas Mavericks basketball team, demonstrates Theory Z principles—sometimes in slightly outlandish fashion. For instance, Cuban has been repeatedly fined by the National Basketball Association ($500,000 in one instance) for criticizing the efforts of referees. His isn't just the usual courtside griping, however. In Cuban's eyes, failure to call penalties on opposing players was endangering the health and safety of his players.[48] By showing that he'll do whatever it takes to protect and support his employees, including everyone from players to coaches to office workers, Cuban embraces the holistic concern for employees that Ouchi promoted.

Equity Theory

Equity theory contributes to the understanding of motivation by suggesting that employee satisfaction depends on the perceived ratio of inputs to outputs. If you work side by side with someone, doing the same job and giving the same amount of effort, only to

Theory X
Managerial assumption that employees are irresponsible, are unambitious, and dislike work and that managers must use force, control, or threats to motivate them

Theory Y
Managerial assumption that employees enjoy meaningful work, are naturally committed to certain goals, are capable of creativity, and seek out responsibility under the right conditions

Theory Z
Leadership approach that emphasizes involving employees at all levels and treating them like family

equity theory
A theory that suggests employees base their level of satisfaction on the ratio of their inputs to the job and the outputs or rewards they receive from it

Which Theory Will Solve the Problem of Employee Theft?

In a world where many managers go out of their way to keep employees happy, the rather bleak assumptions regarding the motives and behavior of the average employee expressed in Theory X almost sound like something from the Dark Ages. After all, today's Theory Y managers are supposed to treat employees with respect, give them plenty of freedom, and trust them to make the right decisions and look out for the best interests of customers and the company.

But there's one small problem: Some employees abuse that trust and steal from their employers. Actually, it's not a small problem at all. Employee theft and embezzlement is a *huge* problem, costing U.S. companies hundreds of billions of dollars a year—that's *billions* with a *b*. (Legally speaking, embezzlement differs slightly from regular theft. The FBI defines it as "misappropriation or misuse of money or property entrusted to one's care, custody, or control," as opposed to simply taking something that doesn't belong to you. A payroll manager who puts fictitious employees on the books, then pockets their paychecks commits embezzlement, for instance.)

Employee thievery ranges from the simple to the complex, from taking office supplies to stealing retail products (in the retail business, theft by employees is usually a much bigger problem than shoplifting) to creating fictitious companies that then bill the employer for equally fictitious goods or services. The financial damage is considerable, although exact amounts are difficult to pin down—partly because some companies are embarrassed to report such losses. In rough terms, simple theft of supplies and inventory costs companies somewhere between $15 billion and $90 billion every year. Throw in intellectual property theft, and the number jumps to $240 billion a year or so. Embezzlement more than doubles that, to some $600 billion a year.

Who pays for all this? You do—you and every other employee, investor, and customer. Not only do companies suffer the direct financial damage, but they also incur billions of dollars in costs for everything from extra insurance to security guards to legal expenses to an array of technological controls. The result is higher costs for customers, less money to spend on employee wages and benefits, and additional restrictions on all employees—including the honest ones. Moreover, some experts estimate that 30 to 50 percent of all business failures are a result of employee theft and embezzlement.

Against those odds, even the most enlightened modern managers may need to exercise some good old-fashioned Theory X skepticism about their workforces.

Questions for Critical Thinking

1. How should managers explain to their workforces the necessity to implement security controls?
2. Could Herzberg's hygiene factors help explain employee theft and embezzlement? Why or why not?

learn that your colleague earns more money, would you be satisfied in your work and motivated to continue working hard? You perceive a state of *inequity*, so you probably won't be happy with the situation. In response, you might ask for a raise, decide not to work as hard, try to change perceptions of your efforts or their outcomes, or simply quit and find a new job; any one of these steps could bring your perceived input/output ratio back into balance.[49] In the aftermath of large-scale layoffs in many sectors of the economy in the past few years, many of the employees left behind feel a sense of inequity in being asked to shoulder the work of those who left, without getting paid more for the extra effort.[50] Equity also plays a central role in complaints about gender pay fairness (see page 351) and many unionizing efforts, whenever employees feel they aren't getting a fair share of corporate profits or are being asked to shoulder more than their fair share of hardships.

Expectancy Theory

Expectancy theory, considered by some experts to offer the best available explanation of employee motivation, links an employee's efforts with the outcome he or she expects from that effort. Like equity theory, expectancy theory focuses less on the specific forces that motivate employees and more on the process they follow to seek satisfaction in their jobs. Expectancy theory expands on earlier theories in several important ways, including linking effort to performance and linking rewards to individual goals (see Exhibit 13.9). The effort employees will put forth depends on (1) their expectations about their own ability to perform, (2) their expectations about the rewards that the organization will give in response to that performance, and (3) the attractiveness of those rewards relative to their individual goals.[51] For example, if a sales representative believes she has the

expectancy theory
Suggests that the effort employees put into their work depends on expectations about their own ability to perform, expectations about likely rewards, and the attractiveness of those rewards

EXHIBIT 13.9

Expectancy Theory

Expectancy theory suggests that employees base their efforts on expectations of their own performance, expectations of rewards for that performance, and the value of those rewards.

The quality of the effort put forth depends on...

...expectations of

...and expectations of

...and the attractiveness of those rewards relative to

| Individual effort | Individual performance | Organizational rewards | Individual goals |

ability to sell her company's products and believes her employer will reward her in a way that supports her personal or professional goals, she'll probably be strongly motivated to sell.

Motivational Strategies

Once managers have some idea of what raises or lowers employee motivation, they can devise policies and procedures that attempt to keep the workforce energized and engaged. The range of motivational decisions managers face is almost endless, from redesigning jobs to make them more interesting to offering recognition programs for high achievers. Whether it's a basic award program for salespeople or an entirely new way to structure the workforce, though, every motivational strategy needs to consider two critical aspects: setting goals and reinforcing behavior.

Setting Goals

As mentioned earlier, successful motivation involves action. To be successful, that action needs to be directed toward a meaningful goal. Accordingly, **goal-setting theory** suggests the idea that goals can motivate employees. The process of setting goals is often embodied in the technique known as **management by objectives (MBO)**, a companywide process that empowers employees and involves them in goal setting and decision making. This process consists of four steps: setting goals, planning actions, implementing plans, and reviewing performance (see Exhibit 13.10). Because employees at all levels are involved in all four steps, they learn more about company objectives and feel that they are an important part of the companywide team. Furthermore, they understand how even their individual job function contributes to the organization's long-term success.

One of the key elements of MBO is a collaborative goal-setting process. Together, a manager and employee define the employee's goals, the responsibilities for achieving those goals, and the means of evaluating individual and group performance so that the employee's activities are directly linked to achieving the organization's long-term goals. Jointly setting clear and challenging—but achievable—goals can encourage employees to reach higher levels of performance.

Reinforcing Behavior

Employees in the workplace, like human beings in all aspects of life, tend to repeat behaviors that create positive outcomes. **Reinforcement theory** suggests that managers can motivate employees by controlling or changing their actions through **behavior modification**. Managers systematically encourage those actions that are desirable by providing pleasant consequences and discourage those that are not by providing unpleasant consequences.

Positive reinforcement offers pleasant consequences (such as a gift, praise, public recognition, bonus, dinner, or trip) for completing or repeating a desired action.

goal-setting theory
Motivational theory suggesting that setting goals can be an effective way to motivate employees

management by objectives (MBO)
A motivational approach in which managers and employees work together to structure personal goals and objectives for every individual, department, and project to mesh with the organization's goals

reinforcement theory
A motivational approach based on the idea that managers can motivate employees by influencing their behaviors with positive and negative reinforcement

behavior modification
Systematic use of rewards and punishments to change human behavior

EXHIBIT 13.10 Management by Objectives

The MBO process has four steps. This cycle is refined and repeated as managers and employees at all levels work toward establishing goals and objectives, thereby accomplishing the organization's strategic goals.

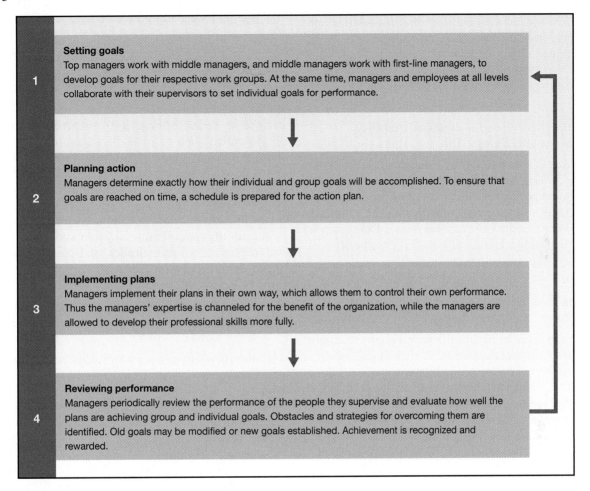

1 Setting goals
Top managers work with middle managers, and middle managers work with first-line managers, to develop goals for their respective work groups. At the same time, managers and employees at all levels collaborate with their supervisors to set individual goals for performance.

2 Planning action
Managers determine exactly how their individual and group goals will be accomplished. To ensure that goals are reached on time, a schedule is prepared for the action plan.

3 Implementing plans
Managers implement their plans in their own way, which allows them to control their own performance. Thus the managers' expertise is channeled for the benefit of the organization, while the managers are allowed to develop their professional skills more fully.

4 Reviewing performance
Managers periodically review the performance of the people they supervise and evaluate how well the plans are achieving group and individual goals. Obstacles and strategies for overcoming them are identified. Old goals may be modified or new goals established. Achievement is recognized and rewarded.

Experts recommend the use of positive reinforcement because it emphasizes the desired behavior rather than the unwanted behavior. By contrast, *negative reinforcement* allows people to avoid unpleasant consequences by behaving in the desired way. For example, fear of losing a job (unpleasant consequence) may move an employee to finish a project on time (desired behavior). For motivated employees, however, negative techniques are likely to be less powerful than encouraging their sense of direction, creativity, and pride in doing a good job.

How This Affects You

1. Does Maslow's theory of the hierarchy of needs make sense in your own life? What if you are a typical college student who doesn't have much financial security at the moment but you're simultaneously trying to fulfill higher-order needs such as social interaction and self-actualization through education—would it make more sense, according to Maslow, to drop out of college and work seven days a week so you could help ensure that your physiological and safety needs are met?

2. Think about McGregor's Theory X and Theory Y in relation to your fellow students. Do you think today's college students more closely match the descriptions of Theory X employees or Theory Y employees? What evidence can you provide to support your conclusion?

3. Do goals motivate you? Why or why not? Does it depend on whether the goals are your own or imposed by someone else?

Summary of Learning Objectives

1 Discuss the function of a company's organization structure.

An organization structure provides a framework through which a company can coordinate and control the work, divide responsibilities, distribute authority, and hold employees accountable. An organization chart provides a visual representation of this framework.

2 Explain the concepts of accountability, authority, and delegation.

Accountability is the obligation to report work results to supervisors or team members and to justify any outcomes that fall below expectations. Authority is the power to make decisions, issue orders, carry out actions, and allocate resources to achieve the organization's goals. Delegation is the assignment of work and the transfer of authority and responsibility to complete that work.

3 Define five major types of organization structure.

Companies can organize in four primary ways: by function, which groups employees according to their skills, resource use, and expertise; by division, which establishes self-contained departments formed according to similarities in product, process, customer, or geography; by matrix, which assigns employees from functional departments to interdisciplinary project teams and requires them to report to both a department head and a team leader; and by network, which connects separate companies that perform selected tasks for a headquarters organization. In addition, many companies now combine elements of two or more of these designs into hybrid structures.

4 Highlight the advantages and disadvantages of working in teams.

Teamwork has the potential to produce higher-quality decisions, increase commitment to solutions and changes, lower stress and destructive internal competition, and improve flexibility and responsiveness. The potential disadvantages of working in teams include inefficiency, groupthink, diminished individual motivation, structural disruption, and excessive workloads.

5 List the characteristics of effective teams.

Effective teams have a clear sense of purpose, communicate openly and honestly, build a sense of fairness in decision making, think creatively, stay focused on key issues, manage conflict constructively, and select team members wisely by involving stakeholders, creative thinkers, and members with a diversity of views. Moreover, effective teams have an optimal size of between 5 and 12 members.

6 Review the five stages of team development and highlight six causes of team conflict.

Teams typically go through five stages of development. In the forming stage, team members become acquainted with each other and with the group's purpose. In the storming stage, conflict often arises as coalitions and power struggles develop. In the norming stage, conflicts are resolved and harmony develops. In the performing stage, members focus on achieving the team's goals. In the adjourning stage, the team dissolves upon completion of its task. Team conflict can arise from competition for scarce resources; confusion over task responsibility; poor communication and misinformation; differences in values, attitudes, and personalities; power struggles; and goal incongruity.

7 Compare Maslow's hierarchy of needs and Herzberg's two-factor theory, then explain their application to employee motivation.

Maslow's hierarchy organizes individual needs into five categories and proposes that the individual must satisfy the most basic needs before being able to address higher-level needs. Based on the assumption that employees want to "climb to the top" of Maslow's pyramid, managers should provide opportunities to satisfy those higher-level needs. Herzberg's two-factor theory covers the same general set of employee needs but divides them into two distinct groups. His theory suggests that hygiene factors—such as working conditions, company policies, and job security—can influence employee dissatisfaction, but an improvement in these factors will not motivate employees. Only motivational factors such as recognition and responsibility can improve employee performance.

8 Explain why expectancy theory is considered by some to be the best description of employee behavior.

Expectancy, which suggests that the effort employees put into their work depends on expectations about their own ability to perform, expectations about the rewards that the organization will give in response to that performance, and the attractiveness of those rewards relative to their individual goals, is considered a good model because it considers the linkages between effort and outcome. For instance, if employees think a linkage is "broken," such as having doubts that their efforts will yield acceptable performance or worries that they will perform well but no one will notice, they're likely to put less effort into their work.

Behind the Scenes

Teaming Up for Success at The Container Store

The Container Store was not started with a modest goal. Founders Garrett Boone and Kip Tindell set out to become the "best retail store in the United States." Judging by feedback from customers and employees, they just might have succeeded.

As millions of frustrated consumers know all too well, though, delivering great customer service in retail environments isn't easy. The Container Store does it with strong company values, respect for employees, and a structure that promotes teamwork over individual competition. The company's values flow from the idea that people are its greatest asset because they are the key to exceptional service. The notion that "people are our greatest asset" is repeated often in the business world, and often without substance to back it up, but The Container Store goes to extraordinary lengths to practice what it preaches.

When selecting new employees, for instance, the company engages in a comprehensive interviewing and selection process to find the perfect person for each position, driven by the belief that one great person equals three good ones. Most employees are college educated, almost half come from employee referrals, and most have been customers of the store. They are also self-motivated, team oriented, and passionate about customer service.

Those traits are enhanced by extensive employee development: New full-time employees receive over 200 hours of training in their first year and nearly that much every year thereafter. In comparison, most retailers give new workers less than 10 hours of training per year. As a result, Container Store employees feel extremely confident in their ability to help customers, and positive feedback from customers continues to build that confidence.

The Container Store also pays three to four times the minimum wage, offering wages as much as 50 to 100 percent above those of other retailers. The financial security builds loyalty and helps keep annual turnover around 20 percent, a fraction of the typical turnover rates in the industry. What's more, salespeople are not paid commissions, unlike retail staffs in many other companies. Without the constant pressure to "make the numbers," it's easier for employees to take their time with customers, using their creative instincts and extensive training to design complete solutions to customers' storage problems. By not paying commissions, The Container Store also helps employees sense that they're all part of a team, rather than being in competition with one another.

That emphasis on teamwork is reinforced twice a day, before opening and after closing, through a meeting called "the huddle." Similar to a huddle in football, it helps to give everyone a common purpose: set goals, share information, boost morale, and bond as a team. Morning sessions feature spirited discussions of sales goals and product applications and may include a chorus of "Happy Birthday" for celebrating team members. Evening huddles include more team building and friendly competitions such as guessing the daily sales figures. Tindell believes that full, open communication with employees takes courage but says, "The only way that people feel really, really a part of something is if they know everything."

The Container Store also differs dramatically from many retail establishments in the way it embraces part-time employees. These workers are essential at the busiest times, such as evenings and holiday seasons, but they are treated as second-class citizens in some companies. Not at The Container Store. To begin with, the company refers to them as "prime-time" employees, not part-time, since these staffers are most valuable in those prime-time rush periods. And these people also receive extensive training and are treated as equal members of the team at each store. As one prime-timer in Houston puts it, "Everyone is treated as an important human being. I don't feel like a part-time employee at all—I feel like a professional. They make belonging easy and a source of pride."

By aligning its corporate values with its management practices and its organization structure, The Container Store paves the way for its employees to deliver great customer service. And by frequently astonishing its employees with enlightened leadership, the company sets a strong example for the people in blue aprons who are expected to astonish customers every day.

People outside the company are starting to notice, too. The Container Store has become a consistent winner in such nationwide forums as the annual Performance Through People Award, presented by Northwestern University, and *Fortune* magazine's annual list of "The 100 Best Companies to Work For."[52]

Critical Thinking Questions

1. Based on what you've learned about the way Container Store employees interact with customers, do you think that the company emphasizes centralized or decentralized decision making? Explain your answer.

2. How might the company's emphasis on teamwork affect accountability and authority?

3. What effect might a change to commission-based compensation have on the team structure at The Container Store?

LEARN MORE ONLINE

Visit The Container Store's website at www.containerstore.com and read about the company's history, its culture, and the benefits it offers employees. What do you think of the company's belief that one great person equals three good people? What kinds of jobs are available in stores, the home office, and the distribution center? (For the latest information on The Container Store and organization structures, teamwork, and motivation, visit www.prenhall.com/bovée and click on "Real-Time Updates.") ■

Key Terms

accountability (324)	free riders (331)	organization chart (322)
authority (324)	functional structure (326)	organization structure (322)
behavior modification (340)	functional teams (329)	problem-solving teams (329)
centralization (325)	goal-setting theory (340)	reinforcement theory (340)
chain of command (324)	hybrid structure (328)	responsibility (324)
cohesiveness (333)	hygiene factors (337)	scientific management (336)
committee (329)	informal organization (323)	self-managed teams (329)
cross-functional teams (329)	line organization (324)	span of management (325)
decentralization (325)	line-and-staff organization (324)	tall organizations (325)
delegation (324)	management by objectives	task force (329)
departmentalization (326)	(MBO) (340)	team (328)
divisional structure (327)	matrix structure (327)	Theory X (338)
engagement (335)	morale (335)	Theory Y (338)
equity theory (338)	motivation (335)	Theory Z (338)
expectancy theory (339)	motivators (337)	virtual teams (329)
flat organizations (325)	network structure (327)	work specialization (323)
formal organization (323)	norms (333)	

Test Your Knowledge

Questions for Review

1. Why is organization structure important?
2. What are the advantages and disadvantages of work specialization?
3. What are the advantages and disadvantages of functional departmentalization?
4. What is motivation?
5. What is expectancy theory?

Questions for Analysis

6. Why would you expect a manager of a group of nuclear physicists to have a wide span of management?
7. How can a virtual organization reduce costs?
8. What can managers do to help teams work more effectively?
9. Why do managers often find it difficult to motivate employees who remain after downsizing?
10. **Ethical Considerations.** You were honored that you were selected to serve on the salary committee of the employee negotiations task force. As a member of that committee, you reviewed confidential company documents listing the salaries of all department managers. You discovered that managers at your level are earning $5,000 more than you, even though you've been at the company the same amount of time. You feel that a raise is justified on the basis of this confidential information. How will you handle this situation?

Questions for Application

11. You are the leader of a cross-functional work team whose goal is to find ways of lowering production costs. Your team of eight employees has become mired in the storming stage. They disagree on how to approach the task, and they are starting to splinter into factions. What can you do to help the team move forward?
12. **How This Affects You.** How do you motivate yourself when faced with school assignments or projects that are difficult or tedious? Do you ever try to relate these tasks to your overall career goals? Are you more motivated by doing your personal best or by outperforming other students?
13. **Integrated.** How do economic concepts such as profit motive and competitive advantage (see Chapter 1) affect today's workforce?
14. **Integrated.** Chapter 12 discusses several styles of leadership, including autocratic, democratic, and laissez-faire. Using your knowledge about the differences in these leadership styles, which style would you expect to find under the following organization structures: (a) tall organization—departmentalization by function; (b) tall organization—departmentalization by matrix; (c) flat organization; (d) self-directed teams?

Practice Your Knowledge

Sharpening Your Communication Skills

Write a brief memo to your instructor describing a recent conflict you had with a peer at work or at school. Be sure to highlight the cause of the conflict and steps you took to resolve it. Which of the three conflict-resolution styles discussed in this chapter did you use? Did you find a solution that both of you could accept?

Building Your Team Skills

What's the most effective organization structure for your college or university? With your team, obtain a copy of your school's organization chart. If this chart is not readily available, gather information by talking with people in administration, then draw your own chart of the organization structure.

Analyze the chart in terms of span of management. Is your school a flat or a tall organization? Is this organization structure appropriate for your school? Does decision making tend to be centralized or decentralized in your school? Do you agree with this approach to decision making?

Finally, investigate the use of formal and informal teams in your school. Are there any problem-solving teams, task forces, or committees at work in your school? Are any teams self-directed or virtual? How much authority do these teams have to make decisions? What is the purpose of teamwork in your school? What kinds of goals do these teams have?

Share your team's findings during a brief classroom presentation, then compare the findings of all teams. Is there agreement on the appropriate organization structure for your school?

Improving Your Tech Insights: Telecommuting Technologies

In simplest form, telecommuting doesn't require much more than a computer, a telephone, and access to the Internet and e-mail. However, most corporate employees need a more comprehensive connection to their offices, with such features as secure access to confidential files, groupware, and web-based virtual meetings that let people communicate and share information over the Internet. Some of the other technologies you'll encounter in telecommuting include broadband Internet connections, some form of file access (including shared workspaces), security (including user authentication and access control), Internet-based telephone service, and wireless networking.

When they're used successfully, telecommuting technologies can reduce facility costs, put employees closer to customers, reduce traffic and air pollution in congested cities, give companies access to a wide range of independent talent, and let employees work in higher-salary jobs while living in lower-cost areas of the country. In the future, these technologies have the potential to change business so radically they could even influence the design of entire cities. With less need to pull millions of workers into central business districts, business executives, urban planners, and political leaders have the opportunity to explore such new ideas as *telecities*—virtual cities populated by people and organizations who are connected technologically, rather than physically.

Telecommuting offers compelling benefits, but it must be planned and managed carefully. Conduct some online research to find out what experts believe are the keys to success. Start with the Telework Coalition, www.telcoa.org. You can also find numerous articles in business publications (search for both "telecommuting" and "telework"). In a brief e-mail to your instructor, provide four or five important tips for ensuring successful telecommuting work arrangements.[53]

Expand Your Knowledge

Discovering Career Opportunities

Whether you're a top manager, first-line manager (supervisor), or middle manager, your efforts will impact the success of your organization. To get a closer look at what the responsibilities of a manager are, log on to the Prentice Hall Student Success SuperSite at www.prenhall.com/success. Click on "Majors Exploration" and then select "Business" and "Management" in the drop-down boxes. Then scroll down and read about careers in management.

1. What can you do with a degree in management?

2. What is the future outlook for careers in management?

3. Follow the link to the American Management Association website, and click on "Research." Then scroll down and click on "Administrative Professionals Current Concerns Survey." According to the survey, what has affected administrative professionals the most in recent years? On which five tasks do managers spend most of their time?

Developing Your Research Skills

Although teamwork can benefit many organizations, introducing and managing team structures can be a real challenge. Search past issues of business journals or newspapers (print or online editions) to locate articles about how an organization has overcome problems with teams.

1. Why did the organization originally introduce teams? What types of teams are being used?

2. What problems did each organization encounter in trying to implement teams? How did the organization deal with these problems?

3. Have the teams been successful from management's perspective? From the employees' perspective? What effect has teamwork had on the company, its customers, and its products?

See It on the Web

Visit these websites and answer the following questions for each one. (Up-to-date links for all websites mentioned in this chapter can be found on the Textbook Resources page for Chapter 13 at www.mybusinesslab.com. Please note that links to sites that become inactive after publication of the book will be removed from the Featured Websites section.)

1. What is the purpose of this website?

2. What kinds of information does this website contain? Please be specific.

3. How is the information provided at this website useful for businesspeople? Consumers?

4. How did you expand your knowledge of organization, teamwork, and motivation by reviewing the material at this website? What new things did you learn about this topic?

Learn from Leaders in Collaborative Work

The Center for Collaborative Organizations at the University of North Texas is a leading research and development center for organizational teamwork and other collaborative work modes. Click on "Information Resources" for links to numerous articles and research papers in communication and collaboration, organizational design, and teamwork www.workteams.unt.edu

Be Direct

The "Group Skills" section of the Free Management Library offers numerous articles to help team members and team leaders work more effectively. Learn more about team building, virtual teams, communities of practice, group dynamics, and more. www.managementhelp.org (click on "Group Skills")

Resolve Conflict Like a Pro

The field of conflict resolution has been growing very quickly and includes practices such as negotiation, mediation, arbitration, international peace building, and more. Learn more about each of these topics along with basic information about conflict resolution by visiting CRInfo. Be sure to check out the web resources, where you'll find links to communication and facilitation skills, consensus building, and more. Find out why BATNA is important. Discover what a mediator does. Learn how to conduct effective meetings. And don't leave without testing your knowledge of common negotiation terms. www.crinfo.org

Companion Website

Learning Interactively

Log onto www.prenhall.com/bovée, locate your text, and then click on its Companion Website. For Chapter 13, take advantage of the interactive Chapter Quiz to test your knowledge of the chapter. Get instant feedback on whether you need additional studying. Also, you'll find an abundance of valuable resources that will help you succeed in this course, including PowerPoint presentations and Web Links.

Video Case

Juicing Up the Organization: Nantucket Nectars

LEARNING OBJECTIVES

The purpose of this video is to help you:

1. Recognize how growth affects an organization's structure

2. Discuss why businesses organize by departmentalization

3. Understand how flat organizations operate

SYNOPSIS

Tom Scott and Tom First founded Nantucket Nectars in 1989 with an idea for a peach drink. In the early days, the two ran the entire operation from their boat. These days, Nantucket Nectars has more than 130 employees split between headquarters in Cambridge, Massachusetts, and several field offices. As a result, management has developed a more formalized organization structure to keep the business running smoothly. The company relies on cross-functional teams to handle special projects such as the implementation of new accounting software. These strategies have helped Nantucket Nectars successfully manage its rapid growth.

Discussion Questions

1. *For analysis:* What type of organization is in place at Nantucket Nectars?
2. *For analysis:* How would you describe the top-level span of management at Nantucket Nectars?
3. *For application:* Nantucket Nectars may need to change its organization structure as it expands into new products and new markets. Under what circumstances would some form of divisional departmentalization be appropriate for the firm?
4. *For application:* Assume that Nantucket Nectars is purchasing a well-established beverage company with a tall structure stressing top-down control. What are some of the problems that management might face in integrating the acquired firm into the existing organization structure of Nantucket Nectars?
5. *For debate:* Assume that someone who is newly promoted into a management position at Nantucket Nectars cannot adjust to delegating work to lower-level employees. Should this new manager be demoted? Support your chosen position.

ONLINE EXPLORATION

Visit the Nantucket Nectars site at www.nantucketnectars.com and follow the links to read about the company and its products. Then use your favorite search engine to find recent news about the company (which is formally known as Nantucket Allserve). Has it been acquired by a larger company or has it acquired one or more smaller firms? What are the implications for the chain of command, decision making, and organization structure of Nantucket Nectars?

CHAPTER 14

Human Resources

LEARNING OBJECTIVES

After studying this chapter, you will be able to

1 Explain the challenges and advantages of a diverse workforce

2 Discuss four staffing challenges employers are facing in today's workplace

3 Discuss four alternative work arrangements that a company can use to address workplace challenges

4 Identify the six stages in the hiring process

5 List six popular types of financial incentive programs for employees

6 Highlight five popular employee benefits

7 Describe four ways an employee's status may change and discuss why many employers like to fill job vacancies from within

8 Define the collective bargaining process

Behind the Scenes

Brewing Up People Policies for Chainwide Success

www.starbucks.com

Hiring, training, and compensating a diverse workforce of 40,000 employees worldwide would be a difficult task for any company. But it was an especially daunting challenge in an industry whose annual employee turnover rate approached 300 percent. It was even more of a challenge for a company that was striving to open a new store every day, despite a tight labor market, an uncertain global economy, and increasingly intense competition.

This was the high-pressure situation facing Starbucks Coffee Company as it set out to spread its gourmet coffee across the world. Already, the rich aroma of fresh-brewed espresso was wafting through neighborhoods all over North America, with new stores planned for the United Kingdom, Japan, China, and many other countries. But Chairman Howard Schultz and his management team knew that good locations and top-quality coffee were just part of the company's formula for success.

By offering benefits to all employees (including part-timers), Starbucks attracts and keeps quality workers.

To keep up with this ambitious schedule of new store openings, Starbucks had to find, recruit, and train hundreds of new employees every month, no easy feat "when there is a shortage of labor and few people want to work behind a retail counter," as Schultz noted. Moreover, Starbucks's employees (known internally as *partners*) had to deliver consistently superior customer service in every store and every market. In other words, Starbucks's employees had to do more than simply pour coffee—they had to believe passionately in the product and pay attention to all the details that can make or break the retail experience for the chain's millions of customers.

Schultz knew it would take more than good pay and company benefits to motivate and inspire employees. But what? If you were a member of Schultz's management team, how would you attract, train, and compensate a diverse workforce? What human resources policies and practices would you implement to motivate employees to give topnotch service?[1] ■

Keeping Pace with Today's Workforce

Howard Schultz (profiled in the chapter opener) knows that hiring the right people to help a company reach its goals and then overseeing their training and development, motivation, evaluation, and compensation are critical to a company's success. These activities are known as **human resources management (HRM)**, which encompasses all the tasks involved in acquiring, maintaining, and developing an organization's human resources, as well as maintaining a safe working environment that meets legal requirements and ethical expectations.[2] You may not pursue a career in HRM specifically, but understanding the challenges and responsibilities of the HRM function will make you a more successful manager.

human resources management (HRM)
Specialized function of planning how to obtain employees, oversee their training, evaluate them, and compensate them

Staffing Challenges

Managers in every organization face an ongoing array of staffing challenges, including aligning the workforce with organizational needs, fostering employee loyalty, adjusting workloads and monitoring for employee burnout, and helping employees balance their work and personal lives:

- *Aligning the workforce.* Matching the right employees to the right jobs at the right time can be a constant challenge. Externally, changes in market needs, competitive moves, advances in technology, and new regulations can all affect the ideal size and composition of the workforce. Internally, shifts in strategy, technological changes, and growing or declining product sales can force managers to realign their workforces. *Rightsizing* is a term used to imply that the organization is making changes in the workforce to match its business needs more precisely. Although rightsizing usually involves *downsizing* the workforce, companies sometimes add workers in some areas even while they eliminate jobs in others.

- *Fostering employee loyalty.* Companies face a considerable dilemma regarding employee loyalty: Most can't guarantee long-term employment, but they want employees to commit themselves to the company. Managers can respond to this challenge in a variety of ways. First and most important, they can manage their companies effectively and ethically; managerial blunders can devastate workforces. Second, they can give employees a stake in the success of the firm through profit sharing and other programs. Third, they can take better care of their employees. Employees who believe they are being treated well will tend to stay—and to stay engaged. Fourth, they can work with employees to align their career goals with the company's goals to create plans that benefit both parties—even if it will be for only a few years.[3]

- *Monitoring workloads and avoiding employee burnout.* As companies try to beat competitors and keep workforce costs to a minimum, managers need to be on guard for *employee burnout*, a state of physical and emotional exhaustion that can result from constant exposure to stress over a long period of time. Other employees cite the inability to ever truly get away from work, now that they're connected via mobile phones, laptop computers, and PDAs with wireless e-mail access.[4] A vital question here is whether all those hours are really necessary—particularly in professional and managerial jobs, where analysis, creativity, and decision-making skills are so important. The *quality* of this work is often more important than the *quantity*. Critics of long work hours also point to European companies such as Airbus and Nokia that compete successfully in world markets, even though Europeans typically work far fewer hours than their North American and Asian counterparts.[5]

- *Managing work-life balance.* The concern over workloads is one of the factors behind the growing interest in **work-life balance**, the idea that employees, managers, and entrepreneurs need to balance the competing demands of their professional and personal lives. Many companies are trying to make it easier for employees to juggle multiple responsibilities with on-site day-care facilities, flexible work schedules, and other options designed to improve **quality of work life (QWL)**. In addition to such benefits, companies can also improve QWL through *job enrichment*, which reduces specialization and makes work more meaningful by expanding each job's responsibilities, and *job redesign*, which restructures work to provide a better fit between employees' skills and their jobs.

Demographic Challenges

The workforce is always in a state of change, whether from a shift in global immigration patterns or from the changing balance of age groups within a country's population. The companies that are most successful at managing and motivating their employees take great care to understand the diversity of their workforces and establish programs and policies that both embrace that diversity and take full advantage of diversity's benefits.

work-life balance
Efforts to help employees balance the competing demands of their personal and professional lives

quality of work life (QWL)
Overall environment that results from job and work conditions

The pressure to get more done with fewer employees is raising concerns about employee burnout.

Workforce Diversity

Today's workforce is diverse in race, gender, age, culture, family structures, religion, sexual orientation, mental and physical ability, and educational backgrounds. Over the past few decades, many innovative companies have changed the way they approach workforce diversity, from seeing it as a legal matter to seeing it as a strategic opportunity to connect with customers and take advantage of the broadest possible pool of talent.[6]

Differences in everything from religion to ethnic heritage to military experience enrich the workplace, but all can create managerial challenges. A diverse workforce brings with it a wide range of skills, traditions, backgrounds, experiences, outlooks, and attitudes toward work—all of which can affect employee behavior on the job. Supervisors face the challenge of communicating with these diverse employees, motivating them, and fostering cooperation and harmony among them. Teams face the challenge of working together closely, and companies are challenged to coexist peacefully with business partners and with the community as a whole. Some of the most important diversity issues today include age, gender, race and ethnicity, and religion in the workplace.

Age   In many companies, it's not uncommon for two or even three generations of people to be working side by side. While this age diversity offers some important benefits—such as keeping a company tuned into different sectors of the consumer market—it also presents two key managerial challenges. The first involves the age composition of the workforce as it relates to supply and demand. For example, higher-than-average birth rates during the two decades following World War II produced the *Baby Boom* generation, which has dominated the U.S. workforce for the past couple of decades. Many middle and upper management positions are now filled by people from this age group, a fact that can be a source of frustration for younger employees hoping to climb the corporate ladder. However, as this generation begins to retire, their exodus from the workplace could have the reverse effect, leaving millions of positions empty starting around 2010.[7]

The second challenge involves attitudes and expectations regarding work, which can differ from one generation to the next. For instance, so-called *Generation X*, those born from the early 1960s through the early 1980s, is the most entrepreneurial generation in U.S. history. A majority of Gen-Xers have expressed an interest in being their own bosses, and many are comfortable working freelance positions on a long-term basis. In contrast, the first wave of *Generation Y*, or the *Millennial Generation*, now entering the workforce has shown a greater interest in job security and cooperative team efforts.[8]

Although there are no official boundaries between generations and much diversity within generations, each generation is shaped by world events and reactions to previous generations. Differing viewpoints among generations can be a source of both strength and conflict in the workplace. As with all other diversity issues, the solution to age-related conflicts can be found in respecting one another and working toward common goals. As Virginia Byrd, a veteran career counselor from Encinitas, California, put it, "It's a real blessing to have different generations in our workplaces. There is so much we can share, if we make the effort."[9]

Gender   By many measures, the United States has made considerable strides toward gender equity in the past 50 years, but significant problems remain. For example, the Equal Employment Opportunity Commission (EEOC) still fields more than 20,000 complaints a year regarding gender discrimination.[10]

The statistical picture of men and women in the workforce is complex, and various parties have sliced and diced the data in order to promote a variety of conclusions. However, nearly a half-century after the Civil Rights Act of 1964 made it illegal for employers to practice **sexism**, or discrimination on the basis of gender, three general themes are clear. First, in virtually every profession in every industry and every stage of their careers, women earn less on average than men. Over the past several decades, the pay gap has closed from less than 60 percent to roughly 70 to 80 percent (depending on the survey), but progress has stalled in recent years. Second, even in occupations that have traditionally been served primarily by women, such as teaching and nursing,

The number of U.S. workers over 65 has been growing in recent years, creating both opportunities and challenges for managers.

sexism
Discrimination on the basis of gender

women still earn less than men on average. Third, the higher up you go in most corporations, the fewer women you'll find in positions of authority. Although women fill roughly half of all managerial and professional positions in the United States, among *Fortune* 500 companies, only 15 percent of board members and fewer than 3 percent of CEOs are women.[11] Almost half of *Fortune* 1000 companies have no women top executives.[12] A lack of opportunities to advance into the top ranks is often referred to as the **glass ceiling**, implying that women can see the top but can't get there.

With laws against employment discrimination, a society that is much more supportive of women in professional roles than it was just a few decades ago, and strong evidence that companies in which women are given opportunities to lead outperform companies that don't, why do these gaps still exist? In addition to instances of simple discrimination, analysts suggest a variety of reasons, including women's lower levels of education and job training, different occupational choices, the need to juggle the heavy demands of both career and parenthood, and the career hit that women often take when they step out of the workforce for extended periods—since more women than men choose to be stay-at-home parents.[13]

Beyond pay and promotional opportunities, many working women also have to deal with **sexual harassment**, defined as either an obvious request for sexual favors with an implicit reward or punishment related to work, or the more subtle creation of a sexist environment in which employees are made to feel uncomfortable by lewd jokes, remarks, or gestures. Even though male employees may also be targets of sexual harassment and both male and female employees may experience same-sex harassment, sexual harassment of female employees by male colleagues continues to make up the majority of reported cases.[14] Most corporations now publish strict policies prohibiting harassment, both to protect their employees and to protect themselves from lawsuits.[15]

glass ceiling
Invisible barrier attributable to subtle discrimination that keeps women out of the top positions in business

sexual harassment
Unwelcome sexual advance, request for sexual favors, or other verbal or physical conduct of a sexual nature within the workplace

Race   In many respects, the element of race in the diversity picture presents the same concerns as gender: equal pay for equal work, access to promotional opportunities, and ways to break through the glass ceiling. And as with gender, the EEOC still receives thousands of complaints every year about racial discrimination.[16] However, while the ratio of men and women in the workforce remains fairly stable year to year, the ethnic composition of the United States has been on a long-term trend of greater and greater diversity. Even the term *minority*, as it applies to nonwhite residents, makes less and less sense every year: In two states (California and New Mexico), several dozen large cities, and one-tenth of all counties across the United States, Caucasian Americans no longer constitute the majority.[17]

Unfortunately, as with average wages between women and men, disparity still exists along racial lines. For instance, African American males earn roughly 75 percent of what white males earn, and that ratio has barely budged in the last decade.[18] One bright spot: African Americans now hold more than 300 board seats in the largest U.S. corporations, leading to expectations that people in these positions will use their influence to level the playing field for minority employees.[19]

Religion   The effort to accommodate employees' life interests on a broader scale has led a number of companies to address the issue of religion in the workplace. As one of the most personal aspects of life, of course, religion does bring potential for controversy in a work setting. On the one hand, some employees feel they should be able to express their beliefs in the workplace and not be forced to "check their faith at the door" when they come to work. On the other hand, companies want to avoid situations in which openly expressed religious differences might cause friction between employees or distract employees from their responsibilities.

To help address such concerns, firms such as Ford, Intel, Texas Instruments, and American Airlines allow employees to form faith-based employee-support groups as part of their diversity strategies. In contrast, some companies don't allow organized religious activities at their facilities.[20] However, the EEOC and other employment experts

Managers have the responsibility to educate their employees on the definition and consequences of sexual harassment.

say that outright bans may not hold up in court. "If there is a possibility of an accommodation, you have to explore it," asserts one EEOC official.[21] As more companies work to establish inclusive workplaces, and as more employees seek to integrate religious convictions into their daily work, you can expect to see this issue being discussed at a wide range of companies in the coming years.

Diversity Initiatives

To respond to these many challenges—and to capitalize on the business opportunities offered by both diverse marketplaces and diverse workforces—companies across the country are finding that embracing diversity in the richest sense is simply good business. In response, thousands of U.S. companies have established **diversity initiatives**, which can include such steps as contracting with more suppliers owned by women and minorities, targeting a more diverse customer base, and supporting the needs and interests of a diverse workforce. For example, IBM established executive-led task forces to represent women, Asian Americans, African Americans, Hispanic Americans, Native Americans, people with disabilities, and individuals who are gay, lesbian, bisexual, and transgender. Today, diversity is embraced at the employee level through more than 100 networking groups that unite people with a variety of talents and interests. As part of a broader effort to include as many employees as possible in its available talent pool, the company views its diversity efforts as a way to produce the best products in a competitive marketplace. For instance, women and minorities are a significant presence in the small-business marketplace, and having women and minorities on product development and marketing teams helps IBM understand the needs of these customers.[22]

diversity initiatives
Programs and policies that help companies support diverse workforces and markets

Alternative Work Arrangements

To meet today's staffing and demographic challenges, many companies are adopting alternative work arrangements to better accommodate the needs of employees—and to reduce costs in many cases. Four of the most popular arrangements are flextime, telecommuting, job sharing, and flexible career paths:

- An increasingly important alternative work arrangement, **flextime** is a scheduling system that allows employees to choose their own hours, within certain limits. Of course, the feasibility of flextime differs from industry to industry and from position to position within individual companies. For instance, jobs that involve customer contact can require fixed working hours.

flextime
Scheduling system in which employees are allowed certain options regarding time of arrival and departure

- **Telecommuting**, working from home or another location using computers and telecommunications equipment to stay in touch with colleagues, suppliers, and customers, helps employees balance their professional and personal commitments by spending less time in transit between home and work. Thanks to the iWork program at Sun Microsystems, thousands of employees work from home or from one of several drop-in *telework* centers at least part of the time—and the company saves millions of dollars a year in real estate costs.[23]

telecommuting
Ability to work from home or other remote locations using telecommunications technology

- **Job sharing**, which lets two employees share a single full-time job and split the salary and benefits, can be an attractive alternative for people who want part-time hours in situations normally reserved for full-time employees. After the British drugstore chain Boots implemented job sharing, the percentage of women who returned to the company after maternity leave jumped from 7 to 77 percent.[24]

job sharing
Splitting a single full-time job between two employees for their convenience

- Perhaps the most challenging of all alternative work arrangements are situations in which employees want to temporarily leave the workforce for an extended period to raise children, volunteer, or pursue other personal interests. For example, nearly half of all women in one survey had left work to raise children, and 93 percent of these women wanted to return to work at some point. Companies such as the investment bank Lehman Brothers (www.lehman.com) are working to change both perceptions and policies to re-recruit these parents and other professionals. Flexible schedules, job sharing, and other tools can help, but accommodating these employees also requires changing perceptions among hiring managers and colleagues who have maintained a traditional career path.[25]

For the latest information on keeping pace with today's workforce, visit http:// introbusinessstudent.com and click on "Real-Time Updates."

Planning for a Company's Staffing Needs

Planning for a company's staffing needs is a delicate balancing act. Hire too few employees, and you can't keep pace with the competition or satisfy customers. Hire too many and you raise fixed costs above a level that revenues can sustain. To avoid either problem, HR managers take steps to (1) forecast the supply and demand for all types of talent and (2) evaluate the requirements of every job in the company (see Exhibit 14.1).

Forecasting Supply and Demand

To forecast demand for the numbers and types of employees who will be needed at various times, HR managers weigh (1) forecast sales revenues; (2) the expected *turnover rate*, the percentage of the workforce that leaves every year; (3) the current workforce's skill level, relative to the company's future needs; (4) impending strategic decisions; (5) changes in technology or other business factors that could affect the number and type of workers needed; and (6) the company's current and projected financial status.[26]

In addition to overall workforce levels, every company has a number of employees and managers who are considered so critical to the company's ongoing operations that HR managers work with top executives to identify potential replacements in the event of the loss of any of these people, a process known as **succession planning**.[27] A **replacement chart** identifies these key employees and lists potential replacements.

With some idea of future workforce demands, the HR staff then tries to estimate the *supply* of available employees. To ensure a steady supply of experienced employees for new opportunities and to maintain existing operations, successful companies focus heavily on **employee retention**.

If existing employees cannot be tapped for new positions, the HR team must determine how to find people outside the company who have the necessary skills. **Contingent employees**, or *temporaries*, can help businesses save money and increase flexibility by augmenting their core workforces as needed, without adding to fixed costs. However, contingent workforces are by no means a simple solution to staffing requirements. The challenges include motivating workers who don't feel they have a stake in the organization's long-term success, investing in training for workers with no clear promise of a

succession planning
Workforce planning efforts that identify possible replacements for specific employees, usually senior executives

replacement chart
A planning tool that identifies the most vital employees in the organization and information about their potential replacement

employee retention
Efforts to keep current employees

contingent employees
Nonpermanent employees, including temporary workers, independent contractors, and full-time employees hired on a probationary basis

---

EXHIBIT 14.1 Steps in Human Resources Planning

Careful attention to each phase of this sequence helps ensure that a company will have the right human resources when it needs them.

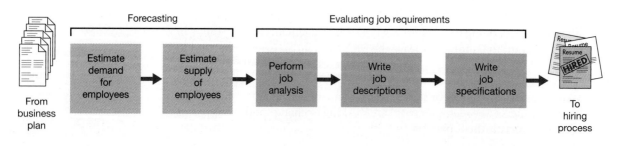

long-term payoff from that investment, and dealing with a variety of legal and taxation issues involved in hiring contingent workers.[28]

In addition to augmenting core staff with contingent workers, companies can also outsource entire business functions, such as sales, product design, or even human resources. In general, outsourcing is used to take advantage of outside expertise, to increase flexibility, or to benefit from the cost-efficiencies offered by firms that specialize in a single business function. Many companies even outsource work to former employees who've set themselves up as independent contractors or started companies that perform the same functions they used to perform for employers.[29]

Evaluating Job Requirements

The second step of the planning function is to evaluate job requirements. Through the process of **job analysis**, employers try to identify both the nature and demands of each position within the firm and the optimal employee profile to fill each position.[30] Once job analysis has been completed, the human resources staff develops a **job description**, a formal statement summarizing the tasks involved in the job and the conditions under which the employee will work. In most cases, the staff will also develop a **job specification**, which identifies the type of personnel a job requires, including the skills, education, experience, and personal attributes that candidates need to possess[31] (see Exhibit 14.2).

> ### Learning from Business Blunders
>
> **Oops:** In a coordinated one-night raid on 61 Wal-Mart locations in 21 states, federal agents rounded up 250 to 300 illegal aliens who worked for companies that Wal-Mart contracted to clean its stores at night. The public and regulators would have probably overlooked one or two instances of this nature, but Wal-Mart has made quite a few headlines in recent years, with several cases of illegal aliens working for cleaning contractors and multiple accusations of violating child labor laws and overtime laws, and discriminating against women. Employees have even complained about being locked in stores at night. (The company claims this policy was intended to protect employees in high-crime areas, but some employees have complained they couldn't get out of the building when they were sick or injured, when hurricanes hit in Florida, or when their wives went into labor.) In all of these cases, Wal-Mart has defended itself by saying that any wrong actions taken on the part of employees or outside firms are against company policy.
>
> **What You Can Learn:** Managing a company as large as Wal-Mart is a complex task, to be sure, and mistakes are bound to happen. Big companies are also big targets, so based on numbers alone, Wal-Mart is going to attract more complaints and more lawsuits than smaller employers. Moreover, Wal-Mart itself wasn't accused of hiring illegal aliens. However, in the court of public opinion, such distinctions are often lost on many people. In addition, the public and government officials aren't always going to accept the defense that company policy forbids all these wrong actions and that the problems were caused by a few rogue managers acting on their own. When mistakes are repeated or occur in multiple places throughout the company, people get suspicious. As Jeffrey Garten, dean of the Yale School of Management, wrote in reference to Wal-Mart's troubles, "For me, there is too much smoke for there not to be a fire." Every business organization needs to clearly communicate explicit policies that forbid illegal activity, and managers need to review the culture of the organization to see if it is intentionally or unintentionally promoting bad behavior. For instance, if a supervisor picks up the message to "cut costs or you'll lose your job," even if it's never expressed in those exact words, he or she might be sorely tempted to cut ethical or legal corners.

Recruiting, Hiring, and Training New Employees

Having forecast a company's supply and demand for employees and evaluated job requirements, the HR manager's next step is **recruiting**, the process of attracting suitable candidates for an organization's jobs. The recruiting function is often judged by a combination of criteria known as *quality of hire*, which measures how closely incoming employees meet the company's needs.[32] Recruiters use a variety of resources, including internal searches, advertising, union hiring halls, college campuses and career offices, trade shows, corporate "headhunters" (outside agencies that specialize in finding and placing employees), and social networking technologies (see Exhibit 14.3).

job analysis
Process by which jobs are studied to determine the tasks and dynamics involved in performing them

job description
Statement of the tasks involved in a given job and the conditions under which the holder of the job will work

job specification
Statement describing the kind of person who would be best for a given job—including the skills, education, and previous experience that the job requires

recruiting
Process of attracting appropriate applicants for an organization's jobs

EXHIBIT 14.2

Job Description and Specification

A well-written job description and specification tells potential applicants what to expect from the job and what employers will expect from them.

Job Title
Director of E-Marketing

Location
Denver, CO

Reports to
Vice President of Marketing

Job Detail

Soccer Scope is a leading retailer of soccer equipment, apparel, and accessories based in Denver, Colorado, with retail locations in 23 states. We seek to expand our online presence under the guidance of a director of e-marketing, a new managerial position to be based in our Denver headquarters.

The candidate who fills this position will be responsible for all nonstore aspects of our retailing efforts, including Soccer Scope's primary U.S. website and our country and region websites around the world, search-related advertising strategies, search engine optimization strategies, e-mail marketing campaigns, clicks-and-bricks integration strategy, affiliate marketing campaigns, customer retention efforts, and all aspects of online marketing research. The director of e-marketing will also work closely with the director of information technology to ensure the successful deployment of e-marketing platforms and with the director of retail operations to ensure a smooth clicks-and-bricks integration of offline and online retailing operations.

In addition to developing e-marketing strategies and directing e-marketing operations, the director is also responsible for leading a team of marketing and technical specialists who will implement and manage various programs.

Responsibilities

- Develop e-marketing strategies and plans consistent with Soccer Scope's overall business strategy and brand imperatives
- Establish and achieve aggressive customer acquisition and retention goals
- Coordinate efforts with technology and retailing counterparts to ensure successfully integrated online and offline marketing operations
- Assemble, lead, and develop an effective team of e-marketing professionals

Skills and Experience

- BA or BS in business, advertising, marketing, or related discipline required; MBA preferred
- Minimum 8 years of marketing experience, with at least 3 years in e-commerce
- Current and thorough understanding of e-marketing strategies
- Demonstrated proficiency in developing and executing marketing strategies
- Excellent communication skills in all media

EXHIBIT 14.3 How Employers and Job Seekers Approach the Recruiting Process

Studies show that employers prefer to fill job openings with people from within their organization or from an employee's recommendation. Placing want ads is often viewed as a last resort. In contrast, typical job seekers begin their job-search process from the opposite direction (starting with reading advertisements).

Most preferred → Least preferred

1. Look for someone inside the organization
2. Rely on contacts and personal recommendations
3. Hire an employment agency or search firm
4. Review unsolicited résumés
5. Solicit résumés through advertising

The Hiring Process

Most companies go through six steps to hire new employees:

1. Recruiters select a small number of qualified candidates from all of the applications and résumés received. Many organizations now use computer-based *applicant tracking systems* to manage the hiring process and identify the most attractive candidates for each job.

2. Recruiters then screen the candidates, typically through phone interviews, online tests, or on-campus interviews. Interviews at this stage are usually fairly structured, with applicants asked the same questions so that recruiters can easily compare responses.

3. Candidates who make it through screening are then invited to visit the company for another round of interviews. This process usually involves several interviews with a variety of colleagues, managers, and someone from the HR department, but the number and format of the interviews vary widely depending on the company and the job in question. At Southwest Airlines, for example, flight attendant candidates are asked to give three-minute speeches about themselves in front of a panel of interviewers and all the other candidates. The interviewers are not just evaluating the speaker—they're also watching the other candidates' behavior. Anyone who acts bored or disrespectful while candidates are speaking is eliminated from further consideration.[33]

4. The interview team compares notes and assesses the remaining candidates. Team members sometimes lobby for or against individual candidates based on what they've seen and heard during interviews.

5. Recruiting specialists check references and research the backgrounds of the top few candidates. Some 80 percent of U.S. employers now conduct criminal background checks, for instance. Other types of background checks look into résumé credentials, credit histories, and even terrorist watch lists.[34] Despite concerns over privacy, many employers believe they have no choice when it comes to background checks, since they can be held liable for the actions of employees who obtained jobs under false pretenses—and lying by job candidates is depressingly common. In one recent survey of more than 2 million job applicants, 44 percent lied about their employment history, 41 percent lied about their education, and 23 percent claimed to have professional credentials or licenses they didn't have.[35]

6. With all this information in hand, the hiring manager selects the most suitable person for the job and tenders a job offer.

In an effort to improve the predictability of the selection process and reduce the reliance on interviewing, many employers now conduct a variety of preemployment tests.[36] These tests attempt to assess such factors as substance abuse, integrity, personality, and job skills. For example, thousands of computer programmers compete in the annual Google Code Jam, vying for valuable prizes and the chance to visit Google to explore job opportunities.[37]

Drug and alcohol testing is one of the most controversial issues in business today. Some employers believe such testing is absolutely necessary to maintain workplace safety, whereas others view it as an invasion of employee privacy and a sign of disrespect. Some companies test only applicants, but not employees.[38] Companies test for three reasons: (1) to cut the costs (approximately $100 billion a year) and reduced productivity associated with drug abuse, (2) to reduce the number of accidents (substance abusers have two to four times as many accidents as other employees, and drug use is linked to 40 percent of industrial fatalities), and (3) to reduce legal liability for negligent hiring

When Employees Turn on Each Other

Few events in a company's history can be as traumatic as extreme workplace violence, when employees exact revenge or take out frustrations by attacking or killing their colleagues. Every year, dozens of employees are killed by their fellow workers, and hundreds more are seriously injured.

Although murders of employees by employees represent a small fraction of workplace violence, they can have a dramatic effect on company morale. "No organization is ever completely the same after a tragedy like this," emphasizes Mary Tyler, a psychologist with the federal government's Office of Personnel Management. Survivors and witnesses of attacks frequently quit, and productivity within the firm can suffer for months afterward. Even when murder isn't involved, assaults and intimidation create a dangerous, poisonous work environment for everyone involved. Moreover, these incidences of violence can subject employers to tremendous legal damages for failing to provide employees with safe workplaces.

What causes workers to explode with such rage? The key to understanding this problem is to recognize that workplace murder is unlike the often-random violence that afflicts society in general. As security consultant Doug Kane explains, "Workplace violence is one of the few types of violent behavior that follows a clear pattern. It is never spontaneous and almost always avoidable." According to the FBI, no specific personality profile can identify potentially violent attackers, but a consistent pattern of circumstances does appear in many cases, including a recent firing, a demotion, or an argument with co-workers or supervisors. In addition, employees who speak openly about suicide should be considered risks as well, since many workplace

murderers take their own lives after killing one or more co-workers.

Experts recommend five steps to protect workers. First, take the problem seriously. Too many workers die because managers don't think violence can happen at their facilities. Second, perform thorough background checks on all potential hires, looking specifically for a history of substance abuse, conflicts with co-workers, or convictions for violent crimes. Third, implement protection policies, such as prohibiting any kind of weapons on company grounds and deciding in advance how to handle conflicts before they escalate into violence. (Most U.S. companies do not have comprehensive, formal programs to prevent workplace violence.) Fourth, train everyone—and particularly frontline supervisors, since they often bear the brunt of attacks—to watch for the telltale warning signs. Fifth, respond instantly to those warning signs. In many cases, attackers made threats or exhibited other evidence of impending disaster, but most of the companies involved failed to respond.

Questions for Critical Thinking

1. Debate continues regarding the use of zero-tolerance policies for aggressive behavior. Some experts say employees who exhibit violent tendencies should be fired immediately, but others say that doing so would discourage co-workers from reporting seemingly minor incidents. What is your opinion?
2. Should a company be held liable for financial damages if an employee kills one or more colleagues? Why or why not?

practices if an employee harms an innocent party on the job.[39] In recent years, as many as 80 percent of U.S. employers have conducted drug testing, but that percentage appears to be declining.[40]

Federal and state laws and regulations govern many aspects of the hiring process (see Exhibit 14.4 for a list of some of the most important employment-related laws). In particular, employers must respect the privacy of applicants and avoid discrimination. For instance, any form or testing that can be construed as a preemployment medical examination is prohibited by the Americans with Disabilities Act.[41]

Training and Development

With the pace of change in everything from government regulations to consumer tastes to technology, employee knowledge and skills need to be constantly updated. Consequently, the most successful companies place a heavy emphasis on employee

EXHIBIT 14.4 Major Employment Legislation

Here are a few of the most significant sets of laws that affect employer-employee relations in the United States.

CATEGORY	LEGISLATION	HIGHLIGHTS
Labor and unionization	National Labor Relations Act, also known as the Wagner Act	Establishes the right of employees to form, join, and assist unions and the right to strike; prohibits employers from interfering in union activities
	Labor-Management Relations Act, also known as the Taft-Hartley Act	Expands union rights; gives employers free speech rights to oppose unions; gives the president the right to impose injunctions against strikes
	Labor-Management Reporting and Disclosure Act, also known as the Landrum-Griffin Act	Gives union members the right to nominate and vote for union leadership candidates
	State right-to-work laws	Gives individual employees the right to choose not to join a union
	Fair Labor Standards Act	Establishes minimum wage and overtime pay for nonexempt workers; sets strict guidelines for child labor
	Immigration Reform and Control Act	Prohibits employers from hiring illegal immigrants
Workplace safety	State workers' compensation acts	Require employers (in most states) to carry either private or government-sponsored insurance that provides income to injured workers
	Occupational Health and Safety Act	Empowers the Occupational Safety and Health Administration (OSHA) to set and enforce standards for workplace safety
Employee benefits	Employee Retirement Income Security Act	Governs the establishment and operation of private pension programs
	Consolidated Omnibus Budget Reconciliation Act (usually known by the acronym COBRA)	Requires employers to let employees or their beneficiaries buy continued health insurance coverage after employment ends
	Federal Unemployment Tax Act and similar state laws	Requires employers to fund programs that provide income for qualified unemployed persons
	Social Security Act	Provides a level of retirement, disability, and medical coverage for employees and their dependents; jointly funded by employers and employees

training and development efforts, for everyone from entry-level workers to the CEO. Overall, U.S. companies now spend more than $50 billion a year on training.[42]

Training usually begins with **orientation programs** designed to ease the new hire's transition into the company and to impart vital knowledge about the organization and its rules, procedures, and expectations. Effective orientation programs help employees

orientation programs
Sessions or procedures for acclimating new employees to the organization

become more productive in less time, help eliminate confusion and mistakes, and can significantly increase employee retention rates.[43]

skills inventory
A list of the skills a company needs from its workforce, along with the specific skills that individual employees currently possess

Training and other forms of employee development continue throughout the employee's career in most cases. Many HR departments maintain a **skills inventory**, which identifies both the current skill levels of all the employees and the skills the company needs in order to succeed. Depending on the industry, some of the most common subjects for ongoing training include problem solving, new products, sales, customer service, safety, sexual harassment, supervision, quality, strategic planning, communication, time management, and team building.[44]

Appraising Employee Performance

performance appraisals
Evaluations of employees' work according to specific criteria

How do employees (and their managers) know whether they are doing a good job? How can they improve their performance? What new skills should they learn? Most human resources managers attempt to answer these questions by developing **performance appraisals** to objectively evaluate employees according to set criteria. The ultimate goal of performance appraisals is not to judge employees but rather to improve their performance. Thus, experts recommend that performance reviews be an ongoing discipline—not just a once-a-year event linked to employee raises. Employees need regular feedback so that any deficiencies can be corrected quickly.

Most companies require regular written evaluations of each employee's work. To ensure objectivity and consistency, firms generally use a standard company performance appraisal form to evaluate employees. The evaluation criteria are in writing so that both employee and supervisor understand what is expected and are therefore able to determine whether the work is being done adequately (see Exhibit 14.5). Written evaluations also provide a record of the employee's performance, which may protect the company in cases of disputed terminations.[45]

The specific measures of employee performance vary widely by job, company, and industry. Most jobs are evaluated in several areas, including tasks specific to the position, contribution to the company's overall success, and interaction with colleagues and customers. For example, a production manager might be evaluated on the basis of communication skills, people management, leadership, teamwork, recruiting and employee development, delegation, financial management, planning, and organizational skills.[46]

Many performance appraisals require the employee to be rated by several people (including more than one supervisor and perhaps several co-workers). This practice further promotes fairness by correcting for possible biases. The ultimate in multidimensional reviews is the *360-degree review*, in which a person is given feedback from subordinates, peers, and superiors. To ensure anonymity and to compile the multiple streams of information, 360-degree reviews are often conducted via computer. Experts also recommend that 360-degree reviews not be used to set salaries and that reviewers be thoroughly trained in the technique.[47]

Evaluating individual performance is a challenge in organizations where employees work in teams. Assessments by the team leader are important, of course, but they can't always sort out what each member contributed to the overall output, particularly in teams that operate with a great deal of autonomy. A good way to address this problem is to have each team member evaluate his or her own contribution and that of every other team member as well. A manager who oversees the team can then compare all the assessments (which are done anonymously) to look for patterns—who contributes the bulk of the new ideas, who's just along for the ride, and so on.[48]

electronic performance monitoring (EPM)
Real-time, computer-based evaluation of employee performance

In addition to formal, periodic performance evaluations, many companies evaluate some workers' performance continuously, using **electronic performance monitoring (EPM)**, sometimes called *computer activity monitoring*. For instance, customer service and telephone sales representatives are often evaluated by the number of calls they complete per hour and other variables. Newer software products extend this

EXHIBIT 14.5 Sample Performance Appraisal Form

Many companies use forms like this (either printed or online) to ensure that performance appraisals are as objective as possible.

Name _____ Title _____ Service Date _____ Date _____

Location _____ Division _____ Department _____

Length of Time in Present Position   Period of Review   Appraised by _____

_____   From: _____ To: _____   Title of Appraisor _____

Area of Performance	Comment	Rating
Job Knowledge and Skill Understands responsibilities and uses background for job. Adapts to new methods/techniques. Plans and organizes work. Recognizes errors and problems.		5 4 3 2 1
Volume of Work Amount of work output. Adherence to standards and schedules. Effective use of time.		5 4 3 2 1
Quality of Work Degree of accuracy–lack of errors. Thoroughness of work. Ability to exercise good judgment.		5 4 3 2 1
Initiative and Creativity Self-motivation in seeking responsibility and work that needs to be done. Ability to apply original ideas and concepts.		5 4 3 2 1
Communication Ability to exchange thoughts or information in a clear, concise manner. Ability to deal with different organizational levels of clientele.		5 4 3 2 1
Dependability Ability to follow instructions and directions correctly. Performs under pressure. Reliable work habits.		5 4 3 2 1
Leadership Ability/Potential Ability to guide others to the successful accomplishment of a given task. Potential for developing subordinate employees.		5 4 3 2 1

5. Outstanding   Employee who consistently exceeds established standards and expectations of the job.

4. Above Average   Employee who consistently meets established standards and expectations of the job. Often exceeds and rarely falls short of desired results.

3. Satisfactory   Generally qualified employee who meets job standards and expectations. Sometimes exceeds and may occasionally fall short of desired expectations. Performs duties in a normally expected manner.

2. Improvement Needed   Not quite meeting standards and expectations. An employee at this level of performance is not quite meeting all the standard job requirements.

1. Unsatisfactory   Employee who fails to meet the minimum standards and expectations of the job.

I have had the opportunity to read this performance appraisal.

How long has this employee been under your supervision?

Signature   Date

Signature of Supervisor   Date

monitoring capability, from measuring data input accuracy to scanning for suspicious words in employee e-mails. As you can imagine, EPM efforts can generate controversy in the workplace, elevating employee stress levels and raising concerns about invasion of privacy.[49]

Somebody's Watching (and Listening and Reading and Monitoring and Recording)

If you've grown accustomed to saying anything about anybody in e-mail and instant messaging, get ready for some major culture shock when you enter (or reenter) the corporate world. For a number of reasons, the majority of mid- to large-size companies now monitor employee e-mail and IM—using both increasingly sophisticated monitoring software and, in some cases, human beings who actually intercept and read outgoing messages. Roughly a quarter of these companies have fired employees for violating e-mail usage policies.

To get an idea of the monitoring capabilities now available, consider just some of the features in TrueActive Monitor, a monitoring product used by nearly 100,000 employers: keystroke logging (records everything a person types), chat room and IM recording, website tracking (records which websites a person visits), text scanning (monitors messages for particular words or phrases), file management activity (can tell if someone deletes or copies files), and webcam control (can activate a webcam for video evidence of who was using a computer at specific times).

Now, if the idea of someone scanning your messages raises your hackles, you're not alone. However, companies have a variety of valid concerns regarding how their employees use information technology:

- Protecting corporate information, including client records, strategic plans, and product design details
- Making sure employees don't inadvertently break the law when communicating with customers
- Protecting company networks from viruses, spyware, and other malware
- Preventing the transmission of pornographic material, which can open a company to lawsuits over sexual harassment
- Making sure employees don't use the Internet for personal reasons when they are on company time

Privacy advocates raise valid concerns about employers going too far to check up on employees. However, the risks of not monitoring are so great—a few poor choices by a single employee can cost millions—that the use of monitoring tools is only going to increase in the coming years.

As an employee, you can avoid trouble by remembering one simple thought: All of the information technology you use at work is company property, provided by your employer for your use in engaging in company business. For anything else, it's best to use your own Internet service and your own personal e-mail and IM accounts.

Questions for Critical Thinking

1. What effect is workplace monitoring likely to have on employee morale? Do you think most workers blame management or their own misbehaving colleagues for the use of these monitoring technologies?
2. At present, only two states (Delaware and Connecticut) require employers to notify employees that their e-mail messages are being monitored. Should all states enact this requirement? Why or why not?

Administering Compensation and Employee Benefits

Pay and benefits are of vital interest to all employees, of course, and these subjects also consume considerable time and attention in HR departments. For many companies, payroll is the single biggest expense, and the cost of benefits, particularly health care, continues to climb. Consequently, **compensation**, the combination of direct payments such as wages or salary and indirect payments through employee benefits, is one of the HR manager's most significant responsibilities.

Salaries and Wages

Most employees receive the bulk of their compensation in the form of **salary**, if they receive a fixed amount per year, or **wages**, if they are paid by the unit of time (hourly, daily, or weekly) or by the unit of output (often called "getting paid by the piece" or "piecework"). The Fair Labor Standards Act, introduced in 1938 and amended many times since then, sets specific guidelines that employers must follow when administering salaries and wages, including setting a minimum wage and paying overtime for time

compensation
Money, benefits, and services paid to employees for their work

salary
Fixed cash compensation for work, usually by yearly amount; independent of the number of hours worked

wages
Cash payment based on the number of hours the employee has worked or the number of units the employee has produced

worked beyond 40 hours a week. However, most professional and managerial employees are considered exempt from these regulations, meaning, for instance, their employers don't have to pay them for overtime. The distinction between *exempt employees* and *nonexempt employees* is based on job responsibilities and pay level. In general, salaried employees are exempt, although there are many exceptions.[50]

Both wages and salaries are, in principle, based on the contribution of a particular job to the company. Thus, a sales manager, who is responsible for bringing in sales revenue, is paid more than a secretary, who handles administrative tasks but doesn't sell or supervise. However, pay often varies widely by position, industry, and location. Among the best-paid employees in the world are chief executive officers of large U.S. corporations.

Compensation has become a hot topic in recent years, at both ends of the pay scale. At the low end, for instance, many businesses, employees, and unions are wrestling with the downward pressure on wages and benefits exerted by Wal-Mart's enormous presence in the economy. With more than a million employees, the company's cost-conscious strategy indirectly affects thousands of people who've never worked there. As other stores try to compete with Wal-Mart, many feel they have no choice but to pay their employees less and offer fewer benefits. Some critics also charge that Wal-Mart employees who can't afford the company's health insurance and those who are on food stamps are increasing the burden on taxpayers. Lower wages also mean Wal-Mart employees themselves are able to spend less on consumer goods and services, and consumer spending is a major factor in the strength of the U.S. economy. As one researcher puts it, "You can't have every company adopt a Wal-Mart strategy. It isn't sustainable."[51] (You can read Wal-Mart's responses to such criticisms at www.walmartfacts.com.)

At the upper end of the pay scale, executive compensation, and the pay of CEOs in particular, has generated its own brand of controversy. CEOs typically receive complex compensation packages that include a base salary plus a wide range of benefits and bonuses, including *golden handshakes* when they join a company and *golden parachutes* when they leave. Annual CEO compensation packages of $10 million to $20 million or more are not uncommon these days. Thirty years ago, the average CEO of a public company made roughly 40 times more than the average hourly worker; today, it's well over 500 times more.[52]

Incentive Programs

To encourage employees to be more productive, innovative, and committed to their work, many companies provide managers and employees with **incentives**, cash payments linked to specific individual, group, and companywide goals; overall productivity; and company success. In other words, achievements, not just activities, are made the basis for payment. The success of these programs often depends on how closely incentives are linked to actions within the employee's control:

- For both salaried and wage-earning employees, one type of incentive compensation is the **bonus**, a payment in addition to the regular wage or salary. Performance-based bonuses have become an increasingly popular approach to compensation as more companies shift away from automatic annual pay increases.[53]

- In contrast to bonuses, **commissions** are a form of compensation that pays employees in sales positions based on the level of sales made within a given time frame.

- Employees may be rewarded for staying with a company and encouraged to work harder through **profit sharing**, a system in which employees receive a portion of the company's profits.

- Similar to profit sharing, **gain sharing** ties rewards to profits (or cost savings) achieved by meeting specific goals such as quality and productivity improvement.

incentives
Cash payments to employees who produce at a desired level or whose unit (often the company as a whole) produces at a desired level

bonus
Cash payment, in addition to regular wage or salary, that serves as a reward for achievement

commissions
Employee compensation based on a percentage of sales made

profit sharing
The distribution of a portion of the company's profits to employees

gain sharing
Plan for rewarding employees not on the basis of overall profits but in relation to achievement of goals such as cost savings from higher productivity

Sales professionals usually earn at least part of their income through commissions; the more they sell, the more they earn.

pay for performance
Incentive program that rewards employees for meeting specific, individual goals

knowledge-based pay
Pay tied to an employee's acquisition of knowledge or skills; also called competency-based pay or skill-based pay

employee benefits
Compensation other than wages, salaries, and incentive programs

cafeteria plans
Flexible benefit programs that let employees personalize their benefits packages

■ A variation of gain sharing, **pay for performance** requires employees to accept a lower base pay but rewards them with bonuses, commissions, or stock options if they reach agreed-upon goals. To be successful, this method needs to be complemented with effective feedback systems that let employees know how they are performing throughout the year.[54]

■ Another approach to compensation being explored by some companies is **knowledge-based pay**, also known as *competency-based pay* or *skill-based pay*, which is tied to employees' knowledge and abilities rather than to their job per se. More than half of all large U.S. companies now use some variation on this incentive.[55]

Employee Benefits and Services

Companies also regularly provide **employee benefits**—elements of compensation other than wages, salaries, and incentives. These benefits may be offered as either a preset package—that is, the employee gets whatever insurance, paid holidays, pension plan, and other benefits the company sets up—or as flexible plans, sometimes known as **cafeteria plans** (so called because of the similarity to choosing items from a menu). The benefits most commonly provided by employers are insurance, retirement benefits, employee stock-ownership plans, stock options, and family benefits. As you read the following sections, you'll begin to understand why the field of benefits has become such a complex area in business today, and why benefits often figure strongly in union contract negotiations, strategic planning decisions, and even national public policy debates.

Insurance

Employers can offer a range of insurance plans to their employees, including life, health, dental, vision, disability, and long-term-care insurance. Although employers are under no general legal obligation to provide insurance coverage (except in union contracts, for instance), many companies view these benefits as a competitive necessity, to attract and retain good employees.

Perhaps no other issue illustrates the challenging economics of business today more clearly than health insurance. With medical costs rising much faster than inflation in general, companies are taking a variety of steps to manage the financial impact, including forcing employees to pick up more of the cost, reducing or eliminating coverage for retired employees, auditing employees' health claims, monitoring employees' health and habits, dropping spouses from insurance plans, or even firing employees who are so sick or disabled that they are no longer able to work. The situation is particularly acute for small businesses, which don't have the purchasing power of large corporations.[56]

The tension is likely to continue, prompting calls for more government intervention, spurring unionizing efforts, pitting healthy employees against their less-healthy colleagues, and extending the reach of companies into their employees' personal lives. For instance, Weyco, a small employer in Okemos, Michigan, forbids its employees to smoke—even on their own time—and enforces the policy through random breathalyzer testing.[57] Other companies require employees who smoke or who are obese to pay a greater share of their health-care costs.[58]

Health-care costs—including the question of how to insure the millions of U.S. residents without health insurance—will continue to be a major topic of discussion in the coming years. In aggregate, the United States spends enough to provide adequate care for everyone, but the system is plagued by waste, inefficiency, and imbalance. Per capita, the United States spends more on health care than any other country, but according to a number of key measures, the quality of care is lower than in many other countries.[59]

EXHIBIT 14.6 Creative Approaches to Skyrocketing Health-Care Costs

For a variety of reasons—cost control, competitiveness, and concern for their employees—U.S. companies are tackling high health-care costs in a variety of ways.

High-deductible insurance	One of the simplest changes is switching to high-deductible insurance, in which the employee must pay more of his or her medical expenses directly before insurance kicks in. This not only lowers insurance premiums, but advocates say it forces employees to use health-care services more carefully.
Health Savings Accounts (HSAs)	Higher deductibles are a feature of the new Health Savings Accounts (HSAs) introduced in 2003. HSAs let employees sock away parts of their salaries tax-free and use the money to pay for medical care or spend it on other things if they stay healthy.
In-house clinics	A few companies have saved by opening their own private clinics on site, giving them more control over costs and removing the insurance layer from the health-care model. However, this option is attractive only to companies with large, geographically concentrated workforces.
Health insurance buying groups	Smaller employers can band together to increase their purchasing power. After joining the employers' group Presidion, the Tampa, Florida, restaurant chain Ragin' Ribs cut its health-care costs by 25 percent. Similar organizations also exist to help independent contractors save on insurance.
Employer-driven quality improvements	An even more comprehensive cooperative effort is the Leapfrog Group, a nonprofit coalition representing a variety of employers and health-care plans; Leapfrog offers incentives to hospitals and health-care providers to reduce preventable medical errors, improve the quality of care, and in doing so also cut costs dramatically.
Insurance for the uninsured	A coalition of large employers recently formed the Affordable Health Care Solution, a giant purchasing cooperative that lowers the cost of insurance for independent contractors, part-timers, and others who can't afford insurance.
Sliding-scale plans	With a sliding-scale program, employers charge for health insurance based on salary, making insurance more affordable for lower-wage workers.
Wellness programs	Many employers have discovered that a great way to cut health-care costs is to keep employees healthier in the first place; wellness programs can include everything from dietary advice to exercise facilities to smoking-cessation classes.

In the true spirit of entrepreneurship, however, U.S. companies aren't just giving up in the face of rising costs. Exhibit 14.6 shows a sample of many creative ways employers, insurers, and public officials are trying to offer adequate coverage at manageable costs.

Retirement Benefits

Many employers offer **retirement plans**, which are designed to provide continuing income after the employee retires. Company-sponsored retirement plans can be categorized as either *defined benefit plans*, in which the company specifies how much it will pay employees upon retirement, or *defined contribution plans*, in which companies specify how much they will put into the retirement fund (by matching employee contributions, for instance), without guaranteeing any specific payouts during retirement. Although both types are technically **pension plans**, when most people speak of pension plans, they are referring to traditional defined benefit plans, in which employers promise to pay their employees a benefit upon retirement based on the employee's retirement age, final average salary, and years of service.[60] Defined benefit plans are far less common than they were in the past, and some of these plans are in serious financial trouble. To meet their current and future obligations to employees, pension fund managers invest

retirement plans
Company-sponsored programs for providing retirees with income

pension plans
Generally refers to traditional, defined benefit retirement plans

some of the company's cash and assume those investments will grow enough to cover future retirement needs. However, dramatic investment losses in recent years have left many plans underfunded, some by billions of dollars, forcing those companies to redirect cash from other purposes.[61]

Defined benefit plans are insured by the Pension Benefit Guaranty Corporation (PBGC), a federal agency that collects money from companies that have pension plans and that takes over payments to retirees whenever one of these companies is unable or unwilling to pay its retirees. After a number of large pension defaults in recent years, the PBGC is paying out more than it takes in, and healthy companies such as IBM and GE are paying far more than unhealthy or bankrupt companies (mostly steel companies and airlines at this point).[62]

Defined contribution plans are similar to savings plans; they provide a future benefit based on annual employer contributions, voluntary employee matching contributions, and accumulated investment earnings. Employers can choose from several types of defined contribution plans, the most common of which is known as a **401(k) plan**. In a 401(k) plan, employees contribute a percentage of their pretax income, and employers often match that amount or some portion of it. In addition to the money their employers invest, employees enjoy tax reductions based on their annual contributions to the fund.[63]

Some 10 million U.S. employees are now enrolled in a type of defined benefit plan known as an **employee stock-ownership plan (ESOP)**, in which a company places a certain amount of its stock in trust for some or all of its employees, with each employee entitled to a certain share. These plans allow employees to later purchase the shares at a fixed price. If the company does well, the ESOP may provide a substantial employee benefit. In fact, many companies report that ESOPs help boost employee productivity since workers perceive a direct correlation between their efforts and the value of the company stock price.[64]

Stock Options

A related method for tying employee compensation to company performance is the stock option plan. **Stock options** grant employees the right to purchase a set number of shares of the employer's stock at a specific price, called the *grant* or *exercise price*, during a certain time period. Options typically *vest* over a number of years, meaning that employees can purchase a prorated portion of the shares every year until the vesting period is over (at which time they can purchase all the shares they are entitled to).

Stock options can be a win-win situation for employers and employees. From the employer's perspective, stock options cost little, provide long-term incentives for good people to stay with the company, and encourage employees to work harder because they have a vested interest in the company doing well. From the employee's perspective, stock options can generate a handsome profit if the stock's market price exceeds the grant price.

Options are particularly common in executive compensation packages, where they offer an incentive for effective corporate management. They were also quite popular in the technology boom in the 1980s and 1990s, when start-ups would frequently lure new employees with low salaries but thousands of stock option shares. However, the popularity of stock options has waned somewhat in recent years, following a change in accounting rules that forced companies to account for the value of outstanding options in their annual financial reports. Before that change, investors and regulators argued that companies were hiding the true costs of options and thereby reporting inflated earnings. Microsoft, which helped make many of its early employees wealthy through stock options, stopped granting them in 2003.[65]

In addition to the question of expensing, a second stock-option controversy involves *backdating*, or fixing the date of the stock option grant on a day in the past

---

401(k) plan
A defined contribution retirement plan in which employers often match the amount employees invest

employee stock-ownership plan (ESOP)
Program enabling employees to become partial owners of a company

stock options
Contract allowing the holder to purchase or sell a certain number of shares of a particular stock at a given price by a certain date

at which the stock's price was at a low point. By lowering the grant price as much as possible, backdating maximizes the profit employees make when they eventually sell the stock. The rules governing backdating used to give companies quite a bit of leeway, but Sarbanes-Oxley (see page 163) requires that companies now report options within two days of the grant date. More than 200 companies have been investigated for backdating in recent years, and at least one CEO has been convicted of criminal charges.[66]

Family Benefits

The Family Medical and Leave Act (FMLA) of 1993 requires employers with 50 or more workers to provide up to 12 weeks of unpaid leave per year for childbirth, adoption, or the care of oneself, a child, a spouse, or a parent with serious illness.[67] Many employees can't afford to take extended periods of time off without pay, but at least the law creates the opportunity for those who can.

Day care is another important family benefit, especially for single parents and two-career couples. In fact, half of all working families rely on day care.[68] Nearly half of all companies now offer some sort of child-care assistance, including flexible savings accounts (which let employees put aside some of their pay for child care and other services), referral programs, discounted rates at nearby child-care centers, and on-site day-care centers.[69] Although the number of companies with on-site day-care centers remains fairly low, recent research led by Bowdoin College economist Rachel Connelly shows that such facilities don't have to be the financial burden many perceive them to be—and can even generate profits. Moreover, day-care facilities also send a message that the company cares about work-life balance.[70]

Another family benefit of growing importance is elder care, assisting employees with the responsibility of caring for aging parents. Many employers now offer some form of elder-care assistance, ranging from referral services that help find care providers to dependent-care allowances. Some companies will even agree to move elderly relatives when they transfer an employee to another location.[71]

Trust Insurance employee Kathy Hatfield gets to spend time with her daughters at the company's on-site day-care center. Such centers reduce costs and stress for employees with children.

Other Employee Benefits

Paid holidays, sick pay, premium pay for working overtime or unusual hours, and paid vacations are other important benefits offered to employees. To provide incentives for employee loyalty, most companies grant employees longer paid vacations after they've been with the organization for a prescribed number of years. Some companies let employees buy additional vacation time or sell unused days back to the employer. Sick-day allowances also vary from company to company and from industry to industry. And rather than separating time off by vacation, sick days, and other reasons, some companies present employees with a block of "general-purpose" time that they are free to use for whatever reason they wish. For example, Agilent Technologies takes this approach with a program called Flexible Time Off.[72]

employee assistance programs (EAPs)
Company-sponsored counseling or referral plans for employees with personal problems

Among the many other benefits that companies sometimes offer are sabbaticals (time off to spend at the employee's discretion, usually after a certain length of service to the employer), tuition loans and reimbursements (U.S. companies contribute roughly $10 billion every year to continuing education for their employees), financial counseling and legal services, and even assistance with buying homes in areas with high housing costs.[73] One of the most cost-effective benefits employers can establish is an **employee assistance program (EAP)**, which offers private and confidential counseling to employees who need help with issues related to drugs, alcohol, domestic violence, finances, stress, family issues, and other personal problems. Studies by the National Council on Alcoholism and Drug Dependence (NCADD) show that these services save between $5 and $16 for each dollar spent as a result of improved safety and productivity, as well as reduced employee turnover.[74]

Overseeing Changes in Employment Status

attrition
Loss of employees for reasons other than termination

Of course, providing competitive compensation and good employee benefits is no guarantee that employees will stay with the company. Every company experiences some level of **attrition**, when employees leave for reasons other than termination, including retirement, new job opportunities, long-term disability, or death. Virtually all companies also find themselves with the need to terminate employment of selected workers from time to time. Whatever the reason, overseeing changes in employment status is another responsibility of the human resources department.

Promoting and Reassigning Employees

As Exhibit 14.3 showed, many companies prefer to look within the organization to fill job vacancies. In part, this "promote from within" policy allows a company to benefit from the training and experience of its own workforce. This policy also rewards employees who have worked hard and demonstrated the ability to handle more challenging tasks. In addition, morale is usually better when a company promotes from within because employees see that they can advance. For example, Enterprise Rent-A-Car, one of the nation's largest employers of new college graduates, has used its strong tradition of promoting from within as a major selling point to potential employees.[75]

However, a possible pitfall of internal promotion is that a person may be given a job beyond his or her competence. The best salesperson in the company is not necessarily a good candidate for sales manager, because managing often requires a different set of skills. If the promotion is a mistake, the company not only loses its sales leader but also risks demoralizing the sales staff. Companies can reduce such risks through careful promotion policies and by providing support and training to help promoted employees perform well.

Terminating Employees

HR managers also have the unpleasant responsibility of **termination**—permanently laying off employees because of cutbacks or firing employees for poor performance or other reasons. **Layoffs** are the termination of employees for economic or business reasons unrelated to employee performance. As Michael Dell, founder and CEO of Dell, puts it, making cuts "is one of the hardest, most gut-wrenching decisions you can make as a leader." Layoffs are "an admission that we screwed up" by over-hiring.[76]

To help ease the pain of layoffs, many companies provide laid-off employees with job-hunting assistance. *Outplacement* services such as résumé-writing courses, career counseling, office space, and secretarial help are offered to laid-off executives and blue-collar employees alike. Large-scale outplacement efforts are often outsourced to specialist firms such as Challenger, Gray & Christmas (www.challengergray.com), which can help laid-off employees find jobs in much less time than they can usually do on their own.[77]

Terminating employment by firing is a complex subject with many legal ramifications, and the line between a layoff and a firing can be blurry. For instance, every state except Montana supports the concept of *at-will employment*, meaning that companies are free to fire nearly anyone they choose. Exceptions to this principle vary from state to state, but in general, employers cannot discriminate in firing, nor can they fire employees for whistle-blowing, filing a worker's compensation claim, or testifying against the employer in harassment or discrimination lawsuits.[78] If a terminated employee believes any of these principles have been violated, he or she can file a *wrongful discharge* lawsuit against the employer. In addition, employers must abide by the terms of an employment contract, if one has been entered into with the employee (these are much more common for executives than they are for lower-level employees). Some employers offer written assurances that they will terminate employees only *for cause*, which usually includes such actions as committing crimes or violating company policy.

termination
Process of getting rid of an employee through layoff or firing

layoffs
Termination of employees for economic or business reasons

Retiring Employees

Companies can face two dramatically different challenges regarding retiring employees. For companies that are short-handed, the challenge is to persuade older employees to delay retirement. Facing a shortage of chemical engineers, Dow Chemical is trying to persuade some of its 20,000 employees who are scheduled to retire by 2012 to continue working. The firm has introduced a variety of programs, including three-day weeks, to entice older employees to stay.[79]

Conversely, companies with too many employees may induce employees to depart ahead of scheduled retirement days by offering them *early retirement*, financial incentives known as **worker buyouts**. In recent years, companies in the U.S. auto industry have offered buyouts to thousands of workers as they attempt to align their workforces with declining revenues.[80]

In the past, **mandatory retirement** policies forced people to quit working as soon as they turned a certain age. However, the Age Discrimination in Employment Act now outlaws mandatory retirement, although some professions, such as airline pilots, are still governed by such rules.[81]

worker buyout
Distribution of financial incentives to employees who voluntarily depart; usually undertaken in order to reduce the payroll

mandatory retirement
Required dismissal of an employee who reaches a certain age

Working with Labor Unions

Although they work toward common goals in most cases, managers and employees do face an inherent conflict over resources: Managers, as representatives of company ownership, want to minimize the costs of operating the business, whereas employees want

labor unions
Organizations of employees formed to protect and advance their members' interests

locals
Relatively small union groups, usually part of a national union or a labor federation, that represent members who work in a single facility or in a certain geographic area

shop steward
Union member and employee who is elected to represent other union members and who attempts to resolve employee grievances with management

business agent
Full-time union staffer who negotiates with management and enforces the union's agreements with companies

national union
Nationwide organization made up of local unions that represent employees in locations around the country

to maximize salaries and benefits. If employees believe they are not being treated fairly or don't have a voice in how the company is run, they may have the option of joining **labor unions**, organizations that seek to protect employee interests by negotiating on behalf of employees. Over the years, labor unions have played an important role in the establishment of worker's compensation, child-labor laws, overtime rules, and minimum-wage laws (see Exhibit 14.7), and they remain an important factor in several major industries.

Union Organization

Many unions are organized at local, national, and international levels. **Locals** represent employees (often referred to as the *rank and file*) in a specific geographic area or facility. Each department or facility also elects a **shop steward**, a regular employee who serves as a go-between with supervisors. In larger locals, an elected full-time **business agent** negotiates with management and works to ensure compliance with union contracts.

A **national union** is a nationwide organization composed of many local unions that represent employees in specific locations; examples are the United Auto Workers of America and the United Steelworkers of America. A national union is responsible for such activities as organizing in new areas or industries, negotiating industrywide contracts, assisting locals with negotiations, administering benefits, lobbying Congress, and lending assistance in the event of a strike. The American Federation of Labor–Congress of Industrial Organizations (AFL-CIO) is a **labor federation** consisting of a variety of national unions and of local unions that are not associated with any other national union.

EXHIBIT 14.7 Key Legislation Relating to Unions

Most major labor legislation was enacted in the 1930s and 1940s. Subsequent legislation amends and clarifies earlier laws.

LEGISLATION	PROVISION
Norris-La Guardia Act of 1932	Limits companies' ability to obtain injunctions against union strikes, picketing, membership drives, and other activities.
National Labor Relations Act of 1935 (Wagner Act)	Gives employees the right to form, join, or assist labor organizations; the right to bargain collectively with employers through elected union representatives; and the right to engage in strikes, picketing, and boycotts. Prohibits certain unfair labor practices by the employer and union. Established the National Labor Relations Board to supervise union elections and to investigate charges of unfair labor practices by management.
Labor-Management Relations Act of 1947 (Taft-Hartley Act)	Amends Wagner Act to reaffirm employees' rights to organize and bargain collectively over working conditions. Establishes specific unfair labor practices both for management and for unions, and prohibits strikes in the public sector.
Landrum-Griffin Act of 1959	Amends Taft-Hartley Act and Wagner Act to control union corruption and to add the secondary boycott as an unfair labor practice. A secondary boycott occurs when a union appeals to firms or other unions to stop doing business with an employer who sells or handles goods of a company whose employees are on strike. The act requires all unions to file annual financial reports with the U.S. Department of Labor, making union officials more personally responsible for the union's elections, the right to sue unions, and the right to attend and participate in union meetings.
Plant-Closing Notification Act of 1988	Requires employers to give employees and local elected officials 60 days advance notice of plant shutdowns or massive layoffs.

The Collective Bargaining Process

In the **collective bargaining** process (see Exhibit 14.8), union and management negotiators work together to forge the policies that will apply to all employees covered by a given contract. In some cases, the two sides can gradually compromise on key points until they reach an overall agreement. If negotiations reach an impasse, outside help may be needed. The most common alternative is **mediation**—bringing in an impartial third party to study the situation and make recommendations for resolution of the differences. However, mediators can only offer suggestions, and their solutions are not binding. When a legally binding settlement is needed, the negotiators may submit to **arbitration**—a process in which an impartial referee listens to both sides and then makes a judgment by accepting one side's view. In *compulsory arbitration*, the parties are required by a government agency to submit to arbitration; in *voluntary arbitration*, the parties agree on their own to use arbitration to settle their differences.

When negotiation, mediation, and arbitration can't bring the parties together, both labor and management are able to draw on several powerful options in an attempt to force resolution. Labor's options include strikes, boycotts, and publicity campaigns:

- *Strikes.* The most powerful weapon that organized labor can use is the **strike**, a temporary work stoppage aimed at forcing management to accept union demands. An essential part of any strike is **picketing**, in which union members positioned at entrances to company premises march back and forth with signs and leaflets, trying to persuade nonstriking employees to join them and to persuade customers to stop doing business with the company. Two less-drastic actions are *slowdowns*, in which employees continue to do their jobs but at a slow enough pace to disrupt operations, and *sickouts*, in which a high number of employees call in sick at the same time.

- *Boycotts.* A less direct union weapon is the **boycott**, in which union members and sympathizers refuse to buy or handle the product of a target company. In fact, the AFL-CIO (www.unionlabel.org) maintains a page on its website that lists companies it would like consumers to boycott.

labor federation
Umbrella organization of national unions and unaffiliated local unions that undertakes large-scale activities on behalf of their members and that resolves conflicts between unions

collective bargaining
Process used by unions and management to negotiate work contracts

mediation
Process for resolving a labor-contract dispute in which a neutral third party meets with both sides and attempts to steer them toward a solution

arbitration
Process for resolving a labor-contract dispute in which an impartial third party studies the issues and makes a binding decision

strike
Temporary work stoppage by employees who want management to accept their union's demands

picketing
Strike activity in which union members march before company entrances to communicate their grievances and to discourage people from doing business with the company

boycott
Union activity in which members and sympathizers refuse to buy or handle the product of a target company

EXHIBIT 14.8 The Collective Bargaining Process

Contract negotiations go through the four basic steps shown here.

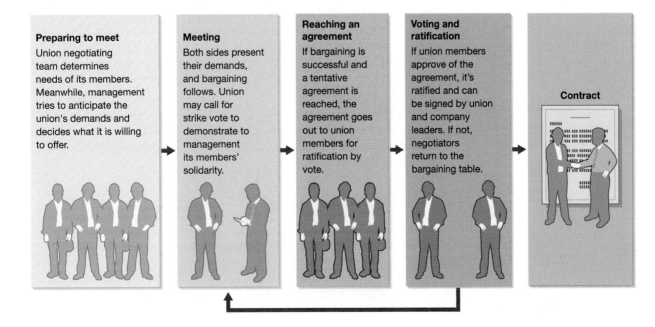

Preparing to meet
Union negotiating team determines needs of its members. Meanwhile, management tries to anticipate the union's demands and decides what it is willing to offer.

Meeting
Both sides present their demands, and bargaining follows. Union may call for strike vote to demonstrate to management its members' solidarity.

Reaching an agreement
If bargaining is successful and a tentative agreement is reached, the agreement goes out to union members for ratification by vote.

Voting and ratification
If union members approve of the agreement, it's ratified and can be signed by union and company leaders. If not, negotiators return to the bargaining table.

Contract

When contract talks broke down between grocery workers and major grocery chains in Southern California, the result was a strike that lasted four and a half months.

■ *Publicity.* Increasingly, labor is pressing its case by launching publicity campaigns, often called *corporate campaigns*, against a target company and companies affiliated with it. For example, the Service Employees International Union is active in Wal-Mart Watch (www.walmartwatch.com), one of a number of publicity campaigns that seek to educate the public about the policies and practices of the retail giant.[82]

From its side, management can use a number of legal methods to pressure unions when negotiations stall:

strikebreakers
Nonunion workers hired to replace striking workers

lockout
Management tactic in which union members are prevented from entering a business during a strike

injunction
Court order prohibiting certain actions by striking workers

■ *Strikebreakers.* When union members walk off their jobs, management can legally replace them with **strikebreakers**, nonunion workers hired to do the jobs of striking workers. (Union members brand them as "scabs.")
■ *Lockouts.* Management's counterpart to a strike is a **lockout**, in which the company prevents union employees from entering the workplace in order to pressure the union. Lockouts are legal only if the union and management have come to an impasse in negotiations and the employer is defending a legitimate bargaining position. During a lockout, the company may hire temporary replacements as long as it has no antiunion motivation and negotiations have been amicable.[83]
■ *Injunctions.* An **injunction** is a court order prohibiting union workers from taking certain actions. Injunctions are legal only in certain cases. For example, the president of the United States has the right, under the Taft-Hartley Act, to obtain a temporary injunction to halt a strike deemed harmful to the national interest, such as a wide-scale transportation strike.

The Labor Movement Today

In certain industries, including transportation, retailing, and manufacturing, unions remain a significant force in employee-management relations in the United States. But overall, union membership has declined, from more than a third of the workforce in the 1950s to less than 15 percent today.[84] True to the often combative nature of the relationship, each side blames organized labor's decline on the other. Some business leaders say unions don't have anything relevant to offer workers in today's environment of more enlightened and supportive management, while union leaders say companies routinely break laws designed to protect unionizing efforts.[85]

Moving into the future, unions continue to push for progress on a number of issues:

- *Membership*. Labor's top priority is reversing the downward trend in union membership. Central to the union message to workers is that membership will assure them of better wages, better health care, and better retirement income.[86]

- *Health-care costs*. Health-care costs and insurance coverage have become a major point of contention in labor negotiations, with employers saying that employees need to pay a larger share of health-care costs and employees saying they can't afford to. You can expect to see unions play a visible role in the continuing debate over how to fix the country's health-care system.

- *Immigration reform*. The Service Employees International Union is among the unions pushing for immigration reform, including creating a path to citizenship for workers who entered the country illegally and protecting immigrant workers from exploitation.[87]

- *Strategic cooperation*. In industries that face vigorous international competition, such as autos, steel, and aircraft, some union and business leaders are trying to work more cooperatively than they have in years past. In the steel industry, for instance, union leaders have made significant concessions and even helped arrange the consolidation of three battered steel companies in the hopes of competing more effectively with overseas suppliers.[88]

How This Affects You

1. Have you ever had a communication breakdown at work or in a school setting that you could attribute to differences in age, gender, ethnic heritage, or religion? How did you and the other person resolve the situation? What did you learn from this experience that you could apply in the workplace in the future?

2. Have you ever left a job interview thinking that the interviewer didn't get a clear picture of your ability to perform the job or contribute to the company? What did you learn from this that you can use in your next job interview?

3. Do you, a family member, or a friend belong to a union? If not, would you consider taking a job that required you to join a union? Why or why not?

Summary of Learning Objectives

1 Explain the challenges and advantages of a diverse workforce.

Smart business leaders recognize that diverse workforces bring a broader range of viewpoints and ideas, they help companies understand and identify with diverse markets, and they enable companies to tap into the broadest possible pool of talent. Supervisors face the challenge of communicating with these diverse employees, motivating them, and fostering cooperation and harmony among them. Teams face the challenge of working together closely, and companies are challenged to coexist peacefully with business partners and with the community as a whole.

2 Discuss four staffing challenges employers are facing in today's workplace.

The four challenges identified in the chapter are (1) aligning the workforce with the organization's needs, (2) fostering employee loyalty in a time when most companies can no longer guarantee lifetime employment, (3) monitoring employee workloads and making sure employees are not in danger of burnout, and (4) helping employees find a balance, at least temporarily, between the demands of their personal and professional lives.

3 Discuss four alternative work arrangements that a company can use to address workplace challenges.

To meet today's staffing and demographic challenges, companies are offering their employees flextime (the ability to vary their work hours), telecommuting (the ability to work from home or another location), job sharing (the ability to share a single full-time job with a co-worker), and flexible career paths (the opportunity to leave the workforce for an extended period then return).

4 Identify the six stages in the hiring process.

The stages in the hiring process are (1) selecting a small number of qualified applicants, (2) performing initial screening interviews, (3) administering a series of follow-up interviews, (4) evaluating candidates, (5) conducting reference and background checks, and (6) selecting the right candidate.

5 List six popular types of financial incentive programs for employees.

The most popular employee incentive programs are bonuses, commissions, profit sharing, gain sharing, pay for performance, and knowledge-based pay.

6 Highlight five popular employee benefits.

The two most popular employee benefits are insurance (health, life, disability, and long-term care) and retirement benefits, such as pension plans that help employees save for later years. Employee stock-ownership plans and stock options, two additional benefits, allow employees to receive or purchase shares of the company's stock and thus obtain a stake in the company. Family benefits programs, also popular, include maternity and paternity leave, child-care assistance, and elder-care assistance.

7 Describe four ways an employee's status may change and discuss why many employers like to fill job vacancies from within.

An employee's status may change through promotion or through reassignment to a different position, through termination (removal from the company's payroll), through voluntary resignation, or through retirement. Employers like to fill vacancies created from such changes by promoting from within for these reasons: The employee has been trained by the company and knows the ropes; it boosts employee morale; and it sends a message to other employees that good performance will be rewarded.

8 Define the collective bargaining process.

First, the union negotiating team determines member needs while the management team tries to anticipate union demands and crafts responses to those demands. Second, the two sides conduct a series of meetings during which they attempt to reach an agreement by compromising as needed. Third, if the negotiating process is successful, union leaders present the proposed contract to the union membership for a vote. Fourth, if the contract is ratified by a member vote, the contract is then signed by the union and the company.

Behind the Scenes

Perking Up the Perfect Blend at Starbucks

On the fast track toward global growth, the Starbucks chain transformed the ordinary cup of coffee into a wide variety of taste choices for millions of coffee lovers. Along the way, the company's astonishing success encouraged competitors to join the fray. To stay on top, Starbucks managers had to ensure that their stores provided the best service along with the best coffee—which meant attracting, training, and compensating a diverse and dedicated workforce.

Guided by the company mission statement, Howard Schultz and his managers designed a variety of human resources programs to motivate Starbucks partners (employees). First, they raised employees' base pay. Next, management bucked the trend in the industry by offering full medical, dental, life insurance, and disability insurance benefits to every partner who worked at least 20 hours per week. These partners were also eligible for paid vacation days and retirement savings plans, benefits not commonly available to part-time restaurant workers. Finally, Starbucks invested in its workforce by providing new hires with 24 hours of training about the finer points of coffee brewing as well as the company's culture and values.

But the most innovative benefit brewed up by management was its Bean Stock, a program offering stock options not just to upper-echelon managers but to all partners who worked 20 or more hours per week. "We established Bean Stock in 1991 as a way of investing in our partners and creating ownership across the company," explained Bradley Honeycutt, vice president of human resource services. "It's been a key to retaining good people and building loyalty." For those who wanted to enlarge their financial stake in Starbucks, management devised a program that permitted partners to buy company stock at a discount. Owning a piece of the company motivated employees to take customer service to an even higher level of excellence. "We do everything we possibly can to get our customers to come back," says Schultz.

To help partners better balance their work and family obligations—another priority for Starbucks—the human resources department designed a comprehensive work-life program featuring flexible work schedules, access to employee assistance specialists, and referrals for child-care and elder-care support. The company also encouraged employees to become involved in their local communities, and it honored employees whose achievements exemplified the company's values. Finally, to encourage open communication and employee feedback, good or bad, management began holding a series of open forums in which company performance, results, and plans were openly discussed. Employees were encouraged to share ideas. "There is a tremendous amount of sharing in the company," notes Schultz. "It makes everybody think like an owner."

While most CEOs say that people are their most important asset, Starbucks lives that idea every day by giving people a stake in the outcome and treating them with respect and dignity. In all, putting employees first has helped Starbucks expand by attracting an energetic, committed workforce and keeping turnover to a minimal 60 percent, much lower than the industry average.[89]

Critical Thinking Questions

1. Why do Starbucks's human resources managers need to be kept informed about any changes in the number and timing of new store openings planned for the coming year?
2. Why does Starbucks offer benefits to its part-time labor force?
3. How does Starbucks's generous employee-benefits program motivate its employees?

LEARN MORE ONLINE

Visit the Starbucks website at www.starbucks.com; click on "About Us" and then click on "Career Center." Explore how Starbucks presents its HR policies to potential employees. Browse the pages that discuss working at Starbucks. Read about company culture, diversity, benefits, and learning and career development. Why would Starbucks post information about company culture in this section of the website? Why would job candidates be interested in learning about the culture as well as the employee benefits and training at Starbucks? (For the latest information on Starbucks, visit www.prenhall.com/bovée and click on "Real-Time Updates.") ■

Key Terms

arbitration (371)
attrition (368)
bonus (363)
boycott (371)
business agent (370)
cafeteria plans (364)
collective bargaining (371)
commissions (363)
compensation (362)
contingent employees (354)
diversity initiatives (353)
electronic performance monitoring (EPM) (360)
employee assistance programs (EAPs) (368)
employee benefits (364)
employee retention (354)
employee stock-ownership plan (ESOP) (366)
flextime (353)
401(k) plan (366)
gain sharing (363)

glass ceiling (352)
human resources management (HRM) (349)
incentives (363)
injunction (372)
job analysis (355)
job description (355)
job sharing (353)
job specification (355)
knowledge-based pay (364)
labor federation (371)
labor unions (370)
layoffs (369)
locals (370)
lockout (372)
mandatory retirement (369)
mediation (371)
national union (370)
orientation programs (359)
pay for performance (364)
pension plans (365)
performance appraisals (360)

picketing (371)
profit sharing (363)
quality of work life (QWL) (350)
recruiting (355)
replacement chart (354)
retirement plans (365)
salary (362)
sexism (351)
sexual harassment (352)
shop steward (370)
skills inventory (360)
stock options (366)
strike (371)
strikebreakers (372)
succession planning (354)
telecommuting (353)
termination (369)
wages (362)
worker buyout (369)
work-life balance (350)

Test Your Knowledge

Questions for Review

1. What do human resources managers do?
2. What are some strategic staffing alternatives that organizations use to avoid overstaffing and understaffing?
3. What is the purpose of conducting a job analysis? What are some of the techniques used for gathering information?
4. Why do some companies use preemployment drug testing while others don't?
5. What is the glass ceiling?

Questions for Analysis

6. How do incentive programs encourage employees to be more productive, innovative, and committed to their work?
7. Why do some employers offer comprehensive benefits even though the costs of doing so have risen significantly in recent years?
8. What are the advantages and disadvantages of 401(k) retirement plans?
9. The 1986 Immigration Reform and Control Act forbids companies to hire illegal aliens but at the same time prohibits discrimination in hiring on the basis of national origin or citizenship status. How can companies satisfy both requirements of this law?
10. **Ethical Considerations.** Corporate headhunters have been known to raid other companies for their top talent to fill vacant or new positions for their clients. Is it ethical to contact the CEO of one company and lure him or her to join the management team of another company?

Questions for Application

11. Assume you are the manager of human resources at a manufacturing company that employs about 500 people. A recent cyclical downturn in your industry has led to financial losses, and top management is talking about laying off workers. Several supervisors have come to you with creative ways of keeping employees on the payroll, such as exchanging workers with other local companies. Why might you want to consider this option? What other options exist besides layoffs?
12. **How This Affects You.** When you begin interviewing as you approach graduation, you will need to analyze job offers that include a number of financial and nonfinancial elements. Which of these aspects of employment are your top three priorities: a good base wage; bonus or commission opportunities, profit-sharing potential; rapid advancement opportunities; flexible work arrangements; good health-care insurance coverage; or a strong retirement program? Which of these elements would you be willing to forgo in order to get your top three?
13. **Integrated.** Of the five levels in Maslow's hierarchy of needs, which is satisfied by offering salary? By offering health-care benefits? By offering training opportunities? By developing flexible job descriptions?
14. **Integrated.** What are some of the human resources issues managers are likely to encounter when two companies (in the same industry) merge?

Practice Your Knowledge

Sharpening Your Communication Skills

A visit to CCH's SOHO Guide at www.toolkit.cch.com can help you reduce your legal liability whether you are laying off or firing a single employee or are contemplating a company-wide reduction in your workforce. Visit the website and scroll down to the "Small Business Guide" and click on "People Who Work for You" followed by "Firing and Termination" to find out the safest way to fire someone from a legal standpoint before it's too late. Learn why it's important to document disciplinary actions. Then use the information at this website to write a short memo to your instructor summarizing how to set up a termination meeting and what you should say and do at the meeting when you fire an employee.

Building Your Team Skills

Team up with a classmate to practice your responses to interview questions. Use the list of common interview questions provided in the Prologue, and take turns posing and responding to those questions. Which questions did you find most difficult to answer? What insights did you gain about your strengths and weaknesses by answering those questions? Why is it a good idea to rehearse your answers before going to an interview?

Improving Your Tech Insights: Assistive Technologies

The term *assistive technologies* covers a broad range of devices and systems that help people with disabilities perform activities that might otherwise be difficult or impossible. These include technologies that help people communicate orally and visually, interact with computers and other equipment, and enjoy greater mobility, along with myriad other specific functions.

Assistive technologies create a vital link for thousands of employees with disabilities, giving them the opportunity to pursue a greater range of career paths and giving employers access to a broader base of talent. With the United States heading for a potentially serious shortage of workers in a few years, the economy will benefit from everyone who can make a contribution, and assistive technologies will be an important part of the solution.

Research some of the technologies now on the market. AssistiveTech.net, www.assistivetech.net, is a great place to search for the many categories of assistive technologies now available; it also provides links to a variety of other sites. The Business Leadership Network, www.usbln.org, "recognizes and promotes best practices in hiring, retraining, and marketing to people with disabilities." For a look at the government's efforts to promote these technologies, visit the National Institute on Disability and Rehabilitation Research, www.ed.gov/about/offices/list/osers/nidrr. Also visit the Rehabilitation Engineering and Assistive Technology Society of North America, www.resna.org. Technology companies such as IBM (www.ibm.com/able) and Microsoft (www.microsoft.com/enable) also devote significant resources to developing assistive technologies and making information technology more accessible. Choose one assistive technology and in a brief e-mail to your instructor, explain how this technology can help companies support employees or customers with disabilities.[90]

Expand Your Knowledge

Discovering Career Opportunities

If you pursue a career in human resources, you'll be deeply involved in helping organizations find, select, train, evaluate, and retain employees. You have to like people and be a good communicator to succeed in HR. Is this field for you? Using your local Sunday newspaper, the *Wall Street Journal*, and online sources such as Monster (www.monster.com), find ads seeking applicants for positions in the field of human resources.

1. What educational qualifications, technical knowledge, or specialized skills are applicants for these jobs expected to have? How do these requirements fit with your background and educational plans?

2. Next, look at the duties mentioned in the ad for each job. What do you think you would be doing on an average day in these jobs? Does the work in each job sound interesting and challenging?

3. Now think about how you might fit into one of these positions. Do you prefer to work alone, or do you enjoy teamwork? How much paperwork are you willing to do? Do you communicate better in person, on paper, or by phone? Considering your answers to these questions, which of the HR jobs seems to be the closest match for your personal style?

Developing Your Research Skills

Locate one or more articles in business journals or newspapers (print or online editions) that illustrate how a company or industry is adapting to changes in its workforce. (Examples include retraining, literacy or basic-skills training, flexible benefits, and benefits aimed at working parents or people who care for aging relatives.)

1. What changes in the workforce or employee needs caused the company to adapt? What did the company do to respond to these changes? Was the company's response voluntary or legally mandated?

2. Is the company alone in facing these changes, or is the entire industry trying to adapt? What are other companies in the industry doing to adapt to the changes?

3. What other changes in the workforce or in employee needs do you think this company is likely to face in the next few years? Why?

See It on the Web

Visit these websites and answer the following questions for each one. (Up-to-date links for all websites mentioned in this chapter can be found on the Textbook Resources page for Chapter 14 at www.mybusinesslab.com. Please note that links to sites that become inactive after publication of the book will be removed from the Featured Websites section.)

1. What is the purpose of this website?

2. What kinds of information does this website contain? Please be specific.

3. How is the information provided at this website useful for businesspeople? Consumers?

4. How did you expand your knowledge of human resource management by reviewing the material at this website? What new things did you learn about this topic?

Explore the Latest Workforce Management Ideas

Visit *Workforce Management* online to see what management leaders are thinking about month by month (requires registration to read most articles, but it's free). The Community Center hosts a number of forums in which you can read questions, answers, and commentary from working HR managers. The Research Center lists a wide range of topics to explore in the HRM field. www. workforce.com

Digging Deeper at the Bureau of Labor Statistics

By now you're probably aware that the U.S. government has an agency for almost every purpose. Many of these agencies gather facts and statistics on trends in the United States, and the Bureau of Labor Statistics (BLS) is no exception. When you need to find detailed information about national or regional employment conditions—such as wages, unemployment, productivity, and benefits—check out the BLS website. www.bls.gov

Maximizing Your Earning Potential

You know you should be making more money. So now what? Log on to Salary.com to find out what you are worth. Then maximize your earning potential by exploring the basics of negotiation. Sharpen your skills so you can get the job, salary, and benefits you want. Contemplating a move? Use the cost-of-living wizard to find out if it makes economic sense. You may even want to prepare for your next performance review by taking one of the site's self-tests. Finally, don't leave without learning how to manage your take-home pay or getting some facts about tuition assistance. Many companies will reimburse you for your career course work. But you may not get it if you don't ask. www.salary.com

Companion Website

Learning Interactively

Log onto www.prenhall.com/bovée, locate your text, and then click on its Companion Website. For Chapter 14, take advantage of the interactive Chapter Quiz to test your knowledge of the chapter. Get instant feedback on whether you need additional studying. Also, you'll find an abundance of valuable resources that will help you succeed in this course, including PowerPoint presentations and Web Links.

Video Case

Channeling Human Resources at Showtime

LEARNING OBJECTIVES

The purpose of this video is to help you:

1. Identify the many ways in which human resource managers can actively develop employees
2. Appreciate the role of mentoring in employee development
3. Understand how a performance appraisal system can be designed and administered

SYNOPSIS

One of the biggest challenges at Showtime Networks Inc. (SNI), as anywhere, is attracting, retaining, and motivating a committed workforce. Demographic changes, work and family issues, and increasing diversities of age, race, and lifestyle call forth the dedication and creativity of its human resource staff. This video introduces various Showtime executives who discuss the company's human resource policies and challenges. The firm is a leader in creating a broad training and career development program that serves many different kinds of employee needs. It also uses a performance appraisal system that employees have helped design and has a formal program for encouraging mentoring.

Discussion Questions

1. *For analysis:* Among the organizational changes recently made at Showtime are the combining of the legal and the human resource departments and the appointment of one particular human resource manager to each SNI division. Comment on the advantages or disadvantages of these changes.
2. *For analysis:* Is Showtime doing a good job of offering its employees chances to develop and improve their skills? Can you suggest additional programs it could undertake to achieve this goal?
3. *For analysis:* Do you think the performance appraisal system at Showtime is an effective one? Why or why not?
4. *For application:* Could you apply Showtime's approach to a company with only three or four employees? Why or why not?
5. *For debate:* Do companies have a responsibility, beyond their own business needs, to mentor and develop employees? Why or why not?

ONLINE EXPLORATION

Showtime is now owned by CBS. Visit the CBS Careers page at www.cbscorporation.com/careers. Consider the information available on this site and the manner in which it is presented. Does CBS sound like the sort of company you'd like to work for? Why or why not? What advice would you give the company to improve recruiting of college graduates, if any?

Appendix A

The U.S. Legal System and Business Law

The U.S. Legal System

Throughout this textbook, you encounter a number of regulatory agencies, such as the FDA, FTC, EPA, and SEC, whose function is to protect society from the potential abuses of business. Federal, state, and local governments work in numerous ways to protect both individu-als and other businesses from corporate wrongdoing. Laws also spell out accepted ways of performing many essential business functions—along with the penalties for failing to comply. In other words, like the average person, companies must obey the law or face the consequences.

As you read this material, keep in mind that many U.S. companies also conduct business in other countries, so executives in these firms must also be familiar with **international law**, the principles, customs, and rules that govern the relationships between sovereign states and international organizations and persons.[1] Successful global business requires an understanding of the domestic laws of trading partners as well as of established international trading standards and legal guidelines.

Global companies, such as Coca-Cola, must have a firm grasp of international law.

Sources of Law

A *law* is a rule developed by a society to govern the conduct of, and relationships among, its members. The U.S. Constitution, including the Bill of Rights, is the foundation for U.S. laws. Because the Constitution is a general document, laws offering specific answers to specific problems are constantly embellishing its basic principles. However, law is not static; it develops in response to changing conditions and social standards. Individual laws originate in various ways: through legislative action (*statutory law*), through administrative rulings (*administrative law*), and through customs and judicial precedents (*common law*). To one degree or another, all three forms of law affect businesses. Moreover, at times the three forms of law may overlap so that the differences between them become indistinguishable. Nonetheless, in cases where the three forms of law appear to conflict, statutory law generally prevails.

Statutory Law

Statutory law is law written by the U.S. Congress, state legislatures, and local governments. One of the most important elements of statutory law that affects businesses is the **Uniform Commercial Code (UCC)**. Designed to mitigate differences between state statutory laws and to simplify interstate commerce, this code is a comprehensive, systematic collection of statutes in a particular legal area.[2] For example, the UCC provides a nationwide standard in many issues of commercial law, such as sales contracts, bank deposits, and warranties.

Administrative Law

Once laws have been passed by a state legislature or Congress, an administrative agency or commission typically takes responsibility for enforcing them. That agency may be called on to clarify a regulation's intent, often by consulting representatives of the affected industry. The administrative agency may then write more specific regulations, which are considered **administrative law**.

EXHIBIT A.1 The U.S. Court System

A legal proceeding may begin in a trial court or an administrative agency (examples of each are given here). An unfavorable decision may be appealed to a higher court at the federal or state level. (The court of appeals is the highest court in states that have no state supreme court; some other states have no intermediate appellate court.) The U.S. Supreme Court, the country's highest court, is the court of final appeal.

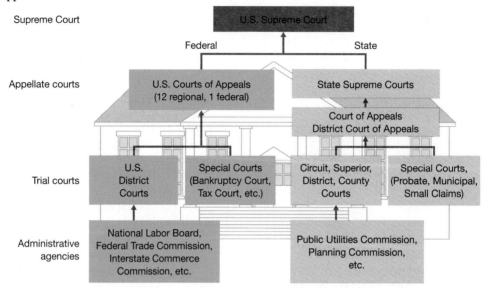

Administrative agencies also have the power to investigate corporations suspected of breaking administrative laws. A corporation found to be misbehaving may agree to a **consent order**, which allows the company to promise to stop doing something without actually admitting to any illegal behavior. As an alternative to entering into a consent order, the administrative agency may start legal proceedings against the company in a hearing presided over by an administrative law judge. During such a hearing, witnesses are called and evidence is presented to determine the facts of the situation. The judge then issues a decision, which may impose corrective actions on the company. If either party objects to the decision, the party may file an appeal to the appropriate federal court. [3]

Common Law

Common law, which originates in courtrooms and judges' decisions, began in England many centuries ago and was transported to the United States by the colonists. It is applied in all states except Louisiana (which follows a French model). Common law is sometimes called the "unwritten law" to distinguish it from legislative acts and administrative-agency regulations, which are written documents. Instead, common law is established through custom and the precedents set in courtroom proceedings.

Despite its unwritten nature, common law has great continuity, which derives from the doctrine of *stare decisis* (Latin for "to stand by decisions"). What the *stare decisis* doctrine means is that judges' decisions establish a precedent for deciding future cases of a similar nature. Because common law is based on what has gone before, the legal framework develops gradually.

In the United States, common law is applied and interpreted in the system of courts (see Exhibit A.1). Common law thus develops through the decisions in trial courts, special courts, and appellate courts. The U.S. Supreme Court (or the highest court of a state when state laws are involved) sets precedents for entire legal systems. Lower courts must then abide by those precedents as they pertain to similar cases.

In most states, business cases are heard in standard trial courts. However, many corporations and states are pushing for the establishment of a network of special business courts. More than a dozen states now have business courts or business-only court sessions. Advocates say that the special nature of business legal disputes requires experienced judges who understand business issues. They also feel that a system of business courts would go a long way toward reducing the expense and unpredictability of business litigation. However, opponents say that business courts are likely to favor local companies in disputes involving out-of-state litigants. Moreover, they say that the courts are likely to come under the influence of powerful business special-interest groups. [4]

Business Law

Although businesses must comply with the full body of laws that apply to individuals, a subset of laws can be defined more precisely as **business law**. This includes those elements of law that directly affect business activities. For example, laws pertaining to business licensing, employee safety, and corporate income taxes can all be considered business law. The most important categories of laws affecting business include torts, contracts, agency, property transactions, patents, trademarks, copyrights, negotiable instruments, and bankruptcy.

Torts

A **tort** is a noncriminal act (other than breach of contract) that results in injury to a person or to property.[5] A tort can be either intentional or the result of negligence. The victim of a tort is legally entitled to some form of financial compensation, or **damages**, for his or her loss and suffering. This compensation is also known as a *compensatory damage award.* In some cases, the victim may also receive a *punitive damage award* to punish the wrongdoer if the misdeed was deemed particularly bad.

Intentional Torts

An **intentional tort** is a willful act that results in injury. For example, accidentally hitting a softball through someone's window is a tort, but purposely cutting down someone's tree because it obscures your view is an intentional tort. Note that *intent* in this case does not mean the intent to cause harm; it is the intent to commit a specific act. Some intentional torts involve communication of false statements that harm another's reputation. If the communication is published in any permanent form, from a newspaper to a book to a television program, it is called *libel;* if it is spoken, it is *slander.*[6]

Negligence and Product Liability

In contrast to intentional torts, torts of **negligence** involve a failure to use a reasonable amount of care necessary to protect others from unreasonable risk of injury.[7] Cases of alleged negligence often involve **product liability**, which is a product's capacity to cause damage or injury for which the producer or seller is held responsible. Product liability is one of the most hotly contested aspects of business law today, with consumer advocates pointing to the number of product-related injuries and deaths every year—some 28 million injuries and 22,000 deaths—and business advocates pointing to the high cost of product-liability lawsuits—as much as $150 billion every year.[8]

A company may also be held liable for injury caused by a defective product even if the company used all reasonable care in the manufacture, distribution, or sale of its product. Such **strict product liability** makes it possible to assign liability without assigning fault. It must only be established that (1) the company is in the business of selling the product, (2) the product reached the customer or user without substantial change in its condition, (3) the product was defective, (4) the defective condition rendered the product unreasonably dangerous, and (5) the defective product caused the injury.[9]

With so much at stake, including the magnitude of legal fees in many cases, it's no surprise that product-liability lawsuits generate so much controversy. Although few people would argue that individual victims of harmful goods and services shouldn't be entitled to some sort of compensation, many people now ask whether the system needs reforms. For instance, a recent survey suggested a majority of U.S. consumers favor such reforms as limiting the fees that lawyers can earn in product-liability lawsuits, placing limits on the amount of money awarded for pain and suffering, and enacting sanctions against attorneys who file frivolous lawsuits.[10] In addition, business leaders point out that the billions of dollars consumed by legal fees and damage awards raise prices for all consumers and, in some cases, limit the product choices available in the marketplace. In the past few years, many states have enacted restrictions on the types of liability cases that plaintiffs can file and on the size of damage awards.[11]

Contracts

Broadly defined, a **contract** is an exchange of promises between two or more parties that is enforceable by law. Many business transactions—including buying and selling products, hiring employees, purchasing group insurance, and licensing technology—involve contracts. Contracts may be either express or implied. An **express contract** is derived from the words (either oral or written) of the parties; an **implied contract** stems from the actions or conduct of the parties.[12]

Elements of a Contract

The law of contracts deals largely with identifying the exchanges that can be classified as contracts. The following factors must usually be present for a contract to be valid and enforceable:

- *An offer must be made.* One party must propose that an agreement be entered into. The offer may be oral or written, but it must be firm, definite, and specific enough to make it clear that someone intends to be legally bound by the offer. Finally, the offer must be communicated to the intended party or parties.

- *An offer must be accepted.* For an offer to be accepted, there must be clear intent (spoken, written, or by action) to enter into the contract. An implied contract arises when a person requests or accepts something and the other party has indicated that payment is expected. If, for example, your car breaks down on the road and you call a mobile mechanic and ask him or her to repair it, you are obligated to pay the reasonable value for the services, even if you didn't agree to specific charges beforehand. However, when a specific offer is made, the acceptance must satisfy the terms of the offer. For example, if someone offers you a car for $18,000, and you say you would take it for $15,000, you have not accepted the offer. Your response is a *counteroffer,* which may or may not be accepted by the salesperson.

- *Both parties must give consideration.* A contract is legally binding only when the parties have bargained with each other and have exchanged something of value, which is called the **consideration**. The relative value of each party's consideration does not generally matter to the courts. In other words, if you make a deal with someone and later decide you didn't get enough in the deal, that result is not the court's concern. You entered into the deal with the original consideration in mind, and that fact is legally sufficient.[13]

- *Both parties must give genuine assent.* To have a legally enforceable contract, both parties must agree to it voluntarily. The contract must be free of fraud, duress, undue influence, and mutual mistake.[14] If only one party makes a mistake, it ordinarily does not affect the contract. On the other hand, if both parties make a mistake, the agreement would be void. For example, if both the buyer and the seller of a business believed the business was profitable, when in reality it was operating at a loss, their agreement would be void.

- *Both parties must be competent.* The law gives certain classes of people only a limited capacity to enter into contracts. Minors, people who are senile or insane, and in some cases those who are intoxicated cannot usually be bound by a contract for anything but the bare necessities: food, clothing, shelter, and medical care.

- *The contract must not involve an illegal act.* Courts will not enforce a promise that involves an illegal act. For example, a drug dealer cannot get help from the courts to enforce a contract to deliver illegal drugs at a prearranged price.

- *The contract must be in proper form.* Most contracts can be made orally, by an act, or by a casually written document; however, certain contracts are required by law to be in writing. For example, the transfer of goods worth $500 or more must be accompanied by a written document. The written form is also required for all real estate contracts.

A contract need not be long; all these elements of a contract may be contained in a simple document (see Exhibit A.2). In fact, a personal check is one type of simple contract.

Contract Performance

Contracts normally expire when the agreed-to conditions have been met, called *performance* in legal terms. However, not all contracts run their expected course. Both parties involved can agree to back out of the contract, for instance. In other cases, one party fails to live up to the terms of the contract, a situation called **breach of contract**. The other party has several options at that point:

- *Discharge.* When one party violates the terms of the agreement, generally the other party is under no

EXHIBIT A.2 Elements of a Contract

This simple document contains all the essential elements of a valid contract.

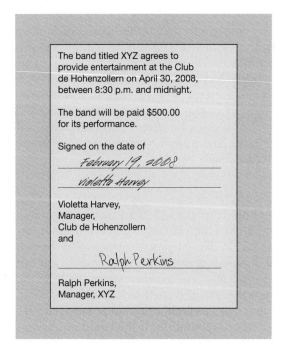

obligation to continue with his or her end of the contract. In other words, the second party is discharged from the contract.

- *Damages.* A party has the right to sue in court for damages that were foreseeable at the time the contract was entered into and that result from the other party's failure to fulfill the contract. The amount of damages awarded usually reflects the amount of profit lost and often includes court costs as well, although figuring out fair amounts is not always easy. When talk-show host Rosie O'Donnell and publisher Gruner + Jahr USA sued each other for more than $100 million each over the collapse of the magazine *Rosie,* a judge determined that neither side deserved anything.[15]

- *Specific performance.* A party can be compelled to live up to the terms of the contract if money damages would not be adequate.

To control the increasing costs of litigation, more and more companies are now experimenting with alternatives to the courtroom. These include independent mediators, who sit down with the two parties and try to hammer out a satisfactory solution to contract problems, and mandatory arbitration, in which an impartial arbitrator or arbitration panel hears evidence from both sides and makes a legally binding decision. However, mandatory arbitration has come under fire by consumer groups because it can wipe out a customer's right to sue.

After the massive "Big Dig" highway project in Boston ran billions of dollars over budget, the state of Massachusetts sued the company in charge of the project, claiming it had withheld financial information that might have changed the state's decision to approve the project.

Warranties

The Uniform Commercial Code specifies that everyday sales transactions are a special kind of contract (although this provision applies only to tangible goods, not to services), even though they may not meet all the exact requirements of regular contracts. Related to the sales contract is the notion of a **warranty**, which is a statement specifying what the producer of a product will do to compensate the buyer if the product is defective or if it malfunctions. Warranties come in several flavors. One important distinction is between *express warranties*, which are specific, written statements, and *implied warranties*, which are unwritten but involve certain protections under the law. Also, warranties are either *full* or *limited*. The former obligates the seller to repair or replace the product, without charge, in the event of any defect or malfunction, whereas the latter imposes restrictions on the defects or malfunctions that will be covered. Warranty laws also address a number of other details, including giving consumers instructions on how to exercise their rights under the warranty.[16]

Agency

Many creative and athletic professionals engage the services of agents to promote their services, negotiate contracts, and conduct other business affairs. These relationships illustrate a common legal association known as **agency**, which exists when one party, known as the *principal*, authorizes another party, known as the *agent*, to act on his or her behalf in contractual matters.[17]

All contractual obligations come into play in agency relationships. The principal usually creates this relationship by explicit authorization. In some cases—when a transfer of property is involved, for example—the authorization must be written in the form of a document called **power of attorney**, which states that one person may legally act for another (to the extent authorized).

Usually, an agency relationship is terminated when the objective of the relationship has been met or at the end of a period specified in the contract between agent and principal. It may also be ended by a change of circumstances, by the agent's breach of duty or loyalty, or by the death of either party.

Property Transactions

Anyone interested in business must know the basics of property law. Most people think of property as some object they own (a book, a car, a house). However, **property** is actually the relationship between the person having the rights to any tangible or intangible object and all other persons. The law recognizes two primary types of property: real and personal. **Real property** is land and everything permanently attached to it, such as trees, fences, or mineral deposits. **Personal property** is all property that is not real property; it may be tangible (cars, jewelry, or anything having a physical existence) or intangible (bank accounts, stocks, insurance policies, customer lists). A piece of marble in the earth is real property until it is cut and sold as a block, when it becomes personal property. Property rights are subject to various limitations and restrictions. For example, the government monitors the use of real property for the welfare of the public, to the point of explicitly prohibiting some property uses and abuses.[18]

Two types of documents are important in obtaining real property for factory, office, or store space: a deed and a lease. A **deed** is a legal document by which an owner transfers the *title*, or right of ownership, to real property to a new owner. A lease is used for a temporary transfer of interest in real property. The party that owns the property is commonly called the *landlord*; the party that occupies or gains the right to occupy the property is the *tenant*. The tenant pays the landlord, usually in periodic installments, for the use of the property. Generally, a lease may be granted for any length of time that the two parties agree on.

Patents, Trademarks, and Copyrights

If you invent a product, write a book, develop some new software, or simply come up with a unique name for your business, you probably want to prevent other people from using or prospering from your **intellectual property** without fairly compensating you. Several forms of legal protection are available for your creations. They include patents,

Trademarked brand names are a valuable element of intellectual property.

trademarks, and copyrights. Which one you should use depends on what you have created. Having a patent, copyright, or trademark still doesn't guarantee that your idea or product will not be copied. However, they do provide you with legal recourse if your creations are infringed upon.

Patents

A patent protects the invention or discovery of a new and useful process, an article of manufacture, a machine, a chemical substance, or an improvement on any of these. Issued by the U.S. Patent Office, a patent grants the owner the right to exclude others from making, using, or selling the invention for 20 years from the date the patent application is filed.[19] After that time, the patented item becomes available for common use. On the one hand, patent law guarantees the originator the right to use the discovery exclusively for a relatively long period of time, thus encouraging people to devise new machines, gadgets, and processes. On the other hand, it also ensures that rights to the new item will be released eventually, allowing other enterprises to discover even more innovative ways to use it.

Trademarks

A trademark is any word, name, symbol, or device used to distinguish the product of one manufacturer from those made by others. A service mark is the same thing for services. McDonald's golden arches and Nike's "swoosh" are two of the most visible of modern trademarks. Brand names can also be registered as trademarks.

If properly registered and renewed every 20 years, a trademark generally belongs to its owner forever. Among the exceptions are popular brand names that have become generic terms, meaning that they describe a whole class of products. A brand-name trademark can become a generic term if the trademark has been allowed to expire, if it has been incorrectly used by its owner (as in the case of Borden's ReaLemon lemon juice, which the Federal Trade Commission ruled was being used by Borden to maintain a monopoly in bottled lemon juice), or if the public comes to equate the name with the class of products, as was the case with zipper, linoleum, aspirin, and many other common terms that started out as brand names.

Trade dress, defined as the general appearance or image of a product, has been easier to legally protect since 1992 when the U.S. Supreme Court extended trademark protection to products with "inherently distinctive" appearances. For instance, General Motors and AM General successfully sued Lanard Toys for selling toy trucks that copied the design of the Hummer SUV (produced by GM) and its original military version, the Humvee (produced by AM General).[20]

Copyrights

Copyrights protect the creators of literary, dramatic, musical, artistic, scientific, and other intellectual works. Any printed, filmed, or recorded material can be copyrighted. The copyright gives its owner the exclusive right to reproduce (copy), sell, or adapt the work he or she has created.

The Library of Congress Copyright Office will issue a copyright to the creator or to whomever the creator has granted the right to reproduce the work. (A book, for example, may be copyrighted by the author or the publisher.) Copyrights issued through 1998 are good for 75 years from the date of publication. Copyrights issued after 1998 are valid for the lifetime of the creator plus 70 years.[21]

Copyright protection on the Internet has become an especially important topic as more businesses and individuals include original material on their websites. Technically, copyright protection exists from the moment material is created. Therefore, anything you post on a website is protected by copyright law. However, loose Internet standards and a history of sharing information online has made it difficult for some users to accept this situation. But the No Electronic Theft Act (enacted in 1998) makes it clear that the sanctity of the copyright extends to online publishing. This law makes it a crime to possess or distribute multiple copies of online copyrighted material for profit or not. Specifically, it closes the loophole that had allowed the distribution of copyrighted material as long as the offender didn't seek profit. Penalties include fines up to $250,000 and five years in prison.[22] To avoid potential copyright infringements, experts suggest that authors include copyright and trademark notices on webpages that contain protected material, include a link on each page to a detailed copyright notice that explains what users can and cannot do, and place disclaimers on all pages that contain links to other sites.[23]

Negotiable Instruments

Whenever you write a personal check, you are creating a **negotiable instrument**, a transferable document that represents a promise to pay a specified amount. (*Negotiable* in this sense means that it can be sold or used as payment of a debt; an *instrument* is simply a written document that expresses a legal agreement.) In addition to checks, negotiable instruments include certificates of deposit, promissory notes, and commercial paper. To be negotiable, an instrument must meet several criteria:[24]

- It must be in writing and signed by the person who created it.
- It must have an unconditional promise to pay a specified sum of money.
- It must be payable either on demand or at a specified date in the future.
- It must be payable either to some specified person or organization or to the person holding it (the bearer).

You can see how a personal check meets those criteria; when you write one, you are agreeing to pay the amount of the check to the person or organization to whom you're writing it.

Bankruptcy

Even though the U.S. legal system establishes the rules of fair play and offers protection from the unscrupulous, it can't prevent most consumers or businesses from taking on too much debt. The legal system does, however, provide help for parties that find themselves in deep financial trouble.

Bankruptcy is the legal means of relief for debtors who are unable to meet their financial obligations.[25] (Consumer bankruptcy, including the 2005 law that makes it more difficult for consumers to file for bankruptcy and to avoid paying debts if they do file, is covered in Appendix B.)

Voluntary bankruptcy is initiated by the debtor; *involuntary bankruptcy* is initiated by creditors. The law provides for several types of bankruptcy, which are commonly referred to by chapter number of the Bankruptcy Reform Act. In a Chapter 7 bankruptcy, the debtor's assets will be sold and the proceeds divided equitably among the creditors. Under Chapter 11 (which is usually aimed at businesses but does not exclude individuals other than stockbrokers), a business is allowed to get back on its feet and continue functioning while it arranges to pay its debts.[26] For the steps involved in a Chapter 11 bankruptcy, see Exhibit A.3. If a company emerges from Chapter 11 as a leaner, healthier organization, creditors generally benefit. That's because once a company is back on its financial feet it can resume payments to creditors. For instance, after Polaroid reorganized it finances during nine months of Chapter 11 bankruptcy protection, the courts approved the sale of substantially all of Polaroid's business to One Equity Partners. Both the secured and unsecured creditors supported the sale in anticipation of receiving payments on their outstanding debt balances.[27]

As Exhibit A.4 shows, a number of Chapter 11 bankruptcies of epic proportions have been filed in the past few years. Banking failures dominated the early 1990s, whereas technology and energy failures dominated in the early years of the new millennium.

EXHIBIT A.3 Steps in Chapter 11 Bankruptcy Proceedings

Chapter 11 bankruptcy may buy a debtor time to reorganize finances and continue operating. However, using this device to evade financial obligations is extremely risky from a legal standpoint, and declaring bankruptcy may severely damage the reputation and credit rating of a firm or an individual.

Step 1: All current legal proceedings against the firm are halted. A decision is made to either liquidate or reorganize the firm, based on the value of the firm's assets. If liquidation is chosen, the firm's assets are transferred to a trustee, who sells them to pay the firm's debts. If reorganization is chosen, go to step 2.

Step 2: The courts may appoint a trustee to operate the firm, or current management may continue to operate it. A reorganization plan is developed either by current management, by the trustee, or by a committee of creditors. When plan is developed, go to step 3.

Step 3: Creditors and shareholders vote on the reorganization plan. Plan is ratified if (1) at least one-half of creditors vote in favor and if their claims against the company represent at least two-thirds of total claims; (2) at least two-thirds of shareholders approve the plan; and (3) the plan is confirmed by the court. When plan is ratified, go to step 4.

Step 4: The plan guarantees creditors new securities, and sometimes cash, in exchange for dismissal of their claims. With the firm discharged from its debts, it is free to start anew without the weight of past failures.

EXHIBIT A.4

Largest U.S. Bankruptcies Since 1980

The largest U.S. corporate bankruptcies in recent years occurred mainly in the airline, energy, financial services, and technology industries.

COMPANY	YEAR OF FILING	ASSETS (PRIOR TO FILING)
WorldCom	2002	$103,914,000,000
Enron	2001	$63,392,000,000
Conseco	2002	$61,392,000,000
Texaco	1987	$35,892,000,000
Financial Corp. of America	1988	$33,864,000,000
Refco	2005	$33,333,172,000
Global Crossing	2002	$30,185,000,000
Pacific Gas and Electric	2001	$29,770,000,000
UAL (parent of United Airlines)	2002	$25,197,000,000
Delta Air Lines	2005	$21,801,000,000
Adelphia Communications	2002	$21,499,000,000
MCorp	1989	$20,228,000,000
Mirant Corporation	2003	$19,415,000,000
Delphi Corporation	2005	$16,593,000,000
First Executive Corporation	1991	$15,193,000,000

Test Your Knowledge

Questions for Review

1. What are the three types of U.S. laws, and how do they differ? What additional laws must global companies consider?
2. What is the difference between negligence and intentional torts?
3. What are the seven elements of a valid contract?
4. How can companies protect their intellectual property?
5. What criteria must an instrument meet to be negotiable?

Questions for Analysis

6. What is precedent, and how does it affect common law?
7. What does the concept of strict product liability mean to businesses?

8. Why is agency important to business?
9. What is the advantage of declaring Chapter 11 bankruptcy? What is the disadvantage?
10. **Ethical Considerations.** Should products that can be used in the commission of a crime be declared illegal? For example, DVD burners can be used to make illegal copies of movies pirated from the Internet. Why wouldn't the government simply ban such devices?

Appendix Glossary

administrative law   Rules, regulations, and interpretations of statutory law set forth by administrative agencies and commissions

agency   Business relationship that exists when one party (the principal) authorizes another party (the agent) to enter into contracts on the principal's behalf

bankruptcy   Legal procedure by which a person or a business that is unable to meet financial obligations is relieved of debt

breach of contract   Failure to live up to the terms of a contract, with no legal excuse

business law   Those elements of law that directly influence or control business activities

common law   Law based on the precedents established by judges' decisions

consent order   Settlement in which an individual or organization promises to discontinue some illegal activity without admitting guilt

consideration   Negotiated exchange necessary to make a contract legally binding

contract   Legally enforceable exchange of promises between two or more parties

damages   Financial compensation to an injured party for loss and suffering

deed   Legal document by which an owner transfers the title, or ownership rights, to real property to a new owner

express contract   Contract derived from words, either oral or written

implied contract   Contract derived from actions or conduct

intellectual property   Intangible personal property, such as ideas, songs, trade secrets, and computer programs, that are protected by patents, trademarks, and copyrights

intentional tort   Willful act that results in injury

international law   Principles, customs, and rules that govern the international relationships between states, organizations, and persons

negligence   Tort in which a reasonable amount of care to protect others from risk of injury is not used

negotiable instrument   Transferable document that represents a promise to pay a specified amount

personal property   All property that is not real property

power of attorney   Written authorization for one party to legally act for another

product liability   The capacity of a product to cause harm or damage for which the producer or seller is held accountable

property   Rights held regarding any tangible or intangible object

real property   Land and everything permanently attached to it

stare decisis   Concept of using previous judicial decisions as the basis for deciding similar court cases

statutory law   Statute, or law, created by a legislature

strict product liability   Liability for injury caused by a defective product when all reasonable care is used in its manufacture, distribution, or sale; no fault is assigned

tort   Noncriminal act (other than breach of contract) that results in injury to a person or to property

Uniform Commercial Code (UCC)   Set of standardized laws, adopted by most states, that govern business transactions

warranty   Statement specifying what the producer of a product will do to compensate the buyer if the product is defective or if it malfunctions

Personal Finance: Getting Set for Life

Will You Control Your Money, or Will Your Money Control You?

In your years as a consumer and a wage earner, even if you've only had part-time jobs so far, you've already established a relationship with money. How would you characterize that relationship? Positive or negative? Are you in control of your money, or does money—and a frequent lack of it—control you? Unfortunately, too many people in the United States find themselves in the second situation, with heavy debt loads, a constant cycle of struggle from one paycheck to the next, and worries about the future. Nearly two-thirds of U.S. adults say they are living paycheck to paycheck, and nearly three-quarters say that getting out of debt is their primary

By establishing positive financial habits now, you can avoid the money worries that plague millions of U.S. consumers.

financial goal.[1] When people get stuck in this mode, money often controls their lives because it's a constant source of worry.

The good news is that with some basic information in hand, you can almost always improve your financial well-being and take control of your money. The timing might seem ironic, but the best time to establish a positive relationship with money is right now, when you're still a student. If you build good habits now, when money is often scarce, you'll be taking a major step toward getting set for life. Conversely, if you fall into bad habits, you could find yourself struggling and worrying for years to come. You'd be amazed at how many graduates think that their financial lives will improve dramatically when they start earning a "real" paycheck, only to discover that their bills and debts increase even faster than their earnings.

This appendix will help you understand the basic principles of personal finances and give you a solid foundation for managing your money. Before exploring some helpful strategies for each stage of your life, you'll learn three lessons that every consumer and wage earner needs to know and get a brief look at the financial planning process.

Three Simple—but Vital—Financial Lessons

If you've ever read a copy of the *Wall Street Journal* or another financial publication, you might have gotten the sense that money management is complex and jargon infested. However, unless you become a financial professional, you don't need to worry about the intricacies of "high finance." A few simple lessons will serve you well, starting with three ideas that will have enormous impact on your financial future: (1) the value of your money is constantly changing, so you need to understand how time affects your financial health, (2) small sacrifices early in life can have a huge payback later in life, and (3) every financial decision you make involves trade-offs. Taking these three ideas to heart will improve every aspect of your money management efforts, no matter how basic or sophisticated your finances.

The Value of Your Money Is Constantly Changing

If you remember only one thing from this discussion of personal finance, make sure this thought stays with you: A dollar today does not equal a dollar tomorrow. If you've successfully invested a dollar, it will be worth a little more tomorrow. However, if you charged a dollar's worth of purchases on a credit card, you're going to owe a little more than a dollar tomorrow. And even if you hold it tightly in your hand, that dollar will be worth a little less tomorrow, thanks to **inflation**—the tendency of prices to increase over time. When prices go up, your **buying power** goes down, so that dollar will buy less and less with each passing day.

These effects are so gradual that they are virtually impossible to notice from one day to the next, but they can have a staggering impact on your finances over time. Put time to work for you, and you'll join that happy segment of the population whose finances are stable and under control. Let time work against you, and you could get trapped in an endless cycle of stress and debt.

A simple example will demonstrate the power of time. Let's say you inherit $10,000 today and have two choices: hide it under your mattress or invest it in the stock market. Now fast-forward ten years. If you hid the $10,000 under your mattress, it'll now be worth only $7,000 or so (assuming today's inflation rates stay about the same). It will still *look* like $10,000, but because of inflation, it'll *spend* like $7,000. On the other hand, if you invested it in the stock market, you could have $15,000 or more, assuming stock market returns track historical patterns. That's a difference of $8,000 between the two choices, almost as much as your inheritance to begin with.

Now let's say you didn't get that inheritance but you did get the urge to treat your best friends to a relaxing vacation. You don't have the cash, but lucky you—a shiny new credit card with a $10,000 limit just arrived in the mail, so away you go. The bill arrives a few days after you return home, and you start paying a modest amount, say $150 a month. At 13 percent interest, which is not unusual for a credit card, it'll take you just about ten years to pay off the $10,000 you borrowed—and you'll end up paying $18,000, nearly twice what you thought that vacation was costing you. Doesn't seem so relaxing now, does it?

Depending on the financial decisions you make, then, time can be your best friend or your worst enemy. The **time value of money** refers to increases in money as a result of accumulating interest.[2] Time is even more powerful when your investment or debt is subject to **compounding**, which occurs when new interest is applied to interest that has already accumulated. Financial planners often talk about the "magic of compounding," and it really can feel like magic—good magic if it's compounded interest on savings, bad magic if it's compounded interest on debt. Saving is about the only legitimate way to earn money by doing nothing.

Small Sacrifices Early in Life Can Produce Big Payoffs

If you're currently living the life of a typical college student, you probably can't wait to move on and move up in life. You'll land that first "real" job, then get a nicer apartment, buy a new car, replace those ratty clothes you've been wearing for four years, and stop eating ramen seven nights a week. This might be the last thing you want to hear, but if you can convince yourself to continue your frugal ways for a few more years, you'll benefit tremendously in the long run.

Let's say that by age 65 you'd like to have a retirement fund of $1 million in *today's dollars,* which means adjusted for inflation. Compare the scenarios in Exhibit B.1 (which assumes 8 percent annual return on your investments, which is in line with historical stock market investments, and 4 percent annual inflation of both the cost of living and the amount you invest). If you start investing at age 25, you'll need to start out investing $946 a month. If you wait until age 35 to start, you'll need to invest $1,585 a month to reach $1 million. Wait until age 45, and you'll need to invest $2,957 a month. In other words, the longer you wait, the more painful it gets.

Of course, saving $946 a month during the early years of your career is no easy task, and it may be impossible, depending on your starting salary. In addition to the endless temptations to spend, you may also face the costs of starting a family, for instance. However, you'd be amazed at how much you can save every month by forgoing that new car, renting a cheaper apartment, buying modestly priced clothes, and watching your entertainment expenses closely. A few simple choices can often free up hundreds of dollars every month. And if you join the growing number of college graduates who plan to move back in with their parents during the initial years of their careers, you can really pile up the savings.[3] Even if you can save only a few hundred dollars a month early in your career, the earlier you start, the better off you'll be. Just keep increasing your monthly investment

EXHIBIT B.1 Building a Million

The longer you wait to pursue a financial goal, the more difficult it becomes to achieve. If you want to amass $1 million (in today's earning power) by age 65, for example, starting at age 25 is much less expensive than starting at age 45.

STARTING AGE	MONTHLY INVESTMENT REQUIRED*
25	$ 946
35	$1,585
45	$2,957

*Assumes 8 percent annual return, 4 percent inflation, and 4 percent increase in amount invested each year.

every time your salary increases, and do everything you can to take advantage of the time value of money.

Every Decision Involves Trade-Offs

By now, you've probably noticed that the time value of money and frugal living involve lots of choices. In fact, virtually every financial decision you make, from buying a cup of coffee to buying a house, involves a **trade-off**, in which you have to give up one thing to gain something else. If your family and friends give you $2,000 for graduation, should you run right out and buy alloy wheels and a custom exhaust system for your car? Or should you invest that $2,000 in the stock market and invest another $200 every month, so that in five or six years you could have enough to buy a new car—in cash, with no monthly payments? If you choose the second option, while your friends are shelling out $400 or $500 in payments for their new cars, you can be investing that amount every month and build up enough money to start your own business or perhaps retire a few years early.

Even the smallest habits and choices have consequences. Addicted to potato chips? Let's say you spend $3.19 for a big bag two or three times a week. Kick that habit now and invest $400 or so a year instead. Over the course of 40 years, you could earn enough to treat yourself to a new car when you retire. Sounds crazy, but over the course of many years, even tiny amounts of money can add up to large sums.

Not all your choices will be so simple, of course. Most of the examples presented so far have involved trading current pleasures and luxuries for future financial gain—a dilemma you'll be facing most of your life, by the way. Other choices involve risks versus rewards. Should you buy life insurance to provide for your family or invest the money and hope it'll grow fast enough to provide your loved ones with enough to get by on in the event of your death? Should you invest your money in a safe but slow-growing investment or an investment that offers the potential for high growth—but the risk that you could lose everything? As you gain experience with financial choices, you'll recognize your own level of *risk tolerance*. For instance, if you're lying awake at night worrying about a high-risk stock you just purchased, you may have a lower level of risk tolerance and you'll probably want to stick with safer, saner investments.

Figuring out the best choice is difficult in many cases, but simply recognizing that every decision involves a trade-off will improve your decision making. Too often, people get into trouble by looking at *only* the risk (which can stop them from making choices that might in fact be better for them in the long run) or *only* the potential rewards (which can lure them into making choices that are too risky). Consider all the consequences of every choice you make, and you'll start making better financial decisions.

You'll pick up many other financial tips as you start investing, buying houses, selecting insurance, and making other financial choices, but these three concepts will always

apply. With those thoughts in mind, it's time to take a look at the financial planning process.

Creating Your Personal Financial Plan

Creating and following a sensible financial plan is the only sure way to stay in control of your finances. A good plan can help you get the most from whatever amount of money you have, identify the funds you'll need in order to get through life's major expenses, increase your financial independence and confidence, minimize the time and energy needed to manage your finances, and answer a question that vexes millions of people every year: Where did all my money go?

Many people discover they'd rather turn the task over to a professional financial planner. Even if you do most of your planning yourself, you may encounter special situations or major transactions in which you'd like the advice of an expert. The right advice at the right time can mean all the difference. Unfortunately, finding the right adviser is not a simple task: Some 250,000 people in the United States offer their services as financial advisers.[4] Before you sign on with anyone, make sure you understand what advice you need and who can provide it. Ask for references, professional credentials, investing strategies, and most important of all, how the adviser is paid.[5]

Fee-only planners charge you for their services, either an hourly rate or a percentage of the assets they're managing for you. In theory, the major advantage of fee-only planners is complete objectivity, as they don't make money on the specific decisions they recommend for you. In contrast, **commission-based planners** are paid commissions on the financial products they sell you, such as insurance policies and mutual funds. While you can certainly receive good advice from a commission-based planner, make sure he or she has a wide range of offerings for you. Otherwise, you're likely to by hampered by limited choices.[6] Of course, since these types of planners are selling you something, make sure their recommendations are really the best choices for your financial needs. If you can't get a good recommendation from family members or colleagues, consider a matchmaker such as www.wiseadvisor. com, an impartial service that helps investors find advisers.

Even if you decide to rely on a full-service financial adviser to guide your decisions, stay informed and actively involved. Lawsuits against financial advisers have risen dramatically in recent years, as clients seek compensation for losses in the stock market, for recommendation of tax shelters (investments designed primarily to reduce tax obligations) that the Internal Revenue Service (IRS) later ruled "abusive," or for other financial missteps. Some observers attribute this trend to clients who are simply angry and frustrated that many stocks crumbled after the dot-com boom. In other cases, however, clients have sued advisers who led them into overly complex or even illegal investment and tax schemes.[7] Keep in mind that even if you get advice, you are ultimately responsible for—and in control of—the choices

EXHIBIT B.2 The Financial Planning Process

The financial planning process starts with an honest assessment of where you are now, followed by setting goals, defining and implementing plans, measuring your progress, then adjusting if needed.

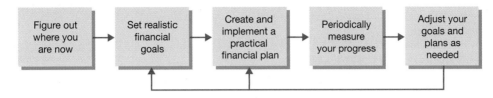

involving your money. Don't count on anyone else to secure your financial future for you.

Planning can be as simple or as complex as you're inclined to make it, as long as you follow the basic steps shown in Exhibit B.2.[8] The following sections discuss each step in more detail.

Figure Out Where You Are Now

Successful financial planning starts with a careful examination of where you stand right now, financially speaking. Before you can move ahead, you need to add up what you own and what you owe, where your money is going, and how you're using credit. You might not like what you see, but if

your finances are heading downhill, the sooner you learn that, the sooner you can fix it.

Start by listing your **assets**—the things you own—and your **liabilities**—the amounts of money you owe. Assets include both *financial assets,* such as bank accounts, mutual funds, retirement accounts, and money that people owe you, and *physical assets,* such as cars, houses, and artwork. Liabilities include credit card debts, car loans, home mortgages, and student loans. After you've itemized everything you own and everything you owe, calculate your **net worth** by subtracting your liabilities from your assets. The **balance sheet** in Exhibit B.3 shows Devon Anderson's net worth. It is currently negative, but that's certainly not uncommon for

EXHIBIT B.3 Devon Anderson's Net Worth

Devon Anderson's net worth is currently negative, driven in large part by her school loans. However, she now knows exactly where she stands and can start working to improve her balance.

ASSETS		
Cash accounts	Checking account	$ 450.67
	Savings account	927.89
Investments	50 shares Microsoft	1,302.50
Retirement accounts	(none)	
Automobiles	2001 Escort	5,500.00
Personal property	Jewelry	1,800.00
	Furniture	2,000.00
	Computer	450.00
Total assets		**$ 12,431.06**

LIABILITIES		
Current bills	Rent	$ 650.00
(due within 30 days)	Visa	120.00
	MasterCard	195.00
	Car payment	327.25
Credit card debt	Visa	1,185.34
	MasterCard	2,431.60
Housing debt	(none)	
Automobile loans	2001 Escort	3,880.10
Other debt	Student loans	22,560.00
Total liabilities		**$31,349.29**
Net worth (total assets − total liabilities)		**($18,918.23)**

EXHIBIT B.4 Devon Anderson's Income and Expense Statement

Devon was surprised to learn that she has been spending over $800 more every month than she takes in. Since she can't work any more hours without compromising her studies and she is reluctant to ask her parents for more, the only solution is to cut expenses. After some careful thought, she realizes that by cutting her mobile phone usage in half (or finding a better deal), dropping the sailing club, economizing on groceries, and cutting way back on entertainment, fast food, and new clothes, she can almost break even every month.

INCOME	
Wages (take home, average per month)	$ 1,230.00
Help from the parents	450.00
Total income	$ 1680.00

EXPENSES (AVERAGE MONTHLY)	
Rent	$ 650.00
Gas bill	34.00
Electric bill	76.00
Mobile phone	98.00
Food	315.00
Misc. household supplies	45.00
School materials & supplies	22.00
Car payment	327.25
Gasoline	38.00
Sailing club	78.25
Clothes	188.00
Entertainment & fast food	325.00
Visa payment	120.00
MasterCard payment	195.00
Total expenses	**$ 2,511.50**
Monthly difference	**($ 831.50)**

college students. The important thing for Devon at this point is that she knows how much she's worth, so she has a baseline to build on.

Your balance sheet gives you a snapshot of where you stand at a particular time. The second major planning tool is your **income and expense statement**, or simply *income statement*. This statement answers that all-important question of where your money is going month by month. Start by adding up all your sources of income from jobs, parents, investments, and so on. If you have irregular income, such as a one-time cash infusion from your parents at the beginning of each semester, divide it by the number of months it needs to cover to give you an average monthly value. Next, list all your expenses. If you're in the habit of using debit cards, credit cards, or a checkbook for most of your expenses, this task is fairly easy, since your statements will show where the money is going. However, if you tend to use cash for a lot of purchases, you'll need to get in the habit of recording those purchases. (Using cash has the major advantage of limiting your spending to money that you actually have, but it doesn't leave a "paper trail," so you have to keep track of the

spending yourself.) Exhibit B.4 shows Devon's income and expense statement.

Assembling your balance sheet and your income and expense statement can be a chore the first time around, but updating it as you make progress is much easier. By the way, software such as Intuit Quicken or Microsoft Money can simplify these tasks, but it's not absolutely necessary. You can do all your recordkeeping in a spreadsheet (the software is probably already on your computer) or simply keep records in a notebook. How you record your data is less important than making sure you do it.

Set Realistic Financial Goals

Now that you've gotten through the chore of assessing your current financial situation, the next step is setting goals. Take some time with this step. Your goals will drive all your financial decisions from here on out, so make sure they're the right ones for you. For instance, saving up for an early retirement requires a different financial strategy than saving up to take a year off in the middle of your career. Think carefully about what you really value in life. Discuss your dreams and plans with family and friends. Is making a million dollars by the time you're 40 your most important goal, and are you willing to work around the clock to get there? Or would you rather accumulate wealth more slowly and live at a more relaxed pace? Do you want to start a family when you're 25? 35? Perhaps being able to take care of an aging relative is important. In spite of what you might hear in TV commercials, you can't have it all, but you can make trade-offs that are compatible with your personal goals and values.

No matter what they might be, effective financial goals have two aspects in common: They are *specific* and they are *realistic*. "I want to be rich" and "I just don't want to have to worry about money" are not good goal statements because both are too general to give you any guidance. For one person, "not worrying about money" could require $100,000 a year, but another person might get by on only $50,000 a year. You can certainly start with a general desire, such as wealth or freedom from worry, but you need to translate that into real numbers so you can craft a meaningful plan.

In addition to making them specific, make sure your goals are realistic. Lots of young people start out life saying they'd like to make $1 million dollars by age 30 or retire by age 40. These are wonderful desires, but for most people, they simply aren't realistic. The problem with having unrealistic goals is that you'll be repeatedly frustrated by your inability to meet them, and you're more likely to give up on your financial plan as a result.[9] While amassing $1 million in the first 10 years of your career is highly unlikely, amassing $1 million in 40, 30, or sometimes even 20 years is quite attainable for many professional wage earners. A few minutes with a financial calculator will help you assess the various possibilities and determine what is reasonable for you. (If you don't have a calculator with financial functions or software such as Quicken or Money, visit www. choosetosave.org, which offers a wide variety of online calculators. In fact, just playing around with the many calculators on this site will teach you a fair amount about financial planning.)

Many people find it helpful to divide financial goals into short, medium, and long term. Your personal time frame for each might vary, but in general, short-term goals will get you through your current financial situation, medium-term goals will get you into the next stage in your life, and long-term goals will get you completely set for life. For some people, this planning might split up into 1 year or less, 2 to 5 years, and 6 years and beyond. For others, short term might be the next 5 years, medium could be 6 to 10, and long term beyond 10 years.[10] The important thing is to consider the phases in your life and establish goals for each phase. Also, think carefully about the type of goals you wish to achieve. For instance, acquiring a ranch might be a significant goal for you, whereas someone who loves to travel may have little interest in real estate. Similarly, if you find that you have a low tolerance for risk or a number of loved ones depend on you, comprehensive insurance coverage might be a

You can find a wide range of free financial planning tools online, such as these calculators offered by the "Choose to Save" program at www.choosetosave.org.

significant goal. So go ahead and earn that million if you want to, but make sure you know *why* you're earning it.

Create and Implement a Practical Plan to Meet Your Goals

You've thought about your goals and defined some that are specific and realistic. You're inspired and ready to start. What's next? For all the thousands of books, television shows, magazines, software products, and websites devoted to money, financial success really boils down to one beautifully—and brutally—simple formula: Earn more, spend less, and make better choices with what you have left over. On the plus side, this is an easy concept to understand. On the minus side, it's completely unforgiving. If you're spending more than you're earning or making bad choices with your savings and investments, you're never going to reach your goals until you can turn things around. The sections on life stages later in this appendix explore some of the details of these three components, but here's a brief overview to put it all in context.

■ *Earn more.* Particularly in the early stages of your career, income from your job will probably provide most or all of your income, so be sure to maximize your earning potential. As you get more established and have the opportunity to invest, you can start earning income from real estate, stocks and other investments, and perhaps businesses that you either own yourself or own a share of. As you move into retirement, your sources of income will shift to returns from your own investments, along with both employer- and government-funded retirement plans. For most people, earning power continues to build to a peak between the ages of 45 and 55, then declines into and through retirement.[11]

- *Spend less.* Regardless of how much control you have over your income (and there are times and circumstances in life when you probably can't expect to change your earning power), you always have some control over how you spend your money. The first and most important step to spending less is maintaining a personal budget. For most people, budgeting sounds like about as much fun as having root canal surgery, but it shouldn't be that way. Don't think of budgeting as a straightjacket that crimps your style; think of it as a way to free up more cash so that you can accomplish those wonderful goals you've set for yourself. When you skip a night out at the clubs or squeeze another year out of your car, think of that ranch in Montana you want to buy or that business you want to start. As with dieting, exercise, and other personal improvement regimes, sticking to a budget is difficult at first, but as you start to see some positive results, you'll be motivated to continue. Another important aspect of budgeting is understanding *why* you spend money, particularly on things you don't need and can't afford.[12] Don't try to spend your way out of depression, for instance. "Retail therapy" never solves anything and only makes financial matters worse. If you're prone to budget meltdowns, try to make everything as automatic as possible. For example, have your employer invest part of your salary in a company-sponsored investment program or have a mutual fund company pull money from your checking account every month.

- *Make better choices.* Now that you've maximized your income and minimized your expenses, success comes down to making better choices with the money you have to save and invest (and the occasional bit of good luck, but you can't control that part, obviously). Investing can be a complex subject, with literally thousands of places to put your money. As with everything else in personal finance, the more you know, the better you're likely to perform (see Chapter 8 for more information). Don't make investments that you don't understand, whether it's some exotic financial scheme or simply the stock of a company that doesn't make sense to you. Proceed at your own pace, such as starting with an *index mutual fund* (which tracks the overall performance of the stock market) instead of trying to pick individual stocks.

In addition to your other healthy financial habits, get in the habit of keeping good records of income, expenses,

Investopedia.com is one of several websites that offer free, self-paced learning materials for people who want to take control of their finances.

investments, and other financial matters. Doing so will not only help you track your progress, but the IRS requires you to keep a variety of tax-related records. For a good overview of both suggested and required records, refer to Publication 552 (for personal records) and Publication 583 (for business records), both of which are available online at www.irs.gov.

Finally, make sure that anyone who plays a role in the plan, whether roommates sharing grocery costs or family members sharing all aspects of finances, buys into the plan. One of the most critical aspects of successful financial planning is discipline, and a plan will fall apart if some people follow it and some don't. Money is one of the most common issues in relationship problems and divorces, so talk things over calmly and honestly with your partner or spouse. Getting everyone to agree to—and commit to—the plan will reduce stress and increase the chances of success.[13]

Periodically Measure Your Progress

To make sure you're on track to meet your goals, get in the habit of periodically checking your progress. Is your net worth increasing? (It might still be moving up toward zero, but that's progress!) Are your expenses under control? However, don't obsess over your finances. Life's too short, and there are too many other pleasurable ways to spend your time. You don't need to check your stock portfolio a dozen times a day or lie in bed every night dreaming up new ways to snip nickels and dimes out of your budget. After a while, you'll get a sense of how often you need to measure your progress to make sure you stay on track toward your goals. In general, check your income and expenses at least once a month to make sure you're staying within budget. For larger assets such as your house, you might want to verify approximate values once or twice a year.

However, don't put off checking your financial health so long that you don't notice problems such as poorly performing investments or small expenses that somehow ballooned into big expenses. If you're using a financial planner, don't wait for an annual statement. Find out where you stand at least once a quarter.

Adjust Your Goals and Plans as Needed

At various points in your life, you'll find that your goals or your financial status have changed enough to require adjustments to your plan. Whenever you pass through one of life's major transitions, such as getting married, having children, changing jobs, or buying a house, chances are you'll need to make some revisions. For instance, many first-time home buyers are surprised by the amount of money it takes to maintain a house, particularly a "fixer-upper" that needs a lot of work. To keep your income and expenses in balance, you may find you need to make sacrifices elsewhere in your budget.

If you're like most college students, you'll go through at least four major stages in your financial life: getting through college, establishing a financial foundation, building your net worth and preparing for life's major expenses, and planning for retirement. (If you're back in college after having been in the workforce for a while, your situation might vary.) The following sections give you an overview of the decisions to consider at each major stage in your life.

Life Stage 1: Getting Through College

The most important financial advice for college students can be summed up in a single phrase: Make sure you graduate. With tuition and expenses rising so rapidly these days, completing your education can be a mammoth struggle, to be sure, but if you leave school early, you will dramatically reduce your earning power throughout your entire career. According to U.S. Census Bureau data, workers with a bachelor's degree earn almost twice as much, on average, as workers with only a high school diploma. Advanced degrees can add even more to your earning power.[14] Multiply those numbers by 40 or 45 years in the workforce, and a college diploma can be worth a half million dollars or more. No matter how desperate things might be, do everything possible to stay in school. Ask for advice—and help—if you need it. Many people find doing so uncomfortable or embarrassing, but you're almost guaranteed to regret it later if you don't ask when you really do need help. Talk to a counselor in your school's financial aid office, and make sure you explore every available option for financial assistance. Ask friends and family for advice. If you have a job, see whether your employer is willing to help with school expenses.

Is it a good idea to borrow money to get through college? Absolutely, with two caveats. First, make sure the money goes toward the essential elements of your education and not toward the weekend's entertainment. Second, make sure you understand the true cost of any loan before you sign on the dotted line. In general, *private loans*, those that aren't guaranteed by a government agency, are more expensive than those that are. In recent years, some students have been stunned to discover they were paying as much as 18 percent interest or more on student loans.[15] If you're not sure what the true cost of a loan is, ask a financial aid counselor or another trusted advisor before you sign. Remember that a loan is not a gift; it's a serious financial and potentially expensive commitment that will affect your life for years.

Speaking of borrowing, every college student needs to be aware of the dangers of credit card debt. Far too many students dig themselves into a giant hole with such debt. If you find yourself in this situation, don't panic—but stop digging any deeper. Your first step to recovery is to recognize that you're at a make-or-break point in both your college career and your life as a whole. No amount of extracurricular fun is worth the damage that a credit card mess can inflict on your life. Excessive credit card debt from college can follow you for decades, limiting your ability to pay off student loans and purchase a car or a house, warns Sophia Jackson, a North Carolina financial adviser who counsels many students from schools in the area. She describes debt problems with college-age consumers as "absolutely epidemic."[16] Too many students drop out of college because of credit card debt, and many more spend years after graduation paying off debt they probably shouldn't have accumulated in the first place. Don't assume you can ring up a big balance during college and easily pay it off when you start working, either. Many graduates entering the workforce are disappointed to find themselves bringing home less and paying out more than they expected. You'll be facing a host of new expenses, from housing to transportation to a business-quality wardrobe; you can't afford to devote a big chunk of your new salary to paying off your beer and pizza bills from the previous four or five years.

Do you really need it? Every purchase you make now means you have less money to save and invest for the future.

Your second step is to compile your income and expense statement as described earlier so you know where all that borrowed money is going. Do a thorough and honest evaluation of your expenses: How much of your spending is going toward junk food, clubbing, concert tickets, video games, and other nonessentials? At first, it won't seem possible that these small-ticket items can add up to big trouble, but it happens to thousands of college students every year. Most colleges and college towns offer a wide spectrum of free and low-cost entertainment options. With a little effort and creativity, anyone can find ways to reduce nonessential expenses, often by hundreds of dollars a month. As noted earlier, a few sacrifices now can make all the difference.

Life Stage 2: Building Your Financial Foundation

Whew, you made it. You scraped by to graduation, found a decent job, and now are ready to get really serious about financial planning. First, give yourself a pat on the back; it's a major accomplishment in life. Second, dust off that financial plan you put together in college. It's time to update it to reflect your new status in life. Third, don't lose those frugal habits you learned in college. Keep your *fixed expenses*, those bills you have to pay every month no matter what, as low as possible. Some of these expenses are mandatory, such as transportation and housing, but others may not be. Such things as gym and club memberships, additional features on your mobile phone service, and subscriptions have a tendency to creep into your budget and gradually raise your expenses. Before you know it, you could be shelling out hundreds of dollars a month on these recurring but often nonessential expenses.

Among the important decisions you may need to make at this stage are paying for transportation and housing, taking steps to maximize your earning power, and managing your cash and credit wisely.

Paying for Transportation

Transportation is likely to be one of your biggest ongoing expenses, if transportation for you means owning or leasing a vehicle. The *true cost* of owning a vehicle is significantly higher than the price tag. You'll probably have to finance it, you'll definitely need to insure it, and you'll face recurring costs for fuel and maintenance. And unfortunately, unlike houses, which often *appreciate* in value, cars always *depreciate* in value (with extremely rare exceptions, such as classic cars). In fact, that lovely new ride can lose as much as 20 percent of its value the instant you drive away from the dealership. If you pay $25,000 for a car, for example, your net worth could drop $5,000 before you've driven your first mile. And if you took out a five-, six-, or seven-year loan, you'll probably owe more than the car is worth for the first

several years, a situation known as having an "upside-down" loan. In fact, 40 percent of new-car buyers now owe more on their cars than those cars are worth.[17]

There is good news, however. Most cars tend not to depreciate much during their second, third, and fourth years, but their value then plummets again after five years. You can take advantage of this effect by looking for a used car that is one year old, driving it for three years, then selling it.[18] Automotive websites such as www.edmunds.com offer a wealth of information about depreciation and other costs, including the true cost of owning any given model. Also check with your insurance company before buying any car, as some models cost considerably more to insure.

Negotiating the purchase of a car ranks high on most consumers' list of dreaded experiences. You can level the playing field, at least somewhat, by remembering two important issues. First, most buyers worry only about the monthly payment, which can be a costly mistake. Salespeople usually negotiate with four or even five variables at once, including the monthly payment, purchase price, down payment, value of your trade-in, and terms of your loan. If you don't pay attention to these other variables, you can get a low monthly payment and still get a bad deal. Experts suggest arranging your financing ahead of time, then negotiating only the purchase price when you're at the dealership.[19] If you're not comfortable negotiating, considering using a car-buying service such as CarsDirect.com (www.carsdirect.com).

Leasing, rather than buying, is a popular option with many consumers. In general, the biggest advantage of leasing is lower monthly payments than with a purchase (or a nicer car for the same monthly payment, depending on how you look at it). However, leases are even more complicated than purchases, so it's even more important to know what you're getting into. Also, leases usually aren't the best choice for consumers who want to minimize their long-term costs. To learn more about leasing, visit www.leaseguide.com.

Paying for Housing

Housing also presents you with a lease-versus-buy decision, although purchasing a house has two huge advantages that purchasing a car doesn't have: Most houses appreciate in value, and the interest on the **mortgage** reduces taxable income. And compared to renting, buying your own place also lets you build **equity**, the portion of the house's value that you own. These three factors mean that real estate is nearly always a recommended investment for anyone who can afford it. However, there are times when renting makes better financial sense. The **closing costs** for real estate—all the fees and commissions associated with buying or selling a house—can be considerable. Closing costs can represent from 3 to 6 percent of the price of a home. Depending on how fast your house's value rises, you may need to stay there two or three years just to recoup your closing costs before selling.

If you think that a job change, an upcoming marriage, or any other event in your life might require you to move in the

Buying a house could be the one of the most important financial decisions you ever make.

near future, plug your numbers into a "rent versus own" calculator to see which option makes more sense. You can find several of these calculators online; two handy examples are at HomeLoanCenter.com (www.homeloancenter.com) and Choose to Save (www.choosetosave.org).

When you are ready to buy, take your time. Buying a house is the most complicated financial decision many people will ever make, involving everything from property values in the neighborhood to the condition of the home to the details of the financial transaction. Fortunately, you can learn more about home ownership from a number of sources. Check local lenders and real estate agencies for free seminars. Online sources include the U.S. Department of Housing and Urban Development (www.hud.gov) and MSN Real Estate (http://realestate.msn.com). Buying your own house can and should be a wonderful experience, but don't let emotional factors lead you to a decision that doesn't make financial sense. Keep in mind that a house is both a home and an investment.

Maximizing Your Earning Power

Why do some people peak at earning $40,000 or $50,000 a year while others go on to earn 2 or 3 or 10 times that much? Because your salary is likely to be the primary "engine" of your financial success, this question warrants careful consideration. The profession you choose is one of the biggest factors, of course, but even within a given profession, you'll often find a wide range of income levels. A number of factors influence these variations, including education, individual talents, ambition, location, contacts, and good old-fashioned luck. You can change some of these factors throughout your career, but some you can't. However, compensation experts stress that virtually everyone can improve his or her earning power by following these tips:[20]

- *Know what you're worth.* The more informed you are about your competitive value in the marketplace, the

better chance you have of negotiating a salary that reflects your worth. Several websites offer salary-level information that will help you decide your personal value, including www.bls.gov, www.salary.com, www.vault.com, and www.salaryexpert.com. (Some of these sites charge a modest fee for customized reports, but the information could be worth many times what you pay for it.)

- *Be ready to articulate your value.* In addition to knowing what other people in your profession make, you need to be able to explain to your current employer or a potential new employer why you're worth the money you think you deserve. Collect concrete examples of how you've helped companies earn more or spend less in the past—and be ready to explain how you can do so in the future. Moreover, seek out opportunities that let you increase and demonstrate your worth.

- *Don't overlook the value of employee benefits, performance incentives, and perks.* For instance, even if you can't negotiate the salary you'd really like, maybe you can negotiate extra time off or a flexible schedule that would allow you to run a home-based business on the side. Or perhaps you can negotiate a bonus arrangement that rewards you for higher-than-average performance.

- *Understand the salary structure in your company.* If you hope to rise through the ranks and make $200,000 as a vice president, for instance, but the CEO is making only $150,000, your goal is obviously unrealistic. Some companies pay top performers well above market average, whereas others stick closely to industry norms.

- *Study top performers.* Some employees have the misperception that top executives must have "clawed their way" to the top or stepped on everyone else on their way up. In most cases, the opposite is true. Employees and managers who continue to rise through the organization do so because they make people around them successful. Being successful on your own is one thing; helping an entire department or an entire company be successful is the kind of behavior that catches the attention of the people who write the really big paychecks.

Managing Cash

When those paychecks start rolling in, you'll need to set up a system of **cash management**, your personal system for handling cash and other **liquid assets**, which are those that can be quickly and easily converted to cash. You have many alternatives nowadays for storing cash, from a basic savings account to a variety of investment funds, but most offer interest rates that are below the average level of inflation. In other words, if you were to keep all your money in such places, your buying power would slowly but surely erode over time. Consequently, the basic challenge of cash management is keeping enough cash or other liquid assets available to cover your near-term needs without keeping so much

EXHIBIT B.5 Places to Stash Your Cash

You can find quite a few places to park your cash, but they're not all created equal.

TYPE OF ACCOUNT	ADVANTAGES	DISADVANTAGES
Checking account (demand deposit)	Convenient, usually no minimum balance needed to open, often provides online banking and access via ATMs, insured against losses due to bank failure	Does not earn any interest
Checking account (NOW account)	Convenience of a regular checking account, plus you earn interest on your balance; insured	Some institutions require a minimum balance to open an account; modest interest rates
Savings account	Slightly higher interest rate than on typical checking account, often linked to a checking account for simple transfers; insured	Low interest rates; not as liquid as checking accounts (except for linked accounts, in which you can easily transfer funds to checking)
Money market deposit account	Higher interest rates than checking or savings accounts; insured	High minimum balances; limited check writing; fees can limit real returns
Money market mutual fund	Higher interest rates than many other cash management options	Not insured (but limited exposure to risk); minimum balance requirements; limited check writing
Asset management account	Convenience of having cash readily available for investment purposes; higher interest rates than regular checking or savings accounts; consolidated statements show most of your cash management and investing activity	Expensive (high monthly fees); large minimum balances; restrictions on check writing privileges (such as high minimum amounts) can limit usefulness as regular checking account; not insured against losses
Certificate of deposit	Higher interest rates that are fixed and therefore predictable; insured	Minimum balance requirements; limited liquidity (your money is tied up for weeks, months, or years)

cash that you lose out on investment growth opportunities or fall prey to inflation. Once again, your budget planning will come to the rescue by showing you how much money you need month to month. Financial experts also recommend keeping anywhere from three to six months' worth of basic living expenses in an *emergency fund* that you can access if you find yourself between jobs or have other unexpected needs.

Chapter 8 introduces the wide variety of financial institutions that offer ways to store and protect your cash. Just as there are a number of alternatives to the traditional bank these days, you can also choose from several different options for holding cash (see Exhibit B.5 for a summary of their advantages and disadvantages):[21]

- *Checking accounts.* Whether it's a traditional checking account from your neighborhood bank, an online

account at an Internet bank, or a brokerage account with check-writing privileges, your checking account will serve as your primary cash management tool. A checking account can be either a demand deposit, which doesn't pay interest, or an interest-bearing or negotiable order of withdrawal (NOW) account.

- *Savings accounts.* Savings accounts are convenient places to store small amounts of money. Many savings accounts can be linked to a checking account for quick access to your cash. Although they're convenient and safe, savings accounts nearly always offer interest rates below average inflation rates, so the buying power of your account steadily diminishes.

- *Money market accounts.* Money market accounts, sometimes called money market deposit accounts, are an alternative to savings accounts; the primary difference is that they have variable interest rates that are usually higher than savings account rates.

- *Money market mutual funds.* Money market mutual funds, sometimes called money funds, are similar to stock mutual funds, although they invest in *debt instruments* such as bonds, rather than stocks.

- *Asset management accounts.* Brokerage firms and mutual fund companies frequently offer **asset management accounts** as a way to manage cash that isn't currently invested in stocks or stock mutual funds.

- *Certificate of deposits.* With a certificate of deposit (CD), you are essentially lending a specific amount of money to a bank or other institution for a specific length of time and a specific interest rate. The length of time can range from a week to several years; the longer the time span and the larger the amount, the higher the interest rate.

No matter which types of accounts you choose, make sure you understand all the associated fees—which might not be clearly labeled as fees, either. Some accounts charge a fee every month, some charge fees when your balance drops below a certain amount or you write too many checks, and so on. For accounts with checking capability, **overdraft fees** can chew up hundreds of dollars if you bounce checks frequently. Also, be sure to verify your account statement every month and **reconcile** your checking account to make sure you and the bank agree on the balance.

Managing Credit

Even if you never want to use a credit card or borrow money, it's increasingly difficult to get by without credit in today's consumer environment. For instance, car rental companies usually require a credit card before you can rent a car, most hotels require a credit card, and landlords want to verify your **credit history**, a record of your mortgages, consumer loans (such as financing provided by a home appliance store), credit card accounts, and bill-paying performance. Banks and other companies voluntarily provide this information to **credit bureaus**, businesses that compile **credit reports**. As you read in Chapter 8, an increasing number of employers are looking into the credit history of job applicants as well. Moreover, you may find yourself in need of a loan you didn't anticipate, and getting a loan without a credit history is not easy. Consequently, building and maintaining a solid credit history needs to be a part of your lifetime financial plan.

To build a good credit history, apply for a modest amount of sensible credit (a credit card, auto loan, or a line of credit at a bank, for instance), use that credit periodically, and make sure that at least some credit is being established in your name. If an account is in someone else's name, such as a parent, spouse, or domestic partner, you won't "get credit" for a good payment history, even if you provide some or all of the money.[22] This situation can be a troublesome

one for married women in households where most of the accounts are in the husband's name. Applying for credit after a divorce or death of the husband can be difficult for women who haven't built up credit in their own names. Most important of all is to pay all your bills on time. If you find that you can't pay a particular bill by the due date, call the company and explain your situation. You may get some leniency by showing that you're making a good faith effort to pay your bill.

Experts also recommend that you verify the accuracy of your credit report once a year. Mistakes do creep into credit reports from time to time, and you also need to make sure you haven't been a victim of *identity theft*, in which someone illegally applies for credit using your name. Actually, you don't have just one credit report. The three major credit reporting agencies in the United States each keep a file on you and provide their own credit reports to lenders, landlords, and others with a valid need to see them. You are entitled to one free credit report every 12 months from each of the three companies; visit www.annualcreditreport.com for more information. You can also visit the three bureaus direction at Experian (www.experian.com), TransUnion (www.transunion.com), or Equifax (www.equifax.com).

Managing your credit wisely will help you avoid one of the most traumatic events that can befall a consumer: **personal bankruptcy**. You have several options for declaring bankruptcy, but none of them is desirable and all should be avoided by every means possible. Declaring bankruptcy, even if for an unavoidable reason such as medical costs or loss of a spouse, is sometimes called "the ten-year mistake" because it stays on your credit record for ten years.[23] Bankruptcy is not a simple cure-all, as it is sometimes presented. If you are considering bankruptcy, talk to a counselor first. Start with the National Foundation for Credit Counseling (www.nfcc.org). Wherever you turn for advice, make sure you understand it thoroughly and understand why the organization would be motivated to give you that particular advice. You've probably seen ads (and a torrent of spam e-mail) offering ways to get out from under your debt. Many of these schemes involve declaring bankruptcy, which may not be the right choice for you.[24]

After years of growing concern about the number of U.S. consumers filing for personal bankruptcy, Congress modified the bankruptcy filing process in 2005—and made it considerably more difficult for many people to file. Consumers seeking bankruptcy protection must first submit to *credit counseling*, which is designed to explore alternatives to bankruptcy. The outcome of credit counseling is likely to depend largely on household income: Those with high incomes will be encouraged to get their spending under control, those with moderate incomes will be encouraged to apply for a *debt-management plan* (an agreement to stop using credit cards and pay off existing balances, possibly in exchange for reduced interest rates), and those with lower incomes and therefore less hope of paying off their debts over time will be directed toward bankruptcy filing. For anyone who still seeks bankruptcy, the popular *Chapter 7* bankruptcy, in which all debts are wiped out, is now more difficult to obtain. Consumers with income above a certain threshold (which varies by state) are now required to file for *Chapter 13* bankruptcy instead, in which debts are consolidated but still must be repaid over a number of years.[25]

Stage 3: Increasing Your Net Worth and Preparing for Life's Major Expenses

With your basic needs taken care of and a solid foundation under your feet, the next stage of your financial life is to increase your net worth and prepare for both expected and unexpected expenses. Some of the major decisions at this stage include investments, taxes, insurance, your children's education, and emergency planning.

Investing: Building Your Nest Egg

The various cash management options described earlier can be an effective way to store and protect money you already have, but they aren't terribly good at generating more money. That's the goal of *investing*, in which you buy something of value with the idea that it will increase in value before you sell it to someone else. You read about the most common financial investment vehicles in Chapter 8: stocks, mutual funds, and bonds. Real estate is the other major category of investment for most people, not only their own homes but also rental properties and commercial real estate. The final category of investments includes precious metals (primarily gold), gems, and collectibles such as sports or movie memorabilia.

The details of successful investing in these various areas differ widely, but six general rules apply to all of them:

- *Don't invest cash that you may need in the short term.* You may not be able to *liquidate* the investment (selling it to retrieve your cash) in time, or the value may be temporarily down, in which case you'll permanently lose money.

- *Don't invest in anything you don't understand or haven't thoroughly evaluated.* If you can't point to specific reasons that the investment should increase in value, you're simply guessing or gambling.

- *Don't invest on emotion.* You might love eating at a certain restaurant chain, shopping at a particular online retailer, or collecting baseball cards, but that doesn't mean any of these is automatically a good investment.

- *Understand the risks.* Aside from Treasury bills and U.S. savings bonds, virtually no investment can guarantee that you'll make money or even protect the money you originally invested. You could lose most or all of your money, thanks to the risk/reward trade-off discussed earlier. To give yourself the opportunity to realize higher gains, you nearly always need to accept higher levels of risk.

- *Beware of anybody who promises guaranteed results or instant wealth.* Chances are that person will profit more by snaring you into the investment than you'll earn from the investment yourself.

- *Given the risks involved, don't put all your eggs in one basket.* Diversify your investments to make sure you don't leave yourself vulnerable to downturns in a single stock or piece of real estate, for instance.

If you plan to invest in a specific area, you would be wise to take a course about it or commit to learning on your own. Most of the websites mentioned throughout this appendix offer information, and some offer formal courses you can take online. Investment clubs are an increasingly popular way to learn and pool your resources with other individual investors, too. In the beginning, don't worry about the details of particular stocks or the intricacies of real estate investment trusts and other more advanced concepts. Focus on the fundamentals: Why do stock prices increase or decrease? What effect do interest rates have on bonds? How can a particular house increase in value dramatically while another in the same neighborhood stays flat?

You can also practice investing without risking any money. This is a smart move early in your career, when you're still getting on your feet and may not have much money to invest yet. After you've learned the basics of stock investing, for instance, set up a "mock portfolio" on one of the many online sites that provide free portfolio tracking. Month by month, monitor the performance of your choices. Whenever you see a big increase or decrease, dig deeper to understand why. By practicing first, you can learn from your mistakes before those mistakes cost you any money.

Taxes: Minimizing the Bite

Taxes will be a constant factor in your personal financial planning. You pay *sales tax* on many of the products you buy (in all but five states); you pay federal *excise taxes* on certain

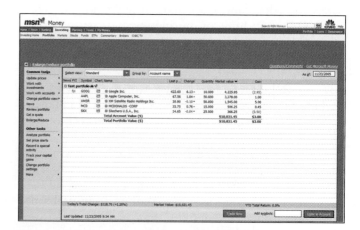

Create a mock portfolio to test your stock market skills before you invest real money in the market.

purchases such as gasoline and phone service; you pay *property tax* on real estate; and you pay *income tax* on both earned income (wages, salaries, tips, bonuses, commissions, and business profits) and investment income. The total taxes paid by individuals vary widely, but you can safely assume that taxes will consume $0.30 to $0.40 of every $1.00 you make.

Your personal tax strategy should focus on minimizing the taxes you are required to pay, without running afoul of the law or harming your financial progress (for instance, you usually don't want to skip an investment opportunity just because you'll have to pay tax on your gains). Put another way, you are expected to pay your fair share of taxes, but no one expects you to pay more than your share.

You can reduce taxes in three basic ways: (1) by reducing your consumption of goods and services that are subject to either sales tax or excise taxes, (2) by reducing your *taxable income,* or (3) by reducing your tax through the use of *tax credits.* Reducing consumption is a straightforward concept, although there are obviously limits to how far you can reduce consumption and therefore this portion of your tax obligation.

Reducing your taxable income (the part of your income that is subject to local, state, or federal income tax, not reducing your overall income level) is more complicated but can have a great impact on your finances. Authorities such as the IRS allow a variety of **deductions**, such as interest paid on home mortgages and the costs associated with using part of your home for office space. Qualifying deductions can be subtracted from your *gross income* to lower your taxable income. A portion of your income is also *exempt* from federal income tax, based on the number of dependents in your household. The more **exemptions** you can legally claim, the lower your taxable income. You can also lower your taxable income by investing a portion of your income in *tax-exempt* or *tax-deferred* investments. With **tax-exempt investments** (which are primarily bonds issued by local governments), you don't have to pay federal income tax on any income you earn from the investment. With **tax-deferred investments**, such as 401(k) plans and individual retirement accounts (IRAs), you can deduct the amount of money you invest every year from your gross income, and you don't have to pay tax on income from the investment until you withdraw money during retirement.

Unlike deductions, which only reduce your taxable income and therefore reduce your tax burden by your tax rate, **tax credits** reduce your tax obligation directly. In other words, a $100 *deduction* reduces your tax bill by $28 (if you're in the 28 percent tax bracket, for instance), whereas a $100 *credit* reduces your tax bill by $100.

Personal tax software such as TurboTax (www.turbotax. com) or TaxCut (www.taxcut.com) can guide you through the process of finding deductions and credits. For more complex scenarios, though, it's always a good idea to get the advice of a professional tax adviser.

Insurance: Protecting Yourself, Your Family, and Your Assets

Unfortunately, things go wrong in life, from accidents to health problems to the death of an income provider. Insurance is designed to protect you, your family, and your assets if and when these unpleasant events occur. In a sense, insurance is the ultimate risk/reward trade-off decision. If you had an ironclad guarantee that you would never get sick or injured, you would have no need for health insurance. However, there's a reasonable chance that you will need medical attention at some point, and major injuries and illness can generate many thousands of dollars of unplanned expenses. Consequently, most people consider it a reasonable trade-off to pay for health insurance to protect themselves from catastrophic financial blows. Exhibit B.6 (page 402) provides a brief overview of your most significant insurance options.

Another vital step to protecting your family, and one that is often overlooked by younger people, is preparing a **will**, a legal document that specifies what happens to your assets (as well as who will be legal guardian of your children, if you have any) in the event of your death.

Stage 4: Plan for a Secure, Independent Retirement

Retirement? You're only 25 years old (or 35 or 45). Yes, but as you saw earlier in the discussion of compound interest, it's never too early to start planning for retirement. It's tempting to picture retirement as a carefree time when you can finally ditch your job and focus on hobbies, travel, volunteer work, and the hundred other activities you haven't had time for all your life. Sadly, the reality for millions of retired people today is much different. Between skyrocketing medical costs, the dot-com devastation in the stock market, and lower than expected company pensions in some cases, retirement for many people is a never-ending financial struggle with little hope for improvement.

Perhaps the most important step you can take toward a more positive retirement is to shed all of the misconceptions that people often have about retirement planning:[26]

- *My living expenses will drop so I'll need less money.* Some of your expenses may well drop, but rising health-care costs will probably swamp any reductions you have in housing, clothing, and other personal costs.

- *I'll live for roughly 15 years after I retire.* The big advantage of that expensive health care is that people are living longer and longer. You could live for 20 or 30 years after you retire.

- *Social Security will cover my basic living expenses.* Social Security probably won't cover even your basic requirements, and the entire system is in serious financial trouble.

EXHIBIT B.6 Understanding Your Insurance Options

You can buy insurance for every eventuality from earthquake damage to vacation interruptions, but the most common and most important types include medical, disability, auto, homeowner's, and life insurance.

CATEGORY	HIGHLIGHTS
Medical insurance	Usually purchased as part of group coverage, such as through an employer or a union; individual or single family is available but often more expensive; most plans offer a variety of cost and coverage options—for instance, to lower your monthly costs you can select a higher deductible, which is the amount you have to pay before insurance coverage kicks in; selecting the right plan requires a careful analysis of your needs and financial circumstances
Disability insurance	Temporarily replaces a portion of your salary if you are unable to work; various policies have different definitions of "disability" and restrictions on coverage and payments
Auto insurance	Most states now have *compulsory liability insurance laws*, meaning that you have to prove that you are covered for any damage you might cause as a driver; coverage for your vehicle can be both *collision* (damages resulting from collisions) and *comprehensive* (other damages or theft); you can also buy coverage to protect yourself from illegally uninsured motorists
Homeowner's insurance	Most policies include both *property loss coverage* (to replace or repair the home and its contents) and *liability coverage* (to protect you in case someone sues you); often required by the lender when you have a mortgage
Life insurance	Primary purpose is to provide for others in the event that your death would create a financial hardship for them; common forms are *term life* (limited duration, less expensive, no investment value), *whole-life* (permanent coverage, builds cash value over time, more expensive than term life), and *universal life* (similar to whole-life but more flexible)

While it's unlikely that political leaders would ever let Social Security collapse, the safest bet is to not count on it at all.

- *My employer will keep funding my pension and health insurance.* Thousands of retirees in recent years have been devastated by former employers who either curtailed or eliminated pension and health coverage.

- *I can't save much right now, so there's no point in saving anything at all.* If you find yourself thinking this, remind yourself of the magic of compounding. Over time, small amounts grow into large amounts of money. Do whatever it takes to get started now.

- *I have plenty of time to worry about retirement later.* Unfortunately, you don't. The longer you wait, the harder it will become to ensure a comfortable retirement. If you're not prepared, your only option will be to continue working well into your 70s or 80s.

In other words, the situation is serious. However, that doesn't mean it's hopeless—not by any means. You control your destiny, and you don't need to abandon all pleasures and comforts now to make it happen. But you do need to put a plan together and start saving now. Make retirement planning a positive part of your personal financial planning, part of your dream of living the life you want to live.

Appendix Glossary

asset management accounts   Cash management accounts offered by brokerage firms and mutual fund companies, frequently as a way to manage cash that isn't currently invested elsewhere

assets   The physical things, such as real estate and artwork, and financial elements, such as cash and stocks, that you own

balance sheet   A summary of your assets and liabilities; the difference between the two subtotals is your net worth

buying power   The real value of money, adjusted for inflation; inflation raises prices, which in turn reduces buying power

cash management   All of the planning and activities associated with managing your cash and other liquid assets

closing costs   Fees associated with buying and selling a house

commission-based planners   Financial advisers who are paid commissions on the financial products they sell you, such as insurance policies and mutual funds

compounding   The acceleration of balances caused by applying new interest to interest that has already accumulated

credit bureaus   Businesses that compile credit information on businesses and individual consumers

credit history   A record of your mortgages, consumer loans, credit card accounts (including credit limits and current balances), and bill-paying performance

credit reports   Reports generated by credit bureaus, showing an individual's credit usage and payment history

deductions   Opportunities to reduce taxable income by subtracting the cost of a specific item, such as business expenses or interest paid on home mortgages

equity   The portion of a house's current value that you own

exemptions   Reductions to taxable income based on the number of dependents in the household

fee-only planners   Financial advisers who charge a fee for their services, rather than earning a commission on financial services they sell you

income and expense statement   A listing of your monthly inflows (income) and outflows (expenses); also called an *income statement*

inflation   The tendency of prices to increase over time

liabilities   Amounts of money you owe

liquid assets   Assets that can be quickly and easily converted to cash

mortgage   A loan used to purchase real estate

net worth   The difference between your assets and your liabilities

overdraft fees   Penalties charged against your checking account when you write checks that total more than your available balance

personal bankruptcy   A condition in which a consumer is unable to repay his or her debts; depending on the type of bankruptcy, a court will either forgive many of the person's debts or establish a compatible repayment plan

reconcile   The process of comparing the balance you believe is in your account with the balance the bank believes is in your account

tax credits   Direct reductions in your tax obligation

tax-deferred investments   Investments such as 401(k) plans and IRAs that let you deduct the amount of your investments from your gross income (thereby lowering your taxable income); you don't have to pay tax on any of the income from these investments until you start to withdraw money during retirement

tax-exempt investments   Investments (usually municipal bonds) whose income is not subject to federal income tax

time value of money   The increasing value of money as a result of accumulating interest

trade-off   A decision-making condition in which you have to give up one or more benefits to gain other benefits

will   A legal document that specifies what happens to your assets, who will execute your estate (carry out the terms of your will), and who will be the legal guardian of your children, if you have any, in the event of your death

References

Notes

Prologue

1. Jeffrey R. Young, "'E-Portfolios' Could Give Students a New Sense of Their Accomplishments," *Chronicle of Higher Education*, 8 March 2002, A31.

2. Brian Carcione, e-portfolio [accessed 20 December 2006] http://eportfolio.psu.edu.

3. Nancy M. Somerick, "Managing a Communication Internship Program," *Bulletin of the Association for Business Communication* 56, no. 3 (1993): 10–20.

4. Fellowforce website [accessed 8 July 2007] www.fellowforce.com.

5. Bureau of Labor Statistics, *2006–2007 Occupational Outlook Handbook* [accessed 16 August 2007] www.bls.gov/oco.

6. Drakeley, "Viral Networking: Tactics in Today's Job Market," 5.

7. Anne Fisher, "Greener Pastures in a New Field," *Fortune*, 26 January 2004, 48.

8. Cheryl L. Noll, "Collaborating with the Career Planning and Placement Center in the Job-Search Project," *Business Communication Quarterly* 58, no. 3 (1995): 53–55.

9. Rockport Institute, "How to Write a Masterpiece of a Résumé" [accessed 16 October 1998] www.rockportinstitute.com/résumés.html.

10. "Resume Fraud Gets Slicker and Easier," CNN.com [accessed 11 March 2004] www.cnn.com.

11. "Resume Fraud Gets Slicker and Easier"; Employment Screening Resources website [accessed 18 March 2004] www.erscheck.com.

12. Pam Stanley-Weigand, "Organizing the Writing of Your Resume," *Bulletin of the Association for Business Communication* 54, no. 3 (September 1991): 11–12.

13. Susan Vaughn, "Answer the Hard Questions Before Asked," *Los Angeles Times*, 29 July 2001, W1–W2.

14. Richard H. Beatty and Nicholas C. Burkholder, *The Executive Career Guide for MBAs* (New York: Wiley, 1996), 133.

15. Adapted from Burdette E. Bostwick, *How to Find the Job You've Always Wanted* (New York: Wiley, 1982), 69–70.

16. Norma Mushkat Gaffin, "Recruiters' Top 10 Resume Pet Peeves," Monster.com [accessed 19 February 2004] www.monster.com; Beatty and Burkholder, *The Executive Career Guide for MBAs*, 151.

17. Rockport Institute, "How to Write a Masterpiece of a Résumé."

18. Beverly Culwell-Block and Jean Anna Sellers, "Résumé Content and Format—Do the Authorities Agree?" *Bulletin of the Association for Business Communication* 57, no. 4 (1994): 27–30.

19. Ed Tazzia, "Wanted: A Résumé That Really Works," *Brandweek*, 15 May 2006, 26.

20. Ellen Joe Pollock, "Sir: Your Application for a Job Is Rejected; Sincerely, Hal 9000," *Wall Street Journal*, 30 July 1998, A1, A12.

21. "Scannable Resume Design," ResumeEdge.com [accessed 19 February 2004] www.resumeedge.com.

22. Kim Isaacs, "Tips for Creating a Scannable Résumé," Monster.com [accessed 19 February 2004] www.monster.com.

23. Sarah E. Needleman, "Why Sneaky Tactics May Not Help Résumé; Recruiters Use New Search Technologies to Ferret Out Bogus Keywords," *Wall Street Journal*, 6 March 2007, B8.

24. Connie Winkler, "Job Tryouts Go Virtual," *HR Magazine*, September 2006, 131–134.

25. Steven Isbitts, "Virtual Interview," *Tampa Tribune*, 20 March 2006 [accessed 13 December 2006] www.ebscohost.com.

26. Robert Gifford, Cheuk Fan Ng, and Margaret Wilkinson, "Nonverbal Cues in the Employment Interview: Links Between Applicant Qualities and Interviewer Judgments," *Journal of Applied Psychology* 70, no. 4 (1985): 729.

27. Amanda Bennett, "GE Redesigns Rungs of Career Ladder," *Wall Street Journal*, 15 March 1993, B1, B3.

28. Robin White Goode, "International and Foreign Language Skills Have an Edge," *Black Enterprise*, May 1995, 53.

29. Joan Lloyd, "Changing Workplace Requires You to Alter Your Career Outlook," *Milwaukee Journal Sentinel*, 4 July 1999, 1; Camille DeBell, "Ninety Years in the World of Work in America," *Career Development Quarterly* 50, no.1 (September 2001): 77–88.

Chapter 1

1. Katie Marsal, "iTunes Store a Greater Cash Crop Than Apple Implies?" Apple Insider blog, 23 April 2007 [accessed 7 June 2007] www.appleinsider.com; "100 Million iPods Sold," Apple press release, 9 April 2007 [accessed 7 June 2007] www.apple.com; Jeff Leeds, "Online Song Sales, Though Rising Fast, Are at Most a Hopeful Blip," *Los Angeles Times*, 1 February 2004, C1; Apple iTunes website [accessed 7 March 2007] www.apple.com/itunes; Pui-Wing Tam and Nick Wingfield, "Apple's iTunes to Fall Short on Song Sales, *Wall Street Journal*, 16 March 2004, B3; Bob Tedeschi, "Music at Your Fingertips, but a Battle Among Those Selling It to You," *New York Times*, 1 December 2003, C21; Gloria Goodale, "'Don't Call Me a Pirate. I'm an Online Fan.' One Girl's Downloading Habits Reveal the Gulf Between the Music Industry and Teens," *Christian Science Monitor*, 18 July 2003, 13; John Schwartz and John Markoff, "Power Players: Big Names Are Jumping Into the Crowded Online Music Field," *New York Times*, 12 January 2004 [accessed 30 March 2004] www.nytimes.com; Peter Lewis, "Gadgets: Drop a Quarter in the Internet," *Fortune*, 14 March 2004 [accessed 30 March 2004] www.fortune.com.

2. Figures computed from data retrieved from Hoover's [accessed 11 June 2007] www.hoovers.com and Amazon.com websites [accessed 11 June 2007] www.amazon.com.

3. IBM 2006 Annual Report [accessed 4 June 2007] www.ibm.com.

4. *Gross-Domestic-Product-by-Industry Accounts*, U.S. Bureau of Economic Analysis website [accessed 6 January 2005] www.bea.doc.gov; "U.S. Service Sector Grows But Factory Orders Decline," *Los Angeles Times*, 4 November 2004, C5; U.S. Bureau of Labor Statistics website [accessed 29 March 2004] www.bls.gov.

5. Robert L. Heilbroner and Lester C. Thurow, *Economics Explained* (New York: Simon & Schuster, 1994), 29–30.

6. Ronald M. Ayers and Robert A. Collinge, *Economics: Explore and Apply* (Upper Saddle River, N.J.: Pearson Prentice Hall, 2005), 97–103.

7. Heilbroner and Thurow, *Economics Explained*, 250.

8. Emily Thornton, "Roads to Riches," *BusinessWeek*, 7 May 2007 [accessed 5 June 2007] www.businessweek.com; Palash R. Ghosh, "Private Prisons Have a Lock on Growth," *BusinessWeek*, 6 July 2006 [accessed 5 June 2007] www.businessweek.com.

9. "European Court Expected to Rule on Microsoft Appeal in September," OUT-LAW News, 7 June 2007 [accessed 7 June 2007] www.out-law.com; Erin Joyce, "Court Upholds EU's Penalties Against Microsoft," *Internetnews.com*, 22 December 2004 [accessed 12 January 2005] www.internetnews.com; Brier Dudley and Kim Peterson, "Microsoft Legal Maneuvers Could Offset EU Sanctions," *Seattle Times*, 25 March 2004 [accessed 27 March 2004] www.seattletimes.com.

10. "FTC Sues to Prevent Whole Foods-Wild Oats Merger," *Birmingham Business Journal*, 6 June 2007 [accessed 7 June 2007] http://sanantonio.bizjournals.com.

11. "Justice Department Requires Divestitures in $1.5 Billion Merger of Monsanto and Delta & Pine Land," press release, 31 May 2007 [accessed 7 June 2007] www.usdoj.gov.

12. Steven Pearlstein, "Deregulation's Unkept Promise," *Washington Post*, 1 June 2007, D1; Jim Rossi, "The Electric Deregulation Fiasco: Looking to Regulatory Federalism to Promote a Balance Between Markets and the Provision of Public Goods," *Michigan Law Review*, May 2002, 1768–1790; Ferdinand E. Banks, "A Simple Economic Analysis of Deregulation Failure," *OPEC Review*, June 2002, 169–181.

13. Christina D. Romer, "Business Cycles," *The Concise Encyclopedia of Economics*, The Library of Economics and Liberty website [accessed 5 June 2007] www.econlib.org.

14. Robert Bixby, "A Fiscal Wakeup Call," Concord Coalition website [accessed 7 June 2007] www.concordcoalition.org; Anna Bernasek, "The $44 Trillion Abyss," *Fortune*, 24 November 2003, 113–116; Mike Allen, "Bush Pledges Effort to Balance Budget by 2004," *Washington Post*, 17 April 2002, A6; Richard W. Stevenson, "2 Parties Predict a Sharp Increase in Spending by U.S.," *New York Times*, 12 May 2002, sec. 1, 1; Martin Kasindorf and Ken Fireman, "The Clinton Budget/2002 Solution," *Newsday*, 7 February 1997, A4; Gilbert C. Alston, "Balancing the Federal Budget," *Los Angeles Times*, 14 February 1997, B8.

15. "Housing's Contribution to Gross Domestic Product (GDP)," National Association of Homebuilders website [accessed 7 June 2007] www.nahb.org; Kathleen Madigan, "Keep Your Nest Egg Safe—Watch Housing Data," *BusinessWeek*, 17 April 2000, 208–210.

16. Sue Kirchhoff, "Delicate Balance Helps USA Battle Deflation, Inflation," *USA Today*, 5 March 2003, B1–B2.

17. U.S. Bureau of Labor Statistics website [accessed 7 June 2007] www.bls.gov; Jyoti Thottam, "Why Aren't Your Prices Falling?" *Time*, 26 May 2003, 53.

18. U.S. Bureau of Labor Statistics website [accessed 7 June 2007] www.bls.gov; Jon E. Hilsenrath, "Producer-Price Drop Signals Change in Inflation Dynamics," *Wall Street Journal*, 13 September 2004, A2.

19. Jessi Hempel, "Friendster: Posed for a Comeback," *BusinessWeek*, 22 August 2006 [accessed 5 June 2007] www.businessweek.com; Robert D. Hof, "There's Not Enough 'Me' in MySpace," *BusinessWeek*, 4 December 2006, 40.

20. Stephen Baker, "Where Danger Lurks," *BusinessWeek*, 25 August 2003, 114–118.

21. See Note 1.

22. Adapted from Robert J. Holland, "Connected—More or Less," Richmond.com, 8 August 2006 [accessed 5 October 2006] www.richmond.com; Vayusphere website [accessed 22 January 2006] www.vayusphere.com; Christa C. Ayer, "Presence Awareness: Instant Messaging's Killer App," *Mobile Business Advisor*, 1 July 2004 [accessed 22 January 2006] www.highbeam.com; Jefferson Graham, "Instant Messaging Programs Are No Longer Just for Messages," *USA Today*, 20 October 2003, 5D; Todd R. Weiss, "Microsoft Targets Corporate Instant Messaging Customers," *Computerworld*, 18 November 2002, 12; "Banks Adopt Instant Messaging to Create a Global Business Network," *Computer Weekly*, 25 April 2002, 40; Michael D. Osterman, "Instant Messaging in the Enterprise," *Business Communications Review*, January 2003, 59–62; John Pallato, "Instant Messaging Unites Work Groups and Inspires Collaboration," *Internet World*, December 2002, 14+.

23. Adam Horowitz, David Jacobson, Tom McNichol, and Owen Thomas, "The 101 Dumbest Moments in Business," *Business 2.0* [accessed 6 June 2007] www.business2.com.

Chapter 2

1. Diane Brady, "Pepsi: Repairing a Poisoned Reputation in India," *BusinessWeek*, 11 June 2007, 46–54; PepsiCo website [accessed 9 June 2007] www.pepsico.com; Diane Brady, "Pepsi's Troubled Water in India" multimedia presentation [accessed 9 June 2007] www.businessweek.com; "PepsiCo's Products Are Safe," press release, 12 August 2006 [accessed 9 June 2007] www.pepsiindia.co.in; Annette Farr, "View from a Farr—Coke and Pepsi See Green," Just-Drinks.com, 15 May 2007 [accessed 9 June 2007] www.just-drinks.com; "'Pepsi-Coke: Quit India Campaign' Coke and Pepsi vs. People of India," Navdanya website, 19 September 2004 [accessed 9 June 2007] www.navdanya.org; Miranda Kennedy, "Coke, Pepsi Fizzling in India?" Marketplace, 14 August 2006 [accessed 9 June 2007] http://marketplace.publicradio.org; Centre for Science and Environment, "CSE Dares Cola Companies to Come Clean," press release, 7 August 2006 [accessed 9 June 2007] www.cseindia.org.

2. Art Kleiner, "Daniel Yankelovich: The Thought Leader Interview," *Strategy+Business*, Fall 2005, 91–97.

3. Tom Krazit, "FAQ: The HP 'Pretexting' Scandal," ZDNet.com, 6 September 2006 [accessed 26 October 2006] www.zdnet.com.

4. Eamon Javers, "Spies, Lies & KPMG," *BusinessWeek*, 26 February 2007, 86–88.

5. John Carey, "How Safe Is the Food Supply?" *BusinessWeek*, 21 May 2007, 40+.

6. Jill Lawless, "Sony: Sorry for Cathedral Shootout Game," *Forbes*, 15 June 2007 [accessed 15 June 2007] www.forbes.com.

7. Paula Lehman, "The Marshall of MySpace," *BusinessWeek*, 23 April 2007, 85–88.

8. "Personal Leadership in Business Ethics," United Technologies website [accessed 10 June 2007] www.utc.com.

9. Betsy Stevens, "Communicating Ethical Values: A Study of Employee Perceptions," *Journal of Business Ethics*, June 1999, 113–120.

10. Milton Bordwin, "The Three R's of Ethics," *Management Review*, June 1998, 59–61.

11. Joanne Sammer, "United Technologies Offers a Model for Reporting Ethical Issues," *Workforce Management*, August 2004, 64–66.

12. Richard Lacayo and Amanda Ripley, "Persons of the Year," *Time*, 20 December 2002–6 January 2003, 60.

13. Mahzarin R. Banaji, Max H. Bazerman, and Dolly Chugh, "How (Un)Ethical Are You?" *Harvard Business Review*, December 2003, 56–64.

14. Michael Porter and Mark Kramer, "Strategy & Society: The Link Between Competitive Advantage and Corporate Social Responsibility," *Harvard Business Review*, December 2006, 78–92.

15. Porter and Kramer, "Strategy & Society: The Link Between Competitive Advantage and Corporate Social Responsibility."

16. Porter and Kramer, "Strategy & Society: The Link Between Competitive Advantage and Corporate Social Responsibility."

17. Milton Friedman "The Social Responsibility of Business Is to Increase Its Profits," *New York Times Magazine*, 13 September 1970 [accessed 15 June 2007] www.umich.edu/~thecore.

18. "Social Responsibility: 'Fundamentally Subversive'?" Interview with Milton Friedman, *BusinessWeek*, 15 August 2005 [accessed 14 June 2007] www.businessweek.com.

19. Milton Friedman, John Mackey, and T. J. Rodgers, "Rethinking the Social Responsibility of Business: A Reason Debate Featuring Milton Friedman, Whole Foods' John Mackey, and Cypress Semiconductor's T. J. Rodgers," *Reason*, October 2005 [accessed 14 June 2007] www.reason.com.

20. Henry G. Manne, "Milton Friedman Was Right," WSJ OpinionJournal, 24 November 2006 [accessed 15 June 2007] www.opinionjournal.com.

21. Alexei M. Marcoux, "Business Ethics Gone Wrong," *Cato Policy Report*, May/June 2000 [accessed 14 June 2007] www.cato.org.

22. "Friedman, Mackey, and Rodgers, "Rethinking the Social Responsibility of Business."

23. Ian Wilhelm, "A Surge in Corporate Giving," *Chronicle of Philanthropy*, 17 August 2006 [accessed 19 June 2007] http://find.galegroup.com.

24. David Grayson and Adrian Hodges, "Forget Responsibility, Think Opportunities," *The Observer*, 4 June 2004 [accessed 19 June 2007] http://observer.guardian.co.uk.

25. Porter and Kramer, "Strategy & Society: The Link Between Competitive Advantage and Corporate Social Responsibility."

26. Porter and Kramer, "Strategy & Society: The Link Between Competitive Advantage and Corporate Social Responsibility."

27. "New Initiative Creates Partnerships on Water Projects Across Africa," Greenbiz.com, 7 June 2004 [accessed 18 June 2007] www.greenbiz.com.

28. Jim Carlton, "Once Targeted by Protesters, Home Depot Plays Green Role," *Wall Street Journal*, 6 August 2004, A1+.

29. "Electric Power Annual," U.S. Department of Energy website [accessed 20 June 2007] www.energy.gov.

30. Mark P. Mills, "Google & Intel: Saving the Climate and Margins," *Forbes*, 15 June 2007 [accessed 19 June 2007] www.forbes.com.

31. Traci Watson, "Smoggy Skies Persist Despite Decade of Work," *USA Today*, 16 October 2003, 6A.

32. Peter Matthiessen, "Rachel Carson," 29 March 1999, *Time* [accessed 20 June 2007] www.time.com.

33. "Human Impacts on Climate," American Geophysical Union website [accessed 20 June 2007] www.agu.org.

34. "Tap Water at Risk: Bush Administration Actions Endanger America's Drinking Water Supplies," Natural Resources Defense Council website [accessed 4 April 2004] www.ndrc.org.

35. "What's on Tap? Grading Drinking Water in U.S. Cities," Natural Resources Defense Council website [accessed 4 April 2004] www.ndrc.org.

36. Elizabeth Weise and Traci Watson, "Mercury in Many Lakes, Rivers," *USA Today*, 25 August 2004, 1A; Traci Watson, "States Looks Harder for Mercury," *USA Today*, 25 August 2004, 3A.

37. Paul Rauber, "Saving the Environment," *The Nation*, 8 March 2004 [accessed 3 April 2004] www.highbeam.com.

38. Katrina Cochran Destée, "Hello Green Moto," *Ethical Company*, October 2006, 42–46.

39. "Report of the World Commission on Environment and Development," United Nations General Assembly, 96th Plenary Meeting, 11 December 1987 [accessed 20 June 2007] www.un.org.

40. Millennium Ecosystem Assessment website [accessed 20 June 2007] www.millenniumassessment.org; Polly Courtice, "What a Sustainable Economy Would Look Like," *Ethical Corporation*, November 2006, 38–40.

41. Pete Engardio, "Beyond the Green Corporation," *BusinessWeek*, 29 January 2007 [accessed 20 June 2007] www.businessweek.com.

42. Engardio, "Beyond the Green Corporation."

43. "About Identity Theft," Federal Trade Commission website [accessed 11 June 2007] www.ftc.gov.

44. Bill Clements, "Subprime Loans and Foreclosures, Anatomy of a Crisis in the U.S.," *Finance & Commerce* (Minneapolis, Minn.) 24 May 2007 [accessed 12 June 2007] www.ebscohost.com; Chris Arnold, "Former Ameriquest Workers Tell of Deception," National Public Radio Morning Edition, 1 May 2007 [accessed 12 June 2007] www.npr.org.

45. Chris Arnold, "Massachusetts Presses Lenders on Foreclosures," National Public Radio Morning Edition, 1 May 2007 [accessed 12 June 2007] www.npr.org; Arnold, "Former Ameriquest Workers Tell of Deception"; Stacy Kaper, "Six Groups Agree to Principles," *American Banker*, 22 May 2007, 4.

46. Action on Smoking and Health website [accessed 15 March 2005] www.ash.org; Chris Burritt, "Fallout from the Tobacco Settlement," *Atlanta Journal and Constitution*, 22 June 1997, A14; Jolie Solomon, "Smoke Signals," *Newsweek*, 28 April 1997, 50–51; Marilyn Elias, "Mortality Rate Rose Through '80s," *USA Today*, 17 April 1997, B3; Mike France, Monica Larner, and Dave Lindorff, "The World War on Tobacco," *BusinessWeek*, 11 November 1996; Richard Lacayo, "Put Out the Butt, Junior," *Time*, 2 September 1996, 51; Elizabeth Gleick, "Smoking Guns," *Time*, 1 April 1996, 50.

47. Lorraine Woellert, "Anger on the Right, Opportunity for Bush," *BusinessWeek*, 7 July 2003 [accessed 24 January 2005] www.businessweek.com; Roger O. Crockett, "The Great Race Divide," *BusinessWeek*, 14 July 2003 [accessed 24 January 2005] www.businessweek.com; Earl Graves, "Celebrating the Best and the Brightest," *Black Enterprise*, February 2005, 16.

48. "Disability Discrimination," Equal Employment Opportunity Commission website [accessed 12 June 2007] www.eeoc.gov.

49. "Injuries, Illnesses, and Fatalities," Bureau of Labor Statistics [accessed 12 June 2007] www.bls.gov/iif.

50. "Health and Safety Report," Intel website [accessed 12 June 2007] www.intel.com; Peter Asmus, "100 Best Corporate Citizens: 2003," *Business Ethics*, Spring 2003, 6–10.

51. Abigail Goldman, "Sweat, Fear, and Resignation Amid All the Toys," *Los Angeles Times*, 26 November 2004, A1, A30–A32.

52. Edward Iwata, "How Barbie Is Making Business a Little Better," *USA Today*, 27 March 2006, B1–B2.

53. "Working with Factories," Gap website [accessed 12 June 2007] www.gap.com; Cheryl Dahle, "Gap's New Look: The See-Through," *Fast Company*, September 2004, 70–71.

54. "Workers in Contract Factories," Nike website [accessed 12 June 2007] www.nike.com.

55. "Independent Monitoring & Assessment," Nike website [accessed 19 January 2005] www.nike.com; Fair Labor Association website [accessed 12 June 2007] www.fairlabor.org.

56. See Note 1.

57. Geanne Rosenberg, "Truth and Consequences," *Working Woman*, June/August 1998, 79–80.

58. Adapted from David LaGress, "They Know Where You Are," *U.S. News & World Report*, 8 September 2003, 32–38; Christopher Elliott, "Some Rental Cars Are Keeping Tabs on Drivers," *New York Times*, 13 January 2004, C6; Kristi Heim, "Microchips in People, Packaging and Pets Raise Privacy Questions," *Seattle Times*, 18 October 2004 [accessed 18 October 2004] www.seattletimes.com; Andrew Heining and Christa Case, "Are Book Tags a Threat?" *Christian Science Monitor*, 5 October 2004 [accessed 7 October 2004] www.csmonitor.com; Corie Lok, "Wrist Radio Tags," *Technology Review*, November 2004, 25; Brian Albright, "RFID Dominates Frontline's Supply Chain Week," *Frontline Solutions*, November 2003, 10–13.

Chapter 3

1. Quentin Hardy, "Hope & Profit in Africa," *Forbes*, 18 June 2007, 92–117; MTV Base website [accessed 16 June 2007] www.mtvbase.com; Diane Coetzer, "Smith, Ludacris Help Launch African MTV Channel," Billboard.com, 21 April 2005 [accessed 16 June 2007] www.billboard.com; Damien Rafferty, "MTV Base (UK):

Championing African Music," Fly Global Music Culture website, 31 May 2007 [accessed 16 June 2007] www.fly.co.uk, "MTV Base Africa on MTV Base UK," Africa on Your Street, BBC website [accessed 16 June 2007] www.bbc.co.uk; "The Road from Soldier back to Child," *Africa Recovery*, October 2001, 10+; "Africa Gets Own MTV Channel Today," Afrol News, 22 February 2005 [accessed 16 June 2007] www.afrol.com; "MTV Music Channels Top Cool Survey Again," BizCommunity.com, 30 May 2007 [accessed 16 June 2007] www.bizcommunity.com.

2. Bob Parks, "Technology Map of the World," *Business 2.0*, August 2004, 111–118.

3. Holley H. Ulbrich and Mellie L. Warner, *Managerial Economics* (New York: Barron's Educational Series, 1990), 190.

4. "Toyota 'World's Largest Carmaker,'" BBC News, 24 April 2007 [accessed 29 June 2007] www.bbc.co.uk.

5. Aaron Bernstein, "Shaking Up Trade Theory," *BusinessWeek*, 6 December 2004, 116–120.

6. "President Bush's Statement on Open Economies," FDCH Regulatory Intelligence Database, 10 May 2007 [accessed 29 June 2007] www.ebsco.com; Vladimir Masch, "A Radical Plan to Manage Globalization," *BusinessWeek*, 24 February 2007, 11; Philip Levy, "Trade Truths for Turbulent Times," *BusinessWeek*, 24 February 2007, 9.

7. "Twelve Myths About Hunger," Institute for Food and Development Policy website [accessed 27 January 2005] www.foodfirst.com.

8. Peter Davis, "Investment and the Development Theory Myth," *Ethical Corporation*, October 2006, 29–30.

9. Steve Stecklow and Erin White, "At Some Retailers, 'Fair Trade' Carries a Very High Cost," *Wall Street Journal*, 8 June 2004, A1, A10.

10. Robert J. Samuelson, "Trading with the Enemy," *Newsweek*, 1 April 1996, 41; Amy Borrus, Pete Engardio, and Dexter Roberts, "The New Trade Superpower," *BusinessWeek*, 16 October 1995, 56–57; David A. Andelman, "Marco Polo Revisited," *American Management Journal*, August 1995, 10–12; John Greenwald, "Get Asia Now, Pay Later," *Time*, 10 October 1994, 61.

11. "Protectionism Fades, So EU Carmakers Must Fight," *Automotive News Europe*, 11 June 2007, 10.

12. "Import Quotas," U.S. Customs and Border Protection website [accessed 29 June 2007] www.cbp.gov.

13. "Bush Announces Sanctions Against Sudan," CNNMoney.com, 29 May 2007 [accessed 29 June 2007] http://money.cnn.com.

14. Eric Schmitt, "U.S. Backs off Sanctions, Seeing Poor Effect Abroad," *New York Times*, 31 July 1998, A1, A6; Robert T. Gray, "Book Review," *Nation's Business*, January 1999, 47.

15. Anne Davies, "McGauran Takes Farm Subsidies Fight to US," *Brisbane Times*, 27 June 2007 [accessed 29 June 2007] www.brisbanetimes.com.au; Bradley S. Klapper, "U.S., Brazil Wrangle over Farm Subsidies," *Forbes*, 19 June 2007 [accessed 29 June 2007] www.forbes.com.

16. John D. Daniels, Lee H. Radebaugh, and Daniel P. Sullivan, *International Business*, 10th ed. (Upper Saddle River, N.J.: Pearson Prentice Hall, 2004), 182.

17. "10 Common Misunderstandings About the WTO," World Trade Organization website [accessed 29 June 2007] www.wto.org.

18. International Monetary Fund website [accessed 29 June 2007] www.imf.org.

19. World Bank Group website [accessed 29 June 2007] www.worldbank.org.

20. "North American Free Trade Agreement (NAFTA)," USDA Foreign Agricultural Service website [accessed 29 June 2007] www.fas.usda.gov.

21. "North American Free Trade Agreement (NAFTA)," Public Citizen website [accessed 28 January 2005] www.publiccitizen.org; Debra Beachy, "A Decade of NAFTA," *Hispanic Business*, July/August 2004, 24–25; Geri Smith and Cristina Lindblad, "Mexico: Was NAFTA Worth It?" *BusinessWeek*, 22 December 2003, 66–72; Charles J. Walen, "NAFTA's Scorecard: So Far, So Good," *BusinessWeek*, 9 July 2001, 54–56.

22. Europa (EU gateway site) [accessed 28 June 2007] www.europa.eu.

23. "About APEC," APEC website [accessed 29 June 2007] www.apec.org.

24. Diana Farrell, "Beyond Offshoring: Assess Your Company's Global Potential," *Harvard Business Review*, December 2004, 82–90.

25. The Business of Touch website [accessed 29 June 2007] www.businessoftouch.com.

26. Daniels et al., *International Business*, 335.

27. "FAQs for Journalists; Facts and Figures on Corruption," Transparency International website [accessed 29 June 2007] www.transparency.org.

28. "FAQs for Journalists."

29. Organisation for Economic Co-Operation and Development website [accessed 29 June 2007] www.oecd.org.

30. Tobias Webb and John Russell, "Stop Paying and They Stop Asking," *Ethical Corporation*, September 2006, 42–43; Zara Maung, "Cross-Continental Road to Honesty," *Ethical Corporation*, October 2006, 14–15.

31. James Wilfong and Toni Seger, *Taking Your Business Global* (Franklin Lakes, N.J.: Career Press, 1997), 289.

32. Hoover's website [accessed 29 June 2007] www.hoovers.com.

33. Geoffrey A. Fowler, "Viacom, Boosting China Toehold, Enter Beijing Television Venture," *Wall Street Journal*, 24 September 2004, B4.

34. Ginny Parker and Robert Guy Matthews, "Carrefour Retreat Points Up Pitfalls of Flying Solo into Japanese Market," *Wall Street Journal*, 13 October 2004, A14.

35. Janet Ong, "Amazon to Boost Spending on China Unit," *Seattle Times*, 5 June 2007 [accessed 5 June 2007].

36. Daniels et al., *International Business*, 253.

37. Tracie Rozhon, "Luxury Market Blooms Near Red Square," *New York Times*, 17 September 2004, C1, C10; Clay Chandler, "China Deluxe," *Fortune*, 26 July 2004, 150–156.

38. Elizabeth Esfahni, "Thinking Locally, Succeeding Globally," *Business 2.0*, December 2005, 96–98.

39. Erin White and Jeffrey A. Trachtenberg, "'One Size Doesn't Fit All': At WPP, Sir Martin Sorrell Sees Limits to Globalization," *Wall Street Journal*, 1 October 2003, B1, B2.

40. Om Malik, "The New Land of Opportunity," *Business 2.0*, July 2004, 72–79.

41. Joel Millman and Ann Zimmerman, "'Repats' Help Payless Shoes Branch Out in Latin America," *Wall Street Journal*, 24 December 2003, B1, B2.

42. Paul Magnusson, "Your Jitters Are Their Lifeblood," *BusinessWeek*, 14 April 2003, 41; Del Jones, "Executives Pessimistic About Disaster Readiness, Survey Finds," *USA Today*, 5 August 2003, 12B; Gary Fields, "FedEx Takes Direct Approach to Terrorism," *Wall Street Journal*, 9 October 2003, A4.

43. Paul Magnusson, "What Companies Need to Do," *BusinessWeek*, 16 August 2004, 26–29.

44. Toni Locy, "Anti-Terror Law Puts New Demands on Business," *USA Today*, 26 February 2004, 5A.

45. Nicholas Stein, "America's 21st-Century Borders," *Fortune*, 6 September 2004, 114–120.

46. Robert Lenzner and Nathan Vardi, "Terror Inc.," *Forbes*, 18 October 2004, 52–54.

47. Kevin Allison, "Gates Warns on US Immigration Curbs," *Financial Times*, 7 March 2007 [accessed 29 June 2007] www.ft.com; "American Idiocracy," *Economist*, 24 March 2007, 40.

48. See Note 1.

49. Adam Zagorin, "The Great Banana War," *Time*, 8 February 1999 [accessed 11 May 1999] www.pathfinder.com.

50. Adapted from "Overview," Telepresence World website [accessed 29 June 2007] www.telepresenceworld.com; Rick Whiting, "Innovation: Videoconferencing's Virtual Room," *InformationWeek*, 1 April 2002, 14;

Teliris website [accessed 29 June 2007] www.teliris.com.

51. "USAJobs: International Trade Specialist," USA Jobs website [accessed 17 June 1999] www.usajobs.opm.gov/wfjic/ jobs/BL2896.htm.

Chapter 4

1. Carvin website [accessed 26 June 2007] www.carvin.com; "Carvin AW175" (product reviews), Harmony Central website [accessed 18 March 2005] www.harmonycentral.com; "Carvin CT6M California Carved Top," *Guitar Player*, December 2004 [accessed 18 March 2005] www.guitarplayer.com; Rich Krechel, "Some Custom-made Guitars Can Cost $4,000 to $8,000," *St. Louis Post Dispatch*, 27 September 2001, 16.

2. Lawrence M. Fisher, "The Prophet of Unintended Consequences," *Strategy+Business*, Fall 2005, 78–89.

3. Adapted in part from Russell L. Ackoff, "Why Few Organizations Adopt Systems Thinking," Ackoff Center Weblog, 7 March 2007 [accessed 23 June 2007] http://ackoffcenter.blogs.com; Daniel Aronson, "Introduction to Systems Thinking," The Thinking Page website [accessed 21 June 2007] www.thinking.net; "What Is Systems Thinking?" The Systems Thinker website [accessed 21 June 2007] www.thesystemsthinker.com; Peter Senge, *The Fifth Discipline: The Art and Practice of the Learning Organization* (New York: Doubleday, 1994) 57–67.

4. "Google Announces First Quarter 2007 Results," Google press release, 19 April 2007 [accessed 21 June 2007] www.google.com.

5. Stephen P. Robbins and David A. DeCenzo, *Fundamentals of Management*, 4th ed. (Upper Saddle River, N.J.: Pearson Prentice Hall, 2004), 405.

6. Peter Fingar and Ronald Aronica, "Value Chain Optimization: The New Way of Competing," *Supply Chain Management Review*, September–October 2001, 82–85.

7. Michael V. Copeland and Andrew Tilin, "The Instant Company," *Business 2.0*, June 2005, 82–94.

8. Tim Laseter and Keith Oliver, "When Will Supply Chain Management Grow Up?" *Strategy+Business*, Fall 2003, 32–36; Robert J. Trent, "What Everyone Needs to Know About SCM," *Supply Chain Management Review*, 1 March 2004 [accessed 16 April 2004] www.manufacturing.net.

9. Mary Schlangenstein, "Southwest Airlines Profit Jumps," *Washington Post*, 15 April 2005 [accessed 24 June 2007] www.washingtonpost.com.

10. Aude Lagorce, "Spirit CEO Sees Ongoing Supply-Chain Strain," MarketWatch, 21 June 2007 [accessed 24 June 2007] www.marketwatch.com.

11. Joann Muller, "A Savior from the East," *Forbes*, 4 June 2007, 112–113; Jeffrey K. Liker and Thomas Y. Choi, "Building Deeper Supplier Relationships," *Harvard Business Review*, December 2004, 104–113.

12. Trent, "What Everyone Needs to Know About SCM."

13. Andrew Feller, Dan Shunk, and Tom Callarman, "Value Chains Versus Supply Chains," BPTrends, March 2006 [accessed 24 June 2007] www.bptrends.com.

14. Lee J. Krajewski and Larry P. Ritzman, *Operations Management: Processes and Value Chains*, 7th ed. (Upper Saddle River, N.J.: Pearson Prentice Hall, 2005), 744.

15. Malcolm Wheatley and Kevin Parker, "Rise in Global Enterprise Deployments Seen as Response to Far-Flung Supply Networks," *Manufacturing Business Technology*, May 2007, 26–27.

16. Krajewski and Ritzman, *Operations Management: Processes and Value Chains*, 299–300.

17. Roberta A. Russell and Bernard W. Taylor, *Operations Management: Focusing on Quality and Competitiveness*, 4th ed. (Upper Saddle River, N.J.: Pearson Prentice Hall, 2003), 161.

18. Krajewski and Ritzman, *Operations Management: Processes and Value Chains*, 244–245.

19. Robert Kreitner, *Management*, 9th ed. (Boston: Houghton-Mifflin, 2004) 202–203.

20. Krajewski and Ritzman, *Operations Management: Processes and Value Chains*, 482–483.

21. Russell and Taylor, *Operations Management: Focusing on Quality and Competitiveness*, 511.

22. Kreitner, *Management*, 576–578; Robert Johnston and Graham Clark, *Service Operations Management* 2nd ed. (Harlow, England: Pearson Education Limited, 2005), 249–251.

23. Alan Young, "Healing Corrupted by Practices of Big Pharma," *Toronto Star*, 11 April 2004 [accessed 17 April 2004] www.highbeam.com; Kathleen Longcore, "Group Aims to Fix Medical Mistakes, Shorten Recovery with Technology," *Grand Rapids Press* (Grand Rapids, MI), 3 April 2004 [accessed 17 April 2004] www.highbeam.com.

24. Mark M. Davis, Nicholas J. Aquilano, and Richard B. Chase, *Fundamentals of Operations Management* (Boston: Irwin McGraw-Hill, 1999), 177–179; Russell and Taylor, *Operations Management*, 131.

25. Russell and Taylor, *Operations Management*, 131.

26. Thomas A. Stewart and Anand P. Ramand, "Lessons from Toyota's Long Drive," *Harvard Business Review*, July–August 2007, 74–83.

27. Dale H. Besterfield, Carol Besterfield-Michna, Glen H. Besterfield, and Mary Besterfield-Sacre, *Total Quality Management*, 3rd ed. (Upper Saddle River, N.J.: Pearson Prentice Hall, 2003), 2–3.

28. Leland Teschler, "TQM Comes Down to Earth," *Machine Design*, 14 September 2006, 8; Besterfield et al, *Total Quality Management*, 10–13.

29. John McQuaig, "Whatever Happened to TQM?" *Wenatchee Business Journal*, October 2004, C8.

30. Tom McCarty, "Six Sigma at Motorola," *EuropeanCEO*, September–October 2004 [accessed 21 March 2005] www.motorola.com.

31. McCarty, "Six Sigma at Motorola"; General Electric, "What Is Six Sigma?" GE website [accessed 21 March 2005] www.ge.com.

32. Timothy Stansfield and Ronda Massey, "A Remedy to Fad Fatigue," *Industrial Management*, March 2007, 26–30; Brian Hindo, "Six Sigma: So Yesterday?" *BusinessWeek*, 11 June 2007 [accessed 26 June 2007] www.businessweek.com.

33. International Organization for Standardization website [accessed 24 June 2007] www.iso.org.

34. Daniel Lyons, "Too Much Information," *Forbes*, 13 December 2004, 110–115.

35. Irma Becerra-Fernandez, Avelino Gonzalez, and Rajiv Sabherwal, *Knowledge Management* (Upper Saddle River, N.J.: Pearson Prentice Hall, 2004), 200.

36. Elizabeth Esfahani, "7-Eleven Gets Sophisticated," *Business 2.0*, January/February 2005, 93–100.

37. Kenneth C. Laudon and Jane P. Laudon, *Management Information Systems*, 8th ed. (Upper Saddle River, N.J.: Pearson Prentice Hall, 2004), 325.

38. Victoria Murphy Barret, "Fight the Jerks," *Forbes*, 2 July 2007, 52–54.

39. Andy Reinhardt, "The Paperless Manual," *BusinessWeek E.Biz*, 18 September 2000, EB92.

40. WebEx website [accessed 26 June 2007] www.webex.com.

41. 37Signals website [accessed 26 June 2007] www.37signals.com; Copeland and Tilin, "The Instant Company."

42. Evolve24 website [accessed 5 October 2006] www.evolve24.com.

43. Spencer E. Ante and Brian Grow, "Meet the Hackers," *BusinessWeek*, 29 May 2006 [accessed 26 June 2007] www.businessweek.com.

44. Sharon Gaudin, "The Move to Web 2.0 Increases Security Challenges," *InformationWeek*, 24 May 2007 [accessed 26 June 2007] www.informationweek.com.

45. "Employee Communication Is Cause for Concern," Duane Morris LLP website, 23 August 2006 [accessed 4 October 2006] www.duanemorris.com.

46. Greg Burns, "For Some, Benefits of E-Mail Not Worth Risk," *San Diego Union-Tribune*, 16 August 2005, A1, A8; Pui-Wing Tam, Erin White, Nick Wingfield, and Kris

Maher, "Snooping E-Mail by Software Is Now a Workplace Norm," *Wall Street Journal*, 9 March 2005, B1+.

47. Jeffrey Gangemi, "Cybercriminals Target Small Biz," *BusinessWeek*, 11 December 2006 [accessed 26 June 2007] www.businessweek.com.

48. Al Senia, "High-Tech Handsets Are Hacker Bait," *BusinessWeek*, 10 January 2007 [accessed 26 June 2007] www.businessweek.com; Ken Belson, "Hackers Are Discovering a New Frontier: Internet Telephone Service," *New York Times*, 2 August 2004, C4; Yuki Noguchi, "Hold the Phone: Hackers Starting to Infect Our Cells," *Seattle Times*, 26 November 2004 [accessed 26 November 2004] www.seattletimes.com; Steven Ranger, "Mobile Virus Epidemic Heading This Way," *Test Bed Blog*, 10 February 2005, [accessed 10 February 2005] www.vnunet.com; Stephanie N. Mehta, "Wireless Scrambles to Batten Down the Hatches," *Fortune*, 18 October 2004, 275–280.

49. Sharon Gaudin, "Thumb Drives Replace Malware as Top Security Concern, Study Finds," *InformationWeek*, 7 May 2007 [accessed 26 June 2007] www.informationweek.com.

50. Sushil K. Sharma and Jatinder N. D. Gupta, "Improving Workers' Productivity and Reducing Internet Abuse," *Journal of Computer Information Systems*, Winter 2003–2004, 74–78.

51. Jack Trout, "Beware of 'Infomania,'" *Forbes*, 11 August 2006 [accessed 5 October 2006] www.forbes.com.

52. Laudon and Laudon, *Management Information Systems*, 208.

53. Stuart Crainer and Des Dearlove, "Making Yourself Understood," *Across the Board*, May/June 2004, 23–27.

54. See Note 1.

55. Adapted from National Nanotechnology Initiative website [accessed 28 June 2007] www.nano.gov; Project on Emerging Nanotechnologies website [accessed 28 June 2007] www.nanotechproject.org; Barnaby J. Feder, "Technology: Bashful vs. Brash in the New Field of Nanotech," *New York Times*, 15 March 2004 [accessed 16 April 2004] www.nytimes.com; "Nanotechnology Basics," Nanotechnology Now website [accessed 16 April 2004] www.nanotech-now.com; Center for Responsible Nanotechnology website [accessed 16 April 2004] www.crnano.org; Gary Stix, "Little Big Science," *Scientific American*, 16 September 2001 [accessed 16 April 2004] www.sciam.com; Tim Harper, "Small Wonders," *Business 2.0*, July 2002 [accessed 16 April 2004] www.business2.com; Erick Schonfeld, "A Peek at IBM's Nanotech Research," *Business 2.0*, 5 December 2003 [accessed 16 April 2004] www.business2.com; David Pescovitz, "The Best New Technologies of 2003," *Business 2.0*, November 2003, 109–116.

Chapter 5

1. Vern Kopytoff, "Google Surpasses Microsoft as World's Most-Visited Site," *San Francisco Chronicle*, 25 April 2007 [accessed 2 July 2007] www.sfgate.com; Hoover's [accessed 2 July 2007] www.hoovers.com; Danny Sullivan, "Major Search Engines and Directories," Search Engine Watch, 28 March 2007 [accessed 2 July 2007] http://searchenginewatch.com; Thomas Claburn, "Google, Yahoo Gain Search Market Share; Microsoft, Time Warner Lose," *InformationWeek*, 21 November 2006 [accessed 2 July 2007] www.informationweek.com; Robert D. Hof and Catherine Holahan, "Behind Those Web Mergers," *BusinessWeek*, 21 May 2007, 46; "FAQ: Google Acquires DoubleClick," Google website [accessed 2 July 2007] www.google.com; Catherine Holahan, "Much Ado About DoubleClick," *BusinessWeek*, 30 May 2007 [accessed 2 July 2007] www.businessweek.com; Catherine Holahan, "Google vs. Microsoft: Vying for DoubleClick," *BusinessWeek*, 3 April 2007 [accessed 2 July 2007] www.businessweek.com; Catherine Holahan, "Google's DoubleClick Strategic Move," *BusinessWeek*, 14 April 2007 [accessed 2 July 2007] www.businessweek.com; Juan Carlos Perez and Robert McMillan, "Update: Google to Buy DoubleClick for $3.1 Billion," *InfoWorld*, 13 April 2007 [accessed 3 July 2007] www.infoworld.com.

2. Norman M. Scarborough and Thomas W. Zimmerer, *Effective Small Business Management* (Upper Saddle River, N.J.: Pearson Prentice Hall, 2000), 84.

3. James W. Cortada, "Do You Take This Partner," *Total Quality Review*, November–December 1995, 11.

4. Emily Thornton, "A Little Privacy, Please," *BusinessWeek*, 24 May 2004, 74–75; John H. Christy and Shlomo Reifman, "The Importance of Being Private," *Forbes*, 29 November 2004, 201–202.

5. "The Fortune 500," *Fortune.com* [accessed 1 July 2007] www.fortune.com.

6. Hoover's [accessed 1 July 2007] www.hoovers.com; U.S. Census Bureau website [accessed 1 July 2007] www.census.gov.

7. Geoffrey Colvin and Ram Charan, "Private Lives," *Fortune*, 27 November 2006, 190–198.

8. Scarborough and Zimmerer, *Effective Small Business Management*, 90.

9. Robert G. Goldstein, Russell Shapiro, and Edward A. Hauder, "So Many Choices of Business Entities—Which One Is Best for Your Needs?" *Insight (CPA Society)*, February/March 1999, 10–16.

10. Hoover's [accessed 1 July 2007] www.hoovers.com.

11. William J. Holstein, "Unlikely Allies," *Directorship*, 3 October 2006 [accessed 1 July 2007] www.forbes.com.

12. Jena McGregor, "Activist Investors Get More Respect," *BusinessWeek*, 11 June 2007, 34–35.

13. Martin Lipton, "Shareholder Activism and the 'Eclipse of the Public Corporation,'" *The Corporate Board*, May/June 2007, 1–5.

14. David A. Nadler, "Building Better Boards," *Harvard Business Review*, May 2004, 102–111.

15. Brent Schlender, "Inside Andy Grove's Latest Crusade," *Fortune*, 23 August 2004, 68–78.

16. Floyd Norris, "Ebbers and Passive Directors Blamed for WorldCom Woes: Board That Made Decisions in Haste with No Questioning," *Wall Street Journal*, 10 June 2003, C1, C2.

17. Cora Daniels, "Finally in the Director's Chair," *Fortune*, 4 October 2004, 42–44; Nadler, "Building Better Boards"; Judy B. Rosener, "Women on Corporate Boards Make Good Business Sense," *Directorship*, May 2003 [accessed 18 February 2005] www.womensmedia.com.

18. Joann S. Lublin, "Back to School," *Wall Street Journal*, 21 June 2004, R3.

19. Joann S. Lublin, Theo Francis, and Jonathan Weil, "Directors Are Getting the Jitters," *Wall Street Journal*, 13 January 2005, B1, G6; Jack Milligan, "Targeting the Board," *Bank Director*, 4th Quarter 2003 [accessed 18 February 2005] www.bankdirector.com.

20. "Mergers & Acquisitions Explained," Thomson Investors Network [accessed 8 April 2004] www.thomsoninvest.net.

21. "Mergers & Acquisitions Explained."

22. *The PSI Opportunity* (online newsletter), PSI website [accessed 8 April 2004] www.psiusa.com.

23. Nancy K. Kubasek, Bartley A. Brennan, and M. Neil Browne, *The Legal Environment of Business*, 3rd ed. (Upper Saddle River, N.J.: Pearson Education, 2003), 691.

24. Irene Macauley, "Corporate Governance: Crown Charters to Dotcoms," Museum of American Financial History website [accessed 8 April 2004] www.financialhistory.org.

25. Brian Hindo, "A Dynamo Called Danaher," *BusinessWeek*, 19 February 2007 [accessed 2 July 2007] www.businessweek.com; Mark Maremont, "More Can Be More," *Wall Street Journal*, 25 October 2004, R4.

26. *PR Newswire*, "Bank of America Completes FleetBoston Merger; Starting Today, Customers Have Access to Full ATM Network" [accessed 8 April 2004] www.highbeam.com.

27. "IBM Acquisition Performance—On Track," IBM website [accessed 1 July 2007] www.ibm.com.

28. "Spring Merger Fever," *Wall Street Journal*, 22 May 2007, A14.

29. "Cheap Sunglasses? Not for Luxottica," *BusinessWeek*, 21 June 2007 [accessed 1 July 2007] www.businessweek.com.

30. "The Contra Team," *Business 2.0*, April 2006, 83.

31. Gregory Cocoran, "How Daimler-Chrysler Stacks Up Against 'Deals from Hell,'" *Wall Street Journal Online*, 14 May 2007 [accessed 1 July 2007] http://blogs.wsj.com.

32. Stephen Labaton, "800-Pound Gorillas," *New York Times*, 11 June 2000, sec. 4, 1; Martin Peers, Nick Wingfield, and Laura Landro, "AOL, Time Warner Set Plan to Link in Mammoth Merger," *Wall Street Journal*, 11 January 2000, A1, A6; Thomas E. Weber, Martin Peers, and Nick Wingfield, "Two Titans in a Strategic Bind Bet on a Futuristic Megadeal," *Wall Street Journal*, 11 January 2000, B1, B12; "AOL and Time Warner Will Merge to Create World's First Internet-Age Media and Communications Company," America Online website [accessed 11 January 2000] media.web.aol.com/media/press.cfm.

33. Dennis K. Berman, Jason Singer, and John R. Wilke, "On the Prowl: As Deal Barriers Fall, Takeover Bids Multiply," *Wall Street Journal*, 8 May 2007, A1+.

34. March Gunther, "A Big Win for the Little Guys," *Fortune*, 16 January 2003 [accessed 19 February 2005] www.fortune.com.

35. Erin White and Jason Singer, "Old-Line Retailer Learns New Tricks to Evade Takeover," *Wall Street Journal*, 19 July 2004, A1, A6.

36. Michael Hickins, "Searching for Allies," *Management Review*, January 2000, 54–58.

37. "TASER International Forms Strategic Alliance with iRobot," press release, 28 June 2007 [accessed 1 July 2007] http://money.cnn.com.

38. Dominic M. Palmer and Patrick Mullaney, "Strategy: Building Better Alliances," *Outlook Journal*, July 2001 [accessed 10 August 2005] www.accenture.com.

39. Adapted from 37Signals website [accessed 2 July 2007] www.37signals.com; Tony Kontzer, "Learning To Share," *InformationWeek*, 5 May 2003, 28; Jon Udell, "Uniting Under Groove," *InfoWorld*, 17 February 2003 [accessed 9 September 2003] www.elibrary.com; Alison Overholt, "Virtually There?" *Fast Company*, 14 February 2002, 108.

Chapter 6

1. GeniusBabies.com website [accessed 4 July 2007] www.geniusbabies.com; "Forbes.com Best of the Web Directory," Forbes website [accessed 20 February 2005] www.forbes.com; Abigail Leichman, "Oh, Baby—Novel Gifts for the Newborn," *The Record* (Bergen County, N.J.), 7 September 2002, F01; Isabel M. Isidro,

"GeniusBabies.com: Turning Passion into a Successful Business," *PowerHomeBiz.com* [accessed 10 November 2002] www.powerhomebiz.com; Isabel M. Isidro, "What Works on the Web? 12 Lessons from Successful Home-based Online Entrepreneurs," PowerHomeBiz website [accessed 10 November 2002] www.powerhomebiz.com; Karen Dash, "Dotcom Moms: Many Parents Have Discovered the Perfect Place to Balance Work and Family—the Web," *Raleigh News & Observer*, 14 May 2000 [accessed online 10 November 2002] www.babyuniversity.com/about_us/raleigh_n_o.shtml; Barbara Whitaker, "For the Small Retailer, Life on the Internet Is One Big Bazaar," *New York Times*, 29 March 2000 [accessed online 10 November 2002] www.nytimes.com.

2. Irwin Speizer, "Going to Ground," *Workforce Management*, December 2004, 39–44.

3. Alan Hughes, "Funny Money," *Black Enterprise*, December 2004, 130–144; Bo Burlingham, "Don't Call Her an Entrepreneur," *Inc.*, September 2004, 97–102.

4. Bernard Stamler, "Redefinition of Small Leads to a Huge Brawl," *New York Times*, 21 September 2004, G8.

5. "Table of Small Business Size Standards Matched to North American Industry Classification System Codes," U.S. Small Business Administration [accessed 3 July 2007] www.sba.gov.

6. "Advocacy Small Business Statistics and Research," U.S. Small Business Administration [accessed 3 July 2007] www.sba.gov.

7. "Advocacy Small Business Statistics and Research," U.S. Small Business Administration [accessed 3 July 2007] www.sba.gov.

8. "Advocacy Small Business Statistics and Research." Malik Singleton, "Same Markets, New Marketplaces," *Black Enterprise*, September 2004, 34; Edmund L. Andrews, "Where Do the Jobs Come From?" *New York Times*, 21 September 2004, E1, E11.

9. Norman M. Scarborough and Thomas W. Zimmerer, *Effective Small Business Management*, 7th ed. (Upper Saddle River, N.J.: Pearson Prentice Hall, 2003), 22.

10. Stacy Perman, "Where the Rubber Is the Roadside," *BusinessWeek*, 11 December 2006, 76.

11. Chondo.net website [accessed 3 July 2007] www.chondo.net; Heidi Dietrich, "Online Radio Venture Bets on African Tunes," *Puget Sound Business Journal*, 27 August–2 September 2004, 14–15.

12. Intrapreneur.com website [accessed 3 July 2007] www.intrapreneur.com.

13. National Association of Women Business Owners website [accessed 3 July 2007] www.nawbo.com.

14. Mary Ellen Egan, "Big Shot in Bangalore," *Forbes*, 18 October 2004, 88–89.

15. "Advocacy Small Business Statistics and Research."

16. Jim Hopkins, "Hispanic-Owned Companies See Strong Growth Spurt," *USA Today*, 2 July 2003, B1.

17. Coastal Enterprises website [accessed 3 July 2007] www.ceimaine.org; David J. Dent, "Coming to America," *Inc.*, November 2004, 100–107.

18. Scarborough and Zimmerer, *Effective Small Business Management*, 16.

19. Stacy Perman, "The Startup Bug Strikes Earlier," *BusinessWeek*, 31 October 2005 [accessed 3 July 2007] www.businessweek.com.

20. Jim Hopkins, "Bad Times Spawn Great Start-Ups," *USA Today*, 18 December 2001, 1B; Alan Cohen, "Your Next Business," *FSB*, February 2002, 33–40.

21. Louise Nicholson and Alistair R. Anderson, "News and Nuances of the Entrepreneurial Myth and Metaphor: Linguistic Games in Entrepreneurial Sense-Making and Sense-Giving," *Entrepreneurship Theory and Practice*, March 2005, 153–172.

22. "Are Your Ready? U.S. Small Business Administration website [accessed 21 February 2005] www.sba.gov; "Entrepreneurial Test," SBA Online Women's Business Center, U.S. Small Business Administration website [accessed 21 February 2005] www.sba.gov; Scarborough and Zimmerer, *Effective Small Business Management*, 4.

23. Zakiyyah El-Amin, "The New Look on the Greens," *Black Enterprise*, June 2004, 64; Urban Golf Gear website [accessed 21 February 2005] www.urbangolfgear.com.

24. Joshua Hyatt, "The Real Secrets of Entrepreneurs," *Fortune*, 15 November 2004, 185–202.

25. Jessica Mintz, "First Things First," *Wall Street Journal*, 29 November 2004, R10–R11.

26. "Buy a Business," U.S. Small Business Administration [accessed 3 July 2007] www.sba.gov.

27. Stacy Perman, "Extending the Front Lines of Franchising," *BusinessWeek*, 12 April 2005 [accessed 3 July 2007] www.businessweek.com; Wendy Harris, "10 Hottest Deals in Franchising," *Black Enterprise*, September 2004, 77–88.

28. Amey Stone, "Before You Ink That Contract..." *BusinessWeek*, 14 April 2005 [accessed 3 July 2007] www.businessweek.com.

29. Harris, "10 Hottest Deals in Franchising."

30. Douglas MacMillan, "Franchise Owners Go to Court," *BusinessWeek*, 29 January 2007 [accessed 4 July 2007] www.businessweek.com; Jill Lerner, "UPS Store Dispute Escalating," *Atlanta Business Chronicle*, 24 February 2006 [accessed 4 July 2007] www.bizjournals.com.

31. Kerry Miller, "The Restaurant Failure Myth," *BusinessWeek*, 16 April 2007 [accessed 4 July 2007] www.businessweek.com.

32. "Study: Restaurant Failure Rate Lower Than Thought," *Baltimore Business Journal*, 10 September 2003 [accessed 21 February 2005] www.bizjournals.com; "McBusiness," *Inc. State of Small Business 2001*, 58.

33. Joseph W. Duncan, "The True Failure Rate of Start-Ups," *D&B Reports*, January–February 1994; Maggie Jones, "Smart Cookies," *Working Woman*, April 1995, 50–52; Janice Maloney, "Failure May Not Be So Bad After All," *New York Times*, 23 September 1998, 12.

34. Hyatt, "The Real Secrets of Entrepreneurs."

35. Daniel McGinn, "Why Size Matters," *Inc. 500*, Fall 2004, 33–36.

36. SCORE website [accessed 11 April 2004] www.score.org.

37. Anne Field, "Management: The A Team," *BusinessWeek SmallBiz Features*, Winter 2006 [accessed 4 July 2007] www.businessweek.com.

38. Christine Comaford-Lynch, "Don't Go It Alone: Create an Advisory Board," *BusinessWeek*, 1 February 2007 [accessed 4 July 2007] www.businessweek.com.

39. National Business Incubation Association website [accessed 21 February 2005] www.nbia.com; Louisiana Technology Park website [accessed 21 February 2005] www.lactechpark.com.

40. Gwendolyn Bounds, "The Great Money Hunt," *Wall Street Journal*, 29 November 2004, R1, R4.

41. Paulette Thomas, "It's All Relative," *Wall Street Journal*, 29 November 2004, R4, R8.

42. Reed Albergotti, "Long Shot," *Wall Street Journal*, 29 November 2004, R4; Scarborough and Zimmerer, *Effective Small Business Management*, 439.

43. Bob Zider, "How Venture Capital Works," *Harvard Business Review*, November/December 1998, 131–139.

44. Amy Chozick, "A Helping Hand," *Wall Street Journal*, 29 November 2004, R9, R11.

45. Association for Enterprise Opportunity website [accessed 4 July 2007] www.microenterpriseworks.org.

46. National Venture Capital Association website [accessed 4 July 2007] www.nvca.org.

47. Arlene Weintraub, "Biotech's Tough New Taskmasters," *BusinessWeek*, 14 June 2004, 42; Turney Stevens, "What Do VC Firms Look For When They Invest?" *Puget Sound Business Journal*, 1–7 October 2004, 48.

48. William Payne, "What to Expect from Angel Networks," *American Venture*, September/October 2004, 38–39; Kaufman Foundation, "Business Angel Investing Groups Growing in North America," October 2002 [accessed 21 February 2005] www.angelcapitalassociation.org.

49. Michael V. Copeland, "How to Find Your Angel," *Business 2.0*, March 2006, 47–49.

50. Perman, "Where the Rubber Is the Roadside."

51. Kent Hoover, "Small SBA Loans Cost More; Large Loans Harder," *Puget Sound Business Journal*, 8–14 October 2004, 18.

52. U.S. Small Business Administration website [accessed 4 July 2007] www.sba.gov.

53. U.S. Small Business Administration website [accessed 4 July 2007] www.sba.gov.

54. See Note 1.

55. Adapted from Spoke website [accessed 5 July 2007] www.spoke.com; LinkedIn website [accessed 5 July 2007] www.linkedin.com; Ryze website [accessed 5 July 2007] www.ryze.com; David Pescovitz, "Technology of the Year: Social Network Applications," *Business 2.0*, November 2003, 113–114.

Chapter 7

1. Adapted from *Microsoft 2004 Annual Report* [accessed 26 April 2005] www.microsoft.com; Elliot Blair Smith, Matt Krantz, and Jon Swartz, "Microsoft's Flush, with Nothing to Splurge On," *USA Today*, 22 July 2004, B1–B2; Brier Dudley, Microsoft Shareholders to Vote on Lucrative Dividend," *Seattle Times*, 7 November 2004 [accessed 26 April 2005] www.ebsco.com; Microsoft teleconference, 20 July 2004 [accessed 26 April 2005] www.microsoft.com; Marcia Vickers, "A Dividend from Microsoft's Dividend?" *BusinessWeek Online*, 22 July 2004 [accessed 26 April 2005] www.businessweek.com; Jay Greene, "Checking Out Microsoft's New CEO," *BusinessWeek Online*, 26 April 2005 [accessed 26 April 2005] www.businessweek.com; Patrice Hill, "Microsoft Lifts Economy," *Washington Times*, 1 February 2005, C6.

2. Robert Stuart, "Accountants in Management—A Globally Changing Role," *CMA Magazine*, 1 February 1997, 5.

3. "Frequently Asked Questions," American Institute of Certified Public Accountants website [accessed 7 July 2007] www.aicpa.org.

4. Jack L. Smith, Robert M. Keith, and William L. Stephens, *Accounting Principles*, 4th ed. (New York: McGraw-Hill, 1993), 16–17.

5. Matt Krantz, "Some Major Companies Still Use Pro Forma Accounting," *USA Today*, 11 August 2003, B1; "Pro Forma" Financial Information: Tips for Investors," SEC website [accessed 9 May 2004] www.sec.gov; David

Henry and Robert Berner, "Ouch! Real Numbers," *BusinessWeek*, 24 March 2003, 72–73.

6. David Henry, "Generally Improvable Accounting Principles," *BusinessWeek*, 20 November 2006 [accessed 6 July 2007] www.businessweek.com.

7. International Accounting Standards Board website [accessed 6 July 2007] www.iasb.org; Kerry Capell and David Henry, "When Bankers Keep Saying *Non*," *BusinessWeek*, 1 March 2004, 54.

8. "Summary of SEC Actions and SEC Related Provisions Pursuant to the Sarbanes-Oxley Act of 2002," SEC website [accessed 9 May 2004] www.sec.gov; "Sarbanes-Oxley Act's Progress," *USA Today*, 26 December 2002 [accessed 9 May 2004] www.highbeam.com.

9. Scott Leibs, "Five Years and Counting," *CFO*, 1 July 2007 [accessed 9 July 2007] www.cfo.com.

10. Hal S. Scott, "Sarbanes-Oxley 404: Will the SEC's and PCAOB's New Standards Lower Compliance Costs for Small Companies?" testimony before the U.S. House of Representatives Small Business Committee, 5 June 2007.

11. Joseph Weber, "SarbOx Isn't Really Driving Stocks Away," *BusinessWeek*, 2 July 2007, 87; Peter Gumbel, "London vs. New York Smackdown," *Fortune*, 6 August 2007, 36–41.

12. Karen E. Klein, "SOX Revisions: A Break for Small Biz?" *BusinessWeek*, 8 June 2007 [accessed 6 July 2007] www.businessweek.com; Jacob H. Zamansky, "Unraveling Wall Street Reforms," *Forbes*, 8 February 2007 [accessed 6 July 2007] www.forbes.com.

13. David H. Bangs, Jr., "Financial Troubleshooting," *Soundview Executive Book Summaries* 15, no. 5 (May 1993).

14. See Note 1.

15. Adapted from Dennis Callaghan, "Sarbanes-Oxley: Road to Compliance," *eWeek*, 16 February 2004 [accessed 8 May 2004] www.eweek.com; Ellen Florian, "Can Tech Untangle Sarbanes-Oxley?" *Fortune*, 29 September 2003, 125–128; Thomas Hoffman, "Big Companies Turn to Packaged Sarb-Ox Apps," *Computerworld*, 1 March 2004 [accessed 8 May 2004] www.computerworld.com.

Chapter 8

1. Adapted from Greg Morcroft, "From Schwab a $3.5 Billion Hint," *Wall Street Journal*, 3 July 2007, C2; "Schwab Announces $3.5 Billion Capital Restructuring, Declares Quarterly Dividend," press release, 2 July 2007 [accessed 12 July 2007] www.schwab.com; "Schwab Passes Out the Cash," *BusinessWeek*, 2 July 2007 [accessed 12 July 2007] www.businessweek.com; John Battelle, "1.2 Trillion Buck Chuck," *Business 2.0*, 101–103;

Sonja Ryst, "Will BofA Put Rivals Out of Commissions," *BusinessWeek*, 11 October 2006 [accessed 12 July 2007] www.businessweek.com; Aaron Pressman, "The Busiest Broker on Earth," *BusinessWeek*, 18 April 2005, 84+; Jim Cole, "Despite Letdown, Schwab Likes Its Bank's Situation," *American Banker*, 18 April 2005, 8; Gaston F. Ceron, "Online Brokers Are Taking Hit from Price War," *Wall Street Journal*, 11 April 2005, C1; Ruth Simon, "Discount Brokers Cut Prices," *Wall Street Journal*, 16 March 2005, D1; "Schwab's Earnings Fall; Big Increase in Profit at Ameritrade," *New York Times*, 19 January 2005, C2; Gregory Bresiger, "Why Did Schwab Sell Capital Markets?" *Traders Magazine*, 1 November 2004, 1; Patrick McGeehan, "Charles Schwab to Give Up Title at Brokerage Firm," *New York Times*, 1 February 2003, C1; "Company News; Charles Schwab Reports a $79 Million Loss in Quarter," *New York Times*, 22 January 2003, C1; Patrick McGeehan, Seeing Long Trading Slump, Schwab Sets More Cutbacks," *New York Times*, 13 August 2002, C2; Louise Lee and Emily Thornton, "Schwab vs. Wall Street," *BusinessWeek*, 3 June 2002, 62–71; Louise Lee, "Will Investors Pay for Schwab's Advice?" *BusinessWeek*, 21 January 2002, 36; Fred Vogelstein, "Can Schwab Get Its Mojo Back?" *Fortune*, 17 September 2001, 93–98; Susanne Craig, "Schwab Unveils a New Service, Chides Brokers," *Wall Street Journal*, 17 May 2002, C1, C13; Charles Gasparino and Ken Brown, "Discounted, Schwab's Own Stock Suffers from Move into Online Trading," *Wall Street Journal*, 19 June 2001, A1, A6; Rebecca Buckman, "Schwab, Once a Predator, Is Now Prey," *Wall Street Journal*, 8 December 1999, C1; Louise Lee, "When You're No. 1, You Try Harder," *BusinessWeek E.Biz*, 18 September 2000, EB88.
2. American Express Blue website [accessed 11 July 2007] www.americanexpress.com/blue; Mandy Andress, "Smart Is Not Enough: Cards Must Also Be Easy and Useful," *InfoWorld*, 16 October 2000, 94; Mary Shacklett, "American Express' Blue is Setting the Pace in U.S. Smart Card Market," *Credit Union Magazine*, September 2000, 16A–17A.
3. MARTA Breeze card website [accessed 11 July 2007] www.breezecard.com; Massachusetts Bay Transportation Authority website [accessed 11 July 2007] www.mbta.com.
4. Daniel Wolfe, "Can New Online Features Find an Audience?" *American Banker*, 2 January 2007, 9.
5. Wolfe, "Can New Online Features Find an Audience?"; Anita Hamilton, "Banking Goes Mobile," *Time*, 2 April 2007 [accessed 11 July 2007] www.time.com; Steve Bills, "Debit at Core of Citi Mobile Banking Push," *American Banker*, 3 April 2007, 10.

6. Don Ogilvie, "Issues That Need Immediate Attention on Hill," *American Banker*, 9 March 2007, 11; Peter Romaniuk, Jeffry Haber, and Gary Murray, "Suspicious Activity Reporting," *CPA Journal*, March 2007, 70–72.
7. John C. Soper, "What's Next for Consolidation in Banking?" *Business Economics*, April 2001, 39.
8. Stephan Labaton, "Accord Reached on Lifting Depression-Era Barriers Among Financial Industries," *New York Times*, 23 October 1999, A1, B4.
9. E*TRADE Financial website [accessed 11 July 2007] www.etrade.com.
10. "Important Banking Legislation," FDIC website [accessed 11 July 2007] www.fdic.gov.
11. Ed Roberts, "Wal-Mart Launches Massive Incursion into Retail Banking," *Credit Union Journal*, 25 June 2007, 1, 27.
12. TreasuryDirect website [accessed 11 July 2007] www.treasurydirect.com.
13. "Closed Fund," Investopedia [accessed 28 July 2007] www.investopedia.com.
14. Vanguard website [accessed 28 July 2007] http://flagship.vanguard.com.
15. Jack R. Kapoor, Les R. Dlabay, and Robert J. Hughes, *Personal Finance*, 7th ed. (Boston: McGraw-Hill Irwin, 2004), 474–477; "Your Specialist and the Auction Market," NYSE website [accessed 4 May 2005] www.nyse.com.
16. Kapoor, Dlabay, and Hughes, *Personal Finance*, 474.
17. NASDAQ website [accessed 1 August 2007] www.nasdaq.com
18. Heidi Moore and Vipal Monga, "NYSE-ArcaEx Confounds Street," The Deal.com [accessed 3 May 2005] www.thedeal.com.
19. *A Guide to the NYSE Marketplace*, NYSE Euronext website [accessed 1 August 2007] www.nyse.com.
20. Adam Shell, "Technology Squeezes Out Real, Live Traders," *USA Today*, 12 July 2007, A1–A2.
21. NYSE Euronext website [accessed 1 August 2007] www.nyse.com.
22. SEC website [accessed 29 July 2007] www.sec.gov.
23. SEC website [accessed 29 July 2007] www.sec.gov.
24. "SIPC Exposes Phony 'Look-Alike' Web Site," SEC website [accessed 1 August 2007] www.sec.gov.
25. "Margin Trading: The Dreaded Margin Call," Investopedia.com [accessed 4 May 2005] www.investopedia.com.
26. Dow Jones Indexes website [accessed 1 August 2007] www.djindexes.com.
27. "Standard and Poor's 500 Index—S&P 500," Investopedia.com [accessed 4 May 2005] www.investopedia.com.
28. See Note 1.

29. Adapted from Kiplinger.com [accessed 9 July 2007] www.kiplinger.com; *SmartMoney* [accessed 9 July 2007] www.smartmoney.com; CNNMoney [accessed 9 July 2007] http://money.cnn.com.

Chapter 9
1. Adapted from Alan Ohnsman and Jeff Bennett, "Toyota Puts Hipness Ahead of Sales for New Scion Cars," Bloomberg.com, 8 February 2007 [accessed 5 August 2007] www.bloomberg.com; Mark Rechtin, "Scion's Dilemma," *AutoWeek*, 23 May 2006 [accessed 5 August 2007] www.autoweek.com; Michael Paoletta, "Toyota's Scion Starts Label," *Billboard*, 26 March 2005, 8+; "2005 Scion tC," Edmunds.com [accessed 12 April 2005] www.edmunds.com; "10 Hottest Cars and Trucks in 2004," *Advertising Age*, 20 December, 28; David Welch, "Not Your Father's… Whatever," *BusinessWeek*, 15 March 2004, 82–84; Daren Fonda, "Scion Grows Up," *Time (Canada)*, 16 August 2004, 61; Katherine Zachery, "The Makings of a Hit," *Ward's Auto World*, June 2004, 42; Christopher Palmeri, "Toyota's Youth Models Are Having Growing Pains," *BusinessWeek*, 31 May 2004, 32; Steven Kichen, "Scion's Smart Moves," *Forbes*, 12 October 2004 [accessed 12 April 2005] www.forbes.com; Norihiko Shirouzu, "Scion Plays Hip-Hop Impresario to Impress Young Drivers," *Wall Street Journal*, 5 October 2004, B1+; Phil Patton, "As Authentic as 'The Matrix' or Menudo," *New York Times*, 25 July 2004, sec. 12, 1+; Dan Lienert, "What's New? With Toyota's Scion, Youth Must Be Served," *New York Times*, 19 October 2003 [accessed 12 November 2003] www.nytimes.com; Fara Warner, "Learning How to Speak to Gen Y," *Fast Company*, July 2003, 36; Daren Fonda, "Baby, You Can Drive My Car," *Time*, 30 June 2003, 46; Christopher Palmeri, Ben Elgin, Kathleen Kerwin, "Toyota's Scion: Dude, Here's Your Car," *BusinessWeek*, 9 June 2003, 44; Jonathan Fahey, "For the Discriminating Body Piercer," *Forbes*, 12 May 2003, 136; George Raine, "Courting Generation Y," *San Francisco Chronicle*, 11 May 2003, I3.
2. "AMA Board Approves New Marketing Definition," *Marketing News*, 1 March 1985, 1.
3. Avon Foundation website [accessed 3 August 2007] http://walk.avonfoundation.org.
4. Philip Kotler and Gary Armstrong, *Principles of Marketing*, 10th ed. (Upper Saddle River, N.J.: Pearson Prentice Hall, 2004), 6.
5. BizXchange website [accessed 3 August 2007] www.bizx.bz.
6. June Lee Risser, "Customers Come First," *Marketing Management*, November/December 2003, 22–26.
7. Ranjay Gulati and James B. Oldroyd, "The Quest for Customer Focus," *Harvard Business Review*, April 2005, 92–101.

8. Peter Kafka, "Sony Sings Off-Key," *Forbes*, 13 December 2004 [accessed 12 April 2005] www.forbes.com.

9. Kotler and Armstrong, *Principles of Marketing*, 12–13.

10. Kotler and Armstrong, *Principles of Marketing*, 19–21.

11. Fiona Haley, "Profitable Player Winner: Progressive," *Fast Company*, October 2004, 84–85.

12. "Two Strikes and You're Out," *Marketing Management*, September/October 2004, 5.

13. Sam Decker, "The Big Idea Behind Social Commerce," iMedia Connection, 14 June 2007 [accessed 3 August 2007] www.imediaconnection.com.

14. Gordon A. Wyner, "The Journey to Marketing Effectiveness," *Marketing Management*, March/April 2004, 8–9; Lawrence A. Crosby and Sheree L. Johnson, "The Three Ms of Customer Loyalty," *Marketing Management*, July/August 2004, 12–13.

15. Alan Middleton, "The Evolution of Marketing," *Marketing*, 28 February 2005, 9.

16. "Marketing Under Fire," *Marketing Management*, July/August 2004, 5.

17. J. Walker Smith, "Permission Is Not Enough," *Marketing Management*, May/June 2004, 52.

18. Robert Berner, "I Sold It Through the Grapevine," *BusinessWeek*, 29 May 2006, 32; "Undercover Marketing Uncovered," *CBSnews.com*, 25 July 2004 [accessed 11 April 2005] www.cbsnews.com; Stephanie Dunnewind, "Teen Recruits Create Word-of-Mouth 'Buzz' to Hook Peers on Products," *Seattle Times*, 20 November 2004 [accessed 11 April 2005] www.seattletimes.com.

19. Teri Agins, "As Consumers Mix and Match, Fashion Industry Starts to Fray," *Wall Street Journal*, 8 September 2004, A1, A6.

20. Dan Hill, "Why They Buy," *Across the Board*, November–December 2003, 27–32; Eric Roston, "The Why of Buy," *Time*, April 2004.

21. Michael R. Solomon, *Consumer Behavior*, 6th ed. (Upper Saddle River, N.J.: Pearson Prentice Hall, 2004), 366–372.

22. James C. Anderson and James A. Narus, *Business Market Management: Understanding, Creating, and Delivering Value*, 2nd ed. (Upper Saddle River, N.J.: Pearson Prentice Hall, 2004), 114–116; Kotler and Armstrong, *Principles of Marketing*, 215, 224–226.

23. Eric Almquist, Martin Kon, and Wolfgang Bock, "The Science of Demand," *Marketing Management*, March/April 2004, 20–26; David C. Swaddling and Charles Miller, "From Understanding to Action," *Marketing Management*, July/August 2004, 31–35.

24. Joseph Pereira, "Spying on the Sales Floor," *Wall Street Journal*, 21 December 2004, B1, B4.

25. Eric Dash, "The Gift That Keeps Giving," *Inc.*, September 2004, 32.

26. Peter Coy, "Another Reason for Those Empty Houses," *BusinessWeek*, 13 August 2007 [accessed 5 August 2007] www.businessweek.com.

27. Kotler and Armstrong, *Principles of Marketing*, 47–48.

28. Gordon A. Wyner, "Pulling the Right Levers," *Marketing Management*, July/August 2004, 8–9.

29. Jennifer Barron and Jill Hollingshead, "Making Segmentation Work," *Marketing Management*, January/February 2002, 24–28.

30. Lawrence A. Crosby and Sheree L. Johnson, "Redefine Your Customer Base," *Marketing Management*," April 2004, 12–13.

31. Michael J. McCarthy, "Granbury, Texas, Isn't a Rural Town: It's a 'Micropolis,'" *Wall Street Journal*, 3 June 2004, A1, A6.

32. Claritas Corporation website [accessed 5 August 2007] www.claritas.com; Haya El Nassar and Paul Overberg, "Old Labels Just Don't Stick in 21st Century," *USA Today*, 17 December 2003; Michael J. Weiss, *The Clustering of America* (New York: Harper & Row, 1988), 41.

33. Duff McDonald, "Best Buy's Brilliant Bouncer," *Business 2.0*, January/February 2005, 60.

34. NetJets website [accessed 5 August 2007] www.netjets.com.

35. Michael E. Raynor and Howard S. Weinberg, "Beyond Segmentation," *Marketing Management*, December 2004, 22–28.

36. Mountain Dew website [accessed 5 August 2007] www.mountaindew.com.

37. Rechtin, "Scion's Dilemma."

38. Kotler and Armstrong, *Principles of Marketing*, 55–56.

39. Kichen, "Scion's Smart Moves."

40. Paul Gillin, *The New Influencers: A Marketer's Guide to the New Social Media* (Sanger, Calif.: Quill Driver Books, 2007), xi.

41. See Note 1.

42. Adapted from Doug Henschen, "IDC Reports on BI Sales: Which Vendors Are Hot?" *Intelligent Enterprise*, 1 July 2007 [accessed 6 August 2007] www.intelligententerprise.com; "TechEncyclopedia," TechWeb.com [accessed 5 August 2007] www.techweb.com; Ganesh Variar, "Only the Best Survive: The Combination of Integration and BI Were the Standouts of the 2003 IT Landscape," *Intelligent Enterprise*, January 2004 [accessed 4 May 2004] www.intelligententerprise.com; Angoss website [accessed 4 May 2004] www.angoss.com.

Chapter 10

1. Adapted from "Botox Has Competition," Carefair.com, 13 July 2007 [accessed 8 August 2007] www.carefair.com; Allergan website [accessed 8 August 2007]

www.allergan.com; Botox Cosmetic website [accessed 8 August 2007] www.botoxcosmetic.com; Amy Howell, "The Latest Wrinkle: Men and Botox," *Cincinnati Enquirer*, 24 July 2007 [accessed 8 August 2007] www.azcentral.com; Jennifer Clark, "Botulinum Toxin Type A Safety Review Remains Positive," *Dermatology Times*, February 2005, 105, 110; Melissa Foss, "Botox and Beyond," *InStyle*, March 2005, 427+; John Jesitus, "Bogus Botox Sounds Wake-Up Call," *Cosmetic Surgery Times*, March 2005, 1, 10; Harriet Tramer, "Docs Detecting How to Boost Botox Profitability," *Crain's Cleveland Business*, 7 March 2005, 17; Julie Schmit, "Medicis Tightens Face of Vanity Race with $2.8 Billion Bid for Inamed," *USA Today*, 22 March 2005 [accessed 14 April 2005] www.usatoday.com; "Smooth Moves: Medical Treatments for Facial Wrinkles," Mayo Clinic website [accessed 14 April 2005] www.mayoclinic.com; David Lipschultz, "When Facial Wrinkles Are Ironed Away for Good," *New York Times*, 11 February 2003, D6; Brian O'Reilly, "Facelift in a Bottle," *Fortune*, 24 June 2002, 101–104; Ronald D. White, "Allergan Bets on Botox Lift," *Los Angeles Times*, 23 May 2002, C1; Michael McCarthy, "Botox Maker Plans $50 Million Ad Campaign," *USA Today*, 29 April 2002, B1; Reed Abelson, "FDA Approves Allergan Drug for Fighting Wrinkles," *New York Times*, 16 April 2002, C4; Carol Lewis, "Botox Cosmetic: A Look at Looking Good," *FDA Consumer*, July–August 2002 [accessed 14 April 2005] www.fda.gov.

2. Stephen H. Wildstrom, "For Puzzled Seniors Only," *BusinessWeek*, 11 December 2006, 24.

3. Beoworld.org [accessed 6 August 2007] www.beoworld.org; Poul Funder Larsen, "Better Is … Better," *Wall Street Journal*, 22 September 2003, R6, R11.

4. "Reshaping Nikon's Film Camera Assortment," Nikon press release, 11 January 2006 [accessed 6 August 2007] www.prnewswire.com.

5. David Kiley, "Fine-Tuning a Brand's Signature Sound," *BusinessWeek*, 13 August 2007, 56.

6. Justin Doebele, "The Engineer," *Forbes*, 9 January 2006, 122–124.

7. David Armstrong, Monte Burke, Emily Lambert, Nathan Vardi, and Rob Wherry, "85 Innovations," *Forbes*, 23 December 2002, 122–202.

8. Michael V. Copeland and Om Malik, "How to Build a Bulletproof Startup," *Business 2.0*, June 2006 [accessed 7 August 2007] www.business2.com.

9. Lev Grossman, "The Quest for Cool," *Time*, 8 September 2003, 48–54.

10. Nicolas Block, Kara Gruver, and David Cooper, "Slimming Innovation Pipelines to

Fatten Their Returns," *Harvard Management Update*, August 2007, 3–5.

11. Nanette Byrnes, "Xerox' New Design Team: Customers," *BusinessWeek*, 7 May 2007, 72.

12. Douglas McGray, "Babes in R&D Toyland," *Fast Company*, December 2002, 46.

13. David Haigh and Jonathan Knowles, "How to Define Your Brand and Determine Its Value," *Marketing Management*, May/June 2004, 22–28.

14. David Kiley, "Best Global Brands," *BusinessWeek*, 6 August 2007, 56–64.

15. David Kiley, "Wagoner's Fighting Chance," *BusinessWeek*, 11 December 2006, 36–39.

16. Janell M. Kurtz and Cynthia Mehoves, "Whose Name Is It Anyway?" *Marketing Management*, January/February 2002, 31–33.

17. "Lenovo to Sell Disney-Branded PCs," *Business Standard* (Mumbai), 7 August 2007 [accessed 7 August 2007] www.business-standard.com.

18. Ezra Dyer, "2006 Ford Harley-Davidson F-150: This Harley's Not a Hog, But It Is a Ham," Edmunds InsideLine, 17 March 2006 [accessed 7 August 2007] www.edmunds. com; Rick Barrett, "Harley-Davidson, Ford Extend Pact; Automaker to Use Harley's Colors, Logos," *Milwaukee Journal Sentinel*, 5 February 2004 [accessed 17 April 2005] www.ebsco.com; Laura Clark Geist, "Licensing Links Brands, People with Goods," *Automotive News*, 16 September 2002, 2M.

19. Margaret Webb Pressler, "Do Not Pry Open Until Christmas: The Hard Truth About Hated 'Clamshell' Packaging," *Washington Post*, 30 November 2006 A1+; Jennifer Saranow, "The Puncture Wound I Got for Christmas," *Wall Street Journal*, 30 December 2004, D1+.

20. Bernard Silver, "Bar Codes Grow in Use at Age 30; Keeping Track of Almost Everything," *Seattle Times*, 3 July 2004 [accessed 17 April 2005] www.ebsco.com.

21. General Mills website [accessed 7 August 2007] www.generalmills.com.

22. Marc Gunther, "Hard News," *Fortune*, 6 August 2007, 80–85.

23. Erik Brynjolfsson, Yu (Jeffrey) Hu, and Duncan Simester, "Goodbye Pareto Principle, Hello Long Tail: The Effects of Search Costs on the Concentration of Sales," research paper, February 2007 [accessed 7 August 2007] http://papers.ssrn.com.

24. Chris Anderson, "The Long Tail," *Wired*, October 2004 [accessed 7 August 2007] www.wired.com.

25. Ken Belson, "Mobile ESPN to End Service Aimed at Sports Customers," *New York Times*, 29 September 2006 [accessed 7 August 2007] www.nytimes.com.

26. Carol Matlack, "What's This? The French Love McDonald's?" *BusinessWeek*,

13 January 2003, 50; Shirley Leung, "Armchairs, TVs and Espresso—Is It McDonald's?" *Wall Street Journal*, 30 August 2002, A1, A6.

27. Mitchell Pacelle, "Growing Profit Source for Banks: Fees from Riskiest Card Holders," *Wall Street Journal*, 6 July 2004, A1+.

28. Dan Milmo, "BA Boss Speaks Out over Price Fixing," *Guardian* (UK), 3 August 2007 [accessed 7 August 2007] www.guardian. co.uk.

29. "Q2 2004 SanDisk Corp. Earnings Conference Call," *Fair Disclosure Wire*, 14 July 2004 [accessed 3 August 2004] www.highbeam.com.

30. Eric Anderson and Duncan Simester, "Mind Your Pricing Cues," *Harvard Business Review*, September 96–103.

31. Thomas T. Nagle and Reed K. Holden, *The Strategy and Tactics of Pricing*, 3rd ed. (Upper Saddle River, N.J.: Pearson Prentice Hall, 2002), 2–4.

32. Lisa Margonelli, "How Ikea Designs Its Sexy Price Tags," *Business 2.0*, October 2002, 106–112.

33. Revionics website [accessed 7 August 2007] www.revionics.com; Amy Cortese, "The Power of Optimal Pricing," *Business 2.0*, September 2002, 68–70.

34. Matthew Maier, "A Radical Fix for Airlines: Make Flying Free," *Business 2.0*, April 2006, 32–34.

35. Diane Brady, "The Twisted Economics of Harry Potter," *BusinessWeek*, 2 July 2007, 38–39.

36. Priceline website [accessed 7 August 2007] www.priceline.com.

37. Aubrey Kent and Richard M. Campbell, Jr., "An Introduction to Freeloading: Campus-Area Ambush Marketing," *Sport Marketing Quarterly*, 2007, Vol. 16, Issue 2, 118–122.

38. Adapted from Desktop Factory website [accessed 8 August 2007] www.desktopfactory.com; Dimension 3D Printing website [accessed 8 August 2007] www.dimensionprinting.com; Stratasys website [accessed 8 August 2007] www. stratasys.com; Z Corporation [accessed 8 August 2007] www.zcorp.com.

Chapter 11

1. Costco website [accessed 18 August 2007] www.costco.com; Michelle V. Rafter, "Welcome to the Club," *Workforce Management*, April 2005, 41–46; David Meier, "It's the Employees, Stupid," MotleyFool.com, 17 September 2004 [accessed 7 October 2004] www.fool.com; Jeff Malester, "Costco Sales Rise 10%, Hit $12.4 Billion in Fis. Q2," *TWICE*, 2005, 53; Ilana Polyak, "Warehouse Sale," *Kiplinger's Personal Finance*, May 2005, 67; Suzanne Wooley, "Costco? More Like Costgrow," *Money*, August 2002, 44–46;

"Costco: A Cut Above," *Retail Merchandiser*, July 2002, 44; Pete Hisey, "Costco.com Means Business," *Retail Merchandiser*, October 2001, 36; Shelly Branch, "Inside the Cult of Costco," *Fortune*, 6 September 1999, 184–188.

2. Ingram Book Group website [accessed 16 August 2007] www.ingrambook.com.

3. Covisint website [accessed 16 August 2007] www.covisint.com; ChemConnect website [accessed 16 August 2007] www.chemconnect.com; Robert M. Grant and Anjali Bakhru, "The Limits of Internationalisation in E-Commerce," *European Business Journal*, 3rd Quarter 2004, 95–104.

4. Supervalu website [accessed 16 August 2007] www.supervalu.com.

5. Dollar General website [accessed 16 August 2007] www.dollargeneral.com; "'Wheel' of Retailing Continues, as Wal-Mart Starts to Move Upstream," *Supply Chain Digest*, 23 September 2005 [accessed 16 August 2007] www.scdigest.com; Robert Berner and Brian Grow, "Out-Discounting the Discounter," *BusinessWeek*, 10 May 2004, 78–79.

6. Walgreens website [accessed 16 August 2007] www.walgreens.com.

7. Target website [accessed 16 August 2007] www.target.com.

8. Montgomery Ward website [accessed 16 August 2007] www.wards.com.

9. Matt Richtel and Bob Tedeschi, "Online Sales Lose Steam as Buyers Grow Web-Weary," *New York Times*, 17 June 2007 [accessed 16 August 2007] www.nytimes.com.

10. Sucharita Mulpuru, "Forty Facts About the US Online Shopper," teleconference and PowerPoint presentation, Forrester Research, 9 November 2006 [accessed 16 August 2007] www.forrester.com.

11. Mulpuru, "Forty Facts About the US Online Shopper."

12. Cate T. Corcoran, "What Works: Retailers Share Strategies for Online Success," *Women's Wear Daily*, 9 March 2005, 6.

13. Maryanne Murray Buechner, "Recharging Sears," *Time*, 27 May 2002, 46.

14. Mulpuru, "Forty Facts About the US Online Shopper."

15. Japan Guide website [accessed 16 August 2007] www.japan-guide.com.

16. Dell website [accessed 16 August 2007] www.dell.com.

17. Philip Kotler and Gary Armstrong, *Principles of Marketing*, 9th ed. (Upper Saddle River, N.J.: Pearson Prentice Hall, 2001), 435.

18. Edward F. Moltzen, "Apple Grows, But So Does Channel Conflict," *CMP Channel*, 27 July 2007 [accessed 16 August 2007] www.crn.com.

19. Adapted from Caterpillar website [accessed 16 August 2007] www.cat.com.

20. Gary Armstrong and Philip Kotler, *Marketing: An Introduction*, 5th ed. (Upper Saddle River, N.J.: Pearson Prentice Hall, 2000), 405.

21. Verne Gay, "Milk, the Magazine," *American Demographics*, February 2000, 32–33.

22. Salesforce.com website [accessed 16 August 2007] www.salesforce.com.

23. Catherine Holahan, "The Sell-Phone Revolution," *BusinessWeek*, 23 April 2007 [accessed 16 August 2007] www.businessweek.com;

24. Bradley Johnson, "TV Still Rules But the Net Is Showing Gains," *Advertising Age*, 25 June 2007, S-6.

25. Henry Blodget, "The Great Ad Share Shift: Google Sucks Life out of Old Media," Silicon Alley Insider, 15 August 2007 [accessed 16 August 2007] www.alleyinsider.com.

26. "Google Adwords," Google website [accessed 18 August 2007] www.google.com; Danny Sullivan, "Major Search Engines and Directories" Search Engine Watch, 28 March 2007 [accessed 2 July 2007] http://searchenginewatch.com; Thomas Claburn, "Google, Yahoo Gain Search Market Share; Microsoft, Time Warner Lose," *InformationWeek*, 21 November 2006 [accessed 2 July 2007] www.informationweek.com.

27. Holahan, "The Sell-Phone Revolution."

28. Efficient Frontier website [accessed 18 August 2007] www.efrontier.com; John Heilemann, "Target: Madison Ave." *Business 2.0*, March 2006, 42–44.

29. "What Is Direct Marketing," Direct Marketing Association website [accessed 27 September 2007] www.the-dma.org.

30. "Direct Hit," *The Economist*, 9 January 1999, 55–57.

31. Heidi Dietrich, "Direct Marketer Steers Away from E-Mail Ads," *Puget Sound Business Journal*, 23–29 April 2004, 28.

32. Mulpuru, "Forty Facts About the US Online Shopper."

33. National Do Not Call Registry [accessed 16 August 2007] https://telemarketing.donotcall.gov.

34. Ellen Neuborne, "Telemarketing After 'Do Not Call,'" *Inc.*, November 2003, 32–34.

35. National Do Not Call Registry [accessed 16 August 2007] https://telemarketing.donotcall.gov; Holahan, "The Sell-Phone Revolution."

36. Karen Krebsbach, "Mobile Phone Texting Rings True for HSBC," *USBanker*, April 2007, 30–31.

37. Armstrong and Kotler, *Marketing: An Introduction*, 409.

38. David Meerman Scott, *The New Rules of Marketing and PR* (Hoboken, N.J.: Wiley, 2007), 62.

39. "A Definition of Social Media," *Technology in Transition* blog, 6 April 2007 [accessed 11 June 2007] http://technologyintranslation.blockwork.org; Robert Scoble, "What Is Social Media?" Scobleizer blog, 16 February 2007 [accessed 11 June 2007] www.scobleizer.com; Paul Gillin, *The New Influencers* (Sanger, Calif.: Quill Driver Books, 2007), xi–xii.

40. Heather Green, "The Big Shots of Blogdom," *BusinessWeek*, 7 May 2007, 66.

41. Evolve24 website [accessed 18 August 2007] www.evolve24.com.

42. Matthew G. Nelson, "Online Brands Rush to Embrace Facebook's 'Widget Platform,'" ClickZ, 19 June 2007 [accessed 18 August 2007] www.clickz.com; Spencer E. Ante, Heather Green, and Catherine Holahan, "The Next Small Thing," *BusinessWeek*, 23 July 2007, 58–62.

43. Emily Steel, "Young Surfers Spurn Banner Ads, Embrace 'Widgets,'" *Wall Street Journal*, July 2, 2007, B3; Jason Lee Miller, "Widgets a Hit with Kids," WebProNews, 2 July 2007 [accessed 16 August 2007] www.webpronews.com.

44. Todd Polifka, "Add Service Element Back In to Get Satisfaction," *Marketing News*, 1 May 2007, 21–24.

45. Dave Kahle, "9 Tips for Dealing with Angry & Difficult Customers," *American Salesman*, October 2006, 15–18.

46. National Advertising Review Council website [accessed 16 August 2007] www.narcpartners.org.

47. William Wells, John Burnett, and Sandra Moriarty, *Advertising: Principles & Practice*, 6th ed., (Upper Saddle River, N.J.: Pearson Prentice-Hall, 2003), 45–53.

48. See Note 1.

49. Adapted from Holahan, "The Sell-Phone Revolution"; Yahoo! website [accessed 16 August 2007] http://advertising.yahoo.com; "Nick Gillespie Discusses the Personalized Cover of Reason Magazine and the Possibilities of Database Technology" (interview), Talk of the Nation, National Public Radio, 4 May 2003 [accessed 6 May 2004] www.highbeam.com; Kevin J. Delaney, "Will Users Care If Gmail Invades Privacy?" *Wall Street Journal*, 6 April 2004, B1, B3; Allison Fass, "Spot On," *Forbes*, 23 June 2003, 140; "Hey You! How About Lunch?" *Wall Street Journal*, 1 April 2004, B1, B5.

Chapter 12

1. Adapted from Wegmans website [accessed 8 August 2007] www.wegmans.com; Matthew Boyle, "The Wegmans Way," *Fortune*, 24 January 2005 [accessed 11 August 2007] www.fortune.com; William Conroy, "Rochester, N.Y.-Based Grocer Tops Magazine's Best Employer Rankings," *Asbury Park* (N.J.) *Press*, 11 January 2005 [accessed 8 March 2005] www.ebsco.com; Matthew Boyle, "The Wegmans Way," *Fortune*, 24 January 2005, 62–68; "UCCNet Designated as U.S. Data Pool of Choice by Leading Retailers," UCCNet website [accessed 8 March 2005] www.uccnet.org; Joy Davis, "Caring for Employees Is Wegmans' Best Selling Point," *Democrat and Chronicle* (Rochester, N.Y.), 6 February 2005 [accessed 8 March 2005] www.democratandchronicle.com; Michael A. Prospero, "Employee Innovator: Wegmans," *Fast Company*, October 2004, 88; Matt Glynn, "Employees of Rochester, N.Y.-Based Grocer Celebrate Firm's Top Ranking," *Buffalo* (N.Y.) *News*, 11 January 2005 [accessed 8 March 2005] www.ebsco.com.

2. Anne Fisher, "Starting a New Job? Don't Blow It," *Fortune*, 24 February 2005 [accessed 26 February 2005] www.fortune.com.

3. Richard L. Daft, *Management*, 6th ed. (Mason, Ohio: Thompson South-Western, 2003), 5.

4. Marvel website [accessed 9 August 2007] www.marvel.com; Melanie Warner, "How a Meek Comic Book Company Became a Hollywood Superpower," *New York Times*, 19 July 2004, C7.

5. Cornelus A. de Kluyver and John A. Pearce II, *Strategy: A View from the Top* (Upper Saddle River, N.J.: Pearson Prentice Hall, 2003), 6–7.

6. Michael C. Mankins, "Stop Wasting Valuable Time," *Harvard Business Review*, September 2004, 58–65.

7. Daft, *Management*, 533.

8. Hydrogen Power Inc., website [accessed 9 August 2007] www.hydrogenpowerinc.com.

9. Translink website [accessed 9 August 2007] www.translink.co.uk.

10. Datamonitor, "Coca-Cola Company SWOT Analysis" [accessed 8 August 2007] www.ebsco.com.

11. Mark Phelan, "New Ford CEO Upbeat, But Says We're 'Not Competitive' Yet," *USA Today*, 10 November 2006 [accessed 8 August 2007] www.usatoday.com.

12. Cirque du Soleil website [accessed 9 August 2007] www.cirquedusoleil.com; W. Chan Kim and Renée Mauborgne, "Blue Ocean Strategy," *Harvard Business Review*, October 2004, 76–84.

13. David Welch, "Staying Paranoid at Toyota," *BusinessWeek*, 2 July 2007, 80–82.

14. Barbara Kiviat, "The End of Management?" *Time Bonus Section: Inside Business*, August 2004.

15. Paul Kaihla, "A New Office Pool," *Business 2.0*, April 2006, 87; Kiviat, "The End of Management?"

16. Julie Schlosser, "How Target Does It," *Fortune*, 18 October 2004, 100–112.

17. de Kluyver and Pearce, *Strategy: A View from the Top*, 55–56.

18. "Throw Out the Old Handbook in Favor of Today's Crisis Drills," *PR News*, 27 January 2003, 1.

19. Daft, *Management*, 13.

20. Daft, *Management*, 514–515.

21. James G. Clawson, *Level Three Leadership: Getting Below the Surface*, 2nd ed. (Upper Saddle River, N.J.: Pearson Prentice Hall, 2003), 112–119.

22. "Sometimes, EQ Is More Important Than IQ," CNN.com, 14 January 2005 [accessed 14 January 2005] www.cnn.com; Daniel Goleman, "What Makes a Leader?" *Harvard Business Review*, November–December 1998, 92–102; Shari Caudron, "The Hard Case for Soft Skills," *Workforce*, July 1999, 60–66.

23. Clawson, *Level Three Leadership: Getting Below the Surface*, 116.

24. Clawson, *Level Three Leadership: Getting Below the Surface*, 118.

25. Patricia Sellers, "eBay's Secret," *Fortune*, 18 October 2004, 161–178; Nick Wingfield, "Auctioneer to the World," *Wall Street Journal*, 5 August 2004, B1, B6.

26. Daniel Goleman, "Leadership That Gets Results," *Harvard Business Review*, March–April 2000, 78–90.

27. Daft, *Management*, 526.

28. Stephen P. Robbins and David A. DeCenzo, *Fundamentals of Management*, 4th ed. (Upper Saddle River, N.J.: Pearson Prentice Hall, 2004), 325.

29. Sonja D. Brown, "Congratulations, You're a Manager! Now What?" *Black Enterprise*, April 2006, 102–106.

30. Cigna website [accessed 9 August 2007] http://careers.cigna.com; Eve Tahmincioglu, "Group Mentoring: A Cost-Effective Option," *Workforce Management*, December 2004 [accessed 10 March 2005] www.workforce.com; Eve Tahmincioglu, "When Women Rise," *Workforce Management*, September 2004, 26–32.

31. David Kiley, "The New Heat on Ford," *BusinessWeek*, 4 June 2007, 33–38.

32. Daft, *Management*, 382; Robbins and DeCenzo, *Fundamentals of Management*, 209.

33. Michael Been and Nitin Nohria, "Cracking the Code of Change," *Harvard Business Review*, May–June 2000, 133–141.

34. Robbins and DeCenzo, *Fundamentals of Management*, 211; Daft, *Management*, 384, 396.

35. Robbins and DeCenzo, *Fundamentals of Management*, 210–211.

36. "The New Heat on Ford."

37. Kevin J. Gregson, "Converting Strategy to Results," *American Venture*, September/October 2004, 16–18.

38. The Benchmarking Exchange website [9 August 2007] www.benchnet.com.

39. "Extreme Benchmarking," *Business 2.0*, April 2006, 81.

40. Robert E. Kaplan and Robert B. Kaiser, "Developing Versatile Leadership," *MIT Sloan Management Review*, Summer 2003, 19–26.

41. Courtland L. Bovée and John V. Thill, *Business Communication Today*, 9th ed.

(Upper Saddle River, N.J.: Pearson Prentice Hall, 2008), 4.

42. Holly Ocasio Rizzo, "Patently Successful," *Hispanic Business*, April 2007, 34–36.

43. Daft, *Management*, 128; Kathryn M. Bartol and David C. Martin, *Management* (New York: McGraw-Hill, 1991), 268–272.

44. Rizzo, "Patently Successful," 34–36.

45. See Note 1.

46. Adapted from Business Intelligence. com [accessed 10 August 2007] www.businessintelligence.com; TechEncyclopedia [accessed 10 August 2007] www.techweb.com/encyclopedia; Business Objects website [accessed 10 August 2007] www.businessobjects.com; Cognos website [accessed 10 August 2007] www.cognos.com.

Chapter 13

1. The Container Store website [accessed 11 August 2007] www.containerstore.com; "2005: Best Companies to Work For," *Fortune*, 24 January 2005 [accessed 11 March 2005] www.fortune.com; Bob Nelson, "Can't Contain Excitement at The Container Store," BizJournals.com [accessed 11 March 2005] www.bizjournals.com; Mike Duff, "Top-Shelf Employees Keep Container Store on Track," *DSN Retailing Today*, 8 March 2004, 7, 49; Bob Nelson, "The Buzz at The Container Store," *Corporate Meetings & Incentives*, June 2003, 32; Jennifer Saba, "Balancing Act," *Potentials*, 1 October 2003 [accessed 15 April 2004] www.highbeam.com; Peter S. Cohan, "Corporate Heroes," *Financial Executive*, 1 March 2003 [accessed 15 April 2004] www.highbeam.com; Margaret Steen, "Container Store's Focus on Training a Strong Appeal to Employees," *Mercury News* (San Jose, Calif.), 6 November 2003 [accessed 15 April 2004] www.highbeam. com; Holly Hayes, "Container Store Brings Clutter Control to San Jose, Calif.," 17 October 2003, *Mercury News* (San Jose, Calif.), 1F; "Performance Through People Award," press release, 10 September 2003; David Lipke, "Container Store's CEO: People Are Most Valued Asset," 13 January 2003, *HFN* [accessed 9 March 2003] www.highbeam. com; Lorrie Grant, "Container Store's Workers Huddle Up to Help You Out," 30 April 2002, *USA Today*, B1.

2. Peter F. Drucker, "Management's New Paradigms," *Forbes*, 5 October 1998, 152–176.

3. Stephen P. Robbins and David A. DeCenzo, *Fundamentals of Management* 4th ed. (Upper Saddle River, N.J.: Pearson Prentice Hall, 2004), 142–143.

4. Charles R. Greer and W. Richard Plunkett, *Supervision: Diversity and Teams in the Workplace*, 10th ed. (Upper Saddle River, N.J.: Pearson Prentice Hall, 2003), 77.

5. Caroline Ellis, "The Flattening Corporation," *MIT Sloan Management Review*, Summer 2003, 5.

6. Jeffrey Pfeffer, "How Companies Get Smart," *Business 2.0*, January/February 2005, 74.

7. Gareth R. Jones, *Organizational Theory, Design, and Change*, 4th ed. (Upper Saddle River, N.J.: Pearson Prentice Hall, 2004), 109.

8. Jones, *Organizational Theory, Design, and Change*, 109–111.

9. Lee Hawkins, Jr., "Reversing 80 Years of History, GM Is Reining In Global Fiefs," *Wall Street Journal*, 6 October 2004, A1, A14; Jonathan Fahey, "Come Home to Momma," *Forbes*, 21 June 2004, 56.

10. Richard L. Daft, *Management*, 6th ed., (Mason, Ohio: South-Western, 2003), 320.

11. Jones, *Organizational Theory, Design, and Change*, 163.

12. Jones, *Organizational Theory, Design, and Change*, 167.

13. Sinead Carew, "Motorola Reshuffles Its Business Units," Reuters, 17 July 2007 [accessed 10 August 2007] http://news. yahoo.com; Don Clark, "Intel Restructures into 5 Units, Putting Focus on Succession Issue," *Wall Street Journal*, 18 January 2005, A3.

14. Daft, *Management*, 324–327.

15. Thomas A. Stewart and Louise O'Brien, "Execution Without Excuses," *Harvard Business Review*, March 2005 [accessed 12 March 2005] www.ebsco.com.

16. Jerald Greenberg and Robert A. Baron, *Behavior in Organizations*, 8th ed. (Upper Saddle River, N.J.: Pearson Prentice Hall, 2003), 558–560; Daft, *Management*, 329.

17. Pete Engardio and Bruce Einhorn, "Outsourcing Innovation," *BusinessWeek*, 21 March 2005, 84–94.

18. Inergy website [accessed 10 August 2007] www.inergy.com.

19. Stephen P. Robbins, *Essentials of Organizational Behavior*, 6th ed. (Upper Saddle River, N.J.: Pearson Prentice Hall, 2000), 105.

20. Greer and Plunkett, *Supervision*, 293.

21. Erin White, "To Make Your Pitch at U.K. Ad Agencies, You'll Need a Partner," *Wall Street Journal*, 3 September 2004, A1, A5.

22. David Kiley, "Can VW Find Its Beetle Juice?" *BusinessWeek*, 31 January 2005, 76+.

23. Daft, *Management*, 594; Robbins and DeCenzo, *Fundamentals of Management*, 336.

24. Steven Wilhelm, "Cutting Edge: 7E7 Program Chief Outlines Plans," *Puget Sound Business Journal*, 15 August 2003 [accessed 12 March 2005] www.bizjournals.com.

25. Daft, *Management*, 618; Robbins and DeCenzo, *Fundamentals of Management*, 262.

26. Robbins and DeCenzo, *Fundamentals of Management*, 257–258; Daft, *Management*, 634–636.

27.   Robert Kreitner, *Management*, 9th ed. (Boston: Houghton Mifflin, 2004), 475–481; Daft, *Management*, 635–636.

28.   "Is Your Team Too Big? Too Small? What's the Right Number?" Knowledge@ Wharton, 14 June 2006 [accessed 10 August 2007] http://knowledge.wharton.upenn.edu.

29.   Nicola A. Nelson, "Leading Teams," *Defense AT&L*, July–August 2006, 26–29; Larry Cole and Michael Cole, "Why Is the Teamwork Buzz Word Not Working?" *Communication World*, February–March 1999, 29; Patricia Buhler, "Managing in the 90s: Creating Flexibility in Today's Workplace," *Supervision*, January 1997, 24+; Allison W. Amason, Allen C. Hochwarter, Wayne A. Thompson, and Kenneth R. Harrison, "Conflict: An Important Dimension in Successful Management Teams," *Organizational Dynamics*, Autumn 1995, 20+.

30.   Jared Sandberg, "Some Ideas Are So Bad That Only a Team Effort Can Account for Them," *Wall Street Journal*, 29 September 2004, B1.

31.   Daft, *Management*, 614.

32.   Mark K. Smith, "Bruce W. Tuckman—Forming, Storming, Norming, and Performing in Groups," Infed.org [accessed 5 July 2005] www.infed.org; Robbins and DeCenzo, *Fundamentals of Management*, 258–259; Daft, *Management*, 625–627.

33.   Jones, *Organizational Theory, Design, and Change*, 112–113; Greenberg and Baron, *Behavior in Organizations*, 280–281; Daft, *Management*, 629–631.

34.   Greenberg and Baron, *Behavior in Organizations*, 418–419.

35.   Daft, *Management*, 631–632.

36.   Kreitner, *Management*, 547–548.

37.   Courtland L. Bovée and John V. Thill, *Business Communication Today*, 8th ed. (Upper Saddle River, N.J.: Pearson Prentice Hall, 2005), 42–43.

38.   Leigh Buchanan, "The Things They Do for Love," *Harvard Business Review*, December 2004, 19–20.

39.   Robbins and DeCenzo, *Fundamentals of Management*, 284.

40.   Edwin A. Locke and Gary P. Latham, "What Should We Do About Motivation Theory? Six Recommendations for the Twenty-First Century," *Academy of Management Review*, July 2004, 388+.

41.   Robbins and DeCenzo, *Fundamentals of Management*, 27–29.

42.   Andrew J. DuBrin, *Applying Psychology: Individual & Organizational Effectiveness*, 6th ed. (Upper Saddle River, N.J.: Pearson Prentice Hall, 2004), 122–124.

43.   Daft, *Management*, 552–553.

44.   "What Is Your Bank's Employee Retention Strategy?" *Community Banker*, February 2007, 18–19.

45.   Daft, *Management*, 547; Robbins and DeCenzo, *Fundamentals of Management*, 283–284; DuBrin, *Applying Psychology: Individual & Organizational Effectiveness*, 15–16.

46.   Cobalt Boats website [accessed 11 August 2007] www.cobaltboats.com; John Grossmann, "Location, Location, Location," *Inc.*, August 2004, 83–86.

47.   Richard L. Daft, "Theory Z: Opening the Corporate Door for Participative Management," *Academy of Management Executive*, November 2004, 117–121.

48.   Todd Raphael, "Think Twice: HR's New Guru? An NBA Bigmouth," *Workforce Management*, 6 July 2004 [accessed 25 March 2005] www.workforce.com.

49.   Daft, *Management*, 554–555.

50.   Eryn Brown, "How to Get Paid What You're Worth," *Business 2.0*, May 2004, 102–110.

51.   Robbins and DeCenzo, *Fundamentals of Management*, 289.

52.   See Note 1.

53.   Adapted from "Benchmarking Study Finds 'Telework' Has Evolved into a Mainstream Way of Working; Now, 'It's Just Work,'" press release, Telework Coalition, 9 March 2006 [accessed 11 August 2007] www.telcoa.org; Rich Karlgaard, "Outsource Yourself," *Forbes*, 19 April 2004 [accessed 24 April 2004] www.highbeam.com; David Kirkpatrick, "Big-League R&D Gets Its Own eBay," *Fortune*, 3 May 2004 [accessed 24 April 2004] www.highbeam.com; Joseph N. Pelton, "The Rise of Telecities: Decentralizing the Global Society," *The Futurist*, 1 January 2004 [accessed 24 April 2004] www.highbeam.com.

Chapter 14

1.   Adapted from "Starbucks Company Fact Sheet," Starbucks website [accessed 18 August 2007] www.starbucks.com; "Mr. Coffee," *Context*, August–September 2001, 20–25; Jennifer Ordonez, "Starbucks' Schultz to Leave Top Post, Lead Global Effort," *Wall Street Journal*, 7 April 2000, B3; Karyn Strauss, "Howard Schultz: Starbucks' CEO Serves a Blend of Community, Employee Commitment," *Nation's Restaurant News*, January 2000, 162–163; Carla Joinson, "The Cost of Doing Business?" *HR Magazine*, December 1999, 86–92; "Interview with Howard Schultz: Sharing Success," *Executive Excellence*, November 1999, 16–17; Kelly Barron, "The Cappuccino Conundrum," *Forbes*, 22 February 1999, 54–55; Naomi Weiss, "How Starbucks Impassions Workers to Drive Growth," *Workforce*, August 1998, 60–64; Scott S. Smith, "Grounds for Success," *Entrepreneur*, May 1998, 120–126; "Face Value: Perky People," *The Economist*, 30 May 1998, 66; Howard Schultz and Dori Jones Yang, "Starbucks: Making Values Pay," *Fortune*, 29 September 1997, 261–272.

2.   Gary Dessler, *A Framework for Human Resource Management*, 3rd ed. (Upper Saddle River, N.J.: Pearson Prentice Hall, 2004), 2.

3.   Lauren Keller Johnson, "The New Loyalty: Make It Work for Your Company," *Harvard Management Update*, March 2005, 3–5.

4.   DuBrin, *Applying Psychology: Individual & Organizational Effectiveness*, 6th ed. (Upper Saddle River, N.J.: Pearson Prentice Hall, 2004), 159.

5.   Jeffrey Pfeffer, "All Work, No Play? It Doesn't Pay," *Business 2.0*, August 2004, 50.

6.   Nancy R. Lockwood, "Workplace Diversity: Leveraging the Power of Difference for Competitive Advantage," *HR Magazine*, June 2005, special section 1–10.

7.   "HR Must Evolve to Meet Needs of Age-Diverse Workforce," *Reliable Plant* [accessed 12 August 2007] www.reliableplant.com.

8.   Neil Howe and William Strauss, "The Next 20 Years: How Customer and Workforce Attitudes Will Evolve," *Harvard Business Review*, July/August 2007, 41–52.

9.   Michael Kinsman, "Respect Helps Mix of Generations Work Well Together," *San Diego Union-Tribune*, 19 September 2004, H2.

10.   "Sex-Based Charges: FY 1997–FY 2006," EEOC website [accessed 13 August 2007] www.eeoc.gov.

11.   "U.S. Women in Business," 22 June 2007, Catalyst website [accessed 13 August 2007] www.catalyst.org; David Leonhardt, "Gender Pay Gap, Once Narrowing, Is Stuck in Place," *New York Times*, 24 December 2006 [accessed 13 August 2007] www.nytimes.com; Louis Uchitelle, "Gaining Ground on the Wage Front," *New York Times*, 31 December 2004, C1–C2; Betsy Morris, "How Corporate America Is Betraying Women," *Fortune*, 10 January 2005, 64–74; Aaron Bernstein, "Women's Pay: Why the Gap Remains a Chasm," *BusinessWeek*, 14 June 2004, 25–59; Judy B. Rosener, "Women on Corporate Boards Make Good Business Sense," *Directorship*, May 2003, 7+; United Press International, "Women Increase Employment, Not Salaries," 8 March 2004 [accessed 29 April 2004] www.highbeam.com; Gary Strauss and Del Jones, "Too Bright Spotlight Burns Female CEOs," *USA Today*, 18 December 2000, 3B.

12.   Constance E. Helfat, Dawn Harris, and Paul J. Wolfson, "The Pipeline to the Top: Women and Men in the Top Executive Ranks of U.S. Corporations," *Academy of Management Perspectives*, November 2006, 42–64.

13.   Gretchen Morgenson, "Working Girls," *New Republic*, 19 March 2007, 56–59; Francine D. Blau and Lawrence M. Kahn, "The Gender Pay Gap: Have Women Gone as Far as They Can?" *Academy of Management Perspectives*, February 2007, 7–23.

14.   "Sexual Harassment Charges: EEOC & FEPAs Combined: FY 1997–FY 2006," EEOC

website [accessed 13 August 2007] www.eeoc.gov.

15. Robert Kreitner, *Management*, 9th ed. (Boston: Houghton Mifflin, 2004), 375–377; "One-Fifth of Women Are Harassed Sexually," *HR Focus*, April 2002, 2.

16. "Race-Based Charges: FY 1997– FY 2006," EEOC website [accessed 13 August 2007] www.eeoc.gov.

17. Stephen Ohlemacher, "Whites Now Minority in 1 in 10 Counties," Yahoo! News, 9 August 2007 [accessed 12 August 2007] http://new.yahoo.com; Kreitner, *Management*, 84.

18. Bruce H. Webster, Jr., and Alemayehu Bishaw, "Income, Earnings, and Poverty Data from the 2005 American Community Survey," August 2006, U.S. Census Bureau [accessed 13 August 2007] www.census.gov; Roger O. Crockett, "For Blacks, Progress Without Parity," *BusinessWeek*, 14 July 2003 [accessed 1 April 2005] www.businessweek.com.

19. Cora Daniels, "Finally in the Director's Chair," *Fortune*, 4 October 2004.

20. Todd Henneman, "A New Approach to Faith at Work," *Workforce Management*, October 2004, 76–77.

21. "Avoid Uniform Policies on Religious Expression at Work," *HR Focus*, July 2007, 10–11.

22. IBM website [accessed 13 August 2007] www.ibm.com; Wendy Harris, "Out of the Corporate Closet," *Black Enterprise*, May 2007 [accessed 13 August 2007] http://integrate.factivia. com; David A. Thomas, "Diversity as Strategy," *Harvard Business Review*, September 2004, 98–108; Joe Mullich, "Hiring Without Limits," *Workforce Management*, June 2004, 53–58; Mike France and William G. Symonds, "Diversity Is About to Get More Elusive, Not Less," 7 July 2003, *BusinessWeek* [accessed 24 January 2005] www. businessweek.com; Anne Papmehl, "Diversity in Workforce Paying Off, IBM Finds," *Toronto Star*, 7 October 2002 [accessed 4 November 2003], www.elibrary.com.

23. "Sun's iWork Program Wins Global Innovators Award," Sun Microsystems website [accessed 13 August 2007] www.sun. com; Samuel Greengard, "Sun's Shining Example," *Workforce Management*, March 2005, 48–49.

24. Clare Brennan, "What Is Job-Sharing?" iVillage [accessed 31 March 2005] www. ivillage.co.uk.

25. Jessica Marquez, "Winning Women Back," *Workforce Management*, 9 April 2007, 1, 20–25; Diane Brady, "Hopping Aboard the Daddy Track," *BusinessWeek*, 8 November 2004, 100–101; Sylvia Ann Hewlett and Carolyn Buck Luce, "Off-Ramps and On-Ramps," *Harvard Business Review*, March 2005, 43–54.

26. Dessler, *A Framework for Human Resource Management*, 74–75.

27. Shari Randall, "Succession Planning Is More Than a Game of Chance," *Workforce Management* [accessed 1 May 2004], www.workforce.com.

28. "Employee or Independent Contractor? How to Tell," *HR Focus*, January 2004, 7, 10.

29. Joellen Perry, "Help Wanted," *U.S. News & World Report*, 8 March 2004, 48–54.

30. Dessler, *A Framework for Human Resource Management*, 66.

31. Dessler, *A Framework for Human Resource Management*, 72.

32. Samuel Greengard, "Quality of Hire: How Companies Are Crunching the Numbers," *Workforce Management*, July 2004 [accessed 8 July 2007] www.workforce.com.

33. Paul Kaihla, "Best-Kept Secrets of the World's Best Companies," *Business 2.0*, April 2006, 81–96.

34. Hope A. Comisky and Christopher P. Zubowicz, "The Law of Criminal Background Checks," *Employee Relations Law Journal*, Vol. 32, No. 3, Winter 2006, 66–85.

35. Thomas A. Buckhoff, "Preventing Fraud by Conducting Background Checks," *CPA Journal*, November 2003, 52.

36. Dino di Mattia, "Testing Methods and Effectiveness of Tests," *Supervision*, August 2005, 4–5.

37. John Sullivan, "A Case Study of Google Recruiting," 5 December 2005 [accessed 7 July 2007] www.drjohnsullivan.com.

38. Andy Meisler, "Negative Results," *Workforce Management*, October 2003, 35+.

39. Tyler D. Hartwell, Paul D. Steele, and Nathaniel F. Rodman, "Workplace Alcohol-Testing Programs: Prevalence and Trends," *Monthly Labor Review*, June 1998, 27–34; "Substance Abuse in the Workplace," *HR Focus*, February 1997, 1, 4+.

40. "Drug Test Company Official Disputes Report Pre-Employment Tests Falling," *Drug Detection Report*, 23 March 2006, 43.

41. Steven Mitchell Sack, "The Working Woman's Legal Survival Guide: Testing," FindLaw.com [accessed 22 February 2004] www.findlaw.com; David W. Arnold and John W. Jones, "Who the Devil's Applying Now?" *Security Management*, March 2002, 85–88.

42. Margery Weinstein, "Learning Dollars," *Training*, April 2007, 6.

43. Carol A. Hacker, "New Employee Orientation: Make It Pay Dividends for Years to Come," *Information Systems Management*, Winter 2004, 89–92.

44. Tammy Galvin, "2003 Industry Report." *Training*, October 2003, 21+.

45. Dessler, *A Framework for Human Resource Management*, 198.

46. PerformanceNow.com website [accessed 2 May 2004] www.performancenow.com;

Dessler, *A Framework for Human Resource Management*, 199.

47. Dessler, *A Framework for Human Resource Management*, 198–199.

48. Andrew E. Jackson, "Recognizing the 'I' in Team," *Industrial Engineer*, March 2005, 38–42.

49. Jeff St. John, "Kennewick, Wash., 'snoop' Software Maker Also Protects Privacy," *Tri-City Herald* (Kennewick, Wash.), 17 April 2004 [accessed 2 May 2004] www.highbeam. com; Dessler, *A Framework for Human Resource Management*, 204–205.

50. Dessler, *A Framework for Human Resource Management*, 223–225.

51. Matthew Grim, "Wal-Mart Uber Alles," *American Demographics*, October 2003, 38–39; Jeffrey E. Garten, "Wal-Mart Gives Globalism a Bad Name," *BusinessWeek*, 8 March 2004, 24; Jerry Useem, "Should We Admire Wal-Mart?" *Fortune*, 8 March 2004, 118–120.

52. Christopher Farrell, "Stock Options for All!" *BusinessWeek*, 20 September 2002 [accessed 18 August 2007] www.businessweek.com; Gary Strauss and Barbara Hansen, "CEO Pay Packages 'Business as Usual,'" *USA Today*, 31 March 2005, B2.

53. Jeff D. Opdyke, "Getting a Bonus Instead of a Raise," *Wall Street Journal*, 29 December 2004, D1–D2.

54. Paul Loucks, "Creating a Performance-Based Culture," *Benefits & Compensation Digest*, July 2007, 36–39.

55. Dessler, *A Framework for Human Resource Management*, 231–232.

56. Gregory Lopes, "Firms Dock Pay of Obese, Smokers," *Washington Times*, 13 August 2007 [accessed 14 August 2007] www.washingtontimes.com; Joseph Weber, "Health Insurance: Small Biz Is in a Bind," *BusinessWeek*, 27 September 2004, 47–48; Joseph Pereira, "Parting Shot: To Save on Health-Care Costs, Firms Fire Disabled Workers," *Wall Street Journal*, 14 July 2003, A1, A7; Timothy Aeppel, "Ill Will: Skyrocketing Health Costs Start to Pit Worker vs. Worker," *Wall Street Journal*, 17 July 2003, A1, A6; Vanessa Furhmans, "To Stem Abuses, Employers Audit Workers' Health Claims," *Wall Street Journal*, 31 March 2004, B1, B7; Milt Freudenheim, "Employees Paying Ever-Bigger Share for Health Care," *New York Times*, A1, C2; Julie Appleby, "Employers Get Nosy About Workers' Health," *USA Today*, 6 March 2003, B1–B2; Ellen E. Schultz and Theo Francis, "Employers' Caps Raise Retirees' Health-Care Costs," *Wall Street Journal*, 25 November 2003, B1, B11; Vanessa Fuhrmans, "Company Health Plans Try to Drop Spouses," *Wall Street Journal*, 9 September 2003, D1, D2.

57. Jeremy W. Peters, "Company's Smoking Ban Means Off-Hours, Too," *New York Times*, 8 February 2005, C5.

58. Lopes, "Firms Dock Pay of Obese, Smokers."

59. Victoria Colliver, "We Spend More, but U.S. Health Care Quality Falls Behind," *San Francisco Chronicle*, 10 July 2007 [accessed 14 August 2007] www.scrippsnews.com; Steve Lohr, "The Disparate Consensus on Health Care for All," *New York Times*, 6 December 2004, C16; Sara Schaefer and Laurie McGinley, "Census Sees a Surge in Americans Without Insurance," *Wall Street Journal*, 30 September 2003, B1, B6; "Half of Health Care Spending Is Wasted, Study Finds," *Detroit News*, 10 February 2005 [accessed 5 April 2005] www.detnews.com.

60. James H. Dulebohn, Brian Murray, and Minghe Sun, "Selection Among Employer-Sponsored Pension Plans: The Role of Individual Differences," *Personal Psychology*, Summer 2000, 405–432.

61. Carroll Lachnit, "The Drowning Pool," *Workforce Management*, October 2004, 12; Keith Naughton, "Business's Killer I.O.U.," *Newsweek*, 6 October 2003, 42–44; Christine Dugas, "Companies Consider Pension Freezes," *USA Today*, 7 January 2004, B1.

62. Pension Benefit Guaranty Corporation website [accessed 14 August 2007] www.pbgc.gov; Mary Williams Walsh, "Taking the Wheel Before a Pension Runs into Trouble," *New York Times*, 30 January 2005, Sunday Money, 5; Amy Borrus, "Will the Bough Break?" *BusinessWeek*, 14 April 2003, 62–63; Barbara De Lollis and Marilyn Adams, "Fed Up with Pension Defaults," *USA Today*, 9 September 2004, B1; Janice Revell, "New Math: Don't Pay As You Go Under," *Fortune*, 4 October 2004, 38.

63. George Van Dyke, "Examining Your 401k," *Business Credit*, January 2000, 59.

64. The ESOP Association website [accessed 14 August 2007] www.esopassociation.org; Dessler, *A Framework for Human Resource Management*, 282.

65. Michelle Kessler, "Fears Subside over Accounting for Stock Options," *USA Today*, 1 January 2006 [accessed 18 August 2007] www.usatoday.com; Robert A. Guth and Joann S. Lublin, "Tarnished Gold: Microsoft Ushers Out Era of Options," *Wall Street Journal*, 9 July 2003, A1, A9; John Markoff and David Leonhardt, "Microsoft Will Award Stock, Not Options, to Employees," *New York Times,* 9 July 2003, A1, C4.

66. Peter Burrows, "New Stock Option Fears in the Valley," *BusinessWeek*, 8 August 2007 [accessed 18 August 2007] www.businessweek.com; "Background on the Options Backdating Scandal," Institutional Shareholder Services website [accessed 18 August 2007] www.issproxy.com; Amanda Cantrell, "Many Firms Seen Dodging The Back-Dating Bullet," CNNMoney.com, 19 July 2006 [accessed 18 August 2007] http://money.cnn.com.

67. Cheeseman, *Contemporary Business and E-Commerce Law*, 4th ed. (Upper Saddle River, N.J.: Pearson Prentice Hall, 2003) 626.

68. Patrick J. Kiger, "A Case for Child Care," *Workforce Management*, April 2004, 34–40.

69. Patrick J. Kiger, "Child-Care Models," *Workforce Management*, April 2004, 38.

70. "Employer-Sponsored Daycare Can Be Profitable, New Study Shows," Bowdoin College website [accessed 6 April 2005] www.bowdoin.edu; Erin L. Kelly, "The Strange History of Employer-Sponsored Child Care: Interested Actors, Uncertainty, and the Transformation of Law in Organizational Fields," *American Journal of Sociology*, November 2003, 606–649.

71. Stephanie Armour, "Employers Stepping Up in Elder Care," *USA Today*, 3 August 2000, 3B.

72. Agilent Technologies website [accessed 6 April 2005] www.agilent.com.

73. Andy Meisler, "A Matter of Degrees," *Workforce Management*, May 2004, 32–38; Stephanie Armour, "More Firms Help Workers Find Home Sweet Home," *USA Today*, 30 August 2004, C1–C2.

74. Atkinson, "Wellness, Employee Assistance Programs"; Kevin Dobbs, Jack Gordon, and David Stamps, "EAPs Cheap But Popular Perk," *Training*, February 2000, 26.

75. Alison Stein Wellner, "The Pickup Artists," *Workforce Management*, July 2004 [accessed 6 April 2005] www.workforce.com.

76. Adam Cohen and Cathy Booth Thomas, "Inside a Layoff," *Time*, 16 April 2001, 38–40.

77. Challenger, Gray & Christmas website [accessed 18 August 2007] www.challengergray.com.

78. John Jude Moran, *Employment Law: New Challenges in the Business Environment*, 2nd ed. (Upper Saddle River, N.J.: Pearson Prentice Hall, 2002), 127; Dan Seligman, "The Right to Fire," *Forbes*, 10 November 2003, 126–128.

79. Pete Engardio, "Managing the New Workforce," *BusinessWeek*, 20 and 27 August 2007, 48–51.

80. Chris Isidore, "GM Offers Workers up to $140K to Leave," CNNMoney.com, 22 March 2006 [accessed 18 August 2007] http://money.cnn.com.

81. Cheeseman, *Contemporary Business and E-Commerce Law*, 649.

82. Wal-Mart Watch website [accessed 18 August 2007] www.walmartwatch.com.

83. Paul D. Staudohar, "Labor Relations in Basketball: The Lockout of 1998–99," *Monthly Labor Review*, April 1999, 3–9; E. Edward Herman, *Collective Bargaining and Labor Relations*, 4th ed. (Upper Saddle River, N.J.: Pearson Prentice Hall, 1998), 61; "NLRB Permits Replacements During Legal Lockout," *Personnel Journal*, January 1987, 14–15.

84. "Trends in Union Membership," AFL-CIO website [accessed 18 August 2007] www.aflcio.org.

85. "Union 101," AFL-CIO website [accessed 18 August 2007] www.aflcio.org.

86. Change to Win website [accessed 18 August 2007] www.changetowin.org.

87. Service Employees International Union website [accessed 18 August 2007] www.seiu.org.

88. Michael Arndt, "Salvation from the Shop Floor," *BusinessWeek*, 3 February 2003, 100–101; Stanley Holmes, "Boeing: Putting Out Labor Fires," *BusinessWeek*, 29 December 2003, 43; Jill Jusko, "Nature Versus Nurture," *IndustryWeek*, July 2003, 40–42; David Kiley, "Foreign Companies Cast Long Shadow on UAW Negotiations," *USA Today*, 6 August 2003, B1.

89. See Note 1.

90. Adapted from IBM Human Ability and Accessibility Center [accessed 15 August 2007] www-3.ibm.com/able; AssistiveTech.net [accessed 15 August 2007] www.assistivetech.net; Business Leadership Network website [accessed 15 August 2007] www.usbln.org; National Institute on Disability and Rehabilitation Research website [accessed 15 August 2007] www.ed.gov; Rehabilitation Engineering and Assistive Technology Society of North America website [accessed 15 August 2007] www.resna.org.

Appendix A

1. Bill Shaw and Art Wolfe, *The Structure of the Legal Environment: Law, Ethics, and Business*, 2nd ed. (Boston: PWS-Kent, 1991), 635.

2. Shaw and Wolfe, *The Structure of the Legal Environment*, 146.

3. George A. Steiner and John F. Steiner, *Business, Government, and Society* (New York: McGraw-Hill, 1991), 149.

4. Paula Burkes Erickson, "Oklahoma Bill Proposes Business Courts," *Daily Oklahoman*, 23 February 2004 [accessed 16 May 2004] www.highbeam.com.

5. Thomas W. Dunfee, Frank F. Gibson, John D. Blackburn, Douglas Whitman, F. William McCarty, and Bartley A. Brennan, *Modern Business Law* (New York: Random House, 1989), 164.

6. Nancy K. Kubasek, Bartley A. Brennan, and M. Neil Browne, *The Legal Environment of Business*, 3rd ed. (Upper Saddle River, N.J.: Pearson Prentice Hall, 2003), 306.

7. Bartley A. Brennan and Nancy Kubasek, *The Legal Environment of Business* (New York: McGraw-Hill, 1990), 184.

8. Kubasek et al., *The Legal Environment of Business*, 325; "Reasonable Product-Liability Reform," *Nation's Business*, 1 September 1997, 88.

9. Dunfee et al., *Modern Business Law*, 569.

10. Michael Ha, "Public Backs Many Tort Reforms," *National Underwriter*, 19 April 2004, 10.

11. Michael Orey, "How Business Trounced the Trial Lawyers," *BusinessWeek*, 8 January

2007 [accessed 20 August 2007] www.businessweek.com.

12. Dunfee et al., *Modern Business Law*, 236.

13. Dunfee et al., *Modern Business Law*, 284–297; Brennan and Kubasek, *The Legal Environment of Business*, 125–127; Douglas Whitman and John William Gergacz, *The Legal Environment of Business*, 2nd ed. (New York: Random House, 1988), 196–197; *The Lawyer's Almanac* (Upper Saddle River, N.J.: Pearson Prentice Hall, 1991), 888.

14. Brennan and Kubasek, *The Legal Environment of Business*, 128.

15. Samuel Maull, "Judge Rules No Damages to Rosie, Publisher," AP Online, 20 February 2004 [accessed 16 May 2004] www.highbeam.com.

16. Richard M. Steuer, *A Guide to Marketing Law: What Every Seller Should Know* (New York: Harcourt Brace Jovanovich, 1986), 151–152.

17. Dunfee et al., *Modern Business Law*, 745, 749.

18. Brennan and Kubasek, *The Legal Environment of Business*, 160; Whitman and Gergacz, *The Legal Environment of Business*, 260.

19. Henry R. Cheeseman, *Business Law*, 4th ed. (Upper Saddle River, N.J.: Pearson Prentice Hall, 2001), 324.

20. Eric Freedman, "Court: Toy Infringes Hummer Trademark," *Automotive News*, 25 December 2006, 10.

21. Cheeseman, *Business Law*, 330.

22. Mike Snider, "Law Targets Copyright Theft Online," *USA Today*, 18 December 1998, A1.

23. Tariq K. Muhammad, "Real Law in a Virtual World," *Black Enterprise*, December 1996, 44.

24. Jerry M. Rosenberg, *Dictionary of Business and Management* (New York: Wiley, 1983), 340.

25. Ronald A. Anderson, Ivan Fox, and David P. Twomey, *Business Law* (Cincinnati: South-Western Publishing, 1987), 635.

26. Brennan and Kubasek, *The Legal Environment of Business*, 516–517.

27. "Polaroid Finalizes Sale, Emerges from Chapter 11," *TWICE*, 8 July 2002, 37; Polaroid website [accessed 29 July 2002] www.polaroid.com.

Appendix B

1. Lawrence J. Gitman and Michael D. Joehnk, *Personal Financial Planning*, 10th ed. (Mason, Ohio: Thomson South-Western, 2005), 27.

2. Jack R. Kapoor, Les R. Dlabay, and Robert J. Hughes, *Personal Finance*, 7th ed. (New York: McGraw-Hill/Irwin, 2004), 18.

3. Anne Kim, "Moving In, Moving On," *Seattle Times*, 8 May 2004 [accessed 13 May 2004] www.seattletimes.com.

4. Kapoor et al., *Personal Finance*, 33.

5. "How to Choose a Financial Advisor," WiserAdvisor.com [accessed 21 May 2004] www.wiseradvisor.com.

6. Arthur J. Keown, *Personal Finance: Turning Money into Wealth*, 3rd ed. (Upper Saddle River, N.J.: Prentice Hall, 2003), 52–53.

7. Albert B. Crenshaw and Brooke A. Masters, "Big Four Face Legal Trouble, Lost Business; IRS, Clients Challenge Tax-Shelter Advice," *Washington Post*, 12 February 2003 [accessed 21 May 2004] www.highbeam.com; Jerry L. Reiter, "The Blame Game," *Registered Rep*, 2 January 2003 [accessed 21 May 2004] www.highbeam.com.

8. Kapoor et al., *Personal Finance*, 11; Gitman and Joehnk, *Personal Financial Planning*, 5.

9. Gitman and Joehnk, *Personal Financial Planning*, 15.

10. Deborah Fowles, "Financial Advice for Your 20s," About.com [accessed 22 May 2004] www.about.com; Gitman and Joehnk, *Personal Financial Planning*, 15.

11. Ana M. Aizcorbe, Arthur B. Kennickell, and Keven B. Moore, "Recent Changes in U.S. Family Finances: Evidence from the 1998 and 2001 Survey of Consumer Finances," *Federal Reserve Bulletin*, January 2003, 4.

12. Deborah Fowles, "The Psychology of Spending Money," About.com [accessed 22 May 2004] www.about.com.

13. Gitman and Joehnk, *Personal Financial Planning*, 15.

14. "College Degree Nearly Doubles Annual Earnings, Census Bureau Reports," press release, 28 March 2005, U.S. Census Bureau [accessed 20 August 2007] www.census.gov; "More College Grads, Fewer Home-Grown," *Seattle Times*, 17 May 2004 [accessed 17 May 2004] www.seattletimes.com.

15. Ben Elgin, "Study Now—and Pay and Pay and Pay Later," 21 May 2007, *BusinessWeek*, 66–67.

16. Lucy Lazarony, "Credit Cards Teaching Students a Costly Lesson," Bankrate.com, 5 June 1998 [accessed 22 May 2004] www.bankrate.com.

17. David Kiley, "Car Buyers Pay More, Owe More Longer," *USA Today*, 17 February 2004, B1; Lucy Lazarony, "It's a Good Time to Be a New-Car Shopper," Bankrate.com, 5 March 2003 [accessed 22 May 2004] www.bankrate.com.

18. Philip Reed, "Drive a (Nearly) New Car for (Almost) Nothing," Edmunds.com [accessed 22 May 2004] www.edmunds.com.

19. Chandler Phillips, "Confessions of a Car Salesman," Edmunds.com [accessed 22 May 2004] www.edmunds.com.

20. Eryn Brown, "Hot to Get Paid What You're Worth," *Business 2.0*, May 2004, 102–110, 134.

21. Keown, *Personal Finance: Turning Money into Wealth*, 143–148; Gitman and Joehnk, *Personal Financial Planning*, 140–147.

22. "How To Establish Credit," CreditInfoWeb.com [accessed 23 May 2004] www.creditinfoweb.com.

23. Kapoor et al., *Personal Finance*, 222.

24. "Ads Promising Debt Relief May Be Offering Bankruptcy," FTC Consumer Alert [accessed 23 May 2004] www.ftc.gov.

25. Christopher Conkey, "Bankruptcy Overall Means Tougher Choices," *Wall Street Journal*, 22 May 2005 [accessed 10 June 2005] www.wsj.com.

26. Kapoor et al., *Personal Finance*, 582.

Illustration and Text Credits

Prologue

1. Exhibit 1, Screenshots used with permission from Claudia Volpi.

2. Exhibit 2, Adapted from Daniel E. Hecker, "Occupational Employment Projections to 2014," *Monthly Labor Review*, November 2005, 70–101.

3. Exhibit 3, The Riley Guide [accessed 16 August 2007] www.rileyguide.com; Bethany McLean, "A Scary Monster," *Fortune*, 22 December 2003, 19+; Alan Cohen, "Best Job Hunting Sites," *Yahoo! Internet Life*, May 2002, 90–92; Richard N. Bolles, "Career Strategizing or, What Color Is Your Web Parachute?" *Yahoo! Internet Life*, May 1998, 116, 121; Tara Weingarten, "The All-Day, All-Night, Global, No-Trouble Job Search," *Newsweek*, 6 April 1998, 14; Michele Himmelberg, "Internet an Important Tool in Employment Search," *San Diego Union-Tribune*, 7 September 1998, D2; Gina Imperato, "35 Ways to Land a Job Online," *Fast Company*, August 1998, 192–197; Roberta Maynard, "Casting the Net for Job Seekers," *Nation's Business*, March 1997, 28–29.

4. Exhibit 8, Adapted from Marilyn Sherman, "Questions R Us: What to Ask at a Job Interview," *Career World*, January 2004, 20; H. Lee Rust, *Job Search: The Completion Manual for Jobseekers* (New York: American Management Association, 1979), 56.

Chapter 1

1. Exhibit 1.2, Adapted from Google website [accessed 6 June 2007] www.google.com; Christopher Caggiano, "Will the Real Bootstrappers Please Stand Up?" *Inc.*, August 1995, 34; Mike Hofman, "Capitalism—A Bootstrappers' Hall of Fame," *Inc.*, August 1997, 54–57; Hoover's [accessed 27 March 2004] www.hoovers.com; Limited Brands website [accessed 6 January 2005] www.limited.com.

2. Exhibit 1.3, Adapted from Amy Gahran, "What Is Conversational Media?" The Right Conversation blog, 1 January 2006 [accessed

7 June 2007] www.rightconversation.com; Monica Kearns, "Whatever Happened to the New Economy?" *State Legislatures*, February 2002, 24–27.

3. Is Web 2.0 the Future or the Past Revisited? Adapted from Aili McConnon and Reena Jana, "Beyond Second Life," *BusinessWeek*, 11 June 2007 [accessed 6 June 2007] www.businessweek.com; Josh Quittner, "Web Boom 2.0," *Time*, 16 December 2006 [accessed 6 June 2007] www.time.com; Russell Shaw, "Web 2.0? It Doesn't Exist," ZDNet blogs, 17 December 2005 [accessed 13 August 2006] http://blogs.zdnet.com; Tim O'Reilly, "What Is Web 2.0? Design Patterns and Business Models for the Next Generation of Software," *O'Reilly*, 30 September 2005 [accessed 13 August 2006] www.oreillynet. com; John Dvorak, "Web 2.0 Baloney," *PC Magazine* online, 1 March 2006 [accessed 13 August 2006] www.pcmag.com; Nicholas Carr, "The Amorality of Web 2.0," (blog entry), 3 October 2005 [accessed 13 August 2006] http://roughtype.com; Shayne Bowman and Chris Willis, "We Media: How Audiences Are Shaping the Future of News and Information," 21 September 2003, Hypergene.net [accessed 4 February 2007] www.hypergene.net.

4. Learning from Business Blunders Adapted from Adam Horowitz, David Jacobson, Tom McNichol, and Owen Thomas, "The 101 Dumbest Moments in Business," *Business 2.0* [accessed 6 June 2007] www.business2.com; "Boston Globe and Telegram & Gazette Circulate Customer Credit Card Numbers by Mistake," Credit-Fraud.com, 31 January 2006 [accessed 6 September 2007] www.card-fraud.com; Paul F. Roberts, "Globe Gaffe Delivers Subscriber Credit Card Data," eWeek.com, 1 February 2007 [accessed 6 September 2007] www.eweek.com.

Chapter 2
1. Exhibit 2.1, Adapted from "eHealth Code of Ethics," Internet Healthcare Coalition website [accessed 20 June 2007] www.ihealthcoalition.org.
2. Exhibit 2.2, Adapted from Manuel G. Velasquez, *Business Ethics: Concepts and Cases* (Upper Saddle River, N.J.: Prentice Hall, 1998), 87; Joseph L. Badaracco, Jr., "Business Ethics: Four Spheres of Executive Responsibility," *California Management Review*, Spring 1992, 64–79; Kenneth Blanchard and Norman Vincent Peale, *The Power of Ethical Management* (Reprint, 1989; New York: Fawcett Crest, 1991), 7–17; John R. Boatright, *Ethics and the Conduct of Business* (Upper Saddle River, N.J.: Prentice Hall, 1996), 35–39, 59–64, 79–86.
3. Exhibit 2.5, "Electric Power Annual," U.S. Department of Energy website [accessed 20 June 2007] www.energy.gov.

4. Exhibit 2.8, "Census of Fatal Occupational Injuries," U.S. Bureau of Labor Statistics website [accessed 20 June 2007] www.bls.gov.
5. Wow, That Sure Was Nice of Kathy to Give Us Those Free Coupons! Adapted from David Meerman Scott, *The New Rules of Marketing and PR* (Hoboken, N.J.: Wiley, 2007), 205; Word of Mouth Marketing Association website [accessed 10 June 2007] www.womma.org; Robert Berner, "I Sold It Through the Grapevine," *BusinessWeek*, 29 May 2006, 32; Melanie Wells, "Kid Nabbing," *Forbes*, 2 February 2004, 84–88; Michelle Conlin, "The Stepford Kids," *BusinessWeek*, 27 September 2004, 26–27; Anick Jesdanun, "How Bloggers Handle Ethics and Disclosure Varies Greatly," *Seattle Times*, 24 January 2005 [accessed 24 January 2005] www.seattletimes.com.
6. Lead Your Team with Ethical Behavior Adapted from Melissa Ingwersen, *Columbus Business First*, 23 January 2004 [accessed 17 January 2005] www.bizjournals.com; Harold Tinkler, "Execs Must Embed Ethics into Company Culture," *Puget Sound Business Journal*, 16 April 2004 [accessed 17 January 2005] www.bizjournals.com; Marc Gunther, "Money and Morals at GE," *Fortune*, 15 November 2004, 176–182; Craig Dreilinger, "Get Real (and Ethics Will Follow)," *Workforce*, August 1998, 101–102; Louisa Wah, "Workplace Conscience Needs a Boost," *American Management Association International*, July–August 1998; "Ethics Are Questionable in the Workplace," *HRFocus*, June 1998, 7.
7. Learning from Business Blunders Adapted from Adam Horowitz, David Jacobson, Tom McNichol, and Owen Thomas, "The 101 Dumbest Moments in Business," *Business 2.0* [accessed 20 June 2007] www.business2.com; Mary Schlangenstein, "Northwest Air Apologizes After Cost-Cutting Advice Irks Workers," Bloomberg.com, 16 August 2006 [accessed 20 June 2007] www.bloomberg.com; Joshua Freed, "Bankrupt NWA Paid CEO $1.8M in '06," *USA Today*, 1 May 2007 [accessed 20 June 2007] www.usatoday.com.

Chapter 3
1. Exhibit 3.1, World Economic Forum, "Global Competitiveness Report 2006–2007," World Economic Forum website [accessed 30 June 2007] www.weforum.org.
2. Exhibit 3.2, U.S. Bureau of Economic Analysis website [accessed 30 June 2007] www.bea.gov.
3. Exhibit 3.3, Adapted from "Strong Dollar, Weak Dollar: Foreign Exchange Rates and the U.S. Economy," Federal Reserve Bank of Chicago website [accessed 29 January 2005] www.chicagofed.org.
4. Exhibit 3.4, Adapted from "Strong Dollar, Weak Dollar: Foreign Exchange Rates and

the U.S. Economy," Federal Reserve Bank of Chicago website [accessed 29 January 2005] www.chicagofed.org.
5. Exhibit 3.5, Courtland L. Bovée and John V. Thill, *Business Communication Today*, 9th ed. (Upper Saddle River, N.J.: Pearson Prentice Hall, 2008), 76. Reprinted by permission of Pearson Education, Inc., Upper Saddle River, N.J.
6. Studying Other Cultures Adapted from P. Christopher Earley and Elaine Mosakowsi, "Cultural Intelligence," *Harvard Business Review*, October 2004, 139–146; Wendy A. Conklin, "An Inside Look at Two Diversity Intranet Sites: IBM and Merck," *The Diversity Factor*, Summer 2005; Craig S. Smith, "Beware of Green Hats in China and Other Cross-Cultural Faux Pas," *New York Times*, 30 April 2002, C11.
7. Learning from Business Blunders Adapted from Mark Landler and Michael Barbaro, "Wal-Mart Finds That Its Formula Doesn't Fit Every Culture," *New York Times*, 2 August 2006 [accessed 23 August 2006] www.nytimes.com.

Chapter 4
1. Exhibit 4.2, Used with permission from isee Systems, Inc., www.iseesystems.com.
2. Exhibit 4.3, Peter Fingar and Ronald Aronica, "Value Chain Optimization: The New Way of Competing," *Supply Chain Management Review*, September–October 2001, 82. Reprinted by permission of the YGS Group.
3. Exhibit 4.6, Adapted from Mark M. Davis, Nicholas J. Aquilano, and Richard B. Chase, *Fundamentals of Operations Management* (Boston: Irwin McGraw-Hill, 1999), 7.
4. Exhibit 4.8, Dashboard visualization created with Xcelsius by Business Objects.
5. Offshoring: Profits, Yes, But at What Cost? Adapted from Michael Mandel, "The Real Costs of Offshoring," *BusinessWeek*, 18 June 2007, 29–34; Jeffrey E. Garten, "Offshoring: You Ain't Seen Nothin' Yet," *BusinessWeek*, 21 June 2004, 28; Jim Hopkins, "To Start Up Here, Companies Hire Over There," *USA Today*, 11 February 2005, B1–B2; Marc Lacey, "Accents of Africa: A New Outsourcing Frontier," *New York Times*, 2 February 2005, C1, C6; Susan Carey and Alex Frangos, "Airlines, Facing Cost Pressure, Outsource Crucial Safety Tasks," *Wall Street Journal*, 21 January 2005, A1, A5; Barbara Hagenbaugh, "U.S. Layoffs Not a Result of Offshoring, Data Show," *USA Today*, 11 June 2004, B1; Jay Solomon, "India's Latest: Debt Collection," *Wall Street Journal*, 6 December 2004, A14; Stephanie Amour and Michelle Kessler, "USA's New Money-Saving Export: White-Collar Jobs," *USA Today*, 5 August 2003, B1–B2; Steve Lohr, "Offshore Jobs in Technology: Opportunity or Threat?" *New York Times*, 22 December 2003, C1, C6; Kris Maher, "Next on the Outsourcing List," *Wall*

Street Journal, 28 March 2004, B1, B8; Jennifer Reingold, "Into Thin Air," *Fast Company*, April 2004, 76–82; Paul Craig Roberts, "The Harsh Truth About Outsourcing," 22 March 2004, 48; Craig Karmin, "'Offshoring' Can Generate Jobs in the U.S.," *Wall Street Journal*, 16 March 2004, B1, B7; Bernard J. La Londe, "From Outsourcing to 'Offshoring'—Part 1," *Supply Chain Management Review*, 1 March 2004 [accessed 16 April 2004] www.manufacturing.net; Paul Kaihla, "Straws in the Wind," *Business 2.0*, 27 April 2004 [accessed 22 July 2004] www.manufacturing. net; Paul Kaihla, "Straws in the Wind," *Business 2.0,* 27 April 2004 [accessed 22 July 2004] www.business2 .com.

6. Advanced Technology on the Factory Floor Beth Stackpole, "Boeing's Brave New World of Product Development," *Design News*, 4 June 2007, 91–94; Tom Lecklider, "Vision Sensors Decide for Themselves," *Evaluation Engineering*, February 2005 [accessed 21 March 2005] www.evaluationengineering.com; Daren Fonda, "Sole Survivor," *Time*, 8 November 2004, 48–49; John Teresko, "Making a Pitch for PLM," *IndustryWeek*, August 2004, 57–62; Online Extra: Porsche's CEO Talks Shop," *BusinessWeek*, 22 December 2003 [accessed 18 March 2005] www.businessweek.com; James A. Senn, *Information Technology: Principles, Practices, Opportunities,* 3rd ed. (Upper Saddle River, N.J.: Pearson Prentice Hall, 2004), 328.

7. Learning from Business Blunders Adapted from "QQ Me . . . But TC* :(," Trend Micro website [accessed 27 June 2007] www.trendmicro.com; Adam Horowitz, David Jacobson, Tom McNichol, and Owen Thomas, "The 101 Dumbest Moments in Business," *Business 2.0* [accessed 27 June 2007] www.business2.com.

Chapter 5

1. Exhibit 5.2, "Business Enterprise," *2007 Statistical Abstract of the United States*, 487.
2. Exhibit 5.3, "The Fortune 500," *Fortune* [accessed 2 July 2007] www.fortune.com. Copyright © 2006 Time Inc. All rights reserved.
3. Learning from Business Blunders Adapted from Ann Keeton, "Merger Mess Stalls US Airways Plans, Savings," *Chicago Tribune*, 1 July 2007 [accessed 2 July 2007] www.chicagotribune.com; Rick Stouffer, "After America West Merger, US Airways Flying Right," *Pittsburgh Tribune-Review*, 19 March 2006 [accessed 2 July 2007] www.pittsburghlive.com; Dan Fitzpatrick, "Bumpy Start to Deal: America West Pilots Angry as Talks Near," *Pittsburgh Post-Gazette*, 21 June 2005 [accessed 2 July 2007] www.post-gazette.com.
4. Hey, Wanna Lose a Few Billion? Do We Have a Deal for You Adapted from "IBM Acquisition Performance—On Track," IBM website [accessed 1 July 2007] www.ibm. com; "Spring Merger Fever," *Wall Street Journal*, 22

May 2007, A14; "The Contra Team," *Business 2.0*, April 2006, 83; Larry Selden and Geoffrey Colvin, "M&A Needn't Be a Loser's Game," *Harvard Business Review*, June 2003, 70–79; Amy Kover, "Big Banks Debunked," *Fortune*, 21 February 2000, 187–194; Erick Schonfeld, "Have the Urge to Merge? You'd Better Think Twice," *Fortune*, 31 March 1997, 114–116; Phillip L. Zweig et al., "The Case Against Mergers," *BusinessWeek*, 30 October 1995, 122–130; Kevin Kelly et al., "Mergers Today, Trouble Tomorrow?" *BusinessWeek*, 12 September 1994; "How to Merge," *The Economist*, 9 January 1999, 21–23; "Study Says Mergers Often Don't Aid Investors," *New York Times*, 1 December 1999, C9.

Chapter 6

1. Exhibit 6.1, http://my.estoresnw.com/countryheritagefarms . Used with permission from Country Heritage Farms.
2. Blueprint for an Effective Business Plan Adapted from "Top 10 Mistakes Entrepreneurs Make When Writing a Business Plan," *Inc.* [accessed 5 July 2007] www.inc.com; Michael Gerber, "The Business Plan That Always Works," *Her Business*, May/June 2004, 23–25; J. Tol Broome, Jr., "How to Write a Business Plan," *Nation's Business*, February 1993, 29–30; Albert Richards, "The Ernst & Young Business Plan Guide," *R & D Management*, April 1995, 253; David Lanchner, "How Chitchat Became a Valuable Business Plan," *Global Finance*, February 1995, 54–56; Marguerita Ashby-Berger, "My Business Plan—And What Really Happened," *Small Business Forum*, Winter 1994–1995, 24–35; Stanley R. Rich and David E. Gumpert, *Business Plans That Win $$$* (New York: Harper Row, 1985).
3. Learning from Business Blunders Adapted from "Amp'd Mobile Files for Bankruptcy," *Los Angeles Business*, 5 June 2007 [accessed 5 July 2007] www.bizjournals. com; Olga Kharif, "Amp'd Mobile Runs Out of Juice," *BusinessWeek*, 6 June 2007 [accessed 5 July 2007] www.businessweek.com.

Chapter 7

1. Learning from Business Blunders Adapted from "Effect of H&R Block Tax Blunder Unclear," CBS News, 24 February 2006 [accessed 9 July 2007] www.cbsnews.com; Peter K. Imber, "H&R Block Underreports Own Corporate Taxes," ABC News, 24 February [accessed 9 July 2007] http://abcnews.go.com.
2. Putting Accountability Back into Public Accounting Adapted from David Reilly and Jennifer Levitz, "PwC Sets Accord in Tyco Case," *Wall Street Journal*, 7 July 2007, A3; Daren Fonda, "Revenge of the Bean Counters," *Time*, 29 March 2004, 38–39; Greg Farrell and Andrew Backover, "Stage Is Set for Auditors, Management to Clash," *USA Today*, 20 February 2003 [accessed 9 May 2004] www.highbeam.com; Thomas A. Fogarty,

"Accounting Oversight Agency Targets Abusive Tax Shelters," *USA Today*, 21 November 2003, 3B; Janice Revell, "The Fires That Won't Go Out," *Fortune*, 13 October 2003, 139–142; Jeremy Kahn, "Do Accountants Have a Future?" *Fortune*, 3 March 2003, 115–116; David Henry and Mike McNamee, "Bloodied and Bowed," *BusinessWeek*, 20 January 2003, 56–57; "Auditors' Methods Make It Hard to Catch Fraud by Executives," *Wall Street Journal*, 8 July 2002, C1, C16; Thaddeus Herrick and Alexei Barrionuevo, "Were Auditor and Client Too Close-Knit?" *Wall Street Journal*, 21 January 2002, C1, C5; Jeremy Kahn, "One Plus One Makes What?" *Fortune*, 7 January 2002, 88–90; Nanette Byrnes, "Auditing Here, Consulting Over There," *BusinessWeek*, 8 April 2002, 34–36; Nanette Byrnes, "Accounting in Crisis," *BusinessWeek*, 28 January 2002, 42–48.
3. How to Read an Annual Report Adapted from Manual Schiffres, "All the Good News That Fits," *U.S. News and World Report*, 14 April 1998, 50–51; Janice Revell, "Decoded," *Fortune*, 25 June 2001, 176; "The P&L: Your Score Card of Profitability," *The Edward Lowe Report*, August 2001, 1–3.

Chapter 8

1. Exhibit 8.1, "Standard and Poor's Ratings Definitions," Standard and Poor's website [accessed 3 August 2007] www.standardandpoors.com; "Bond Ratings," Fidelity website [accessed 3 August 2007] www.fidelity.com.
2. Exhibit 8.4, Amy Feldman, "The Seedy World of Online Stock Scams," *Money*, February 2000, 143–148. Copyright © 2000 Time Inc. All rights reserved.
3. Exhibit 8.5, "Dow Jones Averages," Dow Jones Indexes [accessed 3 August 2007] www.djindexes.com. Used with permission from Dow Jones Indexes, www. djindexes.com.
4. Is an Index Fund Right for Your Financial Future? Adapted from "Index Funds," SEC website [accessed 2 May 2005] www.sec.gov; "The S&P 500 Index Fund" and "Index Fund Anatomy Lesson," Motley Fool [accessed 2 May 2005] www.fool.com; Bill Mann, "Index Funds: Still Your Best Bet," Motley Fool [accessed 2 May 2005] www.fool.com; Nathan Slaughter, "The Case Against Index Funds," Motley Fool [accessed 2 May 2005] www.fool.com; Meir Stratman, "Odds Say You Can't Beat Index Funds," MSN Money [accessed 2 May 2005] http://moneycentral. msn.com.
5. Learning from Business Blunders Adapted from Ben Silverman, "How Buffett Bounces Back," *BusinessWeek*, 2 July 2007 [accessed 2 August 2007] www.businessweek. com; Ben Silverman, "Buffett's Biggest Blunders," *BusinessWeek*, 2 July 2007

[accessed 2 August 2007] www.businessweek. com; Joshua Kennon, "Warren Buffett Biography," About.com [accessed 2 August 2007] www.about.com.

Chapter 9

1. Exhibit 9.1, Gary Armstrong and Philip Kotler, *Marketing: An Introduction*, 5th ed. (Upper Saddle River, N.J.: Pearson Prentice Hall, 2000), 5, Figure 1.1. Copyright © 2000. Reprinted by permission of Pearson Education, Inc., Upper Saddle River, N.J.
2. Exhibit 9.3, Gary Armstrong and Philip Kotler, *Marketing: An Introduction,* 5th ed. (Upper Saddle River, N.J.: Pearson Prentice Hall, 2000), 19. Copyright © 2000, p. 2. Reprinted by permission of Pearson Education, Inc., Upper Saddle River, N.J.
3. Exhibit 9.4, www.yahoo.com. Reproduced with permission of Yahoo! Inc. Copyright © 2007 by Yahoo! Inc. YAHOO! and the YAHOO! logo are trademarks of Yahoo! Inc.
4. Exhibit 9.6, Adapted from Dick Bucci, "Recording Systems Add More Depth when Capturing Answers," *Marketing News*, 1 March 2005, 50; Laurence Bernstein, "Enough Research Bashing!" *Marketing*, 24 January 2005, 10; Naresh K. Malhotra, *Basic Marketing Research,* (Upper Saddle River, N.J.: Pearson Prentice Hall, 2002), 110–112, 208–212, 228–229.
5. Exhibit 9.8, Gary Armstrong and Philip Kotler, *Marketing: An Introduction*, 5th ed. (Upper Saddle River, N.J.: Pearson Prentice Hall, 2000), 201. Copyright © 2000, p. 201. Reprinted by permission of Pearson Education, Inc., Upper Saddle River, N.J.
6. **Mining Your Deepest Secrets** Adapted from "Personal Information: Data Breaches Are Frequent, but Evidence of Resulting Identity Theft Is Limited; However, the Full Extent Is Unknown," *GAO Reports*, 5 July 2007, 1+; Scentric Launches Free Data Privacy Assessment Tool," DMReview.com, 22 February 2007 [accessed 6 August 2007] www.dmreview.com; Paul Magnusson, "They're Watching You," *BusinessWeek*, 24 January 2005, 22–23; Anick Jesdanun, "You're Being Followed—by Web Ads," *Seattle Times*, 14 June 2004 [accessed 14 June 2004] www.seattletimes.com; Harry R. Weber, "Tighter Regulation Sought for Data-Collection Industry," *Seattle Times*, 25 February 2005 [accessed 25 February 2005] www.seattletimes.com; Tom Zeller, "Breach Points Up Flaws in Security Laws," *New York Times*, 24 February 2005, C1, C6; Richard Behar, "Never Heard of Acxiom? Chances Are It's Heard of You," *Fortune*, 23 February 2004, 140–148; Linda Stern, "Is Orwell Your Banker?" *Newsweek*, 8 April 2002, 59; Mike France and Heather Green, "Privacy in an Age of Terror," *BusinessWeek*, 5 November 2001, 83–87; Amy Harmon, "F.T.C. to Propose Laws to Protect Children Online," *New York Times*, 4 June 1998,

C1, C6; Andrew L. Shapiro, "Privacy for Sale," *The Nation*, 23 June 1997, 11–16; Bruce Horovitz, "Marketers Tap Data We Once Called Our Own," *USA Today*, 19 December 1995, 1A–2A; Stephen Baker, "Europe's Privacy Cops," *BusinessWeek*, 2 November 1998, 49, 51.
7. **Learning from Business Blunders** Adapted from Pamela Paul, "It's Mind Vending," *Time*, 15 September 2003; Hallmark website [accessed 4 May 2004] www.hallmark.com; "Every Day, 10,000 Baby Boomers Turn 50; Nobody Said Getting Old Would Be Easy," *Seattle Post-Intelligencer*, 27 March 1997 [accessed 4 May 2004] www.highbeam.com.
8. **Questionable Marketing Tactics on Campus** Adapted from David Ellis, "Credit Card Tips for the College Graduate," CNNMoney.com, 24 May 2007 [accessed 6 August 2007] http://money.cnn.com; Kimberly E. Mock, "Good Credit Skills Are Essential for Georgia's College Students," *Athens Banner-Herald,* 23 February 2004 [accessed 4 May 2004] www.highbeam.com; Charles Haddad, "Congratulations, Grads— You're Bankrupt," *BusinessWeek*, 21 May 2001, 48; Christine Dugas, "Colleges Target Card Solicitors," *USA Today*, 12 March 1999, B1; Lisa Toloken, "Turning the Tables on Campus," *Credit Card Management*, May 1999, 76–79; "Credit Cards Given to College Students a Marketing Issue," *Marketing News*, 27 September 1999, 38.

Chapter 10

1. Exhibit 10.2, Adapted from Philip Kotler and Gary Armstrong, *Principles of Marketing,* 10th ed. (Upper Saddle River, N.J.: Pearson Prentice Hall, 2004), 279.
2. Exhibit 10.3, Adapted from Philip Kotler and Gary Armstrong, *Principles of Marketing,* 10th ed. (Upper Saddle River, N.J.: Pearson Prentice Hall, 2004), 330.
3. **Designing Safer Products** Adapted from Environmental Summit website [accessed 8 August 2007] www.environmentalsummit. org; Chris Ayres and Nicola Woolcock, "America in Rush to Ban Mini-Bikes as Teenage Racers Dice with Death," *Times* (UK), 19 March 2005 [accessed 15 April 2005] www.ebsco.com; Dan Deitz, "A Wider Margin of Safety," *Mechanical Engineering*; March 1995, 68+; Lanny Berke, "Designing Safer Products," *Machine Design*, 17 March 2005, 61; Formula 1 website [accessed 15 April 2005] www.formula1.com.
4. **Learning from Business Blunders** Adapted from Kryptonite Locks website [accessed 8 August 2007] www.kryptonitelocks.com; BikeForums.net [accessed 16 April 2005] www.bikeforums.net; Hannah Hickey, "Many Monterey County, Calif., Cyclists Unaware of Lock Scare," *Monterey County Herald*, 4 October 2004 [accessed 16 April 2005] www.ebsco.com; J.J. Jensen,

"Massachusetts-Based Bike-Lock Maker to Offer Customers Free Upgrades," *Seattle Times*, 23 September 2004 [accessed 16 April 2005] www.ebsco.com.
5. **Ringing Up Business in Creative New Ways** Adapted from Hands-On Mobile website [accessed 8 August 2007] www.hands-on.com; Jyoti Thottam, "How Kids Set the (Ring) Tone," Time, 4 April 2005, 40+; Zingy website [accessed 8 August 2007] www.zingy.com; EA Mobile website [accessed 8 August 2007] www.eamobile. com; "Battling for Mobile iTunes," Om Malik on Broadband (blog), 14 March 2005 [accessed 16 April 2005] www.gigaom.com.

Chapter 11

1. Exhibit 11.1, Adapted from Philip Kotler, *Marketing Management*, 10th ed. (Upper Saddle River, N.J.: Pearson Prentice Hall, 2000), 491.
2. Exhibit 11.3, Used with permission from FramesDirect.com.
3. Exhibit 11.7, (Top) Reprinted by permission of Premier Building Systems; (Middle) Reprinted by permission of Whirlpool Corporation; (Bottom) Copyright © DeBeers group and The Diamond Trading Company Limited. Reproduced with permission.
4. **Learning from Business Blunders** Adapted from Evite website [accessed 6 May 2004] www.evite.com; "Desktop," *Rocky Mountain News* (Denver), 1 September 2003 [accessed 6 May 2004] www.highbeam.com; Adam Horowitz, Mark Athitakis, Mark Lasswell, and Owen Thomas, "The 101 Dumbest Moments in Business," *Business 2.0* [accessed 6 May 2004] www.business2.com.
5. **Hey! Where Did Everybody Go?** Adapted from Mike Drexler, "Media Midlife Crisis: The Changes are Monumental," *Adweek*, 9 February 2004 [accessed 6 May 2004] www.highbeam.com; Kevin J. Delaney and Robert A. Guth, "Beep. Foosh. Buy Me. Pow." *Wall Street Journal*, 8 April 2004, B1, B7; Stuart Elliot, "Advertising," *New York Times*, 14 April 2004, C8; Melanie Wells, "Kid Nabbing," *Forbes*, 2 February 2004, 84–88; Kimberly Palmer, "Highway Ads Take High-Tech Turn," *Wall Street Journal,* 13 September 2003, B5; Brian Hindo, "Ad Space," *Business Week*, 12 January 2004, 14; Ellen Neuborne, "Dude, Where's My Ad?" *Inc.*, April 2004, 56–57; Erin White, "Look Up for New Products in Aisle 5," *Wall Street Journal*, 23 March 2004, B11; Ronald Grover, "Can Mad Ave. Make Zap-Proof Ads?" *BusinessWeek*, 2 February 2004, 36.

Chapter 12

1. Exhibit 12.3, Adapted from Kodak website [accessed 10 August 2007] www.kodak. com. Used with permission from Eastman Kodak Company.
2. Exhibit 12.4, Adapted from Fred Vogelstein, "Mighty Amazon," *Fortune*, 26 May 2003, 60–74; Stuart Crainer, "The 75

Greatest Management Decisions Ever Made," *Management Review*, November 1998, 17–23.

3. Exhibit 12.6, Adapted from and reprinted by permission of Harvard Business Review. From "How to Choose a Leadership Pattern" by Robert Tannenbaum and Warren H. Schmidt, May-June 1973. Copyright © 1973 by the Harvard Business School Publishing Corporation, all rights reserved.

4. Do You Have What It Takes to Be a Leader? Adapted from Peter F. Drucker, "What Makes an Effective Executive," *Harvard Business Review*, June 2004, 58–63; Nicholas Varchaver, "Glamour! Fortune! Org Charts!" *Fortune*, 15 November 2004, 136–148; Carl Robinson, "What They Don't Teach You at Harvard or Kindergarten," *Puget Sound Business Journal*, 16–22 July 2004, 29; Alison Stein Wellner, "Who Can You Trust?" *Inc.*, October 2004, 39–40; Michael C. Mankins, "Stop Wasting Valuable Time," *Harvard Business Review*, September 2004, 58–65; Larry Bossidy and Ram Charan, "Confronting Reality," *Fortune*, 18 October 2004, 225–231.

5. Creating the Ideal Culture in Your Company Adapted from Andrew Bird, "Do You Know What Your Corporate Culture Is?" *CPA Insight*, February, March 1999, 25–26; Gail H. Vergara, "Finding a Compatible Corporate Culture," *Healthcare Executive*, January/February 1999, 46–47; Hal Lancaster, "To Avoid a Job Failure, Learn the Culture of a Company First," *Wall Street Journal*, 14 July 1998, B1.

6. Learning from Business Blunders Adapted from Richard Pérez-Peña and Matthew L. Wald, "Basic Failures by Ohio Utility Set Off Blackout, Report Finds," *New York Times*, 20 November 2003, A1; "US Blackout: Interim Report," *Power Economics*, January 2004, 9; Edward Iwata, "Report: Major Blackout Could Have Been Prevented," *USA Today*, 6 April 2004, A1.

Chapter 13

1. Exhibit 13.8, *Herzberg's Two-Factory Theory of Management*, 4th ed., by Richard L. Daft, 1997. Used with the permission of South-Western, a division of Thomson Learning. All rights reserved.

2. Exhibit 13.9, Adapted from Stephen P. Robbins and David A. DeCenzo, *Fundamentals of Management*, 4th ed. (Upper Saddle River, N.J.: Pearson Prentice Hall, 2004), 289.

3. Learning from Business Blunders Adapted from Clayton M. Christensen and Michael E. Raynor, "Why Hard-Nosed Executives Should Care About Management Theory," *Harvard Business Review*, September 2003, 67–74; Martha McKay, "Lucent Turns Its First Profit in 14 Quarters," *The Record* (Bergen County, N.J.),

23 October 2003 [accessed 14 April 2004] www.highbeam.com.

4. Which Theory Will Solve the Problem of Employee Theft? Adapted from "Common-Sense Measures Preventing Employee Theft," SBA website [accessed 11 August 2007] www.sba.gov; "Embezzlement/Employee Theft," *Business Credit*, February 2005, 41–42; "Shrink Is Shrinking—But So Are the Loss-Prevention Budgets," *IOMA's Security Director's Report*, December 2004, 7–11; James E. Merklin, "Thieves at Work," *Industrial Distribution*, September 2004, 53–54.

Chapter 14

1. Exhibit 14.1, Adapted from Henry R. Cheeseman, *Contemporary Business and E-Commerce Law*, 4th ed. (Upper Saddle River, N.J.: Pearson Prentice Hall, 2003), 628–631.

2. Exhibit 14.6, Adapted from Sarah Rubenstein, "Keeping Coverage," *Wall Street Journal*, 24 January 2005, R5; "Multiple Employer Initiatives: Working for Better Health Care," *HRFocus*, July 2004, 11–15; Traci Purdum, "Health Care for All," *IndustryWeek*, August 2004, 12; Milt Freudenheim, "60 Companies Plan to Sponsor Health Coverage for Uninsured," *New York Times*, 27 January 2005, C1, C17; Michelle Rafter, "The Insider: Health Care Benefits," *Workforce Management*, December 2004, 72; Maryann Hammers, "Sliding-Scale Plans Seeing a Renaissance," *Workforce Management*, January 2005, 22; Vanessa Fuhrmans, "One Cure for High Health Costs: In-House Clinics at Companies," *Wall Street Journal* 11 February 2005, A1, A8; Charlotte Huff, "The Insider: Health Benefits," *Workforce Management*, November 2004, 69–70; Eve Tahmincioglu, "Tackling the High Cost of Health Benefits Takes Some Creativity," *New York Times*, 26 August 2004, C6; Carrie Coolidge, "Saving for Your Health," *Forbes*, 13 December 2004, 240–244; Sara Horowitz, "Ensure They're Insured," *Harvard Business Review*, December 2004, 24; Kris Maher, "Popular . . . but Cheap," *Wall Street Journal*, 24 January 2005, R4.

3. Learning from Business Blunders Adapted from Steven Greenhouse, "Workers Assail Night Lock-Ins By Wal-Mart," *New York Times*, 18 January 2004, 1, 23; Steven Greenhouse, "Wal-Mart Raids by U.S. Aimed at Illegal Aliens," *New York Times*, 24 October 2003, A1, A19; Jeffrey E. Garten, "Wal-Mart Gives Globalism a Bad Name," *BusinessWeek*, 8 March 2004, 24; "Wal-Mart Suit Gets Class-Action Status in Massachusetts," *Wall Street Journal*, 19 January 2004, A2.

4. When Employees Turn on Each Other Adapted from Anne Fisher, "How to Prevent Workplace Violence," *Fortune*, 21 February

2005, 42; "How to Predict and Prevent Workplace Violence," *HRFocus*, April 2005, 10–11; "Threat Assessments Prove Effective and Curbing Violence," *IOMA Security Director's Report*, April 2005, 8–9; Tonya Vinas and Jill Jusko, "5 Threats That Could Sink Your Company," *IndustryWeek*, September 2004, 52+; Laila Karamally, "The Insider: Employee Assistance," *Workforce Management*, September 2004, 60–63; Stephanie Armour, "The Mind of a Killer," *USA Today*, 15 July 2004, A1–A2; Stephanie Armour, "Stopping a Killer," *USA Today*, 16–18 July 2004, A1, 62; Stephanie Armour, "Life After Workplace Violence," *USA Today*, 15 July 2004, 3B.

5. Somebody's Watching (and Listening and Reading and Monitoring and Recording) Adapted from Pui-Wing Tam, Erin White, Nick Wingfield, and Kris Maher, "Snooping E-Mail by Software Is Now a Workplace Norm," *Wall Street Journal*, 9 March 2005, B1, B3; TrueActive website [accessed 4 April 2005] www.winwhatwhere.com; Jon Swartz, "Boeing Scandal Highlights E-Mail Checks," *USA Today*, 11 March 2005 [accessed 3 April 2005] www.usatoday.com; John Schwartz, "Snoop Software Gains Power and Raises Privacy Concerns," *New York Times*, 10 October 2003 [accessed 4 April 2005] www.nytimes.com.

Appendix A

1. Exhibit A.1, Adapted from Bartley A. Brennan and Nancy Kubasek, *The Legal Environment of Business* (New York: Macmillan, 1988), 24; Douglas Whitman and John Gergacz, *The Legal Environment of Business*, 2nd ed. (New York: Random House, 1988), 22, 25.

2. Exhibit A.3, Adapted from Richard A. Brealely and Stewart C. Myers, *Principles of Corporate Finance*, 4th ed. (New York: McGraw-Hill, 1991), 761–765.

3. Exhibit A.4, BankruptcyData.Com [accessed 16 August 2007] www.bankruptcydata.com. Used with permission from New Generation Research, Inc.

Appendix B

1. Exhibit B.5, Adapted from Lawrence J. Gitman and Michael D. Joehnk, *Personal Financial Planning*, 10th ed. (Mason, Ohio: Thomson South-Western, 2005), 139–143; Jack R. Kapoor, Les R. Dlabay, and Robert J. Hughes, *Personal Finance*, 7th ed. (New York: McGraw-Hill/Irwin, 2004), 141; Arthur J. Keown, *Personal Finance: Turning Money into Wealth*, 3rd ed. (Upper Saddle River, N.J.: Prentice Hall, 2003), 150. Used with permission from New Generation Research, Inc.

2. (Choose to Save, page 393). Used with permission from Employee Benefit Research Institute.

3. (Investopedia.com, page 394). Used with permission from Investopedia.com.

Photo Credits

Prologue
xxxi   Mark Richards/PhotoEdit Inc.
xliii   Jon Feingersh/zefa/Corbis NY

Chapter 1
1   AP Wide World Photos
2, 23   AP Wide World Photos
13   Justin Sullivan/Getty Images, Inc.
17   Roy Ooms/Masterfile Corporation
19   Eric Larrayadieu/Getty Images, Inc./
    Stone Allstock
20   Mark Richards

Chapter 2
28   Steve Cole/Getty Images, Inc./
    Photodisc
29, 50   Frank May/AP Wide World Photos
40   Jeff Christensen/Landov LLC
43   Basel Action Network (BAN)
43   Scott Willson/Patagonia, Inc.
46   Gilles Mingasson/Getty Images,
    Inc./Liaison

Chapter 3
56   Susan Van Etten/PhotoEdit Inc.
57, 75   MTV Networks Africa
61   John Van Hasselt/Corbis NY
65   Ramon Espinosa/AP Wide World
    Photos
71   AP Wide World Photos
73   Mehdi Fedouach/Getty Images,
    Inc./Agence France Presse

Chapter 4
80   Peter Arnold, Inc.
81, 105   Carvin Customized Guitars
89   Macduff Everton/Corbis/Bettmann
93   Jeff Morgan/Alamy Images
98   Bernd Auers

Chapter 5
110   Jose L. Pelaez/Corbis/Stock Market
111, 128   R. Magunia/Joker/SV-Bilderdienst/
    The Image Works
113   Jonny Crawford/The Image Works
116   Rudi Von Briel/PhotoEdit Inc.
120   AP Wide World Photos
120   Gary Rothstein/Corbis/Sygma
123   Joe Pugliese/Corbis/Bettmann

Chapter 6
133   Masterfile Corporation
134, 152   Nancy Pierce Photographer
135   Mamoru Tsukada/Aria Pictures
138   Namas Bhojani
143   Subway Restaurants/DAI
147   Tim Barnwell/Native Ground
    Music
151   Thomas Michael Alleman

Chapter 7
158   B. Kraft/Corbis/Sygma
159, 180   Rich Frishman Photography and
    Videograph Inc.
164   AP Wide World Photos
167   Norbert Schewerin/The Image
    Works
177   Michael Newman/PhotoEdit Inc.

Chapter 8
186   John Stuart/Creative
    Eye/MIRA.com
187, 208   Bill Aron/PhotoEdit Inc.
190   Ariel Skelley/Corbis/Bettmann
192   Ariel Skelley/Corbis NY
197   Alan Schein Photography/Corbis
    NY

Chapter 9
213   Leland Bobbe/Corbis NY
214, 237   Reuters Limited
216   AP Wide World Photos
221   Mary Kate Denny/PhotoEdit Inc.
227   G. Fabiano/Sipa Photos/Newscom

Chapter 10
242   AP Wide World Photos
243, 263   Suzanne Dunn/The Image Works
251   David R. Frazier Photolibrary, Inc.
252   Sarah-Maria Vischer/The Image
    Works
256   Colgate-Palmolive Company
257   Spencer Grant/PhotoEdit Inc.
260   Norbert von Groeben/The Image
    Works

Chapter 11
268   The Image Works
269, 291   Mark Richards/PhotoEdit Inc.
274   Mark Matson Photography
277   AP Wide World Photos

278   Chris Salvo/Getty Images, Inc./
    Taxi
282   Peter Hvizdak/The Image Works
286   Michael Newman/PhotoEdit Inc.

Chapter 12
296   Jon Feingersh/Corbis Zefa
    Collection
297, 316   Wegmans Food Markets, Inc.
298   Peter Endig/DPA/Landov LLC
303   Felicia Martinez/PhotoEdit Inc.
307   David McNew/Getty Images, Inc./
    Hulton Archive Photos
309   Hayley Murphy Photography

Chapter 13
321   John Henley/Corbis/Bettmann
322, 343   Joe McDonald
328   Carsten Koall/The Image Works
330   Lockyer, Romilly/Getty Images,
    Inc./Image Bank
333   Christopher Bissell/Getty Images,
    Inc./Stone Allstock
335   Edward Bock/Corbis NY

Chapter 14
349, 374   Michael Newman/PhotoEdit
    Inc.
350   Michael Krasowitz/Getty Images,
    Inc./Taxi
351   Tom McCarthy/PhotoEdit Inc.
352   Jeff Greenberg/Omni-Photo
    Communications, Inc.
364   Jeff Greenberg/The Image
    Works
367   Bob Breidenbach/krt
    photos/NewsCom
372   Fred Greaves/Reuters/Corbis NY
348   Rob Lewine/Corbis NY

Appendix A
379   AGE Fotostock America, Inc.
383   Ed Quinn/Corbis NY
384   Frank May/Corbis NY

Appendix B
388   Rob Lewine/Corbis NY
395   George H. Long/Creative
    Eye/MIRA.com
397   LWA-DannTardif/Corbis NY

Glossary

401(k) plan A defined contribution retirement plan in which employers often match the amount employees invest

absolute advantage A nation's ability to produce a particular product with fewer resources per unit of output than any other nation

accountability Obligation to report results and to justify outcomes that fall below expectations

accounting Measuring, interpreting, and communicating financial information to support internal and external decision making

accounting equation Basic accounting equation that assets equal liabilities plus owners' equity

accounts payable Short-term credit or debt amounts that a company owes its suppliers; the company's "bills" in other words

accounts receivable Amounts that are currently due to a company

accounts receivable turnover ratio Measure of time a company takes to turn its accounts receivable into cash, calculated by dividing sales by the average value of accounts receivable for a period

accrual basis Accounting method in which revenue is recorded when a sale is made and expense is recorded when it is incurred

acquisition Form of business combination in which one company buys another company's voting stock

activity ratios Ratios that measure the effectiveness of the firm's use of its resources

administrative law Rules, regulations, and interpretations of statutory law set forth by administrative agencies and commissions

administrative skills Technical skills in information gathering, data analysis, planning, organizing, and other aspects of managerial work

advertising Paid, nonpersonal communication to a target market from an identified sponsor using mass communications channels

affirmative action Activities undertaken by businesses to recruit and promote members of groups whose economic progress had

been hindered through either legal barriers or established practices

agency Business relationship that exists when one party (the principal) authorizes another party (the agent) to enter into contracts on the principal's behalf

arbitration Process for resolving a labor-contract dispute in which an impartial third party studies the issues and makes a binding decision

artificial intelligence Ability of computers to solve problems through reasoning and learning and to simulate human sensory perceptions

asset allocation Method of shifting investments within a portfolio to adapt them to the current investment environment and investor objectives

assets management accounts Cash management accounts offered by brokerage firms and mutual fund companies, frequently as a way to manage cash that isn't currently invested elsewhere

assets Any things of value owned or leased by a business or an individual

attrition Loss of employees for reasons other than termination

auction Selling method in which the price is set by customers bidding against each other

auction exchange Centralized marketplace where securities are traded by specialists on behalf of investors

audit Formal evaluation of the fairness and reliability of a client's financial statements

authority Power granted by the organization to make decisions, take actions, and allocate resources

autocratic leaders Leaders who do not involve others in decision making

automated teller machines (ATMs) Electronic terminals that permit people to perform basic banking transactions 24 hours a day without a human teller

balance of payments Sum of all payments one nation receives from other nations minus the sum of all payments it makes to other nations, over some specified period of time

balance of trade Total value of the products a nation exports minus the total value of the

products it imports, over some period of time

balance sheet (business) Statement of a firm's financial position on a particular date; also known as a *statement of financial position*; (personal) A summary of your assets and liabilities; the difference between the two subtotals is your net worth

balanced scorecard Method of monitoring the performance from four perspectives: finances, operations, customer relationships, and the growth and development of employees and intellectual property

bankruptcy Legal procedure by which a person or a business that is unable to meet financial obligations is relieved of debt

barrier to entry A critical resource or capability a company must possess before it can enter a particular market or industry

bear market Falling stock market

behavior modification Systematic use of rewards and punishments to change human behavior

behavioral segmentation Categorization of customers according to their relationship with products or response to product characteristics

benchmarking Collecting and comparing process and performance data from other companies

board of directors Group of people, elected by the shareholders, who have the ultimate authority in guiding the affairs of a corporation

bond Method of funding in which the issuer borrows from an investor and provides a written promise to make regular interest payments and repay the borrowed amount in the future

bonus Cash payment, in addition to regular wage or salary, that serves as a reward for achievement

bookkeeping Recordkeeping, clerical aspect of accounting

boycott Union activity in which members and sympathizers refuse to buy or handle the product of a target company

brand A name, term, sign, symbol, design, or combination of those used to identify the products of a firm and to differentiate them from competing products

brand equity The value that a company has built up in a brand

brand extension Applying a successful brand name to a new product category

brand loyalty The degree to which customers continue to purchase a specific brand

brand manager Managers who develop and implement a complete strategy and marketing program for specific products or brands

brand mark Portion of a brand that cannot be expressed verbally

brand names Portion of a brand that can be expressed orally, including letters, words, or numbers

breach of contract Failure to live up to the terms of a contract, with no legal excuse

break-even analysis Method of calculating the minimum volume of sales needed at a given price to cover all costs

break-even point Sales volume at a given price that will cover all of a company's costs

broker An expert who has passed specific tests and is registered to trade securities for investors

budget Planning and control tool that reflects expected revenues, operating expenses, and cash receipts and outlays

bull market Rising stock market

bundling Offering several products for a single price that is presumably lower than the total of the products' individual prices

business A profit-seeking organization that provides goods and services that a society wants or needs

business accelerator Similar in concept to an incubator but focused more on advisory services and (in some cases) financing

business agent Full-time union staffer who negotiates with management and enforces the union's agreements with companies

business cycles Fluctuations in the rate of growth that an economy experiences over a period of several years

business incubators Facilities that house small businesses and provide support services during the company's early growth phases

business law Those elements of law that directly influence or control business activities

business model A company's plan to generate sales revenue and earn a profit based on that revenue

business plan A written document that provides an orderly statement of a company's goals and a plan for achieving those goals

buying power The real value of money, adjusted for inflation; inflation raises prices, which in turn reduces buying power

cafeteria plans Flexible benefit programs that let employees personalize their benefits packages

calendar year Twelve-month accounting period that begins on January 1 and ends on December 31

capacity planning Establish the overall level of resources needed to meet customer demand

capital The physical, human-made elements used to produce goods and services, such as factories and computers; can also refer to the funds that finance the operations of a business

capital budgeting Process for evaluating proposed investments in select projects that provide the best long-term financial return

capital gains Return that investors receive when they sell a security for a higher price than the purchase price

capital investments Money paid to acquire something of permanent value in a business

capital-intensive businesses Businesses that require large investments in capital assets

capitalism Economic system based on economic freedom and competition

cash basis Accounting method in which revenue is recorded when payment is received and expense is recorded when cash is paid

cash management All of the planning and activities associated with managing your cash and other liquid assets

category killers Discount chains that sell only one category of products

cause-related marketing Identification and marketing of a social issue, cause, or idea to selected target markets

centralization Concentration of decision-making authority at the top of the organization

certified management accountants (CMAs) Accountants who have fulfilled the requirements for certification as specialists in management accounting

certified public accountants (CPAs) Professionally licensed accountants who meet certain requirements for education and experience and who pass a comprehensive examination

chain of command Pathway for the flow of authority from one management level to the next

channel conflict Disagreements between channel partners over pricing, product availability, and other distribution matters

checks Written orders that tell the user's bank to pay a specific amount to a particular individual or business

chief executive officer (CEO) Person appointed by a corporation's board of directors to carry out the board's policies and supervise the activities of the corporation

chief information officer (CIO) A high-level executive responsible for understanding the company's information needs and creating

systems and procedures to deliver that information to the right people at the right time

close the books The act of transferring net revenue and expense account balances to retained earnings for the period

closing costs Fees associated with buying and selling a house

coaching Helping employees reach their highest potential by meeting with them, discussing problems that hinder their ability to work effectively, and offering suggestions and encouragement to overcome these problems

co-branding Partnership between two or more companies to closely link their brand names together for a single product

code of ethics Written statement setting forth the principles that guide an organization's decisions

cognitive dissonance Tension that exists when a person's beliefs don't match his or her behaviors; a common example is *buyer's remorse*, when someone regrets a purchase immediately after making it

cohesiveness A measure of how committed the team members are to their team's goals

collective bargaining Process used by unions and management to negotiate work contracts

commercialization Large-scale production and distribution of a product

commission-based planners Financial advisers who are paid commissions on the financial products they sell you, such as insurance policies and mutual funds

commissions Employee compensation based on a percentage of sales made

committee Team that may become a permanent part of the organization and is designed to deal with regularly recurring tasks

common law Law based on the precedents established by judges' decisions

common stock Shares whose owners have voting rights and have the last claim on distributed profits and assets

communication mix Particular blend of personal selling, advertising, direct marketing, sales promotion, and public relations that a company uses to reach potential customers

communism Economic system in which the government owns and operates all productive resources and determines all significant economic choices

comparative advantage theory Theory that states that a country should produce and sell to other countries those items it produces most efficiently

compensation Money, benefits, and services paid to employees for their work

competition Rivalry among businesses for the same customer

competitive advantage Ability to perform in one or more ways that competitors cannot match

compounding The acceleration of balances caused by applying new interest to interest that has already accumulated

conceptual skills Ability to understand the relationship of parts to the whole

conflict of interest Situation in which a business decision may be influenced by the potential for personal gain

consent order Settlement in which an individual or organization promises to discontinue some illegal activity without admitting guilt

consideration Negotiated exchange necessary to make a contract legally binding

consolidation Combination of two or more companies in which the old companies cease to exist and a new enterprise is created

consumer market Individuals or households that buy goods and services for personal use

consumer price index (CPI) Monthly statistic that measures changes in the prices of about 400 goods and services that consumers buy

consumer promotion Sales promotion aimed at final consumers

consumerism Movement that pressures businesses to consider consumer needs and interests

contingent employees Nonpermanent employees, including temporary workers, independent contractors, and full-time employees hired on a probationary basis

contract Legally enforceable exchange of promises between two or more parties

controller Highest-ranking accountant in a company, responsible for overseeing all accounting functions

controlling Process of measuring progress against goals and objectives and correcting deviations if results are not as expected

convertible bonds Corporate bonds that can be exchanged at the owner's discretion into common stock of the issuing company

core competencies Functions in which a company has a distinct advantage over its competitors

corporate culture A set of shared values and norms that support the management system and that guide management and employee behavior

corporate governance In a broad sense, describes the policies, procedures, relationships, and systems in place to oversee the successful and legal operation of the enterprise; in a narrow sense, describes the responsibilities and performance of the board of directors

corporate social responsibility (CSR) The idea that business has obligations to society beyond the pursuit of profits

corporation Legally chartered enterprise having most of the legal rights of a person, including the right to conduct business, to own and sell property, to borrow money, and to sue or be sued; owners of the corporation enjoy limited liability

cost of goods sold Cost of producing or acquiring a company's products for sale during a given period

coupons Certificates that offer discounts on particular items and are redeemed at the time of purchase

credit In bookkeeping, an increase in assets

credit bureaus Businesses that compile credit information on businesses and individual consumers

credit cards Plastic cards that allow the user to buy now and repay the loaned amount at a future date

credit history A record of your mortgages, consumer loans, credit card accounts (including credit limits and current balances), and bill-paying performance

credit reports Reports generated by credit bureaus, showing an individual's credit usage and payment history

crisis management Procedures and systems for minimizing the harm that might result from some unusually threatening situations

critical path In a PERT network diagram, the sequence of operations that requires the longest time to complete

cross-functional teams Teams that draw together employees from different functional areas

currency Bills and coins that make up a country's cash money

current assets Cash and items that can be turned into cash within one year

current liabilities Obligations that must be met within a year

current ratio Measure of a firm's short-term liquidity, calculated by dividing current assets by current liabilities

customer buying behavior Behavior exhibited by consumers as they consider, select, and purchase goods and services

customer loyalty Degree to which customers continue to buy from a particular retailer or buy the products of a particular manufacturer or service provider

customer service Efforts a company makes to satisfy its customers to help them realize the greatest possible value from the products they are purchasing

customized production The creation of a unique good or service for each customer

damages Financial compensation to an injured party for loss and suffering

data Facts, numbers, statistics, and other individual bits and pieces that by themselves don't necessarily constitute useful information

data mining A method of extracting previously unknown relationships among individual data points in a database

database marketing Process of building, maintaining, and using customer databases for the purpose of contacting customers and transacting business

databases Computerized files that collect, sort, and cross-reference data

day order Any order to buy or sell a security that automatically expires if not executed on the day the order is placed

dealer exchange Decentralized marketplace where securities are bought and sold by dealers out of their own inventories

debentures Corporate bonds backed only by the reputation of the issuer

debit An increase in liabilities

debit cards Plastic cards that allow the bank to take money from the user's demand-deposit account and transfer it to a retailer's account

debt financing Acquiring funds through borrowing

debt ratios Ratios that measure a firm's reliance on debt financing of its operations (sometimes called *leverage ratios*)

debt-to-equity ratio Measure of the extent to which a business is financed by debt as opposed to invested capital, calculated by dividing the company's total liabilities by owners' equity

debt-to-total-assets ratio Measure of a firm's ability to carry long-term debt, calculated by dividing total liabilities by total assets

decentralization Delegation of decision-making authority to employees in lower-level positions

decision-making skills Ability to identify a decision situation, analyze the problem, weigh the alternatives, choose an alternative, implement it, and evaluate the results

deed Legal document by which an owner transfers the title, or ownership rights, to real property to a new owner

deductions Opportunities to reduce taxable income by subtracting the cost of a specific item, such as business expenses or interest paid on home mortgages

deflation Economic condition in which prices fall steadily throughout the economy

delegation Assignment of work and the authority and responsibility required to complete it

demand Buyers' willingness and ability to purchase products

demand curve Graph of the quantities of product that buyers will purchase at various prices

demand deposit Money that can be used by the customer at any time, such as checking accounts

democratic leaders Leaders who delegate authority and involve employees in decision making

demographics Study of statistical characteristics of a population

department stores Full-price retailers that sell clothing, housewares, furniture, and related items

departmentalization Grouping people within an organization according to function, division, matrix, or network

depreciation Accounting procedure for systematically spreading the cost of a tangible asset over its estimated useful life

devaluation A move by one government to drop the value of its currency relative to the value of other currencies

direct mail Advertising sent directly to potential customers, usually through the mail

direct marketing Direct communication other than personal sales contacts designed to effect a measurable response

discount pricing Offering a temporary reduction in price

discount stores Retailers that sell a variety of goods below the market price by keeping their overhead low

discretionary order Market order that allows the broker to decide when to trade a security

discrimination In a social and economic sense, denial of opportunities to individuals on the basis of some characteristic that has no bearing on their ability to perform in a job

distribution centers Warehouse facilities that specialize in collecting and shipping merchandise

distribution channels Systems for moving goods and services from producers to customers; also known as marketing channels

distribution mix Combination of intermediaries and channels a producer uses to get a product to final customers

distribution strategy Firm's overall plan for moving products to intermediaries and final customers

diversification Assembling investment portfolios in such a way that a loss in one investment won't cripple the value of the entire portfolio

diversity initiatives Programs and policies that help companies support diverse workforces and markets

dividends Distributions of corporate assets to shareholders in the form of cash or other assets

divisional structure Grouping departments according to similarities in product, process, customer, or geography

double-entry bookkeeping Way of recording financial transactions that requires two entries for every transaction so that the accounting equation is always kept in balance

dumping Charging less than the actual cost or less than the home-country price for goods sold in other countries

dynamic pricing Continually adjusting prices to reflect changes in supply and demand

earnings per share Measure of profitability calculated by dividing net income after taxes by the average number of shares of common stock outstanding

ecology Study of the relationships among living things in the water, air, and soil, their environments, and the nutrients that support them

e-commerce Short for *electronic commerce*; retailing through the Internet and other electronic channels such as mobile phone services

economic indicators Statistics that measure variables in the economy

economic system Means by which a society distributes its resources to satisfy its people's needs

economics The study of how society uses scarce resources to produce and distribute goods and services

economies of scale Savings from buying parts and materials, manufacturing, or marketing in large quantities

electronic business (e-business) Organization in which all major business functions take full advantage of the capabilities and efficiencies of information technology

electronic communication networks (ECNs) Computer-based trading networks that connect buyers and sellers without market makers or other intermediaries

electronic funds transfer systems (EFTS) Computerized systems for completing financial transactions

electronic performance monitoring (EPM) Real-time, computer-based evaluation of employee performance

embargo Total ban on trade with a particular nation (a sanction) or of a particular product

employee assistance programs (EAPs) Company-sponsored counseling or referral plans for employees with personal problems

employee benefits Compensation other than wages, salaries, and incentive programs

employee retention Efforts to keep current employees

employee stock-ownership plan (ESOP) Program enabling employees to become partial owners of a company

empowerment Granting decision-making and problem-solving authorities to employees so they can act without getting approval from management

engagement An employee's rational and emotional commitment to his or her work

enterprise resource planning (ERP) Materials and resource planning systems that encompass the entire organization

entrepreneurship The combination of innovation, initiative, and willingness to take the risks required to create and operate new businesses

equilibrium price Point at which quantity supplied equals quantity demanded

equity The portion of a house's current value that you own

equity financing Acquiring funds by selling shares of a company's stock

equity theory A theory that suggests employees base their level of satisfaction on the ratio of their inputs to the job and the outputs or rewards they receive from it

ethical dilemma Situation in which both sides of an issue can be supported with valid arguments

ethical lapse Situation in which an individual or group makes a decision that is morally wrong, illegal, or unethical

ethics The rules or standards governing the conduct of a person or group

ethnocentrism Judging all other groups according to your own group's standards, behaviors, and customs

euro A unified currency used by roughly half the nations in the European Union

exchange process Act of obtaining a desired object or service from another party by offering something of value in return

exchange rate Rate at which the money of one country is traded for the money of another

exclusive distribution Market coverage strategy that gives intermediaries exclusive rights to sell a product in a specific geographical area

exemptions Reductions to taxable income based on the number of dependents in the household

expectancy theory Suggests that the effort employees put into their work depends on expectations about their own ability to perform, expectations about likely rewards, and the attractiveness of those rewards

expenses Costs created in the process of generating revenues

exporting Selling and shipping goods or services to another country

express contract Contract derived from words, either oral or written

fair trade A voluntary approach to trading with artisans and farmers in developing countries, guaranteeing them above-market prices as a way to protect them from exploitation by larger, more-powerful trading partners

family branding Using a brand name on a variety of related products

fee-only planners Financial advisers who charge a fee for their services, rather than earning a commission on financial services they sell you

financial accounting Preparing financial information for users outside the organization

financial control The process of analyzing and adjusting the basic financial plan to correct for forecasted events that do not materialize

financial management Effective acquisition and use of money

financial plan A forecast of financial requirements and the financing sources to be used

first-line managers Those at the lowest level of the management hierarchy; they supervise the operating employees and implement the plans set at the higher management levels; also called supervisory managers

fiscal policy Use of government revenue collection and spending to influence the business cycle

fiscal year Any 12 consecutive months used as an accounting period

fixed assets Assets retained for long-term use, such as land, buildings, machinery, and equipment; also referred to as *property, plant, and equipment*

fixed costs Business costs that remain constant regardless of the number of units produced

flat organizations Organizations with a wide span of management and few hierarchical levels

flextime Scheduling system in which employees are allowed certain options regarding time of arrival and departure

foreign direct investment (FDI) Investment of money by foreign companies in domestic business enterprises

form utility Customer value created by converting raw materials and other inputs into finished goods and services

formal organization A framework officially established by managers for accomplishing the organization's tasks

franchise Business arrangement in which one business obtains rights to sell the goods or services of the supplier (franchisor)

franchisee Small-business owner who contracts for the right to sell goods or services of the supplier (franchisor) in exchange for some payment

franchisor Supplier that grants a franchise to an individual or group (franchisee) in exchange for payments

free riders Team members who do not contribute sufficiently to the group's activities because members are not being held individually accountable for their work

free trade International trade unencumbered by restrictive measures

free-market system Economic system in which decisions about what to produce and in what quantities are decided by the market's buyers and sellers

functional structure Grouping workers according to their similar skills, resource use, and expertise

functional teams Teams whose members come from a single functional department and that are based on the organization's vertical structure

gain sharing Plan for rewarding employees not on the basis of overall profits but in relation to achievement of goals such as cost savings from higher productivity

Gantt chart A type of bar chart used for project or process scheduling

general expenses Operating expenses, such as office and administrative expenses, not directly associated with creating or marketing a good or a service

general obligation bond Municipal bond that is backed by the government's authority to collect taxes

general partnership Partnership in which all partners have the right to participate as co-owners and are individually liable for the business's debts

generally accepted accounting principles (GAAP) Professionally approved U.S. standards and practices used by accountants in the preparation of financial statements

generic products Products characterized by a plain label, with no advertising and no brand name

geodemographics Method of combining geographical data with demographic data to develop profiles of neighborhood segments

geographic segmentation Categorization of customers according to their geographical location

glass ceiling Invisible barrier attributable to subtle discrimination that keeps women out of the top positions in business

global warming A gradual rise in average temperatures around the planet; caused by increases in carbon dioxide emissions

globalization Tendency of the world's economies to act as a single interdependent economy

goal Broad, long-range target or aim

goal-setting theory Motivational theory suggesting that setting goals can be an effective way to motivate employees

goods-producing businesses Businesses that produce tangible products

green marketing Efforts by companies to distinguish themselves by practicing sustainable development and communicating these efforts to consumers

gross domestic product (GDP) Value of all the final goods and services produced by businesses located within a nation's borders; excludes receipts from overseas operations of domestic companies

gross national product (GNP) Value of all the final goods and services produced by domestic businesses that includes receipts from overseas operations and excludes receipts from foreign-owned businesses within a nation's borders

gross profit Amount remaining when the cost of goods sold is deducted from net sales; also known as *gross margin*

holding company Company that owns most, if not all, of another company's stock but does not actively participate in the management of that other company

hostile takeovers Situations in which an outside party buys enough stock in a corporation to take control against the wishes of the board of directors and corporate officers

human resources All the people who work for an organization

human resources management (HRM) Specialized function of planning how to obtain employees, oversee their training, evaluate them, and compensate them

hybrid structure Structure that combines elements of functional, divisional, matrix, and network organizations

hygiene factors In Herzberg's two-factor model, aspects of the work environment that are associated with dissatisfaction

identity theft Crimes in which thieves steal personal information and use it to take out loans and commit other types of fraud

implied contract Contract derived from actions or conduct

importing Purchasing goods or services from another country and bringing them into one's own country

incentives Cash payments to employees who produce at a desired level or whose unit (often the company as a whole) produces at a desired level

income and expense statement A listing of your monthly inflows (income) and outflows (expenses); also called an *income statement*

income statement Financial record of a company's revenues, expenses, and profits over a given period of time

inflation Economic condition in which prices rise steadily throughout the economy; the tendency of prices to increase over time

informal organization Networks of informal employee interactions that are not defined by the formal structure

information Useful knowledge, often extracted from data

information systems (IS) A collective label for all technologies and processes used to manage business information

information technology (IT) A generally accepted synonym for information systems; many companies use *IT* to refer to the department that manages information systems

initial public offering (IPO) A corporation's first offering of shares to the public

injunction Court order prohibiting certain actions by striking workers

insider trading The use of unpublicized information that an individual gains from the course of his or her job to benefit from fluctuations in the stock market

insight A deep level of understanding about a particular subject or situation

institutional advertising Advertising that seeks to create goodwill and to build a desired image for a company rather than to sell specific products

institutional investors Companies and other organizations that invest significant amounts of money, often funds entrusted to them by others

integrated marketing communications (IMC) Strategy of coordinating and integrating all communications and promotional efforts with customers to ensure greater efficiency and effectiveness

intellectual property Creative outputs with commercial value, such as design ideas, manufacturing processes, brands, artistic creations, computer programs, and chemical formulas

intensive distribution Market coverage strategy that tries to place a product in as many outlets as possible

intentional tort Willful act that results in injury

international law Principles, customs, and rules that govern the international relationships between states, organizations, and persons

interpersonal skills Skills required to understand other people and to interact effectively with them

inventory Goods and materials kept in stock for production or sale

inventory control Determine the right quantities of supplies and products to have on hand and tracking where those items are

inventory turnover ratio Measure of the time a company takes to turn its inventory into sales, calculated by dividing cost of goods sold by the average value of inventory for a period

investment portfolios Assortment of investment instruments

job analysis Process by which jobs are studied to determine the tasks and dynamics involved in performing them

job description Statement of the tasks involved in a given job and the conditions under which the holder of the job will work

job sharing Splitting a single full-time job between two employees for their convenience

job specification Statement describing the kind of person who would be best for a given job—including the skills, education, and previous experience that the job requires

joint venture Cooperative partnership in which organizations share investment costs, risks, management, and profits in the development, production, or selling of products

justice The resolution of ethical questions and other dilemmas in a manner that is consistent with generally accepted standards of right and wrong

just-in-time (JIT) Inventory management in which goods and materials are delivered throughout the production process right before they are needed

knowledge Expertise gained through experience or association

knowledge-based pay Pay tied to an employee's acquisition of knowledge or skills; also called competency-based pay or skill-based pay

labor federation Umbrella organization of national unions and unaffiliated local unions that undertakes large-scale activities on behalf of their members and that resolves conflicts between unions

labor unions Organizations of employees formed to protect and advance their members' interests

labor-intensive businesses Businesses in which labor costs are more significant than capital costs

laissez-faire leaders Leaders who leave the most instances of decision making up to employees, particularly concerning day-to-day matters

layoffs Termination of employees for economic or business reasons

leading Process of guiding and motivating people to work toward organizational goals

lean systems Manufacturing systems that maximize productivity by reducing waste and delays

leveraged buyouts (LBO) Situation in which individuals or groups of investors purchase companies primarily with debt secured by the company's assets

liabilities (business) Claims against a firm's assets by creditors; (personal) Amounts of money you owe

license Agreement to produce and market another company's product in exchange for a royalty or fee

licensing Agreement to produce and market another company's product in exchange for a royalty or fee

limit order Market order that stipulates the highest or lowest price at which the customer is willing to trade securities

limited liability companies (LLCs) Organizations that combine the benefits of S corporations and limited partnerships without the drawbacks of either

limited partnership Partnership composed of one or more general partners and one or more partners whose liability is usually limited to the amount of their capital investment

line of credit Arrangement in which the financial institution makes money available for use at any time after the loan has been approved

line organization Chain-of-command system that establishes a clear line of authority flowing from the top down

line-and-staff organization Line organization that adds functional groups of people who provide advice and specialized services

liquid assets Assets that can be quickly and easily converted to cash

liquidity The level of ease with which an asset can be converted to cash

liquidity ratios Ratios that measure a firm's ability to meet its short-term obligations when they are due

locals Relatively small union groups, usually part of a national union or a labor federation, that represent members who work in a single facility or in a certain geographic area

lockout Management tactic in which union members are prevented from entering a business during a strike

logistics The planning, movement, and flow of goods and related information throughout the supply chain

long-term liabilities Obligations that fall due more than a year from the date of the balance sheet

loss-leader pricing Selling one product at a loss as a way to entice customers to consider other products

macroeconomics The study of "big picture" issues in an economy, including competitive behavior among firms, the effect of government policies, and overall resource allocation issues

mail-order firms Companies that sell products through catalogs and ship them directly to customers

malware Short for *malicious software*; computer programs that are designed to disrupt websites, destroy information, or enable criminal activity

management Process of coordinating resources to meet organizational goals

management accounting Preparing data for use by managers within the organization

management by objectives (MBO) A motivational approach in which managers and employees work together to structure personal goals and objectives for every individual, department, and project to mesh with the organization's goals

management information system (MIS) Computer system that provides managers with information and support for making routine decisions

management pyramid Organizational structure comprising top, middle, and lower management

managerial roles Behavioral patterns and activities involved in carrying out the functions of management; includes interpersonal, informational, and decisional roles

mandatory retirement Required dismissal of an employee who reaches a certain age

manufacturing resource planning (MRP II) An expansion of MRP that links to a company's financial systems and other processes

margin trading Borrowing money from brokers to buy stock, paying interest on the borrowed money, and leaving the stock with the broker as collateral

market A group of customers who need or want a particular product and have the money to buy it

market indexes Measures of market activity calculated from the prices of a selection of securities

market order Authorization for a broker to buy or sell securities at the best price that can be negotiated at the moment

market segmentation Division of a diverse market into smaller, relatively homogeneous groups with similar needs, wants, and purchase behaviors

market share A firm's portion of the total sales in a market

marketable securities Stocks, bonds, and other investments that can be turned into cash quickly

marketing Process of planning and executing the conception, pricing, promotion, and distribution of ideas, goods, and services to create and maintain relationships

marketing concept Approach to business management that stresses customer needs and wants, seeks long-term profitability, and integrates marketing with other functional units within the organization

marketing mix The four key elements of marketing strategy: product, price, distribution, and promotion

marketing intermediaries Businesspeople and organizations that channel goods and services from producers to customers

marketing research The collection and analysis of information for making marketing decisions

marketing strategy Overall plan for marketing a product; includes the identification of target market segments, a positioning strategy, and a marketing mix

mass customization Manufacturing approach in which part of the product is mass produced and the remaining features are customized for each buyer

mass production The creation of identical goods or services, usually in large quantities

matching principle Fundamental principle requiring that expenses incurred in producing revenue be deducted from the revenues they generate during an accounting period

material requirements planning (MRP) Computer system that helps manufacturers get the correct materials where they are needed, when they are needed, without unnecessary stockpiling

materials handling Movement of goods within a firm's warehouse terminal, factory, or store

matrix structure Structure that uses functional and divisional patterns simultaneously

media Communications channels, such as newspapers, radio, and television

mediation Process for resolving a labor-contract dispute in which a neutral third party meets with both sides and attempts to steer them toward a solution

mentoring Experienced managers guiding less-experienced colleagues in nuances of office politics, serving as role models for appropriate business behavior, and helping to negotiate the corporate structure

merchant wholesalers Independent wholesalers that take legal title to goods they distribute

merger Combination of two companies in which one company purchases the other and assumes control of its property and liabilities

microeconomics The study of how consumers, businesses, and industries collectively determine the quantity of goods and services demanded and supplied at different prices

middle managers Those in the middle of the management hierarchy; they develop plans to implement the goals of top managers and coordinate the work of first-line managers

mission statement A statement of the organization's purpose, basic goals, and philosophies

monetary policy Government policy and actions taken by the Federal Reserve Board to regulate the nation's money supply

money Anything generally accepted as a means of paying for goods and services

monopolistic competition Situation in which many sellers differentiate their products from those of competitors in at least some small way

monopoly Market in which there are no direct competitors so that one company dominates

morale Attitude an individual has toward his or her job and employer

mortgage A loan used to purchase real estate

motivation The combination of forces that moves individuals to take certain actions and behaviors and avoid other actions or behaviors

motivators In Herzberg's two-factor model, factors that may increase motivation

multichannel retailing Coordinated efforts to reach customers through more than one retail channel

multinational corporations (MNCs) Companies with operations in more than one country

municipal bonds Bonds issued by city, state, and government agencies to fund public services

mutual funds Financial organizations pooling money to invest in diversified blends of stocks, bonds, or other securities

NASDAQ (National Association of Securities Dealers Automated Quotations) National over-the-counter securities trading network

national brands Brands owned by the manufacturers and distributed nationally

national union Nationwide organization made up of local unions that represent employees in locations around the country

natural resources Land, forests, minerals, water, and other tangible assets usable in their natural state

need Difference between a person's actual state and his or her ideal state; provides the basic motivation to make a purchase

negligence Tort in which a reasonable amount of care to protect others from risk of injury is not used

negotiable instrument Transferable document that represents a promise to pay a specified amount

net income Profit earned or loss incurred by a firm, determined by subtracting expenses from revenues; also called the *bottom line*

net worth The difference between your assets and your liabilities

network structure Virtual organization in which a company relies on multiple external partners to complete its business model

news conference Gathering of media representatives at which companies announce new information; also called a press conference or press briefing

news release Brief statement or video program released to the press announcing new products, management changes, sales performance, and other potential news items

nongovernmental organizations (NGOs) Nonprofit groups that provide charitable services or promote social and environmental causes

nonprofit organizations Firms whose primary objective is something other than returning a profit to their owners

norms Informal standards of conduct that guide team behavior

objective Specific, short-range target or aim

oligopoly Market dominated by a few producers

online display advertising Larger visual and multimedia ads that appear on websites

open order Limit order that does not expire at the end of a trading day

operating expenses All costs of operation that are not included under cost of goods sold

operational plans Plans that lay out the actions and the resource allocation needed to achieve operational objectives and to support tactical plans

organization chart Diagram showing how employees and tasks are grouped and where the lines of communication and authority flow

organization structure Framework that enables managers to divide responsibilities, ensure employee accountability, and distribute decision-making authority

organizational market Businesses, nonprofit organizations, and government agencies that purchase goods and services for use in their operations

organizing Process of arranging resources to carry out the organization's plans

orientation programs Sessions or procedures for acclimating new employees to the organization

outsourcing Contracting out certain business functions or operations to other companies

overdraft fees Penalties charged against your checking account when you write checks that total more than your available balance

over-the-counter (OTC) market Network of dealers who trade securities on computerized linkups rather than a trading floor

owners' equity Portion of a company's assets that belongs to the owners after obligations to all creditors have been met; called shareholders' or stockholders' equity in publicly traded companies

parent company Company that owns most, if not all, of another company's stock and that takes an active part in managing that other company

participative management Philosophy of allowing employees to take part in planning and decision making

partnership Unincorporated business owned and operated by two or more persons under a voluntary legal association

pay for performance Incentive program that rewards employees for meeting specific, individual goals

penetration pricing Introducing a new product at a low price in hopes of building sales volume quickly

pension plans Generally refers to traditional, defined benefit retirement plans

performance appraisals Evaluations of employees' work according to specific criteria

permission marketing Promotional campaigns that send information only to those people who've specifically asked to receive it

permission-based marketing Marketing approach in which firms first ask permission to deliver messages to an audience and then promise to restrict their communication efforts to those subject areas in which audience members have expressed interest

personal bankruptcy A condition in which a consumer is unable to repay his or her debts; depending on the type of bankruptcy, a court will either forgive many of the person's debts or establish a compatible repayment plan

personal property All property that is not real property

personal selling Personal communication between a seller and one or more potential buyers

persuasive advertising Advertising designed to encourage customers to try new products or to switch brands

philanthropy The donation of money, time, goods, or services to charitable, humanitarian, or educational institutions

physical distribution All the activities required to move finished products from the producer to the customer

picketing Strike activity in which union members march before company entrances to communicate their grievances and to discourage people from doing business with the company

place marketing Marketing efforts to attract people and organizations to a particular geographical area

place utility Customer value added by making a product available in a convenient location

planned system Economic system in which the government controls most of the factors of production and regulates their allocation

planning Establishing objectives and goals for an organization and determining the best ways to accomplish them

point-of-purchase (POP) display Advertising or other display materials set up at retail locations to promote products to potential customers as they are making their purchase decisions

positioning Using promotion, product, distribution, and price to differentiate a good or service from those of competitors in the mind of the prospective buyer

possession utility Customer value created when someone takes ownership of a product

power of attorney Written authorization for one party to legally act for another

preferred stock Shares that give their owners first claim on a company's dividends and assets after paying all debts

premiums Free or bargain-priced items offered to encourage customers to buy a product

price The amount of money charged for a product or service

price elasticity A measure of the sensitivity of demand to changes in price

price-earnings ratio Ratio calculated by dividing a stock's market price by its earnings per share over a 12-month period (usually the previous 12 months)

primary market Market where firms sell new securities issued publicly for the first time

principal Amount of money a corporation borrows from an investor through the sale of a bond

private brands Brands that carry the label of a retailer or a wholesaler rather than a manufacturer

private corporation Company owned by private individuals or companies

privatization The conversion of public ownership to private ownership

problem-solving team Informal team that meets to find ways of improving quality, efficiency, and the work environment

producer price index (PPI) A statistical measure of price trends at the producer and wholesaler levels

product Good or service used as the basis of commerce

product advertising Advertising that tries to sell specific goods or services, generally by describing features, benefits, and, occasionally, price

product liability The capacity of a product to cause harm or damage for which the producer or seller is held accountable

product life cycle Four basic stages through which a product progresses: introduction, growth, maturity, and decline

product line A series of related products offered by a firm

product mix Complete list of all products that a company offers for sale

production The creation of goods and services

production and operations management Overseeing all the activities involved in producing goods and services

production forecasts Estimates of future demand for a company's products

productivity The efficiency with which an organization can convert inputs to outputs

profit Money left over after expenses and taxes have been deducted from revenue generated by selling goods and services

profit sharing The distribution of a portion of the company's profits to employees

profitability ratios Ratios that measure the overall financial performance of a firm

program evaluation and review technique (PERT) A planning tool that managers of complex projects use to determine the optimal order of activities, the expected time for project completion, and the best use of resources

promotion Wide variety of persuasive techniques used by companies to communicate with their target markets and the general public

promotional strategy Statement or document that defines the direction and scope of the promotional activities that a company will use to meet its marketing objectives

property Rights held regarding any tangible or intangible object

protectionism Government policies aimed at shielding a country's industries from foreign competition

proxy Document authorizing another person to vote on behalf of a shareholder in a corporation

psychographics Classification of customers on the basis of their psychological makeup, interests, and lifestyles

public accountants Professionals who provide accounting services to other businesses and individuals for a fee

public corporation Corporation that actively sells stock on the open market

public relations Nonsales communication that businesses have with their various audiences (includes both communication with the general public and press relations)

pull strategy Promotional strategy that stimulates consumer demand, which then exerts pressure on wholesalers and retailers to carry a product

purchasing The acquisition of the raw materials, parts, components, supplies, and finished products required to produce goods and services

pure competition Situation in which so many buyers and sellers exist that no single buyer or seller can individually influence market prices

push strategy Promotional approach designed to motivate wholesalers and retailers to push a producer's products to end users

quality A measure of how closely a product conforms to predetermined standards and customer expectations

quality assurance A more comprehensive approach of companywide policies, practices, and procedures to ensure that every product meets quality standards

quality control Measuring quality against established standards after the good or service has been produced and weeding out any defective products

quality of work life (QWL) Overall environment that results from job and work conditions

quick ratio Measure of a firm's short-term liquidity, calculated by adding cash, marketable securities, and receivables, then dividing that sum by current liabilities; also known as the *acid-test ratio*

quotas Limits placed on the quantity of imports a nation will allow for a specific product

radio frequency identification (RFID) Inventory tracking system that uses small antenna tags attached to products or shipping containers and special sensors to detect the presence of the tags

ratio analysis Use of quantitative measures to evaluate a firm's financial performance

real property Land and everything permanently attached to it

rebates Postsales reductions in price; must be applied for by the purchaser

recession Period during which national income, employment, and production all fall

reconcile The process of comparing the balance you believe is in your account with the balance the bank believes is in your account

recovery Period during which income, employment, production, and spending rise

recruiting Process of attracting appropriate applicants for an organization's jobs

reinforcement theory A motivational approach based on the idea that managers can motivate employees by influencing their behaviors with positive and negative reinforcement

relationship marketing A focus on developing and maintaining long-term relationships with customers, suppliers, and distribution partners for mutual benefit

reminder advertising Advertising intended to remind existing customers of a product's availability and benefits

replacement chart A planning tool that identifies the most vital employees in the organization and information about their potential replacement

responsibility Obligation to perform the duties and achieve the goals and objectives associated with a position

retail theater Offering entertainment and education opportunities in addition to shopping

retailers Firms that sell goods and services to individuals for their own use rather than for resale

retained earnings The portion of shareholders' equity earned by the company but not distributed to its owners in the form of dividends

retirement plans Company-sponsored programs for providing retirees with income

return on investment (ROI) Ratio between net income after taxes and total owners' equity; also known as *return on equity*

return on sales Ratio between net income after taxes and net sales; also known as *profit margin*

revenue bond Municipal bond backed by revenue generated from the projects it is financing

revenues Amount earned from sales of goods or services and inflow from miscellaneous sources such as interest, rent, and royalties

S corporation Corporation with no more than 75 shareholders that may be taxed as a partnership; also known as a subchapter S corporation

salary Fixed cash compensation for work, usually by yearly amount; independent of the number of hours worked

sales promotion Wide range of events and activities (including coupons, rebates, contests, in-store demonstrations, free samples, trade shows, and point-of-purchase displays) designed to stimulate interest in a product

Sarbanes-Oxley Comprehensive legislation, passed in the wake of Enron and other scandals, designed to improve integrity and accountability of financial information

scientific management Management approach designed to improve employees' efficiency by scientifically studying their work

scrambled merchandising Strategy of adding products unrelated to a store's original product mix

search advertising Online ads that are linked to search engine results or website content

secondary market Market where subsequent owners trade previously issued shares of stocks and bonds

secured bonds Bonds backed by specific assets that will be given to bondholders if the borrowed amount is not repaid

securities Investments such as stocks, bonds, options, futures, and commodities

selective distribution Market coverage strategy that uses a limited number of outlets to distribute products

self-managed teams Teams in which members are responsible for an entire process or operation

selling expenses All the operating expenses associated with marketing goods or services

service businesses Businesses that perform useful activities for customers

sexism Discrimination on the basis of gender

sexual harassment Unwelcome sexual advance, request for sexual favors, or other verbal or physical conduct of a sexual nature within the workplace

shareholder activism Advocacy by individual or institutional shareholders, using their status as shareholders to influence management policies and decisions

shareholders Owners of a corporation

shop steward Union member and employee who is elected to represent other union members and who attempts to resolve employee grievances with management

short selling Selling stock borrowed from a broker with the intention of buying it back later at a lower price, repaying the broker, and keeping the profit

Six Sigma A quality management program that strives to eliminate deviations between the actual and desired performance of a business system

skills inventory A list of the skills a company needs from its workforce, along with the specific skills that individual employees currently possess

skim pricing Charging a high price for a new product during the introductory stage and lowering the price later

small business Company that is independently owned and operated, is not dominant in its field, and meets certain criteria for the number of employees or annual sales revenue

smart cards Cards with embedded computer chips that store bank account amounts and personal data

social audit Assessment of a company's performance in the area of social responsibility

social commerce The creation and sharing of product-related information among customers and potential customers

social media Electronic media that invite participation by the general public

socialism Economic system characterized by public ownership and operation of key industries combined with private ownership and operation of less-vital industries

sole proprietorship Business owned by a single individual

span of management Number of people under one manager's control; also known as span of control

specialty advertising Advertising that appears on various items such as coffee mugs, pens, and calendars, designed to help keep a company's name in front of customers

specialty store Store that carries only a particular type of goods

speculators Investors who make risky investment decisions in anticipation of making large profits quickly

stakeholders Individuals or groups to whom business has a responsibility

standards Criteria against which performance is measured

stare decisis Concept of using previous judicial decisions as the basis for deciding similar court cases

start-up companies New business ventures

statement of cash flows Statement of a firm's cash receipts and cash payments that presents information on its sources and uses of cash

statistical process control (SPC) Use of random sampling and control charts to monitor the production process

statistical quality control (SQC) Monitoring all aspects of the production process to see whether the process is operating as it should

statutory law Statute, or law, created by a legislature

stealth marketing The delivery of marketing messages to people who are not aware that they are being marketed to; these messages can be delivered by either acquaintances or strangers, depending on the technique

stereotyping Assigning a wide range of generalized attributes, which are often superficial or even false, to an individual based on his or her membership in a particular culture or social group

stock certificate Document that proves stock ownership

stock exchange Location where traders buy and sell stocks and bonds

stock options Contract allowing the holder to purchase or sell a certain number of shares of a particular stock at a given price by a certain date

stock split Increase in the number of shares of ownership that each stock certificate represents, at a proportionate drop in each share's value

stop order An order to sell a stock when its price falls to a particular point to limit an investor's losses

strategic alliance Long-term relationship in which two or more companies share ideas, resources, and technologies in order to establish competitive advantages

strategic CSR Social contributions that are directly aligned with a company's overall business strategy

strategic marketing planning The process of examining an organization's current marketing situation, assessing opportunities and setting objectives, then developing a marketing strategy to reach those objectives

strategic plans Plans that establish the actions and the resource allocation required

to accomplish strategic goals; they're usually defined for periods of two to five years and developed by top managers

strict product liability Liability for injury caused by a defective product when all reasonable care is used in its manufacture, distribution, or sale; no fault is assigned

strike Temporary work stoppage by employees who want management to accept their union's demands

strikebreakers Nonunion workers hired to replace striking workers

subsidiary corporations Corporations whose stock is owned entirely or almost entirely by another corporation

succession planning Workforce planning efforts that identify possible replacements for specific employees, usually senior executives

supply Specific quantity of a product that the seller is able and willing to provide

supply chain A set of connected systems that coordinates the flow of goods and materials from suppliers all the way through to final customers

supply chain management (SCM) The business procedures, policies, and computer systems that integrate the various elements of the supply chain into a cohesive system

supply curve Graph of the quantities that sellers will offer for sale, regardless of demand, at various prices

sustainable development Operating business in a manner that minimizes pollution and resource depletion, ensuring that future generations will have vital resources

system An interconnected and coordinated set of *elements* and *processes* that converts *inputs* to desired *outputs*

tactical plans Plans that define the actions and the resource allocation necessary to achieve tactical objectives and to support strategic plans

tall organizations Organizations with a narrow span of management and many hierarchical levels

target markets Specific customer groups or segments to whom a company wants to sell a particular product

tariffs Taxes levied on imports

task force Team of people from several departments who are temporarily brought together to address a specific issue

tax credits Direct reductions in your tax obligation

tax-deferred investments Investments such as 401(k) plans and IRAs that let you deduct the amount of your investments from your gross income (thereby lowering your taxable income); you don't have to pay tax on any of the income from these investments until you start to withdraw money during retirement

tax-exempt investments Investments (usually municipal bonds) whose income is not subject to federal income tax

team A unit of two or more people who share a mission and collective responsibility as they work together to achieve a common goal

technical skills Ability and knowledge to perform the mechanics of a particular job

telecommuting Ability to work from home or other remote locations using telecommunications technology

telemarketing Selling or supporting the sales process over the telephone

termination Process of getting rid of an employee through layoff or firing

test marketing Product-development stage in which a product is sold on a limited basis—a trial introduction

Theory X Managerial assumption that employees are irresponsible, are unambitious, and dislike work and that managers must use force, control, or threats to motivate them

Theory Y Managerial assumption that employees enjoy meaningful work, are naturally committed to certain goals, are capable of creativity, and seek out responsibility under the right conditions

Theory Z Leadership approach that emphasizes involving employees at all levels and treating them like family

time deposits Bank accounts that pay interest and require advance notice before money can be withdrawn

time utility Customer value added by making a product available at a convenient time

time value of money The increasing value of money as a result of accumulating interest

top managers Those at the highest level of the organization's management hierarchy; they are responsible for setting strategic goals, and they have the most power and responsibility in the organization

tort Noncriminal act (other than breach of contract) that results in injury to a person or to property

total quality management (TQM) A management philosophy and strategic management process that focuses on delivering the optimal level of quality to customers by building quality into every organizational activity

trade allowance Discount offered by producers to wholesalers and retailers

trade deficit Unfavorable trade balance created when a country imports more than it exports

trade promotions Sales-promotion efforts aimed at inducing distributors or retailers to push a producer's products

trade surplus Favorable trade balance created when a country exports more than it imports

trademarks Brands that have been given legal protection so that their owners have exclusive rights to their use

trade-off A decision-making condition in which you have to give up one or more benefits to gain other benefits

trading blocs Organizations of nations that remove barriers to trade among their members and that establish uniform barriers to trade with nonmember nations

transaction Exchange of value between parties

transparency The degree to which affected parties can observe relevant aspects of transactions or decisions

Treasury bills Short-term debt securities issued by the federal government; also referred to as *T-bills*

Treasury bonds Debt securities issued by the federal government that are repaid more than ten years after issuance

Treasury notes Debt securities issued by the federal government that are repaid within one to ten years after issuance

U.S. savings bonds Debt instruments sold by the federal government in a variety of amounts

Uniform Commercial Code (UCC) Set of standardized laws, adopted by most states, that govern business transactions

Universal Product Codes (UPCs) A bar code on a product's package that provides information read by optical scanners

unlimited liability Legal condition under which any damages or debts attributable to the business can also be attached to the owner because the two have no separate legal existence

utilitarianism A decision-making approach that seeks to create the greatest good for the greatest number of people affected by the decisions

utility Power of a good or service to satisfy a human need

value chain All the elements and processes that add value as raw materials are transformed into the final products made available to the ultimate customer

value webs Multidimensional networks of suppliers and outsourcing partners

variable costs Business costs that increase with the number of units produced

venture capitalists (VCs) Investors who provide money to finance new businesses or turnarounds in exchange for a portion of

ownership, with the objective of reselling the business at a profit

virtual teams Teams that use communication technology to bring geographically distant employees together to achieve goals

viruses Invasive programs that reproduce by infecting legitimate programs

vision A viable view of the future that is rooted in but improves on the present

wages Cash payment based on the number of hours the employee has worked or the number of units the employee has produced

wants Specific goods, services, experiences, or other entities that are desirable in light of a person's experiences, culture, and personality

warehouse Facility for storing inventory

warranty Statement specifying what the producer of a product will do to compensate the buyer if the product is defective or if it malfunctions

wheel of retailing Evolutionary process by which stores that feature low prices gradually upgrade until they no longer appeal to price-sensitive shoppers and are replaced by new low-price competitors

whistle-blowing The disclosure of information by a company insider that exposes illegal or unethical behavior by others within the organization

wholesalers Firms that sell products to other firms for resale or for organizational use

widgets Small software programs that provide part of the functionality of a website

will A legal document that specifies what happens to your assets, who will execute your estate (carry out the terms of your will), and who will be the legal guardian of your children, if you have any, in the event of your death

word of mouth Informal communication between customers and potential customers

work specialization Specialization in or responsibility for some portion of an organization's overall work tasks; also called division of labor

worker buyout Distribution of financial incentives to employees who voluntarily depart; usually undertaken in order to reduce the payroll

working capital Current assets minus current liabilities

work-life balance Efforts to help employees balance the competing demands of their personal and professional lives

Name/Organization/Brand/ Company Index

A

Accenture, 88
Actuate, 318
Acxiom, 220
Adelphia Communications, 387
Adobe Systems, 138
Agilent Technologies, 368
Airbus, 13, 58, 350
Albertson's, 119
Alca, 87
Alexander, Bill, 40
Alexander Book Company, 261
Alka-Seltzer Plus, 255
Allen, Robert, 338
Allergan, 243, 263
Altria Group, 118
AM General, 384
Amazon.com, 2, 5, 7, 71, 219, 272, 278, 302
America West, 123
American Airlines, 325, 352
American Express, 189
American Federation of Labor–Congress of Industrial Organizations (AFL-CIO), 370, 371
American Geophysical Union, 43
American Idol, 285
American Institute of Certified Public Accountants (AICPA), 162
American International Group, 118
American Marketing Association, 215, 240
American Red Cross, 4, 54–55
American Society for Quality (ASQ), 108
Ameriquest, 45–46
Amp'd Mobile, 146
Amy's Ice Creams, 131
Angoss, 239
AOL Time Warner, 124
Apple, 2, 13, 23, 151, 217, 277
aQuantive, 128
Arrington, Michael, 288
Arthur Andersen, 162
AssistiveTech.com, 377
Association for Enterprise Opportunity, 150
Audi, 329
Austin, Bob, 247
Avon, 216
Ayotte, Daniel, 147
Azua, Maria, 313

B

Ballmer, Steve, 159, 180
Bang & Olufsen, 245
Bank of America, 118, 123, 147
Barron's, 202
Barton, Clara, 54
Bed, Bath & Beyond, 272, 273
Beijing Television, 70
Berkshire Hathaway, 118, 200
Best Book Buys, 266
Best Buy, 229
Better Business Bureau, 54
Bezos, Jeff, 7
Bill and Melinda Gates Foundation, 180
Biocon, 137
BizXchange, 216
BMW, 92, 119, 231
BMW Motorcycles, 295
Body Glove, 109
Boeing, 13, 58, 90, 92, 329
Boone, Garrett, 322, 343
Boots, 353
Borden's ReaLemon, 384
Boston Globe, 21
Botox Cosmetic, 243, 263
Branson, Sir Richard, 138
Breeze card, 189
Brin, Sergey, 7, 111
British Airways, 257
Brunnings, Susannah, 222
Buffet, Warren, 200
Business 2.0, 148
Business Leadership Network, 377
Business Objects, 239, 318
BusinessIntelligence.com, 318
BusinessWeek, 148, 202
Buyer Persona, 240
Byrd, Virginia, 351

C

Calloway, 303
Campus Athletics, 107
Cape Cod Cooperative Bank, 338
Cardinal Health, 118
CarsDirect.com, 396
CareerBuilder.com, xxx
Carrefour, 71, 272
Carson, Rachel, 42
Carvin Guitars, 81, 93, 105–106
Caterpillar, 279
Catholic Church, 325

CBS, 378
Center for Collaborative Organization, 346
Centre for Science and Environment, 29, 50
CFO, 183
CFO IT, 183
Challenger, Gray & Christmas, 369
Chandler, Asa, 7
Charles Schwab, 187, 192, 208–209
CharlieCard, 189
Cheerios, 254
ChemConnect, 270
Chevron, 118
ChoicePoint, 220
Chondo, 135
Choose to Save, 393, 397
Chrysler, 251
Church of England, 32
Cigna, 309
CIO, 108, 183
Cirque du Soleil, 301
Citibank, 191
Citigroup, 74, 118
Claritas Corporation, 229
Clawson, James, 307
Clorox, 7
CNN, 302
CNN/Money.com, 203
Coastal Enterprises, 138
Cobalt Boats, 338
Coca-Cola, 7, 251, 285, 301, 302, 379
Cognos, 318
Coke, 29, 50
Colgate toothpaste, 256
College Entrepreneurs Organization, 138
College Nannies and Tutors, 138
CollegeGrad.com, xxv
CollegeRecruiter.com, xxx
Compaq Computer, 138
Computer Central Services, 167
Computerworld, 183
Connelly, Rachel, 367
ConocoPhillips, 118
Conseco, 387
Consumer Reports, 311
Container Store, The, 322, 343
Cooper, Cynthia, 34
Cooper, Peter, 150
Costco, 269, 272, 291
Country Heritage Farms, 137
Covisint, 270
Cox, Christopher, 164

CPAnet, 184
Creative Age Publications, 319–320
Crest toothpaste, 255
CRInfo, 346
Crowell, Joel G., 338
Cuban, Mark, 338

D
DaKAH, 237
Danaher, 123
dELiA*s, 217
del.icio.us, 5, 235, 287
Dell, 88, 138, 275, 302, 327
Dell, Michael, 302, 369
Deloitte & Touche, 34, 161
Delphi Corporation, 387
Delta & Pine Land Company, 14
Delta Airlines, 387
Desktop Factory, 265
Diamond Trading Company, 280
Dice.com, xxx
DiFranco, Ani, 135
Digg, 5, 235, 287
Diligence, 30
Dimension 3D Printing, 265
Diners Club, 302
Discman, 217
Disney, 73
Dix, Julie, 147
Dollar General, 272
Donahue-Arpas, Michelle, 134, 136, 152–153
Double Click, 111, 128
Dow Chemical, 44, 369
Drucker, Peter, 323
Dun & Bradstreet, 173

E
E*TRADE, 192, 208
EA Mobile, 250
Eastman, Michael, 135
eBay, 2, 261, 307
Efficient Frontier, 284
eHealth, 33
Eli Lily, 303
Enron, 33, 34, 162, 387
Enterprise Rent-A-Car, 368
Equifax, 220, 399
Erbsen, Wayne, 147
Ernst & Young, 161
Esnips, 20
ESPN, 255
Euronext, 198
eVenturing, 148
Evite, 279
Evolve24, 100, 288
eWeek, 183
Experian, 399
Exxon Mobil, 118

F
Facebook, 154, 287
Fair Labor Association, 49
FedEx, 98, 141, 151, 278
FedEx Ground, 134
FeedDigest, 150

Fellowforce, xxv
Fidelity Investments, 208
Financial Corp. of America, 387
First Executive Corporation, 387
First, Tom, 346
FirstEnergy, 312
Fisher-Price, 250
FleetBoston, 123
Flickr, 249
Forbes, 202
Ford, Henry, 229
Ford Motor, 118, 248, 251, 252, 301, 309, 311, 352
Fortune Small Business, 148
Fortune, 202
FramesDirect.com, 274
Friedman, Milton, 38, 39
Friendster, 20, 154

G
Gap, 48–49
Garten, Jeffrey, 356
Gates, Bill, 40, 74, 138, 159, 180
General Electric (GE), 44, 118, 122, 251, 366
General Mills, 253, 254
General Motors (GM), 87, 118, 237, 247, 251, 326, 384
GeniusBabies.com, 134, 136, 152–153
Giannulli, Mossimo, 303
Gladiator GarageWorks, 280
Global Crossing, 387
Global Healthcare Intelligence Platform, 99
Global Hyatt, 116
GMAC, 119
Goldman Sachs Group, 118
Goldstone, Steve, 46
Goleman, Daniel, 307
Google, 7, 13, 85–86, 111, 128, 125, 135, 138, 284, 357
Govender, Rogers, 32
Graham, Donald, 254
Great America amusement park, 53
Greenspan, Alan, 34

H
H&R Block, 160
Hallmark Cards, 116, 223
Hands-On Mobile, 250
Harley-Davidson, 252
Hatfield, Kathy, 367
Heckmann, Dick, 123
Heilbroner, Robert, 9
Herzberg, Frederick, 337
Hewlett-Packard. *See* HP
Hewlett, William, 138
HNC Software, 220
Holiday Inn, 302
Home Depot, 41, 73, 118, 120, 273
HomeLoanCenter.com, 397
Honda, 88, 232, 251, 302
Hoover's, 85
HP (Hewlett-Packard), 88, 118, 138, 301, 303, 312
Huberman, Bernard, 301
Hummer SUV, 384

Humvee, 384
Hyatt hotels, 116
Hydrogen Power, 299–300
Hyundai, 58

I
Iacocca, Lee, 247
IBM, 6, 67, 88, 118, 123, 126, 239, 251, 313, 353, 366
IKEA, 258
iLike, 288
IMDiversity, xxx
Inc., 148, 150
Inc.com, 131, 319
Indeed.com, xxx
Industry Week, 108
Inergy Automotive Systems, 328
Information Builders, 318
InformationWeek CFO, 183
Insightful, 239
Institute of Management Accountants, 161
Intel, 48, 151, 352
Intelligent Enterprise, 239
Interbrand, 251
Interfaith Center on Corporate Responsibility (ICCR), 120
Internet Healthcare Coalition, 33
Internship Programs.com, xxx
Intuit, 191
Investopedia 203, 394
Investors' Business Daily, 202
IPOC, 30
iPod, 2, 13, 23, 248
iRobot, 127
iTunes, 2, 13, 23

J
Jackson, Sophia, 395
Jacobsen, Dean and Darlene, 147
Japanese Streets, 58
JC Penney, 272
Jeep, 252
Jiffy Lube, 13
Jitterbug phone, 244
Jobs, Steve, 2, 23
Johnson & Johnson, 302
Jones, Jennifer, 240
Joyo, 71
J.P. Morgan Chase & Co., 118

K
K2 Sports, 123
Kane, Doug, 358
Kauffman eVenturing, 148
Keeley, Joseph, 138
Keen Footwear, 87
Kennedy, John F., 44
Kettle Valley Fruit Snack, 217
Khan, Shahrukh, 73
Kidrobot, 100
Kiernan, Matthew J., 44
Kiplinger's, 211
Knight, Philip, 7
Kodak, 300
Kohler, 117

Korn/Ferry International, xxxiv
Koyanagi, Risa, 135
KPMG, 30, 161
Kraft, 32
Kramer, Mark, 37, 40
Kroger, 272
Kryptonite locks, 248

L

Lanard Toys, 384
Land Rover, 252
Landes, Chuck, 162
Lands' End, 79
Lehman Brothers, 353
Lenovo, 252
LensCrafters, 217
LexisNexis, 220
Lexus, 229, 233–234
LG Electronics, 72
Limited, The, 7
LinkedIn, xxix, 155
Liveris, Andrew, 44
Liz Claiborne, 48
London Stock Exchange, 198
Looney Tunes, 252
Lotus Development, 138
Loughridge, Mark, 123
Louisiana Technology Park, 148
Lucent Technologies, 326
Luxottica, 123

M

Mac, Bernie, 135
MacHeads, 277
Mackey, John, 39
Management Assistance Program for
    Nonprofits, 319
Marcoux, Alexei, 39
Mark & Spencer, 126
Marketing Voices, 240
MarketingSherpa, 294
MarketWatch, 203
Marriott, 7, 40, 73
Marriott Marquis hotels, 255
Marriott, Willard, 7
Marshall's, 272
Marvel Enterprises, 298–299
Maslow, Abraham, 336
Massachusetts Bay Transportation
    Authority, 189
Mattel, 48
Mazumdar-Shaw, Kiran, 137, 138
MCCI, 266–267
McDonald's, 70, 101, 184, 256
McDowell, Ross, 149
McGregor, Douglas, 338
McKesson, 118
McNamara, Frank, 302
MCorp, 387
Megaputer Intelligence, 239
Meisburger, Dave, 218
Mercedes-Benz, 231, 167
Merrill Lynch, 118
Metropolitan Atlanta Rapid Transit
    Authority, 189

Microsoft, 14, 37, 40, 88, 128, 138, 147, 159,
    180, 239, 251, 285, 303, 366
Microsoft Windows, 14
Millennium Ecosystem Assessment, 43
Miller, Amy, 131
Mills, Mark H., 41
Mirant Corporation, 387
Mizrahi, Isaac, 303
Money, 211
Monsanto, 14
Monster.com, xxx, xxxi
MonsterTrak, xxx
Montgomery Ward, 273
Moody, 194
Mootry, Aisha, 308, 309
Morgan Stanley, 118
Morita, Akito, 302
Morningstar, 203
Motley Fool, 203, 212
Motorola, 43, 96, 250, 327
Mountain Dew, 230
MSN, 284
MSN Real Estate, 397
MTV, 146
MTV Base Africa, 57, 75–76
Mulally, Alan, 301, 309, 311
MyBabyShops.com, 152
MySpace, 20, 32, 101, 154, 287

N

Nabisco, 32, 252
Nantucket Nectars, 346–347
Narain, Sunita, 29, 50
National Association of Securities Dealers
    Automated Quotations (NASDAQ),
    197, 204
National Basketball Association (NBA),
    250, 338
National Business Incubation Association,
    148
National Consumers League, 54
National Council on Alcoholism and Drug
    Dependence, 368
National Credit Union Association, 191
National Foundation for Credit Counseling,
    399
National Fraud Information Center, 54
Native Ground Books and Music, 147
Nesbit, Robert, xxxiv
NetJets, 229
Net-Temps, xxx
New York Stock Exchange (NYSE), 197, 198,
    211–212
Nidetch, Jean, 302
Nigam, Hemanshu, 32
Nike, 7, 48, 49, 251, 303
Nike outlet stores, 272
Nikon, 248
Ning, 20, 288
Nokia, 43, 350
Nolo, 131
Nooyi, Indra, 29, 51
Nordstrom, 272, 311
Nordstrom Rack, 272
Northwest Airlines, 47

O

Oakley, 123
O'Connor, Kelly, 241
Office Depot, 272
Okosi, Alex, 57, 75
One Equity Partners, 385
Oracle, 239, 318
Ouchi, William, 338
Oxley, Michael, 164

P

Pacific Gas and Electric, 387
Packard, David, 138
Page, Larry, 7, 111
Partovi, Ali, 288
Patagonia, 43, 48
Payless, 73, 272
Pemberton, John, 7
PepsiCo, 29, 50, 231
Pepsi-Cola, 73
Pinchot, Gifford, 136
Podcast Alley, xxviii
Polaroid, 385
Porsche, 92, 231, 298
Portfolios.com, xxv
Porter, Michael, 37, 40, 86
Pottruck, David, 187, 208
Premiere Building Systems, 280
Priceline.com, 261
PricewaterhouseCoopers, 161, 162
Procter & Gamble, 31, 118, 285
Progressive Insurance, 218
Project on Emerging Nanotechnologies, 107
Prudential Financial, 244
Pure Logicol, 263

Q

QuickBooks, 191
Quicken, 191
Quinn, Jane Bryant, 172

R

Raytheon, 249
ReaLemon, 384
RealNetworks, 2, 217
Real-Time Updates, xv–xvi
Reebok, 48
Refco, 387
Rehabilitation Engineering and Assistive
    Technology Association of North
    America, 377
REI.com, 272
Revella, Adele, 240
Rhapsody, 217
Right Media, 111, 128
Riley Guide, xxix, xxx
RJR Nabisco, 46
Robert Morris Associates, 173
Roche Laboratories, 99
Rolls Royce, 247
RRSat Global Communications
    Network, 164
Rubbersidewalks, 135, 151
Ryanair, 260
Ryze, xxix, 148, 155

S

Safeway, 272
Saks Fifth Avenue, 274
Salary.com, 378, 397
salaryexpert.com, 397
Sam's Club, 272
Samsung Jitterbug, 244
SAP, 318
SAS, 239, 318
Saturn, 237, 326
Schmidt, Eric, 128
Schultz, Howard, 349, 374
Schwab, Charles, 208–209
Scion, 214, 229, 230, 233, 237
Scott, David Meerman, 31, 287
Scott, Tom, 346
Sears, 239, 252, 272, 273
Service Corps of Retired Executives
      (SCORE), 147
Service Employees International Union, 372,
      373
7-Eleven, 98, 272
Sharper Image, 266
Showtime Networks, 378
Silicon Graphics, 138
SimplyHired.com, xxx
Sinegal, Jim, 269
Singapore Airlines, 248
Skechers USA, 240–241
Skype, 100
Smart Money, 211
Smith, Adam, 7
Smith, Fred, 141
Smith, Lindsay, 135, 151
Sony, 217, 302
Southwest Airlines, 13, 87, 126, 229, 311,
      325, 357
Sozzi, Ray, 156
Specific Media, 111
Spirit AeroSystems, 87
Spivak, Katy, 234
Spoke, 155
SPSS, 239
Standard & Poor's, 194
Staples, 273
Starbucks, 349, 374–375
StartSmart, 138
Steenland, Doug, 47
Stratasys, 265
Street, The, 203
Student Advantage, 156
Stuppin, Bonnie, 261
Subway, 143
Sub-Zero refrigerators, 276
Sun Microsystems, 138, 353
SunDisk, 257
SunTrust, xl
Supervalu, 270

T

Taggies, 147
Tanner, Craig, 139

Tapestry Partners, 308, 309
Target, 5, 272, 273, 291, 303
Taser International, 127
Taurus, 248
TaxCut, 401
Taylor, Frederick W., 336
TaylorMade, 303
TD Ameritrade, 208
Technorati, xxviii
Telegram & Gazette (Worcester, MA), 21
Telework Coalition, 345
Templin, Mark, 214, 231
Tendulkar, Sachin, 73
Teva, 87
Texaco, 387
Texas Instruments, 352
Thames Water, 40
Thompson, Samuel, 126
Thurow, Lester, 9
Time Warner. *See* AOL Time Warner
Tindell, Kip, 322, 343
Tinkler, Harold, 34
T.J. Maxx, 272
T-Mobile, 285
Today Show, 288
Tommy Armour, 303
Toro, 126
Toyota, 40, 58, 88, 93, 95, 214, 229, 230, 233,
      237, 251, 301, 303
Translink, 300–301
Transparency International, 68
TransUnion, 399
Tremor, 31
Trickle-Up, 150
Trust Insurance, 367
Tuckman, Bruce, 332
TurboTax, 401
Turner, Ted, 302
Turning Heart, Rene, 150
Tylenol, 302
Tyler, Mary, 358

U

United Airlines (UAL), 387
United Technologies, 33, 122
UnitedHealth Group, 118
UPS, 7, 278
Urban Golf Gear, 139
US Airways, 123, 200
U.S. Army, 325
U.S. Rubber Recycling, 135
U.S. Trust, 187, 209
USA Jobs, xxx

V

Valero Energy, 118
Van Dine, Jim, 87
Vandebroek, Sophie, 249
vault.com, 397
Velveeta, 252
Verizon, 118, 146
Viacom, 57, 75, 70

Virgin, 138
Virgin Airways, 257
Virgin Cola, 255
Virginia Horse Journal, 147
Vocalpoint, 31
Volkswagen, 120
Volpi, Claudia, xxv
Volvo, 231
Vox, 20

W

Walgreens, 272
Walkman, 217, 302
Wall Street Journal, 202, 204
Wal-Mart, 5, 72, 117, 118, 192, 261, 272, 273,
      278, 291, 297, 303, 356, 372
Warner Brothers, 252
Washington Post, 254
Watanabe, Katsuaki, 95
Watkins, Sherron, 34
WebCPA, 183
WebEx, 100
Wegman, Danny, 297, 307, 316
Wegmans, 297, 316
Weight Watchers, 302
Wexner, Leslie, 7
Weyco, 364
Whitman, Meg, 307
Whole Foods Markets, 14, 39, 274
Wiedeking, Wendelin, 298
Wild Oats, 14
Williams-Sonoma, 303
Wilson, Kemmons, 302
Windows, Microsoft, 14
Woodruff, Robert, 302
Woods, Tiger, 139
Word of Mouth Marketing Association
      (WOMMA), 31
Workforce Management, 377
WorldCom, 33–34, 120, 121, 387
Wrigley's Gum, 7

XYZ

Xerox, 249
Yahoo!, 79, 126, 128, 284
Yahoo! Finance, 203
Yahoo! HotJobs, xxx
Yahoo! Japan, 71
Yahoo! Shoposphere, 219
Yankelovich, Daniel, 30
Young Entrepreneur, 148
Young Entrepreneurs Organization, 148
YouTube, 5, 235, 287
Z Corporation, 265
Zingy, 250

Subject Index

A

absolute advantage, 58
accelerators, business, 148
accountability, of employees, 324
accountants
   budgeting and, 177
   types of, 160–161
accounting, 159–164
   careers in, xxvii
   fraud in, 162
   functions of, 160–161
   principles of, 164–166
   rules of, 161–164
   types of, 160
accounting equation, 164–165
accounting process, 166
accounts payable, 169
accounts receivable, 168
accounts receivable turnover ratio, 174, 175
accrual basis, 165
accrued expenses, 169
acid-test ratio, 173, 174
acquisitions, 121–126
   defenses against, 125–126
   effects of, 126
   government approval of, 14
   trends in, 124–125
   See also mergers
action plans, 304
actively managed funds, 196
activists
   environmental, 39
   shareholder, 120
activity ratios, 174–175
additive fabrication, 265
administrative law, 379
administrative skills, 313
advantage
   absolute, 58
   comparative, 58
   competitive, 8, 13
advertising, 235, 279
   core message of, 279
   deceptive, 289
   ethics in, 220–221, 289
   individualized, 293
   in marketing mix, 282–284
   media for, 282–283
   online, 85, 111, 128, 219, 283–284
   specialty, 286
   types of, 282

advertising exchange, 284
advisory boards, for small business, 147
adware, 101
affirmative action, 47
Africa, 57, 75–76
African Americans, earnings of, 352
age composition, of workforce, 351
Age Discrimination in Employment Act, 369
agencies, regulatory, 15
agency relationships, 383
agenda, for meetings, 334
agents, 271
air pollution, 43
airline industry, 257, 260, 261
Alcohol Labeling Legislation, 45
alcohol, employee problems with, 368
alcohol testing, 357–358
alien corporation, 119
American Automobile Labeling Act, 45
Americans with Disabilities Act, 47, 358
anchors, in shopping malls, 273
angel investors, 150
angel networks, 150
annual reports, 172, 182, 184
antitrust legislation, 13–14
appeals, logical vs. emotional, 279–281
applicant tracking systems, 357
application letters, xxxvii–xl
arbitration, labor, 371
arbitrators, 382
artificial intelligence, 99
Asia-Pacific Economic Cooperation (APEC), 64, 65
asset management account, 399
assets, 391
   in accounting equation, 164–165
   liquid, 397–398
   types of, 167–168
assistive technologies, 376–377
Association of Southeast Asian Nations (ASEAN), 64
attrition, of employees, 368
at-will employment, 369
auction exchange, 197
auction pricing, 261
audiences, reaching, 285
audits, 161, 162, 163
authority, 324
   delegation of, 307
authorized stock, 193
auto industry, 58, 369

auto insurance, 402
autocratic leaders, 307
automated teller machines (ATMs), 190, 192
automatic vending, 274
automotive industry, 247
avatars, 274

B

Baby Boom generation, 6, 351
backdating, of stock options, 366–367
background checks, for job applicants, xxxiii, 357, 359
balance of payments, 59
balance of trade, 59
balance sheet, 167–169
   personal, 391
balanced funds, 196
balanced scorecard, 311
bank accounts, 398
Bank Holding Act, 192
Bank Insurance Fund, 191
banking
   deregulation of, 190
   electronic, 190–191
   evolving environment for, 191–192
   terrorism and, 74
Banking Act of 1933, 191
bankruptcy, 385–386
   personal, 399–400
banks, 189
   business loans from, 149–150
   failure of, 191, 385
   fees charged by, 399
barriers to entry, 5
Barron's, 202
bartering, 216
Basic Guide to Exporting, 78
batch-of-one production, 93
Bean Stock, 374
behavior modification, 340–341
behavioral segmentation, 228
behavioral targeting, 293
benchmarking, 312
benefits. *See* employee benefits
beverage industry, 29
Big Four accounting firms, 161
big picture, systems thinking for, 83
"bigger hammer" syndrome, 85
bill of rights, for consumers, 44
billboards, 285

blogs, 5, 287
    company, 235
    for small-business advice, 147–148
    for stealth marketing, 31
blue-chip stocks, 204
board of directors, 46, 115–116, 119,
    120–121, 131
bond quotations, 206
bond ratings, 194
bonds, 169
    corporate, 194
    government, 17, 195
    investing in, 193–194
bonuses, 363
bookkeeping, 160
    double-entry, 165–166
borrowing, 178–179
    See also loans
bottom line, 169
boycotts, 371
brand awareness, 251
brand equity, 232, 251
brand extension, 255
brand insistence, 251
brand loyalty, 251, 301
brand manager, 253
brand marks, 251
brand names, 232, 251
brand preference, 251
brand sponsorship, 252
brands, 251
    global, 72–73
    protecting, 277
breach of contract, 382
break-even analysis, 257, 259
break-even point, 233, 257–258, 259
bribery, 68
brokerage business, 187, 208–209
brokerage firms, 190, 192
    discount, 187, 202
brokers
    as marketing intermediaries, 271
    securities, 201–202
budgeting, 176–177
    personal, 394, 398
bull market, 203
bundling, of products, 261–262
Bureau of Labor Statistics, 378
burnout, 350
business
    careers in, xxvi–xxvii
    defined, 3–4
    social responsibility of, 21, 30, 38–49
business accelerators, 148
business agent, 370
business analysis, 249–250
business analysis tools, 318
business courts, 380
business cycles, 16
business ethics, 30
business-format franchises, 143
business incubators, 148
business intelligence (BI) systems, 318
business law, 380–386
business loyalty, 30

business management, study of, 3
business mind-set, 2–4
business model, as system, 85–86
business ownership, forms of, 111–121
business plan, 140–141, 142
business services, 246
business-to-business marketing, 221,
    223–224, 270
business units, 327
businesses
    buying, 141–143
    types of, 4–5
BusinessWeek, 202
buy-and-sell investors, 201
buyer's remorse, 222
buyers, 9
    industrial, 246
buying behavior
    consumer, 222–223
    organizational, 223–224
buying power, 216, 389
buzz marketing, 31

C
cafeteria plans, 364
calendar year, for accounting, 167
Canada, 63, 72, 74
CAN-SPAM, 45
capacity planning, 90–91
capital
    cost of, 177–178
    as factor of production, 6
    start-up, 149
capital budgeting, 177
capital gains, 195
capital-intensive businesses, 5
capital investments, 177
capital items, 245
capital structure, 177
capitalism, 8
    See also free-market systems
career counseling, xxxi
career planning, xxii–xxxi
career success, business knowledge and,
    2–3
cars, purchasing, 396
cash basis bookkeeping, 166
cash equivalents, 159
cash flow, monitoring, 176
cash management, 397–398
catalogs, mail order, 273, 274
category killers, 272, 273
cause-related marketing, 41, 216
CE (Conformité Européenne), 65
centralization, 325, 326
CEOs. See chief executive officers
certificate of deposit (CD), 188, 398, 399
certified management accountants (CMAs),
    161
certified public accountants (CPAs),
    160–161
CFO. See chief financial officer
change, managing, 309–310
change quotient (CQ), 307
channel conflict, 275, 277

channels
    communication, 282–284
    distribution, 233, 269, 275–277
Chapter 7 bankruptcy, 385, 399
Chapter 11 bankruptcy, 385, 400
charisma, 306
checking accounts, 188, 398
checks, 385
chief ethics officer, 33
chief executive officers (CEOs), 117, 119, 305
    compensation of, 363
    gender gap in, 352
chief financial officer (CFO), 119, 160, 176
chief information officer (CIO), 97, 119
chief technology officer (CTO), 119
child-care assistance, 367
China, 9, 43
chronological résumés, xxxiv, xxxv
Cigarette Labeling Act, 45, 46
cigarettes, 46
CIO. See chief information officer
circular flow of money, 17, 19
civil law, 68
Civil Rights Act of 1964, 351
Civil Rights Act of 1991, 47
Clayton Antitrust Act, 13
Clean Air Act, 42, 43
Clean Water Act, 43
clicks and mortar, 274
click-through rates, 128
closed corporations, 116
closely held companies, 116
closing, of sales, 282
closing costs, for real estate, 396
closing the books, 166–167
coaching, 308–309
COBRA, 359
co-branding, 252
code of ethics, 33
cognitive dissonance, 222
cohesiveness, in teams, 333
collaboration
    groupware for, 130
    information systems and, 98
    Internet for, 100
collateral, 178–179
collective bargaining, 371–372
collectivism, 39
college degree, earnings and, 395
college placement office, xxxi
college students, credit card debt of, 234, 395
combination résumés, xxxiv
command teams, 329
commercial banks, 189
commercialization, 250
commercials, TV, 285
commissions, sales, 363
committees, 329
Commodity Futures Trading Commission
    Act, 198
common law, 68, 380
common stock, 115–116, 193
communication
    careers in, xxvii
    crisis, 287

customer, 8, 235
   defining message for, 279
   ethical, 289
   etiquette in, 289
   information systems and, 98
   in-person, 104
   leadership and, 306
   postsales, 236, 289
   in teams, 331, 334
   truthful, 31
   web-based, 100
   See also customer communication
communication mix, 281–289
communication skills, 313
communism, 9
community banks, 192
comparative advantage, 58
comparison shopping engines, 274
compensation, 362–364, 397
compensatory damages, 381
competency-based pay, 364
competition
   evaluating, 226, 303
   fair, 30
   monopolistic, 13
   pure, 12
competitive advantage, 8, 13
compliance management software, 183
components, 246
compounding, of interest, 389
compromise, 334
computer activity monitoring, 360
computer-aided design (CAD), 92
computer-aided engineering (CAE), 92
computer-aided manufacturing (CAM), 92
computer chip technology, 189
computer-integrated manufacturing
      (CIM), 92
computer simulations, 83
computer systems, 100
   security of, 101
computers, power usage and, 41
concentrated marketing, 229, 230
concept testing, 249
conceptual skills, 313
conflict, managing, 332, 333–334, 346
conflict of interest, 32
   in accounting firms, 162
Conformité Européenne, 65
conglomerates, 122
conscientiousness, 39
consensus, decision by, 331
consent order, 380
consideration, in contracts, 382
Consolidated Omnibus Budget
      Reconciliation Act, 359
consolidation, 122, 124
Consumer Guide to Buying a Franchise, 144
consumer market, 222
consumer price index (CPI), 19
Consumer Product Safety Act, 45
Consumer Product Safety Commission
      (CPSC), 15, 44, 45
consumer products, 244–245
   See also products

consumer promotion, 286
Consumer Protection Credit Act, 45
consumerism, 44
consumers
   benefits from business for, 36
   bill of rights for, 44, 45–46
   business's responsibility toward, 44–46
   feedback from, 46
content management systems, 98
contingency leaders, 308
contingent employees, 354–355
contracts, 381–383
control
   information systems and, 98
   span of, 325
control charts, 95
control cycle, 311
controller, 160
controlling function, of management,
      311–312
Controlling the Assault of Non-Solicited
      Pornography and Marketing Act, 45
convenience products, 245
convenience stores, 272
convertible bonds, 194
convertible preferred stock, 193
cooperative advertising, 282
copyrights, 384–385
core competencies, 86–87
corporate accountants, 160
corporate bonds, 194
corporate campaigns, 372
corporate culture, 96, 310–311
   mergers and, 124
corporate hierarchy, 305
corporate reform, 120–121
corporate social responsibility (CSR), 30
   approaches to, 38–39
   global, 49
   strategic, 40
   toward consumers, 44–46
   toward employees, 46–49
   toward environment, 41–42
   toward investors, 46
corporations, 115–121
   advantages of, 117
   characteristics of, 112
   disadvantages of, 117
   governance of, 119–121
   number of, 114
   ownership of, 115–116
   private, 116
   private vs. public, 116
   shareholders' equity in, 169
   stocks in, 193
   taxing of, 117
   types of, 116, 118–119
cosmetic medicine, 263
cosmetic procedures, 243
cost accounting, 160
cost-based pricing, 257–258
cost leadership, 303
cost of goods sold, 170
cost-of-living increases, 19
cost-plus pricing, 233, 257

costs, controlling, 99–100
countries, trade between, 58–59, 63–65
coupons, 286
court system, U.S., 380
CPAs. *See* certified public accountants
creative thinking, 331
credibility, lack of, 34
credit
   in bookkeeping, 165
   managing personal, 399
credit bureaus, 399
credit cards, 188–188, 399
   for college students, 234, 395
   to finance start-ups, 151
   monitoring of, 234
credit control, 17
credit counseling, 399
credit history, 399
credit ratings, 178
credit reports, 399
credit unions, 189
creditors, 160, 178, 385
crime, computer-based, 101
criminals, banking and, 191
crisis communication planning, 287
crisis management, 304
critical paths, 91, 92
cross-functional teams, 326, 329
cross-promotion, 286
crowdsourcing, xxv
CSR. *See* corporate social responsibility
CTO. *See* chief technology officer
Cuba, 61
cultural differences
   business ethics and, 32
   buying behavior and, 222
   conducting business and, 66–68
   See also diversity; international business
cultural diversity, 21
culture clash, 124
cultures, studying, 67, 69
cumulative preferred stock, 193
currency, 188
   exchange rates for, 65–66
current assets, 167, 168
current ratio, 173, 174
curriculum vitae, xxxi
customer buying behavior, 222–223
   organizational, 223–224
customer communication, 8
   in marketing mix, 234–236
   strategies for, 278–290
   vs. promotion, 234
customer-focused companies, 217
customer-led innovation, 249
customer loyalty, 217, 228
customer relationship management (CRM)
      systems, 99, 282
customer satisfaction, 20, 96, 218, 279, 289
customer service, 215, 218, 343
   distribution and, 277
   international, 72
customers
   buying behavior of, 222–223
   complaints of, 218

customers (*continued*)
  data mining of, 220
  data on, 21
  delighting, 218
  involving in marketing process, 218–219
  online conversations among, 287–288
  service delivery and, 93–94
  understanding, 221–225
customization, 72, 81, 256
  mass, 93, 105
customs, of other cultures, 67, 68
Customs and Trade Partnership Against
    Terrorism, 74
CV. *See* curriculum vitae
cycles, business, 16
cynicism, 38–39

D
damages, court, 381, 382
Darfur, 61
data, collection of, 97, 235
data marts, 239
data mining, 97, 220, 239
data mining systems, 239
data visualization, 102
data warehouses, 239
database marketing, 234
databases, 97
day care, 367
day order, 202
dealer exchange, 197
deals, merger and acquisition, 124, 125
debentures, 194
debit cards, 189
debits, 165
debt financing, 149, 178–179
debt-management plan, 399
debt, national, 18
debt ratios, 174, 175
debt-to-equity ratio, 172, 174, 175
debt-to-total-assets ratio, 174, 175
decentralization, 325–326
deception
  in bookkeeping, 162
  by job applicants, xxxiii
Deceptive Mail Prevention and Enforcement
    Act, 45
deceptive pricing, 257
decision making
  computers for, 99
  ethical, 34–35, 36
  financial, 390
  by managers, 298, 314
  about purchases, 222–223
  in teams, 328, 330, 332, 334
decision-making meetings, 334
decision support system (DSS), 99, 318
decline phase, of product life cycle, 232, 248
deductions, 401
deeds, 383
defined-benefit plans, 365–366
defined-contribution plans, 365–366
deflation, 19
delegation, 324
demand, 9–10, 257

demand curve, 9
demand deposits, 188
democratic leaders, 307
demographics, 228
Denmark, 59
department stores, 272, 273
departmentalization, 326–328
dependent-care allowances, 367
deposit institutions, 189
Depository Institutions Deregulation and
    Monetary Control Act, 190
depreciation, 166, 396
deregulation, 14, 190
design, product, 92
devaluation, 66
differentiated marketing, 229, 230
differentiation, of products, 303
digital cameras, 248
digital products, 265, 273
digital rights management (DRM), 102
digital theft, 102
direct deposit, 190
direct mail, 284
direct marketing, 235, 284–285
direct-to-consumer news releases, 287
Directory of Angel-Investor Networks, 150
disabilities
  employees with, 376–377
  equal treatment and, 47–48
disability insurance, 402
disclosure, financial, 199
discount pricing, 261
discount rate, 16–17
discount stores, 272, 273
discretionary order, 202
discrimination
  economic, 47
  employment, 352
  price, 257
disinflation, 19
display advertising, online, 111, 128, 284
disposable income, 6
disruptive technologies, 227
distribution
  international, 70
  in marketing mix, 233–234
  physical, 277–278
  terrorism's effect on, 73–74
distribution centers, 278
distribution channels
  choosing, 275–277
  control of, 275, 277
  cost of, 275, 277
distribution mix, 275–277
distribution strategies, 269–278
distributors, 271
  trade allowances for, 286–287
diversification, 201, 227
diversity
  in entrepreneurship, 136–137
  in workforce, 21, 313, 351–353
diversity initiatives, 47, 353
divesting, 14
dividends, 116, 159, 169, 180, 193
division of labor, 323

divisional structure, 327
DMAIC, 96
dollar, U.S., 65, 66
domestic corporation, 119
dot-com boom and crash, 5, 85–86
double-entry bookkeeping, 165–166
Dow Jones Industrial Average, 204
downloading
  inappropriate, 101
  music, 2
downsizing, 138, 350
drop shippers, 271
drug testing, 357
dumping, 62
durable goods orders, 19
dynamic pricing, 261, 262

E
early adopters, 260
earning power, 394
  maximizing, 397
earnings per share, 172, 173
earnings, retained, 166–167, 169
e-business, 100
ECNs, 197–198
ecology, 42
e-commerce, 21, 99, 100, 273, 274
  small business and, 136
economic conditions, marketing activities
    and, 226–227
economic contraction, 15
economic expansion, 15
economic fluctuations, 16
economic indicators, 18–19
  international, 59
economic performance, 18–20
Economic Statistics Briefing Room, 26
economic systems, 6–9
economics, 6
  careers in, xxvii
  free-market systems, 8
  macroeconomics, 6, 12–18
  microeconomics, 6, 9–12
  monitoring economic performance,
    18–20
  planned systems, 9
economies of scale, 58, 93, 123
economy
  global, 20–21
  role of small business in, 135–136
  stability of, 15–16
  U.S., 6
EDGAR, 199
EEOC, 15, 47, 351, 352–353
EFTS, 190
elder care, 367
electricity
  deregulation of, 14
  generation of, 41
electronic business. *See* e-business
electronic commerce. *See* e-commerce
electronic communication networks (ECNs),
    197–198
Electronic Data Gathering, Analysis, and
    Retrieval (EDGAR) database, 199

electronic funds transfer systems (EFTS), 190
electronic networking, 87
electronic performance monitoring (EPM), 360–361
electronic waste, 43
e-mail
  misuse of, 101
  monitoring of, 103, 362
  targeted, 285
embargoes, 61
embezzlement, 339
emotional appeals, 279–281
emotional quotient (EQ), 307
empathy, in managers, 307
employee assistance programs, 368
employee benefits, 364–368
  laws regarding, 359, 362–363
employee performance management systems, 99
employee retention, 354
Employee Retirement Income Security Act, 359
employee stock-ownership plan (ESOP), 366
employee turnover, 316
employees
  accountability of, 324
  burnout of, 350
  coaching of, 308–309
  compensation of, 362–364
  contingent, 354–355
  corporate social responsibility toward, 46–49
  with disabilities, 47–48, 376–377
  dissatisfaction of, 337
  empowerment of, 308, 340
  equal treatment of, 47–48
  exempt vs. nonexempt, 363
  family benefits for, 367
  firing of, 362, 369
  hiring of, 357–358
  incentive programs for, 363–364
  insurance for, 364–365
  involving in decision making, 307
  as knowledge workers, 7
  loyalty of, 350
  mentoring of, 309
  misuse of e-mail by, 101
  monitoring of, 103, 360–361, 362
  motivating, 335
  orientation programs for, 359–360
  performance appraisal of, 360–362
  personal use of Internet by, 362
  promotion of, 368, 397
  quality of work life for, 350
  reassignment of, 368
  recruiting of, xl, 355, 356
  responsibilities of, 324
  retirement of, 369
  retirement benefits for, 365–366
  safety of, 48–49
  satisfaction of, 337
  sexual harassment of, 352
  termination of, 369
  theft by, 339

  training of, 343, 358–360
  use of unauthorized software by, 101
  work hours of, 350
  work-life balance of, 350
  workloads of, 330, 350
  See also teams
employers
  hiring practices of, xxxiii, 357–358
  motivational strategies of, 335–341
employment contract, 369
employment discrimination, 352
employment interviews, xl–xliv
employment, laws regarding, 352, 358, 359
employment portfolio, xxiv
empowerment, of employees, 308, 340
energy industry, 41
engagement, of employees, 335
engineering, computer-aided, 92
enhanced 911, 53
enterprise IM, 25
enterprise resource planning (ERP), 89
enterprise systems, 98
entrepreneurs, 135, 136
  characteristics of, 138–139
  as factor of production, 6
  in free market, 9
  global economy and, 21
  minority, 137
  women, 136–137
environment
  business's responsibility toward, 41–42
  marketing activities and, 227
environmental activists, 39
Environmental Protection Agency (EPA), 15, 42, 43, 54
EPM, 360–361
Equal Opportunity Employment Commission (EEOC), 15, 47, 351, 352–353
equilibrium price, 11–12
equipment, 246
equity financing, 149, 178–179
equity, homeowner's, 396
equity theory, 338–339
ergonomics, 48
ERP, 89
ESOP, 366
ESS, 99
ethical behavior
  to avoid harming others, 31–32
  factors influencing, 32–34
ethical dilemma, 35
ethical lapse, 35
ethics hotline, 33
ethics
  in business, 21, 30–35
  in communication, 31
  in competition, 30
  in decision making, 34–35, 36
  in marketing, 220–221
  in marketing communications, 289
  in marketing research, 234
ethnocentrism, 67
etiquette
  in marketing communications, 289
  in networking, xxix–xxx

euro, 65
European Union (EU), 63–65
  Microsoft and, 14
exchange, medium of, 188
exchange process, 216
exchange rates, 65–66
excise taxes, 18, 400–401
exclusive distribution, 276
executive dashboards, 102, 103
executive information systems, 318
executive support system (ESS), 99
exemptions, tax, 401
exit strategy, 142
expense items, 245
expenses
  accrued, 169
  on income statement, 169–170
  types of, 170–171
expensing, of stock options, 366
experiments, in marketing research, 235
export management companies, 70
export trading companies, 70
exports/exporting, 59, 70, 78
express contracts, 381
external auditors, 161–162, 163
extranets, 100
extrinsic rewards, 338

F
fabrication, digital, 265
facilities, location of, 90
facility layout, 90
factories, working conditions in, 48–49
factors of production, 6–7
factory outlets, 272
failures, business, 145–146
Fair Labor Standards Act, 362
Fair Packaging and Labeling Act, 45
fair trade, 61
faith-based employee support groups, 352
family benefits, 367
family branding, 255
Family Medical and Leave Act (FMLA), 367
farm subsidies, 62
fashion industry, 221–225
FCC, 15, 290
FDA, 15, 32, 290
feasibility studies, 249
features, product, 217
Federal Aviation Administration, 15
Federal Communications Commission (FCC), 15, 290
Federal Deposit Insurance Corporation, 191
Federal Energy Regulatory Commission, 15
Federal Highway Administration, 15
Federal Reserve Board, 16–17, 191
Federal Sentencing Guidelines, 33
Federal Trade Commission Act, 13
Federal Trade Commission (FTC), 14, 15, 44, 128, 143, 290, 293, 384
Federal Unemployment Tax Act, 359
Federal Water Pollution Control Act, 42

feedback
    from consumers, 46
    to employees, 360
    in systems, 85
file management activity, 362
finance, careers in, xxvii
finance companies, 190
finance department, 161, 176
finances, personal, 388–402
financial accounting, 160
Financial Accounting Standards Board
    (FASB), 163
financial advisers, 390
financial analysis, 160
financial control, 177
financial disclosure, 117
financial information, 159
financial institutions, 189–192
financial management, 175–179
financial news, xxvii–xxviii
    analyzing, 202–206
financial plan, 176
    personal, 390–395
financial reporting, 163–164, 199
    compliance software for, 183
Financial Services Modernization Act, 192
financial statements, 166–175
    analyzing, 172–175
    balance sheet, 167–169
    income statement, 169–171
    statement of cash flows, 171
financial strategy, 8
financing
    from marketing intermediaries, 270
    of new businesses, 149–151
    securing, 177
Finland, 59
firewalls, 102
firing, 362, 369
first-line managers, 305
fiscal policy, 16, 17–18
fiscal year, 167
fixed assets, 167, 168
fixed costs, 233, 257
fixed expenses, 396
flat organizations, 325
flexible manufacturing systems (FSM), 92
flextime, 353
floating exchange system, 65
flogs, 287
floor brokers, 197
focus groups, 235
focus strategy, 303
Food and Drug Administration (FDA), 15,
    32, 290
Food, Drug, and Cosmetic Act, 45
Forbes, 202
forecasting, 301–303
    of new-product sales, 249
    production, 90–91
    of staffing needs, 354–355
foreign corporation, 119
Foreign Corrupt Practices Act, 68
foreign direct investment, 71–72
foreign distributors, 70

foreign exchange rates, 65–66
forensic accounting, 160
form utility, 217
formal organization, 323
Fortune, 202
Fortune 500, 131
401(k) plan, 366
four Ps, 232
France, 71, 256
franchisee, 143
franchising, 143–145
    international, 70
franchisor, 143
fraud
    accounting, 162
    securities, 199–200
free-market systems, 8–9
    competition in, 12–13
    government's role in, 13–18
    monitoring economic performance in,
        18–20
    supply and demand in, 9–12
free riders, 331
free trade, 59–61
FSM, 92
FTC. See Federal Trade Commission
FT-SE 100 Index, 204
full and fair disclosure, 199
functional résumé, xxxiv
functional structure, 326
functional teams, 329

G
GAAP, 161–162, 163
GAFTA, 64
gain sharing, 363
Gantt chart, 91
GATT, 62
GDP, 16, 20
gender, pay gap and, 351–352
General Agreement on Tariffs and Trade
    (GATT), 62
general obligation bond, 195
general partnership, 112, 114
generally accepted accounting principles
    (GAAP), 161–162, 163
Generation X, 351
Generation Y, 286, 351
generic products, 252
geodemographics, 228
geographic segmentation, 228
Germany, 72
gift cards, 235
glass ceiling, 352
Glass Steagall Act, 191, 192
global positioning system (GPS), 53
global warming, 43
globalization
    challenges of, 20–21
    corporate social responsibility and, 49
    See also international business
GNP, 20
goals
    communication, 279
    company, 303

for personal finances, 392–393
goal-setting theory, 340
going public, 116–117, 151
golden handshakes, 363
golden parachutes, 363
Golden Rule, 35
goods, inventory of, 89
goods-producing businesses, 4–5
goodwill, as asset, 167
government
    court system of, 380
    in free-market system, 8, 13–18
    homeland security by, 73
    as market for goods and services, 18
    monetary policy of, 16–17
    in planned systems, 9
    See also specific government agencies
government bonds, 17
government regulation, 15, 379–380
    affecting competition, 13–14
    of banking, 191
    of industries, 14, 15
    of marketing, 289–290
    of marketing communications, 289–290
    of securities markets, 198–199
    of small business, 146–147
Greater Arab Free Trade Area (GAFTA), 64
green marketing, 43–44
greenwash, 39
grocery business, 297
gross domestic product (GDP), 16, 20
gross national product (GNP), 20
gross profit, 170
groups. See teams
groupthink, 330
groupware, 100, 130
growth
    business failures and, 146
    economic, 59
growth funds, 196
growth phase, of product life cycle, 232, 248
growth stocks, 180, 205
guitars, custom, 81, 105

H
H-1B visa, 74
harm, causing, 31–32
headhunters, 356
health-care costs, 364–365, 373
health insurance, 364, 365, 401, 402
Health Savings Accounts (HSAs), 365
hierarchy of needs, 336–337
high-growth ventures, 135
high-yield bonds, 194
hiring process, xl, 357–358
Hispanic-owned businesses, 137
holding company, 119
holidays, paid, 368
home, working from, 353
homeland security, 73
homeowners' insurance, 402
honesty, in competition, 30
horizontal structure, 326
horizontal teams, 329
hostile takeovers, 122, 125

housing demand, 227
housing, paying for, 396–397
housing starts, 18–19
HSAs, 365
human resources
    careers in, xxvi
    as factor of production, 6
    planning of, 354–355
    staffing challenges for, 350
human resources management, 349–354
hybrid stock market, 198
hybrid structures, 328
hygiene factors, 337
hypermarkets, 272

I
ideas, generating, 249
identity theft, 21, 44–45, 220, 399
ignorance, ethics and, 32
IMC, 281
IMF, 63
immigrants, in small business, 138
immigration, 74, 373
imports/importing, 32, 59, 70
    restrictions on, 61, 62
incentive programs, 363–364
income funds, 196
income instruments, 201
income statement, 169–171
    personal, 391
income stocks, 180
income taxes, 17–18, 401
incubators, business, 148
index funds, 196
India, 29, 50, 72, 73, 88, 137
industrial and commercial products,
    245–246
industrial espionage, 30
industry funds, 196
inflation, 16, 19, 389
information, defined, 97
information overload, 102, 103
information systems, 96–104
    managing, 100–101
information technology (IT), 98, 99
    careers in, xxvi, 37
informational meetings, 334
informed, right to be, 45–46
initial public offering (IPO), 151, 156, 164,
    197
injunctions, 372
injury, on the job, 48
inkjet fabrication, 265
insider trading, 32
Insider Trading and Securities Fraud Act,
    198
insight, 97
installations, 246
instant messaging, 25
institutional advertising, 282
institutional investors, 120, 203
insurance, 401, 402
    for employees, 364–365
insurance companies, 189
intangible assets, 167

integrated marketing communications
    (IMC), 281
intellectual property, 102, 383–384
    theft of, 339
intelligence, leadership and, 306–307
intelligence quotient (IQ), 306
intensive distribution, 276
interest
    on bonds, 194
    compounding of, 389
    on credit cards, 188–189
    on savings accounts, 188
interest rate
    in cost of capital, 177–178
    discount, 16–17
    prime, 17
intermediaries
    for international trade, 70
    marketing, 269, 270–275
internal auditors, 163
Internal Revenue Service (IRS), 162, 394, 401
International Accounting Standards Board,
    163
international business
    environment for, 66–73
    forms of, 68–72
    quality standards in, 96
    strategic approaches to, 72–73
    terrorism and, 73–74
international funds, 196
International Monetary Fund (IMF), 63
International Organization for
    Standardization (ISO), 96
international trade, 57–66
International Trade Administration, 70, 78
international trade agreements, 62–63
Internet
    advertising on, 111, 219, 283–284
    banking services on, 190–191
    bartering on, 216
    business and, 21, 99–100
    business information on, xxvii–xxx
    business models for, 85–86
    communication with customers on, 235
    copyright protection on, 384
    financial advice on, 203
    job information on, xxix, xxx
    service businesses and, 5
    small business and, 136, 147–148
    trading hubs on, 270
    Web 2.0 and, 5
    See also websites
Internet Public Library, 26
Interstate Commerce Commission (ICC), 15
interviews
    in marketing research, 235
    job, xl–xliv, 357
intranets, 100
intrapreneurship, 136
intrinsic rewards, 338
introduction phase, of product life cycle,
    232, 247, 260
inventory, 89
    marketing intermediaries and, 270
inventory control, 89, 278

inventory management, 93
inventory turnover ratio, 174–175
investing
    in business start-ups, 150
    in franchises, 144
    hazards of, 199–200
    in mutual funds, 195–196
    personal, 400
    in securities, 193–196
    strategies for, 200–206
investment banks, 190, 197
Investment Company Act, 198
investment funds, private equity, 125
investment portfolio, 201
investors
    angel, 150
    in corporations, 115
    institutional, 120, 203
    rights of, 46
Investors' Business Daily, 202
"invisible hand," 8
IPO Central, 156
IPOs, 151, 156, 164, 197
IQ, 103, 306
IRS, 162, 394, 401
ISO standards, 96
issued stock, 193
IT systems, 98, 99
    total cost of ownership of, 103–104

J
Japan, 58, 71, 72, 88, 95, 101, 274
JIT, 93
job analysis, 355
job applicants, 357–358
job boards, online, xxix
job description, 355, 356
job interviews, xl–xliv
job redesign, 350
job requirements, 355
job responsibilities, 323–324
job search, xxiii–xliv
job sharing, 353
job specifications, 355, 356
jobs
    in business, 3
    outsourcing of, 88
    in small business, 135
    joint ventures, 127
    international, 71
junk bonds, 194
justice, 35
just-in-time (JIT) inventory management,
    93

K
kaizen, 95
kakushin, 95
keiretsu, 88
Keirsey Temperament Sorter, xxxi, 317
key word summary, on résumés,
    xxxvi–xxxviii
keywords, auctioning of, 284
kiosks, interactive, 274–275
knowledge, as factor of production, 6–7

knowledge-based pay, 364
knowledge workers, 7

L
labels, product, 252–253
labor federations, 370
labor-intensive businesses, 5, 59
Labor-Management Relations Act, 359, 370
Labor-Management Reporting and
    Disclosure Act, 359
labor unions, 369–373
    laws regarding, 359
    membership in, 372–373
    organization of, 370
lagging indicators, 18
laissez-faire leaders, 307–308
laissez-faire management, 316
landlord-tenant relation, 383
Landrum-Griffin Act, 359, 370
Lanham Trademark Act, 251
law
    business, 380–386
    ethics and, 35
    international, 379
    types of, 379–380
    See also legal aspects
laws, fostering competition, 13–14
lawsuits
    against tobacco companies, 46
    negligent-hiring, 359
    product-liability, 44
    wrongful discharge, 369
layoffs, 369
LBOs, 122
lead time, 89
leaders, team, 329, 334
leadership
    ethical, 34
    skills needed for, 306
    styles of, 307–308
leading function, of management, 305–311
leading indicators, 18
lean systems, 91, 93
leases, 169, 383
    for vehicles, 396
legal aspects
    of corporations, 117
    of employee compensation, 362–363
    of employee termination, 369
    of employment, 352
    of franchising, 144
    of global business, 68
    of hiring practices, 357–358, 359
    of marketing activities, 227
    of product labeling, 252–253
    of securities markets, 198–199
    of sole proprietorships, 113
legislation
    antitrust, 13–14
    relating to labor unions, 370
    See also government
leverage point, 83
leverage ratios, 174, 175
leveraged buyout (LBO), 122
liabilities, 391

in accounting equation, 165
on balance sheet, 168–169
liability
    of board of directors, 121
    limited, 117, 118–119
    product, 381
    unlimited, 113
liability exposure, with forms of business
    ownership, 112, 114–115, 117
liability insurance, auto, 402
libel, 381
Library of Congress Copyright Office, 384
licensing
    international, 70
    of products, 252
life cycle, product, 232, 246–248
life insurance, 402
lifestyle businesses, 135
lifestyle trends, 6
limit order, 202
limited liability companies (LLCs), 118–119
limited liability partnerships (LLPs), 114
limited partnerships, 112, 114
line-and-staff organization, 324
line extension, 255
line filling, 255
line of credit, 190
line organization, 324
line stretching, 255
lines of authority, 324
liquid assets, 397–398
liquidity, 116, 117, 168, 201
liquidity ratios, 173, 174
living wage, 61
LLCs, 118–119
LLPs, 114
loans, 190
    bank, 149
    family, 149
    home, 45–46
    as long-term liabilities, 169
    secured vs. unsecured, 178–179
    students, 395
local advertising, 282
location and tracking technologies, 53
location, importance of, 7, 8
lockouts, 372
logical appeals, 279–281
logistics, 277
long tail, 255
loss-leader pricing, 260–261
loyalty
    brand, 251, 301
    customer, 217, 228
    employee, 350
luxury products, 277
lying, 30
    by job applicants, xxxiii, 357

M
macroeconomics, 6, 12–18
magazines, advertising in, 283
Magnuson-Moss Warranty Act, 45
mail order, 273, 274
malicious software, 101

mall intercept, in marketing research, 235
Maloney Act, 198
malware, 101, 362
management, 297
    careers in, xxvi
    of change, 309–310
    controlling function of, 311–312
    during a crisis, 304
    functions of, 297–312
    leading function of, 305–311
    organizing function of, 304–305
    participative, 307
    planning function of, 298–304
    project, 313
    span of, 325
management accounting, 160
management by objectives (MBO), 340, 341
management information systems (MIS), 99
management pyramid, 305
managers
    conceptual skills of, 313
    decision-making skills of, 314
    emotional quotient in, 307
    hierarchy of, 305
    interpersonal skills of, 312–313
    roles of, 298
    technical skills of, 313
Manchester Cathedral, 32
mandatory retirement, 369
manufacturers, 6
manufacturers' representatives, 271
manufacturing, 59, 90
    computer-aided, 92
    purchasing for, 246
    quality control in, 95
manufacturing franchises, 143
manufacturing resource planning (MRP II),
    89
margin call, 202
margin requirements, 17
margin trading, 202
market, 8, 228
market approach, 281–289
market coverage, 275, 276
    strategies for, 229, 230
market development, 227
market intelligence, 234
market managers, 197
market order, 202
market penetration, 227
market segmentation, 228
marketable securities, 168
marketing, 215–221
    accountability of, 219
    careers in, xxvi
    cause-related, 41
    concentrated, 229, 230
    core concepts in, 215
    differentiated, 229, 230
    ethics in, 220–221
    etiquette in, 220–221
    green, 43–44
    information systems and, 98
    international, 72–73
    involving customers in, 218–219

objectives for, 227
permission-based, 221
product life cycle and, 246–248
role of, 216–217
social commerce in, 219
stealth, 31, 221
strategies for, 225–236
technology in, 219–220
test, 250
undifferentiated, 229, 230
viral, 31
marketing channels, 233, 269, 275–277, 282–284
marketing communication, 281
etiquette in, 289
regulation of, 289
marketing concept, 217–218
marketing intermediaries, 233, 234, 269, 270–275
choosing, 275–277
functions of, 270
marketing manager, 253
marketing mix, 231–236
marketing objectives, pricing and, 256
marketing plan, 225
marketing research, 234–235
marketing strategy, 142
mass communication media, 282
mass customization, 93, 105
mass e-mailing, 285
mass media, 285
mass merchandisers, 273
mass production, 93
master production schedule (MPS), 91
matching principle, 165
material requirements planning (MRP), 89
materials handling, 278
matrix structure, 327
maturity phase, of product life cycle, 232, 248
MBO, 340, 341
m-commerce, 274
media, advertising, 282–284
media mix, 283
mediation, 371
mediators, 382
medical care, mistakes in, 95
medical insurance. See health insurance
meetings, productive, 334–335
mentoring, 309
for small business, 147
merchant wholesalers, 270–271
mercury pollution, 43
mergers, 121–126
advantages of, 123
defenses against, 125–126
disadvantages of, 124
effects of, 126
government approval of, 14
mistakes in, 123
success rate for, 126
trends in, 124–125
types of, 122–123
message, defining, 279
Mexico, 49, 63

microeconomics, 6, 9–12
microelectromechanical systems (MEMS), 107
microlenders, 149
micropolis, 228
middle managers, 305
Millennial Generation, 351
minimum wage, 362
minorities, 352
minority-owned businesses, 137
MIS, 99
mission statement, 142, 300–301
mistakes, as opportunities, 85
mixed capitalism, 8
mixed economy, 8
mobile banking, 191
mobile commerce, 274
mobile phones, 244, 250
advertising on, 286
banking via, 191
monetary policy, 16–17
money, 187–189
circular flow of, 17
money management, personal, 388
money-market deposit account, 188, 398–399
money-market mutual funds, 196, 398, 399
money supply, 16–17
monitoring, of performance, 360–361, 362
monopolies, 13
monopolistic competition, 13
morale, of employees, 335
mortgage, 396
mortgage bonds, 194
mortgage loans, subprime, 45–46
motivation, 335–336
of employees, 335–341
equity theory of, 338–339
expectancy theory of, 339–340
of leaders, 307
strategies for, 340–341
teams and, 330
theories of, 336–340
two-factor theory of, 337–338
motivators, 337
MPS, 91
MRP, 89
MRP II, 89
multichannel retailing, 274
multinational corporations, 71–72
multiplier effect, 17
municipal bonds, 195
murders, in workplace, 358
music industry, 2, 23, 57
mutual funds, 195–196, 207, 398, 399

N
NAFTA, 63, 64
nanotechnology, 107
NASDAQ composite, 196, 197, 204
national advertising, 282
national brands, 252
national debt, 18
National Do-Not-Call Registry, 286
National Environmental Policy Act, 42

National Institute on Disability and Rehabilitation Research, 377
National Labor Relations Act, 359, 370
national unions, 370
nations, trade among, 58–59, 63–65
natural resources, 58
as factor of production, 6
needs, 216
customer, 20
hierarchy of, 336–337
human, 335
information, 97
negative reinforcement, 341
negligence, 381
negotiable instruments, 385
negotiation(s)
of car purchase, 396
labor, 371
net income, 169–170
net operating income, 170
net worth, 391
increasing, 400
Netherlands, 72
network structures, 327–328
networking
by job applicants, xxix–xxx
for small businesses, 148
social, xxix, 32, 154–155, 287
networks, electronic, 87
new economy, 8
new-product development, 249–250
new products, from small business, 135
news conferences, 287
news releases, 287
newsfeeds, 5, 100
newspapers
advertising in, 283
bond quotations in, 206
stock quotations in, 205
niches, marketing to, 229
Nikkei 225 Index, 204
"9 effect," 257
No Electronic Theft Act, 384
Noise Control Act, 42
nongovernmental organizations, 38
nonprofit organizations, 4, 148
norms, group, 333
Norris–La Guardia Act, 370
North American Free Trade Agreement (NAFTA), 63, 64
North American Securities Administrators Association, 203
NOW accounts, 188, 398
Nutrition Education and Labeling Act, 45

O
objectives, company, 303–304
observation, in marketing research, 235
Occupational Outlook Handbook, xxvi
occupational safety, 48–49
Occupational Safety and Health Act, 48, 359
Occupational Safety and Health Administration (OSHA), 15, 48
occupations, business, xxvi–xxvii, xxviii
office automation systems, 98

Office of Consumer Affairs, 289
Office of the Comptroller of the Currency, 191
Office of Thrift Supervision, 191
off-price stores, 272
offshoring, 88
Oil Pollution Act, 42
oligopoly, 13
online analytical processing, 318
online banking, 190–191
online retailers, 272, 273, 274
open-market operations, 17
open order, 202
operating budget, 177
operating expenses, 170
operational plans, 304
operational systems, 98–99
operations management, 90–93
operations plan, 142
opportunities, assessing, 301, 314
optimal pricing, 259–260
optimum price point, 233
opt-in e-mail, 285
options, analyzing, 314
order processing, 278
organization chart, 322–323
organization
    centralized vs. decentralized, 325
    departmental, 326–328
    divisional structures, 327
    flat vs. tall, 325
    formal vs. informal, 323
    functional structures, 326–327
    horizontal vs. vertical, 326
    hybrid structures, 328
    matrix structures, 327
    network structures, 327–328
Organization for Economic Co-Operation
    and Development (OECD), 68
organizational behavior, ethics and, 33
organizational culture, 310–311
organizational market, 222, 223–224
organizational structure, 305, 322–328
organizing function, of management,
    304–305
orientation programs, 359–360
OSHA, 15, 48
outplacement services, 369
outsourcing, 87, 88, 138, 328, 355
overdraft feeds, 399
over-the-counter stock market, 197
overtime, 362–363
owners' equity, 165, 169
ownership
    business, 111–121
    private vs. government, 9
    total cost of, 103–104

P
Pacific Rim, 65
packaging, 252
parent company, 119
participative management, 307
partnership agreement, 115
partnerships, 112, 113–115, 169

passbook savings accounts, 188
patents, 384
pay, 362–363
pay for performance, 364
payroll taxes, 18
penetration pricing, 233, 260
Pension Benefit Guaranty Corporation
    (PBGC), 366
pension funds, 190
pension plans, 365–366
performance appraisal, 360–362
performance appraisal form, 361
performance, measuring, 312
performance metrics, 318
permission-based marketing, 221, 285
personal property, 383
personal selling, 235, 281–282
persuasive advertising, 279
PERT, 91, 92
pesticides, 42
pharmaceutical companies, 70
philanthropy, 39–40
phishing, 199–200
picketing, 371
place marketing, 216
place utility, 217, 270
planned system, 9
planning
    capacity, 90–91
    career, xxii–xxxi
    crisis communication, 287
    information systems and, 98
    materials, 89
    for money needs, 175–176
    personal financial, 390–395
    resource, 89
    for staffing needs, 354–355
    strategic, 298–304
    strategic marketing, 225–236
planning function, of management, 298–304
plans
    activity, 304
    business, 140–141, 142
    crisis management, 304
    strategic, 298–304
Plant-Closing Notification Act, 370
pocket bikes, 247
podcasting, 5, 287
point-of-purchase (POP) displays, 286
poison pill, 125–126
pollution, 42–43
portable storage devices, 102
portfolio tracking, 400
position power, 306
positioning, product, 230–231, 253
positive reinforcement, 340–341
possession utility, 217, 270
power, in organizations, 306
power industry, 312
power of attorney, 383
power struggles, 333
PPI, 19–20
predatory pricing, 260
prediction market, 303
preemployment tests, 357

preferred stock, 116, 193
premium pricing, 233
premiums, for sales promotion, 286
press releases, 287
pretexting, 30
price(s)
    changes in, 19–20
    demand curve and, 10
    equilibrium, 11–12
    inflation and, 16
    in marketing mix, 233
    supply curve and, 11
price-based pricing, 258–259
price controls, 8
price discrimination, 257
price-earnings ratio, 205–206
price elasticity, 233, 257
price fixing, 256–257
price indexes, 19–20
price wars, 261
pricing, 233, 256–262
    adjustment strategies for, 261–262
    auction, 261
    cost-based, 257–258
    decisions about, 233
    discount, 261
    dynamic, 261, 262
    government regulation of, 256–257
    international, 73
    loss-leader, 260–261
    optimal, 259–260
    penetration, 260
    predatory, 260
    price-based, 258–259
    skim, 260
    types of, 257–261
    value, 258–259
primary market, 197
prime interest rate, 17
principal, on bonds, 194
privacy
    of computer networks, 101–102
    of employees, 361, 362
    employer background checks and, 357
    marketing and, 289
    online, 44
    regulations regarding, 220
private brands, 252
private corporations, 116
private enterprise, 8
private equity, 125
Private Securities Litigation Reform Act, 198
privatization, 9
PRIZM NE system, 229
problem solving
    computers for, 99
    in systems thinking, 83
problem-solving teams, 329
problems, defining, 314
process control systems, 98
procurement, 89
procurement auctions, 261
producer price index (PPI), 19–20
product advertising, 282
product concept, 218

product development, 227, 249–250
  considering safety in, 247
product expansion, strategies for, 255
product identity, 232
product launch, 250
product liability, 44, 381
product life cycle, 232, 246–248
  pricing and, 260
product life-cycle management, 92
product-line extensions, 255
product lines, 232, 253
product managers, 253
product mix, 232, 253–254
product placement, 285
production
  customized, 93
  defined, 86
  forecasting for, 90–91
  quality control in, 94–96
  scheduling of, 91
  transformation process in, 94
production and operations management,
    90–93
production control systems, 98
production systems, 86–96
productivity, 91, 93
  monitoring, 103
products
  augmenting of, 244, 245
  branding of, 251–253
  bundling of, 261–262
  characteristics of, 243–249
  customization of, 72, 93, 105, 256
  design of, 92
  development of, 249–250
  differentiation of, 303
  digital, 265, 273
  distribution of, 269–278
  enhancements for, 248–249
  features of, 217
  generic, 252
  identities for, 251–253
  importing and exporting, 70
  for international markets, 72, 256
  labeling of, 252–253
  licensing of, 252
  long tail of, 255
  luxury, 277
  makeovers of, 248–249
  in marketing mix, 232–233
  mass production of, 93
  packaging of, 252
  positioning of, 230–231, 253
  right to choose, 46
  safety of, 44–45, 247, 381
  samples of, 286
  service, 244
  standardization of, 72, 229, 256
  tangibility of, 244
  types of, 244
professional corporations, 116
profit, 4
  on income statement, 169–170
profit motive, 4, 36–37
profit sharing, 350, 363

profitability ratios, 173, 174
program evaluation and review technique
    (PERT), 91, 92
project collaboration systems, 130
project management, 313
promotion
  international, 72–73
  in marketing mix, 234–236
  See also customer communication
promotional mix, 235, 281–289
promotional strategy, 279–290
promotional support, 270
promotions, job, 368, 397
property, 383
property loss, 402
property rights, 102, 383
property taxes, 18, 401
prospecting, for leads, 282
protection policies, 358
protectionism, 61–62
prototype development, 250
proxy fight, 125
proxy voting, 120
psychographics, 228
public accountants, 161
Public Company Accounting Oversight
    Board, 163
Public Company Accounting Reform and
    Investor Protection Act, 163, 198
public corporations, 116
  financial statements of, 163
public relations, 235, 287
publicly held corporations, 116, 117
pull strategy, 281
punitive damages, 381
purchasing, 89, 223–224, 246
purchasing power, 19
pure competition, 12
push strategy, 281

Q
QQPass Trojan horse, 101
qualitative forecasts, 302
quality
  defined, 311
  globalization and, 20
  pricing and, 257
  in production process, 94–96
  subjectivity of, 94
quality assurance, 95
quality control, 95
quality of hire, 356
quality of work life (QWL), 350
quantitative forecasts, 302
quick ratio, 173, 174
quotas, 61

R
race, affirmative action and, 47
racial discrimination, 352
radio, advertising on, 283
radio frequency identification (RFID), 53,
    89, 253
ratio analysis, 173–175
rational model of buyer decisions, 222

raw materials, 246
real estate, 227, 396
real property, 383
Real-Time Updates, xv–xvi
reassignment, of employees, 368
recession, 16
reciprocation, 221
recommendation engines, 274
reconciling, of checking account, 399
recovery, economic, 16
recruiting process, xl, 355, 356
recycling, 43
reference groups, buying behavior and,
    223
regulation. *See* government regulation
Regulation FD, 199
reinforcement theory, 340–341
relationship managers, 324
relationship marketing, 217
religion, workplace and, 352–353
reminder advertising, 279
replacement chart, 354
reputation analysis, 100, 288
reputation, public relations and, 287
research
  business, 100
  marketing, 234–235
research and development, 97
reserve requirement, 16
resource planning, 89
Resource Recovery Act, 42
respect, in intercultural business, 67
responsibility, of employees, 324
restaurant business, 145
restrictive import standards, 62
résumés, 357
  preparing, xxxi–xxxvii
retail stores, Internet and, 5
retail theater, 273–274
retailers, 234, 270, 271–275
  banking services from, 192
  functions of, 270
  online, 255, 272, 273, 274
  pricing by, 271–272
  push strategy to, 281
  trade allowances for, 286–287
  types of, 272, 273
retained earnings, 166–167, 169
retention, employee, 354
retirement, 369
  misconceptions about, 401–402
  planning for, 401–402
retirement benefits, 365–366
return on investment, 173, 174
return on sales, 173, 174
revenue bond, 195
revenues, on income statement, 169, 170
reverse auctions, 261
RFID, 53, 89, 253
Riegle-Neal Interstate Banking and
    Branching Efficiency Act, 192
rights
  of consumers, 44
  of stakeholders, 40
rightsizing, 350

right-to-work laws, 359
ringtones, 250
risk(s)
    by entrepreneurs, 135
    of investments, 400
    managing, 87
    marketing intermediaries and, 270
RSS feeds, 100
rumors, crisis management and, 304

S
S corporations, 118
sabbaticals, 368
Safe Drinking Water Act, 42
safety
    product, 44–45, 247, 381
    in workplace, 48–49, 359
safety cells, 247
salaries, 362–363, 397
sales
    careers in, xxvi
    information systems and, 98
sales promotion, 235, 286–287
sales support, 270
sales taxes, 18, 400
sales transactions, 383
salespeople, 282
samples, of products, 286
sanctions, economic, 61
Sarbanes-Oxley, 121, 163–164, 198, 367
Saudi Arabia, 72, 74
savings, 389, 402
savings accounts, 188, 397, 398
savings and loan associations, 189
Savings Association Insurance Fund, 191
savings bonds, 195
SBA, 151, 156
scams, investment, 199–200
scandals, corporate, 30, 120, 162, 163
scheduling, 91
scientific management, 336
scrambled merchandising, 272
search advertising, 111, 128, 284
search engines, advertising and, 111
seasoned customer exemption, 191
SEC, 198, 199
secondary boycott, 370
secondary market, 197
Section 404 (Sarbanes-Oxley), 164
sector funds, 196
secured bonds, 194
securities
    buying and selling, 201–202
    fraud involving, 199–200
    government, 195
    investing in, 193–196
Securities Act, 198
Securities and Exchange Commission (SEC),
    15, 117, 161, 163
securities brokers, 201–202
Securities Exchange Act, 198
Securities Investor Protection Act, 198
Securities Market Reform Act, 198
securities markets, 197–200
    regulation of, 198–199

security
    of computer systems, 101
    of consumer information, 220
seed money, 149
segmentation, market, 228
selective credit control, 17
selective distribution, 276
self-actualization, 337
self-awareness, 307
self-employment, 138
self-image, buying behavior and, 223
self-managed teams, 329
self-regulation, 307
sellers, 9
selling concept, 218
selling expenses, 170–171
service businesses, 5
service delivery, 93–94
service products, 244
service sector, growth of, 6
services, exporting of, 60
sexism, 351
sexual harassment, 352
shared workspaces, 130
shareholder activism, 120
shareholder value, mergers and, 126
shareholders, 115, 119–120, 193
shareholders' equity, 168, 169
shares, of stock, 193
shark repellent, 126
shelf space, 254
Sherman Antitrust Act, 13
shipping companies, 278
shop steward, 370
shopping malls, 273
shopping products, 245
short selling, 202
sick pay, 368
Silent Spring (Carson), 42
simulations, computer, 83
situational leaders, 308
Six Sigma, 96
skill-based pay, 364
skills inventory, 360
skim pricing, 233, 260
slander, 381
slowdowns, labor, 371
small business(es), 134–138
    assistance for, 146–148
    business partners for, 147
    business plan for, 140–141, 142
    characteristics of, 136
    defined, 135
    economic roles of, 135–136
    increase in number of, 136–137
    ownership options for, 141–145
    starting, 138–148
Small Business Administration (SBA), 135
Small Business Investment Companies, 151
small business networks, 148
smart cards, 189
smog, 42
smoking, by employees, 364
social audit, 41
social bookmarking, 235–236, 287

social class, buying behavior and, 223
social commerce, 219, 221
social intelligence, 307
social media, 235–236, 240, 287–288
social networking sites, xxix, 32, 154–155,
    287
social responsibility. *See* corporate social
    responsibility
Social Security Act, 359
Social Security payments, 19
social skills, in managers, 307
social trends, marketing activities and, 227
socialism, 9
socioemotional roles, in teams, 330–331
Solid Waste Disposal Act, 42
sole proprietorships, 112, 113, 169
    number of, 114
South Korea, 72
spam, 285
span of control, 325
span of management, 325
specialization, work, 323–324
specialty advertising, 286
specialty funds, 196
specialty products, 245
specialty stores, 272, 273
speculators, 201
spying, 30
spyware, 101, 362
staffing
    challenges of, 350
    for international business, 73, 74
stakeholders
    ethical decision making and, 36
    protecting, 14–15
    rights of, 40
Standard & Poor's 500 index, 196, 204
standardization, 72, 229, 256
standards
    control, 311–312
    measuring choices against, 35
stare decisis, 380
start-ups, 138–148
    business plan for, 140–141, 142
    checklist for, 140
    failure of, 145–146
    financing of, 149–151
    pros and cons of, 141, 143
statement of cash flows, 171
statement of financial position, 167
statistical process control (SPC), 95
statistical quality control (SQC), 95
statistics, economic, 18
statutory law, 379
stealth marketing, 31, 221
steel industry, 77
stereotyping, 67
stock certificate, 115
stock exchanges, 164, 197–198
stock market, 197–200
    fluctuations in, 204
stock market indexes, 196, 203–204
stock options, 366–367
stock quotations, 205–206
stock specialists, 197

stock split, 193
stocks, 193
    blue-chip, 204
    buying and selling, 201–202
    common, 115–116
    listing of, 197
    manipulation of, 199
    preferred, 116
stop order, 202
stores. *See* retailers
strategic alliances, 127
    international, 70–71
strategic marketing planning, 225–236
strategic plans, 298–304
strengths, evaluating, 226, 301
strikebreakers, 372
strikes, 371
student loans, 395
subchapter S corporations, 118
subprime home loans, 45–46
subsidiary corporations, 119
subsidies, 62
subsystems, 82
succession planning, 354
Sudan, 61
suicide, in workplace, 358
supercenters, 273
Superfund program, 43
supermarkets, 272
supervisory managers, 305
supplies, business, 246
supply, 9, 11
supply chain, 87, 291
supply chain management, 87–89, 277
Surgeon General, 46
surveys
    in marketing research, 235
    web-based, 100
suspicious activity reports, 191
sustainable development, 43
sweatshops, 48
Sweden, 59
Switzerland, 59
SWOT analysis, 301
synergies
    in mergers, 123
    in teams, 328
system, defined, 81–82
systems
    information, 96–104
    lean, 91, 93
    professional and managerial, 99
    supply chain, 89
systems diagram, 84
systems dynamics, 83
systems thinking, 81–86
    for service delivery, 93–94

T
tactical plans, 304
Taft-Harley Act, 359, 370, 372
tagging, 5, 287
takeovers, hostile, 122, 125
tall organizations, 325
tangibility, of products, 244

target markets, 229
tariffs, 61
task forces, 329
task-specialist role, 330–331
tax accounting, 160, 162
tax considerations, in business ownership
    choice, 112, 117
tax credits, 401
tax-deferred investments, 401
tax-exempt investments, 401
tax rates, 17–18
tax shelters, 162, 390
tax strategy, 401
taxable income, 401
taxes, 400–401
    of corporations, 117
    income, 17–18
    investments and, 201
    payroll, 18
    property, 18
    sales, 18
teams, 328–335
    advantages of, 329-330
    conflict in, 333-334
    developmental stages of, 332–333
    disadvantages of, 330
    effective, 330–331, 332
    goals of, 329
    meetings of, 334–335
    roles in, 330
    size of, 330
    types of, 329
technical skills, 313
technology
    balancing with human touch, 219-220
    challenges of, 21
    information, 37, 98, 99
    Internet, 99–100
    location and tracking, 53
    manufacturing, 92
    marketing activities and, 227
    new economy and, 8
    for social networking, 154–155
telecommuting, 345, 353
telemarketing, 285–286
telepresence, 77
television, advertising on, 283, 285
temporary workers, 354
tender offer, 125
termination, of employees, 369
terrorism
    banking and, 191
    global business and, 73–74
test marketing, 235, 250
testing, preemployment, 357
text scanning, 362
Thailand, 49
theft, by employees, 339
theocratic law, 68
Theory X, 338, 339
Theory Y, 338, 339
Theory Z, 338
threats, assessing, 301
3D printing, 265
360-degree review, 360

thrifts, 189
time deposits, 188
time utility, 217, 270
time value of money, 389
tobacco companies, 46
top managers, 305
torts, 381
total cost of ownership, 103–104
total quality management (TQM), 95–96
Toxic Substances Control Act, 42
toxic waste, 43
Toyota Production System, 93, 123
tracking technologies, 53
trade allowances, 286–287
trade deficit, 59, 60
trade dress, 384
trade, international, 57–66
trade-offs
    in financial decisions, 390
    in product safety, 247
    in supply chain, 87
trade promotions, 286–287
trade restrictions, 61–62
trade secrets, 30
trade shows, xxix
trade surplus, 59, 60
trademarks, 232, 251, 266, 384
trading, 216
trading blocks, 63
trading hubs, online, 270
training, of employees, 343, 358–360
transaction costs, 201
transaction processing systems (TPS), 98
transactional leaders, 308
transactions, 216
    banking, 191
    monitoring of, 234
    property, 383
    recording of, 166–167
    sales, 383
transformation, in production systems, 94
transformational leaders, 308
transparency, 31
transportation
    of products, 278
    terrorism and, 73–74
transportation costs, personal, 396
Transportation Security Administration
    (TSA), 15
travel, business, 67
Treasury bills, 195
Treasury bonds, 195
Treasury notes, 195
trend analysis, 172–173
Trojan horses, 101
trusts, 13
truth, in business communication, 31
Truth-in-Lending Act, 45
turnover rate, 354

U
undifferentiated marketing, 229, 230
unemployment, 18
Uniform Commercial Code (UCC), 379
Union of South American Nations, 64

unions. *See* labor unions
United Kingdom, 72
United Nations, 63
United States
  currency of, 65, 66
  exports and imports of, 60
  foreign direct investment in, 72
  legal system of, 379–380
  in NAFTA, 63
Uniting and Strengthening America by
  Providing Appropriate Tools Required to
  Intercept and Obstruct Terrorism (USA
  PATRIOT) Act, 73, 191
Universal Product Codes (UPCs), 253
unsought products, 245
U.S. Bureau of Labor Statistics, xxvi, 19, 26,
  378
U.S. Census Bureau, 228
U.S. Chamber of Commerce, 147
U.S. Constitution, 379
U.S. Department of Commerce, 26–27,
  70, 78
U.S. Department of Housing and Urban
  Development, 397
U.S. Department of Justice, 14
U.S. Department of Labor, 370
U.S. Government Export Portal, 78
U.S. government securities, 195
U.S. Patent and Trademark Office, 251, 266,
  384
U.S. savings bonds, 195
U.S. Supreme Court, 380
U.S. Treasury, 211
USB flash drive, 102
user-generated content, 5, 235
utilitarianism, 35
utilities, four, 216–217, 270

V

vacations, paid, 368
value, bundle of, 231
value chains, 86–97, 88–89, 92
value pricing, 258–259
value web, 87, 138
Vanguard 500 index, 196
variable costs, 233, 257, 258
vending machines, 274
venture capitalists, 150
vertical structure, 326
vertical teams, 329
vesting, of stock options, 366

video mining, 234
video news release, 287
video sharing, 5, 287
videoconferences, 77
Vietnam, 49
violence, in workplace, 358
viral marketing, 31
virtual meetings, 100
virtual office, 130
virtual organization, 328
virtual reality, 92, 274
virtual teams, 329
virtual workspaces, 100
virtual worlds, 5
viruses, computer, 101, 102, 362
vision statement, 299–300

W

wages, 61, 362–363
  gender gap in, 351–352
Wagner Act, 359, 370
Wall Street, 197
Wall Street Journal, 202
Wal-Mart Watch, 372
wants, 216
warehouse clubs, 272
warehousing, 278
warranties, 383
waste, toxic, 43
water
  pollution of, 43
  safety of, 29
weaknesses, evaluating, 226, 301
Web 2.0, 5, 101
web-based communication, 100
webcam control, 362
webcasts, 287
website tracking, 362
websites
  advertising via, 85, 283, 284
  copyright notices on, 384
  financial, 203
  for investment advice, 211
  job boards on, xxix, xxx
  networking, 148
  for small-business information, 148
  social bookmarking, 235–236
  for social media, 287
  Web 2.0 and, 5
  widgets for, 288
  See also Internet

web-tracking technology, 220, 284, 293
wellness programs, 365
wheel of retailing, 271
whistle-blowing, 33–34, 369
white knight, 126
white papers, 221
whiteboards, virtual, 130
wholesalers, 234, 270–271
  functions of, 270
  push strategy to, 281
widgets (website technology), 288
wikis, 5, 235, 287
will, legal, 401
women
  job bias and, 47
  pay of, 351–352
  time off from work, 353
  in workforce, 351–352
word of mouth, 218, 288
work arrangements, alternative, 353–354
work, attitudes toward, 351
work hours, 350
work specialization, 323–324
worker buyouts, 369
workforce
  aligning, 350
  changing demographics of, 350–353
  diversity in, 21, 313
  global, 46
  in new economy, 8
  older workers in, 351
  organizing, 326–328
  turnover in, 354
  women in, 351–352
  See also employees
working capital, 190, 172, 173
work-life balance, 350, 367
workloads, 330, 350
workplace
  safety in, 48, 359
  violence in, 358
workspaces, virtual, 100, 130
World Bank, 63, 78
World Trade Organization (WTO), 62–63
worms, computer, 101
wrongful discharge lawsuits, 369

Y

yield management, 262
yield management software, 10
young people, as entrepreneurs, 138